THE DEATH PENALTY

A DEBATE

THE DEATH PENALTY

A DEBATE

PRO
Ernest van den Haag

CON
John P. Conrad

Plenum Press • New York and London

Library of Congress Cataloging in Publication Data

Van den Haag, Ernest.

The death penalty.

Includes bibliographical references and index.
1. Capital punishment—United States—Addresses, essays, lectures. I. Conrad, John Phillips, 1913–   . II. Title.
HV8699.U5V36 1983   364.6'6'.0973   83-11079
ISBN 0-306-41416-3

© 1983 Ernest van den Haag and John P. Conrad
Plenum Press is a Division of
Plenum Publishing Corporation
233 Spring Street, New York, N.Y. 10013

Printed in the United States of America

Foreword

From 1965 until 1980, there was a virtual moratorium on executions for capital offenses in the United States. This was due primarily to protracted legal proceedings challenging the death penalty on constitutional grounds.

After much *Sturm und Drang*, the Supreme Court of the United States, by a divided vote, finally decided that "the death penalty does not invariably violate the Cruel and Unusual Punishment Clause of the Eighth Amendment."

The Court's decisions, however, do not moot the controversy about the death penalty or render this excellent book irrelevant.

The ball is now in the court of the Legislature and the Executive. Legislatures, federal and state, can impose or abolish the death penalty, within the guidelines prescribed by the Supreme Court. A Chief Executive can commute a death sentence. And even the Supreme Court can change its mind, as it has done on many occasions and did, with respect to various aspects of the death penalty itself, during the moratorium period.

Also, the people can change their minds. Some time ago, a majority, according to reliable polls, favored abolition. Today, a substantial majority favors imposition of the death penalty. The pendulum can swing again, as it has done in the past.

More importantly, the death penalty involves moral as well as legal questions. The law may temporarily decide but the ultimate resolution of this issue, in my opinion, will rest on moral rather than purely legal considerations. Law and morality often are in tandem, but not always or invariably.

There are now about one thousand persons convicted of capital crimes on death row and the number is steadily increasing.

Despite the green light by the Supreme Court, there have only been a handful of executions. After all, an execution is the supreme and final sanction. It is a testimonial to human compassion that all involved on a governmental level recoil from its imposition.

Under the given circumstances, this book in the format of a debate, pro and con, about the death penalty is timely. And it is most interesting and informative, dealing, as it does, with all aspects of this grave problem.

I know of no other book or article which treats the subject so comprehensively and with such erudition.

During my tenure on the Supreme Court, I read many briefs concerning the death penalty by distinguished lawyers. Many of these briefs cannot hold a candle to this book, written by two non-lawyer scholars. Even in treating the constitutional issues, the opposing views in the debate are presented with keen analysis frequently lacking in the writings and arguments of members of the Bar.

I personally am opposed to the death penalty and believe with Camus that we should take the "great civilizing step" of abolishing it.

But, although I have not changed my mind, I learned much from both of the participants in the debate, Professors van den Haag and Conrad.

This book is must reading for all concerned, pro and con, with the death penalty.

I commend this dialogue as an outstanding example of a dialogue on a subject of transcendent importance—a dialogue conducted with the scholarship, civility, and passion which this debated issue fully warrants.

Arthur J. Goldberg

Preface

This is a debate about capital punishment, an issue that is not likely to fade from public attention in the foreseeable future. Most Americans have made up their minds one way or another. So have we, adversaries with decided and unshaken views. Perhaps one or the other of us may draw some uncommitted readers to his side. Perhaps we may even shake the convictions of a few who have thought themselves settled on their positions as to the death penalty. Our intent, however, is to reach the thoughtful citizen who is concerned about the condition of criminal justice—its effectiveness, its humaneness, and its fairness. We hope to help readers to think more clearly about at least one of the many issues in criminal justice.

To understand what we hope to accomplish in this debate, the reader should know its genesis. At a seminar in New York in the summer of 1980, Conrad (the abolitionist) met Linda Regan, who was to become our editor. In discussing common interests in the problems of criminal justice, Regan enquired about the feasibility of a book on capital punishment. Conrad replied that everything that could be said about capital punishment had been said—over and over again. It was improbable that new facts or arguments would be discovered to justify the publication of yet another book.

Reflecting on this conversation on the airplane going home to California, Conrad noted that although there was a plethora of books and articles that take stands on the death penalty, two coherent sets of opposing views have never been presented within the covers of one book. A debate might clarify the discourse, which suffers from exaggerations, misconceptions, and sentimentality to such an extent that rational consideration of the issues is hopelessly obscured. He suggested to Regan that a debate between himself and van den Haag might be of value in adding to the rigor of thought about punishment in general and capital punishment in particular. Van den Haag is famous in criminal justice circles for his unflinching adherence to the position that the death penalty must be retained in the criminal justice armory. Conrad, on the other hand, firmly holds to the position that capital punishment accomplishes no useful purpose that cannot be achieved by extended incarceration. Both of us were prepared to argue from these positions with vigor and at length—as we think will be evident in this book.

On enquiry, Regan found that van den Haag was willing. Vague rules of engagement were agreed upon in a meeting in San Francisco, where both of us happened to be in the fall of 1980. We agreed that the rigid structure of a college debate would be inappropriate. No proposition for an affirmative and a negative; no simplification of the many issues revolving around capital punishment in the United States. Instead of using the single-issue structure so familiar in sporting debates, we would try to debate all the significant issues, arguing their significance from the different viewpoints we were to occupy.

We have been engaged in the exchange of position statements, rebuttals, and rejoinders ever since. Progress was interrupted on several occasions by competing obligations that kept us away from the battle, sometimes for extended periods, but neither of us lost enthusiasm for the combat in which we have been engaged. Each of us hopes to prevail in the minds of our readers, though not to convince the other. Each of us hopes that at least we will sharpen thought about the death penalty regardless of our readers' convictions.

Our rules are simple. We have written basic chapters that outline the various elements of our positions. Responses to these chapters lead to rejoinders and more responses, all carried to the point where there is nothing further to say, and the issue must go to the reader. Our intent has been to present logically and empirically buttressed arguments leading to a rational resolution in the minds of reasonable readers.

We solemnly covenanted to abstain from *ad hominem* stratagems. At the outset we agreed that this debate would be conducted with civility and respect for each other's integrity. We have dealt out sharp blows, but the basic context is amicable. We part as friends, perhaps to resume battle on another day and about other issues.

The reader is warned that although we have meticulously documented our sources in the footnotes, neither of us intended to offer an exhaustive bibliography. Other writers—e.g., Hugo Adam Bedau, among others[1]— have performed that service. Those who want to know what others have thought and written will have to look elsewhere; we have cited our references only when we needed them to support a point we wished to make. Neither of us pretends to have read the whole of the enormous literature on this subject. We confront each other as gladiators equipped with the weapons of scholarship, not as encyclopedists or cataloguers. If we succeed in stimulating the reader to look further for facts and arguments, we will have achieved one of our lesser aims. Our main objective, however, is the furtherance of responsible discourse on a topic that is too often clouded by error, sentimentality, exaggeration, and various forms of obscurantism and prejudice—on both sides of the issue.

Ernest van den Haag
John P. Conrad

Note

1. Hugo Adam Bedau, *The Death Penalty in America,* 3rd ed. (New York and Oxford: Oxford University Press, 1982), pp. 383–406.

Acknowledgments

Knowing that I was engaged in writing a book about an unpleasant subject, many friends extended their sympathy, their understanding of my need for more than the ordinary amount of solitude, and their assurances that they would read the book once it became available in bookstores and libraries. When requested, other friends read some of my salvos against my doughty opponent and made suggestions to increase their firepower. Among them were Henry Schwarzchild, of the American Civil Liberties Union; Egon Bittner, of Brandeis University; Frank Fair, of Sam Houston State University; and Floyd Feeney, of the University of California at Davis. I am particularly grateful to Brian Forst and Hans Zeisel for their discussion of the faults in Isaac Ehrlich's statistical contention that each execution saves seven or eight innocent lives. Sarah Dike, until the summer of 1982 the editor of *Crime and Delinquency,* provided materials that I could not easily obtain from my usual library sources. My colleagues at the Criminal Justice Center of the Sam Houston State University listened attentively to my chapter, "The Retributivist's Case against Capital Punishment," as a colloquium lecture, and some helpful suggestions emerged. While I profited from these and many other discussions, all the mistakes and failures of grace and erudition belong to me alone.

No one could ask for a more graciously persistent editor than Linda Regan, at whose suggestion this book had its beginning. Gently candid with her criticism, she pointed out gaps in my arguments and thereby augmented their cogency. She was patient and understanding with delays and procrastinations, and appropriately pleased when chapters arrived on time. Her encouragement has been an indispensable ingredient to the completion of this book. I have only myself to thank for all the typing of first, second, and third drafts and the emendations of apparently completed statements; I am also responsible for all the typographical errors that I hope will be caught before this volume reaches the public. Finally, I must thank my wife, Charlotte Conrad, for her forbearance during an endless test of her good humor.

John P. Conrad

Nobody assisted me in writing my part of this book. I am delighted though to acknowledge my debt to my mother who bore me and bore with me. I am grateful also to my assistant Lois A. Aiello for her diligent help in research and typing, and for bearing with me.

Ernest van den Haag

Contents

Introduction: Before the Killing Stopped
John P. Conrad   1

Introduction: Death but Not Torture
Ernest van den Haag   13

1. The Retributivist's Case against Capital Punishment   17

2. The Purpose of Punishment   53

3. The Deterrent Effect of the Death Penalty   63

4. More on the Deterrent Effect of the Death Penalty   67

5. Does Deterrence Need Capital Punishment?   83

   Appendix   131

6. Deterrence, the Death Penalty, and the Data   133

7. The Constitutional Question   157

   Appendix   201

8. Discrimination and Justice   203

9. Justice and Equality   223

10. Special Cases   233

11. Popular Arguments   241

12. Crimes of Passion   253

13. Death, Rehabilitation, the Bible, and Human Dignity   257

14. The Symbolic Meaning of the Death Penalty.............   273

    Appendix   283

15. The Abolitionist Rests   289

16. The Advocate Advocates   297

    Index   301

Before the Killing Stopped

JOHN P. CONRAD

When I started work at San Quentin in 1947, I was employed as a psychiatric social worker in the prison hospital. The Chief Psychiatrist, my immediate superior, had a wide variety of assignments for me, but one on which he set great store was the preparation of psychiatric social histories of the men who were admitted to Condemned Row. They had to be seen as soon as possible after their arrival—"while they were still labile," as the Chief liked to explain. By that he meant that they would be responsive to my inquiries and not influenced by the other condemned men, by their lawyers (of whom the Chief had a low opinion), or by their families. As soon as the newly admitted condemned man had had a physical examination, I was to make haste to the Row and conduct my interview.

The objective was to gain a full account of the prisoner's family, his mental and emotional history, and such information as I could obtain about his criminal activities. I was also responsible for initiating correspondence with his family, with his employers, and with anyone else who seemed likely to tell us anything significant. After I was through with him, the clinical psychologist took his turn and administered the usual battery of tests: the Wechsler-Bellevue for an estimate of intelligence, the Bender-Gestalt for clues to brain damage or other neurological disorder, and the Rorschach and the Thematic Apperception Test to plumb the emotional depths. There might then be further physical examinations, based on what the psychologist and I had discovered. ("What's the point of this?" I heard one consultant ask in the presence of the man he was about to examine. "This guy's health problems are going to disappear soon enough.") Lastly, there was the climactic examination for which all else was preparation. A team of three psychiatrists went together to the Row for an examination in which a determination of legal sanity, by the criteria of the McNaughtan rule, would be made. Although several of the men seen during my time in the hospital were close to psychotic, none were so far out of touch with reality that they qualified as legally insane under the strict rule of McNaughtan's Case. There was one man whose condition on the day before his scheduled execution was so obviously psychotic that he had to be transferred to the State Hospital for the Criminally Insane. He never recovered sufficiently to be returned to San Quentin for execution.

All this elaborate scrutiny was for the benefit of the Governor in considering the exercise of executive clemency. I always explained my mission in terms of the Governor's need to know as much as possible about the men he was to consider for reprieve or commutation. However, condemned men were free to reject the ministrations that we proposed to lavish on them, and a number chose not to be interviewed. One such was Caryl Chessman, later to achieve international renown as an author, a resourceful litigator, and a *cause célèbre*. He was scornful of the Chief Psychiatrist, for whom he had worked as an inmate-clerk during a previous commitment, and whose professional attainments did not impress him. He impatiently dismissed my proposal that I should interview him, pointing out that his old file contained all the information about his mental condition that the Governor could possibly need.

Most prisoners readily agreed to be interviewed. Their manner usually suggested that they were grasping at any straw of hope that came in sight. Although some were diffident about discussing their offenses, most of them disregarded their lawyers' advice to say nothing about their immediate legal situation. I had no need to press them on the subject of the charge against them; the one set of information about these men that was complete on arrival was a full statement of the offense, including all the versions known to the probation officer who wrote the preliminary report.

My interviews with condemned men were always conducted on the Row. There was no question of bringing a man down the elevator from the North Block security unit to the yard and then across the yard to the hospital for the convenience of the psychiatric staff. The Row was in the upper reaches of the North Block, accessible only by elevator. Usually I interviewed my subjects in the disciplinary hearing room, a dirty, unswept place adjoining the isolation cellblock as well as the Row. The furniture was ancient, unrepaired, and hand-me-down, as though to impress the prisoners with their unimportance. Sometimes the hearing room was in use for disciplinary committee proceedings, and then I had to talk to my man in an empty cell. Once, when all the cells were full, the interview took place in an unused shower bath. The sergeant in charge of the Row did not consider my discourse with condemned men a high-priority activity. Some correctional officers said it was a waste of time and pointed out that some of these fellows wouldn't mind taking me along with them.

The first man I interviewed was a young Chicano named Rodriguez. He had been convicted of raping and then killing a young woman in a small San Joaquin Valley town. He had arrived on the previous day, and he was agitated and nervous, anxious to convince me that the charge was false, that he had been somehow convicted on the evidence of a former girl friend who was angry after he had broken off with her.

"That bitch . . . that bitch—" He was choking with fury.

Then there was a loud voice from a cell nearby:

" . . . and you shall be taken to the gas chamber next *Friday* and there you shall *die!*"

Rodriguez's lips tightened, and he could not complete his denunciation of the vengeful young woman whom he had jilted. His Friday was far in the future—eventually it came—but there was indeed to be an execution on the impending Friday.

After I had sent Rodriguez back to his cell, the sergeant in charge of the Row explained the interruption:

"That was McMonigle. He bullies the rest of these poor bastards, and there's not a hell of a lot I can do about him. Nearly all these guys would like to have a chance at him, but I can't allow it, of course. But sometimes I wish I could turn my back."

Two of the men I interviewed insisted from first to last that they wanted to get it over with as soon as possible; they told me that if they could, they would waive the automatic appeal to the Supreme Court that was required by law in all death penalty cases. One was a middle-aged Indian who had killed his wife—he couldn't tell me why. He said he didn't deserve to live, and could see no reason why his execution should be delayed.

The other man was a youth, not yet twenty, who had hacked his land-lady to death with an ax, apparently on impulse. He had had a previous commitment to the California Youth Authority and was convinced that he could not manage a life sentence. He wanted me to understand that he wished no commutation of his sentence. All he wanted was the gas chamber, as soon as it could be opened to him.

Those two were exceptions. The others in my Condemned Row clientèle were eager to escape the death to which they had been sentenced, and at any cost. The example of Caryl Chessman inspired many of them to emulation, though none managed to protract their stay on the Row to the length that Chessman contrived. But several humbler men received commutations from the Governor and descended to the San Quentin yard, there to become members of the elite fraternity of lifers.

Most of the men whom I interviewed went to the gas chamber, always after a long stay for the Supreme Court review and any other legal maneuvers that their lawyers could arrange. When their time came, they usually went quietly and with a semblance of dignity. We could be grateful for that. The brisk, impersonal procedures scheduled for the last two days assumed a prisoner who was at peace with the world and resigned to his fate. His role required him to cooperate with the team of professional correctional officers assigned to the task of killing him.

I witnessed only one execution. Three years after my initiation at San Quentin I was transferred from the Psychiatric Department to the Reception–Guidance Center, and now I was under the supervision of an elderly psychiatrist, a clinician steeped in world-weariness. Noting one day that I had interviewed a great many condemned men at the time of their admission to the Row, he remarked that I ought to complete the cycle and witness "the ultimate in therapy." I am sure that he had nothing more in mind than to shock me, whom he saw as a naïve young idealist, with his sage realism. Nevertheless, I applied to the Warden's office for permission to witness the next execution. Readily granted. Warden Clinton Duffy was famous for his passionate opposition to capital punishment—the ceremony over which he was required by law to preside—and thought that all San Quentin employees should see the procedures for themselves. Perhaps he was a naïve old idealist, but he never yielded in his insistence that the death penalty was wrong under all circumstances.

I was signed on as an official witness. There were a dozen of us listed in compliance with the law that required each death to be observed, recorded, and duly certified to the court that passed sentence and to the Governor. Some were regulars; I had heard that there were several men who applied to be witnesses to each execution and that they were not denied. Some others might be law enforcement officers who had been involved in the apprehension of the murderer who was now to be executed.

On the appointed day, a colleague and I joined the ten other official witnesses. We assembled in the Warden's office, where we were reminded that our presence was necessary for the completion of this proceeding. The officer who briefed us went on to say that experience showed that not everyone was able to stay to the finish. If any of us should feel faint while in the observation room, he was to leave quietly. It was hoped that no one would complicate a difficult procedure by collapsing in the observers' area.

We marched silently out of the administration building, across the street to the visitors' gate, and down the South Block wall to the small building that housed the gas chamber. Some nonofficial observers had already gathered. There were reporters from the San Francisco press and a handful of newly employed guards, who had been instructed to stand on a bench at the rear of the room so that they could see over our heads. We, the official observers, were ranged immediately outside the glassed-in chamber. There was a rail that stretched under the window at waist level. Most of us grasped it.

Immediately after our arrival—that was the cue, I suppose—the door from the death-cell unit, the special pair of cells in which condemned men spent their last night, was opened, and one of the two young men to be killed was briskly led in by two guards. He was dressed in a white shirt and dark trousers; I knew that he wore no underwear because of the danger that the lethal gas might be trapped in a fold of clothing when his corpse was removed for delivery to an undertaker.

He was seated in one of the two steel chairs in the middle of the chamber. Deftly each of the attending guards grasped an arm and fastened it to the chair with a leather strap. Then his ankles were fastened. His shirt was then unbuttoned so that a stethoscope chest-piece could be taped to his ribs. Once that was done, the second man was brought in, and the same quick fastening procedures were carried out. Everything was done rapidly and as though rehearsed in a carefully prepared drill.

Both of the condemned men were black. The first was a small, nervous-looking fellow who smiled toward the Warden, as though in friendly farewell. He had waited for nearly two years for this day; the waiting was over. I read into the pitch of his head, the plaintive smile that I could see only in profile, the relief that I thought he must be feeling. Perhaps he was pleased with these moments at the center of attention. I suspected that our indefatigable chaplain had persuaded him to repent, and perhaps he believed that in a few moments he would be in the presence of his Savior, forgiven for the fearful crime for which he was now to die. Simple inferences from a tilt of the head and a slight smile. Who could say how near the mark they were? I hoped that my speculations were correct. To die without emotion, in mute stolidity, would be to lose one's humanity in advance of death. It would be to die like an animal being put to sleep. But who can say how a man should feel at the time and on the occasion of his officially scheduled death?

His crime partner was a large, dull-looking man, a few years older, much more muscular, and without expression as he was strapped into his chair. No hint of a last message to anyone, no notice taken of these spectators of his last minutes. Maybe he was dying like an uncomprehending animal; maybe he was denying us the satisfaction of guessing his thoughts.

I had not interviewed either of these men. I did not know them, but I had looked up their case files before coming to see them die. The information was meager and perfunctory. There had been an armed robbery in a Los Angeles shopping center. Someone had tried to interfere, a pistol had been fired, and the victim had been instantly killed. Both these men had had prior records of robbery and assault. Other condemned men had become celebrities, either because of the heinous quality of the murders they had committed or because of the tortuous legal strategies by which they had so far evaded execution. Neither of these men had found his way into the headlines. On the next day, their deaths would not even be reported in the San Francisco newspapers.

The door to the chamber was shut. I could not see the Warden, who must have signaled immediately. It was five minutes after ten in the morning; although the execution was scheduled for ten o'clock, it was always delayed for a few minutes in case there was a last-minute message from the Governor's office. The men would have been told that if they wanted to go fast, they should breathe deeply as soon as the door closed. Evidently they had followed that advice. Their heads sank. They were unconscious, but still alive. My colleague, who had been standing beside me, turned and left the room quickly. Looking around me, I saw the witnesses grouped at the observation window, solemn and motionless. Inside the chamber, the two men now seemed to be dead, but none of us moved. Minutes passed, and then a large muscle in the older man's shoulder twitched in a spasm. It was over. Seconds later, the attending physician removed the stethoscope from his ears and confirmed that the prisoners' hearts had stopped beating. We started to move out of the observation area and into the sunlight outside. The Warden's administrative assistant passed around a clipboard with a form for the witnesses to sign. We all left quickly; there was no conversation.

Later I found my colleague.

"What was the matter? Are you all right?"

"Oh, I'm all right. I had to leave, I was so angry. It came over me that it was all so senseless, and I was allowing myself to be a part of that senseless rigamarole."

That was how it was when all the procedures went smoothly, when the men to be killed cooperated by dying without resistance. Usually executions went smoothly like that, but not always.

There was the execution of Leanderess Riley, a young man whom I had interviewed with some difficulty. Scared, at best borderline defective in intelligence, unaccustomed to a neutral interchange with a white official, he had been unable to tell me anything about himself. He was in his early twenties, slight and fragile. Again, it was a routine murder committed by handgun in the course of a robbery in Los Angeles. There have been many like Riley before him and since, but I do not think that many have died in such peculiar agony.

His execution took place a year or so after my departure from San Quentin. One of my colleagues in the Sacramento headquarters of the Department of Corrections had wished to see an execution and was invited to witness Riley's killing. My friend returned to Sacramento shaken and distressed. Riley had not cooperated. When the time came for him to leave the death cell and proceed to the chamber where he was to die, he had screamed and resisted the guards every inch of the way. Forced into the chair, he was strapped down while kicking and screaming. Finally, the gas chamber door was closed, and before the pellets could be released into the acid, he slipped his slender arms and ankles free of the restraining straps. He ran to the chamber door screaming his demand that the door be opened. No one knew what should be done; there was nothing in the procedures to meet such an emergency. The guards were sent in again to strap him down more firmly, but when the door was closed, he slipped loose again, repeating his demand for release. This time the cyanide pellets were dropped into the vat of acid and Riley fell to the floor and soon was dead.

It was said that Riley did not die like a man. Some uttered the opinion that his death was like that of a caged animal—imagery that was neither original nor appropriate. Frenzy had seized him in the face of the death he had had to anticipate for so many months. Reality had robbed the witnesses of their equanimity. I have always wondered why executioners think that a condemned man has an obligation to make the task of killing easy.

It was different in the days when the killers were hanged. Old Jack Brennan, the prison records officer, had had to attend all the hangings in the line of his duties. He told me how it was:

> We hung them at midnight instead of ten in the morning. The gallows was set up in the big room on the second floor of the gym. When it was close to time, they'd bring the man in, make him walk the steps to the trap, where he had to stand. Once the noose was around his neck, the executioner would nod to the warden, who would signal back to spring the trap. My God! What a noise that trap made! Everything was so still you could hear the guy breathing, and then *bang!* went the trap. It sounded like a cannon going

off. No matter how often I heard it, it always shocked me out of my skin. Then in the dim light we would see the poor bastard plunge out of sight.

Sometimes the drop wasn't long enough, and the guy being hung would thrash around under the scaffold, choking. Then somebody would have to get in there and grab his legs and pull so that he wouldn't take forever dying. But if the drop was too long, the guy might be decapitated. I never saw that happen, but they always said that was the worst thing.

That explained a routine entry in the execution register that I had inspected. The register had been kept since the 1870s, with a page for each man hanged. There was a photograph of the person executed—there had been a sprinkling of women—and under the picture, the name, age, county of commitment, and the charge. Then the four last entries:

Height _____
Weight _____
Length of Drop _____
Results _____

Sometimes the results were reported as "satisfactory" and sometimes "unsatisfactory." Obviously the hangman's art depends on an empirical correlation of the data. I had been puzzled by the assessment of the "results," but Jack Brennan's account clarified the matter.

Abolitionists writing about capital punishment sometimes elevate the condemned into an oppressed brotherhood, more sinned against than sinning. Most of those whom I knew were poor men, perfunctorily defended in court by appointed counsel. Many were blacks or Chicanos or Indians. Some were unstable men whose lives on the margins of society kept them in poor touch with reality—or maybe it was the other way around: Their instability had lodged them on that margin.

The lifers were also sentenced for first degree murder. Except for a few who had been ably defended by private counsel, it was hard to account for the difference in their fates. Those who had gone to the gas chamber had been unlucky. Those who argue the case for abolition sometimes seize on this bad luck, attributing the misfortune of the condemned to race discrimination, to the incompetence of the bench or bar, or to the use of the criminal law to discipline the poor. In such an argument, it is a short step to the exaggeration of the virtues of the condemned men as a group. Qualities are attributed that had never been perceived in them as individuals before their admission to the Row.

These men had committed terrible crimes. It was natural that in their preoccupation with their own fate they seldom expressed regret for the killing of their victims or concern for their families. The prospect of death had indeed wonderfully concentrated their minds, as Dr. Samuel Johnson supposed; they could think only of themselves and their scheduled deaths.

A few took a perverse pride in the viciousness of their crimes, as though the notoriety conferred on them by the press had somehow brought them a distinction that eluded common men. In another essay, I have related the apparent pleasure that one of them took in reciting the details of the numerous strangulations he had performed on helpless derelicts during his few brief months of liberty spent on the Skid Row of San Francisco.[1] I had known him well before his release from prison, after which he conducted a single-handed holocaust on men like himself. He had known right from wrong as well as the next man, but preferred the wrong. Years of insignificance must have convinced him that he could never come to notice by doing right.

Other prisoners on the row amused themselves by tormenting their fellows. Zatzke, a homosexual prostitute, had been terrorized by stronger men contemptuous of his weakness. The San Quentin Condemned Row was no oasis of fraternity and mutual concern. A sentimental view of these men is possible only for those who have never spent a few hours with them. The reality of their murders, and the continuing danger that some of them would have presented to society if they had been released must be conceded if a rational argument for the abolition of capital punishment is to be made.

I have heard moral philosophers express the view that although capital punishment could not be approved, its abolition is an impossible political goal. To struggle in behalf of the vicious and wicked requires more tolerance than most people can muster. There are other and more attractive battles to fight. The cause of these ugly and deformed human beings is one that pushes altruism to an ultimate limit.

That point of view expresses an undeniable part of the truth. Nevertheless, this is a cause that I must take up, partly because of a lifelong immersion in prisons and their problems, and a sense that nothing distinguishes the men who go to the Row from their fellow murderers who spend their lives in prison—or indeed from prisoners who are not murderers. And partly I must oppose capital punishment because I cannot accept killing as a permissible action for anyone, even a civil servant acting as an agent of the state. Killing demeans the state, and a society that insists on killing its murderers violates the precepts that make it possible for us to live together.

Inevitably the state is a teacher, as Justice Brandeis once asserted,[2] and when it kills it teaches vengeance and hatred. Murderers are not to be loved, nor may their acts be disregarded. But in allowing them to live, the state reminds all citizens that no man is always and only a murderer. Discourse with men on the Row will be colored by the absorption of the individual in his imminent fate. Rationalizations, recriminations, and self-pity pervade their thoughts and monopolize their words. It is the lifer who becomes a man, leaving gradually his preoccupation with self as the routine of prison life removes the stress of programmed death. Some of them achieve a sort of goodness, as though atonement for atrocities committed in the past can be achieved in the calm monotony that is possible for life prisoners.

But perhaps the most important argument to be made is that in twentieth-century America, so violent a nation, so vulnerable to the anger of the envious and the frustrations of the poor, the state must teach that killing anyone deliberately, for whatever reason, is needless and wrong.

When I began work on this debate, a close colleague urged that I should not overlook the predicament of prison personnel who must administer the death penalty. For years he had been the official in charge of his state's condemned row. He had attended many executions and presided over a few. He thought that too little attention has been given to the procedures that prison officials must carry out in accomplishing an execution.

Whether the prisoner goes to the chamber with becoming dignity or whether, like Leanderess Riley, he resists with might and main, a distressing process must be completed. The guards must escort him to the chamber, sometimes manhandling him along the way; another guard must push the lever that lowers the cyanide into the acid; the warden must signal the guard at that lever when the time has come to perform this fateful act.

This almost mechanical, almost impersonal set of procedures would be the conclusion of months of waiting. The warden and the guards would have had regular contacts with the condemned man and his family—and with scores of other condemned men and their families. In the consciousness of the warden and his staff the months and years preceding the execution have been full of occasions in which the humanity of the man to be killed enlarges far beyond the criminality of the murderer. It is not possible to signal the man at the cyanide lever without being keenly conscious that one is about to kill a man whom one knows well, sometimes intimately—often hoping that the court or the governor would spare him. The sense that killing people is wrong will rise in the mind of a decent man, no matter what the condemned man has done to merit his execution.

It is always possible to hire tough and callous men to do this work. It is wrong to delegate these functions to such men. No one, not even a professional executioner, should enjoy or take pride in this job.

My opposition to capital punishment begins with moral revulsion at the notion of the state being engaged in premeditated homicide. I know that this position can be opposed by retentionists who claim as firm an allegiance to basic morality as mine. No doubt my opponent's arguments will be firmly grounded in moral principles; it is not for me to state those principles for him.

The burden of proof must be on him to show that a punishment so grave and so irrevocable should be retained. The factors that argue so powerfully against capital punishment in this country have been suggested by the great legal philosopher H. L. A. Hart,[3] and I will restate them here as follows:

1. To take any life is to impose suffering not only on the criminal but also on many others. That is an evil to be justified only if some good end is achieved thereby that could not be achieved by any other means.

2. Although the danger is small, the death penalty cannot be expunged if it is discovered that an innocent man has been executed. This possibility is an intolerable risk.

3. The nature of the death penalty distorts the entire criminal justice system. Trials become interminable and in spite of all precautions, elaborate appellate processes preoccupy the courts at vast expense not only of money but also of public confidence in the judicial process. The inevitably protracted waiting for death mocks the fundamental purpose of justice, the swift and sure imposition of the penalty for the crime. The procedures of American justice require inordinate delays in the punishment of any criminal, but where the death penalty is demanded, the delay is interminable.

Unless it can be shown that a social good can be achieved by capital punishment that cannot be accomplished by a lesser punishment, these powerful considerations call for an end to the practice. Obviously, I do not think that any such showing can be made. In the exchanges that will follow, I shall deal with the argument that the killing of murderers discourages murder, and therefore capital punishment should be resumed. I consider this argument untenable. I shall show that capital punishment does not deter, and accomplishes nothing more than an expression of horror of the premeditated homicide.

Writing of the peculiar literature created by witnesses of executions, George Orwell defined the paradox that confronts my opponent and myself:

> I watched a man hanged once. There was no question that everyone concerned knew this to be a dreadful, unnatural action. I believe it is always the same—the whole jail, warders and prisoners alike, is upset when there is an execution. It is probably the fact that capital punishment is accepted as necessary, and yet instinctively felt to be wrong, that gives so many descriptions of executions their tragic atmosphere.[4]

Now, and again at the end, I will rest my case on the proposition that an execution is a needless tragedy, an anachronism whose survival does great harm to society without accomplishing any comparable good. Orwell's instinct was correct. An execution is both wrong and tragic.

Notes

1. "What Happened to Stephen Nash? The Important Questions About Dangerousness," in *In Fear of Each Other*, John P. Conrad and Simon Dinitz (Lexington, Massachusetts: Lexington Books, 1977), pp. 1–12.
2. In *Olmstead* v. *U.S.* (1928), 277 U.S. 438, at 485.
3. H. L. A. Hart, *Punishment and Responsibility* (Oxford: Clarendon Press, 1968), p. 89.
4. Sonia Orwell and Ian Angus, eds., *The Collected Essays, Journalism and Letters of George Orwell*, vol. 3 (New York: Harcourt, Brace & World, 1968), p. 267.

Death but Not Torture

ERNEST VAN DEN HAAG

Until approximately the eighteenth century, death was not the harshest punishment available for law enforcement in civilized countries. Torture was. People found guilty of major crimes (often minor crimes by our lights) were not executed: They were tortured to death, and torture was so cruel that death came as a relief. Condemned persons were commonly boiled, burned, roasted on spits, drawn and quartered, broken on wheels, disemboweled, slowly dismembered, or torn apart by horses. Infinitely elaborate and breathtakingly cruel tortures lasted for days, with those subjected to them begging for death, sometimes granted—as a form of leniency. Often the tortures of criminals served as public spectacles and family entertainments. (Although no fan, I regard TV as an improvement. Less gripping, it also is less painful.)

For the sake of historical perspective, it should be noted that until the nineteenth century, when anesthetics were invented, pain was far more common, and more commonly inflicted and accepted than it is today. Even surgical operations had to take place without anesthetics. Further, the notion of human solidarity was very restricted: The suffering of any one person was not much felt by others—religious rhetoric to the contrary notwithstanding—and it was socially quite acceptable to be amused by their pain. Death at an early age was common. Life expectancy was short, and infectious diseases were ever present, whereas today the degenerative diseases of old age are the major threat to life. Since it happens to all of us, death was not regarded as much of a punishment. The mere shortening of the life-span was thought insufficient to deter or punish crimes.

In the last two centuries capital punishment—originally beheading, from the Latin *caput* (head) or *capitis* (of the head)—has become the ultimate penalty. Few now think that death is not harsh enough, or that the threat of it is insufficient. Many indeed think that death is too much of a punishment for any crime. Is it? To answer this question we will have to consider the purpose of punishment in general and ask whether the death penalty is useful, or needed, to achieve it, and whether, apart from usefulness, it can be morally justified, whether it can be just. Let me consider a few subsidiary issues before turning to these questions.

1. Once a person has been sentenced to death, waiting for execution is likely to be psychologically painful. We all live both in the present and at least partly in the future. Expectations of the future play a major role in our present happiness or unhappiness. Obviously a condemned person has little to look forward to. Waiting for the end, while in prison, is hardly a happy experience. Therefore, there should be as little waiting as possible. Yet at present, the period of waiting and uncertainty is usually very long—up to ten years in some cases until all appeals are exhausted. Of the civilized countries that have retained the death penalty, the United States is the only one that permits or even insists on these long and profitless delays. Although the death penalty is constitutional if imposed by due process, well-meaning judges do, in effect, sabotage it by permitting and inviting infinite appeals and delays. The result is that in 1982 there were about one thousand convicts on death row. Nobody knows how many of them will actually be executed and who will be spared, after expecting execution for years. Most convicts on death row are kept in conditions far worse than those imposed on other prisoners. They are isolated in minuscule cells, with nothing to do but wonder about their fate.

The cruelty is gratuitous. It is not inherent in the death penalty or in any way required by it. Rules and practices mandating a reduction and a speedup of appeals and making sure that persons under death sentence are treated no worse than other persons confined to prison are entirely compatible with the death penalty. Abolitionists and retentionists alike should favor the elimination of unnecessary cruelty. A person sentenced to death is not sentenced to any additional and gratuitous suffering.

2. Death should be inflicted as painlessly as possible. The punishment consists of being deprived of life at a date certain—not of suffering pain beyond this. At present, executions take place by means of electrocution, shooting, gassing, and lethal injections. It seems that shooting is painless (pain occurs only some time after a bullet hits and is not suffered by a person who dies on being hit). Injections, too, are painless.* A condemned man

---

*Injections, though they need not be provided by physicians, nonetheless have a medicinal air about them, and the act is reminiscent of "putting to sleep" an animal. Shooting seems more directly, explicitly, and uniquely punitive, without being more painful.

ought to be allowed to choose, and methods of execution that may be painful, such as electrocution, or present an avoidable psychological burden, such as gassing, ought not to be used. If this were done, unnecessary cruelty (a redundant phrase since cruelty is by definition unnecessary pain) would be avoided. But death itself remains a terrifying thing for most of us.

3. Death is not so terrifying that some people do not volunteer for it. They may fast to death to foster a cause more important to them than their own lives. (Hunger strikers have been known to do so.) Or they may commit suicide because unhappy with life.

However, most people condemned to death, or guilty of crimes that may bring the death penalty, fear death. They do all they can to avoid execution. They assiduously try to avoid apprehension, conviction, and, finally, the death penalty. Only a very small minority—much less than one percent of the condemned—resign themselves to death, or welcome it. They refuse to appeal their sentences, greatly disappointing their lawyers and the American Civil Liberties Union. The latter has argued that convicts should not have the right *not* to appeal their death sentences, a novel civil liberty.

Some opponents of the death penalty have maintained that convicts resigned to execution may have committed their crimes for the sake of being executed, using the law as a means of committing suicide, wherefore the death penalty ought to be abolished: It may lead to crimes and suicides. This argument is unimpressive. According to it, high buildings ought to be abolished as well. They may serve a purpose, as does the death penalty, but also can be abused for suicide; and they may lead to crimes that would not be committed in their absence. Anyway, the idea that people commit crimes for the sake of execution is highly speculative. It seems much more likely that a convict who refuses to appeal his sentence does so because he does not wish to face the agony of waiting, or because he prefers death to a life in prison. It is even possible that he feels guilty enough about his crimes to agree with the sentence according to which he does not deserve to live. There is no serious evidence demonstrating that murders were committed for the sake of execution; and nearly all convicts do what they can to avoid it.

4. We are all sentenced to death—it is part of our life sentence. Unlike a prison sentence, which deprives one of a freedom one would otherwise keep, the death sentence does not deprive one of a life one would otherwise keep. We all die even without a legally imposed sentence. But without the death sentence, we live indefinitely, though not permanently. The death sentence orders execution at a date certain and, in many minds, makes death certain as though it otherwise could have been eluded. What the sentence actually does is to hasten it, to shorten life. But this shortening is feared. Since life is a good, one wishes to continue and prolong it. Death defeats

this wish. However, death also expunges the wish: The dead neither wish nor fear; nor do they suffer. They do not feel.* They do not miss life any more than the nonexistent or unborn do. Hence, it is hard to see how one can rationally fear *being* dead. One is afraid not of death but of dying, conflated with death and pictured as a painful process.

But execution is probably less physically painful than most natural ways of dying. Dying by disease is usually more painful and often more humiliating. Yet when execution is described in detail, one is moved to pity the condemned man. One is made to feel that without the death sentence, he somehow would have been spared dying. And descriptions of executions nearly always give the impression that the sordid, undignified, or moving details of dying are details of execution and would have been avoided if the condemned man had lived, or (if one remembers that he would not have lived forever) if he had died in a hospital rather than by execution. Yet hospital death would have been no more barren of pain or of undignified details. On the contrary. It is misleading, then, to picture the indignities of dying, or of death, as though indignities of execution. Execution is neither more painful nor more sordid than dying usually is.

Whatever can be said against the death penalty, it cannot be said that it causes an otherwise avoidable death, or that it must make death physically more painful or sordid or less dignified than it otherwise would be. However, there is an important psychological difference between being put to death by one's fellow men, as a punishment, and dying from natural causes. To this we will turn anon. And the death penalty is intended to hasten death. We as yet have to consider whether this can be justified as a punishment for any crime.

---

*The religious belief in an afterlife refers to an immortal soul that lives on. But the joys and pain of that soul are not produced in an earthly body and are not relevant to the discussion in the text.

CHAPTER 1

The Retributivist's Case against Capital Punishment

JOHN P. CONRAD

Imagine a society without rewards or punishments. Neither merit nor effort will be recognized. Honors will not go to the worthy. Emoluments will not be increased to encourage those who give more unstintingly or more wisely than others for the good of the community. Advance in an occupation will not depend on excellence or even on faithful service. Whatever a good citizen might deserve he will not get. If solidarity can be maintained at all, it will depend on general altruism and enlightened self-interest. There will be a sort of egalitarian quality of life, but it will be an egalitarianism without reason for hope. Better things to come cannot be expected by any member of this strange society.

No one will have anything to fear from the state, if in such a society a political organization could exist at all. Neither the denial of rewards nor the dread of punishment will enter into anyone's decisions about his conduct. Just as the good will have to find their reward in contemplation of their own goodness, the only punishment of the wicked will be a bad conscience and the memory of evil done. Whatever their transgressions against others might be, the consequences to the transgressors will be, at the most, the affliction of guilt and shame and, perhaps, the ostracism imposed by the virtuous.

Anthropologists report that there are societies like this. The forest pygmies of Central Africa manage happily and harmlessly in communities in which social organization is limited to the necessities of food-gathering and food-sharing. At a higher level of social organization, the Melanesians and the Polynesians of the Pacific islands seem to have relied mainly on the tabu to enforce custom. Solidarity was created through ceremony and magic and by the expulsion of those who violated the simple norms that tradition imposed. Eighteenth-century philosophers inferred from what little was then known of these societies that they were composed of noble savages who lived in a special state of grace. It was thought that the urgencies of civilization had destroyed the natural goodness of man. The simple needs of justice in the primitive tribe were stifled in procedures—so it was thought—when the complexities of civilization required a division of labor, an ever-increasing dependence on technology, and the creation of social, political, and religious hierarchies.

More rigorous anthropological studies have revealed the naïveté of these romantic inferences. Although human beings have lived and perhaps still do live in the societies so nostalgically described, no one has thought of a way for an industrial society to return to these primeval simplicities. There are many ways to account for the foundations of twentieth century society, but all of them provide for formal external controls sustained by rewards and punishments. In its ideal form, this system of controls calls for the fair and certain apportionment of benefits to those who deserve them and in accordance with the expectations that the system creates. At the same time, the system also depends on the expectation that those who violate its laws will be punished according to their desert.

The system does not function ideally, and never has. These are times when the hope of reward and the fear of punishment are uncertain and subject to human caprice and blind chance as well as to actual desert. Rewards go to people who deserve little or nothing from society, whereas many who deserve punishment are punished inappropriately or not at all.

Social control is sustained by establishing consequences for actions of significance to others. With the consequences awarded to effort and worth we are not concerned here, except to note that the solidarity of society depends on a symmetry between rewards and punishment. In capitalist society, most rewards are administered through the economy, whereas formal punishments are reserved to the state. The utopia in which everyone gets his just deserts, whether reward for merit or punishment for harm done, has always been far from realization. To those without a sense of history, this utopia seems more remote than ever, although any social historian must wonder why this impression seems to be so general.

In a society that depends on the administration of punishment for the maintenance of order, we must take this distasteful topic very seriously. Because of my sense of the importance of a rational and just sentencing system, I am an unabashed retributivist. Only after we are assured that justice has been done to the criminal and for society can we turn our attention to the traditional utilitarian objectives of intimidation, incapacitation, and reformation.

As a retributivist, I view punishment as the proper immediate consequence of the criminal act, a stage in the criminal justice process that winds its way from the crime itself through apprehension, arrest, arraignment, prosecution, conviction, and sentencing. Later in this chapter, I will argue that punishment must be administered in such a way that the criminal's reconciliation to the community is not impeded, but that is a step in our consideration of punishment for which I must set the stage with care.

In this sequential process of criminal justice may be found the justification of actions by the state that violate all the accepted precepts of behavior. For punishment must be the infliction of pain or humiliation or deprivation on a fellow human being. All the doctrines of religion and morality are clear that human beings must not harm one another, nor should they do to others what they would not have others do to them. Alone among our social institutions, the criminal justice system requires that these fundamental dictates be violated. No amount of rationalization of motives or appeal to noble objectives or repugnance for the criminal act can transform the deliberate infliction of harm upon an offender into a benign process.

How is it, then, that criminals may be subjected to harm of an extreme and protracted nature, including the penalty of death? Although there is a general belief that has persisted since the late eighteenth century that punishment must have an aim—that it is not enough merely to justify it—there is no clear evidence that in two centuries of trying, any society has succeeded in achieving any of the aims that have been expected of the punishments it imposes. In another chapter, I shall consider the failure of the criminal justice system to reach any of the goals that legal philosophers have set for it. Here, I am concerned only with retribution as the proper consequence of the conviction of a crime. The crime itself justifies the punishment, and the punishment has no other purpose than to be imposed as the legal consequence of guilt. This is the retributivist position on punishment, stated in its simplest form. It provides the advocate of capital punishment with the strongest support for his side of the argument—a support on which I will not elaborate lest I give aid and comfort to my resourceful antagonist.

More needs to be said about the stark simplicity of the retributivist's view of punishment. It is customary in the consideration of this topic to assign two approaches to the rationalization of punishment. Utilitarians would punish because they hope to prevent crime by the intimidation, incapacitation, or reform of the criminal, and by presenting his fate to the general public so that the like-minded may see what the consequences of a criminal act will be. Retributivists punish because the criminal is guilty.

Opposition between the utilitarian and the retributivist is fallacious. In his strict and logical consideration of the whole subject, the Danish jurist, Alf Ross, wrote:

> The traditional opposition of retribution and prevention . . . is meaningless because the opposing answers are not concerned with the same question. To maintain that punishment is imposed *in order to* prevent crime is to offer an answer to the question of the *aim of penal legislation*. To say that punishment is imposed *because* the criminal has incurred . . . guilt is to offer an answer to the question of the . . . *justification for imposing penalties.*[1] (Ross's italics)

This logic requires us to examine capital punishment from both standpoints, as retributivists and as utilitarians. This is the chapter for considering the retributivist position on capital punishment.

It is a position full of problems to make the social scientist uncomfortable. What is a criminologist to do with a theory that calls for no comparisons, no measurement of the achievement of objectives, no analysis of alternatives? Nothing in this approach to the treatment of criminals is susceptible to the scientific method that we consider central to our discipline. The justification of punishment can be discussed only on ethical grounds; there is no room for the empiricist in such a discourse. We are left with the imperative that the guilty must be punished. Actions must have consequences, but there is nothing in that principle to occasion an empirical test, nor are there rules whose effectiveness a criminologist might verify. If retribution is justified by the criminal act that preceded it, social science comes to an end in confronting this proposition. There is no measurement by which we can establish whether this simple equivalence is or is not a reasonable and proper justification.

But if the criminologist can be dismissed at this point, there is plenty of work for the moral philosopher. He must consider now why it is right that the guilty must be punished. What is this equivalence between the crime and the sanction and why should it be allowed to determine the nature and quality of criminal justice? On what principles can a scale of penalties proportionate to the crimes to be punished be constructed?

For Immanuel Kant, the answer lay in an uncharacteristically superficial discussion of the problem. He flatly held that punishment is a categorical imperative; the guilty criminal must be punished, and the moral order demands that the punishment be proportionate to the gravity of the offense.[2] That kind of argument is nothing more than the insistence that punishment is right and requires no justification other than the determination of guilt by a constituted authority. As Honderich points out, "it is pointless to argue in such a way that one's argument reduces to the assertion that something is right because it is right."[3]

Kant lived in an age when enlightenment had enthroned reason and Germany was emerging from an age of disorder. It was natural that even a great philosopher should resist ideas such as those of Beccaria (whom he dismissed as a sentimental humanitarian), which threatened the hard-won stability of Prussian society. Two centuries later we view the administration of justice in the light of a great deal of experience and see complications that had not been manifest from Kant's perspective in Koenigsberg.

So I began this discussion of the retributivist case against capital punishment by asking my readers to consider an imaginary community in which rewards and punishments were not administered. It follows from that example that the significance of punishment is in the establishment of a collective sense about right and wrong conduct. Punishment is right because we have thought of no other way to assure that wrong will be clearly defined. In the language of H. L. A. Hart:

> Criminal punishment . . . defers action till harm has been done; its primary operation consists simply in announcing certain standards of behavior and attaching penalties for deviation, making it less eligible, and then leaving individuals to choose. This is a method of social control which maximizes individual freedom within the coercive framework of law in a number of different ways. . . .[4]

That brings us closer to a justification of punishment than the mere assertion that right is right, but to me a more complete and satisfying justification was made by William Temple, the late Archbishop of Canterbury, in his remarkable lecture, *The Ethics of Penal Action.*

> It is, as I believe, the first moral duty of the community, or of the State on its behalf, to reassert the broken moral law against the offender who has broken it. For this reason, it must affirm his guilt and deal with him in accordance with it. . . . [I]t is the first point in the retributive theory of punishment that the penalty must be visited on the guilty party, and though it is very easy to exaggerate the proportion of individual to corporate responsibility, yet to deny individual responsibility is to deny personality. Retributive punishment, even in brutally vindictive forms, does at least treat its victims as persons and moral agents. . . . The moral approbation which we give to a penal action, when carefully distinguished from all satisfaction in it as an act of vengeance, is due . . . to its expression of the repudiation by the community of the crime. To forgive may be right; to condone (as the word is ordinarily understood) is always wrong. The first

duty of the State is to dissociate itself from the act of its own member; to do this it must act, not only upon, but against that member. . . . The community must exhibit no antagonism in its will against the will of the offending member. This is necessary for the preservation of its own character, on which the characters of its citizens largely depend.[5]

It is beyond the scope of this chapter, and certainly beyond my philosophical capabilities, to rehearse all of the retributivist justifications that have been advanced by contemporary moral philosophers. Whether or not one adopts a retributivist position (and this is the position that I will maintain throughout this debate), the retributivist justification cannot be ignored. The contemplation of unpunished crimes is disturbing, especially those crimes in which a victim has suffered death or a grievous injury. It is not possible for me to assert that my own disturbance over the great number of unpunished crimes that occur in this country during these troubled years is occasioned by the reflection that the great utilitarian objectives of intimidation, incapacitation, and reformation are not being attained by the scofflaws who keep out of the reach of criminal justice. My first reaction to this state of affairs is that society has not succeeded in repudiating the wrongs done by criminals. The moral order is eroded; the social bonds that make community life possible are loosened. The retributivist position as to criminal justice is all I need to justify punishment. Criminal acts must not be condoned, the criminal must be punished. Anything else that punishment can accomplish is an added benefit that is not required to support my position.

If only retributivist considerations are to be admitted to this discourse, what rules should apply in deciding the nature and degree of the punishment to be administered? Kant, who was a retributivist who did not bother with justifications for his categorical imperative (in spite of the complexity of his thought on other matters), insisted that the Roman *jus talionis,* the "law of retaliation," was the reference point at which to begin. That law goes back to the most ancient times. It calls for the infliction upon the wrongdoer of the same injury that he caused to his victim. Necessity required Kant to modify this principle; he called for thieves to become "slaves of the state, . . . either for a certain period of time or indefinitely, as the case may be."[6] For Kant, there could be no elasticity as to the punishment of murderers: "If . . . he has committed a murder, he must die. . . . [T]here is no substitute that will satisfy the requirements of legal justice. . . . There is no equality between the crime and the retribution unless the criminal is judicially condemned and put to death."[7]

Advocates of capital punishment will find Kant an unreliable patron. His invocation of the *jus talionis* as the foundation for the allocation of punishments was an uncharacteristic resort to an easy answer to a difficult question. The *lex talionis,* to use the proper term in Roman law, was the basis for early criminal legislation in nearly every society for which we have recorded history. At the point when it was adopted, the state took vengeance out of the hands of the victim or his kin and reserved it to its courts. In its original form it required the infliction on the criminal of the same wrong he caused the victim.

From the earliest years of the Roman Republic, the application of this principle caused serious difficulties. The Roman judiciary could apply fines for thefts, usually in multiples of the amount stolen. In personal injury cases, the victim was originally entitled to retaliation in kind—the pure *lex talionis*—but it was decided that he could instead accept a money compensation.[8] The law of delicts was contained in the eighth of the Twelve Tables of early Roman law. The tables have long since been shattered, but scholars have pieced them together and have a fair idea of what they contained. Under the Eighth Table, there were twenty-six crimes of which the state took notice. Each of the crimes is stated without definition but with a penalty prescribed in such form that later commentators suppose that Roman judges must have enjoyed wide discretion in imposing sanctions. The death penalty was liberally allowed. For example:

24. Whoever knowingly and maliciously kills a free man must be put to death. Let him who uses wicked enchantments, or makes or gives poisons, be deemed a parricide.
25. If a man kills his parent, veil his head, sew him up in a sack, and throw him into the river.
26. No one is to make disturbances at night in the city under pain of death.[9]

Many laws succeeded the Twelve Tables, but in commenting on them, Sir James Fitzjames Stephen observed that "the notion of extracting from the works of jurists a set of definite, well stated, and duly qualified principles, and arranging them in their natural order in a complete, coherent system does not seem to have presented itself. . . ."[10]

As the Roman criminal law was the basis for the Prussian criminal law that governed the society in which Kant lived, it was natural that he should use it as his point of reference in developing his principles of justice. He gave little consideration to its particulars or to the complexities and absurdities that would arise in their application. It was clear to him that the *lex talionis* supported the death penalty for murder. He preferred to make no exceptions: "even in sentences imposed on a number of criminals in a plot, the best equalizer before the bar of public legal justice is death."[11]

Kant wrote when it was acceptable for the state to enslave a convicted thief as an oarsman in the king's galleys, but the application of the *lex talionis* to the violent criminal called for much more than hard labor. Flogging, branding, mutilation, and torture were commonly inflicted. The scale was complete with the death penalty for murder and high treason. Of this list of sanctions, only the death penalty survives in civilized societies.

If we are to cling to the *lex talionis* as the basis for our system of punishment, there can be no doubt that the death penalty is the appropriate and indeed the only justifiable response to murder. Nothing becomes a premeditated killing so well as another premeditated killing. The law of retaliation, by which our ancestors from the most remote, prehistoric times set such great store, is satisfied, and those who think that retribution is necessarily the same as retaliation will also be satisfied.

Capital punishment is the last vestige of the law of retaliation. With rare exceptions, it is reserved for the crime of murder with malice aforethought. The long project of criminal justice reform that began with the reconsiderations of the law by Montesquieu, Beccaria, and Bentham may be seen, without undue simplification, as the creation of alternatives to the unworkable and unjust law of retaliation. No serious legal philosopher would now follow Kant in the notion that thieves should become slaves of the state for an indefinite period of time. It is hard to defend our capricious treatment of thieves under the present operation of the correctional apparatus, in which labor of any kind is the exception, but their punishment is far from the law of retaliation. Why, then, should retributive justice demand death as the penalty for murder?

So far as the law is concerned in nearly all the countries of Europe, with the exception of the Soviet Union and the insecure regimes that that nation has imposed on its satellites, that question has been clearly answered. Retributive justice does not require the death penalty to maintain its credibility. Fourteen of our fifty states have arrived at this same conclusion, many of them a long time ago. The puzzle is the persistence of thirty-six states and the federal government in including capital punishment on their list of sanctions, despite the enormous difficulties and great expense involved in its actual imposition.

When a capital case is docketed, the courts must begin a long chain of judicial operations that are hardly ever duplicated in other proceedings. Scrupulous care must be taken to assure that fairness is observed in every respect. Evidence must be collected not only to establish the defendant's guilt but also with respect to his legal sanity at the time of the offense and later at the time of the trial. If the verdict is guilty and the sentence is death, then months, and sometimes years must be spent in the automatic appellate review required in most states—all at great public expense. Even if the verdict and the sentence are upheld, appeals to the executive authority for commutation of sentence will occupy the attention of the public and those actors in the criminal justice system who must schedule and carry out the sentence.

If we are to impose the death penalty, would we have it any other way? The sordid spectacle of summary executions in contemporary Iran has revolted the most hardened Western sensibilities. But what safeguards against such unfairness and indecency can be removed when the issue is whether a man shall live or die? None of the traditional precautions of the common law and the constitution have been removed in any of the jurisdictions in which the death penalty still survives. Because of the risks of error, caprice, prejudice, and bigotry, the Supreme Court has required the installation of still more safeguards. Some may interpret this solicitude for the rights of defendants in murder cases as a failure of nerve. I ascribe it to the continuing primacy that we allot to the value of human life, even a life that was lived with vicious disregard for the lives of others.

It is a dilemma without a civilized resolution. Once a prosecutor demands the death penalty, a game begins that must be played for life or death. The values that retributive justice is intended to further are transformed. Victory is the objective, not justice, not retribution for wrong done. The prosecutor wins if he obtains sanction for the defendant's death; the defense wins if it can save the life of a wretched and often dangerous client. The crime itself sinks gradually into a sort of oblivion as the proceedings drag on. We are asked to consider instead the personality of the defendant, his social and emotional handicaps, the possibility that mitigating circumstances have been overlooked, and the question of his mental status. Psychiatrists are pitted against each other, each side exaggerating the significance of its appraisal of the mental condition of the defendant. All the while the chief aim of retributive justive, the repudiation of the wrong done by the criminal, is suppressed in the excitement of the game and its aftermath. In the end, most of our recent executions have been administered to men who insisted on death, thereby bringing to an end the lives in which they could see no future meaning. For them, a penalty worse than death before a firing squad or in an electric chair would be an unpredictably long term of years in prison. For society, can we claim a forthright repudiation?

A life in prison is a severe punishment, just as the men who choose execution as a form of suicide conclude. Manhood and vigor ebb, and years after the murder has been forgotten there may remain a living body sunk in senility. That is one outcome, and no sure way has been found to elude it, whether for murderers in prison cells or saints in convents. The years in prison contribute to apathy for some, but surely apathy is not the response that is appropriate to retributive justice, nor is the defiance implicit in the notion of paying a debt to society by suffering death in return for having caused the death of another. The response that the criminal should seek and that the state should encourage is atonement. For atonement for a wrong done to another is the foundation of the reconciliation between society and the offender that should conclude the long process of retributive justice.

For crimes much less grave than murder, some judges will impose a sentence that provides for unpaid public service rather than servitude, or for restitution to a victim, or for personal services to the victim when monetary restitution is not feasible. For first degree murder, retribution must be more severe or the danger will exist that the most serious of crimes will be seen as condoned by the court. But I have seen many murderers who have chosen service to others—as best they could with limited opportunities—as their way of expiating guilt for an offense, a guilt with which they must live for the rest of their lives. The most famous such case is that of Nathan Leopold, convicted of a crime of the utmost atrocity, who dedicated himself to the education of criminals and to research leading to their better understanding.[12] Less gifted murderers have chosen to make their lives as useful as possible to others—to fellow prisoners, to a larger society when they can. It is a path that they cannot follow when they must go to a scheduled death.

To some it may be surprising that a great clergyman like Archbishop Temple was uncompromising in his assignment of primacy to retribution in the administration of criminal justice. I am no theologian, and I cannot match the language of that great priest; I will quote again from his lecture on the *Ethics of Penal Action:*

> The essential element in . . . retributive punishment is . . . the assertion of the good will of the community against his evil will, whereby in one act it condemns the evil will and reminds him that the good will of the community is also his own, or at least that his duty and welfare consist in making it so. . . .
>
> But he is never only criminal and nothing else. And while the community is bound for his sake to treat him as a criminal if he is proved to be one, it is also under an equal obligation to treat him as a human being whose lapse into crime is no more than an incident even though it be the

chief incident in question. Unless a man is wholly identified with evil, which only God can know him to be, it must be immoral and unjust to treat him as if he were.[13]

The criminal who has many other traits as well as the criminal disposition that brought him to commit a terrible offense is also a man or a woman who is capable of change and will continue to change for the better or for the worse until the day of death. To curtail his life by a scheduled death is to presume a total identification with evil, a presumption that Archbishop Temple reserved to God and that a less religious man will still deny to men. In arrogating to the state the right to abridge life, the law denies to the criminal the right to those changes that are the consequences of remorse, introspection, or the desire for expiation. We are all the losers then. We all need to be reminded that whatever we have done for which we must accept guilt, we, too, are capable of veering toward the good.

As a theologian, Archbishop Temple laid down the principle that in the administration of retributive punishment men should not assume those prerogatives that must be reserved to God. As a criminologist and a moralist of less standing and authority, I hold that the execution of the most contemptible murderer conflicts with the true functions of retributive justice—the repudiation of evil done and the prospective reconciliation of the criminal with the community he has wronged. When punishment lapses into mere retaliation, the criminal's total criminality is affirmed; there can be no reason to expect reconciliation. When that retaliation takes the form of execution, the community makes it clear that it expects neither atonement nor reconciliation. The unreconciled criminal was our enemy; once he is executed he is still unreconciled, a dead enemy.

The scales of punishment that should compose the structure of retributive justice do not require retaliation, even at the apex where murderers must be punished. Capital punishment can be justified only by retaliatory justice as practiced in ancient Greece and Rome. For retributive justice, long imprisonment, sometimes life imprisonment, is the response that fits the continuity of punishments to which modern society is now committed.

By adhering to that limit on the punishment that is permitted to the state, reconciliation becomes the final phase of retributive justice. There should be no exceptions. When made, exceptions to retributive justice are always in the direction of retaliation toward an enemy, never toward retribution imposed on a fellow citizen who has offended the community and with whom the community hopes to be reconciled. The death penalty is an anachronism of which society must purge itself so that the process of retributive justice may contribute to order and solidarity rather than to the inflammation of hostility.

Notes

1. Alf Ross, *On Guilt, Responsibility and Punishment* (London: Stevens and Sons, 1975), p. 44.
2. Immanuel Kant, "The General Theory of Justice," in *The Metaphysical Elements of Justice,* trans. John Ladd (Indianapolis: Bobbs-Merrill, 1965), pp. 99–107.
3. Ted Honderich, *Punishment: The Supposed Justifications* (London: Hutchinson, 1969), p. 29.
4. H. L. A. Hart, *Punishment and Responsibility* (Oxford: Clarendon Press, 1968), p. 23.
5. William Temple, *The Ethics of Penal Action* (London: The Clarke Hall Lecture, 1934), pp. 28–30.
6. Kant, pp. 101–102.
7. Ibid., p. 102.
8. Barry Nicholas, *Introduction to Roman Law* (Oxford: Clarendon Press, 1962), p. 209.
9. Sir James Fitzjames Stephen, *A History of the Criminal Law of England,* vol. 1 (London: Macmillan, 1883), pp. 10–11.
10. Ibid, p. 50.
11. Kant, p. 104.
12. Nathan F. Leopold, *Life Plus 99 Years* (Garden City, New York: Doubleday, 1958).
13. Temple, pp. 31–32.

ERNEST VAN DEN HAAG

I cannot bring myself to regard retributionism as a theory of punishment, or of anything. Any factual "theory" must tell us something about what the world, or any part thereof, is like or has been or will be like. Or at the least, a theory must explain why any part of the world is, was, or will be, whatever the theory says it is, was, or will be. A theory must tell or explain something in ways that ultimately can be tested by experiment or by observation such that the theory is found to be correct or incorrect.

Retributionist "theory" does none of these things. It does tell us that people want retribution. But this psychological fact is not what is called "retributionism." "Retributionism" does not just describe this feeling but tells us that we should act on it by imposing specific punishments on people who "deserve" them. Nothing of the sort follows from the correct assertion that people feel vindictive. Retributionism turns out to be no more than a feeling articulated through a metaphor presented as though a theory. Retributionism is the problem (why should we punish?) pretending to be the solution (because we feel like it; because we want to retribute; punishment is deserved). Theories may or may not justify feelings. But feelings themselves justify no more than other feelings; they may be necessary to a justification, but never sufficient. Feelings, if we are to act on them, are what is to be justified, not the justification but, at best, the explanation of action.

All this does not make retribution wrong. Retributionists ask an interesting question: "What is the moral justification of punishment?" But their answer merely restates the question as an assertion: "Punishment is justified because (and when) deserved." Clearly retributionism cannot be right or wrong: It is a feeling and feelings just are. Unlike judgments or theories, they are neither right nor wrong. Conclusions may be. But the only thing retributionism offers as evidence for its conclusion is feeling.

In contrast, deterrence theory is, whether right or wrong, a theory: It asks what the effects are of punishment (does it reduce the crime rate?) and makes testable predictions (punishment reduces the crime rate compared to what it would be without the credible threat of punishment). The questions asked by retributionism (does it feel right?) and by deterrence theory (does it have the desired effects?) differ, as do the answers. The answers cannot be inconsistent with one another because they are concerned with different subjects. The moral question asked by retributionists demands a moral answer, the factual one a factual answer given by deterrence theories. Alf Ross is right in stressing as much, even though he might have been clearer.

To reiterate, retributionists ask what is morally deserved by criminals and answer: punishment. Deterrence theorists ask what will reduce crime rates and answer: credible threats of punishment.

Because it is not inconsistent with deterrence, and because "retributionism" is an expression of an emotion universally felt, and which all societies must gratify, its coexistence with deterrence theory is useful. Retributionism makes people accept the punishments needed to control the crime rate. Retributionism cannot be proved right. But things may be right even if they cannot be proved so scientifically. Whereas only what is true can be demonstrated scientifically to be true, it does not follow that only what can be demonstrated scientifically to be true is true. Science is concerned with demonstrable truths, not with all truth. Retributionism may be morally true even if, in the nature of the matter, moral truths cannot be demonstrated. It is certain, at any rate, that the law must to some extent gratify the retributionist sentiment, the desire to see crime punished—even if it were useless (as it is not) to do so. If the law did not punish criminals who harm others, the victims would want to do so. (This venerable argument is consequentialist; it is not a retributive argument, since it is independent of the moral issue.)

The desire to see crime punished is felt by noncriminals because they see that the criminal has pursued his interests or gratified his desires by means they, the noncriminals, have restrained themselves from using for the sake of the law and in fear of its punishments. If criminals could break the law with impunity, the self-restraint of noncriminals would have been in vain. They would have been fooled. Thus, the punishment of the criminal is needed to justify the restraint of the noncriminal. To put it another way, the offender, unlike the nonoffender, did not play by the legal rules and took advantage of those who did. He must be deprived of his illicit advantage if others are to continue to play by the rules. His advantage must be nullified in the minds of nonoffenders by the punishment the offender suffers. Punishment is at least psychologically restorative; it returns the advantage to those who play by the legal rules. This nonretributionist explanation of retributionist sentiment does not justify it. It does not warrant retributionism or make it unwarranted. The explanation is irrelevant to moral justification. It merely explains the genesis and the effects of retributionism.

Psychologically, the universal desire for retribution is not hard to explain, then, nor is the social need to gratify it from a consequentialist viewpoint. But contrary to Professor Conrad, retributionism, although it may tell us why we do punish, does not tell us why we *should* punish. It does not yield the moral argument it presumes to offer. Retributionism also tells us little about which penalties to apply, and nothing at all as to whether or not to impose the death penalty.

Let me consider now Professor Conrad's remarks in some detail. In a society without legal punishment, he tells us, "the only punishment of the wicked will be a bad conscience . . . the affliction of guilt and shame. . . ." I don't think a society without punishment could exist. But if it did, I doubt that "the wicked" would have a "bad conscience." Sir James Fitzjames Stephen discussed this matter. He wrote: "Some men, probably, abstain from murder because they fear that if they committed murder they would be hanged. Hundreds of thousands abstain from it because they regard it with horror. *One great reason why they regard it with horror is that murderers are hanged"* (italics added).*

Sir James points out that "one great reason" for horror (and obviously for guilt feelings and for having a bad conscience) is punishment. Something may be punished because felt to be in itself wicked *(malum in se),* but, as Sir James stresses, a crime also tends to be regarded as wicked because it has been punished since time immemorial, because it is a *malum prohibi-*

*J. F. Stephen, *A History of the Criminal Law in England* (London: Macmillan, 1863).

tum. At any rate, conscience is not likely to be very effective as a punitive agent unless there is the accepted custom of legal punishment. At the least, conscience is no more independent of law than law is of conscience. Professor Conrad's view that one can exist without the other seems doubtful to me.

I don't believe that social solidarity depends on "a symmetry between rewards and punishment." No historical evidence is offered, and I know of none, unless "symmetry" is so vaguely defined as to include whatever happened in any society. I am not sure that even the perception of "symmetry" is needed. The Hindus tolerated what we would regard as injustice—a caste system—thinking that people ultimately will be treated according to what they deserve through metempsychosis (transmigration of souls). They did not much object to lack of "symmetry" visible in this life. They expected "symmetry," as many religions did, to occur afterwards. There must indeed be some feeling of social justice—but it is quite elastic: Nazis thought Nazism just. At any rate, "social solidarity" was certainly present in Nazi society.

I can't see why Professor Conrad writes, "To those without a sense of history this utopia [where everybody gets what he deserves] seems more remote than ever." Was it ever nearer? When? And why must you lack "a sense of history" to believe that utopia "seems more remote than ever"? My sense of history tells me that utopia is always infinitely remote, being a fantasy. And why must the "social historian wonder why this impression seems to be so general"? Is it? Should it not be? When was the impression less general? Do those with a "sense of history" think differently and why? Are they right?

Conrad goes on: "Alone among our social institutions, the criminal justice system requires that these fundamental dictates [not to harm others] be violated." I know of no "fundamental dictate" opposed to punishment. We punish (inflict pain, deprivation, or humiliation) children or anyone thought guilty of wrongdoing. I know of no doctrine of "religion and morality" opposed to this practice or to punishing criminals. I think it would be unjust and immoral not to punish them—as well as counterproductive.

Surely Professor Conrad is wrong in asserting, as though there were a consensus, that "no amount of rationalization of motives or appeal to noble objectives or repugnance for the criminal act can transform the deliberate infliction [of punishment] into a benign process." I am not sure what is meant by "benign process," but I am quite willing to argue that the social effects of punishment are "benign," helpful, and salutory for society, just as painful surgery might be, even if here the benefit does not, or not mainly, go to the patient himself. Actually, the consequences of suffering punishment, for a child or for many adults, may well be benign. Religion, which thought of God as punishing the wicked (for rehabilitation in purgatory, and permanently in hell), certainly also taught that God is benevolent.

As for criminals, retributionists—and Conrad claims to be one—usually have thought punishment to be required for the sake of the criminals as much as for the sake of social morality. Utilitarians thought of punishment as a necessary evil imposed for the sake of the social good it is meant to produce. Not so retributionists. They have usually thought of punishment as good in itself. Immanuel Kant even thought that society has a moral obligation to impose punishment, including death, on criminals, an obligation above all to the criminal as a moral being (as a fellow human).* The criminal, Kant thought, must recognize rationally (if he were to draw up laws, would he permit murder, theft, or fraud?) the wrongness of his own acts, which demands the punishment deserved by him. Society has the duty to impose it. To deprive criminals of punishment, Kant implied, would deprive them of their right to be treated as rational and responsible human beings, entitled to what they deserve. Now, I don't agree with Kant. I am not a retributionist. But Professor Conrad is. He cannot, as a retributionist, approve punishment as deserved by guilt, and on the other hand deplore it as unbenign or, as I read him, as immoral.

Conrad regards as "superficial" Kant's view that punishment is demanded by the moral order as a "categorical imperative," that punishment cannot and need not be further justified. Yet Kant at least states clearly and simply what William Temple, whom Professor Conrad quotes with admiration, states in derivative and muddled form: that retributive punishment "treats its victims as . . . moral agents" and repudiates their crimes, so as to uphold the moral order. This is indeed what, according to Kant, legal punishment must do *inter alia*. But how Temple's justification of retributive punishment goes beyond the one Kant gave, rightly or wrongly, escapes me. Moreover, to say, as Temple does further, that punishment is socially useful, that it preserves the character of the community, is at best a utilitarian argument. A retributionist argument must justify punishment regardless of whether it is useful, and in this respect the archbishop is more verbose but not better than Kant.

Professor Conrad asserts, "The retributivist position . . . is all I need to justify punishment . . . the criminal must be punished." Conrad does not

*G. W. F. Hegel thought explicitly that the criminal had the right to be punished.

seem to realize that this is not the proof he wants but rather a statement of what is to be proved. But here he also betrays a profound misunderstanding in adding that the "utilitarian objectives are not being attained" (as though, if they were, it would make retributionism correct) . . . "because there are many who go unpunished." Insufficient punishment does not make punishment either wrong or useless. Moreover, in stating that they are not being attained, Professor Conrad mistakes the utilitarian objectives. The objective is not the impossible one of preventing all crimes or of preventing all persons from committing any by means of punishing all criminals but merely of deterring, by the credible threat of punishment, most persons from committing most crimes most of the time. They are deterred by the threat of punishment that is actually imposed on the few members of the criminal minority who are convicted. That objective is attained—most people most of the time do not commit crimes—though not as fully as may be, in part because punishment, including the death penalty, is imposed insufficiently, on too few persons, too late and too leniently.

Professor Conrad derives Kant's support of the retributive death penalty from the *lex talionis,* which, Conrad believes, influenced Prussian law under which Kant lived. But the *lex talionis* was very widely accepted as the preferred, though not the only, measure of retribution. Thus, in his 1779 *Bill for Proportioning Crimes and Punishments,* Thomas Jefferson, neither a Prussian nor a Kantian, wrote:

> Whosoever shall be guilty of rape, polygamy, sodomy with man or woman, shall be punished, if a man, by castration, if a woman by cutting through the cartilage of her nose a hole of one half inch in diameter at the least. [And] whosoever shall maim another, or shall disfigure him . . . shall be maimed, or disfigured in the like sort; or if that cannot be, for want of some part, than as nearly as may be, in some other part of at least equal value.

Professor Conrad is right: The *lex talionis* cannot be literally applied. Yet for a retributionist it remains a standard by which to measure punishment: Its severity should be proportioned to the seriousness of the crime, though its form may differ from the form of the crime, since we can't steal from burglars, rape rapists, or defraud those who commit fraud. Still, for some crimes we can do something of the kind. It is in the nature of the retributionist view to try. Thus, we may fine those whose crimes are pecuniary and execute those who murder. But the argument, retributive or not, for executing murderers—to be discussed anon—though it finds support in the *lex talionis,* does not rest on it.

I cannot give much weight to the argument suggested by Professor Conrad that, because many countries have abolished the death penalty, we too should abolish it. If many countries follow the Soviet lead and institute cruel concentration camps, should we follow? Should our national decisions follow international fashions, or should they be based on reasoning we accept, whether or not other nations do?

An equally doubtful argument against the death penalty is the cost of imposing it, which Professor Conrad stresses. This cost is not inherent in the penalty but is imposed by judges, who, for reasons of which later, tend to sabotage capital punishment. The cost could be reduced without in any way vitiating the ascertainment of guilt or innocence and the proper application of the laws. Moreover, contrary to Conrad's suggestion, it is not cheaper to keep a criminal confined for all or most of his life than to execute him. He will appeal just as much, causing as many costs as a convict under death sentence. Being alive and having nothing better to do, he will spend his time in prison conceiving of ever new *habeas corpus* petitions, which, being unlimited, in effect, cannot be rejected as *res judicata*. In all likelihood, the cost is higher. But I do not believe that cost, either way, should be a decisive argument here.

Professor Conrad also makes what seems to me a reasonable argument against the adversary system, or at least the length to which it has been pushed. But he neglects to tell why the argument applies specifically to capital trials and not to all criminal proceedings. More important, he does not offer any alternatives to the adversary system of our courts. The only alternative I know of is the continental European system of preliminary inquisitorial proceedings by a magistrate.* There is much to be said for (and against) either system—but why in a debate about the retributive justification of the death penalty?

Professor Conrad also assumes, somewhat gratuitously, that the convicted murderers who volunteered for the death penalty instead of life imprisonment must have thought life imprisonment worse. Perhaps. But why should it be impossible to believe, particularly for a retributionist such as Professor Conrad, that some convicts actually think that death is indeed worse than life in prison but that they deserve it for this very reason, because their crimes do?

Conrad believes that the criminal justice system should aim for atone-

---

*"Inquisitorial" here comes from *inquiry* and should not be confused with the ill-reputed "inquisition."

ment and for restitution. *Atonement* certainly is desirable from a religious, or even a moral, viewpoint, but I cannot see how the government can produce or ascertain it. I do not think atonement is a legal task. In the past, the attempt to produce it has led to cruelties that Professor Conrad deplores no less than I do. *Restitution,* on the other hand, is not punishment—it may compensate the victim, or society, for the harm done, but it does not, from the retributionist viewpoint, punish the doer. Unlike Professor Conrad, I cannot see how Nathan Leopold's educational activities were a punishment for the murder he committed, or a restoration. To return what you have taken is compensation, not punishment. And how do you return the life you have taken?

Professor Conrad concludes with a series of logically questionable assertions. He writes, "For retributive [as distinguished from retaliatory] justice, long imprisonment . . . is the response that fits the continuity of punishments to which modern society is now committed." Are we? Should we be? Why must we be committed to the "continuity of punishments"? Would it not make sense to mark off murder by a discontinuous punishment since it is unlike other crimes, such as fraud or burglary? Should we really treat murder as an aggravated form of pickpocketing? Why can other punishments be justified as retribution but not capital punishment?

"[With] execution, the community makes it clear that it expects neither atonement nor reconciliation." The community does not make it clear by execution that it expects "neither atonement nor reconciliation." Both may occur before execution and even be produced by the imminence of it. Neither is a reason to forgo it.

"In arrogating to the state the right to abridge life, the law denies to the criminal the right to . . . changes. . . ." The state's right to execute does indeed deny the criminal's "right to change," i.e., to live. He has forgone this right by denying it to his victim, and the law therefore denies it to him, just as it denies freedom to other criminals. Professor Conrad does not tell us why the law should not regard such rights as forfeited by crime.

"To curtail [the convict's] life . . . is to presume [his] total identification with evil, . . ." But from the retributionist standpoint, execution does not presume the "total identification" of the criminal "with evil." Execution merely presumes an identification sufficient to disregard what good qualities the convict has (he may be nice to animals and love his mother). If the crime is that serious, if it is a capital crime, other things become immaterial. No total identification with evil—whatever that means—is required; only a sufficiently wicked crime.

JOHN P. CONRAD

Theories come in many sizes and shapes, serving the advance of knowledge in many ways. Along with most writers on criminal justice, I have referred to retributivism as a theory of punishment. I will not retract that usage here. For whatever purpose a theory is formulated and however complex its structure may be, it must share with all other theories the purpose of explanation. By that definition, retributivism is a theory. I expect to show in this rejoinder that it is a more complicated theory than Dr. van den Haag seems to believe.

There are many ways to articulate the theory; the object is to explain why we punish. The shortest possible answer is that given by Anthony Quinton in his essay "On Punishment."[1] Quinton emphasizes that the retributivist position is logical—*not* moral—and goes on to argue that punishment is entailed by guilt. If an offender is found guilty of a crime, he is to be punished.

The truth of this proposition is not self-evident to me. I need reasons to uphold it, not a merely verbal symmetry. Therefore, I will add four complications to this assertion, hoping that it will become more explanatory,

First, I follow the great French sociologist Emile Durkheim in the view that the solidarity of society requires that criminal acts must be repudiated.[2] If no consequences are attached to a verdict of guilt, then the criminal act has been condoned and solidarity has been impaired. The regular condonation of crime will end in the disintegration of standards of conduct. I think it is evident that this process is at work in some of our principal cities, where the volume of crime has overwhelmed the criminal justice system. Crime is condoned when serious charges must be bargained down to fictitious and less serious charges so as to relieve a court docket, or where a district attorney must plead *nolle prosequi* because the police have been unable to complete an investigation that would make a successful prosecution possible. To my knowledge, no one has done a rigorous analysis of the consequences of these lapses of justice, but they certainly do not contribute to the general effectiveness of the system.

I grant that this emphasis on the consequences of law violation verges on utilitarian doctrine. No matter. To denounce criminal acts, as Durkheim required, is also to deter them. I will assign precedence to denunciation because I believe that the solidarity of the community on the criminal nature of certain acts is the first priority of justice. Others, including my opponent, will disagree. I will defer until another chapter my reservations about the utilitarian objectives of intimidation, incapacitation, reformation, and deterrence, but I will readily grant that if the criminal law deters, it will certainly denounce in the same breath.

The second complication is consequentialism. Professor van den Haag complains that it is not a retributive argument since it is independent of the moral issue. This objection is obscure to me, expecially if the logical nature of the retributive position is allowed. But consequentialism is essential to my argument on retributivism, and I will not readily yield on its salience. Any stable society must rely on the distribution of incentives for conformity and achievement and of punishments for those who choose not to comply with the laws. If social values must be supported by consequences for compliance and noncompliance, then retribution for crime must be a part—but only a part—of a larger system of social justice. Retribution is not merely what the people want—and want in every known society—but it is an essential support to the values of any society.

The third complication to the theory of retributivism has to do with the status of the offender. The retributivist assumes that the offender was able to choose between right and wrong if he is in a mental condition fit to stand trial. He is a moral agent, a full partaker in the human condition. He is not sick, he is not irresponsible, he is not an object of reform unless he chooses reform himself. Retributivism affirms the full humanity of the offender, except, of course, in the case of children and insane persons, whose responsibility for their offenses is "diminished."

The fourth consideration is that retributivism requires that the offender shall not benefit from his crime. By sufficient punitive action, the criminal justice system assures that whatever advantage the criminal gained or hoped to gain is nullified by the punishment.

My opponent may dismiss retributivism as a theory in good standing if he chooses. I argue that the universality of punishment cannot be accounted for without this theoretical approach. I grant that it is hard to think of methods for the empirical refinement of this theory. Indeed, this theory probably falls into the class of truths that are true even though—as my antagonist correctly points out—they cannot be scientifically demonstrated.

So far, retributivism is a logical system of thought, entailing no moral justification at all. We punish because the offender has been found guilty of a crime, and we justify the punitive act by the need for a system of consequences if society is to maintain its solidarity.

But once we have established the priority of the retributivist position over all other considerations, we are led straight into the thorny ethical problems with which we are concerned in this debate. If it is permissible for the state to inflict harm on citizens for the reasons I have outlined, what limits must be imposed on the harm that will be done in the name of punishment? All states punish people whom they identify as criminals. All states concede that a rule of law must limit the kinds of punishment that can be allowed, even though it is well known that many states do not and will not observe their own rules. But what rules shall be imposed?

Kant began with the rule of proportionality, relying on the *lex talionis*. He recognized that the ancient Roman law might be a satisfactory justification of capital punishment for murder, but that there would be great difficulties in carrying this principle further. He stressed that "the death of the criminal must be kept entirely free of any maltreatment that would make an abomination of the humanity residing in the person suffering it."[3] He also conceded that many crimes do not allow the simple reciprocation he saw between murder and capital punishment. Neo-Kantians have found ways of reconciling crimes to a system of punishment. Among them, Jeffrie Murphy points out that Kant's reliance on the *lex talionis* leads to the concept of proportionality in the administration of justice—in effect, the rule that underlies all modern penal legislation.[4]

This principle is nothing more than the idea that the punishment must fit the crime. On a scale on which murder is the most serious of crimes, a ranking can be worked out by the legislator by which punishments for lesser crimes can be scaled to lesser penalties. I suspect that Kant would be shocked by this derivation and might disown neo-Kantians on this score alone. Nevertheless, there is nothing in the rule of proportionality that requires that murder must be punishable by death. All that proportionality requires is that murder must be punished with the maximum severity on the scale of punishments. Strict adherence to the *lex talionis* was not practical even for the early Romans; it was ridiculed by Hegel.[5]

Professor van den Haag has challenged me specifically on several scores in his rebuttal. Some of these challenges are better suited for debate on the issues of deterrence, and I will reserve discussion on them until that chapter. As to some others, I have nothing to add to my original argument. But I have chosen twelve objections for further discourse in the interest of clarification and reinforcement of my basic argument. I now proceed to these objections, taking them in the order in which they appear in my opponent's rejoinder.

Can Conscience Exist without Law? This point is not essential to my argument, but it deserves an answer. The universality of guilt and shame in cultures at every stage of development suggests that beyond the law there is a morality that does not depend on formal legislation. Morality emerges from the interactions within a society. Because of the shifts in the nature and quality of those interactions there are changes in the emphases of morality. Readers of Homer, of the Greek tragedies, or of the Aeneid will constantly hear the warnings of conscience and the pains of its violation, but there is nothing about the law. In our own time, the law says nothing about lying or betrayal among families or friends, but those who deceive must answer to their consciences. Throughout history, murder has always been murder. The murderers I have known have had to neutralize their consciences, not because of the law but because of guilt or shame or both. I have always been impressed with Kant's aphorism: "Two things fill the mind with ever new and increasing wonder and awe . . . the starry heavens above me and moral law within me."[6] We may account for the moral law in many ways, but we are answerable to it independently of the formal laws enacted by legislatures. If this were not so, our social order would be even more precarious than it is now.

The Symmetry between Rewards and Punishments. I do not claim an exact or even an approximate symmetry between rewards and punishments in this or any other society. I do argue that the quality of social justice depends on a rough symmetry between the distribution of rewards and punishments. Social stability declines with the uneven distribution of gains and losses to individual citizens.

On the Infliction of Harm. There is no fundamental dictate opposed to punishment. But one of the universals common to all religions is the principle that we should do to others as we would have others do to us. Not even the secularism of our times has eroded the Golden Rule. We have to reconcile punishment with this dictate; those who wish to justify the penal law cannot escape this task. We may inflict harm as a means of denouncing violations of the law, but in doing so we have to set careful limits on the harm we may inflict. These limits depend on principles toward which we must find our way, as I have been trying to do.

The limits of punishment also depend on the collective tolerance of the official infliction of harm. On this point, Durkheim is instructive. In his article *Two Laws of Penal Evolution,* he proposed that any perspective on the history of the criminal law led to two conclusions: (a) The number of severe punishments "is greater insofar as societies belong to a less advanced type— insofar as the central power has a more absolute character." (b) "Deprivation of liberty and of liberty alone, for periods of time varying according to the gravity of the crime, tends increasingly to become the normal type of repression."[7]

Both these "laws" seem to me to be obviously tenable. We have only to look at the use of punishment in the Soviet Union and consider the absolute character of its central power for confirmation of (a). As to (b), consider the 208 offenses for which the penalty of death could be administered in early nineteenth century England, compared with the complete elimination of capital punishment in that nation today.

Durkheim had an explanation for these propositions:

> That which tempers the collective anger which is the soul of punishment is the sympathy we feel for every man who suffers, the horror which all destructive violence produces in us. . . . The same mental state drives us to punish and to moderate the punishment. . . . [T]here is a real and irremediable contradiction in avenging the human dignity offended in the person of the victim by violating it in the person of the criminal. The only way, not of removing the antimony (for it is strictly insoluble), but of alleviating it, is to alleviate the punishment as much as possible.[8]

Prisons are kept out of sight so far as possible, and executions, once public occasions, are now private affairs, limited to the necessary participants. Whether everybody wishes to alleviate punishment in contemporary America is doubtful at best, but the vitality of prison reform movements and the drive to abolish capital punishment testifies to the existence of the "real and irremediable contradiction" in the minds of a large number of American citizens.

Can Punishment Be Benign? In the sense proposed by Hegel and implied by Kant, a criminal has a right to be punished. That right (one that few criminals wish to invoke) is that of the human being who is treated as a moral agent, a person who chooses between right and wrong because he is capable of choice—as compared with a child or an insane person, who is not. If the preservation of that right in the retributivist imposition of punishment is benign, I suppose punishment might be considered to be benign—though I have known few, if any, criminals who sense this benignity. For nearly all criminals of my acquaintance, imprisonment is an experience to be survived without expectation of palpable benefits.

For society, of course, punishment is—or should be—a benign process. I will concur with Professor van den Haag that the retributivist position must concede its benignity. In short, punishment is necessarily adverse to the interests of the criminal himself (except as to the technical observance of his right to be punished), but it is necessarily benign to society.

In Defense of Archbishop Temple. I thought the archbishop was admirably clear in comparison with Kant's diffuse and rambling statements in the *Metaphysics of Justice.* If Dr. van den Haag thought his ideas were muddled or derivative, he did not identify the muddle or tell us from whom Temple's ideas were derived. I detect a close resemblance to the retributivist arguments of Emile Durkheim, to whom I have already alluded at length. For me, and I think for most readers, Temple's lucid prose is more easily digestible than the turgid analyses of Durkheim.

So far as I can make out from my reading of Kant and Hegel on these subjects, their retributive theories are based on the idea that punishment "negates" the criminal's "negation of the law." Temple's refinement is much more rewarding: The state repudiates the criminal act by punishing the criminal. The criminal may be forgiven, but his action cannot be condoned. When punishment does not follow the crime, the crime is implicitly condoned. Temple was not the first to make this assertion, I suppose, but he made it well and lucidly.

The Failure to Attain the Utilitarian Objectives. Much more will be said about the utilitarian theories in our chapters on that subject. Here I will limit myself to repeating that these objectives are certainly not being attained with evident impact on the crime rates. That does not mean that the effort is futile. It does mean that the criminal justice system is not as effective as the general public expects it to be. Probably that level of effectiveness could not be attained by any increase in the system's efficiency. I repeat, what disturbs me more than the apparent inefficiency of the system is that by not repudiating crime, we seem to condone it.

On the Adversarial System. It is ominous that the adversarial system is being stealthily eroded by the necessities of plea bargaining and other negotiations. The classic adversarial confrontation now takes place most prominently in murder trials in which the life of the defendant is at stake. It is not the economic cost of such trials that is their most objectionable feature—though in this country these costs have risen to disgraceful absurdity—but the protracted game that's played for the media and the entertainment of the public. Serious consideration of the crime and the appropriate disposition of the criminal is obscured by the tactics of the opposing litigants.

Far from wishing to do away with the adversary system (for which I cannot see a bright future), I would strip it of its present excrescences, emulating the English courts, where the same principles govern but the abuses so characteristic of our trials are generally avoided. I do not deny that justice can be done under the inquisitorial system of the continental law, but I do not see how that system can be successfully transplanted to countries committed to the Anglo-Saxon common law.

On the Comparison between Death and a Life in Prison. It is not impossible for me to believe that some criminals think that they deserve the death penalty, even though they consider it worse than a life in prison. This point of view has been expressed to me by several condemned men, and I have believed them. Exceptional cases. By far the greater number of murderers of my acquaintance have eagerly accepted a commutation to a life in prison when it was offered to them. Whatever they thought they deserved, they rejected the necessity of the death penalty in their cases.

On Atonement. No, atonement is not a legal task, nor can the government compel it. If the criminal lives—as in the cases of Nathan Leopold and a good many others—he may atone—or make amends—by the quality of his life and his contributions to the general welfare. In the case of the murderer, that is all he can do; he cannot restore the life he has taken. But by his atonement, a murderer can demonstrate to us that wickedness is not necessarily an irremovable condition. If those who have committed the worst of crimes can atone, there is hope that the rest of us, whose shortcomings are less conspicuous, may also change our lives for the better.

The Continuity of Punishments. This continuity is a reality that has existed for a long time in the United States. Only a small minority of convicted murderers make their way to the condemned rows of our prisons, and many of them ultimately escape the gallows, the electric chair, the gas chamber, or—now, God save us!—the lethal hypodermic. The death penalty is already an exception to our commitment to the continuity of incarceration. It is an exception that depends too often on caprice, prejudice, and incompetent counsel. By establishing a "continuity of punishments" with a life term in prison at the apex, we can rule out the injustices that capital punishment makes possible and irrevocable, without in any way diminishing the denunciation of the crime as required by the retributivist.

The Denial of Atonement and Reconciliation. Professor van den Haag supposes that while awaiting execution the criminal can atone and reconcile himself to his fate, if not to society. In a spiritual sense, I agree, this is possible. Reconciliation and atonement under these circumstances must be very private, experiences that are known only to the convict himself and to his pastoral guide. It should be apparent from my essay that I do not mean atonement and reconciliation in this unworldly sense.

The Presumption of Evil. A "total identification with evil" is an irremediable condition. Archbishop Temple was unwilling to allow that it is given to human judgment to make that identification. Only God can say who is irreversibly evil. That is a matter of theology, and as one who is not learned in that discipline, I cannot say how general would be the agreement among theologians on this point. But as a criminologist, I think the point is well taken even when transposed from the theological context. The whole enterprise of criminology must be based on the optimistic assumption that all of us, even the most vicious, can be improved. If we deny that assumption as to a few whose actions have especially horrified us, we call into question its applicability to everyone else.

Retributivist thought has gone far from the Twelve Tables of republican Rome and the stringencies of Leviticus. It has refined its arguments beyond the positions of the redoubtable Kant and Hegel. A truly retributivist system of justice needs no executioners. On the contrary, justice is disfigured by the barbarous actions that are committed in its name.

Notes

1. Anthony M. Quinton, "On Punishment," in *The Philosophy of Punishment,* ed. H. B. Acton (London: Macmillan, 1969), pp. 55–64.
2. Emile Durkheim, *The Division of Labor in Society,* trans. George Simpson (New York: The Free Press, 1933), pp. 85–96.
3. Immanuel Kant, *The Metaphysical Elements of Justice,* trans. John Ladd (Indianapolis: Bobbs–Merrill, 1965), p. 102.
4. Jeffrie G. Murphy, *Retribution, Justice, and Therapy* (Dordrecht, Holland: D. Reidel Publishing Company, 1979), pp. 232–233.
5. Georg Wilhelm Friedrich Hegel, *The Philosophy of Right,* trans. T. M. Knox (Oxford: Oxford University Press, 1942) p. 72. "It is easy enough . . . to exhibit the retributive character of punishment as an absurdity (theft for theft, robbery for robbery, an eye for an eye, a tooth for a tooth, and then you can go on to suppose that the criminal has only one eye or no teeth). But the concept (of retributivism) has nothing to do with this absurdity, for which . . . the introduction of this specific equality is solely to blame."
6. Immanuel Kant, *Critique of Practical Reason,* trans. Lewis White Beck (Indianapolis: Bobbs–Merrill, 1956), p. 166.
7. Quoted in Steven Lukes, *Emile Durkheim; His Life and Work* (London: Allen Lane The Penguin Press, 1973), pp. 258–259.
8. Ibid., p. 261.

ERNEST VAN DEN HAAG

Conrad correctly, but all too indirectly, implies that Anthony Quinton does not provide a theory of punishment but merely indicates that we use the word *punishment* so as to be entailed by the word *guilt.* Interesting, but not helpful in justifying retributionism or anything else.

Conrad is correct in paraphrasing Emile Durkheim, who suggests that punishment is required to maintain social solidarity, which would be eroded if laws were not enforced by punishing violators. But this, as Conrad half admits, has nothing to do with the retributionist theory of which he declared himself to be an adherent. Durkheim showed that punishment is socially useful, not, as retributionists must, that it is morally required. As does Conrad, I agree with Durkheim. But Conrad should realize that from a retributionist viewpoint Durkheim's argument is not relevant. No consequence is relevant to the morality of punishment when morality is conceived to be independent of consequences including usefulness. It is so conceived by retributionists. They think of punishment as a moral requirement, not as a useful device for reducing the crime rate. At the least, they think the need for punishment is independent of its usefulness.

Conrad goes on to explain that although he is a retributionist, he also favors looking at the consequences of punishment, as utilitarians do. This reminds me of a friend of mine, a fervent atheist, who would casually add, "I also believe in God, of course." Well, "a foolish consistency is the hobgoblin of little minds," as Ralph Waldo Emerson put it.* Professor Conrad is not guilty, being neither foolish nor consistent.

I agree with Conrad's views on the responsibility of offenders, on the need to support the values of society, on denying offenders the advantage they hope to gain from their crimes. These views are shared by deterrence and retributionist theories. Unless would-be offenders are responsible—unless they are able to restrain themselves—they could not be deterred; the law exists only to support society's values; if offenders gain from their crimes, would-be offenders will not be deterred. Conrad is right also in arguing that proportionality does not require the death penalty, or, for that matter, any particular penalty. It requires only that penalties be proportional to one another. Proportionality to crimes—unless interpreted as proportionality to other punishments—is meaningless. How can X days in jail be proportional to burglary? The reasons for the death penalty, or any other specific penalty, cannot then be logically derived from proportionality, which is required by both deterrence and retributionist theories. Yet proportionality certainly suggests a need for the death penalty: If we impose life imprisonment for crimes other than murder, does not proportionality suggest a more severe punishment for murder? And what could it be?

I do not think it fruitful to attempt to refute the 12 points Professor Conrad makes. I agree with some and not with others. However, there is

*Ralph Waldo Emerson, "Self-Reliance," 1841.

one point I do not want to leave unchallenged. Conrad states, "The whole enterprise of criminology must be based on the optimistic assumption that all of us, even the most vicious, can be improved." I fail to see why. Criminology is interested in understanding crime and in controlling crime rates. The "improvement" of offenders is, at best, marginal to these tasks. Even if successful, it won't make much difference.*

The assumption that we can improve everybody is not based on evidence. It is a religious assumption at best, based on faith, not a scientific one. (Even the Christian religion, however, does not believe in the infinite perfectability of man. It only urges efforts.) I admire, even envy, Professor Conrad's optimism; but personal temperament must not be confused with scientific theory. The evidence I am aware of indicates that some (rather few) offenders can be improved and others not, just as some people can be cured of disease and others are not helped even by the best medical treatment. Criminology assumes only that crime can be studied and that the results can be applied so as to control it. Rehabilitation is certainly not the most effective way of doing so. Rehabilitationist theories may assume that everybody can be improved, but criminology does not. I think that Professor Conrad confused one with the other.

JOHN P. CONRAD

There comes a point in the debate of any issue when further argument will advance the cause insufficiently to warrant the effort. That may be true with respect to the Retributivist's Case Against Capital Punishment. The main contentions have been laid out, and Professor van den Haag has ably responded. Nevertheless, there are too many loose ends left in his notes. I cannot allow them to dangle.

Thomas Jefferson and the *Lex Talionis*†

Was our third president, the framer of the Declaration of Independence, a believer in the *lex talionis?* No Jeffersonian scholar myself, I have always venerated his memory. I believe that he deserved his reputation as a wise, courageous, and humane statesman, and that he was—and is—one of

---

*See my "Could Successful Rehabilitation Reduce the Crime Rate?" *Journal of Criminal Law and Criminology* (Fall 1982).
†See Ernest van den Haag, p. 33.

the most powerful influences ever exercised by any one man on American political and cultural life. How could he have supported the *lex talionis,* so thoroughly discredited by the philosophers of the French Enlightenment whom he had admired and followed? How could he have submitted to the Virginia House of Delegates a measure that called for castration and mutilation?

Professor van den Haag discovered the Jefferson excerpt in Walter Kaufmann's *Without Guilt and Justice,* a passionately argued and visionary denunciation of the very concept of justice. Kaufmann held that without justice the world could be changed into a utopia in which all human beings would be autonomous. At one point he allows that the state must take action to deter crime, but he cannot bring himself to say what that action should be.

Kaufmann was a scholar who was justly renowned for his translations and commentaries on Hegel and Nietzsche. Without his contributions, many American readers, including myself, would have found these formidable Germans quite inaccessible. His treatment of Jefferson is a shameful lapse into the distortion of an easily reviewed historical record. To set this matter straight is an obligation to the memory of one of the greatest Americans and at the same time an example of one of the most persistent obstacles to criminal justice reform.

Far from being a zealot for retaliation, Jefferson was fully persuaded by the humane arguments of Beccaria and wished to incorporate their spirit into Virginia law. The ugly excerpt from his Bill for Proportioning Crimes and Punishments was a concession to the times and to his colleagues who had undertaken with him the task of revising the laws of Virginia. In 1779 the Virginia House of Delegates, no longer subordinate to the English crown, wished to discard the burdensome accumulation of English statutes and start afresh. Jefferson, then a member of the House of Delegates, moved for the appointment of a committee to draft the revisions; the motion carried, and, of course, Jefferson was appointed, with four others, to take on this immense task.

It is instructive to read Jefferson's own account of the "Revisors'" work on the topic of concern to us:

> On the subject of the Criminal law, all were agreed, that the punishment of death should be abolished, except for treason and murder; and that, for other felonies, should be substituted hard labor in the public works, and in some cases the *Lex talionis.* How this last revolting principle came to obtain our approbation, I do not remember. There remained, indeed, in our laws, a vestige of it in a single case of a slave; it was the English law, in the time of the Anglo-Saxons, copied probably from the Hebrew law of "an eye

for an eye, a tooth for a tooth," and it was the law of several ancient people; but the modern mind had left it far in the rear of its advances.[1]

That was written forty-two years later, when all the events of an exceptionally busy life were no longer clear in his memory. But in his commentary on the bill for the benefit of his fellow revisors at the time of its drafting, Jefferson referred to capital punishment as the "last melancholy resource against those whose existence is become inconsistent with the safety of their fellow citizens." His definitive biographer, Dumas Malone, observed that Jefferson "believed the experience of all ages and countries had shown that cruel and sanguinary laws defeated their own purpose."[2] Commenting further on Jefferson's inability to recall why he had allowed the *lex talionis* to seep into his bill, Malone noted that contemporary records "show that it was partly because of his own policy of going back to simple ancient precedents and partly because of the judgment of his fellow revisors."[3] Jefferson wrote to one revisor, George Wythe, as follows: "I have strictly observed the scale of punishments settled by the Committee, without being entirely satisfied with it. The *lex talionis,* altho' a restitution of the Common law to the simplicity of which we have generally found it so advantageous to return will be revolting to the humanised feelings of modern times. . . . This needs reconsideration."[4]

Whether it was further considered or not, the revolting section appeared in the bill submitted to the legislature. The bill was narrowly defeated, not because traces of the *lex talionis* had survived, but rather because its replacement was not thought sufficiently severe. The vote was taken in 1786, when Jefferson was in France. James Madison sent him the unwelcome news, adding that "our old bloody code is by this event fully restored."[5]

Commenting on this failure, Jefferson wrote in his *Autobiography:*

Beccaria, and other writers on crimes and punishments, had satisfied the reasonable world of the unrightfulness and inefficacy of the punishment of crimes by death; and hard labor on roads, canals and other public works, had been suggested as a proper substitute. The Revisors had adopted these opinions; but the general idea of our country had not yet advanced to that point. The bill, therefore, for proportioning crimes and punishments was lost in the House of Delegates by a majority of a single vote. I learned, afterwards, that the substitute of hard labor in public, was tried (I believe it was in Pennsylvania) without success. Exhibited as a public spectacle, with shaved heads and mean clothing, working on the high roads produced in the criminals such a prostration of character, such an abandonment of self-respect, as, instead of reforming, plunged them into the most desparate and hardened depravity of morals and character.[6]

Rather than stand as an implacable advocate of the ancient law of retaliation, Jefferson was determined to moderate the terrible excesses of eighteenth century English law. A political realist as well as a philosopher, he pushed moderation to the contemporary limit of public acceptance. He committed himself to the novel principle of a scale of punishments proportioned to the gravity of the offense. It was a principle for which the people of Virginia were not yet ready. Ten years after the House of Delegates rejected Jefferson's bill, the state built its first prison, and the death penalty was eliminated for all crimes other than murder and treason.

Kaufmann's misunderstanding of American history is tangential to the major issues of our debate. I have summarized the real story of this episode in Jefferson's great career to rectify a wrong done to his reputation (unwittingly, I hope) by an eminent philosopher. This historical note illustrates the gap that stretched between an ugly tradition and the vision of a more rational, more compassionate future. That gap still exists.

Durkheim and the Moral Foundation of Retributivism

A retributivist requires that the criminal act be denounced and that the form of the denunciation be appropriately punitive. As a moralist, I hold that moral choices are not made in isolation. Moral conduct consists of the interactions of human beings with each other. It is vital that social solidarity, which Durkheim saw as the principal benefit of punishment, should firmly support the moral and the good and reject the immoral and the wicked. Morality is the active choice of the virtues and the rejection of wrongdoing.

As a retributivist, I hold that all men and women are moral agents. They are ends in themselves, never to be used as the means to the ends of the state or of other persons. A moral agent is a person capable of choosing courses of action with due reference to the distinctions between right and wrong. Justice is served to the extent that the distribution of rewards and punishments supports those principles. Dr. van den Haag's citation of the Indian caste system as an example to the contrary is surely off the target; the lower castes consist of people under the most contemptible kind of coercion who have historically had no choice but submission.

Distributive justice will never approach perfection, nor is it possible that rewards and penalties will ever be gauged by merit and demerit alone. We can only try. In a world that can never be perfected but that can be improved, perseverance in the direction of justice is critical to the survival of order.

I am steadfast in support of proportionality in the administration of penalties. Serious deviations from that principle erode solidarity in support of criminal justice. If there is a sense that burglary and larceny are about equally serious, but that robbery with a handgun is much more serious, then the scale of penalties should reflect that consensus; I do not think that proportionality can be more precisely prescribed. If there is an impression of caprice in the administration of the system, if it is seen to be unpredictable or influenced by prejudice, or if serious crimes are leniently punished, then the system is in poor working order and its value in support of morality is impaired. In this sense, the justification of punishment offered by Durkheim is fundamental to the continuing maintenance of a moral society. Nothing in that justification entails the infliction of death on criminals.

Criminology and Optimism

Professor van den Haag stultifies criminology when he restricts it to "understanding crime and . . . controlling crime rates." This view is characteristically conservative in all considerations of the social sciences. It assumes that nothing can be done about a problem except to endure it. On that perception, all that we need to know about crime are its rates of incidence and prevalence. Annual crime rates must be computed so that the workloads of the police, the courts, and the prisons can be projected.

I am not so sanguine as to suppose that the "solution" to the crime problem will be its eradication. Nevertheless, I am sure that the social sciences can contribute much to its diminution. The history of the Western nations over the last two centuries demonstrates that with the spread of social justice, the improved understanding of human nature and social organization, and the fair administration of reasonable laws, a society changes for the better as time goes on, and so do the people who compose that society. Criminology is a policy science, a hybrid mixture of disciplines. The purposes of understanding crime proceed from the hopeful assumptions that something can be done to prevent crime more effectively and to reconcile criminals to the social order in which we must all live together. If these assumptions are untenable, as I fear Dr. van den Haag is inclined to believe, then the study of crime is a sterile occupation, of interest only to budget officers, personnel directors, systems analysts, and those who must run the system from month to month and year to year.

Finally, I must reject the imputation that my opponent conveys with respect to my views about the rehabilitation of criminals. As these programs are now administered in prisons and elsewhere, they are not specific remedies for criminality but at best opportunities for self-improvement for those who wish to take advantage of them. Hope is the essential condition for the reconciliation of the criminal with the society he has offended. It is for the prison to provide the basis for hope—not enforced "rehabilitation."[7] There is plenty of work for scientific criminology to do in improving the settings in which crimes are committed and in encouraging the reintegration of offenders without further engagement in bogus research to find magic cures for criminality.

The Invocation of Sir James Fitzjames Stephen, Bart., K.C.S.I.

It is not surprising that Dr. van den Haag summons Sir James Fitzjames Stephen (1829–1894) in support of his contention that hanging causes people to abstain from murder. Until my opponent arrived on the scene, Sir James was by far the doughtiest advocate of capital punishment. Some account of him and his ideas will shed light on the conceptual course of one line of support for the death penalty.

Stephen was an upper-middle-class Englishman with a conventional education at Eton, Cambridge, and the Inns of Court. He was almost an archetype of the small group of confident and commanding men who made the British Empire possible and brought it to the height of its power. An intimidating barrister, an indefatigable civil servant, a severe and immensely learned judge, a prolific and articulate writer on many topics, Sir James was sure of the superiority of Victorian English values. He also thought he had reason to be concerned about the security of the social order supporting those values.

Remorseless analysis of theological arguments had convinced him that afterlife is improbable and that it is dishonest to preach the promise of heaven and the dread of hell in support of morality. He asked himself how the stability of society could be assured if religion could not be invoked to assure the unquestioning support of the intricate hierarchy of the empire. His view of the alternative to the supernatural sanctions provided by nineteenth century Christianity is represented in this excerpt from his book *Liberty, Equality, Fraternity,* a title that was not chosen because of any sympathy with the ideals of the French Revolution:

> Abolish the gaoler and the hangman and your criminal law becomes empty words. . . . Consider men as a multitude of independent units, and the problem occurs, How can they be bound into wholes? What must be the principle of cohesion? Obviously some motive must be supplied which will operate on all men alike. Practically that means a threat in the last resort of physical punishment. The bond, then, which keeps us together in any tolerable order is ultimately the fear of force. Resist, and you will be crushed. The existence, therefore, of such a sanction [as hanging] is essential in

every society, or as it may otherwise be phrased, society depends on coercion.[8]

Sir James led the insulated life of the English secure classes. His only contacts with less fortunate people were with the murderers, cutthroats, and thieves whom he prosecuted for the crown or, sometimes, defended with a barrister's professional vigor—and later with the criminals who were tried before him and whom he often sent off to be hanged. There is nothing in his prodigious output of books and essays on the criminal law, nor in his brother's not uncritical biography, that faintly suggests that he thought himself subject to the social coercion that he believed to be so necessary for others. He was one of the coercers. He knew that the reins of control had to be in firm hands. There was no question in his mind but that some people—not always murderers, either—should be destroyed because of their wickedness. To his logical and well-trained legal mind, the only reason for "hundreds of thousands" in the English lower classes to abstain from murder was their horror of the act, as emphasized by the hangman. The notion did not occur to Stephen that there might be other forces at work among the lower orders to account for the cohesion and general peace that prevailed in Victorian England.

Sir James Fitzjames Stephen set his stamp on the administration of criminal justice in England for many decades past his time. But in 1965 the death penalty was abolished. Eighteen years have passed without the dire consequences that he would have predicted, even though the economic and social changes that have taken place since his time have greatly modified the cohesion of all classes. In recent years the incidence of all forms of homicide, after many years of relative stability, has begun to decline. I cannot claim a cause-and-effect relationship, and no one else does, but it is apparent that the hangman was not the necessary functionary that Sir James thought he was.

Notes

1. Thomas Jefferson, "Autobiography," in *The Life and Selected Writings of Thomas Jefferson,* ed. Adrienne Koch and William Peden, (New York: Modern Library, 1944), p. 46.
2. Dumas Malone, *Jefferson the Virginian* (Boston: Little, Brown, 1948), p. 270.
3. Ibid., p. 271.
4. Ibid., pp. 271–272.
5. Ibid., p. 269.
6. Jefferson, pp. 47–48.
7. For a further statement of my views on the "rehabilitative ideal," see John P. Conrad, "A

Lost Ideal, A New Hope: The Way Toward Effective Correctional Treatment," *Journal of Criminal Law and Criminology* (Winter 1981), pp. 1699–1734.
8. Quoted in Sir Leslie Stephen, *The Life of Sir James Fitzjames Stephen, Bart., K.C.S.I., A Judge of the High Court of Justice* (London: Smith, Elder, 1895), p. 318. Far from a devotional family memorial, this is a distinguished biography by Sir James's at least equally remarkable brother, the editor of the Dictionary of National Biography and many historical and philosophical essays. I am not sure what significance to attach to the fact that Sir Leslie was the father of Virginia Woolf; it is hard to imagine anyone in sharper intellectual contrast to Sir James than this sensitive niece.

ERNEST VAN DEN HAAG

In his customary, gentlemanly, and generous fashion, Professor Conrad offered to let me withdraw my quotation and comment on Thomas Jefferson's upholding of the *lex talionis*. It seems obvious to me that Conrad is right, my quotation misrepresents Jefferson's actual view, which was opposed to the *lex talionis*. I do not withdraw it simply because I think that readers can learn from the exchange, as I did. I was misled by the misuse that the late Walter Kaufmann made of the quotation in his *Without Guilt and Justice*. This is a wild and woolly book. But it never occurred to me that Kaufmann, who has a well-deserved reputation as a historian of philosophy and who taught at Princeton for many years, would use a quotation misleadingly. I should have been more careful.

My basic argument remains untouched by my mistake. Though rejecting the *lex talionis* himself, Jefferson thought it wise to incorporate it in his proposed bill in order to make the bill acceptable. In short, the *lex talionis* was overwhelmingly accepted in Jefferson's time though he himself opposed it.

Professor Conrad misunderstands me when he believes that to assert as I do that criminology is concerned with understanding crime and controlling crime rates is to "stultify" criminology. "Controlling crime rates" means to reduce crime as much as possible. I cannot see how Professor Conrad really disagrees that this is the ultimate, albeit often indirect, aim of criminological investigation. I am not as optimistic as Professor Conrad is about success by the means he advocates. But I hope Conrad is right—even though present evidence does not justify his optimism.

As for Sir James Fitzjames Stephen, he needs no defense from me. His *Liberty, Equality, Fraternity* is the most vigorous dissent available from John Stuart Mill's *On Liberty*. Everyone interested in political philosophy should read both books.

CHAPTER 2

The Purpose of Punishment

ERNEST VAN DEN HAAG

"Life, liberty, and the pursuit of happiness . . . to secure these rights governments are instituted among men," the Declaration of Independence tells us. How do governments secure rights? Governments prohibit interference with rights by law, and to make the legal prohibitions stick, governments threaten punishment to anyone who violates them. This is what the criminal law does. It prohibits taking life, liberty, or property (part, at least, of the pursuit of happiness as amendments V and XIV to the Constitution make clear) without due (legal) process and specifies the punishments threatened to those who break the law. When the law violation is very serious, the punishment may be death. The intended effect of all legal threats obviously is to deter from doing what the law prohibits, from committing the crimes threatened with punishment. And needless to say, the threatened punishments must be carried out—otherwise the threats are reduced to bluffs and become incredible and therefore ineffective. Thus, the primary purpose of legal punishment is to deter from crime.

Over the years, theorists have agreed on three additional purposes of punishment, although they disagree on the comparative importance of each purpose and therefore on the weight each should have in determining the punishment of criminals.

1. *Rehabilitation* is the bringing about of changes in the character of the convict in order to produce law-abiding behavior upon release.

For a while, this purpose was quite prominent. It is with this purpose in mind that prisons were called "correctional institutions" and guards "correctional officers." Rehabilitation is less fashionable now because no effective method to achieve it has been found. If one compares convicts subjected to any of the many current rehabilitation or treatment programs with convicts not subjected to any program (taking care, of course, that the two groups of convicts are similar, except that one was and the other was not subjected to treatment), one finds no significant differences in behavior after release. The rate of recidivism does not seem to be affected by rehabilitation programs either in this country or abroad in such countries as Sweden. Thus, rehabilitation for the time being remains an ideal, at best, with no realistic method of achieving it.

Even if rehabilitation could be achieved, it would be unlikely to affect the rate at which most crimes are committed. Criminals, unable to commit crimes because incapacitated (by imprisonment or execution), or unwilling because rehabilitated, are likely to be replaced by others who are able and willing. The rate at which most crimes are committed depends on the net benefit, psychic or material, the criminal expects: the benefit less the cost, including the risk of punishment. Rehabilitation does not affect the expected net benefit. Just as the rate at which dentistry is committed would not ultimately change if many practicing dentists retired, so with the rate of crime. Rehabilitation affects the individual criminal rather than the crime rate. Finally, rehabilitation is not very relevant to the rate at which crimes that may be threatened by the death penalty are committed. Murder, for instance, is mainly committed by first offenders. Even if not punished, most offenders guilty of crimes of passion are unlikely to commit other crimes. If we punish them, it cannot be for the sake of rehabilitation.

Note also that if rehabilitation is given priority, justice and punishment become irrelevant. Once the criminal is thought of as a sick person in need of treatment, his crime as a symptom of sickness, he does not deserve punishment. Disease is no crime, and treatment or cure is not justice according to what is deserved. Treatment for crime can only be effective or not. It can be neither just nor unjust, any more than treatment for measles can be. For the strict rehabilitationist, the notion of crime is as irrelevant as the notion of justice or punishment. All he sees is sick persons in need of treatment. Since they do not volunteer for treatment, it is forced on them, and not easily distinguished from punishment, except that, unlike punishment, it must go on for an indeterminate time until cure is achieved. Most rehabilitationists, unlike medical men, seem to assume that everybody is curable.

There is, however, no proof that criminals are more often sick than noncriminals, unless their crimes are taken for evidence, in which case they are sick by definition. Independent evidence indicates that offenders are not more frequently sick than nonoffenders in their socioeconomic group. In practical terms, the law regards as sick—and not responsible for their acts—only those who can be shown by independent evidence (independent of the crime itself) not to understand the nature and effects of their acts or the wrongness thereof.

Finally, many criminals do not need rehabilitation. Their crime (e.g., murdering a spouse) "rehabilitates" them. Yet we might be reluctant to let them go without punishment—to do so might encourage other persons, similarly tempted, and it is felt to be unjust.

2. *Incapacitation* (also referred to as isolation from society, confinement, or imprisonment) is a second purpose of punishment. At least while confined, the convict cannot commit crimes outside. Death incapacitates totally and permanently, imprisonment partially and temporarily. Imprisonment and execution are likely to affect the crime rate by deterring others. But the incapacitation of convicts itself is unlikely to affect most crime rates, since the convicts usually are replaced by others.

3. *Justice* is, without a doubt, one of the main reasons for punishment, although many people are uneasy about acknowledging as much. Justice may be defined as the attempt (a) to punish persons guilty of crime, (b) not to punish innocent persons, and (c) to punish the guilty according to what is deserved by the seriousness of the crime and the culpability of the persons guilty of it. Punishment is defined as a deprivation or suffering inflicted by a court of law, as specified by the law broken by the convict.

The criminal is thought to have done something wrong, which he could have avoided, and therefore to deserve punishment—a repayment (retribution) for the wrong he did, which should offset any advantage, benefit, or pleasure he might have derived from breaking the law. This idea of justice, although repudiated by many persons, has a strong hold on all of us. We would not like to see wrongdoers get away with impunity, even if they do not need rehabilitation or incapacitation. Nor would we want people to suffer undeserved punishments, even if such injustice were somehow socially useful. (It is not.)

One of the most persuasive arguments used against the death penalty is that innocent people may suffer it, owing to some mistake. This is an argument squarely based on justice—it objects to a possible injustice. However rare, such miscarriages of justice are likely to occur. They weaken the argument of retentionists who favor the death penalty for the guilty because it is just. They have to admit that the execution of the guilty necessarily implies the unintended execution of some innocents, which is unjust. However, these miscarriages of justice are irrelevant to the arguments of abolitionists (although they seldom realize as much) since they oppose the death penalty regardless of guilt or innocence. For abolitionists all executions are, in a sense, miscarriages of justice, regardless of guilt. Hence, whether the man to be executed is actually guilty of a crime or not becomes irrelevant.

4. *Deterrence* is the main purpose of the threats of punishment and of punishment itself. A threat is not actually a threat unless it is meant to be carried out. Thus, punishment is implied in the legal threat of punishment. If the purpose of the threat is to deter, this must also be the purpose, or at least one purpose, of punishment. Were it not so, the threat would lose credibility and effectiveness; it would become a pseudothreat, a threat not meant to be carried out as promised.

All criminal laws contain threats of punishment and therefore purport to deter from crime. Does the threat of punishment succeed in this? Certainly not everybody is deterred. Perhaps the threat is not great enough to deter; or it is not carried out often enough, so that the risk of suffering the threatened punishment seems small; or the crime appears so attractive to the criminal that he is willing to bear the risk of punishment. On the other hand, most people learn that crime does not pay and most of the time refrain from committing crimes, even when the opportunity presents itself.

Some scholars doubt the effectiveness of deterrent threats and of punishment. There is no basis for such doubts. Just as credible promises of reward do function as effective incentives, so do credible threats of punishment function as disincentives. They may be material (e.g., money as a reward; deprivation of money, or of freedom, as a punishment) or psychological (love, prestige, or popularity as rewards; unpopularity, contempt, humiliation as disincentives). A moment of reflection illustrates the deterrent effectiveness of threats. How many people would go to the movies—however entertaining they may be—if they had to pay a $500 fine when caught? How many would go if effectively threatened by five years in prison?

While there can be no doubt that credible threats deter in general, there can be legitimate doubts about the deterrent effectiveness of specific threats meant to deter from specific crimes. The factors determining effectiveness are (a) the credibility of the threats (How great is the risk for the offender of being apprehended, convicted, and punished as threatened? How does he perceive the risk? What proportion of offenders are actually punished?); (b) the size of the threatened punishment (Punishment will not deter if it is trivial, any more than it will deter when incredible); (c) the attractiveness of the crime from which the threat is to deter.

Estimates of risk and estimates of attractiveness vary from person to person. Obviously a criminal normally hopes he will not be caught. Yet he is also aware of a risk. Obviously the crime is attractive to the criminal, but the degree of attractiveness depends on his personality and situation. A hungry man will run great risks for food. Drug dealing is so profitable to wholesalers that it is hard to think of any threat that would deter them. And a man in a paroxysm of hate may well disregard any threat of punishment to gratify his anger.

Threats of punishment cannot and are not meant to deter everybody all of the time. They are meant to deter most people most of the time. If sizable and credible, they do. But they are not great enough to deter every genuinely hungry person from stealing food, or every angry person from assaulting another, or every greedy person from stealing. No threat could be great and credible enough to do so. Thus, in considering a legal threat, the basic question is not "Will it deter everybody?" but rather "Will it deter enough additional crimes, compared to a milder threat, to warrant the additional severity?" A second question, no less important, is "Is the threatened punishment just, is it deserved by the seriousness of the crimes that it is meant to punish?"

These questions are relevant when one considers any punishment. But they are particularly relevant—indeed, they are central issues—concerning capital punishment.

JOHN P. CONRAD

In this chapter, Professor van den Haag has staked out some of the issues on which he intends to do battle. Much more will be said about most of them as this debate progresses, but this is the right time to establish my positions with respect to those that he will defend. There are five topics on which I must elaborate, not always in dissent:

On "Rehabilitationism." This is a moribund issue. Only the most naïve fancy that criminals can be sent to prison and eventually be returned to the community as crisp new citizens because carefully selected rehabilitative programs have been administered to them. Some administrators and some academics find it advantageous to profess that with more research and a lot more resources methods can be found to cure nearly all criminals of their criminality.

Such a cure is a will-o'-the-wisp that should no longer be pursued. The wonder is that the pursuit ever began, or that anyone ever thought that rehabilitation should be a goal of the system that administers punishment. Surely, no one needs research to be convinced that a prison is a poor place to relieve the troubled in mind and spirit, or to change the attitudes of the wayward. Nevertheless, the rehabilitative ideal has been given more than lip service for generations. The realities are not simple, in spite of the unflinching enthusiasm of some and the grim nihilism of others.

The history of the rehabilitative ideal depends on three belief systems. In the early days of the penitentiary movement, when criminals began to be sent to prison rather than to the scaffold, it was thought that if the wicked could be offered the comfort of religion and the counsel of upright pastors, many, if not most, could be reclaimed. This theme persists to this day, and I have seen for myself the benign influences that selfless chaplains can exercise over men who seemed beyond the reach of change. Not enough clergymen have changed enough prisoners to make a dent in the statistics of recidivism, or even in the social condition of prison cell blocks. It is good that there are still priests and ministers who are willing to try.

Nineteenth-century faith in education led prison reformers to believe that if only prisoners could be relieved of their illiteracy and taught respectable trades, they would emerge from the darkness of vice and predation to become honest artisans. And again, cases of such transformations are often seen, to the gratification of all who witness them. And again, the means to effect such changes in sufficient numbers to make a statistical difference have eluded penal administrators and educators.

The twentieth century mirage has been the hope that psychotherapy and the belief system emanating from the therapeutic ideal would cure the evils lurking in the criminal consciousness. Numerous therapies with credentials spreading from the most prestigious psychiatrists to the most transparent charlatans have been tried and found wanting. And again, many prisoners have benefited from the experience of therapy—but not enough.

From all these disappointments—most of which were predictable—statistically minded social scientists have drawn the lesson that "treatment" does not bring about rehabilitation. This is true—in the sense that treatment could be planned and prescribed in the same way that a physician can prescribe a medicine with the expectation of a positive result. But it is a mistake to conclude that rehabilitative programs should therefore be abandoned. On the contrary, they must be available in sufficient variety and quality to afford hope of self-improvement to men and women who have no other realistic reason to hope for a change in their fortunes. Without such hopes, a prison lapses into a hell.

I will not argue that the death penalty must be abolished because murderers can be rehabilitated—although that is a legitimate expectation for many. In a prison that is properly administered, many convicts, including many murderers, will live hopeful and meaningful lives, returning eventually to their communities as productive citizens. It is not necessarily inevitable that a life term in prison must consist of years of unrelieved misery and uselessness.

On Incapacitation. My opponent is correct in his conclusion that the incapacitation of criminals can have little effect on the crime rates. I have myself engaged in research on this topic.[1] My colleagues and I found that even with the application of the most stringent penalties, more severe than any that could be enacted by any legislature, crime rates could not be reduced by more than 25%. With the level of sanctions now in general use, incapacitation will affect the crime rates by less than 5%.

Retributivism. Like most of my contemporaries in the administration of prisons, I began with a utilitarian belief that the criminal justice system should rehabilitate as many as possible, should protect the public from those who could not change, and, if all else failed, should deter the unchangeable by subjecting them to an austere but humane experience of deprivation. We also thought that the existence of the penal system undoubtedly deterred many potential criminals from committing crimes—but there was no agreement on how many potential criminals were thus prevented from doing harm to others.

Utilitarianism no longer makes sense to me, for reasons that will become apparent in the course of this debate. I now hold that the prime responsibility of the prison is to carry out the sentence of the court, or, in other words, to punish the criminal for the offense he committed. The punishment must be carried out in strict observance of humane standards of care. If the traditional goals of reform, incapacitation, and intimidation are achieved, so much the better. We have reason to know that each of these approaches is effective with some categories of criminals, but we cannot count on the effectiveness of any.

But the first social function of the prison is to punish. To expect more is to invite the reputation for failure that critics of criminal justice unfairly and unwisely ascribe to it.

The Execution of the Innocent. Professor van den Haag obviously senses that he is on shaky ground when he recognizes that the arguments of the retentionists are weakened by the inevitability that innocent men may be occasionally executed in a miscarriage of justice. He hastily moves away from this concession and observes that this concern is none of the abolitionists' business—because we oppose the execution of anyone, whether innocent or guilty.

This argument is a sophistry. Despite his regret that there will be fatal miscarriages of justice, my opponent is willing to accept on behalf of the state—which is to say, all of us—an occasional injustice of the worst kind so that the killing of authentic murderers may proceed. He does not trouble to address the obvious alternative to this injustice—a life term in prison. When the verdict of the court is in error, it can be corrected with a pardon if the innocent man is in prison. A posthumous pardon is of no value to anyone.

Why cannot the abolitionist object to the processes of capital punishment on the ground that innocent men are sometimes hanged? An act by the state of such monstrous proportions as the execution of a man who is not guilty of the crime for which he was convicted should be avoided at all costs. There are many reasons for urging that capital punishment must be abolished. Not the least of them is the avoidable risk of the ultimate injustice. The prevention of injustice is the business of every good citizen. The abolition of capital punishment is the certain means of preventing the worst injustice. Perhaps the retentionist can resign himself to killing the innocent with the consoling reflection that omelets cannot be made without breaking eggs. More squeamish persons will stare at the gallows and urge their removal from a society that does not need them.

On Deterrence. Throughout this debate, the reader can expect that much will be said about the deterrence of potential offenders. Here I wish to make clear my position. The system of sanctions should be scaled according to the seriousness of the crimes, *not* according to opinions about the severity required to deter them. This point should be obvious. If a fine of $1000 were to be imposed for overtime parking, nearly everyone would be deterred from committing this most trivial of all offenses. Such a sanction cannot be imposed because of the injustice of the perceived disproportionality. The actual penalty for this misdemeanor is small because we do not see it as a serious offense and will not allow it to be treated as such.

The other end of the scale is murder in the first degree, the most serious of all offenses. Often we are appalled at the depraved and vicious nature manifest in the offense, and it is sometimes said that hanging is too good for the perpetrator. I shall contend throughout this debate that a long term of confinement in prison is sufficient to establish the denunciation of the crime and the deterrence of its potential emulators. To kill the offender is to respond to his wrong by doing the same wrong to him. He thus becomes a victim himself, and all too often he enjoys a perverse and undeserved sympathy that trivializes his crime.

I shall not contend that punishment does not deter. Of course it does— for people we think of as normal, like ourselves. For the confirmed criminal, whatever the punishment may be, it is part of the cost of his chosen career. In the days when men and boys were hanged for stealing sheep in England, the offense continued to be committed; the fateful risk could be accepted by those who wished to steal.

We have to measure the punishment according to the desert of criminal, not according to what we think will deter others. Elsewhere in this discourse I shall have more to say in support of this principle.

Note

1. Stephan Van Dine, John P. Conrad, and Simon Dinitz, *Restraining the Wicked* (Lexington, Massachusetts: Lexington Books, 1979).

ERNEST VAN DEN HAAG

Responding to my Chapter 2, Professor Conrad states, "The system of sanctions should be scaled according to the seriousness of the crimes, *not* [italics his] according to opinions about the severity required to deter them." Two points:

1. About "the seriousness of crimes" one may have opinions; unfortunately, one can have nothing else. About "the severity required to deter them" one can have facts, not opinions. Conrad himself implies as much when he continues, "If a fine of $1000 were to be imposed for overtime parking, nearly everyone would be deterred. . . ." Conrad states, correctly, that "nearly everyone would be deterred." This is not an opinion but a testable fact. He goes on to object that the fine "cannot be imposed because of the injustice of the perceived disproportionality." This is a nonissue. The "injustice," in deterrence terminology, simply means that the community prefers a certain amount of overtime parking to imposing so severe and "disproportionate" (to the harm done by the offense) a sanction, i.e., the high fine would not be imposed even if "justice" is disregarded and only deterrence is considered. For the same reason we do not sentence a car thief to death. If we did, what punishment would we give a murderer?* On the other

---

*See my "Punishment as a Device for Controlling the Crime Rate," *Rutgers Law Review* 33 (1981), pp. 711–713, for an explanation as to why a deterrence system must scale penalties no less than a justice system.

hand, the community does prefer executing some murderers rather than not deterring (or risking not to deter) others by failing to execute those who have been convicted. This is where the community differs from Professor Conrad. So do I.

2. Of course, contrary to Conrad's view, execution does not "respond to [the offender's] wrong by doing the same wrong to him." It is not a wrong to punish a criminal for his wrong by imposing on him a physically identical punishment. It cannot always be done (you cannot defraud the defrauder). But there is no reason not to punish with death a man who intentionally and with malice aforethought took the life of another. The killing of the innocent victim is a wrong. The execution of the criminal corrects it and deters others from committing it. The difference between a wrong (a crime) and a lawful act is that the former is unlawful and the latter is not.

Perhaps confirmed criminals are difficult to deter, as Conrad says. But we can deter people from *becoming* confirmed criminals. In this we have been relatively successful, and, if our punishments were more regular and severe, we would be more successful.

JOHN P. CONRAD

If parking violators are fined $1000 for each offense, if that fine is unflinchingly collected, and if, as a result, parking violations sharply diminish in frequency, a satisfactory test of that oppressive, hypothetical sanction would be complete. Professor van den Haag believes that the deterrent effect of sanctions for more serious crimes—especially murder—can be just as easily tested. The fact that no such test has been successfully applied to the superior deterrence of the death penalty does not perplex him. I am not surprised. The simple arguments of the retentionists are so self-evident to them that evidence of their invalidity is dismissed rather than refuted.

"The difference between a wrong and a lawful act is that the former is unlawful and the latter is not." Other differences come to mind, but the implication that the state can do no wrong comforts oppressive regimes throughout our troubled world, as it has throughout all history.

CHAPTER 3

The Deterrent Effect of the Death Penalty

ERNEST VAN DEN HAAG

Crime is going to be with us as long as there is any social order articulated by laws. There is no point making laws that prohibit some action or other (e.g., murder or theft) unless there is some temptation to commit it. And however harsh the threats of the law, they will not restrain some people, whether because they discount the risk of punishment or because they are exposed to extraordinary temptation. They may hope for an immense profit; or be passionately angry or vindictive; or be in such misery that they feel they have nothing to lose. Thus, I repeat, the problem every society must attempt to solve (in part by means of punishment) is not eliminating crime but controlling it.

That threats will not deter everybody all the time must be expected. And it must also be expected that persons committed to criminal activity—career criminals—are not likely to be restrained by threats; nor are persons strongly under the influence of drugs or intoxicated by their own passions. However, if threats are not likely to deter habitual offenders, they are likely to help deter people from *becoming* habitual offenders.

People are not deterred by exactly calculating the size of the threat and the actual risk of suffering punishment against the likely benefit of the crime they consider committing. Few people calculate at all. Rather, the effect of threats is to lead most people to ignore criminal opportunities most of the time. One just does not consider them—any more than the ordinary person sitting down for lunch starts calculating whether he could have Beluga caviar and champagne instead of his usual hamburger and beer. He is not accustomed to caviar, and one reason he is not accustomed to it is that it costs too much. He does not have to calculate every time to know as much. Similarly, he is not accustomed to breaking the law, and one reason is that it costs too much. He does not need to calculate.

It is quite a different matter if one asks, not: "Do threats deter?" but rather: "How much does one threat deter compared to another?" Does the more severe threat deter significantly more? Does the added deterrence warrant the added severity? Thus, no one pondering the death penalty will contend that it does not deter. The question is: Does it deter more than alternative penalties proposed, such as life imprisonment or any lengthy term of imprisonment?

In the past many attempts were made to determine whether the death penalty deters the crimes for which it was threatened—capital crimes—more than other penalties, usually life imprisonment, mitigated by parole (and amounting therefore to something like ten years in prison in most cases). Most of these attempts led to ambiguous results, often rendered more ambiguous by faulty procedures and research methods. Frequently, contiguous states—one with and the other without the death penalty—were compared. Or states were compared before and after abolition. Usually these comparisons were based on the legal availability or unavailability of the death penalty rather than on the presence or absence of executions and on their frequency. But what matters is whether the death penalty is practiced, not whether theoretically it is available. Finally, nobody would assert that the death penalty—or any crime-control measure—is the only determinant of the frequency of the crime. The number of murders certainly depends as well on the proportion of young males in the population, on income distribution, on education, on the proportion of various races in the population, on local cultural traditions, on the legal definition of murder, and on other such factors.

Comparisons must take all of these matters into account if they are to evaluate the effect threatened penalties may have in deterring crimes. In contiguous states, influential factors other than the death penalty may differ; they may even differ in the same state before and after abolition. Hence, differences (or equalities) in capital crime frequencies cannot simply be ascribed to the presence or absence of the death penalty. Moreover, one does not know how soon a change in penalties will make a difference, if it ever does, or whether prospective murderers will know that the death penalty has been abolished in Maine and kept in Vermont. They certainly will know whether or not there is a death penalty in the United States. But in contiguous states? Or within a short time after abolition or reinstatement?

Theoretically, experiments to avoid all these difficulties are possible. But they face formidable obstacles in practice. If, for instance, the death penalty were threatened for murders committed on Monday, Wednesday, and Friday, and life imprisonment for murders committed on Tuesday, Thursday, and Saturday, we would soon see which days murderers prefer, i.e., how much the death penalty deters on Monday, Wednesday, and Friday over and above life imprisonment threatened for murders committed on the other days. If we find no difference, the abolitionist thesis that the death penalty adds no deterrence over and above the threat of life imprisonment would be confirmed.

In the absence of such experiments, none of the available studies seems conclusive. Recently such studies have acquired considerable mathematical sophistication, and some of the more sophisticated studies have concluded, contrary to what used to be accepted scholarly opinion, that the death penalty can be shown to deter over and above life imprisonment. Thus, Isaac Ehrlich, in a study published in the *American Economic Review* (June 1975), concluded that, over the period 1933–1969, "an additional execution per year . . . may have resulted on the average in 7 or 8 fewer murders."

Other studies published since Ehrlich's contend that his results are due to the techniques and periods he selected, and that different techniques and periods yield different results. Despite a great deal of research on all sides, one cannot say that the statistical evidence is conclusive. Nobody has claimed to have *disproved* that the death penalty may deter more than life imprisonment. But one cannot claim, either, that it has been proved statistically in a conclusive manner that the death penalty does deter more than alternative penalties. This lack of proof does not amount to disproof. However, abolitionists insist that there ought to be proof positive.

Unfortunately, there is little proof of the sort sought by those who oppose the death penalty, for the deterrent effect of any sort of punishment. Nobody has statistically shown that 4 years in prison deter more than 2, or 20 more than 10. We assume as much. But I know of no statistical proof. One may wonder why such proof is demanded for the death penalty but not for any other. To be sure, death is more serious a punishment than any other. But 10 years in prison are not exactly trivial either.

If there is no statistical proof of added deterrence, is there any other argument to lead us to think the death penalty adds deterrence and, if so, enough deterrence to warrant imposing it?

JOHN P. CONRAD

Dr. van den Haag continues the discussion of deterrence, raising a number of issues that I will discuss as fully as I can in my Chapter 6, "Deterrence, the Death Penalty, and the Data."

He suggests that experiments might be conducted to assess the superior deterrent effect of the death penalty, and gives as an example a research design calling for alternating the death penalty with life imprisonment according to the day of the week on which the offense was committed. I suspect that my empirically minded opponent knows that he will have to wait a long time before the judiciary will be willing to cooperate in this experiment.

That is a farfetched example of the difficulty that faces those who would scientize the solution of problems that do not lend themselves to the scientific method. Not only is the ethical problem of creating a research design insuperable on the face of it, but the improbability of arriving at a clear-cut result discourages such a misuse of statistics. That is another topic on which I shall have more to say at a later point in this discourse.

As to the relative deterrent effects of different severities of punishment, I think my opponent is wrong in stating that no one is interested in whether four years in prison deters more offenders than two years. All those cost–benefit analysts who have tried to apply their skills to the ballooning costs of incarceration are deeply interested in this question. It has not been answered. I doubt that it will ever be answered to everyone's satisfaction. I have never seen any reason to believe that the death penalty is more deterrent than a life term in prison, but I will agree with my opponent that it is unlikely that this question will be successfully answered, either.

My inventive opponent's last sentence in this chapter, in which he implies another argument to support the deterrent effect of the death penalty, leaves me with bated breath. If the proof cannot be statistical, as he all but concedes, which way to the truth of this matter will he choose?

CHAPTER 4

More on the Deterrent Effect of the Death Penalty

ERNEST VAN DEN HAAG

If it is difficult, perhaps impossible, to prove statistically—and just as hard to disprove—that the death penalty deters more from capital crimes than available alternative punishments do (such as life imprisonment), why do so many people believe so firmly that the death penalty is a more effective deterrent?

Some are persuaded by irrelevant arguments. They insist that the death penalty at least makes sure that the person who suffered it will not commit other crimes. True. Yet this confuses incapacitation with a specific way to bring it about: death. Death is the surest way to bring about the most total incapacitation, and it is irrevocable. But does incapacitation need to be that total? And is irrevocability necessarily an advantage? Obviously it makes correcting mistakes and rehabilitation impossible. What is the advantage of execution, then, over alternative ways of achieving the desired incapacitation?

More important, the argument for incapacitation confuses the elimination of one murderer (or of any number of murderers) with a reduction in the homicide rate. But the elimination of any specific number of actual or even of potential murderers—and there is some doubt that the actual murderers of the past are the most likely future (potential) murderers—will not affect the homicide rate, except through deterrence. There are enough potential murderers around to replace all those incapacitated. Deterrence may prevent the potential from becoming actual murderers. But incapacitation of some or all actual murderers is not likely to have much effect by itself. Let us then return to the question: Does capital punishment deter more than life imprisonment?

Science, logic, or statistics often have been unable to prove what common sense tells us to be true. Thus, the Greek philosopher Zeno some 2000 years ago found that he could not show that motion is possible; indeed, his famous paradoxes appear to show that motion is impossible. Though nobody believed them to be true, nobody succeeded in showing the fallacy of these paradoxes until the rise of mathematical logic less than a hundred years ago. But meanwhile, the world did not stand still. Indeed, nobody argued that motion should stop because it had not been shown to be logically possible. There is no more reason to abolish the death penalty than there was to abolish motion simply because the death penalty has not been, and perhaps cannot be, shown statistically to be a deterrent over and above other penalties. Indeed, there are two quite satisfactory, if nonstatistical, indications of the marginal deterrent effect of the death penalty.

In the first place, our experience shows that the greater the threatened penalty, the more it deters. *Ceteris paribus,* the threat of 50 lashes, deters more than the threat of 5; a $1000 fine deters more than a $10 fine; 10 years in prison deter more than 1 year in prison—just as, conversely, the promise of a $1000 reward is a greater incentive than the promise of a $10 reward, etc. There may be diminishing returns. Once a reward exceeds, say, $1 million, the additional attraction may diminish. Once a punishment exceeds, say, 10 years in prison (net of parole), there may be little additional deterrence in threatening additional years. We know hardly anything about diminishing returns of penalties. It would still seem likely, however, that the threat of life in prison deters more than any other term of imprisonment.

The threat of death may deter still more. For it is a mistake to regard the death penalty as though it were of the same kind as other penalties. If it is not, then diminishing returns are unlikely to apply. And death differs significantly, in kind, from any other penalty. Life in prison is still life, however unpleasant. In contrast, the death penalty does not just threaten to make life unpleasant—it threatens to take life altogether. This difference is perceived by those affected. We find that when they have the choice between life in prison and execution, 99% of all prisoners under sentence of death prefer life in prison. By means of appeals, pleas for commutation, indeed by all means at their disposal, they indicate that they prefer life in prison to execution.

From this unquestioned fact a reasonable conclusion can be drawn in favor of the superior deterrent effect of the death penalty. Those who have the choice in practice, those whose choice has actual and immediate effects on their life and death, fear death more than they fear life in prison or any other available penalty. If they do, it follows that the threat of the death penalty, all other things equal, is likely to deter more than the threat of life in prison. One is most deterred by what one fears most. From which it follows that whatever statistics fail, or do not fail, to show, the death penalty is likely to be more deterrent than any other.

Suppose now one is not fully convinced of the superior deterrent effect of the death penalty. I believe I can show that even if one is genuinely uncertain as to whether the death penalty adds to deterrence, one should still favor it, from a purely deterrent viewpoint. For if we are not sure, we must choose either to (1) trade the certain death, by execution, of a convicted murderer for the probable survival of an indefinite number of murder victims whose future murder is less likely (whose survival is more likely)—if the convicted murderer's execution deters prospective murderers, as it might, or to (2) trade the certain survival of the convicted murderer for the probable loss of the lives of future murder victims more likely to be murdered because the convicted murderer's nonexecution might not deter prospective murderers, who could have been deterred by executing the convicted murderer.

To restate the matter: If we were quite ignorant about the marginal deterrent effects of execution, we would have to choose—like it or not—between the certainty of the convicted murderer's death by execution and the likelihood of the survival of future victims of other murderers on the one hand, and on the other his certain survival and the likelihood of the death of new victims. I'd rather execute a man convicted of having murdered others than to put the lives of innocents at risk. I find it hard to understand the opposite choice.

However, I doubt that those who insist that the death penalty has not been demonstrated to be more deterrent than other penalties really believe that it is not. Or that it matters. I am fairly certain that the deterrent effect of the death penalty, or its absence, is not actually important to them. Rather, I think, they use the lack of statistical demonstration of a marginal deterrent effect to rationalize an opposition to the death penalty that has nonrational sources yet to be examined. In fact, although they use the alleged inconclusiveness of statistical demonstrations of deterrence as an argument to dissuade others from the death penalty, it can be shown that most abolitionists are not quite serious about the relevance of their own argument from insufficient deterrence.

In numerous discussions I have asked those who oppose capital punishment because, in their opinion, it will not deter capital crimes enough, whether they would favor the death penalty if it could be shown to deter more than life imprisonment does. My question usually led to some embarrassment and to attempts to dodge it by saying that additional deterrence has not been shown. However, when I persisted, conceding as much but asking abolitionists to give a hypothetical answer to a hypothetical question, they would admit that they would continue to oppose the death penalty—even if it were shown to deter more than life imprisonment. Which is to say that the argument based on the alleged lack of superior deterrence is factitious.

At times I have pursued the question. I would ask: "Suppose it were shown that every time we execute a person convicted of murder, ten fewer homicides are committed annually than were otherwise expected—would you still favor abolition?" The answer has been "yes" in all cases I can recall. I would persist: "Suppose every time we execute a convicted murderer, 500 fewer persons are murdered than otherwise would be expected to be murdered; suppose that, by executing the convicted murderer, we so much more deter others, who are not deterred by the threat of life imprisonment, that 500 victims will be spared?" After some hesitation, such staunch abolitionists as Professor Hugo Adam Bedau (Tufts University); Ramsey Clark, attorney general of the United States under President Johnson; Professor Charles Black (Yale); and Mr. Henry Schwarzchild, capital punishment project director of the American Civil Liberties Union, admitted that if they had the choice, they would rather see 500 innocents murdered than execute one convict found guilty of murder.* This leads me to doubt the sincerity of abolitionist arguments based on the alleged lack of significant additional deterrent effect of capital punishment.

I also wonder why anyone would hold more precious the life of a convicted murderer than that of 500 innocents, if by executing him he could save them. But about this more anon.

JOHN P. CONRAD

On three points made by Professor van den Haag in this chapter I am in contented agreement:

1. The incapacitation of murderers will not reduce the murder rate. I
   am pleased that this issue is removed from our debate; it is too often

*Professors Bedau and Black at a public debate at the University of Arizona, Tempe, Arizona; Ramsey Clark in private communication; Henry Schwarzchild in various public debates.

advanced by retentionists as a sound commonsense argument in support of capital punishment.

2. It is difficult to find an empirical proof that capital punishment deters potential murderers. I would have said that this search is impossible, but in the vocabulary of the unproved, *difficult* is an acceptable term.

3. The death penalty is unlike other penalties. True; it can be inflicted only once on any offender. Many other differences will come to mind, but they need not be labored here.

It is on the points of our disagreement that more must be said. I have found three issues in this chapter on which argument may be joined. Two of them are "commonsense" arguments advanced by my opponent; the third is a speculative challenge. I shall take them up in order.

Common Sense and Deterrence

Conceding as he does that statistical proof of the deterrent effect of the death penalty is wanting, Professor van den Haag asks us to rely on common sense. Summoning the famous paradoxes of Zeno of Elea in an intellectual sleight of hand, my ingenious antagonist invites us to make a leap of faith. Look, he says, for centuries science showed that motion is impossible, even though the good sense of the man on the street could see to the contrary. Why not rely on the same good sense in considering the validity of the deterrent effects of punishment? Maybe science, logic, and statistics can't detect these effects in their present primitive state, just as no one was able to unsettle Zeno until Georg Cantor's mathematics of the infinite opened up new possibilities of thought. Our best course when science fails us is to call on the stout common sense of ordinary men.

We can admire Professor van den Haag's magic without being entirely taken in. After all, Zeno was scarcely the only scientist or logician to consider the problem of motion. For centuries it has been observed, measured, and codified into physical laws. Zeno's paradoxes are the curiosa of logic, puzzles that still perplex some philosophers, but by no stretch of the imagination are they elements of a theory of motion.

Now consider the situation as to deterrence. Here we have no Zeno proposing a logical anomaly that has gone unresolved for three millennia. We have the common sense of the ages telling us that if the consequences of our actions are predictably unpleasant, we will be moved to refrain from engaging in them. Everyone who has driven an automobile in sight of a police car, everyone who has ever filled out an income tax return, and everyone who has put his baggage through an airport inspection apparatus knows that he has been deterred from doing what he otherwise might do. It is an anomaly that social scientists have never been able to show that similar processes are effective in deterring criminals. Professor van den Haag obviously hopes that social science will eventually produce a Georg Cantor who will prove what the ordinary man knows so well. While waiting for his arrival, we are asked to put our faith in common sense and to disregard the blandishments of social science, statistics, and such knowledge as we have been able to assemble with regard to the behavior of abnormal personalities.

The argument from Zeno's paradoxes to the impact of deterrence on potential murderers is a stunning feat of legerdemain but ends with an untenable analogy. Let us put it to one side and consider the claims of common sense. Two such claims are presented to us. First, we hear that there is experience to show that "the greater the threatened penalty, the more it deters." In another chapter, I shall consider the limited empirical data that relate to this assertion. Here I want to respond to the commonsense argument in the terms of common sense.

Like a good economist, my opponent concedes that a law of diminishing returns must take effect on the deterrence presented by increased penalties. To the calculating criminal, a thirty-year sentence will not seem 50% more deterrent than a twenty-year sentence. If criminals were economists, a calculus of deterrence could be created and charted on graphs, thereby vastly simplifying criminal legislation.

But I repeat: Criminals are not economists, and the calculation of risks does not take place in their minds along recognizably rational lines. The homicidal robber is a creature of impulses and drives that are not readily diagrammed on a blackboard. He shoots, pistol-whips, or stomps his victim not out of a coolly concerted plan that has taken into account the risks of such behavior but out of infuriated frustration. To suppose that any scale of penalties, including or excluding the death penalty, will affect his actions is to ignore the nature of the man with whom we have to cope. So long as this country harbors a pool of pistol-carrying muggers, we can expect that there will be fatal muggings regardless of the penalties we may establish for this kind of offense.

The second commonsense claim made by Dr. van den Haag is based on the unquestioned fact that prisoners under sentence of death—with some notable exceptions—generally pursue every channel they can to seek a commutation of their sentence to life imprisonment. For the sake of the argument, I concede my opponent's unattributed estimate that about 99% of the men on condemned row prefer life in prison to the execution they face. My opponent asks us to conclude from this state of condemned men's minds that the death penalty is more deterrent than life imprisonment.

I do not think that this conclusion follows at all. We are not entitled to make any inference about the deterrent effect of the death penalty on the hypothetical person considering murder. He will prefer not to be suspected, not to be arrested, not to be tried, and not to be sentenced to anything. The distant contingency that as a result of the murder he is considering he might someday be on death row trying to get a reversal of the verdict or a commutation of the sentence is not likely to enter his thoughts. As to the prisoner on death row, whose plans, such as they were, have gone awry, the choice is between life and death. Most condemned men will make what efforts they can to get a change in their circumstances. Abolitionists will agree with retentionists that condemned men would rather not be condemned. No matter how irrational they may be, most people in trouble will try to improve their condition. As Dr. van den Haag remarks, "Life in prison is still life, however unpleasant."

Common sense is the wisdom of the common man. It rises up from the general experience of ordinary people. It does not depend on specialized education, on the acquisition and manipulation of data, or on the subtleties of the logician. The common man knows a lot about the requirements of decent behavior and how to meet those requirements. He tends to apply the Golden Rule as best he can, and to observe the necessities of self-control. But he will have no experience of the most uncommon decision of whether to kill or not to kill, nor is he likely to meet people who have ever made such decisions. Common sense does not illuminate the dark recesses of abnormal psychology. It has nothing to do with the reasons for committing a criminal act, and probably almost nothing to do with the reasons for abstaining after serious consideration of committing a crime.

Trading the Execution of the Murderer for the Survival of Future Victims

Dr. van den Haag now edges off the shaky ground of common sense to juggle some highly speculative hypotheses. Suppose, he asks us, that the execution of one murderer will prevent by deterrence the deaths of one or more potential victims of murder; does not the acceptance of this contingency justify that execution? He cites the willingness of my fellow abolitionists, the Messrs. Bedau, Black, and Clark, to contemplate the violent deaths of 500 innocent victims rather than to allow the execution of one single convicted murderer. Obviously we abolitionists are insincere in maintaining our opposition to capital punishment.

Citation of Immanuel Kant's dictum that "judicial punishment can never be used merely as a means to promote some other good for the criminal himself or for civil society; . . . a human being can never be manipulated merely as a means to the purposes of someone else"[1] reminds us of a principle that is basic to human freedom and that is violated throughout the Communist world as a matter of applied Marxist doctrine. It is quite true that the passage I have quoted is juxtaposed with a ringing defense of capital punishment in which Kant tried to show that anyone convicted of killing another must die. However, my opponent has already rejected Kant's retributivist argument. That argument and Kant's defense of capital punishment have no necessary relationship to the position that *human beings must never be treated as means to someone else's end.* That position was directly derived from Kant's analysis of the essential requirements for maintaining individual liberty in an organized social order. It contrasts with the familiar Marxist–Leninist position that the safety of the state requires the liberal and frequent use of the death penalty. We have seen the sincerity of that belief grotesquely demonstrated to an appalled world for the last sixty-five years.

But I have not answered Professor van den Haag's supposititious question. He may push me to the wall, he may disallow my protests that the question is unfair—because there is no evidence at all that such a "trade" represents a reality—and he may insist on a yes-or-no answer. I will sincerely answer no. I will lock up that murderer for many years, maybe the rest of his life, and let those 500 innocent victims shift for themselves. Killing people is wrong, and the state may not engage in wrongful acts.

I will ask Dr. van den Haag to look down the winding path along which he invites us to follow him. If he persuades us to establish the principle that killing a murderer can be justified if we can suppose that 500 innocent victims may thus be spared, then there is no way out of the position that we may also torture him, in the presence of official witnesses and the press, to accomplish the same end. If death in the gas chamber will save 500, then death on the rack, perhaps with a preliminary disembowelment, might save a thousand. And why limit the deterrent examples to convicted murderers? If a certified psychiatrist will testify that a man is clearly dangerous, even if he has not yet killed anyone, his execution may well be an even more telling example to the pool of potential murderers. The absurdity of these examples should be enough to demonstrate the risks in violating Kant's precept on using people as a means to an end.

Let me sum up here my response to Dr. van den Haag's commonsense case for deterrence. We cannot allow deterrence to be the object of capital punishment for two overwhelmingly sufficient reasons. There is not a jot of evidence that the deterrence of the death penalty affects the populations of potential murderers that it is intended to deter. Even if there were some evidence to that effect, capital punishment is unacceptable as a preventative of murder because in accepting it the legislator has no basis for not using it for other and lesser purposes, or for not using even more grievous forms of punishment in the interest of public safety.

ERNEST VAN DEN HAAG

I can do little but reiterate that by conjuring up the criminal as a creature of impulses and drives who "shoots, . . . or stomps his victim . . . out of infuriated frustration," Professor Conrad once more relies on those who have not been, and perhaps could not be, deterred. We don't want to add to their number. Wherefore we need laws that can deter the deterrables—most of us. This includes the death penalty, which, being the most severe punishment we have, is likely to deter, not all, but some murderers. Which is quite worthwhile.

Professor Conrad quotes Immanuel Kant correctly the first time, but the second time he paraphrases Kant incorrectly: "human beings must never be treated as means to someone else's end." Kant wrote *"merely* as means." The *merely* is of surpassing importance because we do treat each other as means all the time. I treat the physician as a means for my health, the taxi-driver for my transportation, the salesman for my purchases. People are willing to be used as means by others because it serves their ends (e.g., to make an income). To *merely* use a person for my ends, to do so without his consent, is wrong according to Kant. To make use of one another with mutual consent is legitimate. I can use the taxidriver for transportation, and he can use me as a passenger to increase his income.

Now, criminals do not consent to be punished to deter others, any more than police officers consent to being shot at by criminals. However, the police officer volunteered to take that risk by becoming a police officer. And the criminal volunteered to take the risk to be punished for the sake of deterring others. He volunteered by becoming a criminal. He consented, not to the punishment, but to the risk of being punished, for the sake of obtaining whatever gains he hoped to obtain through his crime. He could have avoided the risk of punishment by not becoming a criminal, just as the policeman could have avoided the risk of being shot at by not becoming a policeman. Both are used by society for its purposes, and both volunteered to take the risks involved in the activity in which they engaged for the sake of their purposes. Hence, neither is used *merely* as a means for the purposes of others.

Finally, Professor Conrad writes, "Killing people is wrong, and the state may not engage in wrongful acts." I'm not sure he is serious. Killing innocent people surely is wrong. But murderers? Murderers do wrong and forfeit their lives. Surely it is not enough to say, "Killing murderers is wrong." We should be told why. We are not. Nor is it correct to say that "the state may not engage in wrongful acts." The state at times must. It often does so in war. And surely if killing innocent people is wrong, it would follow that if the state can save the lives of 500 innocents by killing one murderer, the state should not let these prospective "victims shift for themselves." It should protect them by executing the murderer. It would be wrong of the state to allow these 500 to be murdered to cater to Professor Conrad's principles, when the state could have stayed the murderer's hand by executing those who were convicted by due process. It is to secure our lives—not those of murderers—"that governments are instituted among men."

About torture. If I were convinced that innocent lives could be saved by torturing guilty men, I should favor torture. I am not. Wherefore I oppose torture. (Not always: If I am certain that my prisoner knows where the bomb is hidden that will kill ten people when it explodes two hours from now, and if I believe that he will tell only under torture, I will favor torturing him. The ten innocent lives are worth it. And, again, he volunteers: He could tell without torture if he so wanted. If he has to be motivated by torture, so be it. But such cases are exceptional. For punitive purposes, I do not think that torture increases the deterrent effect of death, wherefore I oppose it.)

The psychiatrist, certified or otherwise, who in Professor Conrad's illustration shows that "a man is clearly dangerous" belongs in the loony bin. *Dangerous* is a vague term. We all may be. No psychiatrist can know with certainty what anyone will do in the future. If future behavior could be predicted with certainty, on any basis, we would have to rethink our whole legal system. It is now based on what people have done, not on what they will do. If we knew what people will do, we could replace punishment by appropriate preventive restraints, and we would not have to worry about crime or punishment.

JOHN P. CONRAD

In his rejoinder, Professor van den Haag makes five points to which I must respond. I shall take them in order, scraping away the confusion as best I can.

The Deterrables and the Undeterrables

In my rebuttal, I wrote about muggers, some of whom commit murder in the course of their crimes. My opponent objects to the application of generalizations about the undeterred to the mysterious population of the deterred. Those who speculate about general deterrence assume that there must be a difference between those who stay their hands because of the prospect of punishment and those who proceed with their crimes anyway. That assumption depends on the realistic probability that those who rob and kill will be severely punished. In short, to adopt my opponent's terminology, there must be a population of deterrables out there who refrain from crime solely because they might be punished if caught.

The crime with which we are concerned at this point in our discourse is robbery. It is a popular crime among the unskilled and underemployed youth of our large cities, and it is usually committed with a threat of violence made credible with a weapon. Ordinary citizens have learned to dread it as one of the most serious risks of urban life. If we can deter it by severe and efficient law enforcement, we should.

The beginning of deterrence as to any crime is the apprehension of offenders. As to robbery, the situation is discouraging. The clearance rates hover in the neighborhood of 30% nationally; in many cities the rates are even lower. Clearance rates for murder are about 75% across the nation, lower in some of the large cities. It is the stranger-to-stranger murders that are least likely to be cleared.

At this level of effectiveness, we must conclude that deterrence is not working. The reason is not because the death penalty is in abeyance but rather because muggers, even lethal muggers, are not being arrested rapidly and surely. There are many who believe that the police catch up with nearly all of them eventually. No one can be sure that this is so, but if it is true, then the clearance rates still show that many muggers can get away with their crimes for enough time to make the commission of these offenses worth their while.

If we assume, as I think we must, that in any large city there is a pool of men and boys who see robbery as a remunerative and exciting activity, the consensus in such a pool must be that the chances of getting away with any given mugging are pretty good, even if the victim is hurt in the process. Before we blame the prevalence of robbery on the infrequent infliction of capital punishment, we have to find ways to arrest a much higher percentage of robbers. If it were known that nine times out of ten a guy who mugs a citizen will do some time, the robbery rates would decline. It would be clear that the community takes robbery seriously enough to assure that the consequences would be serious.

Our police are far from such a level of efficiency. At present, with the ready availability of pistols, the high rate of unemployment among unskilled young men, and the low clearance rate for robbery, it is idle to talk about how heavy the penalty should be for those few who are caught. Our society is terribly vulnerable to unskilled crime. Until all three of the conditions that make it so easy to commit are corrected, we can expect that vulnerability to continue. No procession of killer-robbers to the executioner is going to affect the frequency of robbery. Within that pool of potential robbers, there are some who may be tempted but refrain. It is hard for me to believe that the prospect of joining that procession to the scaffold or the electric chair would seriously increase the number of deterrables, given the present or probable future state of law enforcement. And if the arrest rates were to improve substantially, I would be steadfast in maintaining that a life term for the killer-robber will do just as well in deterring his kind as his execution, however administered.

The Kantian Merely[1]

Professor van den Haag wants to talk about the interdependence of ends and means among ordinary people in ordinary life. Professor Kant had a much larger and more difficult issue in mind when he used that adverb *merely* in the paragraph I quoted. In considering the purposes of punishment, Kant wanted to make a stoutly antiutilitarian stand. To his way of thinking, the utilitarian position that corresponded to Bentham's approach to criminal law put the state in the position of using a human being as a means to an end. He reasoned that when this principle governs the relation between a state and its citizens, the freedom of the people is endangered. As I stressed in my rebuttal, the experience of the Marxist–Leninist states has amply proved his point.

I will expand further on Kant's retributivism. When a state punishes a man because that is his desert for the conviction of a crime, the criminal is deprived of any benefit from his offense, and the crime itself is denounced. But when the state uses punishment for the purpose of scaring potential criminals, the desert of the criminal being punished becomes secondary to other aims. And there is the significance of Kant's *merely*. He did not object to the deterrent effect of punishment, so long as it was a secondary effect to the punishment that the state is bound to inflict under the categorical imperative that Kant insisted on. To put a subtle issue into as concrete terms as I can, Kant would hold that if the penalty for robbery should be five years in prison, then those five years should be imposed on *all* convicted robbers. He would strongly object to raising or lowering the penalty according to the rate at which robbery is committed or—worse still from his point of view—according to the availability of prison space.

But Professor van den Haag does not seem to be interested in the fine points of Kantian principles of justice. He argues that the criminal must submit to whatever social ends the community may require of him because he volunteered for the risk of punishment inflicted for any purpose that the state may choose. In effect, the judge is free to use the criminal to deter potential muggers just as Professor van den Haag uses his physician to treat an illness. The analogy is interesting but farfetched through some logically fatal flaws.

The professional arrangement between Dr. van den Haag and his physician has a mutuality in which each party is free to decide on the limits. If he thinks it advisable, the physician may refuse to perform a treatment that the patient may desire, and may terminate the relationship. If Dr. van den Haag decides that he is not getting the benefits he expected or considers that the physician's fees are exorbitant, he, too, is free to end the relationship.

This kind of mutuality exists in each of the examples he gives. It does not and cannot exist between the criminal and the state. The policeman can turn in his badge if he thinks his assignment is too dangerous. The criminal goes to the gallows because he deserves punishment and may not be excused his desert. The policeman gets the pay he deserves as long as he patrols his beat, and he gets nothing when he quits because he deserves nothing. The criminal gets the punishment he deserves when he is convicted of a crime—no more and no less. Once we allow his punishment to be determined by other considerations—the deterrence of other criminals, or his need for rehabilitation—we allow the state to make decisions with respect to his fate that *merely* manipulate him for ends that are at best speculative.

At this point I will welcome back Professor Kant, in spite of his well-known insistence on hanging *all* murderers.

Killing People Is Wrong

Strictly speaking, this mandate must be qualified. No one questions the right of a person to kill in self-defense, and the law tends to be indulgent in allowing this defense. Except for the most adamantly uncompromising pacifists, the duty of the soldier to fight and kill in defense of his country or in a just war has always been accepted by theologians and moral philosophers. What I object to, along with other abolitionists, is killing people—even the most odious criminals—in cold blood. The state cannot teach the people that killing people in cold blood is wrong by killing anyone in cold blood.

As for Professor van den Haag's hypothetical salvation of 500 innocents by executing one miserable murderer, I have pointed out the dangerous direction in which adherence to that principle will lead us. Nevertheless, I am interested in his reluctant admission that he would proceed with torture if it could be shown that 500 more innocents could be saved. He doubts that torture is more deterrent than the electric chair, and I doubt that the electric chair is more deterrent than the life sentence in prison. In the absence of any evidence that salvation by electrocution can be achieved on the scale that my imaginative opponent suggests—or on any scale at all—I cannot see what point he has proved. Those who must resort to speculations as absurd as this are hard pressed to justify their position. Those who believe that the sincerity of abolitionists is successfully tested in this way may be easily led to believe anything.

On Torture

Now what about that man who knows where the bomb is but won't tell unless his demands are met? Professor van den Haag would, as a last resort, put him to some kind of torture. Out of delicacy, I will refrain from asking what method he would choose. As for me, I would keep in mind that information given under this kind of duress is generally unreliable. I would much prefer to arrange for a sodium pentothal interview, which would take less time, would require less repulsive methods, and could be expected to elicit better information.

That has nothing to do with the topic of our debate, of course, but I could not let this *obiter dictum* pass without challenge.

On the Predictions of Certified Psychiatrists

I wholly agree that psychiatrists have no business predicting anything other than the probable effectiveness of the treatment they administer. It is unfortunate that the courts have encouraged the professional specialty of forensic psychiatry to spread like a weed on the nation's witness stands. But forensic psychiatrists do predict freely, and their predictions are taken very seriously, especially if it is a prediction of future violence or criminality. Last year we saw the Supreme Court dispose of a Texas practitioner whose predictions of criminality determined whether or not a convicted murderer should be subjected to the lethal injections that Texas now prefers as its method of execution.[2] I will agree that such a psychiatrist—and he is far from the only one—should be locked out of the courtroom, though perhaps not committed to the "loonybin," as my skeptical opponent recommends.

Unfortunately, in a credulous and anxious world, it is not impossible to believe that some legislators and some judges may be willing to give undue weight to forensic seers. They line up along the winding path down which Dr. van den Haag would lead us.

Notes

1. For a more thorough discussion of this passage in the Kantian text, including a consideration of the significance of *merely*, see Jeffrie G. Murphy, *Kant: The Philosophy of Right* (London: Macmillan, 1970), pp. 140–144.
2. *Estelle* v. *Smith*, (1981) 451 U.S. 454.

ERNEST VAN DEN HAAG

I certainly agree that unless offenders are apprehended they cannot be punished, or others deterred. I am all for apprehension—why does Professor Conrad imply that I am not?—but also for severe punishment, including capital punishment, for those apprehended and convicted. No point apprehending them for a slap on the wrist. Indeed, I think there is a population of deterrables who are not deterred—who will commit crimes—when crime pays, either because offenders are not caught or because they are not sufficiently punished. There is, as Professor Conrad points out, a pool of men and boys in every big city who go around mugging law-abiding citizens. But the pool would be smaller if there were more frequent and severe punishment—including capital punishment for those who commit murder while robbing.

I leave the reader to detect by himself how badly or well Professor Conrad succeeds in escaping from the logical consequences of a very obvious proposition: Punishment is threatened to deter crime and inflicted because threatened.

JOHN P. CONRAD

And I will leave it to the reader to judge whether my steadfast opponent has demonstrated that the logical consequences of his obvious proposition necessarily entail the infliction of capital punishment.

CHAPTER 5

Does Deterrence Need Capital Punishment?

JOHN P. CONRAD

Let us be clear about deterrence. No one can doubt that punishment prevents some crime by intimidating the offender who is punished and by its example to persons who might consider committing a similar offense. Deterrence is implied in the criminal codes, it is made visible by police patrols, it becomes a clearly communicated threat when an offender is convicted and sentenced. Along with many other students of the criminal justice system, Professor van den Haag entertains the opinion that the more severe the sentence, the more effective the threat will be in the prevention of crime. Because the death penalty seems to him and to many others an incomparably more severe sentence than any term of imprisonment, even imprisonment for life, he holds that for the crime of murder it should be resumed in the general administration of justice.

The evidence will never be certain about the effectiveness of deterrence. For the present argument, we can disregard the deterrence of the offender who is being punished; presumably, if he is sentenced to death, he will never offend again. But we have no way of knowing how much crime is prevented by deterring potential criminals through the administration of the various punishments that governments have devised. We cannot even verify or falsify Professor van den Haag's belief that the more severe the punishment, the more crime will be deterred. That does not prevent moral and legal philosophers, social scientists, and plain men on the street from thinking about this question, and they have thought about it for centuries.

There is, of course, a simple logic that convinces reasonable men. If an act is punishable as a crime, then the punishment should be severe enough to cancel out the potential gain that a person considering a crime might expect. It follows that the more severe the punishment, the more people would be deterred from the commission of criminal acts.

This reasoning assumes that potential criminals are rational men, rather like the economists' model of economic man. They will want to maximize gains and minimize losses, and they will arrange for all the information they can get so that they can achieve this goal of the rational economic man. I contend that the rational criminal man, if he exists at all, seldom commits murder, and when he does, his crime is usually impossible for the police to detect.

Professor van den Haag will allow that it is unrealistic to expect that every member of the potentially criminal public is equally deterred by each penalty in the array of punishments that confronts that public. He correctly states that not everyone is deterred, sometimes when the threat of punishment is not credible because it is not consistently imposed, and sometimes when the crime is so attractive to the criminal that he is willing to run the risks of a severe penalty. But, "on the other hand, most people learn that crime does not pay. . . . "

Is this an adequate analysis? I think not. It is true that for some crimes the threat of punishment is barely credible. The police clearance rates in most major cities for burglary, robbery, and the lesser forms of larceny are so low as to present a reasonable prospect of impunity to a criminal with a moderate degree of competence. The excitement of the crime itself, the peer pressure that is often exerted, the compelling need for money for narcotics will counterbalance any serious reflection about the risks attendant on committing it.

Likewise, Professor van den Haag has learned that crime does not pay. In this respect he belongs to a considerable majority of citizens who share this opinion. I think we all learn a good deal more than that. Not only is the threat of punishment and the incommensurable gain from a criminal act sufficient to deter us, but we also have commitments to our concept of ourselves as moral actors, to our self-respect, and to our sense of honor that rule out decisions to act as predators on fellow citizens.

Much more powerful in the prevention of crime than the prospect of death on the gallows or years in a prison cell is the psychological continuity of a human life that builds like a narrative with meaning over the years during which it is lived. Alasdair MacIntyre, one of the most profound of contemporary moral philosophers, discusses this concept of continuity as the essence of personal identity in this way:

We live out our lives, both individually and in our relationships with each other, in the light of certain conceptions of a possible shared future, a future in which certain possibilities beckon us forward and others repel us, some seem already foreclosed and others perhaps inevitable. There is no present which is not informed by some image of some future and an image which always presents itself in the form of a . . . variety of ends or goals—toward which we are either moving or failing to move in the present. Unpredictability and teleology therefore coexist as part of our lives; like characters in a fictional narrative we do not know what will happen next, but none the less our lives have a certain form which projects itself towards our future.[1]

I think MacIntyre has described the way identities are formed with great relevance to our problem in understanding deterrence. As the process of commitment to a future shared with others takes hold, wide categories of decisions, by no means only decisions to commit a crime, are eliminated from consideration. It is inconsistent with my concept of myself as a scholar of criminal justice, and inconsistent with Professor van den Haag's conception of himself as a social philosopher, to adopt certain courses of action. Just as neither of us is likely to decide to become a racing driver, a microbiologist, or an operatic tenor, neither of us will decide to become a mugger, an embezzler, or a member of an organized criminal conspiracy. Our resistance to criminal recruitment has much more to do with our commitments to the continuity of our personal identity than to the fear of punishment for criminal acts. I think this kind of commitment accounts for the crime-free lives that are led by the overwhelming majority of Americans.

It also accounts for the enormous difficulty that confronts penologists in their attempts to divert the recidivist adult offender from a continuing life of crime. Once the picaresque narrative of the career criminal has taken hold of a man's identity, his conception of himself becomes more and more fixed. The chances of a big score are always beckoning, and the choice of a conforming life with a wife, kids, and a steady but boring job will become repellent. Years ago an English career criminal approaching the end of a well-deserved 14-year sentence of preventive detention put it to me with trenchant candor: "A life in the suburbs is not for me. I'm not going to take the train into the city to work as a clerk at regular hours for a bloke who can run my life because he's a boss. I know I'll be in jail again, but it's worth it to be free to do as I please when I'm out."

On one end of the continuum are those to whom the deterrent intent of the law is irrelevant because of their commitments to lives that are in accord with civic values. On the other end of this continuum are those to whom deterrence means just as little as it does to good citizens; they accept criminal values as part of their personal identity, and the risks of punishment are accepted with few qualms.

But it is a continuum. Shading off from the law-abiding citizen are those who will violate selected laws, usually because they see the threat as no great danger to themselves and they can rationalize the violation of the law as no violation of their sense of integrity. Some will cheat judiciously on their income tax returns; some will buy cocaine or marijuana from distributors who are surely scofflaws; some will decide that though they are unsteady after an evening of drinking, they are not too drunk to drive an automobile. Shading off from the committed criminals, most of whom are available for a wide variety of crimes, there are those whose sense of identity is inconsistent with crimes of violence, sex crimes, or crimes involving narcotics.

It is to the middle stratum of the continuum, a band of the spectrum containing young men and women with elastic identities, that deterrence must apply. Because no one can be sure how large a section of society can be placed in this middle stratum, we have no way of coming to any sense of the precise effectiveness of a deterrent sanction. I see no prospect that these difficulties will be surmounted in the years to come. This kind of measurement does not lend itself to census-taking or to the most sensitive and oblique methodologies of survey research. In this state of affairs, vigorous assertions of opinion take the place of facts that cannot be obtained through the methods of science. When policy of such great moment rests on the choice between competing assertions, it becomes necessary to examine these assertions critically, as I intend to do in this chapter.

I do not doubt that the deterrent actions taken by the criminal justice system have a positive effect in reducing crime rates. They could be even more effective if the decisions of judges in these matters were more predictable than they generally are. But it is a narrower question that we must analyze when we consider the deterrence of murder. Unlike the clearance rates for the crimes against property, the clearance rates for homicide are high, and those who kill are usually subjected to the full process of adversary law. A murderer who has been convicted of having killed with malice aforethought or in the course of committing a felony or as an accomplice to a criminal committing a murder under such circumstances can be sure of a prison sentence, and usually a long one. This prospect is well known, even to the stupidest and least stable criminals, no matter how they may choose to rationalize their crimes.

But once again, we can divide the population of murderers according to the sense of personal identity that prevails among people with criminal continuities. I do not think that it can be maintained that everyone is a potential killer, despite the notions that literal-minded psychoanalysts have derived from their understanding of the Freudian id. It is closer to the mark to say that the vast majority of Americans are in no danger at all of being murdered by each other. Those who are in danger are those whose lives are led in a hostile and impoverished environment where hope is a stranger and resignation to misfortune is general. In this environment, violence is overt and considered natural. Those whose lives are lived at the bottom see themselves as unlikely to lose much in losing a life with little meaning. When they choose violence, there is little to move them to stay their hands.

As a retributivist, I make one concession to deterrence, the same concession that I must make to all utilitarian concepts of the criminal justice system. Deterrence is a secondary function of punishment, secondary to an efficient and just administration of retribution. To punish the guilty because punishment is the proper consequence of the conviction of a crime may also deter some potential criminals, just as the criminal's detention in prison will incapacitate him for the commission of crimes for so long as he is locked up, and the exposure he may get from vocational training while in prison may enable him to lead a more constructive life when he gets out.

But deterrence is an intention whose accomplishment no one can measure. Speculations on the proper amount of punishment to inflict so that the maximum amount of crime can be deterred are speculations that are not open to conclusive scientific investigation. Of two things we can be sure: Deterrence is irrelevant to those who are committed to law-abiding lives. It is also irrelevant to those who are committed to careers in which criminal acts must be accepted as natural and necessary. The former have better reasons to refrain from crime than the dread of prison or the electric chair. The latter don't care.

Leaving to one side for a while the primacy of retributivism in the philosophy of punishment, let us consider the claims of deterrence advanced by Professor van den Haag. What kinds of murder are deterred when the death penalty is imposed?

Recalling my years at San Quentin and my observations of the administration of capital punishment at that facility since that time, I find that the occupants of Condemned Row, as I knew them, fell into three general categories. There were two significant exceptions, to whom I shall return presently. First, I will define the categories.

There were several who were peculiarly repellent sex-murderers, men who abducted children or sometimes adult women, raped them or otherwise molested them sexually, and then killed them. A second category consisted of murderers of wives or girl friends; most men convicted of these offenses received life terms instead of the death sentence. The third category was composed of robbers, men who killed the persons they were robbing or the police officers who attempted to arrest them. The first degree murderers who had, for one reason or another, been sentenced to life terms fell into these categories.

Now, one peculiarity of these crimes is that they are not open to deterrence. A sex-murderer is not a calculating offender by any rational standard. He may scheme to seize his victim at a time when he is unlikely to be caught in the act, but usually that exhausts his capability for planning. He does what he feels he has to do, and if he kills his victim, it is in the apparent hope that he can prevent her—or him—from giving evidence. The shame and self-disgust that is so evident in the postconviction statements of many of these men suggests that a half-conscious motive for killing the victim was the desire for a death in the gas chamber. No one can know if such a killer might have spared his victim if he had known that the worst that could happen was a lifetime with his memories in the state penitentiary.

The man or woman who kills a spouse, a lover, or a rival is the perpetrator of the classic *crime passionel*. Neither I nor Professor van den Haag, I am sure, would be willing to condone this kind of murder by allowing the killer the benefit of some "unwritten law," whereby deceit and betrayal in love might justify the taking of the betrayer's life. But in these matters, the killer gives little or no long-range consideration to the consequences of his act. I remember only one spouse-killer whose decisions were rational, and her passion was not amatory nor were her murders deterred. She was executed shortly before my arrival at San Quentin; I never had the opportunity to hear her side of the story. Years before, she had been convicted of second degree murder for poisoning her first husband to collect his insurance. She served her term, was released on parole, and married again. She poisoned her second husband, perhaps supposing that the worst that could happen would be another manageably short term in prison. Instead she was sentenced to death. I suppose that of all the murderers I knew—or knew of— during my San Quentin days, she would have been the most rational. I will never know what kind of miscalculation she thought she had made.

Most spouse-killers kill in anger; the most important influence on their action is the desire for revenge. Professor van den Haag may suppose that deceitful husbands, wives, and lovers will be safer if those they betray are fully aware that the executioner will await them if they carry out their murderous intent. I must doubt it. The furies in such people are implacable and revenge must be carried out. Once in prison serving life terms or awaiting the gas chamber or the electric chair, they are docile, guilty—the survivors of an irreversible tragedy. I have never heard of one who, when released on parole, repeated his offense, though I suppose that may have occurred. In an earlier chapter I mentioned one wife-killer who insisted that he had no right to live and demanded that the death penalty be expedited. I am sure that his was not a singular case, but I do not think that the state should be an accomplice to suicide.

For so long as handguns are readily available in the United States, this country will lead the world in the rate at which robbery is committed. Some experienced robbers take the precaution of not loading their weapons before going to work, but most robbers are not experienced, and most are young men who are burdened with hostility toward a world in which they have no secure and accepted place. They are not only inexperienced as robbers, they are angry, and they know very little about the weapons they carry. Most of them are rather stupid, most of them are easily frightened or confused by an unexpected response from a victim. It is little wonder that sometimes their guns are fired, and at close range it is to be expected that there will be fatalities. The mugger does not expect to be arrested, even when his gun goes off, and unfortunately he is often able to escape. The prospect of an arrest, a trial, and a sentence to prison or to death is not going to enter into such calculations as he is able to make. He has little to lose. He comes from a part of town where violence is pervasive and expected. His life consists of daily frustrations and few satisfactions. For some robbers, though certainly not a majority of them, the need for money with which to pay a dealer for narcotics overwhelms every other consideration.

Robbery is an unskilled criminal's *métier*. It is absurd to think of the young men who commit most of the nation's muggings as crafty schemers capable of engaging in the calculations assumed by social scientists accustomed to predicting the behavior of the reasonable, prudent man. Professor van den Haag and I, if we were minded to plan a day of mugging, would consider the potential gains, the best place to find a suitably affluent victim, the reliability of our crime-partners, if any, the risks of arrest, and the division and disposition of the loot, and would probably decide that with all the variables considered, no plan could be made that would promise enough success to offset the risks. The classic robberies like the Great Train Robbery in England, or some of the expert bank robberies that have claimed the headlines from time to time in this country, require equipment and coordination that are beyond the means and skill of the robber-murderer. Although even these masterpieces of criminality have usually ended in a solution by the police, they have seldom included a homicide, simply because there was nothing in the plan that required extreme violence.

But planning is not a feature of the mugger's work. With a gun in the criminal's hand, any victim will do. In the not infrequent case that the victim is low in cash or unwisely puts up a resistance, he may be punished with a beating or a shooting; the mugger will then go on to try his luck on someone else. How can it be expected that the prospect of the most extreme punishment available to the criminal law will affect the behavior of such a criminal?

There were two exceptions that did not fit any of the three categories of condemned prisoners I have described. Neither was a murderer. One was Caryl Chessman, condemned for kidnapping and raping a woman motorist whom he had flagged down by simulating a police officer's red spotlight. The other was Wesley Wells, a black prisoner with a record of predatory violence in and out of prison that culminated in an incident in which he brained a guard with a spittoon, causing such damage as to incapacitate his victim for life.

Chessman was executed after nearly ten years of clever legal maneuvers that he personally contrived. There were writs upon writs in both state and federal courts; there were worldwide petitions with thousands of signatures addressed to the Governor of California; and, most influential of all, there was a series of well-written autobiographical and semiautobiographical manuscripts that he managed to write on condemned row and get into the hands of publishers. They became best-sellers. A vast amount of sympathy was created for an unpleasant young man with a gift for narrative prose.

He always claimed his innocence of the crime of which he was convicted; the evidence was circumstantial, but a long record of violent crime made his arrest and conviction plausible. I have always thought that he was guilty, but whether he was or not is beside the point I want to make. Because he was sentenced to death, a *cause célèbre* came into being. For ten years Chessman was a celebrity whose predicament raised questions about the administration of criminal justice in California. It is inconceivable that he could have become the symbol that he was—the friendless ex-convict defying the might of the criminal justice establishment—had he been sentenced to an appropriate term in prison.

Chessman was an experienced recidivist. He knew the law, he knew the system, and he also thought he knew that he was cleverer and more adroit than those who made the laws and administered the system. For him, as for some other intelligent career criminals, the fascination of the game he played with the authorities was an obsession. I think he was fully aware of the risks he was running, and in a sort of Dostoyevskian gamble, he lost a game in which winning was not really the objective. Deterrence did not contribute to his commitment to crime; it was irrelevant. Chessman was the most famous of his kind; there are many more gamblers like him in our prisons and on our streets, playing a game with fate and the executioner.

Wesley Wells was more familiarly known as Bob, a hard-bitten black convict with a fancy for young white prisoners. He was feared by everyone around him. Like so many convicts of his generation and to this day, his most important asset was a reputation for violence, and he did everything possible to maintain it. Some such convicts bring their reputation to prison; as violent celebrities, they have made front-page headlines with their exploits. Other convicts achieve their charisma of dread in prison by acts or threats of violence. I never knew Wells's background in sufficient detail to be certain what reputation he had had on the streets, but it is likely that his fame was an artifact of the prison culture. He spent many years on death row. Eventually his sentence was commuted to life imprisonment; he returned to the general population of San Quentin and to his intimidation of weaker prisoners until one day he misjudged his victim and was severely beaten. He then subsided into an innocuous elder of the prison yard and was eventually released on parole. He died two years later, a harmless old man.

Wells was the classic case of the dangerous prisoner, a man who, in his prime, used fear as his instrument for personal satisfaction. The satisfaction of his reputation, so carefully cultivated, led to a culmination in administrative segregation, a carefully controlled lockup in which the prisoner is allowed no movement at all. When a man is so confined, the prison authorities unavoidably certify the authenticity of his reputation. The viciousness of the circle thus completed is not to be broken by deterrence. Wells was a paradigm case of the prison predator and thug, the kind of man who is a danger to others wherever he goes. There are always some men like Bob Wells in every maximum-custody prison, men who attain a peak reputation for violence from which they find it virtually impossible to descend gracefully, even if they wished to do so. The deterrent threat of further punishment has never been known to subdue them.

So far my argument has been that the kinds of murderers who are executed are drawn from the types that are least deterrable. Moved by psychological demons, by furies summoned by real or fancied betrayals, or by the momentum of a robbery, they kill. These are not the men or women whose rationality is sufficient to take into account an estimate of the probabilities of ending in a gas chamber or an electric chair. Pathological sex offenders, betrayed spouses and lovers, and pistol-wielding muggers constitute the population that the executioner is expected to influence. I think it is clear that this is a small population that is invulnerable to reason or the intimidation of the law.

But there are two other populations of killers that might be influenced by deterrence but that are unrepresented on the nation's condemned rows. In my twenty years of employment in the California Department of Corrections, I never met or heard of a contract hit man who had been sentenced to death. There were occasional representatives of organized crime in prison, and, of course, in the federal prisons there were and still are a considerable number, beginning with such famously murderous characters as Scarface Al Capone and Machine Gun Kelly in the 1920s and 1930s. It is startling to read in Sarah Dike's marshaling of the facts about capital punishment that "during 1919–1968, there were 1,004 gangland murders in Chicago, 23 convictions, 4 sentences to life imprisonment, and no death sentences imposed."[2] Admittedly the arrest, trial, and conviction of an organized crime "enforcer" presents special difficulties to the whole criminal justice system. However, it might be supposed that in view of the calculative rationality to be expected of a professional criminal, when such a man is caught he would be tried and whisked off to his execution as conspicuously as possible so as to deter his colleagues. Obviously this does not happen, and I do not venture an explanation. Nevertheless, if the advocates of the death penalty were serious in their argument for deterrence, the hit man would be the most likely candidate for execution.

The second type of deterrable killers are the drunken drivers, responsible, in California at least, for more homicides than all other forms of homicide combined.[3] Those who commit vehicular homicide have a short series of decisions that lead up to their crime. They decide to drink, or rather, they decide not to refrain from drinking even though they are driving. Drunk, they convince themselves that they are fit to drive, and their friends do not dissuade them, although the risk to themselves and to others has been widely and frequently publicized. The people they kill are as dead as those killed by a first degree murderer and as grievously mourned by their families. These victims are more numerous than those who are killed in first and second degree murders, manslaughters, and "nonnegligent" homicides combined.

It is not unreasonable to suppose that, normally, most of these killers are more rational than the killers who risk execution. They come from a large population of people who drive when drunk, knowing that the worst that can happen is a relatively brief prison sentence, if there is a fatality, and really the chances of any punishment at all are slim. There were over 1,200,000 arrests for drunk driving throughout the nation in 1978, surely only a fraction of all the drunk driving that occurred. It is not unreasonable to suppose that the threat of a death penalty for killing anyone while driving under the influence would be more influential with this population, mostly noncriminals in other respects, than it is with the unusual human beings on whom it is normally imposed. Yet I have seldom met men or women serving time on a charge of drunk driving or vehicular homicide, and never have I encountered one on a condemned row. Indeed, such offenders will usually receive rather minimal penalties, sometimes no more than a requirement to perform some public service during their free time.

Of course, I do not advocate the death penalty for the drunken automotive killer, but surely if deterrence is really the objective of the criminal law, more vigorous punishment of those who kill in this irresponsible manner might save lives more consistently than the electrocution of spouse-killers and lethal muggers.

In another chapter I shall deal with the empirical data that relate to the efficacy of capital punishment in the deterrence of murder. None of the information constitutes firm support for the retention of the death penalty, and I think the reasons for its inconclusive tendency are clear when the nature of homicide is considered. The kinds of killings for which society responds with the death penalty are simply not deterrable by the rational processes assumed by such advocates as Professor van den Haag.

All this has been known for centuries. The debate in which my opponent and I are engaged was preceded by an eloquent debate in the *agora* of Athens 2400 years ago, reported by that incomparable historian, Thucydides, who was almost certainly present for the occasion. Because the argument cannot be understood without the background, a brief note on the situation must be made at this point.

The debate took place in 428 B.C. Athens was three years into the Peloponnesian War, which she was eventually to lose to Sparta. Hard pressed but convinced of eventual victory, the city was infuriated when the government of Mitylene, one of its tributary city-states, decided to revoke its alliance with Athens and cast its lot with Sparta. Athens immediately dispatched a naval fleet to subdue the rebellious Mitylenians. The mission was a success; the Mitylenian officials and a Spartan military adviser were captured and brought back to Athens. It was decided to execute all of them immediately, and that was done.

In the assembly that made this decision, Cleon, the son of Cleaenetus, described by Thucydides as "the most violent man in Athens," advocated further action. He persuaded the assembly to issue an order that the entire adult male population of Mitylene should be put to death and that the women and children should be enslaved. A ship was sent off to notify the commander of the occupying forces of the assembly's decision, with orders to carry out the decision without delay.

On the following day, Diodotus, the son of Eucrates, introduced a

motion to rescind this decision. The ensuing debate was recorded by Thucydides, and it dwells on the same issues that have resounded over the centuries from that time to this—though seldom so eloquently.

Cleon opened the debate with a speech opposing the motion before the
assembly. After a denunciation of Mitylenian treachery, he ridiculed the
sentimentality of the intellectuals who supposed that they were wiser than
the laws. He concluded on a theme that combined deterrence of further
defection from the alliance with unashamed vindictiveness:

> Punish them as they deserve, and teach your other allies by a striking exam-
> ple that the penalty of rebellion is death. Let them once understand this
> and you will not so often have to neglect your enemies while you are fighting
> with your confederates.

Opposing Cleon, Diodotus took the floor. After commenting on the evils
of demagoguery and urging that the city's decision in such a matter should
be based on its best interests, he went on to say:

> All, states and individuals, are alike prone to err, and there is no law that
> will prevent them, or why should men have exhausted the list of punish-
> ments in search of enactments to protect them from evil-doers? It is prob-
> able that in early times the penalties for the greatest offenses were less
> severe, and that as these were disregarded, the penalty of death has been
> by degrees in most cases arrived at, which is itself disregarded in like man-
> ner. Either some means of terror more terrible than this must be discovered,
> or it must be owned that this restraint is useless; and that as long as poverty
> gives men the courage of necessity, or plenty fills them with the ambition
> which belongs to insolence and pride, and the other conditions of life remain
> under the thraldom of some fatal and master passion, so long will the
> impulse never be wanting to drive men into danger. Hope also, and cupid-
> ity, the one leading and the other following, the one conceiving the attempt
> and the other suggesting the facility of succeeding, cause the widest ruin,
> and, although invisible agents, are far stronger than the dangers that are
> seen. . . . In fine, it is impossible to prevent, and only great simplicity can
> hope to prevent, human nature doing what it has once set its mind upon,
> by force of law or by any deterrent force whatsoever.[4]

Diodotus's motion won by a narrow margin; a second vessel was sent
off to Mitylene and arrived in the nick of time to prevent the order for the
mass execution of Mitylenians from being carried out.

It is obviously one thing to administer the death penalty to a large and
probably innocent population and quite another to kill a convicted mugger,
but it is probable that deterrence would have been more likely to result from
the former than from the latter. Whether we examine the situation of the
Mitylenians or that of the mugger, a reasoned consideration of deterrence
must lead those who have the best interest of the state at heart to conclude

that whatever deterrent influence the law can exert to prevent murder does not require the threat of death. In another chapter, I shall show that the empirical data assembled by statisticians and social scientists support this analysis.

Notes

1. Alasdair MacIntyre, *After Virtue: A Study in Moral Theory* (Notre Dame, Indiana: University of Notre Dame Press, 1981), pp. 200–201.
2. Sarah Dike, *Capital Punishment in the United States* (Criminal Justice Abstracts, vol. 13, no. 3, September 1981), p. 438.
3. In California in 1977, there were 2626 people killed by drunken drivers. In that year there were 2564 homicides ranging from first degree murder to "nonnegligent" manslaughter.
4. Thucydides, *The Peloponnesian War,* trans. R. Crawley (New York: Modern Library, 1934), pp. 167–170.

ERNEST VAN DEN HAAG

Once more I shall pick out a few disagreements with Professor Conrad. But I want to make it clear that I agree with much of what he so eloquently says in this chapter.

According to Professor Conrad, deterrence theory "assumes that potential criminals are rational men, rather like the economists' model of economic man." No such assumption is made by deterrence or, for that matter, by economic theory. The economic model of rational man is useful in helping us to understand what means would be most rational to maximize whatever ends we want maximized. Economists are quite aware, as are deterrence theorists, that people seldom calculate. Most behavior is habitual, and much depends on emotions and not calculations. Moreover, people usually have multiple ends and are not fully cognizant of all of them. We seldom know everything we want. Finally, we rarely act in the most rational way to achieve what we know we want. All this is hardly news.

The rational model is certainly not meant to be a realistic portrayal of man. It merely makes explicit how people would, or should, act if they wanted to achieve rationally any given set of ends. How helpful are such models? They are misleading if one assumes that they portray all the motivations people actually and individually have. They are not meant to. But if we do not make that silly assumption, models can be as helpful as computers can be, or as the physicist's model of gravity without atmospheric friction. After all, although customers may not, merchants do calculate. They try to anticipate the behavior of customers and to influence it. Merchants are quite rational in believing that when they lower prices, it acts as an incentive for buyers, and that higher prices are disincentives. That much is true even though the customers hardly ever calculate. Why should the criminal law not count on higher costs of crime (punishments are prices paid by offenders) acting as a disincentive?

Rational models are helpful even in describing the behavior of rats. Rats certainly do not calculate, and we do not speak of rational rats. Yet in learning experiments it can be shown that rats tend to respond to incentives and disincentives as though calculating. We can predict their behavior by *our* calculations without assuming that they calculate, for rats do what is rewarded and avoid what is punished—for instance, by electric shocks— just as humans do. Students come somewhat nearer humans, including criminals, than rats do. Consider the following.

Multiple-choice "quizzes" were given to groups of students who were then asked to calculate their own grades by checking to see if they had given the correct answers.* They cheated (by changing their original answers) about one-third of the time. This level of cheating remained unchanged throughout the experiment in a control group that was neither exhorted to honesty nor threatened with punishment.

When students were exhorted to be honest, the rate of cheating was not reduced. On the contrary, it rose: Students took 41% of all opportunities to cheat instead of the previous 34%. The rise is puzzling. "Educating or exhorting people" is often favored as a means of reducing offenses: It costs the least, morally and financially. It also is ineffective and, here, counter-productive: Perhaps students felt that exhortations excluded sanctions.

When a threat was made, and was made credible, to punish cheaters, the cheating level was reduced from 34% to 12%. The reduction—nearly two-thirds—was somewhat less when the threat was made less credible.

It was also found that cheating was most frequent, and threats of punishment least effective, with students whose actual performance fell most below the grades they expected or needed. They had the most to gain from cheating.

This experiment supports three tentative conclusions:

1. Moral exhortation can be useless or counterproductive even in a population presumed to have internalized the moral norms it is exhorted to follow.

---

*See Charles Tittle and Alan R. Rowe, "Fear and the Student Cheater," *Change* (April 1974). Also, "Moral Appeal, Sanction, Threat and Deviance," *Social Problems* 20 (1973), p. 48.

2. Threats of punishment can be very effective, the more so the more credible they are.
3. Temptation is least resisted by those who have most to gain from offenses. The threat of punishment is least effective with them. The greater the advantage the offender can expect from the offense, the greater the threat needed to deter him. By and large, then, the needy are more tempted and less easily deterred than the prosperous, the ambitious than the satisfied.

With all that, Professor Conrad may well be right about some criminals. Some may be altogether irrational, impervious alike to incentives and disincentives. The proportion of these undeterrables in the criminal population is unknown. Whenever our legal system permits us to identify and confine them, the best we can do is to isolate them from society for as long as they may be active. But most people are responsive to incentives and disincentives, and if these are structured well, most people won't become criminals. They can be deterred. Even now, most people do not become criminals, although punishment is so rarely imposed and so lenient that fear of it has greatly decreased.

However, the crime rate has steadily increased although people have become more prosperous and more educated. This testifies to the fact that people are responsive to incentives and disincentives and that disincentives—punishments—are needed, although they are currently used rarely and capriciously by our criminal justice system. Many people now find that criminal activity has become quite rational: Crime is paying better and better; that is why more crimes are being committed. The abolition of the death penalty in practice in the United States certainly has contributed to the unfortunately correct perception that the risk–reward ratio of crime has become very favorable to the criminal. Contrary to what Professor Conrad believes, I think that many criminals are quite rational. They have realized that crime pays, whereas Professor Conrad has not. It is society that is irrational. It allows crime to pay well by punishing so few criminals so leniently as to make crime virtually costless in many cases—only to complain about irrational criminals and rising crime rates.

Take a mundane matter such as burglary. More than 100,000 burglaries were committed in New York in 1980. Yet only 19 persons were serving prison terms for burglary in 1981. Could it be that the low punishment rate is a cause of the high burglary rate? Or consider auto theft. More than 100,000 cars were stolen in New York in 1980, to be resold or to be dismantled with the parts being sold. Yet in 1981 there were altogether 8 persons serving terms for car thefts in New York prisons.* There were 625,222 felony complaints in 1980, and 87,000 felony arrests. Fewer than 9000 felons were sent to prison.† Unfortunately, criminals are right in perceiving that crime pays. Of course, how well it pays depends on one's situation. If you make a reasonable living and have a reasonably pleasant social status, it may not pay for you to risk your lawful income and status by criminal activity even if it pays well by the standards of the poor. But if your income and status are low, you may find that crime can improve your position in life with very little risk. You may take that risk unless you have too many moral scruples. Quite a number of people don't.

Crime rates will continue to rise until crime becomes indeed irrational for most people. Once relatively unimportant crimes are not seriously punished, criminals will think they can get away with murder. After all, murder is often committed during the commission of comparatively trivial crimes that we hardly punish anymore. A man who resists a mugging or a robbery, or who discovers his car being stolen, may very well run the risk of being murdered. So does a man suspected of not sharing the booty as agreed, or of being willing to testify against his partners. And murderers can plead uncontrollable passion, insanity, and now even their inability to appreciate the wrongfulness of their crime. What a marvelous excuse: If they did appreciate the wrongfulness of their act, they probably wouldn't commit murder. So, in a sense, committing the crime serves as an excuse for it.‡ We have nearly 20,000 murders a year, and most murderers apprehended and convicted serve only a few years. If we wanted to encourage crime, including murder, our present practices would be perfect. I do not know how rational criminals are, but I suspect they are more rational than criminologists.

Yet Professor Conrad states "the rational criminal man, if he exists at all, seldom commits murder, and when he does, his crime is usually impossible for the police to detect." To take the last part of his extraordinary statement first, surely Professor Conrad does not mean that such rational murders are never detected. Anyway, in his formulation, Professor Conrad's statement is not testable: We cannot know how many undetected murders there are. We know only of the murders we did detect. But if rational murders are only sometimes detected, and not as often as one might wish, why

---

*See Michael Kramer, "Keeping Bad Guys Off the Street," *New York Magazine,* 8 February 1982.

†*New York Times,* 18 April 1982.

‡To be sure, the law demands proof independent of the act itself for the inability of the offender to appreciate its wrongfulness. But in practice, the act itself often serves as proof.

should this be an argument against imposing the death penalty on the murderers who have been detected? The difficulty, or rarity, of detection hardly is a mitigating circumstance.

Surely the rational murderer does exist: What else are we to call murders for insurance, contract murders, murders by hit men, murders for inheritance, premeditated murders by a wife to remove a husband (or vice versa) in favor of a lover—indeed, most premeditated murders?

At any rate, it seems to me that Professor Conrad looks in the wrong direction. Those who have committed murder may or may not be rational. The threat of the death penalty is addressed to those who, as yet, have not committed murder. If it helps restrain them to such an extent that only those who are not rational do commit murder, the death penalty is exceedingly successful. The increase in "stranger-murders"* indicates that with the waning of the threat of the death penalty an increasing proportion of murders are committed by rational people—as good a reason as any to reinstate the death penalty not only in theory but in actual practice.

I do agree with Professor Conrad that if our self-image does not include criminal activity, we are less likely to engage in it than otherwise. But how is the self-image formed? Why does it not include criminal activity? We may be reluctant to admit it, but the threats of the criminal law are among the factors that shaped our self-image. Even after it has been formed, we may engage in at least some, usually nonviolent, criminal activities if the threats of the criminal law are withdrawn. On the self-image, let me quote Sir James Fitzjames Stephen once more: "Some men, probably, abstain from murder because they fear that if they committed murder they would be hanged [i.e., they fear the cost]. Hundreds of thousands abstain from it because they regard it with horror [i.e., they have rational or emotional internal restraints]. One great reason why they regard it with horror is that murderers are hanged [i.e., the threat formed a habit, which becomes part of the self-image]."† In short, I don't disagree with Professor Conrad on the importance of the self-image in becoming or remaining law-abiding. But I believe that the threats of the law, including the threat of the death penalty, play an important—though seldom conscious—role in forming and maintaining a law-abiding self-image.

Without these threats of the law, the most upright citizens might

---

*Murders in which murderer and victim did not know one another, as in many murders committed during robberies. In 1968 20% of all murders were stranger-murders, whereas by 1974 the stranger-murder rate increased to 34% of all murders, according to the *New York Times,* 23 March 1974, p. 41, column 6. This is an increase of more than 50%.

†J. F. Stephen, *A History of the Criminal Law in England* (London: Macmillan, 1883).

engage in criminal activity. Consider: Nearly everyone, when flying some-where, pays for his ticket and hands it to a ticket taker before entering the plane. Very few people try to cheat. Suppose, now, the airline, believing in the restraining effect of self-images, as Professor Conrad does, decided to do without the ticket taker. People still would be expected to buy tickets but nobody would check on them. What would happen? At first most people would continue to buy tickets. But as word spread that one could ride the plane without a ticket and without fear of punishment, with injury only to one's self-image, I am sure that more and more people would "forget" to buy their ticket while only a few fanatically honest people would continue to do so.*

Crimes of violence are less likely to be committed. Yet if it were not for the threats of the law (or, absent the law, of one's friends), what would prevent the bully or just the strong person from getting his way by imposing it on the weak by force? Yes, Professor Conrad would not become a mugger. Given his talents, and given the law, he does better as a professor. But sup-pose either were lacking? He is right about the self-image but ignores the forces, including the law, that fashion it. Incidentally, in several famous epi-sodes, such as police strikes, criminals were rational enough to commit far more crimes than usual, figuring, correctly, that they would not be appre-hended and punished.

The career criminal, who became one because "A life in the suburbs is not for me," was not, and probably could not be, deterred. But most people, if threatened with sufficient risk of severe punishment, would find noncri-minal activities adventurous enough. They may avoid "a life in the suburbs" and yet not become criminals. It can be done. Nonetheless, apart from unfortunate illustrations, Professor Conrad is right: There are some people who cannot be deterred by the threats of the law; and on the other hand, there are some people who need not be deterred. However, the deterrent threats of the law are meant for the great mass of people who both can be and need to be deterred. Perhaps Leo Tolstoy, who, long before Freud, wrote that the "seeds of every crime are in each of us," exaggerated. There may be congenitally law-abiding people among us. But not many. However, I believe that Tolstoy's "seeds" develop in only a few of us: They need a favor-able environment to develop. It is the task of the law to make the environ-

---

*Incidentally, I think this may not necessarily be true for a city bus. Most people may prefer to be honest—if the amount at issue is small. If it is sizable, controls and the threat of punishment are needed.

ment unfavorable to crime by making crime costly* and the purpose of capital punishment to make it unfavorable to the murderous impulses we all occasionally may feel, however inchoately and dimly.

It is remarkable that, throughout, Professor Conrad illustrates his thesis—that we don't need capital punishment because punishment in general does not deter criminals—by describing or quoting criminals. But these obviously are the people who have not been deterred. The point is to deter those who have not, or have not yet but may, become criminals. So what if "the killer gives little or no long-range consideration to the consequences of his act," if a sex-murderer is not a calculating offender. That is why he became a killer or a sex-murderer. The point of deterrence is to restrain those who are a little more rational, yet tempted to kill in some occasions. It may be "absurd," in Professor Conrad's words, "to think of the young men who commit most of the nation's muggings as crafty schemers capable of engaging in the calculations assumed by social scientists. . . . " It is also unnecessary. Muggers seem to be crafty enough to know they are unlikely to be caught or punished, which is why they mug away, as they did not when they had reason to believe that they would be caught and severely punished.

Whether or not muggers do calculate (those I have known seem quite rational), the law still manages to deter most young men from becoming muggers. Because the law now is lenient in practice and barely enforced, it is not very effective, as any New Yorker can tell. But surely the remedy is not to assume that muggers don't know what they are doing anyway. The remedy is to teach them—and above all to teach prospective muggers—that mugging does not pay, because the punishment is too severe and too likely. Right now, rational muggers know that mugging pays.

Professor Conrad is right on another point: If he and I planned a robbery, we would probably desist after calculating the risks. But not, as he believes, because we calculate more, or better, than actual robbers. Rather, because our risk would be greater than theirs: We have a great deal to lose—position and income—and comparatively little to gain. Robbers with low incomes and positions may calculate just as much as we do, and as well, but reach different results, quite as correct as ours. The risk–reward ratio is different. For them the risk is less (they have only a low income to lose and no status) and the reward bigger (the lower your income, the more sig-

---

*Surely other factors contribute to a favorable or unfavorable environment. But society can do little to influence, say, early family environment. Social work, housing, schooling, or income supplements have not proved effective in reducing crime rates.

nificant any addition to it). Criminals need not calculate less, or less correctly, than middle-class people. They just are not middle-class people and, therefore, if they are as rational as Professor Conrad, will come to a different result.

Over and over Professor Conrad reiterates that convicts he has known were not, and could not be, deterred. But that is evident. Had they been deterred they would not be convicts. Deterrence is meant to prevent noncriminals from becoming criminals. It has not worked with criminals. It will not work with all noncriminals. But it has, does, and will restrain most people from becoming offenders if the law is severe enough and the probability of punishment high enough.

Finally, Professor Conrad points out that nearly half of the 55,000 people killed by or in cars every year are killed by drunken drivers. He advocates more severe punishment for them. I could not agree more. However, this is one of the points where retributionist and deterrence theory differ. Conrad, a self-proclaimed retributionist, should advocate mild punishment for the drunken drivers, for, unlike murderers, they lack the intention to kill. Their victims are just as dead, the harm is just as great. But the drivers were negligent or reckless—they did not have the *mens rea,* the intention to kill, wherefore they are not blamed and punished as the murderer is. Many are law-abiding citizens who just had one too many—and the misfortune of running over somebody. However, from the viewpoint of deterrence, severe punishment is indicated to deter drunken driving, even though the people engaged in it meant no harm. The harm to be prevented is more important than the blameworthiness of the offender. I am glad to see Professor Conrad is with me on the side of deterrence here.

JOHN P. CONRAD

I must enter a sporting complaint about Professor van den Haag's version of my basic thesis. Toward the end of his well-argued rebuttal, he says, "Professor Conrad illustrates his thesis—that we don't need capital punishment because punishment in general does not deter criminals—. . . ." My thesis is much more complicated than that. At the outset of this chapter, I acknowledged as explicitly as I could that punishment does prevent some crime by intimidating some offenders and by an admonitory example to potential offenders. I am not so simple as to think that no one is deterred by the criminal law, or that a predictable consequence of punishment—capital or otherwise—will not prevent many people from proceeding with a criminal plan, or even from acting on a violent impulse.

Punishment certainly deters some potential offenders, but we must not rely on increasing severity to make a corresponding decrease in the number of crimes committed. If we cannot do more to reduce the economic and social causes of crime, we must increase the risks of apprehension by the police. With crime clearance rates as low as they are, it is idle to suppose that dramatic increases in the severity of punishment will seriously affect the incidence of any type of crime.

My theory of deterrence, such as it is, allows for the irrelevance of the criminal law to the majority of citizens who have lifelong commitments to noncriminal careers, and likewise for its irrelevance as a deterrent to men and women whose criminal careers are well established. I concede that between these two ends of a spectrum of behavior we can discern bands of undetermined width composed of people whose commitments are shaky and who are undoubtedly influenced by fears of what would happen to them if they committed crimes and were caught. I am completely unimpressed with the research that I have seen that attempts to measure the dimensions of these spectral bands—especially when it is research that is done in or to a class of social science undergraduates.

Knowing so little about the dimensions of the population of deterrables, whose attitudes and inclinations must vary widely with regard to the items in the catalog of crimes, I contend that there is no evidence at all that capital punishment is needed in making deterrence more effective. What is much more important is that criminals must be apprehended, booked, and prosecuted and that the penalties for crime should be predictable. Everyone, including the criminal population, knows that only a small minority of all the felonies committed are punishable by death, even supposing that the death penalty were more rigorously applied than has ever been the case in this country.

My thesis, then, if it must be compressed into a sentence, would run as follows: It is true that the administration of punishment deters some potential criminals from committing some crimes, but there is no reason to believe that capital punishment adds anything at all to the deterrent effect of the law.

Of course, that is not all that I have to say in my insistence that capital punishment must be abolished; all that I have done here is to clarify as best I can a position that puts deterrence into its proper perspective. In the sections to follow I want to disentangle some of the misunderstanding that results from my deft opponent's oversimplification of my position on deterrence.

The Disincentives of the Criminal Law

Professor van den Haag poses the econometric question: *Why should the criminal law not count on the higher costs of crime (punishments are prices paid by offenders) acting as a disincentive?*

Taken literally, this question suggests the answer that as long as crime rates continue to rise, we should make corresponding increases in the severity of punishments. That throws a harsh light on the practical dilemma of criminal justice in the United States. The response to that answer is simple: We can't afford it. The failure of the police to apprehend more burglars and car thieves, rightly deplored by my opponent, is not attributable to inefficiency or indifference. There is too much crime in the large cities, far more than the resources of any police department can clear. Even if the police in New York City could arrest all the burglars, car thieves, and muggers, there are not enough courts to try them and not enough prison cells to keep them. How can the resumption of capital punishment for an occasional murderer—or even for all first degree murderers—affect this crowding of the system? Some unthinking citizens may be persuaded by soapbox politicians that at last the law is getting tough with these hoodlums. The hoodlums know better. The odds against them will not have changed for the worse.

Rats, Students, and Behavior Modification

I am not an uncritical follower of B. F. Skinner's extrapolations from animal behavior to the human condition,[1] but my opponent's citation of the response of laboratory rats to learning experiments opens an issue that deserves examination. It is true that rats don't calculate. The behavior the experimenter wants is positively reinforced with food, and that which he doesn't want is negatively reinforced with an electric shock. Skinner also allows that undesired behavior can be extinguished by no reinforcement at all; neither rats nor human beings will persist in activities from which there is no gain of any kind. I follow Skinner in the belief that generally human beings are responsive to the reinforcements they receive, though the reinforcement process is much more complex with us than it is with rats. Skinner has always held that negative reinforcement is an inefficient method of behavior modification. When a rat gets nothing from his environment but negative reinforcement, his appropriate response is to curl up into immobility in a position where electric shocks will not be inflicted.

Human beings are more complicated than rats. When the environment provides no positive reinforcement for any kind of socially approved behavior, we can expect that when reinforcement is available for some kind of socially disapproved behavior, then that behavior will be manifested. This hypothesis accounts for a lot of the hustling, prostitution, dope peddling, and outright crime that we observe in the social underclass. Dr. van den Haag is quite right; it is not entirely rational behavior in that it is behavior that is largely conditioned by the environment and not rationally chosen to the extent that would be the case with him or me.

Dr. van den Haag cites in support of his views about deterrence an experiment reported by Tittle and Rowe in what seems to have been an undergraduate class in one of the social sciences. The experiment was carried out with enough deception so that the students undoubtedly didn't know what was going on. Many of them cheated, but when a threat of sanctions was made, some of them desisted. From this sequence of events, my opponent makes three tentative conclusions that, in his view, might be applicable to much more serious offenses than fudging on a quiz. But the authors of this article themselves cautioned:

> ... [I]t would be a mistake to draw sweeping conclusions from these results. We were testing the effect of a particular kind of sanction—one to be imposed formally by an authority figure. The experiment used a particular type of subject (young adults) and was concerned with obedience to a non-legal norm with little moral or normative support. In addition, the behavior under consideration was instrumental behavior (oriented to long-range goals) and probably episodic; that is, it did not involve deep personal commitments to a style of behavior around which one could form an identity. . . . [2]

Dr. van den Haag's three tentative conclusions are of the sweeping kind against which Tittle and Rowe warned. After all, cheating is endemic in most American institutions of higher learning, as my adversary must have observed for himself. To vault from the effects of an unspecified penalty administered in such a normative environment to an assertion about the relative deterrent value of the electric chair is a feat of intellectual agility that few social scientists can match.

The difficulty encountered by my opponent in using this odd illustration of deterrence illustrates the special obscurity in which deterrence research must function. The experiments that can be ethically conducted are of a trivial nature from which generalizations about serious crime problems cannot be safely made. On the other hand, statistical comparisons over time or from jurisdiction to jurisdiction are invariably open to some kind of challenge. I shall have more to say about this matter in a separate chapter on the evidence that supports claims about the value of capital punishment. In the meantime, I cannot accept inferences about the usefulness of the death penalty that are drawn from experiments on college classroom cheating or the behavior of rats and pigeons. Retentionists who rely on empiricism to bolster their arguments stand on precarious scaffolding.

Does Crime Pay?

We must fix our attention on those crimes that might be deterred by the death penalty. The most lucrative crimes, those that can be and sometimes are committed by bankers and corporation officers, are not and should not be subject to the death penalty. The street crimes that are open to the underclass citizen—robbery, burglary, auto theft, and various other kinds of larceny—are lucrative to varying degrees. I am not aware of any authoritative study of the comparative economic returns from these forms of enterprise, but observation and common sense lead me to the conclusion that robbery is the least remunerative. It is the only one of the property crimes that relies on the threat and infliction of force, and consequently it is the only crime in which the death penalty is seriously relevant—except, of course, for those situations where homicide is intended and carried out. (I know that some burglars and perhaps a few auto thieves commit murder in the course of their crimes, but it's uncommon and the threat of force is not a necessary part of these offenses.) Does crime pay? It certainly does, but those crimes that pay best are least likely to be prevented by the deterrent impact of the death penalty. Mugging is a mug's game, to be engaged in out of excitement and because of the lack of sufficient skill and opportunity to engage in safer and more profitable criminal arts.

And this is the kind of confusion that econometrically inclined criminologists must disentangle before they make statements about the disincentives and their operation in the crime market. Some crimes pay very well, and apparently they can be committed with relative impunity, but they are the very crimes that are chosen on those accounts. A burglar with a reliable fence can do very well for himself, assuming that he has the tools and the skill to prepare for his exploits. A mugger or a liquor store holdup man will get away with a few offenses before the word gets around about his successes. The occasional big score will make him more visible to the police; the paradox is that the better a crime pays him, the more likely it is that he will have to pay for it.

What does the death penalty have to do with the economic returns of crime? Apparently my opponent would like us to believe that if the state would only invoke that penalty more often, the economic returns of crime would somehow be effectively offset. It seems to me that in any conceivable condition of the criminal justice system this is a highly suspect argument, which has to dismiss the realities of all kinds of crime.

The Free Flying Analogy

I quite agree with my opponent that if that charming stewardess were not waiting at the entrance to the plane, ready to take our tickets, there would be a lot of knaves who would take advantage of her absence to fly for nothing at all. Neither of us would be so unscrupulous, but I readily concede that there are marginally scrupulous people who would fly incessantly if such opportunities were open to them. There are also marginally honest people who would steal and commit other crimes if they knew that there was absolutely no chance of their being caught. Indeed, some of the crimes that such people might commit would include homicide. The tragic overloading of the system as the consequence of an increasingly large and fecund underclass for whom the society has no economic use has overwhelmed the entire apparatus of criminal justice. Until we can reorganize the economy to provide a productive place in it for all citizens, the administration of the death penalty, no matter how frequently, will be a bloody but futile gesture.

Law Observance Is Not Congenital

On this point, I am even less sanguine than my opponent. The will to abide by the law is the indubitable product of nurture, not nature. Had either of us been born in the miserable circumstances of the American underclass, we might well have discovered the seeds of crime germinating within us; we might have become criminals and perhaps successful criminals. Throughout this discourse, I have insisted on the powerful influence of positive incentives in shaping not merely the image but the actuality of a career in which crime is a minimal contingency, if not entirely excluded. The influence of the criminal law is irrelevant to such people—unless we are considering such offenses as income tax fraud and reckless driving, to neither of which does the death penalty ever apply. I agree with Dr. van den Haag's observation that "even now, most people do not become criminals, although punishment is so rarely imposed . . . that the fear of it has greatly decreased." The reason for the general abstinence from crime has much more to do with who "most people" are than with what the law requires of them. Not many boys and girls learn the provisions of the penal code at their mother's knee.

Deterring the Driving Drunk

I hope that neither Professor van den Haag nor anyone else will infer that I advocate the death penalty for the drunken driver who kills someone in an accident. I present my question about the use of the death penalty in such situations because I want to understand better his insistence on the effectiveness of deterrence in saving innocent lives.

Let us forget *mens rea* for the moment, and also the misfortune of the driving drunk who was not dissuaded from driving home after a night on the town. In the spirit of my inventive opponent's hypothetical questions, I want to know why he would not punish this kind of homicide with the ultimate penalty. Suppose that I could show him that for every drunken driver-killer executed there would be 500 innocent victims spared because of the deterrence of other potentially drunken drivers in the future? He concedes that "the harm to be prevented is more important than the blameworthiness of the offender." He allows that "severe punishment" is indicated to deter drunken driving. How severe? A year in a county jail? Five, ten, fifteen years in prison? Why not the death penalty—especially when we bear in mind that it is likely that if it were inflicted, it would have much more impact on the potential drunken driver than it will have on that street criminal with a cheap pistol under his belt?

I ask these questions because of my desire to know more about how and why utilitarians like Professor van den Haag expect punishment to prevent serious offenses. As a retributivist—perhaps "self-proclaimed," whatever is implied by that modifier—I think this offense should be very seriously regarded. The penalty should be severe, not so much because of its deterrent effect as to indicate that it is an extremely detestable form of homicide, and not merely the misfortune of a man or woman who had one too many. Maybe the people who engage in drunken driving "meant no harm," but I suggest that they meant nothing at all. By punishing them as lightly as we do, we minimize the seriousness of the offense and indulge the irresponsibility of those who endanger the lives of all good citizens. If Dr. van den Haag feels that the death penalty is suitable for an irresponsible young man with a pistol who kills at a moment of high tension in a robbery, why is it unsuitable for the young man with an automobile who lurches down the freeway? Sober, he would know just as well as the young mugger how wrongful his conduct is. We will agree that a severe penalty is appropriate for both young men. But Dr. van den Haag, stern advocate of severity though he is, will let off the driving drunk from the final severity in his inventory but not the pistol-bearing hoodlum. He takes this position, even though I suggest that the deterrent effect of the death penalty in such cases might be even greater than with muggers and hit men. I am still unclear as to his reasons.

Notes

1. B. F. Skinner, *Science and Human Behavior* (New York: The Free Press, 1965).
2. Charles R. Tittle and Alan R. Rowe, "Moral Appeal, Sanction, Threat, and Deviance: An Experimental Test," *Social Problems* 20 (1973), p. 496.

ERNEST VAN DEN HAAG

There are a number of questionable points here on which I shall comment *seriatim*. Professor Conrad writes: "we must not rely on increasing severity [of punishment] to make a corresponding decrease in the number of crimes committed." Who does? We do not know by how much increased severity will reduce the crime rate; nobody expects a *"corresponding"* decrease. I, for one, expect *some* decrease—just as I expect some decrease in parking violations when the fine in increased, though not a "corresponding" one.

I do not know what Conrad's "economic and social causes of crime" are. Neither does anyone else. In the United States crime has risen with prosperity and with education, although all those who allegedly know "the causes" of crime expected it to fall. In contrast, in Japan crime has fallen as prosperity and education have risen. In the United States, a comparatively egalitarian society, crime is much higher than in Spain, Greece, Portugal, France, or England, all much less egalitarian societies.

Professor Conrad wishes to increase the rate "of apprehension by the police." Who doesn't? But why in his mind this is a substitute for, rather than a supplement to, higher penalties we are not told. Nor does Professor Conrad mention that apprehension is of little help if conviction even of the clearly guilty is made as difficult as the courts are making it. The courts now exclude evidence, however probative, when seized without sufficient "probable cause" (which in the minds of some judges nearly requires witnessing the crime), when in excess of a warrant too narrowly formulated, or when found because of a confession made when the offender was unaware that he could have a lawyer—who would tell him not to admit to his crime unless he could make a bargain for low punishment. If the defense questions his sanity, federal courts may require that the prosecution prove the defendant sane beyond a reasonable doubt—almost always an impossible task. (Fortunately, juries often have more common sense than judges.)

As for state courts, the following may shed some light on what some of them are doing*:

> Steve Grogan pleaded guilty to a grand theft auto charge stemming from the Barker raid. Van Nuys Judge Sterry Fagan heard the case. He was aware of Grogan's lengthy rap sheet. The prosecutor also informed the judge that Grogan was exceedingly dangerous; and that he had not only been along on the night the LaBiancas were killed, but we also had evidence that he had beheaded Shorty Shea. Yet unbelievably enough, Judge Fagan gave Grogan straight probation!
>
> On learning that Grogan had returned to the Family at Spahn Ranch, I contacted his probation officer, asking him to revoke Grogan's probation. There was more than ample cause. Among the terms of the probation were that he maintain residence at the home of his parents; seek and maintain employment; not use or possess any narcotics; not associate with known narcotics users. Moreover, he had been seen on several occasions, even photographed with a knife and a gun.
>
> His probation officer refused to act. He later admitted that he was afraid of Grogan. [Many probation and parole officers are simply afraid of their charges. Most do not like to "make waves." Wherefore the most dangerous people seldom have probation or parole revoked.] . . .
>
> The eighteen year old Grogan's rap sheet read as follows: 3-23-66, Possession dangerous drugs, 6 mos. probation; 4-27-66, Shoplifting, Con't on probation; 6-23-66, Disturbing the peace, Con't on probation; 9-27-66, Probation dismissed; 6-5-67, Possession marijuana, Counseled & released; 8-12-67, Shoplifting, Bail forfeiture; 1-22-68, Loitering, Closed after investigation; 4-5-69, Grand theft money & Prowling, Released insuff. evidence; 5-20-69, Grand theft auto, Released insuff. evidence; 6-11-69, Child molesting & Indecent exposure . . . †
>
> Grogan had been observed exposing himself to several children, ages four to five years. "The kids wanted me to," he explained to the arresting officers who caught him in the act. "I violated the law, the thing fell out of my pants and the parents got excited," he later told a court-appointed psychiatrist. After interviewing Grogan, the psychiatrist ruled *against* committing him to Camarillo State Hospital, because "the minor is much too aggressive to remain in a setting which does not provide containment facilities."

*Excerpted from Vincent Bugliosi, *Helter Skelter* (New York: Bantam, 1975), pp. 180–181;419–420. Bugliosi prosecuted the Manson gang.
†This "rap sheet" excludes acts committed when a "juvenile."

The court decided otherwise, sending him to Camarillo for a ninety-day observation period. He remained a grand total of two days, then walked away.

His escape had occurred on July 19, 1969. He was back at Spahn in time for the Hinman, Tate and LaBianca murders. He was arrested in the August 16 Spahn raid, but was released two days later, in time to behead Shorty Shea.

Professor Conrad thinks there is something wrong with deterrence theory. I think there is something wrong with the judiciary and the law that permits it to act as just described. Conrad thinks the police do not apprehend enough. True. But I think the judiciary releases too much and does not punish enough. The reader will have to make his own decision. Apprehension is also made difficult by the many limits the courts have placed on police investigation. I should think that opposing some of these nonsensical limits would be more useful than lamenting the low apprehension rate as though it were an act of God.

Professor Conrad writes, "With crime clearance rates as low as they are, it is idle to suppose that dramatic increases in the severity of punishment will seriously affect the incidence of any type of crime." This is a *non sequitur*. There is no reason to believe that "dramatic increases in the severity of punishment will seriously affect . . . crime" only if (a) a given clearance rate is achieved, (b) we have not achieved this clearance rate. Actually, (c) severity may affect crime rates at any clearance rate above zero. Higher clearance rates are desirable. They cannot replace severity, but they may increase the effectiveness of the whole criminal justice process. Professor Conrad's statement remains an unjustifiable *non sequitur*.

"My theory of deterrence . . . ," Conrad writes, "allows for the irrelevance of the criminal law to [1] the majority of citizens who have lifelong commitments to noncriminal careers, and likewise . . . as a deterrent to [2] men and women whose criminal careers are well established." Irrelevance? Does that not go too far? There are two ways of understanding this sentence: It may be intended as a definition or as a statement of fact. Either way, I can't see the point.

Consider it a definition. If a member of the first group, [1], does commit a crime, well, perhaps then there was no "lifelong commitment" to noncriminal careers. He's redefined. If a member of the second group, [2], is actually deterred by the threat of punishment, well, then his criminal career was perhaps not "well established." He's redefined. Clearly such a definition is useless.

But if Professor Conrad wanted to make a factual statement, he has not told us about the facts on which his dichotomy is based. He does "concede" that there are people in the middle "influenced by fears of what would happen to them if they committed crimes and were caught." Well, I think that 95% of the population are in the middle—some nearer one, some nearer the other end of the spectrum. Most of us are capable of committing crimes and can be pushed to do so by various situations; fortunately, most of us, too, are capable of being deterred by legal threats, wherefore most of us do not commit crimes. All Conrad has told us is that some people don't need, others don't heed the law. But the important thing is that most people need and heed it.

Throughout, Professor Conrad insists that many people are committed to noncriminality, so that the threats of the criminal law are "irrelevant" in keeping them on the straight and narrow: "Not many boys and girls learn the provisions of the penal code at their mother's knee," Conrad says. Sure. Conrad writes as though people were born lawabiding. Aren't they educated and conditioned? Didn't societal rules play any role in governing their conduct? And aren't these confirmed, sanctioned, accepted, and respected with the aid of the criminal law and of its punishments? I thought James Fitzjames Stephen said all that needs to be said about this and have quoted him previously, apparently to no avail: "Some men, probably, abstain from murder because they fear that if they committed murder they would be hanged [i.e., they fear the cost, they are deterred]. Hundreds of thousands abstain from it because they regard it with horror [i.e., they have rational or emotional internal restraints, lifelong commitments to noncriminal careers]. One great reason why they regard it with horror is that murderers are hanged [i.e., the threat formed a habit, which becomes part of the self-image; it led, however indirectly, to the lifelong commitment"].* Wherefore the criminal law becomes irrelevant to those committed to noncriminal careers only because it was relevant to forming the commitment.

Professor Conrad goes on to tell us that we cannot afford to catch, convict, and punish more criminals: It would be too costly. Indeed, it is far more costly than it should be. Our criminal justice system, including the correctional system, is a costly scandal. The cost could be greatly reduced without moral loss by means on which, I suspect, Professor Conrad and I would largely agree. Yet even if crime control stays as costly as it is, it is still much cheaper to catch and punish criminals than not to do so. Crime is far more costly than its control. The trouble is that the cost of crime control is borne

---

*J. F. Stephen, *A History of the Criminal Law in England* (London: Macmillan, 1883).

by taxpayers, whereas the cost of crime is borne by the victims and tends to be discounted or ignored by such as Professor Conrad. Still, any criminal behind bars saves society more than it costs to put and keep him there. As for Conrad's "the hoodlums know better," that is, they feel that the law won't be "getting tough" with them, even if there is a death penalty, I agree that capital punishment is not sufficient. But it is a beginning. If we stick to it, even the hoodlums will get the message. It may take a while because they have learned to expect the treatment Professor Conrad favors. But it won't take forever.

Professor Conrad reacts to my mention of rats, used in learning experiments throughout the world, by a disquisition on the psychologist B. F. Skinner, whom I did not mention because there is no need to. This reference gives Professor Conrad an occasion to state, "Skinner has always held that negative reinforcement [punishment] is an inefficient method of behavior modification." He has. On the basis of one (1) experiment, which is often quoted by uninformed do-gooders. However, those fond of quoting Skinner's experiment have overlooked that many experiments since have shown that negative reinforcement [punishment] works well, and often better than positive reinforcement [reward]—with rats as well as with people. A summary of the relevant experiments may be found in Barry F. Singer's *Psychological Studies of Punishment.** There are literally hundreds of experiments showing, not that Skinner's experiment, but that the sweeping and unwarranted conclusions drawn from it by Skinner himself and by others are wrong. The frequent quotation of the solitary experiment reflects ideology, not fact.

Conrad goes on to say that when there is no reinforcement for social, while there is for antisocial, behavior, the latter will prevail. I doubt that this theory, propounded originally by Edwin H. Sutherland, is very meaningful. It certainly is not useful. But if one grants it to be a meaningful and correct theory, it still does not answer these questions: Why is there reinforcement for antisocial behavior in that group and not for socially acceptable conduct? Why do other groups in similar circumstances generate reinforcement for prosocial conduct? And why do some persons in either group become criminals while others do not? Most important, would there be positive reinforcement for criminal conduct if it were punished seriously enough to be disadvantageous to offenders? I think not. Group reinforcement depends on incentives and disincentives. It is a dependent, not an independent, variable. In short, the theory shows the need for disincentives to crime,

California Law Review 58 (1970), pp. 405–443.

not, as Conrad seems to think, the futility thereof. Sufficient disincentives will overcome and change "positive reinforcement" for crime.

This brings me to Conrad's assertion that there is "tragic overloading of our system [of criminal justice] as the consequence of an increasingly large and fecund underclass for whom the society has no economic use . . . [that will remain] until we can reorganize the economy to provide a productive place in it for all citizens. . . ." In short, it is all society's fault, not the criminal's. There are three implications: (1) The underclass is "increasingly large and fecund" (2) because society fails to provide "economic use" for it; (3) this causes, or contributes to, the high crime rate, "the tragic overloading," (4) which can be remedied only if we "reorganize the economy to provide a productive place in it for all citizens."

This discredited theory was originally presented by Richard A. Cloward and Lloyd E. Ohlin in *Delinquency and Opportunity*.* President Johnson's Great Society, following Cloward's theory, tried to provide a "productive place" for the unemployed young. The crime rate did not fall. It rose. What makes crime attractive is not that people are poor or have nothing to do, but that crime is thought to pay better than the jobs available. I can think of no reorganization to remedy that situation, other than to make crime pay less well.†

As to the facts: If we take the poverty line set by the Department of Labor Statistics (in July 1982 a family of four with an income of less than around $9287 was regarded as poor) and correct for the effects of inflation (i.e., if we consider only the actual purchasing power) and project backward, we find the proportions of all families in the United States living below the poverty line at various times listed in Table I. In other words, there has been an unprecedented reduction in poverty. If one monetizes support by food stamps, Medicaid, and a myriad other "in kind" programs, the number of families below the poverty line approaches zero. If the crime rate has been reduced in any degree since 1900, it is a well-kept secret. Actually it rose. Crime rose most in the last thirty years as poverty was reduced to the vanishing point.

It is not, contrary to Cloward and to Conrad, that people can't find jobs that leads them to resort to crime. Some are unemployable. Others become unemployable because they prefer crime to legitimate activities, because it

---

*New York: The Free Press, 1960.

†An interesting discussion of the whole issue is found in Daniel P. Moynihan, *Maximum Feasible Misunderstanding* (New York: The Free Press, 1969).

TABLE I. Proportion of All Families in the
United States Living Below the Poverty Line,
1900–1982[a]

Year	Percent living below poverty line
1900	90
1920	50
1930	33
1962	20
1966	15–16
1970	11
1982	Probably between 11 and 14 owing to the recession

[a]Source: U.S. Bureau of Labor Statistics

seems more rewarding. Our social policy probably helped; welfare parents, or more likely, mothers, bring up children without offering models of employment and of nonwelfare legitimate income. Many are on welfare not because there are no jobs but because they preferred to be welfare mothers rather than employees. (The welfare rolls increased even in periods of low unemployment.)

I am in favor of reorganizing not society—all the "reorganized" societies I know are worse than ours—but our welfare, educational, and penal policies. Currently we make crime (and welfare) pay. And then lament that there is so much of it. Or we take seriously Professor Conrad's simplistic theory: It is really the fault of society, criminals are not to blame, and more employment would solve the problem. When we had practically no unemployment our crime rates did not fall. And during the Great Depression of the 1930s they were lower than they are now. Old liberal ideas never die. They don't even seem to fade away.

Now about the experiments with students. Conrad objects that my conclusions are to sweeping, because "after all, cheating is endemic" among students; hence, my demonstrating that it can be greatly reduced by the credible threat of punishment does not show that punishment deters. Why not? After all Professor Conrad wrote about positive environmental reinforcement of antisocial behavior, against which punishment is alleged to be useless. Thus, if cheating is "endemic," I should have thought that Professor Conrad would predict that the threat of punishment would not be effective. It was effective. Conrad's theory does not work. Whereupon Conrad complains that my conclusions are "sweeping." They are correct. His are not, according to his own theory. He seems to use the word *sweeping* as a synonym for *correct*.

Of course, it is easier to stop a student from cheating than a burglar from burglarizing. But all I meant to demonstrate is that threats deter most people. The utterly honest student does not need them, and the committed cheater may not heed them. Both are marginal. Most students will. So will most people most of the time.

About drunken drivers: Professor Conrad asks, "Suppose that I could show . . . that for every drunken driver-killer executed there would be 500 innocent victims spared because of the deterrence of other potentially drunken drivers . . ." would you (Ernest van den Haag) favor the death penalty? The answer is yes, I would. I should always be in favor of saving 500 lives by the execution of one offender, whatever his offense. But here I would demand much more conclusive proof of the size of the deterrent effect on drunken driving than is now available even for the effect of the death penalty on murder, since I would inflict the death penalty on the drunken driver only because of the deterrent effect, whereas I believe the murderer deserves it in any case. (I share retributionist feelings about what is deserved morally although, unlike Professor Conrad, I do not think they amount to a theory.)

However, I do not think that the death penalty for drunken driving is as needed as it is for murder. A year in prison for driving while drunk, three years for seriously and culpably harming anyone, five to ten years for very serious harm or for culpably, although unintentionally, killing anyone would reduce the drunken driving rate as much as it can be reduced.

Even this will be politically very difficult, although desirable. Drunken drivers have many politically influential friends. In fact, they themselves often are influential persons. Murderers, fortunately, have few friends. Which is why the death penalty for murder is politically feasible and why it is not for drunken driving.

One reason murderers have few friends is that unlike drunken drivers, at least those murderers for whom capital punishment is meant—those who murder with premeditation or during commission of another crime, those who murder for money, rape murderers *et al.*—are a rightly despised lot, who morally would deserve execution even if it did not deter anyone. In contrast, drunken drivers are careless and reckless but not necessarily evil people. Since their conduct is very harmful, they should be deterred. Far stronger punishment would be required than is now imposed. But since drunken drivers do not intend the evil they bring about, juries would not be likely to allow the more severe punishment Professor Conrad and I both would desire. And if they don't want the punishment imposed, juries can find a guilty person not guilty. They don't have the authority to act in this way, but they have the power.*

JOHN P. CONRAD

One of the benefits of this debate is the lesson I have learned about the difficulties of achieving unambiguous clarity. My dauntless opponent's second batch of comments on this chapter calls for further elaboration of positions that I had innocently thought to be clear. I count no less than eleven points in Dr. van den Haag's response on which I must expound further. I cannot hope to satisfy him, but at least I may resolve such doubts as he may have raised in the minds of uncommitted readers.

A Note on the Economic and Social Causes of Crime

Like most conservative social philosophers, my skeptical opponent professes not to know the social and economic causes of crime. Leaving aside the subtle epistemological issues that can always be summoned to cloud the obvious, I hold that a large volume of crime, including most violent crime, can be traced to the structural poverty that has created an immobilized underclass in the great cities of this nation.

No news there. Large cities have always contained threats to the safety of the comfortable classes. The threats are to be found among the dispossessed, those who live at the bottom of the social pyramid. They are resentful of a predicament for which they do not feel they are to blame. In the United States, more than in most countries, economic distress tends to be ascribed to unworthiness—the poor are generally thought to be undeserving.

For those who are born into families living at the bottom, there are not many options for survival and gratification. Such careers as hustling, prostitution, and the various forms of street crime seem most promising to the young. These are careers with little appeal to those who are born into the more secure classes; these latter lack proximity to role-models for pimping and whoring and mugging, even if they have no particular moral objections to these styles of life. For the underclass, the conventional values of hard work and saving money cannot have much meaning. Boys and girls learn to take what they can get, and when an opportunity such as a street riot or an urban power failure comes along, they show what they have learned.

*See Appendix to this chapter.

Historians have only recently begun to assemble materials that show how violent city life has been in most cultures throughout the centuries. Those familiar with the autobiography of Benvenuto Cellini or the diaries of Samuel Pepys, to cite only two examples at random, need not be reminded of the violence of sixteenth century Florence or seventeenth century London. The violence of our great cities has many precedents. The underclass that generates so much of it is not an urban novelty peculiar to our times.

What is different about our underclass, I fear, is that the hopelessness of deprivation is combined with an awareness of racism and a belief that one's race accounts for one's economic condition. The Irish, the Italian, and the Polish minorities who were once deprived subjects of discrimination have become assimilated in the white majority. The process of assimilation is not so easy for the black and Hispanic poor. The circle is vicious, and it is by no means clear how it will be broken.

It is trite to say these things, and trite to add that in addition to the sense of deprivation in the underclass, its members share with the rest of us profound changes in the routines of family life, the common loss of confidence in our public institutions, and the erosion of religious authority. That makes for a formidable set of economic and social causes of crime. The insistence of doctrinaire conservatives that poverty and deprivation have little or nothing to do with our urban miseries flies in the face of realities that they can see for themselves in New York—and I can see for myself in Los Angeles or San Francisco. We must keep our attention fixed not only on young men and women who are unemployed (the unemployment statistics count only those who are looking for work and who think they might find it) but on the able-bodied unemployable. These are people who have never worked, who have never been subjected to the discipline of a job for which they can be paid. This is the class from which the most alarming criminals are recruited. To suppose that their criminality is unrelated to their economic status requires the most stubborn commitment to an ideology that ignores inconvenient facts.

Dr. van den Haag quite reasonably inquires why it is that in spite of universal education and general affluence the United States has been afflicted with this burden of crime, whereas other well-educated and affluent countries—Japan and France and Germany—have been so much less affected. There are differences of opinion about these matters, but if I must offer my speculations, I would cite the homogeneity of the population in all these countries, the relative security of the working class, the significantly lower unemployment rates (until quite recently in France and Germany), and the unavailability of handguns. I cannot believe that the threat of capital punishment (no longer in force in France and Germany) has anything at all to do with the low crime rates in any of these countries.

The Importance of the Police

I had thought that my point about the incredibility of punishment as a deterrent when the crime clearance rates are low was both obvious and telling. But Dr. van den Haag does not see how I can maintain that if clearance rates are low it does not matter how severe the punishment may be for the unlucky scoundrels who are caught. Somehow this argument seems to him to be a *non sequitur.* I must try again.

Let us suppose that in an unfortunate but hypothetical city the clearance rate for street robbery is an abysmal 10%. (Although I am writing in a hypothetical mode, there are some cities that are not far above this disgraceful rate.) A disciple of Professor van den Haag persuades the legislature to get tough on street crime, and a statute is enacted increasing the penalty for robbery from five years to ten years in prison—a mandatory term, too! Nothing is done to add to the resources of the police; after all, additional police officers are going to cost the city a lot of money. The clearance rates remain at 10% of all reported robberies. Is it to be believed that the increased severity of the punishment is going to make a difference? I submit that there is nothing in the dismal statistics of urban crime that suggests that any improvement will occur. Legislatures continue to enact more and more severe statutory penalties for street crimes, but if any positive results have ensued I have not been told about them.

Consider the reality of street crimes. A young man who is engaged in robberies is deeply concerned not to be caught. If he knows that the chances are that he won't be apprehended—or even if he merely *thinks* he knows that the police can't catch muggers—a tough law on the books is an abstraction of no significance. Combined with vastly increased police effectiveness, such a law would no doubt deter all but the most reckless muggers. Until the achievement of such effectiveness, the deterrent effect of penal severity is a cheap illusion—easy to write into a statute, easy to run through a legislature to show that the hard line on crime is indeed hard. Its meaning on the street is slight. The inclusion of the death penalty in such a code is an irrelevance, satisfying a legislator and his anxious constituents that the lawmakers are tough, doing all they can to prevent violence.

Steve Grogan on Probation

The appalling account of Steve Grogan's career on probation impugns the good sense of Judge Sterry Fagan as well as the professional competence of the probation officer who did not set in motion the machinery for Grogan's revocation. It is a shocking reminder that the criminal justice system must depend on fallible mortals to administer it. However, I refuse to generalize from this episode to the judiciary as a whole, nor will I accept the inference that "most [probation officers] do not like to 'make waves.'" As in most states, California judges are elected; they are well aware that undue leniency extended to violent offenders will jeopardize their tenure on the bench. What possessed Judge Fagan to make the absurd decisions reported by Mr. Bugliosi I cannot imagine. Generally, California judges err on the other side of leniency in such cases.

As to the courage and competence of probation officers, I contend that the officer in this incident was atypical and in all likelihood responsible for an exceptional case, the kind that few probation officers have to supervise. That does not excuse him; he should have been fired. My opponent does not explain what makes him think that the pusillanimity of this officer is characteristic of this much maligned profession. Dangerous people seldom get on probation; if they do, they don't remain when their propensities become evident. In the parole systems with which I am familiar, the paroles of dangerous offenders are revoked with much less cause than is the case with parolees who have no record of violence.

My Theory of Deterrence

Dr. van den Haag does not like my theory of deterrence. He attacks it on four discernible grounds. I don't think he has toppled the structure of my theory, but to be sure that confusion is not compounded I will respond to his critique.

First, he is troubled by my contention that the criminal law is irrelevant to those who are confirmed noncriminals as well as to those who are set in their criminal ways. That proposition contains a definition and a set of facts. There is a class of people who are committed to careers and values that rule out the commission of any crimes, especially the crime of murder, with which we are concerned in this debate. How large this class may be will always be a matter of speculation. Optimist that I am, I think it includes most of the American people. Less sanguine than I, my skeptical opponent believes that if such a class exists, it constitutes a small fraction.

I also hold that there is a criminal class whose members accept the penalties of the law as a part of the cost of the careers to which they are committed. I suspect that this class is unwholesomely large, perhaps as much as 5% of the adult population—far more than our prisons and jails and community correctional programs can accommodate. I am afraid that this percentage is growing.

My theory also allows for a considerable class of people who are indeed subject to the deterrence of the criminal justice system. They are men and women who are uncertain of their values, uncertain of their chances of getting away with a criminal act, and inexperienced in crime and the criminal justice system. If they feel fairly sure of not being caught, they will prefer some form of larceny to violent crimes or crimes that call for planning. Desperate, they may attempt a bank robbery or the holdup of a gas station. Very few have murder in their minds or hearts.

Now, it seems impossible to me to make an empirically defensible distribution of the three classes of people that I hypothesize. My gloomy opponent thinks that 95% of the population is in the middle. If he is right, the nation is in even more trouble than most of its leaders suppose. The law would then be our only bulwark against the anarchy of criminal values. My more hopeful estimate is that the class of deterrables is about 25% of the adult male population and much less of the female population. Exceedingly few of these people are ever minded to commit a violent crime.

The third issue to which I must respond is the misinterpretation that Dr. van den Haag attaches to my assertion that not many boys and girls learn the criminal code at their mother's knee. Somehow this statement sounds to him as though I mean that there is a congenital condition of law-abidingness—a genetic absurdity. What children *do* learn at their mother's knee are values and attitudes toward others. I think of this process as moral learning, and the sooner it gets under way in a child's life, the better it is for him and everyone around him. Some mothers are good guides for their children; too many are not. The failure of mothers and fathers to impart the elements and advantages of decent behavior to their children accounts for a great deal of the crime that distresses both my opponent and myself—as well as our readers.

Finally, Dr. van den Haag summons once more the ghost of Sir James Fitzjames Stephen, whose personality and views I have discussed elsewhere in this discourse. The hundreds of thousands who abstained from murder because they regarded it with horror was the estimate of a man who led the peculiarly sheltered life of a Victorian judge. Unlike some of his fellow judges, however, Sir James was an unbeliever, who thought that divine sanctions could not be honestly promised to sinners and wrongdoers. Therefore, the only source of morality was the criminal law—our mighty fortress against crime. Sir James had been exposed to testimony in court about the terrible crimes of the murderers whom he sentenced to hang. Nothing brought him into any other contact with the social stratum from which these murderers came, and he generalized from them to the whole class of ordinary Englishmen. He inferred that only the horror inspired by hanging prevented those "hundreds of thousands" from also committing homicide. Whatever one thinks about this more than Hobbesian notion, it is certainly not "all that needs to be said" about the criminal law and its punishments.

The Message to the Hoodlums

I do not agree that the resumption of capital punishment is even a beginning toward a tough response to crime. It is a needless distraction from the program that must be adopted if a credible message is to be delivered to the hoodlums. That message must consist of news of efficient policing in all sections of our cities, the adoption of strict standards for negotiated justice, and the availability of fair and proportionate sanctions for all crimes. This formulation implies a commitment to a difficult and expensive program. Many politicians who wish to be seen as champions of law and order—without going to the trouble and incurring the cost of a realistic program of legislation—correctly suppose that a vigorous support of capital punishment will convince the public that they are not "soft on crime." This kind of humbug is the deceptive leadership that makes the control of contemporary crime so difficult. The hoodlums know that they are beyond the reach of the executioner. Unthinking and uninformed citizens seem to be unable to appreciate that very few crimes involve a killing or even the threat of a killing. If politicians and professors tell them otherwise, who can blame them for supposing that capital punishment is a sovereign remedy for street crime?

Negative Reinforcement

My opponent cited a 1970 report in the prestigious *California Law Review,* written by Professor Barry Singer, which is supposed to set me aright on the effectiveness of negative reinforcement. Singer does indeed explode the experiment reported by Skinner from which the ineffectiveness of negative reinforcement was originally inferred. He then reviews numerous other animal experiments, a study conducted by the California Youth

Authority, and concludes that properly administered punishment can extinguish criminal behavior, "provided it is sufficiently severe." The essay ends with a consideration of the potential effectiveness of various kinds of punishment, both incarcerative and otherwise. He supposed that the revival of the ducking stool, the pillory and the stocks, and, possibly, badges of shame like Nathaniel Hawthorne's scarlet letter might be effective with some kinds of criminals.

But I was not relying on Skinner's early experiment with rats to support his contention—and mine—that punishment is an inefficient method of behavior modification. As Skinner put the matter, "A person who has been punished is not thereby simply less inclined to behave in a given way; at best, he learns how to avoid punishment. Some ways of doing so are maladaptive or neurotic. . . . Other ways include avoiding situations in which punished behavior is likely to occur and doing things which are incompatible with punished behavior."[1] What punishment does, then, is to communicate to the person punished what he must not do if he is not to be punished again. It does not suggest an alternative toward personal satisfaction or survival.

One does not need to swallow Skinner's utopian notions about freedom and dignity to accept the good sense of his generalization about negative reinforcement. As I said in the first place, human beings are more complicated than rats and pigeons, but like all animate creatures, we respond to incentives and disincentives.

Professor van den Haag wants to know why underclass young men differ in their responses to illegal incentives. Some commit crimes; others do not. That question has puzzled social theorists for generations, and I will not be lured into a quick and superficial solution. If it will make my dubious opponent feel better about my theory of deterrence, I will certainly agree that society needs better disincentives for crime. I wish he would agree with me that it also needs better incentives for choosing noncriminal careers. If the youth in American ghettos and *barrios* and slums were given incentives for conformity that they could believe, our need for sufficient disincentives would not be so desperate.

All of this is interesting discourse about a topic of vast social importance. It has virtually nothing to do with the topic of our main concern: murder and how those who commit it may be most appropriately punished.

The Underclass

The failure of President Johnson's Great Society is a favorite with conservative writers. The underclass had its chance and look what happened!

Crime rates stayed up. That must show any fair-minded citizen that poverty and deprivation have nothing to do with the incidence of delinquency.

To borrow a phrase from the Duke of Wellington, anyone who can believe that can believe anything. The Great Society flourished for four or five years and then collided with the distracting imperatives of the war in Vietnam. Just as the fiscal mistakes in running the American economy during the last thirty-five years cannot be rectified in a year or so, neither can centuries of racial oppression, decades of structural poverty, and years of social neglect be remedied in a few years. The Great Society was an aborted beginning. It would have amazed no one more than Cloward and Ohlin if in the short span of its course there had been a noticeable decline in the crime rates.

I doubt that any of the academic theorists responsible for the Great Society ever supposed that its achievement would be accompanied by a curtailment of the incidence of homicide.

Crime and the Poverty Line

My opponent offers a table that purports to show that between 1900 and 1982 the percentage of people living below the poverty line has declined from 90% to "between 11 and 14% owing to the recession." This is indeed a dramatic time series. How am I to explain the more or less concomitant rise in the crime rates?

The general answer is that responses to poverty vary from generation to generation. The variance may be attributed to changes in expectations, the quality of social solidarity among the poor, their confidence in the country's leadership, and many other influences. We have no reliable statistics on the incidence of crime before the late 1940s but it is certainly not true that crime was an insignificant problem until the recent past. Those who can remember what it was like in the 1920s and 1930s can recall the ominous burgeoning of organized crime that grew out of our foolish experiment with Prohibition. A lot of poor people saw their chance to get rich and took it, disregarding the both sumptuary and traditional criminal law and the penalties attached.

The present generation of the poor is disproportionately composed of racial minorities. It is a mobile generation that has learned to move around the country in search of opportunity. In a sense this mobility is exactly what conservative economists wish the working class to accept when hard times come along. Most of the opportunities sought are legitimate, but some are not. But the mobility that has characterized working-class life since the beginning of World War II has also created a social anonymity; people no longer know each other as they used to do in neighborhoods in which resi dence was lifelong. Personal reputations for many such people no longer matter so much. Combine these trends with the all too general loss of confidence in and respect for authority and the wonder is that we do not have more crime. The measures to counteract this depressing condition are not apparent to any informed student of the problem. It is most unlikely that the revival of capital punishment will have any effect at all.

The "Reorganization of the Economy"

My opponent objects to the reorganization of society, and so do I. All I want is a reorganization of the economy. I have the same antipathy for revolutionary solutions that Dr. van den Haag claims. We do not need to contemplate a vast social reorganization in order to minimize economic redundancy. Until we achieve the economic conditions that prevail in more stable capitalist societies, I will continue to maintain that "the administration of the death penalty, no matter how frequently, will be a bloody but futile gesture."

Are criminals to blame? We have no choice but to act as though they were. A retributivist such as I must uphold the law by requiring that criminals be punished according to their just desert. If a man is found guilty of a crime, he must be punished; this sequence is essential to the maintenance of social solidarity.

But social scientists and public policy-makers must search for ways that will reduce the inclination of men and women to commit crimes. I cannot yield on the proposition that we must accept a considerable crime rate as one of the many undesirable consequences of creating a large class of people who survive outside of the working economy as unemployed and unemployable. That is by no means the only trouble that accounts for crime; throughout my contributions to this debate I have mentioned many others. So long as we limit our consideration of crime to the means for its control and punishment, we cannot expect that it will be reduced by much. Let me emphasize again that I will insist as loudly as my opponent that crime must be controlled and criminals must be punished.

But crime is also a symptom. The kinds of crime committed and the kinds of people who commit them are indicators of the malfunctions of the social system. To say that a malfunctioning social system is the cause of crime is an oversimplification for which many of my fellow liberals have been responsible. I shall be specific here, because Dr. van den Haag would like to smother me in a stereotype that is dear to conservatives of every stripe. The reason why it is an oversimplification to claim that the malfunctions of society compose the major cause of crime is that it follows from this proposition that the criminal should not be held guilty and then punished.

The questions that crime poses for liberal thought are these: To what correctible condition does the prevalence of this or that kind of crime point? How may that condition be corrected? To neither of these questions is capital punishment a responsible answer.

The Deterrence of Cheaters

It is not I who objected that extrapolations from the Tittle–Rowe experiments on college examination cheating should not be too sweeping. This cautionary note was expressed by the experimenters themselves. I said that I would not accept inferences about the effectiveness of the death penalty as a deterrent from the results of an experiment conducted in a college classroom. Were I a teaching colleague of Dr. Tittle or Dr. Rowe, I would try to apply their model of deterrence in my own classrooms. I would not be in the least surprised to discover that it worked. It would not occur to me that this discovery had any significance for the deterrence of potential murderers.

The Deterrence of Drunken Driver-Killers

I will accept the proposed scale of punishments offered by Dr. van den Haag for the offense of drunken driving. I do not believe it is possible to show that 500 lives might be saved by the execution of one drunken driver-killer, but I have little doubt that mandatory prison terms for second degree murder in such cases would significantly reduce the number of such homicides. I am sure that such legislation would be much easier to get through a legislature than the death penalty.

I raised this question because I think it is no less preposterous than my dogged opponent's insistence on the 500 innocent lives that might, hypothetically of course, be saved by executing one murderer. If the choice lay between turning the killer free and executing him, there might be some sense to the dilemma presented to me and to the other adversaries with whom Dr. van den Haag has debated. But that is never the choice. The distinction has to be made between a life term in prison and a "short pang" administered by the executioner. I say that until my opponent can show that the executioner can save more victims than the life sentence, we can do without the executioner.

Note

1. B. F. Skinner, *Science and Human Behavior* (New York: The Free Press, 1965).

ERNEST VAN DEN HAAG

Contrary to what Conrad implies, I do not deny that poverty plays a major role in motivating crime. I deny that poverty in the sense of destitution, of lacking the minimum requirements of life, plays a major role in the United States. There hardly is such destitution in the United States as distinguished from, say, India, or China (where, incidentally, the crime rates are lower than they are here). It is relative poverty, "living at the bottom," as Conrad puts it, that often motivates crime in the United States. But relative poverty cannot be avoided. Wherever there is a top there is a bottom; wherever some people have more others have less; some necessarily have least—they are "at the bottom." They are most tempted to commit crimes, to get what others have. Others got what they have in legitimate ways. Some of those "at the bottom" (a minority) feel they can and may get things by crime. The temptation is strong for them, but it must be counteracted by punishing those who commit crimes and deterring everybody through the threat of punishment.

If indeed "boys and girls learn to take what they can get" through crime, the law should—and unfortunately does not now sufficiently—teach them that this is not a good idea. The punishment should outweigh the expected advantages and the risk should be great enough to deter. Yes, Conrad is right, there are "unemployable" members of the "underclass." They are unemployable because they find that they can make a reasonable living by committing crimes instead of working. But that living is reasonable only because the law does little about them. In New York State in 1981 there were altogether six persons in prison for stealing cars. But more than 100,000 cars were stolen in New York during that year. No wonder car thieves prefer to make their living by crime and to be "unemployable." It is practically riskless and their income is high—so why be a dishwasher and make much less money?

Professor Conrad writes that the absence of handguns and low unemployment help account for low crime rates in Germany. But the crime rates there were low even when there was high unemployment. And in Switzerland, guns, including handguns, are available to practically everybody—and the crime rate is low. What accounts for differences in crime rates—very low in Japan, very high in the United States, somewhere in between in most of Europe—is not so simple. Certainly no single factor, such as unemployment or handguns, does. Professor Conrad here is carried away, uncharacteristically, by simplistic notions.

I do agree with Professor Conrad that higher arrest rates would help reduce crime. But I think it would help even more if conviction and punishment rates were higher and more severe. There are some interesting statistics on this. Comparing crime and punishment rates (which differ from state to state) among American states, holding constant a number of variables such as the percentage of young males in the population, race, poverty, and unemployment, Professor Isaac Ehrlich concluded that "the rate of specific crime categories, with virtually no exception, varies inversely with estimates of the probability of apprehension and punishment by imprisonment and with the average length of time served in state prisons."* In other words, the higher the risk of punishment and the more severe the punishment, the less crime will be committed. Statistics (and Ehrlich's are quite elaborate) confirm what common sense knew all along.

Professor Conrad wants to know what makes me think that many (not all) probation officers, and the system as a whole, do not do their job well (I'm not sure it can be done well) and what makes me think that many state judges are less than competent and protect criminals more than they protect society from them. The answer is simple. I know many of them. Although not a few do the best job that can be done under the circumstances, far too many are less than adequate.

Finally, I believe that it has been shown by Professor Ehrlich and others† that "the executioner can save more victims than the life sentence." His conclusions—that each execution saves between seven and eight victims who would have been murdered by others if there were no execution—seems to me well proven. Criminologists, sociologists, and economists, shocked that a fellow scholar would attack what has become a dogma to them—that the death penalty is futile—have set upon Ehrlich and in numerous papers tried to disprove his views. He responded and, in my view, got the better of the

---

*Isaac Ehrlich, "Participation in Illegitimate Activities: A Theoretical Investigation," *Journal of Political Economy* (May/June 1973), p. 545.
†See Isaac Ehrlich, "The Deterrent Effect of Capital Punishment: A Question of Life and Death" *American Economic Review* (June 1975).

argument. But at this time, at least, the matter is still controversial. Professor Conrad's view has scholarly support, as does mine. Nevertheless, I shall favor the death penalty as long as there is even a slight chance—neither certainty nor even high probability is needed (although I think the latter is realistic)—as long as there is any chance that by executions we can deter some future murders of future victims. The life of these victims is valuable to me, whereas, in my eyes, the murderer has forfeited his life by taking that of another. That much from the viewpoint of deterrence. Need I add, further, that I share the popular feeling that murder deserves the death penalty, although I do not call this feeling a theory?

Appendix to Chapter 5

ERNEST VAN DEN HAAG

The issue of drunken drivers and the 55,000 persons who perish as a result of traffic accidents every year, half of which are caused by drunken drivers, is too important to let it go without further consideration.

I'm not sure that the death penalty—if it were a practical possibility—would be very useful: The drunken driver, after all, seems to be willing to risk his life (and unfortunately those of others) to begin with. The chances that he will be killed by a traffic accident are greater, as of now, than the chances of a murderer being executed.

With all that, punitive measures will have some deterrent effect. However, the experience in England and in Scandinavia is that when greater punishments were introduced there was a reduction in drunken driving—at first. But it didn't last long. The effect of harsher punishment seems to wear off. I am in favor of it nonetheless, since it does some good.

Given the above, I am in favor also of as yet untried remedies, which may perhaps be effective. I would promise rewards to anyone who notices that a person under the influence of alcohol is about to drive and calls the police. I would make sure of a prompt police response. I would make sure that anyone convicted of drunken driving twice in a two-year period will be deprived of his license for two years, the license to be returned only after he has been certified as a nonalcoholic by a psychiatrist or a group such as Alcoholics Anonymous. I would deprive anyone of a driver's license for a period of no less than five years if convicted three times or more of driving under the influence of liquor. I would greatly increase the penalties for driving without a license by persons who have been deprived of a driving license. (All these measures should be equally applied to persons driving under the influence of drugs.)

As Professor Conrad has pointed out, the problem is a very serious one in terms of the harm done. On the other hand, there is usually no malevolent intent, and strongly punitive measures are likely neither to be used nor, if they are used, to be all that effective. Under the circumstances, preventive measures, measures that place some liability on those who abet or tolerate the drunken driving, and stricter licensing perhaps may be of use.

CHAPTER 6

Deterrence, the Death Penalty, and the Data

JOHN P. CONRAD

A conceptual error common to many criminological writers is the assumption that deterrence prevents all crimes in about the same way. Prove that college sophomores are deterred from cheating by the threat of severe academic discipline, and it follows that potential killers will hold their fire because the law promises an end on the gallows to all murderers. The absurdity of the parallel is ignored by those who would like to justify severity of punishment as the sovereign preventative of crime.

Deterrence is a hydra-headed problem. Its complexity as a problem—disregarding the formidable difficulties in its solution—was crisply stated by the Norwegian criminologist Johannes Andenaes in his slim but wide-ranging treatise, *Punishment and Deterrence:* "Deterrence should not be treated as a monolithic problem. General propositions accepting or rejecting deterrence ought to belong in the past. The question is not whether punishment has deterrent effects, but rather under what conditions and to what extent the deterrent purpose is effected."[1]

Having stated the problem in this form, Andenaes proceeded to consider the deterrence of a wide variety of offenses, ranging from murder to parking violations. I do not agree with all his conclusions, nor is it appropriate to summarize them here. However, the principle stated in the paragraph quoted is obvious, if often violated for polemic effect.

The proposition that we have under consideration in this debate is a narrow item in the deterrence agenda. Our question is whether there is a deterrent effect in the administration of capital punishment to a convicted

murderer that significantly exceeds the effect of incarcerating such a murderer for a long period of years. We are not to argue whether capital punishment is more deterrent than no punishment, or a nominal punishment
such as a stretch of probation. There are abolitionists who will argue that
punishment does not deter homicide, but I am not one of them, and I see no
way of testing this extreme hypothesis. What we are assessing here is the
difference between swinging on the gallows and serving many years, perhaps
the rest of one's life, in prison. So far as I am concerned, the outcome of
this debate does not hinge on the deterrent effectiveness of the death penalty—I hold that it is unnecessary and immoral in the retributivist justification of punishment. Nevertheless, it is a reinforcement of the abolitionist
case that *there is no empirical support for the deterrent effect of the death
penalty as superior to that which is exerted by long incarceration.*

In this chapter I shall present a brief and far from exhaustive summary
of the extensive literature bearing on this proposition. Several full-scale literature reviews are available; I commend those of Glaser[2] and Waldo[3] as
comprehensive and authoritative. Here I want to present the empirical situation as it now stands and to consider its implications for any argument on
the deterrent effect of capital punishment.

The Background

With one major exception, to which I shall come presently, retentionists rely on common sense for the support of their belief that executions are
significantly more deterrent than life terms in prison. The vigorous language
of writers like Sir James Fitzjames Stephen have provided them with col-
orful support for a position that is not nearly as self-evident as they have
claimed. It is customary to assert that although the statistical proof of this
belief is wanting, nevertheless no one has proved that capital punishment is
not more deterrent than extended incarceration. Some retentionists, more
attuned to social science epistemology than others, will observe correctly
that not all the variables that bear on the utility of capital punishment are
susceptible of quantification. But the argument usually is compressed into a
sequence of simplifications of this nature: (a) Everyone knows that human
beings fear death more than any other eventuality. (b) Therefore, the fear
of death is the ultimate deterrent. (c) Although the fear of long-term incarceration is also a deterrent, there is a margin of increased deterrence presented by the threat of the death penalty. (d) Because murder is the crime
of crimes, resulting in irreversible harm to the victim, the state is justified

in taking the murderer's life to assure that deterrence of homicide is maximized.

It will be seen that if the death penalty is *not* the deterrent that retentionists claim, this case collapses. The argument, then, must go into the retributivist arena.

Thorsten Sellin and the Comparative Statistics

Until the early 1970s, studies of the deterrent effect of capital punishment rested on comparisons of the data on homicide. These comparisons were of two general kinds. First, a time series could be constructed for jurisdictions in which the laws had changed. Usually such a situation could be studied where a state had abolished capital punishment and then reinstated it, but the reverse might also be studied. I shall report on one case of the latter kind in this chapter. The second kind of comparison could be made between jurisdictions of which one had retained capital punishment and others had abolished it. Such comparisons obviously have to be made with caution to maintain comparability, so far as possible, as to all variables that might bear on the incidence of homicide.

Many such comparisons have been made by Professor Thorsten Sellin, for many years and still a preeminent criminologist. For me, his most telling comparison was based on the homicide rates in Michigan, Ohio, and Indiana. Michigan has not enjoyed the benefits of capital punishment since 1846, but Ohio and Indiana have consistently used the death penalty throughout their histories. Table I, taken from Sellin's recent volume, *The Penalty of Death*,[4] presents the comparison.

It will be seen that the homicide rates in Michigan from 1920 to 1964 were approximately the same as those in Ohio and Indiana. From 1964 to 1974 the rates rose substantially in Michigan, while the rates in Ohio and Indiana made much more modest gains.

Now, it is frequently said that these comparisons between states are statistically crude because they cannot take into account many intangible variables such as cultural differences, economic conditions, the effectiveness of law enforcement in apprehending and prosecuting offenders, and, no doubt, many other features of the social landscape that do not lend themselves to measurement. I think this point is not well taken with respect to Michigan and Ohio. These states are of about the same size in population, about the same distribution among residents of very large cities, smaller towns, and rural districts, about the same distribution of racial minorities,

TABLE I. Crude Homicide Death Rates, with Numbers of Executions, Michigan, Ohio, and Indiana, 1920–1974 (Mean Annual Rates per 100,000 Population)

		Ohio		Indiana	
Quinquennia	Michigan	Rate	Number of executions	Rate	Number of executions
1920–1924	5.5	7.4	45	6.1	5
1925–1929	8.2	8.4	40	6.6	7
1930–1934	5.6	8.5	43	6.5	11
1935–1939	3.9	5.9	29	4.5	22
1940–1944	3.2	4.3	15	3.0	2
1945–1949	3.5	4.8	36	3.8	5
1950–1954	3.8	3.8	20	3.7	2
1955–1959	3.0	3.4	12	3.0	0
1960–1964	3.6	3.2	7	3.2	1
1965–1969	6.6	5.1	0	4.7	0
1970–1974	11.3	7.8	0	6.4	0

Source: National Office of Vital Statistics, *Vital Statistics of the United States;* William J. Bowers, *Executions in America* (Lexington, Massachusetts: D. C. Heath, 1974), Appendix A.

and about the same distribution of wealth. If capital punishment were an effective deterrent of murder, we would expect that the homicide rate in Ohio during the last sixty years would have been consistently lower than the rate in Michigan—but this is not the case. Nor are the Indiana data any more helpful to the retentionist case.

But what happened in 1965? The Michigan rate soared from 3.6 to 6.6 in five years, and in five years more it was 11.3. In 1974 Ohio wound up the quinquennium with a rate of only 7.8, and Indiana's rate was even better at 6.4. Is that not a significant difference that we see for these two retentionist states?

It certainly is a major change in the data, but it is impossible to conclude that capital punishment had anything to do with it. If capital punishment were indeed the deterrent that retentionists claim, we would expect that the rates in Ohio and Indiana would have soared because of the moratorium from about 1960 to 1974. They did not. Potential murderers do not seem to have been significantly less intimidated by a law under whose terms life imprisonment was the worst that could happen. The modest increases in the homicide rates have to be attributed to factors about which we can only guess. As to Michigan, whatever the influence was that accounted for the vault from 3.6 per 100,000 to 11.3 within the span of a decade, it must have been something other than the status of capital punishment, which never was a factor in that state. But in all three states, as in the whole country, social and political strains of an unprecedented nature were unraveling authority and pulling apart social cohesiveness. The race riots of the 1960s, the Vietnam war, the growing instability of the economy must have had their effect on the crime rates—effects to which numbers cannot be assigned.

Quibbles about mysterious variables that cannot be provided for in such comparisons have never impressed me as anything more than quibbles. The various economic and demographic intangibles that cannot be measured to distinguish Michigan from Ohio do not seem likely to offset the similarities. I am sure that if the comparisons had consistently shown that Ohio and Indiana had enjoyed much lower homicide rates than Michigan over the last 60 years, I would be at a loss to rebut the deterrent effect of the electric chairs that are in use in those states. I suspect that the retentionists would have little patience with any reservations I might have to offer about the comparability of the data from state to state.

I think it is important to note that Sellin made numerous other comparisons between contiguous states. Not one has shown a significant difference over time in favor of a retentionist state.[5]

The Canadian Experience

At least as impressive a demonstration of the irrelevance of capital punishment to murder rates is shown in the homicide statistics of Canada. I shall not review the whole history of capital punishment in Canada, which has taken a different course from that in most American states. Rather, I shall present as much background as seems necessary to appreciate the significance of the data in Table II in support of the abolitionist case.[6]

From 1892 to 1961, the Criminal Code provided for only two classes of homicide: murder, always punished by death, and manslaughter, which carried a maximum penalty of life imprisonment. During much of this time, revision of the code to establish two categories of murder, capital and noncapital, was under debate in the federal parliament. This revision finally was put into effect in 1961. Capital murder was defined as the killing of a police officer or prison guard, planned murder, or murder in the commission of a felony. In 1967 this law was amended to restrict the death sentence to conviction of the murder of police or prison guards only. This amendment also provided that persons committed to life imprisonment could be released on parole only with the approval of the provincial governor in council. In July

TABLE II. Number and Rate (per 100,000
Population) Murder Incidents, Canada,
1961–1980

Year	Murder incidents	Rate
1961	172	0.94
1962	196	1.05
1963	192	1.01
1964	199	1.03
1965	216	1.10
1966	206	1.03
1967	239	1.17
1968	292	1.41
1969	320	1.52
1970	354	1.66
1971	395	1.83
1972	414	1.90
1973	448	2.03
1974	500	2.23
1975	569	2.50
1976	561	2.43
1977	575	2.47
1978	554	2.36
1979	537	2.27
1980	459	1.92

Source: Canadian Center for Justice Statistics, *Homicide Statistics, 1980* (Ottawa, 1980), p. 27, Table 1.

1976 Parliament enacted a law abolishing capital punishment altogether, replacing the death penalty with a mandatory life sentence for first degree murder. First degree murder is limited to "planned or deliberate murders, murder of a police officer or custodial officer who is killed in line of duty, murder committed in the course of certain criminal acts (hijacking, kidnapping or sexual offenses), or murder committed by a person who has been previously convicted of first or second degree murder."[7]

No one has been subjected to capital punishment in Canada since 1962. The stability of the murder rates over a period of twenty years speaks for itself. Note also that for the last four years there has been a decline in the incidence of murder and in the rate per 100,000. I am not so simple as to suppose that the abolition of capital punishment was responsible for the decline—which is of doubtful statistical significance, anyway. It seems at least possible that increasingly strict control of firearms is partly responsible for the decline in the number of murders. Between 1976 and 1980, the annual numbers of murders committed by shooting declined from 194 to 159, with an intervening peak, in 1977, of 221.[7] But however we account for the course of the homicide rates, it is unarguable that they have not been increased by the 1976 legislation. If there were anything of substance to the retentionist hypothesis, we would expect a sharp increase in the number of murders and the rates of their commission.

No doubt some retentionists will patiently explain to me that Canada is very different from the United States. Smaller population. Much more homogeneous. No large racial minorities. All these and more quibbles can be freely granted—as well as the contrast between an averaged murder rate for the last five years of 2.87 per 100,000 for Canada as compared with a rate of 8.49 per 100,000 in the United States. I do not see any challenge that obviates a declining homicide rate in the face of a nationwide abolition of capital punishment that has been in effect for six years.

Isaac Ehrlich's Sophisticated Analysis

In 1975 Professor Isaac Ehrlich published his doctoral dissertation in economics and immediately acquired national prominence. He had subjected the data on homicide and executions since 1930 to the statistical procedure of regression analysis. This is a method for establishing a mathematical equation that best describes the relationship between a dependent variable and predictor variables. In this study, Ehrlich had tried to estimate the deterrent effect of the death penalty by measuring other factors that might affect the homicide rate, determining the extent to which the death penalty was used, and trying to account explicitly for the reverse effect of the number of homicides on the demand for executions. The final result of his statistical labors was the finding that each execution deterred about eight potential murders.

This was the first publication in the relatively brief history of empirical work on capital punishment that found a definite deterrent effect attributable to capital punishment beyond the effect that might be produced by life imprisonment.[8] Retentionists seized on this finding with the delighted alacrity of a starving man presented with a banquet. With my own ears I have heard prosecutors and conservative candidates for office proclaim that science had now proved what plain men with common sense had known all along—executions save lives.

More informed retentionists were more cautious. They hoped that there would be successful replications, carried out with data of better integrity than some of the dubious statistics on which Ehrlich had had to rely in testing his model.

A considerable literature has followed on the publication of Professor Ehrlich's famous paper. I shall not review it here; those who are interested in a tortuous but technical controversy should review Ehrlich's original paper together with critical essays by the National Academy of Sciences,[9] a replication by Brian Forst,[10] and an acerbic exchange of views between Beyleveld[11] and Ehrlich published recently in England.[12]

The upshot of the numerous studies that have been undertaken is that no one has been able to produce findings similar to Ehrlich's, and the general view is that regression analysis does not produce any results that differ in implications from those obtained by Sellin's simpler methods. Indeed, the Panel on Research on Deterrence of the National Academy of Sciences flatly stated:

> "In undertaking research on the deterrent effect of capital punishment ... it should be recognized that the strong value content associated with decisions regarding capital punishment and the high risk associated with errors of commission make it likely that any policy use of scientific evidence on capital punishment will require extremely severe standards of proof. The nonexperimental research to which the study of the deterrent effects of capital punishment is necessarily limited almost certainly will be unable to meet these standards of proof. Thus, the Panel considers that research on this topic is not likely to produce findings that will or should have much influence on policy-makers."[13]

It is now as clear as a consensus of econometricians can make it that there is no reason to believe that executions have any effect in deterring murder.

Responding to the Ehrlich episode, Bowers and Pierce, two sociologists who make no bones of their opposition to capital punishment, undertook a statistical study of the "brutalization" hypothesis.[14] This proposition asserts that the net effect of capital punishment is to stimulate murder in the minds of people who hope to achieve a notoriety that they could never gain by more conventional means. Using the New York data for their base, they wound up with a finding that each execution was responsible for two to three additional murders. Because this study has not been replicated or followed by other investigations of the "brutalization" hypothesis, I cannot accept it as a contribution to the abolitionist argument. It is, however, a much more intact study than Ehrlich's battered research, which has had signally little success in accumulating responsible replications.

The State of Empirical Knowledge

No studies yet exist that provide unchallenged support for the narrow hypothesis of deterrence. It is not likely that the deterrent effect of capital punishment can be established, but, as retentionists wistfully argue, the fact that no one has ever succeeded in this statistical effort doesn't mean that success is impossible. Of this assertion, Zimring and Hawkins, in their exhaustive survey of the whole topic of deterrence remarked: "On a most charitable interpretation this is a highly attenuated form of utilitarian justification."[15] I cannot improve on Sellin's response to this lament: "It is impossible to prove that there are no unicorns. All that we can prove is that we've found none so far. If the end result of a long argument . . . is nothing more than a statement that a particular theory can't be disproved, you are probably safe in putting it in the same class as unicorns."[16]

Notes

1. Johannes Andenaes, *Punishment and Deterrence* (Ann Arbor: University of Michigan Press, 1974), p. 84.
2. Daniel Glaser, "Capital Punishment—Deterrent or Stimulus to Murder? Our Unexamined Deaths and Penalties," *University of Toledo Law Review* 10 (Winter 1979), pp. 317–333.
3. Gordon P. Waldo, "The Death Penalty and Deterrence: A Review of Recent Research," in *The Mad, the Bad, and the Different: Essays in Honor of Simon Dinitz,* ed. Israel L. Barak-Glantz and C. Ronald Huff (Lexington, Massachusetts: D.C. Heath, 1918), pp. 169–178.
4. Thorsten Sellin, *The Penalty of Death* (Beverly Hills and London: Sage, 1980), p. 144.
5. Ibid., pp. 156–174.
6. Canadian Centre for Justice Statistics, *Homicide Statistics, 1980* (Ottawa: Statistics Canada, January 1982), pp. 125–131.
7. Ibid., p. 130.
8. Isaac Ehrlich, "The Deterrent Effect of Capital Punishment: A Question of Life or Death," *American Economic Review* 65 (1975), p. 397.
9. Alfred Blumstein, Jacqueline Cohen, and Daniel Nagin, eds., *Deterrence and Incapacitation: Estimating the Effects of Criminal Sanctions on Crime Rates* (Washington, D.C.: National Academy of Sciences, 1978), pp. 59–63, a summary of the findings of the Panel on Research on Deterrent and Incapacitative Effects relative to capital punishment. See also in the same volume, Lawrence Klein, Brian Forst, and Victor Filatov, "The Deterrent Effect of Capital Punishment: An Assessment of the Estimates," pp. 336–360, a paper commissioned by the panel for inclusion in this report.
10. Brian E. Forst, "The Deterrent Effect of Capital Punishment: A Cross-State Analysis," *University of Minnesota Law Review* 61 (1977), pp. 743–767.
11. Deryck Beyleveld, "Ehrlich's Analysis of Deterrence," *British Journal of Criminology* 22 (April 1982), pp. 101–123.

12. Isaac Ehrlich, "On Positive Methodology, Ethics and Polemics in Deterrence Research," *British Journal of Criminology* 22 (April 1982), pp. 124–139.
13. Blumstein *et al.,* eds., p. 63.
14. William J. Bowers and Glenn L. Pierce, "What Is The Effect Of Executions: Deterrence or Brutalization" (Unpublished paper, Center for Applied Social Research, Northeastern University, n. d.).
15. Franklin E. Zimring and Gordon J. Hawkins, *Deterrence* (Chicago and London: University of Chicago Press, 1973), p. 16.
16. Sellin, p. 178.

ERNEST VAN DEN HAAG

I do not think that deterrence is a "hydra-headed problem." All the theory says is that threats are likely to deter if the disadvantages threatened sufficiently outweigh the advantages perceived in the threatened act and if the threats are credible. Increasing a threat deters from crime, just as increasing a price deters from purchasing. To be sure, we still have to learn what price increases or decreases lead to what changes in sales. What threats are likely to deter from what acts to what extent? We can only go by experience with some occasional experimentation with students, parking rule violators, or criminals. From this, of course, we cannot (directly) infer what threats would suffice to reduce the burglary rate. But we can infer that some threats will.

It is at this point that Professor Conrad's argument becomes odd. He insists (1) that "there is no empirical support" for the superior deterrent effect of the death penalty over alternatives such as long incarceration. (He is wrong on that, but let me come to this in a moment.) Yet he neglects to mention (2) that there is no "empirical support," either, for the superior effect of "long incarceration" over short incarceration or, for that matter, no incarceration.

Why, then, does he advocate "long incarceration"? The answer is simple. Conrad is not entirely bereft of common sense. Yet he does not like (simply abhors) the death penalty. So, "long incarceration" seems an acceptable substitute, although there is no proof for its deterrent effect.

Conrad knows (and chooses to deny only when the death penalty is at issue) that a greater threat deters more. He knows also that there is no "empirical support," i.e., statistical proof, for this commonsense observation. But he chooses to demand it for the death penalty—although he does not demand it for "long incarceration." Yet I know of no statistical proof that the threat of "long incarceration" deters more than the threat of shorter imprisonment. I think it does. But I base myself on the common sense that Conrad rejects when the death penalty is at stake.

Now to Sellin's tables quoted by Professor Conrad: In my opinion they prove nothing, other than that compiling such tables is an idle pastime. There is no evidence in these tables for the homicide rate having much to do with execution rates. How can this happen? There are many possible explanations; the figures are much too small to reach conclusions. But there are no explanations, either, for the wild gyrations that, for instance, led to a near doubling of the Michigan homicide rate within five years—without any changes in the threatened punishment.

About the Canadian data: Professor Conrad is correct in what he suggests at first and then dismisses. Canada, which always has had a much lower crime rate than the United States, is not comparable to it. Professor Conrad points out that the homicide rate has not greatly changed in Canada regardless of whether there were executions or not. (There weren't any since 1962.) Yet the rate more than doubled, according to Conrad's table, from 1961 (were there many executions in that year?) to 1980. Surely this is not, as Professor Conrad has it, evidence against the death penalty. Is it evidence for it? I cannot say, for we are not told about many other factors that influence the homicide rate and that may have changed over 20 years (e.g., the number of young males in the population, the degree of urbanization and of income inequality, the ethnic composition of the population). Nobody, to my knowledge, has ever maintained that the death penalty is the only factor determining the homicide rate. It is one of many influences. If it were shown that Canada imposes much shorter prison sentences for auto theft than the United States (not the case, incidentally) and yet the rate of auto theft is higher in the United States despite longer sentences—would Conrad conclude that longer sentences are useless? He would be foolish if he were to so conclude. For there are many factors other than the threatened punishment that influence the rate of auto theft; these factors may change over time, and they may differ between Canada and the United States. So with homicide rates. Comparisons are not impossible. But they require far more statistical sophistication and caution than displayed by Sellin or Conrad.

About Isaac Ehrlich's pioneering work Professor Conrad is, shall we say, selective. He mentions Ehrlich's 1975 paper in the *American Economic Review*, a longitudinal study, which related homicide rates to executions in the 30 years preceding the suspension of executions in the 1960s. Ehrlich found that each execution had saved between seven and eight lives. Conrad does not mention (could it be that he did not read?) Ehrlich's cross-sectional paper in the *Journal of Political Economy* (1977) in which he compared homicide rates in execution and nonexecution states (over a three year period) and concluded that "capital punishment has a differential effect over and above the actually enforced imprisonment terms." In fact, "although the results have been obtained through different procedures" they are "in essence the same as those derived from the analysis of time series data." This shows that the idea that time series results were somehow freakish and depended on the period chosen is wrong.

Conrad fails even to mention this paper with its important corroboration of the original results. Further, in suggesting, correctly, that Ehrlich's 1975 paper gave rise to "considerable literature," Conrad mentions, with one exception, only attacks on Ehrlich, and not his quite persuasive replies. (Ehrlich replied to practically every scientifically plausible attack and to some implausible ones.) Thus, Ehrlich's reply to the National Academy of Sciences report (which strikes me as altogether persuasive) is not mentioned.* Nor is any of the literature on Ehrlich's side quoted.

Finally, Conrad mentions—admittedly with reservations—a silly paper by Bowers and Pierce finding that "each execution was responsible for two to three additional murders." This paper was never published. Conrad fails to mention a paper by David P. Phillips† published in the American Journal of Sociology (July 1980) which shows that "there is a statistically significant tendency for the number of homicides to drop below the number expected in the week of publicized execution" and "in the two weeks following . . . the frequency of homicides drops by 35%." Phillips's paper has merit. But it is not relevant to the basic controversy. Nor is the paper quoted by Conrad, which, unlike that by Phillips, has no serious claims on our attention. It is remarkable that Conrad quotes an unpublished paper stating that executions raise the murder rates but neglects to notice a published paper that came to the opposite conclusion.‡

JOHN P. CONRAD

As expected, my combative opponent has found plenty in my chapter with which to disagree. His assertions are mostly supported by his shrewd

---

*See Isaac Ehrlich and Randall Mark, "Fear of Deterrence" *Journal of Legal Studies,* (June 1977).

†"The Deterrent Effect of Capital Punishment: New Evidence on an Old Controversy," *American Journal of Sociology* 86 (July 1980), pp. 139–148.

‡For an additional discussion of the Phillips paper, see *American Journal of Sociology* 88 (July 1982), pp. 161–172.

speculations rather than solid facts, but facts are seldom kind to the retentionist cause. Advocates of the death penalty must depend on the reduction of complexity to the most extreme oversimplification.

Take, for example, the rejection of complexity in the deterrence problem. Along with writers like Andenaes,[1] Gibbs,[2] and Zimring and Hawkins,[3] I perceive difficulties and differences where my rough-and-ready opponent sees none. I observe that some crimes are highly sensitive to deterrents, as for example, income tax violations. Others are almost entirely insensitive, such as narcotics law violations and crimes committed to enable an addict to get his fix. We know rather little about the elements of the state's response to the criminal that have deterrent effects, as contrasted with those obviously empty threats that political charlatans enjoy so much. Nevertheless, if I may indulge in some *a priori* logic that goes back to Beccaria and his contemporaries,[4] I believe that the celerity and the certainty of apprehension is the indispensable foundation of effective deterrence. It does no good to threaten terrible consequences to our criminals if it is well known that we can't catch them, and catch them as soon as possible after the commission of their crimes. To put the matter as bluntly as I can, deterrence is effective only insofar as the consequences of crime are predictable. The experienced contract killer can predict to himself—and has good reason to know—that the chances of his being apprehended, prosecuted, and convicted of his crime are negligible. If he acts on that prediction, the comparative deterrent effects of capital punishment and life imprisonment are irrelevant. At the other extreme, the betrayed husband who kills his faithless wife and her paramour will know, if he reflects at all on his prospects, that he will almost certainly be apprehended, prosecuted, and convicted, but the nature of his punishment would be the unpredictable element. In some states, a clever lawyer can get him off with a fine and a couple of years of probation. Most men in this situation do not reflect on their prospects and proceed with the dictates of their impulses.

Therefore, I maintain that the application of deterrence to the practice of sentencing is a "hydra-headed problem." Threats to parking violators are completely credible, but how much of a consequence must be threatened for effective deterrence? What will happen if the sanction is too severe? To what extent can we adapt our experience with parking violators to drunken drivers? If the threat is only marginally credible, as with burglary in most large cities, what measures can be taken to increase its significance to the ordinary criminal?

I could go on, but I hope that enough has been said to persuade the reader that deterrence is not the simple problem that my opponent supposes it to be. Let us go on, then, to one of the yawning gaps in criminological research that Professor van den Haag has discovered. In spite of the obviousness of the problem, in spite of its openness to solution, we do not have empirical data to delineate the differential effects of differing periods of incarceration. Does a five-year term deter more than a six-month term? Does a life sentence deter more than a ten-year term? Why on earth do I believe that a murderer should get a life sentence when I can't prove that a five- or ten-year term would do just as well?

I could retort that in this welter of noninformation, speculations, and nineteenth century dogmas, Professor van den Haag has inadvertently conceded that he can't show that the gallows is more effective than a long stretch in the penitentiary. Of course, he is a devout believer in the econometric solution to the capital punishment problem propounded by Dr. Ehrlich; *that* question is resolved forever! (I will come back to Dr. Ehrlich presently.)

I would be disingenuous to claim that my basis for fixing the sentence for first degree murder has anything to do with its deterrent effect. I have insisted that I am a retributivist. The sentences I would impose on murderers are based on their desert, not on the deterrence of others. I say that this crime deserves the utmost in severity that it is proper and moral for the state to inflict: a long term in prison. It is the standard of depravity by which all other crimes must be measured. It is beyond question that when a man is locked up for twenty or thirty years to satisfy retributivist purposes, the utilitarian aims will also be served. He will be incapacitated, he will be intimidated, and no doubt the select public of potential murderers will be to some extent deterred. But the court decides that he should be locked up for a long time because that is what he deserves. The sentence incidentally may deter some, but that is not its basic purpose. If Professor van den Haag should someday announce that he has data that demonstrate that a two-year sentence will satisfy the law of diminishing returns in the deterrence of murder, he will find me intransigently severe. Regardless of who is deterred by what, we must lock up the first degree murderer for a life sentence or its equivalent in years. If a murderer is to be released on parole, that release cannot be allowed until a minimum of ten years has been served. For some specially heinous murderers, the day of release may never come.

The Interstate Comparisons

Dr. van den Haag's disdainful dismissal of Sellin's comparisons between abolitionist and retentionist states is natural enough, and typical of retentionist argumentation. Such comparisons have never been useful to his cause. The only response he can make to them is to deplore the lack of rigor that can be maintained in a scientific experiment but that never can be arranged for in the punishment of serious criminals. It is easy to declaim that without rigor there is no knowledge, and then go on to show that the numbers are too small, the data are not as reliably collected as they should be, the death penalty is in the statutes but seldom pronounced, and in any event it is impossible to control all the variables between two differing states.

Quibbles. If the death penalty had the deterrent consequences that Dr. van den Haag claims for it, whereby numerous (500?) innocent victims are saved by each execution, this significant effect should show up in the data. It does not. None of the explanations that Dr. van den Haag offers accounts for the absence of any fluctuations in any of the mountains of data that can be attributed to the death penalty. Whatever the reason for the "wild gyrations" in the Michigan time series, these gyrations cannot be fastened onto the absence of the death penalty. Indeed, the Michigan homicide experience strongly suggests that other influences are at work on the homicide rates. Perhaps it was the increasing violence in the narcotics traffic in and around Detroit. Perhaps it had something to do with the increasing size and despair of the metropolitan underclass. Whatever it was, the restoration of the death penalty—not in effect since the middle of the nineteenth century—was not considered a likely remedy, and certainly had nothing to do with the elevation in the murder rates. It is also impressive to note that the moratorium on capital punishment did nothing to the homicide rates in the adjacent states of Indiana and Ohio, which remained remarkably stable throughout the 1970s.

The Deterrence of Homicide in Canada

I am pleased to read that Professor van den Haag does not suppose that the death penalty is the only variable affecting the homicide rate. That is a point that I have been stressing throughout this debate. But if we are to retain the death penalty, as my steadfast opponent advocates, there ought to be some evidence of its benign influence in the protection of innocent victims. I am sure that Dr. van den Haag does not seriously believe that each execution will save 500 lives—after all, not even the dogged Isaac Ehrlich foresees such a benefit from the return of the executioner—but there should be some statistical manifestation in support of his argument based on general deterrence. An oscillation from 0.94 murders per 100,000 in 1961 to 1.92 per 100,000 in 1980 cannot easily be explained by the failure to use the gallows when there are so many other explanations for a slight gain in the incidence of homicide that also must be considered.

In a comprehensive review of the Canadian abstinence from executions, published in 1972, when nearly ten years had passed without any executions but before the final abolition of capital punishment in 1976, Fattah concluded that "the increase in criminal homicide in Canada during recent years cannot be attributed to the suspension of capital punishment. . . ."[5] He went on to assign ten supporting reasons for this conclusion.[6] His final words on the topic are: "Nothing emerges from the study of trends in violent crimes that would support or even suggest the proposition that the suspension of capital punishment has caused an increase in the homicide rate. Although the data show that there has been a slight increase in recent years, it indicates [sic] at the same time that this increase cannot be attributed to any one cause. . . . [I]t can safely be claimed that the suspension is unlikely to have played a part in this increase."[7]

Fattah compared the number of murder charges with the number of executions in Canada for the years 1881–1960. The percentage of charges that led to executions varied from a high in the quinquennium 1931–1935 of 35.9% to a low of 7.9% in 1956–1960. In the ten-year period 1951–1960, there were 398 murders charged, resulting in 56 executions. At no time in the history of capital punishment in Canada did the rate of executions approach half the number of charges. Fattah commented, "The slight actual risk of execution during the entire period, and in particular during the 10 years preceding the legal suspension of the death penalty, speaks against any deterrent effect this punishment may have had and indicates that any such effect is obviated by the odds against execution."[8]

If he pleases, Professor van den Haag may argue that if only more executions had been imposed, the threat would have been more credible. But eighty years of data show that many influences must have limited the Canadian courts in the frequency with which the death penalty was pronounced. It is unreasonable to suppose that the considerations that caused the courts to limit the number of executions could have been put aside. It is even more unreasonable to argue that there was a judicial conspiracy to "sabotage" capital punishment. Just as the death penalty is not the only variable to consider in accounting for the homicide rate, the requirements of deterrence can never be the first consideration in sentencing any criminal to any punishment—but especially when the sentence is death.

Dr. Ehrlich's Fading Magic

Dr. Ehrlich never fails to corroborate himself, even though hardly anyone else has joined him in his opinion of his infallibility on the issue that he has explored so persistently for so many years. I am not an economist. I approach econometric solutions to noneconomic problems with suspicion and skepticism. The performance of economists in their own domain of understanding and improving the performance of the economy has not been so impressive as to overwhelm the other social sciences with their reputation for superior methods and insights. When they invade criminology with methods designed for explaining the markets, I want to know what their assumptions are that justify the application of their analytic methods to the data of crime.

The underlying assumption is that murder rates can be understood in terms of supply-and-demand theory. That notion is preposterous. It is supposed that as the price of murder rises (as quoted in the statutory penalties), the demand (as measured by the homicide rate) will decline. Double the price of shoes and neither Dr. van den Haag nor I will buy shoes so often— though a shoe fetishist might well feel compelled to ignore the behavior of the market. But double the penalty for murder and tell me who these potential murderers are who will refrain from killing.

In a review of Ehrlich's peculiar doctrines, Baldus and Cole wrote what might well be the last word: "There is no reason to think that economics or any other discipline has yet identified the determinants of the murder rate with enough confidence to rely on results obtained from regression analysis."[9] Exactly.

In addition to the eminent authorities who have done what they could with Ehrlich's methodology and found it wanting, I have found a devastating critique of all the variant statistical methodologies that have been applied to the capital punishment data. In an article on the deterrent effect of capital punishment, Arnold Barnett examined the articles by Passell and Forst, as well as the numerous articles by Ehrlich, and concluded that "Ehrlich's model, like Passell's and Forst's, sustained systematic errors of greater magnitude than the effect it ascribed to capital punishment."[10]

My irreverent view of Ehrlich's ponderous maneuvers with the data of homicide was, I concede, an intuitive reluctance to accept his basic postulate about the supply of murders and the demand for committing them. I have been heartened by the authority of Professor Wassily Leontief, a Nobel laureate, a past president of the American Economic Association, and himself an econometrician of august credentials. In a recent letter to *Science,* Leontief wrote,

> As an empirical science, economics dealt from the outset with the phenomena of common experience. Producing and consuming goods, buying and selling, receiving income and spending it are activities engaging everyone's

attention practically all the time. Even the application of the scientific principle of quantification did not have to be initiated by the analyst himself—measuring and pricing constitute an integral part of the phenomena that he sets out to explain. Herein lies, however, the initial source of the trouble in which academic economics finds itself today.

By the time the facts of every day experience were used up, economists were able to turn for bits and pieces of less accessible, more specialized information to government statistics. However, these statistics—compiled for administrative or business, but not for scientific purposes—fall short of what would have been required for concrete, more detailed understanding of the structure and functions of a modern economic system.

Not having been subjected from the outset to the harsh discipline of systematic fact-finding, traditionally imposed on and accepted by their colleagues in the natural and historical sciences, economists developed a nearly irresistible predilection for deductive reasoning. . . ."[11]

Professor Leontief was certainly not thinking of Professor Ehrlich when he wrote this letter, but his strictures apply. Like anyone else studying crime in America, Ehrlich has had to rely on the Uniform Crime Reports compiled by the Federal Bureau of Investigation. These data are not compiled with the social scientist's need for precision as a principal objective. We are welcome to use them if we choose, but we have always been discontented with their organization, their lack of systematic audit, the gross inaccuracies that have sometimes required the FBI to exclude data from such large reporting agencies as the New York City police, and, most exasperating to us, the lack of discrimination within crime categories. It is fair to say that the FBI has made many corrections in its methods of collection and tabulation, but the unreliability and the incompleteness of the data during the earlier years of Dr. Ehrlich's study period were notorious. Even now, arrests are far more systematically recorded than convictions and dispositions of offenders. No differentiation is made for the various degrees of homicide; we never have any way to distinguish between capital murders and the lesser degrees of homicide. To apply so finely tuned an instrument as regression analysis to data that are so defective is a waste of time and statistical talent. The wonder is that Dr. Ehrlich has attracted so much attention from economists and statisticians who should know better.

It is not surprising at all that he exerts a special fascination for retentionists. When he fades away for good, who will take his place?

The Insignificance of Phillips

My argus-eyed opponent has spotted an odd article by Professor David Phillips, a sociologist, and wonders why I have not discussed it. In Dr. van den Haag's opinion, it is not relevant to our basic controversy, even though it seems to him to say something about the deterrent powers of the hangman.[12] Dr. van den Haag does not tell us why he thinks the article is irrelevant, but I can face its implications with equanimity.

Phillips's finding is exquisitely ambiguous: He thinks he has shown that after a well-publicized execution, the number of murders decline significantly during the three weeks that follow the event as compared with the three weeks before. The decline does not, however, affect the murder rate over time. In a comment on Phillips's article, Hans Zeisel remarked that the relationship between the executions and the incidence of murder hardly warrants the term *deterrence*—the more appropriate word would have been *delay*.[13]

For my part, I wonder why Phillips bothered. His study is based on twenty-two executions occurring in England between the years 1857 and 1921 that were deemed notorious enough to receive the attention of the London *Times*. He counted up the column inches that the *Times* allocated to each execution and then counted up the murders committed in what he called the "experimental" and the "control" periods. The willingness to undertake such a dusty enquiry (how dusty may only be judged by those who have dug into ancient newspaper files) testifies to Phillips's perseverance, though not to his epistemological judgment. I am not surprised that Dr. van den Haag mentions this study so diffidently. Why, indeed, mention it at all?

Notes

1. Johannes Andenaes, *Punishment and Deterrence* (Ann Arbor: University of Michigan Press, 1974).
2. Jack P. Gibbs, *Crime, Punishment and Deterrence* (New York, Oxford, and Amsterdam: Elsevier, 1975).
3. Franklin E. Zimring and Gordon J. Hawkins, *Deterrence: The Legal Threat in Crime Control* (Chicago: University of Chicago Press, 1973).
4. Cesare Beccaria, *On Crimes and Punishments,* trans. Henry Paolucci (Indianapolis: Bobbs-Merrill 1963). (Originally published, 1764.)
5. Ezzat Abdel Fattah, *A Study of the Deterrent Effect of Capital Punishment with Special Reference to the Canadian Situation* (Ottawa: Information Canada, 1972), p. 191.
6. Fattah's ten supporting reasons are of considerable relevance to our debate. They may be found in his report on pp. 191–193. I shall summarize them, all too briefly, here.
   (1) During the years of suspension of capital punishment, the homicide rate rose more slowly and less than any other crime of violence.
   (2) There is no consistent trend in the moderate increase in the murder rates between 1962 and 1970, the study years.
   (3) The years during which capital punishment was administratively suspended did not

witness an increase in criminal homicide over 1962. "Furthermore, in many Canadian provinces the first year of legal suspension did not mark an increase in [the] criminal homicide rate over the previous year. In . . . Nova Scotia, Ontario, Saskatchewan, and Alberta, homicide rates actually declined after capital punishment was legally suspended."

(4) The increase in criminal homicide should be at an identical rate in all the provinces if the abolition of capital punishment is a determining independent variable. This was not the case. The increase in British Columbia was 5.1% during the eight-year period of the study; in Alberta it was 82.4%.

(5) If the suspension of capital punishment had led to an increase in criminal homicide, this increase should have been most apparent in the most populous and industrialized province—Ontario. But the homicide rate in that province was unchanged throughout the study period.

(6) "There are reasons to believe that homicide and suicide are complementary phenomena and that they are affected by the same factors. This explains why the proportion of one to the other in any country remains fairly constant over the years. If the suspension of the death penalty leads to an increase in criminal homicide, such an abolition would tend to upset the balance . . . since the increase in homicide would necessarily be higher than that of suicide. . . . Actually, the increase in suicide during the past years has been at a higher rate than that of homicide. . . ."

(7) If the increase in criminal homicide were due to the suspension of capital punishment, then the categories of murder for which this punishment has been retained should not show an increase. Actually, the largest number of police murders took place when capital punishment was in effect and in a year when two murderers were executed (1962). The presence of the death penalty did not prevent the slaying of 11 policemen that year. "The murder of policemen has been on the increase since the legal suspension of capital punishment in 1968, in spite of the fact that it has been retained for this type of killing."

(8) "Our data show that during the years preceding the administrative suspension of capital punishment, the probability of a murderer being hanged was less than one in 10. When legal suspension . . . follows it cannot drastically change the situation. If such a suspension is followed by an increase in homicide, then the causes should be sought elsewhere."

(9) "Our data clearly show that there are substantial differences in the criminal homicide rates among the Canadian provinces. This fact alone indicates . . . that homicide rates are determined by factors that are beyond the control of the criminal law, and hence not in the least affected by the frequency of legal executions."

(10) Homicide is not an isolated phenomenon but an integral part of violent criminality. Provinces with high rates of violent crimes have high rates of homicide, while provinces with low rates of violent crimes have low rates of homicide. The homicide rate is therefore influenced by the same social factors that affect other crimes of violence. Changes in punishment can have a negligible effect on the homicide rate—if any at all.

7. Fattah, p. 193.
8. Fattah, p. 180.
9. David C. Baldus and James W. L. Cole, "A Comparison of the Work of Thorsten Sellin and Isaac Ehrlich on the Deterrent Effect of Capital Punishment," *Yale Law Journal* 85 (1975), pp. 170–186.

10. Arnold Barnett, "The Deterrent Effect of Capital Punishment: A Test of Some Recent Studies," *Operations Research* 29 (March/April 1981), pp. 346–370.
11. Wassily Leontief, "Academic Economics," *Science* 217 (9 July 1982), pp. 104–107.
12. David P. Phillips, "The Deterrent Effect of Capital Punishment: New Evidence on an Old Controversy," *American Journal of Sociology* 86 (July 1980), pp. 139–148.
13. Hans Zeisel, "A Comment on 'The Deterrent Effect of Capital Punishment' by Phillips," *American Journal of Sociology* 88 pp. 167–169; David P. Phillips, "Reply to Zeisel," (July 1982), pp. 170–172.

ERNEST VAN DEN HAAG

Professor Conrad stresses "difficulties and differences about deterrence" where I do not. The difficulties he stresses are not relevant to the issue at hand, or are altogether misperceived, wherefore I ignored them. To wit: Professor Conrad is wrong when he says that narcotics law violations are "entirely insensitive" to deterrents. Although irrelevant to the death penalty, this matter is so often brought up that it may as well be clarified.

A threat deters only if most of those tempted by the crime are likely to perceive the threatened penalty as severe enough and probable enough to make the threatened criminal act unrewarding. No penalty will deter drug dealers as long as the income from drug dealing is high enough to make the crime seem rewarding despite any penalty. If one were to put $1,000,000 in the middle of Times Square in New York announcing that anyone who tries to take the money will suffer the death penalty, and if there is a 50% chance of not being apprehended, there will be many takers—not because the crime is "insensitive" to deterrence but because the reward held out (the $1,000,000) is such as to dwarf the risks of death in the perceptions of people to whom $1,000,000 means a lot. And actually, chances of apprehension for drug dealers are much less than 50%. Now, if we were to threaten drug takers (consumers) with five years in prison and if we were to carry out the threat for an indefinite time, none but inveterate addicts would *take* drugs. Newcomers would be deterred. The market that relies on a stream of newcomers would dry up. Few would try the drug out of curiosity just once— yet they are the ones who become new addicts—if there is a high chance of five years in jail. (There is no penalty currently.) Ordinary people, nonaddicts, would be deterred, and the problem would be solved for there would be no *new* addicts. It would matter little how dealers would be punished— their business would no longer be profitable.

There is nothing wrong with the theory of deterrence, but one must know how to apply it—just as there is nothing wrong with the theory of gravitation: Those who know how to apply it realize that the flying of air-planes is not inconsistent with it.

I agree with Professor Conrad that empty threats not implemented by a sufficient rate of apprehension and conviction will not deter. I wonder why he thinks that there is a complexity to the "hydra-headed problem" of deterrence I overlooked. Threats deter only when credible. (I did not realize this was "complexity.") I know literally of no one writing about crime who has ever overlooked the problem of credibility. It is an important part of the "econometric solution to the capital punishment problem propounded by Dr. Ehrlich." He certainly did not ignore it, although he criticizes others for doing so by drawing conclusions from death penalty laws rather than from executions.

Professor Conrad at length reiterates Fattah's conclusion from the Canadian data, but the data do not support it, as I pointed out. Wherefore we might as well leave Canada and Fattah.

Professor Conrad tells us that he approaches "econometric solutions to noneconomic problems* with suspicion and skepticism." An autobiographical fact of interest to psychologists. It sheds no light whatever on whether the "econometric solutions" here, or elsewhere, are correct. Specifically, Professor Conrad simply assumes what he means to prove: that the demand for murder will not decline if the price rises. It is no proof to quote others (such as Baldus and Cole) who say the same and have no more evidence than Professor Conrad. Ehrlich actually did show by means of statistical data that the demand for crime decreases when the price goes up. That Professor Conrad does not like economics and feels it should not invade what he regards as his turf does not make the data incorrect.

Why Professor Conrad cites Leontief escapes me. His view seems irrelevant not only, as Conrad concedes, to Ehrlich and to the death penalty but to anything I can think of.

JOHN P. CONRAD

My dogmatic opponent has left a few loose ends behind him in what appears to have been his terminal contribution to this chapter. In the interest of perfect clarity, if not in the interest of the reader's patience, I will try again to straighten out the wandering strands of this phase of the argument.

---

*Since economics is simply a method of analysis, more or less fruitfully applicable to anything, what is a "noneconomic problem"?

On the Complexities of Deterrence. I have stressed these complexities because Dr. van den Haag insists on extrapolating from the deterrent effects discovered in experiments with sophomore students to the deterrence of potential and actual murderers. If he would stick to the topic of murder in his discussion of deterrence, I would concede that we are dealing with a much simpler question, though it is certainly not free of complexity.

I referred to crimes committed to enable an addict to get his fix. I must doubt that such crimes are deterrable by raising the penalty or even by increasing the risk of apprehension. They are not as frequently violent as some people suppose, but muggings, some of them fatal, certainly occur for such purposes. The point is that it is an absurdity to assert that deterrence is relevant for such offenses; that is one of Hydra's heads.

And that is the point I wished to make in arguing that such crimes are insensitive to deterrence. As to my opponent's digression on the topic of addiction in general, I can agree that if he has the magic for apprehending all addicts and locking them all up for five years, the business of the peddler and his suppliers will fall off sharply. As the courts and the legislatures have agreed with the moral philosophers that addiction should not be treated as a crime, nor should mere possession of addictive drugs, the solution to the narcotics problem proposed by my draconian opponent is not feasible. Even if such a drastic reversal of the law were to be put into effect, Professor van den Haag would be hard put to it to assure that all the purchasers of drugs were arrested, convicted, and put behind bars for five years or any significant portion of such a term. Another of Hydra's heads. In proposing his simple solution, my adversary has set for himself a task that far exceeds in difficulty any of the labors of Hercules, even the slaying of the monstrous Hydra. He may be excused from proceeding. The narcotics problem is important but certainly is not germane to our discourse.

On the Canadian Data. My imperious opponent waves aside Professor Fattah's analysis of eighty years of statistics of the death penalty in Canada. He is satisfied that in his earlier dismissal of these data he has shown that they do not support Fattah's ten conclusions. Is it possible that Dr. van den Haag finds these conclusions beyond empirical refutation? That is the only explanation I can imagine for his precipitate dismissal of what seems to me to be a closely reasoned argument.

On Econometric Solutions. So far as I know, Dr. van den Haag is the first to suggest that economics is the universal social science, and that the methods of economic analysis are "fruitfully applicable to anything." The times are hard for orthodox economists, and this note of cheer will be generally welcome.

But I had in mind a discussion of the assumptions that entitle an economist to apply his methods of analysis to the problems of murder. As Baldus and Cole remarked, these assumptions rely on a certainty of the determinants of murder rates that no one except Isaac Ehrlich and his acolytes can claim. Throughout Dr. Ehrlich's prolific writing on the topic there is an underlying claim that murder rates behave in accordance with the laws of supply and demand. As Professor Leontief pointed out in his acerbic but brief critique of the reliance of economists on deductive reasoning, the real world is not as simple as the conclusions of economists drawing on their models. I am not sure how an economist should go about the task that Dr. Ehrlich set for himself, but I suggest that it would be useful for him to begin with some attention to the categorization of the homicide data by a study of murder bookings by a selection of police departments. A significant variation in the homicide rates for a specific category as found in Detroit—where the death penalty cannot be invoked—and Chicago or Cleveland—where it can—might lead to clues on deterrence and its utility. Much more hard labor than programming a computer to accept all the suspect data on which Dr. Ehrlich has contentedly relied.[1]

Note

1. One of the first doubters of the Ehrlich *oeuvre* was Gordon Tullock, "Does Punishment Deter Crime?" *The Public Interest* 36 (Summer 1974), p. 108. Tullock, an enthusiastic utilitarian, was rightly dubious about Ehrlich's reliance on "the data available for this study [*which*] were not what one would hope for...." I am not aware that Dr. Ehrlich has found ways to obtain more satisfactory data.

CHAPTER 7

The Constitutional Question

ERNEST VAN DEN HAAG

The death penalty poses a legal as well as a moral question. Thus, many lawyers in the United States have tried to get the Supreme Court to declare capital punishment unconstitutional mainly on the basis of the Eighth Amendment, which prohibits "cruel and unusual punishment," or of the Fourteenth, which requires "the equal protection of the laws" for all the inhabitants of the United States. Let us consider the constitutional question then.

The Eighth Amendment, which prohibits "cruel and unusual punishment" was enacted in 1791. However, so was the Fifth Amendment, which requires that no one shall be "deprived of life, liberty or property without due process of law." The Fifth Amendment implies that *with* "due process of law" one may be deprived "of *life,* liberty or property"—i.e., that the death penalty is a legitimate punishment. Since the prohibition of "cruel and unusual punishment" was enacted at the same time, obviously it was not meant to repeal the death penalty, which at the time was imposed frequently.

If the framers did not consider the death penalty "cruel and unusual," do we? If we do, is what we consider "cruel and unusual" today to determine whether laws imposing the death penalty are constitutional—or should we be guided by what the framers of the Constitution meant by "cruel and unusual"? If we are to be guided by what they thought, the Constitution binds us until it is amended, and the death penalty is constitutional.* If we are to be guided by what we want and not by what the framers of the Constitution decided, why have a Constitution? Why pretend to adhere to a rule made in the past when we mean to be bound only by the rules we make? To have a Constitution means to wish to adhere to rules made in the past. Else we can leave everything to the rules we currently decide on.

It is interesting nonetheless to ask: Do we today consider the death penalty cruel? Certainly Professor Conrad does. But the majority of Americans do not. According to polls, something like 70% are in favor of the death penalty. When the Supreme Court objected to some aspects of state laws imposing capital punishment, more than two-thirds of all the states reenacted them so as to remove putative constitutional defects. All this does not show that the death penalty is a good thing. But it does show that the majority of Americans and of their state representatives favor it at this time.† Indeed, if the majority in any state does not want the death penalty, it can abolish it (and in the past often has). Why then make it a federal and a constitutional matter? Indeed, why make the retention or abolition of capital punishment a judicial matter at all?

If standards of cruelty did evolve, so that what was not thought "cruel and unusual" when the Fifth and Eighth Amendments were passed now is perceived to be, should the death penalty become unconstitutional? One first must ask: Perceived by whom? The people? If so, why not let them vote? The judges of the Supreme Court? They were not elected. Their task certainly is *not* to interpret popular feeling or perception. They do not take polls and are not *meant* to respond to popular feelings. They are meant to interpret the law independently. Nor are the judges meant to enact their own moral theories into law. It is not the task of the Supreme Court to discover or to reveal new moral standards. Their task is to interpret the laws, including the Constitution. If the voters want to accept new moral standards, if, for instance, they now consider the death penalty wrong, they can vote

---

*Of course, we can abolish it anyway: Although we can't make laws the Constitution prohibits, we need not make all the laws the Constitution permits. Legislatures can abolish the death penalty or retain it. Courts must respect either decision as long as it does not violate the Constitution.

†P. C. Ellsworth, and L. Ross, "Public Opinion and Capital Punishment: A Close Examination of the Views of Abolitionists and Retentionists" (Unpublished manuscript, 1980). The authors report that two-thirds of their respondents would support the death penalty— even if it were proven to be no better a deterrent than life imprisonment. The Gallup poll reported in March 1981 that 66% of the public favor the death penalty for persons convicted of murder.

accordingly to elect representatives who will repeal it. Courts are not meant to be legislatures. Our Constitution distinguishes the making (or repealing) of laws, through the political process, from the interpretation of laws through the judicial process. The judges are supposed to interpret laws. Legislators are to make them.

To be sure, sometimes an interpretation is hard to distinguish from a new law, but at other times that distinction is easy. In the case of the death penalty it certainly is. Neither a consensus (which is absent anyway) nor a moral discovery by judges can be a ground for judicial repeal of the death penalty, which the Constitution says plainly can be imposed, provided there is due process. Wherefore the court has concentrated on the dueness of the legal process.* Repeal requires the enactment of laws through the political process. Those who insist on judicial repeal ask the Supreme Court to do the work of legislators, and to assume their function. The very fact that opponents of the death penalty wish to use the judicial rather than the political process for repeal suggests that they know quite well that they do not have popular backing.

Judges dislike the death penalty more often than the average person. They are college-educated. Usually they were told by their professors that the death penalty is cruel and obsolete: According to polls, the majority of the college-educated does oppose the death penalty, whereas the majority of voters does not. There are two reasons for this difference. First, the college-educated, including judges, usually do not move in circles in which violence, including murder, is a daily threat. Not feeling threatened by murder, they can afford to treat it leniently. They can be philosophical about it. Less well-educated and poorer people threatened by violence feel they cannot. Second, whatever the advantages of college education, it has one disadvantage. Students tend to absorb and to be victimized by the intellectual fashions of their college days. Uneducated people more often accept tradition and their own experience. The death penalty is traditional. The idea of the criminal as a sick victim of society thrives among intellectuals. The fashion in intellectual circles for the last fifty years has been to regard criminals as victims of society, sick people who should be treated and rehabilitated. People who are executed cannot be rehabilitated.

It is because of his all too reasonable suspicion of intellectual fashions that William F. Buckley, Jr., declared some time ago that he would rather be governed by the first thousand people listed in the phone directory—a random selection in all relevant respects—than by the Harvard faculty. His-

---

*See *Furman* v. *Georgia* (1972), 408 U.S. 238.

torical experience shows that he has a good point. Take just one instance. The average man in the United States never fell for totalitarianism. He was anti-Communist. So were the labor unions. So were the popular magazines such as the *Reader's Digest*. However, many intellectuals were, until quite lately, entranced by communism. So were many college teachers (some of whom are intellectuals). So were the magazines they read.*

I do not deny that intellectuals have an important role to play in our society, nor do I wish to deny that many of them have been anti-Communist all along. Rather, I wish to insist that the views of the best educated are not always the best views. Education does not necessarily produce judgment or stability.† We live in a democracy. This means that intellectuals, or any other minority elite group, cannot and should not impose their views on the majority. They can try to persuade, but they should not try to impose their views on the majority by judicial decree. The majority of the people at this point show no disposition to repeal the death penalty. To me it seem undemocratic to try to get around this fact by attempting to repeal the death penalty through judicial means. Yet the attempt has not ceased. The judiciary has not abolished the death penalty by declaring it unconstitutional. The words of the Constitution are too plain. Nonetheless, the judiciary has connived with those who wish to abolish it by, in effect, sabotaging the death penalty.

If voters had repealed Prohibition and ten years after repeal only three liquor stores a year were licensed in the United States to sell liquor, might one conclude that the licensing authorities were sabotaging the repeal? *Furman* v. *Georgia,* which removed doubts about the constitutionality of the death penalty—doubts rather frivolously raised by abolitionists, was decided in 1972. (The death penalty never had been prohibited as the sale of alcohol was during Prohibition. *Furman* merely settled doubts that had led to a suspension of executions.) Last year, ten years later, three executions took place. Two of the convicts executed had insisted on execution. They were tired of the sabotage judges and lawyers were engaged in. Finally, despite last-minute attempts to deny the government the right to carry out the sentence of the court confirmed in numerous appeals, and despite attempts to deny the prisoners the right to renounce further appeals, the executions took place. Three executions in one year out of nearly 1000 persons on death row—all this ten years after *Furman* reconfirmed the constitutionality of the death penalty. The case for sabotage seems unrebuttable.

---

*See Paul Hollander, *The Political Pilgrims* (New York: Oxford University Press, 1981).
†*Corruptio optimi pessima,* as Seneca put it: "The corruption of the best is worst."

The Supreme Court has ruled that the death penalty cannot be imposed mandatorily. When the law permits it, the death penalty must be imposed in each case at the discretion of the court. The court also has found that the Constitution requires limitations to the discretion of trial courts. The courts must consider in each case mitigating and aggravating factors, which must be stated in the laws that permit the imposition of the death penalty.* But it is the procedures that follow the imposition of a death sentence that amount to sabotage.

Once a trial court imposes the death penalty, the defendant can and usually will appeal. The American Civil Liberties Union, which regards the death penalty as a violation of civil liberties, has gone so far as to try to deny people sentenced to death the right *not* to appeal their sentences. The ACLU feels that anyone who does not agree with them must be crazy. If, finally, the state's highest court confirms the sentence, the defendant can start all over again by appealing to the federal courts, alleging that there was a violation of some constitutional provision in the process by which the sentence was imposed. I do not know of any case where the appeal to the federal judiciary has been rejected without going all the way to the Supreme Court, which rarely declines a hearing. The process may take many years. If a defendant succeeds on any collateral issue—for instance, by claiming that certain evidence should not have been admitted by the trial court, or that a juror was improperly seated, or that the defense lawyer was incompetent and so on *ad infinitum*—the matter can be retried all over in state court and the appeals processes can be invoked once more if the defendant is resentenced to death.

The total result at the present time is that we have about 20,000 murders a year. We also have fewer than 1000 persons on death row, which means that only a very small percentage of all convicted murderers are sentenced to death. In the last decade we have executed at most zero to three persons a year. This means that most of the criminals on death row are likely to die of old age. It is hard to deny that the judiciary is successful in sabotaging the death penalty to death, to coin a phrase. If sabotage must be shown by existence of intention to sabotage, I do not believe it can be shown. If sabotage can be shown by regarding the results of judicial proceedings as probative, there seems little doubt that sabotage is occurring, as shown by the fact that executions are extremely rare.

In affirmative action cases, the courts have often held that the number of minority employees actually hired (or not hired) is probative of discrim-

---

*In many states, after a guilty finding, there is a special hearing that leads to a death sentence or to a lesser one.

ination regardless of intention or hiring procedure. I see no reason why this kind of evidence should not be used to suggest that the courts are sabotaging the law with respect to the death penalty.

JOHN P. CONRAD

In this phase of our discourse, the reader is treated to the spectacle of two nonlawyers venturing on some of the most treacherous ground in jurisprudence. Whatever our valid credentials may be, neither of us has been admitted to the bar. To justify our audacity, we might paraphrase Georges Clemenceau and assert that constitutional law is much too serious a matter to leave to judges and lawyers.

An aphorism is not enough; there are better reasons. The Constitution of the United States is the foundation of our laws, but it was also the product of eighteenth century thought and experience. Not only that, but over two centuries of use many adaptations have had to be made. Alexander Hamilton, James Madison, and the other framers knew nothing of railroads, airplanes, or the intricacies of a national social security system. More to the point, they had no inkling of the quality of life in a multiracial industrial metropolis like New York or Chicago. The modern city police department had yet to be organized. There were no prisons. Crime had yet to be identified as a major national problem.

The Constitution was and remains a remarkable instrument for defining and preserving the liberties of American citizens. That elaborate adaptations have had to be made by inference to carry out the intentions of the framers does not in the least detract from the wisdom of those astonishing men. To enact laws and to decide lawsuits consistently with the expectations of those eighteenth century lawyers calls for a level of wisdom comparable to theirs. Such wisdom must be informed by history; the constitutional lawyer must take into account the changes in values, ideas, and the human condition over the twenty decades that have elapsed since our system of government began.

Unlike lawyers engaged in less exalted practice, the constitutional lawyer must wrestle with language that cannot be made precise. Good statutory draftsmanship requires definitions of the significant terms to be used, and these definitions are rigorously written into the opening sections of well-prepared legislation. Even in criminal law, where such terms as *murder, rape,* and *theft* are in reality concepts that go far back into antiquity, definitions are essential to the creation of a code.

The Constitution presents a vastly different situation. The framers and their colleagues who drafted the Bill of Rights did not provide us with a glossary. They left it to the courts to define and redefine their terms. Perhaps this is one of the reasons for Chief Justice Hughes's remark to Justice Douglas when the latter joined the Supreme Court: "Justice Douglas, you must remember one thing. At the constitutional level where we work, ninety percent of any decision is emotional. The rational part of us supplies the reasons for supporting our predilections."[1]

Anglo-American lawyers have built their profession on the ambiguities of their language. These ambiguities are nowhere so troublesome as those found in our Constitution. Emotions derived from education and experience cannot be prevented from influencing the interpretation of such terms as *the right to bear arms, due process of law,* and, most significant for this confrontation, *cruel and unusual punishment.* A good lawyer can always construct a line of reasoning that will justify his chosen definition of these terms. A great judge can make the great contribution to the preservation of the Constitution that Justice Douglas attributed to Hughes: "putting into imperishable words the tolerance which government must show even the most lowly of us."

In the sense that Chief Justice Hughes meant, I will not deny a substantial emotional basis for my opposition to the death penalty. I will suppose that Dr. van den Haag will make a reciprocal concession. What is important to both sides in this dispute is the precise articulation of the rational arguments that support our predilections. If these arguments can be shown by one side or the other to be lacking in rigor, the advantage goes to the side with the more rigor.

It is now important to state the propositions on which we can agree. I have found three such points of agreement in my tenacious opponent's chapter. I proceed from them in entirely different directions from Dr. van den Haag's reasoning.

1. When the Bill of Rights was added to the Constitution, there was no intention to prohibit capital punishment on the ground that it was cruel and unusual.
2. The most recent opinion polls and actions by the state legislatures show that the majority of the American people now favor the retention of capital punishment.
3. Few murderers have been executed in recent years.

There can be no challenge to these facts. Our differences begin with the interpretation of their meaning. I shall now open a skirmish over our divergent interpretations and then move on to the main battleground where fundamental differences on policy and perspective must be fought out.

The Meaning of "Cruel and Unusual"

Unlike the rest of the Constitution, the Eighth Amendment was transplanted, almost word for word, from the English Bill of Rights of 1689. That declaration read:

> And thereupon the said lords spiritual and temporal, and commons . . . do in the first place, (as their ancestors in like cases have usually done), for the vindication and asserting their ancient rights and liberties, declare . . .
>
> 10. That excessive bail ought not to be required, nor excessive fines imposed; nor cruel and unusual punishments inflicted."[3]

Except for the substitution of "shall" for "ought," the Eighth Amendment is identical to this clause. No one I know of has claimed that this difference is of any substantive significance. Because of the peculiar durability of this vague constitutional mandate, we must examine its historical antecendents. There is plenty of uncertainty here, too, as we shall see.

The English Bill of Rights was one of the enduring outcomes of the "Glorious Revolution" of 1688, when James II was forced off the British throne and William III became king. One of the conditions of his coronation was his acceptance of the Bill of Rights, which Parliament enacted in 1689. The tenth clause, quoted above, was written into the bill in the aftermath of two horrifying events during the closing years of the Stuart regime. First was the brutal punishment of a clergyman, Titus Oates, for the crime of perjury, during which he was dragged behind a horse through the streets of London, being whipped along the way by the public executioner. The second event was the "Bloody Assizes," in the course of which Lord Chief Justice Jeffreys sentenced to grisly execution hundreds, perhaps thousands of men who had participated—or who were thought to have participated—in the abortive Monmouth Rebellion of 1685.

Parliament's aim in enacting the cruel and unusual punishment clause seems almost certainly to have had two objectives. First, the English courts were to be prevented from inflicting any excessive or legislatively unauthorized punishments, as had been the case in the sentences imposed on Titus Oates and on the victims of the Bloody Assizes. Second, penalties for all offenses were to be proportionate. Under no circumstances should a perjurer be whipped through the city streets, as was done with the Reverend Titus Oates, nor were persons to be executed because they were convicted of being away from home on the night when a rebellion was afoot. But capital punishment, with all the embellishments of disembowelment, drawing, quartering, and beheading, was preserved in the law, if not often in practice, until 1814, when execution was limited to hanging without any attendant horrors.[4]

When Virginia, along with the other twelve colonies, declared itself independent (well in advance of July 4, 1776), one of the first orders of business was the drafting of a Declaration of Rights, which was passed in June 1776. The ninth section was a verbatim transcription of the cruel and unusual punishment clause of the English Bill of Rights. When the first ten amendments were added to our Constitution in 1791, the identical language was incorporated in the Eighth Amendment.

What did the Virginia House of Delegates and, later, our Congress and the ratifying states mean by this loose term, *cruel and unusual punishment?* In a thorough, but not entirely persuasive article, Anthony F. Granucci argued that whereas the English Parliament meant to prevent unauthorized and disproportionate punishment, the American legislators misinterpreted that clause to mean the prohibition of torturous punishments.[5] That may be so, but it is not clear from Granucci's account that the original purpose of the prohibition was not also preserved. In his historical review of the antecendents of the Eighth Amendment in *Furman* v. *Georgia,* Justice Brennan probed the legislative history further.[6] Noting that there is little direct evidence of the framers' intention in providing against cruel and unusual punishment, Brennan quoted Holmes of Massachusetts and Patrick Henry of Virginia as demanding that the power of Congress to fix sentences by legislation must be severely restricted to the principles of rationality. They vigorously argued that without such limits in a constitutional restraint there would be nothing to prevent a legislative body from enacting any whimsically and outrageously disproportionate penalty for any crime whatsoever. Without a constitutional provision limiting the authority of a legislature to proportionate penalties, and a Supreme Court to enforce the limits, the freedom of the people would always be in jeopardy. Forty years later, Justice Joseph Story wrote, "The provision [the Eighth Amendment], would seem to be wholly unnecessary in a free government, since it is scarcely possible that any department of such a government should authorize or justify such atrocious conduct."[7] This sentence has been frequently quoted by writers inclined to view the amendment as superfluous. However, Story continued in the next sentence, "It was adopted . . . as an admonition to all departments of national government to warn them against such violent proceedings. . . . Mr Justice Blackstone has wisely remarked that sanguinary laws are a bad symptom of the distemper of any state, or at least of its weak constitution."

Justice Story took an optimistic view of the blessings of democracy. No one familiar with the administration of punishment in American prisons and jails will be so sure of the needlessness of constitutional recourse against the abuses that have taken place in very recent years.

Over seventy years have passed since the Supreme Court decided, in *Weems* v. *United States,* that the state legislatures had to comply with the Eighth Amendment.[8] Later in this response, I shall consider the propriety of the Supreme Court's intervention in capital punishment questions. Here the question is what meaning should be attached to the cruel and unusual punishment clause in judicial review of these matters. There are only two choices of a basis for interpretation. One is to assume that the constitutional interpretation must be restricted to outlawing only those punishments that were considered torturous and excessive in 1791. I understand my opponent to favor this rule of interpretation; disembowelment and thumbscrews are not to be permitted, but branding and ear-cropping might be allowed, as well as the death penalty, since the former two punishments were administered in several states at that time.

I prefer the Supreme Court's view, as phrased in *Trop* v. *Dulles,* that the words of the Eighth Amendment are not precise and their scope is not static. The cruel and unusual punishment clause "must draw its meaning from the evolving standards of decency that mark the progress of a maturing society."[9]

How can the "progress of a maturing society" be discerned? I do not see this task as particularly obscure. In 1791 there were no police and no prisons as we know them now. Justice had to be rough. Capital punishment was administered more freely than even the most vigorous of its contemporary advocates would approve. Where the gallows might be considered excessive for one of the lesser crimes, nostrils could be slit or ears cropped to establish forever the villainy of the convicted offender. The great nineteenth century reform was the prison, one of whose intended effects was the reduction of the barbarities of criminal justice. Those who believe that the prisons of today are modern barbarities that must be abolished or radically reformed may be entitled to their opinion, but the monstrosities that they replaced in the early nineteenth century were incomparably worse.

To testify to the change that incarceration made possible, I will summon Dr. van den Haag's great Victorian precursor, Sir James Fitzjames Stephen, whose apologia for capital punishment, as it was formerly administered, included the following historical review:

> The means now available for disposing of criminals, otherwise than by putting them to death, are both more available and more effectual than they formerly were. In the days of Coke, it would have been impossible practically to set up convict establishments like Dartmoor or Portland, and the expense of establishing either police or prisons adequate to the wants of the country would have been regarded as exceedingly burdensome, beside which the management of prisons was not understood. Hence, unless a criminal was hanged, there was no way of disposing of him. Large numbers of criminals accordingly were hanged whose offences indicated no great moral depravity. The disgust excited by this indiscriminate cruelty ought not to blind us to the fact that there is a kind and degree of wickedness which ought to be regarded as unpardonable.[10]

A judge with Sir James's unlimited self-confidence had no difficulty in discriminating the degree of depravity that required the death of the offender on the gallows. Modern judges are not always so sure. The burden of making this discrimination has resulted in a rather small minority of the potentially eligible murderers receiving a sentence of death. Capital punishment has become unusual, and its very exceptional imposition has raised the question of cruelty. To ignore the prison in which life sentences can be and are served, to ignore the professed uncertainties of those who must pronounce the sentence of death is to ignore also "the progress of a maturing society." It is the nature of a conservative view of the idea of progress to be skeptical of such a notion as the maturation of a society. We do well to maintain our doubts, but not to the exclusion of hope.

Public Opinion and Capital Punishment

For many years the Roper Poll has enquired into the state of public opinion regarding capital punishment. In 1965, 47% of those surveyed were reported as opposed, 38% were in favor, and 15% were uncertain. This abolitionist distribution has shifted in the retentionist direction ever since. In 1978, 66% were in favor, 28% were opposed, and only 6% unsure.[11] I do not doubt that this distribution of public opinion reflects current public sentiment. It must be directly attributable to the growing anxiety about the volume of violent crime and the expressed opinion of many eminent public men that there might be less crime if more liberal use were made of the death penalty. It is impressive that in the Harris Survey of 1977 the following question was asked: "Suppose that it could be proven to your satisfaction that the death penalty was NOT more effective than long prison sentences in keeping other people from committing crimes such as murder, would you be in favor of the death penalty or opposed to it?" And the answers were then quite different from the overwhelming majority reported in the Roper Poll of 1978: The percentage in favor declined from 66% to 46%, whereas the percentage of abolitionists rose to 40% and the unsures rose to 14%. Among the black respondents, opposition rose from 48% to 51%, and the white respondents opposing the death penalty rose from 25% to 39%.[12]

What *does* the public want? In the first place, this is an issue about which few people have firsthand knowledge. The Harris and Roper data make it clear that there is a substantial fraction of the public that doesn't know but supposes that its leaders do. Throughout the Nixon years, a very hard line was taken with respect to criminal justice. The president himself frequently expressed his view that the death penalty was an essential element in the deterrence of crime. It is important to remember that neither the president nor his principal legal advisers, nor the attorney general and his deputies and assistants had had any extensive experience with criminal justice before taking office. It is impossible to conclude that such men as President Nixon, Vice-President Agnew, John Ehrlichmann, the chief domestic counsel, John Dean, the chief legal counsel, John Mitchell, the attorney general, or Richard Kleindienst, the deputy attorney general, had direct knowledge of the crime problem that could lead them to a reasoned position that capital punishment deters crime. What is far more probable is the inference that the death penalty belonged in the "hard-line package" that these leaders of the people wanted as a demonstration of their toughness. Their success was considerable.

One other footnote to the opinion poll matter: My opponent supposes that opposition to the death penalty is strongest in the comfortable suburbs, where the dangers of street crime are minimal, but plain people living in daily fear of their lives in the inner cities strongly support a penalty that they believe will protect them from violence. Dr. van den Haag does not cite his authority for this supposition, and the facts, so far as I can discover, point in the opposite direction. If the Gallup Poll is to be believed, a distribution of opinion about capital punishment according to income produced the results given in Table I. I am not at all sure what these percentages mean, but I am certain that they don't mean that opposition to the death penalty is a predilection of the comfortable.

Further evidence suggesting that the real support for capital punishment is to be found among the more fortunate classes of society is in the background of its abolition in the United Kingdom and France. For many years, opposition to capital punishment was an issue with firm support in the Labour party of Great Britain. The vigorous opposition to the abolition of the death penalty came vociferously from the Conservative party. Abo-

TABLE I. Question: Are You in Favor of the
Death Penalty for Persons Convicted of
Murder?

Income	Percent favoring
$20,000 and over	65%
$15,000 to $19,999	67%
$10,000 to $14,999	63%
$7,000 to $9,999	71%
$5,000 to $6,999	60%
$3,000 to $4,999	50%
Under $3,000	36%

Source: George H. Gallup, *The Gallup Opinion Index,*
Report No. 158 (Princeton, New Jersey: Gallup Poll, September 1978), pp. 22–25.[13]

lition took place in 1965, when the Labour party was in office. Similarly, abolition of the death penalty was hardly considered in France until 1981, when a socialist government took office. In both nations, opposition to the death penalty was a predilection of the working classes, the plain people on whose common sense and perception of the realities of violence Professor van den Haag sets such great store.

The Declining Number of Executions

In spite of the firm support that capital punishment has always enjoyed in the United States, its use has steadily declined since 1930. As a good deal of the exchange of views taking place in this chapter concerns this trend and the reasons for it, I will present in Table II the data, collapsed into five-year intervals, for the entire country.

The number of executions between 1965 and 1979 was sharply curtailed by the constitutional litigation that was under way, and by the Supreme Court's requirement that state legislation had to be modified to meet the strict criteria laid down in *Furman* v. *Georgia* and certain other decisions. Despite the virtual moratorium on executions between 1965 and 1980, the courts have not refrained from imposing the death sentence, as Table III shows.

The lack of correlation between the decline in the frequency of executions and the increasing number of death sentences pronounced by the courts is most easily explained by the responsiveness of the inferior courts to public opinion supporting the death penalty, and by the compunction of

TABLE II. Executions in the United States, 1930–1979

Years	Executions
1930–34	776
1935–39	891
1940–44	645
1945–49	639
1950–54	413
1955–59	304
1960–64	181
1965–69	10
1970–74	0
1975–79	3

Source: Bureau of Justice Statistics, U.S. Department of Justice, *Capital Punishment 1979* (Washington, D.C.: U.S. Government Printing Office, 1980), p. 16.

TABLE III. Number of Death Sentences, Number of Sentencing Jurisdictions, Numbers of Persons under Death Sentence, United States, 1968–1980

Year	Total sentenced to death	Number of jurisdictions sentencing	Total under death sentence at year end
1968	138	25	517
1969	143	24	575
1970	133	26	631
1971	113	24	642
1972	83	19	334
1973	42	7	134
1974	165	18	242
1975	320	27	484
1976	249	30	416
1977	150	20	410
1978	183	23	445
1979	159	25	567
1980	187	25	718

Sources: For years 1968–1978, Bureau of Justice Statistics, U.S. Department of Justice, *Capital Punishment 1979* (Washington, D.C.: U.S. Government Printing Office, 1980), p. 20. Distribution by race and disposition omitted. For 1980, see Bureau of Justice Statistics Bulletin, July 1981.

the appellate courts to authorize executions in the face of serious constitutional obstacles. I do not suppose that my opponent will resist this explanation, but I shall return to it with my own interpretive remarks at a later point in this response.

I now turn to six matters discussed in this chapter by Professor van den Haag on which our differences have no identifiable points of agreement on the facts. In each case, I shall argue that my opponent is wrong in his understanding of the Constitution and judicial process, in his interpretation of recent social and political history, and, in some matters, as to both.

Should Capital Punishment Be a Judicial Matter?

Professor van den Haag asks why the question of abolition or retention should be decided in the courts. Here he confronts the long-settled system of constitutional government in the United States. Unlike the constitutional system of any other country, our government depends on an intricate apparatus of checks and balances that originated in the framers' distrust of unregulated power. It is an inconvenient system. In no other country may the courts overturn legislation because it violates the Constitution. This is the system in this country. Until we have a new Constitution that works in a different way, the courts have a duty to rule on the constitutionality of legislation whenever such a question is raised in pleading a case.

In effect, the courts exercise a limited but powerful role in supervising the executive and legislative branches of government. The courts may not judge the wisdom or propriety of executive regulations or legislative statutes, but they must rule on questions of constitutionality. This arrangement is not a necessary feature of democratic government. The British parliamentary system works well with the roles reversed; Parliament can and does supervise the courts.

Many political scientists will agree with Professor van den Haag. Ours is an inefficient and counterproductive system that prevents administrators from getting things done and may often thwart the will of the people. I don't agree. Our system preserves liberty, and it deters all branches of government from violations of standards of fairness to all citizens. Considering the state of freedom and personal autonomy in most other countries, Americans are naturally cautious about fundamental changes in our Constitution to gain some theoretical advantage of governmental efficiency. That requires us to maintain the power of the Supreme Court to rule on constitutional questions whenever they are presented. Some of those rulings will be unpopular; I have been disturbed by many decisions handed down by the Supreme Court throughout its long history, just as Dr. van den Haag regrets its intervention in the capital punishment cases. Looking back on that history, I prefer to view the succession of decisions as events in the endless progress of a maturing society. In such a society change takes place, and nothing is unchangeable, not even the established precedents in the interpretation of the Constitution.

Does the Supreme Court Usurp the Powers of the Legislature?

Again, Professor van den Haag has misunderstood the peculiar role that the Supreme Court must play in our system of checks and balances. He supposes that when the Supreme Court is asked to overturn a death penalty law, it is expected to repeal it. There is a distinction, and it is important. When a legislature decides to repeal a previously enacted statute, it does so for a variety of reasons that are constitutionally acceptable. It may consider that experience has shown that the law was unwise. It may conclude that it did not produce the expected result, or that it did produce unexpected results that cannot be accepted. It may even decide to repeal a good law because the insistent pressure of a special interest has induced it to act against good judgment. Sometimes it may repeal a statute because it is thought to be unconstitutional, even though the Supreme Court has not declared it so.

When the Supreme Court overturns a law, it does so in the context of adversary litigation in which one or more of the issues at stake is the constitutionality of the law. One of the parties to the lawsuit argues that compliance with the law is inconsistent with the Constitution. As to the question of capital punishment, there are only three provisions of the Constitution that matter: the Fifth, Eighth, and Fourteenth Amendments. So long as these provisions remain in the Constitution, the argument *for* capital punishment must rest on the principle that my opponent wishes to establish: The language of the Constitution can be construed only by the concepts available to the framers, men of the late eighteenth century and of the reconstruction era of the nineteenth century. That is to embalm the Constitution in a mausoleum for admiration where it is of relevance only as an obstacle to change. That is the implication of his notion that "to have a Constitution means a wish to adhere to rules made in the past. Else we can leave everything to the rules we currently decide on."

This is not the theory on which the Supreme Court has acted since the days of Chief Justice Marshall. One of the most eloquent pronouncements against Professor van den Haag's notion is contained in the 1883 case of *Hurtado* v. *California:*

> ... a process of law, which is otherwise forbidden, must be taken to be due process of law, if it can show the sanction of settled usage both in England and in this country; but it by no means follows that nothing else can be due process of law. ... To hold that such a characteristic is essential to due process of law would be to deny every quality of the law but its age and to render it incapable of progress or improvement. It would stamp upon our jurisprudence the unchangeableness attributed to the laws of the Medes and the Persians.[14]

Later, in the far-reaching decision in *Weems* v. *United States,* which established the Supreme Court's authority to intervene in state legislation violating the Eighth Amendment, Justice McKenna carried the principle in *Hurtado* a good deal further:

> Legislation, both statutory and constitutional, is enacted, it is true, from an experience of evils, but its general language should not, therefore, be necessarily confined to the form that evil had theretofore taken. Time works changes, brings into existence new conditions and purposes. Therefore, a principle to be vital must be capable of wider application than the mischief which gave it birth. This is peculiarly true of constitutions. They are not ephemeral enactments, designed to meet passing occasions. They are, to use the words of Chief Justice Marshall, "designed to approach immortality as nearly as human institutions can approach it." The future is their care and provision for events of good and bad tendencies of which no prophecies can be made. In the application of a constitution, therefore, our contemplation cannot be only of what has been but of what may be. Under any other rule, a constitution would be as easy of application as it would be deficient in efficacy and power.[15]

For my opponent to argue that when the courts declare a statute in violation of the Eighth Amendment that statute is *repealed* is to misconstrue the role that the Supreme Court has played throughout all of American history. To urge that lawyers should not use the Eighth Amendment to attack death penalty statutes is to require that constitutional advocates should disregard their duties to the courts and to their clients. If there is good enough reason to argue that a law is unconstitutional, then that argument must be heard by the courts and refuted by opposing counsel if it can be refuted.

On the Antipathies of Judges

My intuitive opponent thinks that judges dislike the death penalty more than "the average person." He then goes on to advance two reasons for this state of affairs. This presents me with a complex position to attack, particularly complex because the facts are not readily verifiable. I will do what I can with what seems to me to be a wholly untenable argument.

First, there are judges and judges. Many criminal court judges are former prosecutors, seldom known for squeamishness in their demands for the ultimate penalty. Above them are appellate judges, some of whom take a position like that of Justice Blackmun of the present Supreme Court: "I yield to no one in the depth of my distaste, antipathy, and, indeed abhorrence for the death penalty, with all its aspects of physical distress and fear and of moral judgement exercised by finite minds. That distaste is buttressed by a belief that capital punishment serves no useful purpose that can be demonstrated. . . ."[16] But Justice Blackmun wrote one of the dissenting opinions in *Furman* v. *Georgia,* believing, as does Dr. van den Haag, that it is for the legislatures to act in such a matter, not for the federal courts. I suspect that there are many other appellate judges who feel much as does Justice Blackmun, and a good many who feel as did Justice Douglas and Justice Marshall, both of whom rose from poverty and disadvantage to their later eminence, and both of whom vigorously denounced the death penalty in *Furman.*

Neither my opponent nor I can know how the matter really stands. The only hard evidence is that a lot of trial judges are pronouncing a lot of death sentences, as shown in my Table III, above. What is unconscionably soft are the reasons that my ingenious opponent advances in support of his contention about judicial attitudes toward capital punishment.

First he says that judges can afford to treat murder leniently because they are well insulated from violence, whereas the poor are not. Without mentioning his source, he cites "polls" that show that college-educated people oppose the death penalty whereas the majority of voters do not. In an earlier portion of this response, I have cited polls that indicate that the affluent favored capital punishment somewhat more than the less comfortable classes. Rather consistently, blacks have either opposed the death penalty or have piled up the largest minority vote against it. There are relatively few blacks in the affluent classes. Blacks are the most frequent victims of violence. If there were any validity to my opponent's offhand hypothesis, blacks should be the group most vigorously in favor of the retention of capital punishment.

The second reason advanced for the supposed perversity of judges is the disadvantage of a college education, as seen by my well-educated and learned opponent. The fashion in intellectual circles in which judges are educated is said to be adherence to the notion that the criminal is a "sick victim of society." It is true that criminologists, sociologists, and psychologists try to account for the destructive behavior of violent offenders. In doing so, they cannot ignore the influences of deprivation, racial discrimination, relegation to an unemployed and unemployable underclass, the poor quality of education provided for the disadvantaged, and so on. Most of us would prefer to avoid the use of the term *sick,* but no one can claim that the conditions from which most criminals come are those of blooming social health.

It would be natural for a socially sensitive judge to take these matters into account, and it is fortunate that some judges do. Most do not—or if they have, their predilections have not come to my attention. In a complicated series of decisions in the early 1970s, a five-to-four majority opposing the death penalty was patched together in the Supreme Court. Perhaps three of the five had anchored their opinions in social science. The rest looked elsewhere for their rationales. Wherever their reasons came from, they were sincerely held, and I do not believe that their origins can be found in university classrooms, especially when the insulation of law schools from the rest of their universities is kept in mind. If Professor van den Haag has knowledge to the contrary, that knowledge should be stated in explicit terms rather than in the form of obviously unverifiable hypotheses.

The Intellectuals and Democracy

I will yield to the temptation to ascribe Mr. William Buckley's aversion for the Harvard faculty to the natural inclination of any loyal Yale man. Dr. van den Haag wants to make a much more important point, and presently I will deal with it. Unfortunately, on the way to his point, Dr. van den Haag refers to a notion that has long befuddled conservative circles: Intellectuals are "entranced"—or were until recently—by communism. That is intended to show the unreliability of intellectuals, especially when it is compared to the stout common sense of the "average man," who belongs to a union and reads the *Reader's Digest.*

I have always modestly aligned myself with the intellectuals, hoping to be taken for one. I have tried to practice the special distinguishing activity of the intellectual—thinking as rationally as I can about the society around me, its history, and its prospects. Neither I nor most of the intellectuals I have known have ever been "entranced" with communism as it has been applied in those countries that have tried it or as it has been formulated by its theoreticians. For me the Moscow trials of the mid-1930s were enough to immunize me from the entrancement of communism. Some of my friends kept an open mind until the Ribbentrop–Molotov treaties of 1939. It has been a long time since I have met a really entranced but genuine intellectual. American Marxists, particularly, are a vulgar breed, given to slogans and obfuscations rather than to rational thought. No one, especially judges and lawyers, is likely to be taken in by their absurdities.

What is especially ironic in my opponent's advocacy of capital punishment is its widespread and frequent use in the Communist countries and its universal abandonment in the other Western democratic nations. When I have challenged Communist acquaintances on the liberal use of capital punishment in the Soviet Union, in Maoist China, and in Castro's Cuba, I am loftily told that the anger of the masses requires this response to the crimes of their oppressors. The proof of this assertion is as hard to find as the proof of the effectiveness of the death penalty in deterring violent crime. In both cases I am assured that the need for the death penalty is self-evident common sense.

But the point that Dr. van den Haag wants to reach after his detour into anticommunism is the notion that there is a strategy of the intellectuals to rid the country of capital punishment by imposing their views on the inarticulate but much more sensible majority. By resort to the courts rather than to the polls, this strategy, it is supposed, will unfairly deprive the silent masses of the treasure of the death penalty.

The chain of reasoning that Dr. van den Haag has forged seems to run as follows: Intellectuals oppose the death penalty. They have been most successful in their opposition by constitutional litigation. Therefore, they have been imposing their views on the less alert and less resourceful majority. What intellectuals should do is to take to the hustings and let the people decide.

But the courts are open to the intellectual retentionists, of whom my opponent is only one of many. Their reasoning often prevails over that of the abolitionists, as witness the united opposition of the Nixon-appointed justices in *Furman* v. *Georgia.* As long as the courts are open to reason and as long as constitutional issues are adjudicated in the federal courts, there is no reason why the abolitionist should abstain from constitutional litigation. His victories in court should be regarded as the consequence of the better case at the time it was argued.

As to the unimpressive performance of the abolitionists in the state legislatures, we can only plead that intellectuals are not very good at emotional polemics, which usually win in legislative battles in which they are the principal weapons. It is a remarkable testimony to the diversity of American cultures that as many as fourteen states have abolished the death penalty, some for many years. However, it is evident that intellectuals have much to learn from English and French legislators, who have resoundingly responded to reason on this issue.

The Sabotage of Death

We now come to the crowning assertion to which Dr. van den Haag's tortuous argument has led. We are asked to believe that the infrequency with which the death penalty is imposed is the consequence of—indeed, the indirect evidence of—deliberate sabotage by misuse of the appellate procedures. The principal villain in this conspiracy is the American Civil Liberties Union (ACLU), but the various state and federal appellate courts cannot escape my opponent's blame.

It is contended that the extremity to which the ACLU has gone can be seen in its insistence on litigating the cases of men who have demanded that they should be executed, as in the celebrated case of Gary Gilmore, shot by a state firing squad in Utah at his insistence, in spite of the ACLU's last-ditch attempt to save him through appeals to the federal courts. "Butt out," Gilmore said to the ACLU, but the ACLU persisted anyway. Is this not unreasonable sabotage of the law?

Not at all. The ACLU position is clear and consistent. This principled opposition to the death penalty is not based on sentimental sympathy for a vicious and contemptible killer. The ACLU position is that killing people is wrong, even when the state does the killing. It must be prevented through every constitutional and legal means available. It is just as wrong for the state to kill Gary Gilmore—even though he wanted to be killed—as it was for Gilmore to kill his victims. The execution of a Gilmore is just as wrong as the execution of a man who prefers a life sentence.

Knowing that prejudice, caprice, and trial errors take place very frequently in capital cases, the ACLU searches the transcripts for such discrepancies and, when they are found, litigates them, sometimes successfully. In every such case, the state that is to proceed with an execution is represented in open court. I do not see how this process can be defined as sabotage. In the usual context in which sabotage occurs, it is a clandestine deed performed by taking advantage of an inattentive victim. That is hardly the case here. The decline in the number of executions that Dr. van den Haag deplores is open to much more credible explanations.

Looking at the most recent data available to me: In 1979, fifty-six persons were removed from condemned status. Of this number, twenty-six were commuted to reduced sentences, nearly all to life imprisonment. Four died during the year, including three who were executed. Seven were awaiting a new trial, their plea for a new trial having been granted. Twelve were awaiting resentencing, one was found not guilty when tried again, and six were relieved of the death penalty although their disposition had not been decided.[17]

If in these data there is evidence that there is a conspiracy to sabotage capital punishment, the largest blame must be assigned to the governors who exercise their prerogative of mercy by commuting death sentences to life terms.

One final point: Dr. van den Haag does not "know of any case where the appeal to the federal judiciary has been rejected without going all the way to the Supreme Court, which rarely declines a hearing." This is a misunderstanding of procedure. Many death penalty cases are sent to the Supreme Court with a plea for a stay, usually on a writ of *certiorari.* In the vast majority of these cases the plea is read by the circuit justice responsible for the judicial circuit in which the case originated and is denied *without* a hearing. That part of the process takes place with celerity. The years of litigation take place at much lower levels.

How to Reduce the Volume of Murder?

"The total result at the present time is that we have about 20,000 murders a year." The cause of which this is the "total result," presumably, is the infrequent use of the death penalty, which my suspicious opponent attributes to sabotage. We are to infer that this appalling volume of homicides would be reduced if the death penalty were more liberally applied.

The aggregation of murders and "nonnegligent homicides" compiled annually by the Federal Bureau of Investigation reached the figure of 21,509 known to the police in the calendar year 1980.[18] In every case, someone died as the result of a criminal action by someone else. Some of these killings could not conceivably be subject to the death penalty because of mitigating circumstances or diminished responsibility on account of age or insanity. Others were the most flagrant and callous murders. The FBI does not attempt to determine a distribution of its homicide data according to the various degrees of murder and manslaughter; no one can say what the distribution might be. I am not certain from Professor van den Haag's argument which murderers he would insist on executing for the purpose of deterrence and which ones might be spared for a lesser penalty. Let us suppose that he would allow no exceptions. All killers, irrespective of age or mental condition, must be killed.

Among those 21,509 homicides there were some multiple killings. Let us assume that there were really only 15,000 murderers who were responsible for this fearful total of homicide. According to the Uniform Crime Reports, the clearance rate for homicide was 72.3%. Thus, only 10,845 murderers would be convicted and sentenced. If there are 250 working days in a year, we would have 43.4 men, women, and children to kill every day. This is an execution rate that would far exceed the 75,000 hanged during the thirty-eight year reign of Henry VIII. The statistics of executions in those countries where it is most frequently used—Russia, Iran, the South African Republic—are not made known to international data collectors. I doubt that an execution rate as high as I have projected here could be sustained for long even in the USSR or the Islamic Republic of Iran.

Let us suppose that Dr. van den Haag will allow that only a quarter of the men and women committing murder and nonnegligent homicide would qualify for execution, and that no one would be executed who was under the age of eighteen. That might reduce the number of executions to ten per working day. Perhaps my opponent can tolerate this daily body-count, perhaps the country—which seems to be increasingly able to accustom itself to a violent routine—can inure itself to this rate of extermination. After all, if Dr. van den Haag's expectations are realized, this process will lead to a radical reduction in the number of murders committed.

After how many working days of bureaucratically administered death?

Notes

1. William O. Douglas, *The Court Years, 1937–75* (New York: Random House, 1980), p. 8.
2. Ibid., p. 9.
3. 1 Wm. and Mary (1689), 2d Sess., c. 2.
4. Sir Leon Radzinowicz, *A History of English Criminal Law and Its Administration from 1750* (London: Stevens and Sons, 1948), pp. 518–520.
5. Anthony F. Granucci, "'Nor Cruel and Unusual Punishments Inflicted:' The Original Meaning," *California Law Review* 57 (October 1969), pp. 839–865.
6. *Furman* v. *Georgia* (1971), 408 U.S. 238, at 257–306.
7. Joseph Story, *On the Constitution* (Boston: Hilliard and Gary, 1833), p. 710.

8. *Weems* v. *United States* (1909), 217 U.S. 349.
9. *Trop* v. *Dulles* (1957), 356 U.S. 86.
10. Sir James Fitzjames Stephen, *A History of the Criminal Law of England* vol. 3 (London: Macmillan, 1883), p. 383. From the last sentence of this excerpt I infer a retributivism of the most rigorous kind; the really depraved must be exterminated. After all, it was Stephen who minted the curious comparison "the criminal law stands to the passion of revenge in much the same relation as marriage to the sexual appetite." *A General View of the Criminal Law of England* (London: Macmillan, 1863), p. 99.
11. Michael J. Hindelang, Michael R. Gottfredson, and Timothy Flanagan, eds., *Sourcebook of Criminal Justice Statistics—1980,* U.S. Department of Justice, Bureau of Justice Statistics (Washington, D.C.: U.S. Government Printing Office, 1981), pp. 200–201.
12. Ibid., p. 202.
13. Ibid., p. 202. For convenience I have omitted the percentages in the original table that related to the crimes of rape, airplane hijacking, and treason, all of which were substantially lower than the percentages favoring capital punishment for murder.
14. *Hurtado* v. *California* (1883), 110 U.S. 516, at 529.
15. *Weems* v. *United States* (1909), 217 U.S. 349, at 373.
16. *Furman* v. *Georgia,* at 403.
17. Hugo Adam Bedau, *The Death Penalty in America,* 3rd ed. (New York and Oxford: Oxford University Press, 1982), p. 63.
18. United States Department of Justice, the Federal Bureau of Investigation, *Uniform Crime Reports, 1980* (Washington, D.C.: U.S. Government Printing Office, 1981), p. 182. All the data in this section are drawn from this table.

ERNEST VAN DEN HAAG

I agree with many of the skillfully argued points in Professor Conrad's comment, and I will confine myself to attempting to refute only those arguments with which I am not satisfied.

On Justice Douglas's quoting Chief Justice Hughes on the Supreme Court: "Ninety percent of any decision is emotional. The rational part of us supplies the reasons for supporting our predilections." This applies not just to the Supreme Court but to any decision anywhere. Reason does not motivate us. Emotional "predilections" do. However, reasonable people, when "the rational part" of them does not supply sufficient reasons to support their predilections, abandon them. Were it not so, there would be no point at all to having a Supreme Court, or indeed, in being rational. Reason tells us whether, when, and to what extent to follow our emotional predilections. Only a deranged persons follows "predilections" without regard to reasons pro and con. I don't believe that justices are altogether deranged.

As to the idea that the Eighth Amendment's prohibition of cruel and unusual punishment "must draw its meaning from the evolving standards of decency that mark the progress of a maturing society," it sounds fine. But I cannot see why judges, rather than legislators, should determine what these standards are or ought to be, and how they are evolving. Nor do I see how judges could. By popular vote? In that case, why not leave it to the legislatures in the first place?* By revelation? By consulting Professor Conrad or me? We don't agree. But why not rely on the Constitution, which clearly authorizes the death penalty when proportionate and imposed by due process? What is the use of having a Constitution if we follow "evolving standards," invented, decided upon, and imposed by judges, instead of following the constitutional amendments that we have committed ourselves to follow until and unless they are amended further?† Our Constitution does not outlaw the death penalty. But it does permit the death penalty to be outlawed by any legislature that wishes to outlaw it. Why, then, insist that judges make a decision that the Constitution clearly reserved for legislatures? Because legislatures don't decide what abolitionists want them to decide? Professor Conrad is fond of noting that the death penalty has been abolished in many foreign countries. To my knowledge it has been abolished by law, never by judicial reinterpretation of the Constitution.

Professor Conrad points out that, although according to the Roper poll 66% of the population supported the death penalty in 1978, according to the Harris poll in 1977 only 46% would support it if it were shown that the death penalty is "not more effective than long prison sentences" in deterring people from murder. This means that 20% of the population (66 − 46 = 20) support the death penalty because of its deterrent effect and the remaining 46% for retributionist reasons. If people support the death penalty because of its deterrent effect and are asked whether they would support it if there were no deterrent effect, what answer is one to expect? The 20% who support capital punishment for its deterrent effect quite logically would not support it if it were proven that the death penalty has no more deterrent effect than a very long prison sentence. So what? There is no such proof. If there were, a massive plurality of the population (46%) would remain in favor of the death penalty, obviously for retributionist reasons. Of course, the 20%

---

*The popular vote, according to all polls, favors the death penalty, which is why the legislatures do.

†About "branding and ear-cropping," Professor Conrad is somewhat unfair (it happens occasionally to the best of us). I am opposed to these penalties whether or not the Constitution does permit them. Not everything the Constitution permits is right, nor does it outlaw everything wrong. I am opposed to these penalties not because they are unconstitutional but because they are revolting. Thus, if they were applied, I should favor outlawing them even if constitutionally permissible.

would have opposed imprisonment, or any punishment, if it were shown not to have deterrent effects. But it does. So does the death penalty. The 20% are not abolitionists. They are people who believe in punishment for deterrent rather than retributionist reasons.

Professor Conrad also presents a table to indicate that high-income groups do not favor the death penalty less than low-income groups do, as he alleges I believe. However, the Conrad table shows nothing of the kind. It does show that the lowest income groups—up to an income of $5000—do favor the death penalty least. However, the rich ($20,000 plus) do favor the death penalty by less (65%) than the most numerous group of the nonrich (earning $7000–10,000): 71% do.* Anyway, I think it is education that matters: The college-educated favor the death penalty less than those who were not indoctrinated. Which says more about colleges than about the death penalty. That the Labour party in England opposed capital punishment, as Professor Conrad correctly points out, is neither here nor there. The majority of the English people favor it. The majority of Parliament outlawed it. Traditionally the English Parliament has not felt bound by the views of the voters on "questions of conscience." Parliament in England largely consists of college-educated people. Many, despite their education, are members of the Labour party.

Professor Conrad quotes the cases of *Hurtado* and *Weems,* implying that they contradict my view of constitutional interpretations by the Supreme Court. They do not, and Professor Conrad has not attempted to show otherwise. Wisely, for there is nothing in the quoted passages inconsistent with my views, which are shared by the present Supreme Court. It has ruled the death penalty constitutional if due process is observed. Professor Conrad also accuses me of not understanding the difference between repealing a law—something voters or legislatures can do—and overturning it—something courts can do if the law is unconstitutional. I don't understand why I am so accused. I plead not guilty. The burden of proof is on the accuser. Finally, Professor Conrad writes that to follow the Constitution as I advocate is "to embalm the Constitution in a mausoleum." But I do not think it is dead—the very fact that it prevents Professor Conrad from abolishing capital punishment by judicial decree shows that it is quite alive. It would be dead—useless, ripe for a mausoleum—only if it were interpreted according to the judges' views of "evolving standards," for then it would lose all meaning and we could do without it.

---

*Professor Conrad does not indicate the size of the groups.

Professor Conrad is materially wrong (and should know better) when he writes that I am "one of many intellectual retentionists." There are few. In the academic world, including the major law schools, in social science and humanities departments, the overwhelming majority wish to abolish the death penalty. I wish I were "one of many." Moreover, abolitionists are supported by powerful and well-funded organizations such as the ACLU. Retentionists have no support other than truth and logic.

Now to the Gilmore case. Professor Conrad writes, "It is just as wrong for the state to kill Gary Gilmore—even though he wanted to be killed—as it was for Gilmore to kill his victims." Really? The victims did not want to be killed. They were murdered by Gary Gilmore—which may be why he wanted to be executed. The victims were innocent. Gilmore was guilty of murder. Is it really just as wrong to execute Gilmore as it was for him to kill his victims? It is an odd morality that asserts that it is as wrong to kill a killer who wants to be killed as it is for the killer to kill an innocent who wants to live. I don't share that morality. I hope Professor Conrad doesn't in his less polemic moments.

The Gilmore case brings to mind an argument lately used by abolitionists, namely, that execution is invited by some murderers because they wish to commit suicide by means of being executed. I want to consider this argument once more. It does not seem a serious argument. Few murderers invite executions. Most do everything in their power to avoid capture, and if captured, to avoid conviction, and if convicted, to avoid the death penalty. Those who are willing to be executed do not commit suicide. They are willing to be executed. It is hard to ascertain actual motives in each case. Some may prefer death to life imprisonment. The great majority obviously does not, but neither choice seems irrational. Others may feel that they deserve execution. They may be right. In Professor Conrad's words, they may wish to "reconcile" themselves to society and to its moral norms by accepting the punishment they deserve.

Finally, it is argued that some murderers commit their crime for the sake of the punishment they expect and that, in this way, the punishment becomes an incentive to the crime. Such cases, if they exist at all (and the evidence is quite tenuous), are altogether exceptional, so much so that it would be silly to tailor the law to fit them. Incidentally, since this reasoning may apply to imprisonment as much as to the death penalty (more, since it is hard to imprison oneself and comparatively easy to kill oneself), how could the law fit these exceptional cases? By abolishing all punishments so as not to give an incentive to crimes?

JOHN P. CONRAD

Professor van den Haag's adroit rejoinder gives me a lot of work to do. Some of the points he has made reflect disagreements on issues where I have nothing further to say. The reader must decide who has the better case. Those whose predilections coincide with my opponent's views will hardly be shaken by the reasoning I have advanced in support of my positions. I must hope that readers whose views are consistent with mine will find no fatal flaws in my supporting arguments.

On other points I must return my opponent's fire. With consummate skill he has introduced some new issues in responding to my rebuttal. There are some misunderstandings—surely not deliberate—that amount to more than quibbles over semantics. I hope that the reader's patience will not be unduly tried as I attempt to straighten out the abolitionist argument, perhaps laboring the obvious all too obviously.

"The Progress of a Maturing Society." Professor van den Haag does not see how judges can be expected to determine the evolving standards of a maturing society. Along with the entire federal and state judiciaries, the Supreme Court must undertake this task in our system of government. It is not an enviable responsibility. Stand-pat conservatives will complain of activism that moves in directions of which they disapprove, whereas liberals will deplore the court's decisions as representing the dead hand of the past. As to matters of freedom of religion, freedom of speech, the nature of due process, the scope of interstate commerce, to mention only a few of the most difficult constitutional issues, the courts must scan the changes that have taken place in the social and economic structure of the nation and interpret the Constitution accordingly.

As an example of the evolution of our standards, consider the system of sanctions that prevailed in eighteenth century America. For several major felonies, hanging seemed proper to our ancestors, and for minor crimes, branding and ear-cropping were allowed. The times have changed. The Supreme Court has ruled out the death penalty for rape, although for over a century it had been inflicted on rapists in many states.[1] It is now considered that the penalty of death is disproportionate to rape and therefore inconsistent with the Eighth Amendment. Under the "evolving standards of decency" principle, capital punishment for rape has evolved into the scope of cruel and unusual punishment. Evolution of standards is a process of which the courts have taken notice and on which they have acted. Does this process apply to the death penalty for *any* crime? If so, on what basis can the Supreme Court intervene to overturn all capital punishment statutes?

As I indicated in my rebuttal, the most obvious indication of this evolution took place within a quarter-century of the ratification of the Eighth Amendment. The practice of incarceration as punishment for felonies seems to many now to be an abhorrent exercise of the state's power over the individual. I do not share this view, although I concede that American prisons fall far short of attainable standards of order and decency. When sentences to prison replaced the physical punishments common in the eighteenth century, a major reform took place, and it was a reform in the interest of humane exercise of the state's power. Although jails and involuntary servitude had existed for centuries before the innovation of the penitentiary, they had not been part of our system of control of criminals. Jails were for the detention of persons awaiting trial or pending payment of indebtedness. They were not available for punishment, as Sir James Fitzjames Stephen explained in the passage I quoted in my rebuttal. Involuntary servitude under excruciatingly callous circumstances was frequently used in some continental countries, and transportation to remote colonies was an option open to English courts. Neither of these sanctions was used in the American colonies or in the years immediately preceding the adoption of the Constitution.

The framers could not have had in mind the possibility of large penal establishments when the Eighth Amendment was proposed. Agreeing with my opponent for once, I must doubt that they would have excluded the death penalty if they had foreseen the evolution of the prison from its beginnings in Philadelphia to its present ubiquitous use throughout the country. Contemporary Americans have learned to accept the principle that a sentence to prison is an appropriate sanction for even the gravest crimes. That includes murder in the first degree. Its inclusion in the list of crimes that may be punishable by imprisonment in itself demonstrates the evolving standards of a maturing nation. Where we have learned to accept life imprisonment as the usual punishment for murder, it cannot be denied that changes in our standards have occurred. Professor van den Haag may deplore this change, and so may many others. The point is that it has happened.

How can the intervention of the federal courts be justified? It is clear to me—and to the courts as well—that the responsibility for interpreting the Eighth Amendment is a judicial function, just as the courts must interpret the interstate commerce clause of the Constitution in the light of changing business patterns. There are many arguments that can be presented to the courts in support of the abolition of capital punishment. Some of them deserve little respect; others are, in my lay opinion, compelling. If the majority of the justices are convinced by any argument, the court must act. It is a unique system, and one that has served the country well.

As to the underlying principle of the Eighth Amendment, its history clearly indicated that its terms have applied to different forms of punishment throughout the years during which that clause has been used. Throughout those years, the purpose has been to set limits on the power of the state to punish. In eighteenth century America, capital punishment was the only possible disposition for the gravest felonies. In twentieth century America, it is an option that has to be justified by tortuously involuted reasoning. To my mind, that state of affairs alone would justify the abolition of the death penalty.

We go to the Supreme Court with an Eighth Amendment argument because under this unusual system of government we may. Such a course would be unavailable in any other country that I know of. Dr. van den Haag correctly points out that in the countries where the death penalty has been abolished, it has always been through a legislative action. That is an irrelevant point in this country. The Supreme Court has a constitutional responsibility to check the other branches in their actions to assure that those actions are in compliance with a reasoned interpretation of the Constitution. It is the nation's protector against the tyranny of the majority. Long ago Alexis de Tocqueville, defining this role stated: "the power vested in American courts of justice of pronouncing a statute to be unconstitutional forms one of the most powerful barriers that have been devised against the tyranny of political assemblies."[2]

That tyranny is of peculiar significance with respect to capital punishment. We live in an age when the numbers of crimes committed increases nearly every year. To many citizens, the incidence and prevalence of violent crime is the most serious issue facing a troubled nation. No one really has a program for the abatement of urban violence. But activist legislators, unwilling to concede impotence, and eager to display toughness, can and do urge the increased application of the death penalty as a solution to the problem. Their stentorian pleas for the return of the executioner distract the public and the legislatures from a serious consideration of the difficult and often unattractive measures that might be taken with better prospects of success. Their fulminations also create a hysterical climate in which it is impossible to argue reasonably about the death penalty. No state legislator, no congressman dares to be seen as "soft on crime" or deficient in the easy but spurious common sense that says that killers ought to be killed.

In principle, I will join my opponent in a preference for legislative solutions to the capital punishment problem. Some day, I believe, it will be possible to legislate the death penalty out of existence. In the present climate of opinion, with politicians encouraging the public to demand a resumption of electrocution, gassing, and hanging, it is not reasonable to expect that reason will prevail on the floors of our legislatures. From the time of Thucydides in ancient Athens, legislative assemblies have been easily swayed by passionate arguments that persuade sensible men and women to discard reason in making their judgments. The courts are supposed to immunize themselves against passion—though not always with success—and to insist on tightly rational arguments as the basis for their decisions. Abolitionists firmly believe that reason is on their side. It is no wonder that we choose to go to the courts.

An Apologetic Note about Ear-Cropping. In a footnote, Professor van den Haag complains that I was unfair in my reference to branding and ear-cropping as acceptable penalties under his interpretation of the Eighth Amendment. I certainly did not wish to imply that these punishments are acceptable to him. I only said that under his interpretation of the Eighth Amendment it would be impossible for the Supreme Court to outlaw them. Aside from that not particularly important point, I note with great curiosity that my adversary would oppose the application of these sanctions because they are "revolting." Indeed they are. The question that leaps into my mind is this: If the death penalty is not also revolting, why not?

Public Support of the Death Penalty. Let us take note of a conceptual problem that will be discussed at greater length elsewhere in my contributions to this discourse. Professor van den Haag observes that there is no proof that the death penalty is not more deterrent than a prison sentence. But where should the burden of proof lie? I have yet to see any proof that the death penalty is *more* deterrent than a life sentence, and Professor van den Haag has not attempted to present any empirical proof of this theorem.

With all the centuries of experience that we have had with capital punishment, the best that its advocates can do to justify its retention is to make assertions that it must be an effective deterrent because it is the most severe sanction possible. If 20% of the population would not support the death penalty if it were shown to be no more deterrent than imprisonment, I interpret their vote for the death penalty as based on reliance on assertions like those of my opponent, which constitute an act of faith. Even though we cannot prove that the death penalty is a significantly more effective deterrent, we should believe it is anyway. That may be stout common sense to my adversary. It looks like blind faith to me.

What Are the Statistics Saying? Table I in my rebuttal is not in any way mine; it belongs to the Gallup Poll. I introduced it into evidence because Dr. van den Haag would have us believe that judges oppose the death penalty because they live protected lives in the suburbs among the rich and comfortable, whereas the poor and threatened have no way of escaping predators in the ghettos and barrios, and therefore desire the retention of capital punishment.

Whatever this table may mean—and, as I said earlier, I am not sure what it means—the middle classes are more in favor of a return of the executioner than the less affluent. So the first reason for ascribing opposition to the death penalty to insulation against the perils of the inner city collapses.

Dr. van den Haag falls back on the evils of a college education to account for the reluctance of judges to execute offenders. He thinks that the college-educated favor the death penalty less than "those who were not indoctrinated." No data in support of this proposition, but, for the sake of argument, let us assume that somehow exposure to higher learning inclines young men and women to oppose capital punishment. How are we to account for such a result? Dr. van den Haag suspects that malleable young men and women are convinced by intellectually chic professors that the death penalty is wrong because murderers are the victims of a sick society and cannot be rehabilitated after they are dead.

How all that is imparted to the impressionable young is hard to make out. It sounds like a plunge into wishful thinking. Because college-educated people don't think the way Dr. van den Haag thinks they should, he concludes that their views say "more about colleges than about the death penalty." I have never made the kind of enquiry for which Dr. Gallup is renowned, and I cannot say for sure why educated men and women tend to dislike capital punishment. It makes at least as much sense to ascribe their distaste for executioners to a wider knowledge of history, to more settled habits of reflection, and to broader information than is available to their less-educated fellow citizens. If that inference is to be defined as evidence of elitism, I will accept it. I prefer to believe that education is not a crippling process that disables its victims from thinking for themselves.

Hurtado and Weems. If the quotation from *Hurtado* v. *California* is read with care, it will be seen that the Supreme Court in an *obiter dictum* said that it is wrong to render the law incapable of progress or improvement; unchangeableness is not a virtue of American jurisprudence, however pleasing it was to the Medes and Persians. *Weems* went much further in establishing the Eighth Amendment as applying to the states as well as to the federal government, and therefore entitling the federal courts to intervene in matters of cruel and unusual punishment. The court's recognition that "time works changes, brings into existence new conditions and purposes" is consistent with my argument that the Supreme Court cannot be bound by the conditions and purposes that prevailed in the time of the framers. I hope that in the not too remote future, the Supreme Court will consider the death penalty in the light of this principle.

How Many "Intellectual Retentionists?" My rueful opponent charges me with knowing better than to claim that he is one of "many intellectual retentionists." That depends on the definition of an "intellectual." I know plenty of academic retentionists, I know of many retentionist judges and lawyers, most of whom have credentials entitling them to be considered "intellectual." Nevertheless, I will concede that few—if any—have been so articulate, so zealous in this cause as my tireless opponent.

But having given credit where credit is due, I must enter a disclaimer of any support from the American Civil Liberties Union for my role as an abolitionist. Although I have been a member of the ACLU for many years, I have never been given any reason to suppose that it is either "powerful" or "well funded."

Gary Gilmore. Dr. van den Haag must be an ethical relativist, unlikely though it may seem to his readers. He holds that to kill a guilty murderer is less wrong than to kill an innocent victim. I hold that it is wrong to kill anyone, even Gary Gilmore—a ruthless and irresponsible killer—in cold blood, and I will make no distinction as to who is killed. That makes me an ethical absolutist, I suppose. If Dr. van den Haag cannot share that morality, I must contemplate the intricacies of his relativism with deep concern.

Suicide by Execution? In a sort of postscript, Dr. van den Haag deals with an argument that I have heard from some abolitionists to the effect that some murderers kill because they hope to commit suicide in the electric chair or the gas chamber. I will say that this argument does not impress me, either. Although I have known condemned men who wanted to be executed, the motive for the murders they committed certainly was not a desire for suicide.

Nor have I met any condemned men who committed their crimes in a quest for punishment. Until more evidence is furnished by those who advance this hypothesis, I see no need to abolish punishment so as to remove the incentive to crime.

It is pleasant to conclude this surrebuttal on a note of complete agreement with my opponent.

Notes

1. *Coker* v. *Georgia* (1977), 433 U.S. 485.
2. Alexis de Tocqueville, *Democracy in America,* vol. 1, trans. Henry Reeve, Francis Bowen, and Phillips Bradley (New York: Knopf, 1945), p. 103.

ERNEST VAN DEN HAAG

I resist temptation to comment on most of the points raised once more by Professor Conrad, confining myself to two.

Noting that I find "ear-cropping" revolting, Professor Conrad asks, "If the death penalty is not also revolting, why not?" The answer is simple. We all must die. But we must not have our ears cropped. Ear-cropping is a human invention, and it strikes me as a revolting one. Death is not a human invention, and I find nothing revolting about it. Nor do I find it revolting to "hasten death," in the words of John Stuart Mill. On the contrary, I would find it revolting if we were to allow a person to live among us who has forfeited his right to life by killing an innocent other.

One other comment: Professor Conrad calls me an "ethical relativist" because I hold that "to kill a guilty murderer is less wrong than to kill an innocent victim." I hold it not only to be less wrong but to be right and a moral duty. In this I agree with the philosopher Immanuel Kant. He is not usually called a relativist; nor am I. (I wish we had more in common.)

There is a difference between guilt and innocence that, despite my efforts, Professor Conrad resists appreciating. That difference is relevant to any punishment. I would hold it wrong to imprison an innocent, but right to punish a guilty person by imprisonment. If paying heed to the difference between innocence and guilt makes me a relativist, I am. But I must say that this is a rather peculiar use of the term. Usually *relativist* is a term applied to those who blur the distinction between guilt and innocence, as Professor Conrad attempts to do, not to those who stress it, as I do. When the crime is grave enough, I believe that for those guilty of it the death penalty is justified. I believe so precisely because I think that nobody has the right to kill an innocent person, i.e., to murder. This rule can be enforced only, in my view, by making it clear that the murderer himself will forfeit his life.

JOHN P. CONRAD

No less than the procedures for ear-cropping, the gallows, the electric chair, the gas chamber, and the rifles raised by a firing squad are all human inventions. They all succeed in "consigning a man to the short pang of a rapid death," as John Stuart Mill elegantly summed up the hideous event of an execution.* In his day and until the abolition of the death penalty in 1965, English murderers were hanged. I have never witnessed this procedure, but the unvarnished accounts I have heard and read leave little doubt

---

*My opponent's citation of John Stuart Mill's advocacy of capital punishment calls for a discussion of that great man's views on this topic. They will be found in a speech delivered in Parliament in 1868 in which the abolition of capital punishment was debated; the abolitionist lost. The full exchange is found in Gertrude Ezorsky's *Philosophical Perspectives on Punishment* (Albany: State University of New York Press, 1972), pp. 271–278.

Old-fashioned liberals like myself venerate the name and example of Mill as a paragon of reasoned enlightenment on the conduct of human affairs. Those who are unfamiliar with this particular contribution to parlimentary discourse may be surprised that this farsighted man should have adopted a position that is rejected by nearly all contemporary liberals.

It must be said that Mill was eloquent but hardly at his usually persuasive level of argumentation. His case for the death penalty relied on two points. First, he held that execution was less cruel than the alternative, lifelong incarceration. "What comparison can there really be, in point of severity, between consigning a man to the short pang of a rapid death, and immuring him for life in a living tomb, there to linger out what may be a long life in the hardest and most monotonous toil . . . ?" This reasoning is scarcely consistent with the usual insistence that the great benefit of the death penalty is the deterrent value of the horror attendant on that "short pang." The reference to the "living tomb" exaggerated the conditions of English prisons, even at that time, and certainly for our own time.

Mill's second point was expressed in these words, strangely coming from the mouth of one of the earliest and most ardent advocates of women's rights: "what else than effeminancy *(sic)* is it to be more shocked by taking a man's life than by depriving him of all that makes life desirable or valuable? Is death then the greatest of all earthly ills?" It should have been obviously inappropriate to assign a sexual orientation to the values attendant on taking a life; virility and effeminacy have nothing to do with the awful decision.

Surely Mill was not at his best in this debate—even though his side won decisively.

that it is a revolting spectacle. The alternatives—the electric chair, the gas chamber, and the firing squad—are only marginally less repulsive. Concerned about the seemliness of the death penalty, legislators in Texas, Oklahoma, and Idaho have innovated; they have enacted statutes specifying injections of lethal poisions as the method of execution. The objections of the medical profession to this procedure raise questions as to its practicality that have not yet been resolved in an execution.*

Killing people in cold blood should be seen as intolerably revolting, whether done on a side street during a robbery or in the antiseptic conditions that can be arranged for anesthesiological extinction of life. There is no method of execution that is not an unnatural human invention, no matter what pains we take to euphemize the deed. We refer to the criminal as submitting to the "supreme penalty," or "paying his debt to society," but in plain words, we have killed him deliberately and aforethought. We are grateful to him if he takes this bitter medicine "like a man" and commend him for his "stoicism."† In the act of killing, itself, and in all the words used to justify it, to explain it, and to describe it, the state expects to teach those who need such a lesson that killing people is wrong. There are more effective ways of conveying this simple element of morality that do not require the state to administer horror.

My half-serious suggestion that my unflinching opponent is an ethical relativist was based on his conviction that killing some people is less wrong than killing others. I hold, of course, that killing anyone is wrong, no matter what kind of person he may be. Any other position is surrounded by a moral quagmire. Death penalty advocates must concede that not all murderers are

---

*For a full but sanitized account of the various methods of execution now considered acceptable, see the *Report of the Royal Commission on Capital Punishment, 1949–1953* (London: Her Majesty's Stationery Office, Reprinted 1973, Cmd. 8932), pp. 246–273. After a detailed review of experience in England and other countries, the Royal Commission concluded that hanging is the speediest and most humane method of killing murderers. The three other prevailing alternatives—electrocution, gas, and shooting—were rejected for reasons that seem convincing. Lethal injections were considered. Although the painless aspect of the process held some appeal, the medical objections were considered insuperable.

For a skeptical commentary on the commission's account of hanging, see Arthur Koestler, *Reflections on Hanging* (London: Victor Gollancz, 1956), pp. 9–10, 139–145.

†The Royal Commission took special note of the good behavior of condemned men in England, who spared onlookers the experience of "distressing and unseemly scenes of panic and resistance. Those of our witnesses who have the duty of attending executions gave striking and unanimous testimony to the stoicism with which condemned men—and women— almost always face death on the scaffold." Ibid., pp. 260–261.

equally deserving of the ultimate penalty. They must choose who goes to the gallows or the chair, and agreement will seldom be unanimous. Fine and tenuous distinctions must be made between those who are to be executed and those who may be spared, to be justified by the argument that one is more contemptible, more dangerous, or more outrageous than the other—a sort of relativism that confounds values and leads to uncertainties about the rightness and wrongness of behavior. A culture that is already too much inclined to an ethical relativism that understands all and therefore condones all should not be encouraged to make these morbid distinctions or to attempt to learn from them.

Even if Professor van den Haag could have his way and capital punishment could be resumed in the exceptional administration that was characteristic in this country for the two or three decades preceding the *de facto* moratorium, it would never be made "clear that the murderer himself would forfeit his life." The distinctions in culpability may be based on honest differences of opinion, on the quality of the prosecution and the defense, on the vagaries of a jury, or on public hysteria. The occasional execution that will take place (I say "occasional" because, although there may soon be many as a result of the exhaustion of appellate procedures, the number of executions will be small compared to the number of homicides) will make nothing clear.

And if there is any quality that the muddled administration of criminal justice in America requires more than any other, it is clarity—the certainty that evenhanded justice will be done.

ERNEST VAN DEN HAAG

Once more I shall correct only a few mistaken arguments.

1. Professor Conrad writes, "There is no method of execution that is not an unnatural human invention." What is a natural human invention? Is it natural to do anything that is not instinctive, e.g., to read books? to wear pants? If only that which is prevented by nature is unnatural, no need to worry. We can't do anything unnatural anyway. However, if all that nature permits is natural, "unnatural" merely indicates Professor Conrad's disapproval. Well, nature has permitted executions since biblical times, indeed since the beginning of that "unnatural human invention" (?) the law, and long before that other human invention (natural? unnatural?) prison. Exe-

cutions are, if not more natural, surely more traditional than abolition of the death penalty is.*

Because Professor Conrad is so worried about the dignity of executions, let me insert here a description of the execution of Marin Falier in 1355. Falier, who had been elected doge of Venice, was thereafter convicted of a conspiracy to make himself hereditary prince and dictator of that republic.

> Falier did not attempt to deny the charges. He made a full confession, pleaded guilty and proclaimed himself both deserving of and fully prepared for the supreme penalty. Sentence was passed on 17 April; the next morning, at the hour of tierce, the old man was brought from his private apartments to the Council Chamber and thence to the top of the marble staircase that descended from the first-floor loggia into the inner corner of the Palace. The insignia of office were stripped from him, his ducal *corno* being replaced by a plain round cap. In a brief speech, he asked the Republic's pardon for his treachery and confirmed the justice of his sentence. Then he laid his head upon the block. It was severed with a single stroke.†

Crimes are, if not "unnatural human inventions," unjust and lacking in dignity. Executions need be neither.

2. "Not all murderers are equally deserving of the ultimate penalty," Professor Conrad writes. He's right. So? The courts determine which murderers are *sufficiently* deserving of the death penalty. It is not required, or possible, that they be equally deserving.

3. However, according to Conrad, to separate the "more contemptible, more dangerous, or more outrageous" who deserve the death penalty from those who do not is a "fine and tenuous distinction" and "relativism" a sort of selectivity that "confounds values and leads to uncertainties about the rightness and wrongness of behavior."

The opposite is true. To determine that one criminal is more deserving of any punishment, including the death penalty, than another certainly is not "relativism." On the contrary, "relativism" consists of denying the possibility of such distinctions, of saying that they are "relative", i.e., uncertain, "fine and tenuous," and subjective, that ultimately none of us is much worse than any other and none deserving of death. I think some criminals are. Wherefore I am not a "relativist."

---

*Which is neither here nor there. A legal sense of "natural" (as in natural rights) is possible, but here too Professor Conrad is out of luck. Practically all traditional legal theorists, including the framers of our Constitution, thought of the death penalty as consistent with natural rights and laws.

†Taken from John Julius Norwich, *A History of Venice* (New York: Alfred A. Knopf, 1982), pp. 227–228.

I am not sure whether Professor Conrad believes that, as Mme de Staël said, *"tout comprendre c'est tout pardonner,"* when he paraphrases that to understand all is therefore to condone all. At any rate I don't. The more I understand some people—Nazis, Communists, criminals (even some others)—the less I condone what they have done or are doing.*

4. Professor Conrad faults John Stuart Mill for not agreeing with him. It does not follow that Mill is wrong. Anyway, Conrad's point rests on a confusion. Conrad suggests that Mill's view, that death is less cruel or severe a punishment than life imprisonment, is "scarcely consistent" with the "usual insistence" that the death penalty is more deterrent than life imprisonment. There is no inconsistency. Death may indeed be less cruel or painful than life imprisonment, as Mill thought, yet more deterrent, because more feared. People often fear the lesser pain or deprivation more than the greater one. (But I am not as sure as Mill was that death is the lesser punishment.)

5. The fear of death—and I have already pointed out that it is not necessarily rational (see Introduction: Death but not Torture pp. 13–16)— is strong in all of us. Even a criminal who cannot expect anything better than life imprisonment when caught *in flagrante delicto* will surrender when he sees the policeman's gun pointed at him. He prefers anything to death. From which one may conclude that the threat of death will deter him more than any other threat can.

JOHN P. CONRAD

I had thought that my previous comments on this chapter would be terminal, but I reckoned without the murk spread by Professor van den Haag in his rejoinder. I shall try to clear it up by responding to his comments in the order in which he has made them.

1. As to "unnatural" human inventions and a doge's dignity, my opponent contended that ear-cropping is not an acceptable form of punishment because it is a "revolting"—or, as I put it, an "unnatural"—human invention. I argued that the gas chamber, the gallows, the firing squad, and the lethal needle—the methods of execution now commonly in use—are also "unnatural" or "revolting." They have supplanted some even more hideous methods that both my opponent and I have discussed in earlier chapters.

*The idea that all conflict is   ·understanding so that understanding always
                                        ·se. Some conflict is produced by misun-

But capital punishment was unnatural in biblical times, it was unnatural in ancient Athens and Rome, and it is unnatural now. To kill another human being is an unnatural act, prohibited in the sacred books of most religions and justified by feats of ethical and theological casuistry throughout the ages. That tradition sanctions capital punishment does not clean up a bloody and demeaning practice.

On the gallows, stoical murderers earn the gratitude of the witnesses by sparing them the distress that resistance would cause. The condemned man can retain shreds of human dignity on the scaffold; the state cannot. Consider the execution of Marin Falier, so glowingly cited by my polymathic opponent. Here was a septuagenarian public servant, a man who had served the Venetian state long and well. He had been a victorious admiral, a successful diplomat, and a respected magistrate. An irascible old man, nearing eighty, with his judgment apparently impaired, he allowed himself to conspire against the Venetian constitution. The facts are by no means clear, but even if we suppose that the secret Council of Ten that condemned him had been correct in their verdict, the beheading of this old man was a dreadful act, one that besmirched Venetian justice. The account of the execution quoted by Dr. van den Haag reflects honor on the doge, but none on the Venetian state.

In a footnote, my perseverant opponent again alludes to the "traditional legal theorists" who thought of the death penalty as "consistent with natural rights and laws." For Dr. van den Haag, time and thought stood still in the distant past. I respond to the twentieth century and to the prospects ahead. We have a lot of hard thinking to do. We may respectfully consider the principles laid down by our ancestors, but we must not be bound to the ways in which they put those principles into practice. Ear-cropping was indeed an awful way to punish thieves, and I respect Dr. van den Haag's rejection of this ugly practice. The deliberate killing of a criminal is also a revolting act, and I wish my opponent would concede that even though he considers it necessary, it is also hideous, no matter how it is done.

2. On the comparative deserts of murderers, I objected to the distinction that judges and juries must make between murders that call for the execution of the defendant and murders that do not. All killings are wrong if willfully done, and the distinctions that are made between willful killings introduce artificial and morbid considerations that blur morality. It is especially objectionable that the decision of the court may be, and often is, influenced by public hysteria or may be determined by the relative effectiveness of the lawyers trying the case. There is indeed an artificial relativism that

seeps into trials for murder when the defendant's life is at stake. Much of that fine and tenuous distinction-making would vanish if we limited punishment to a life term in prison for all those who commit willful murder.

3. If Dr. van den Haag can infer from my language that I believe that "to understand all is to condone all," he is capable of inferring anything from anyone's statements, no matter how unambiguously they are stated. I have expressed my aversion for ethical relativism in this last response, and I think it is both explicit and implicit in everything else I have written in this debate. To make distinctions between levels of contemptibility of the various kinds of murder is no way to lead people away from this kind of relativism. I maintain that there must be an absolute prohibition of willful killing, to be enforced by punishment consisting of a life term under the state's control, most of it in prison.*

4. My sensitive opponent has discovered a distinction between cruelty and horror that to his way of thinking supports John Stuart Mill's position on capital punishment. He has a point and he is welcome to it. If horror is really more deterrent than cruelty, it was not apparent to Mill. His view of the death penalty was expedient and utilitarian. He saw no reason for subjecting murderers to lifelong imprisonment when they could be hanged.

I will agree with Professor van den Haag that death is not a lesser punishment than life imprisonment, but I doubt that my concession will mollify him.

5. We all prefer not to be killed. Does that prove that the threat of death will deter more than life imprisonment? We all prefer not to be locked into a prison cage, and the prospect of spending the rest of one's life so confined troubles anyone who has seen men and women living behind bars. To me the most pathetic prisoners are those who have found a kind of contentment in the daily routines of their cellblocks.

Professor van den Haag's methods of proof are curious indeed. It seems to him that the fact that criminals caught in the act will usually surrender to a police officer armed with a pistol shows that the threat of death is greater than the threat of life imprisonment. So what else is a criminal to do? If he shoots it out with the police, as so many do, he will almost certainly

---

*Actually, Mme de Staël wrote, *"Tout comprendre rend très indulgent,"* or, "To understand everything makes one very indulgent." Nobody seems to know who improved that sentence to read, *"Tout comprendre, c'est tout pardonner."* But I hope Dr. van den Haag recognizes that there is a large difference between pardoning a man who has done wrong and condoning the wrong he had done.

lose—and most of them do. The criminal who surrenders instinctively knows that he has less to lose. The fear of death plays a part in his decision, but its connection with the relative deterrence of the electric chair and the life term is not probative.

ERNEST VAN DEN HAAG

I must repeat that, Conrad not withstanding, "the sacred books of most religions," far from prohibiting the death penalty, encourage it. The Bible repeatedly prescribes it. The "sacred books" prohibit only killing an innocent human being—not punishing, by death, a person for doing so. The difference between innocence and guilt is not important, or not important enough, for Professor Conrad to justify this punishment. To me it is as important as the difference between life and death.

About Marin Falier: Oddly, Conrad writes that "even if we suppose that the secret Council of Ten that condemned him had been correct in their verdict, . . ." The council, the Venetian executive, was not secret, although its proceedings were not public, as was usual in the 14th century and as is usual for the executive to this day. In the Falier case the responsibility appeared too heavy and the council was joined by twenty additional noblemen, as constitutionally provided in such cases. Others joined *ex officio*. Falier was not tortured or threatened with torture. He fully confessed. Anyway, the structure of the conspiracy made his participation evident. Nonetheless, Conrad mistrusts the Venetian judgment—perhaps because he was not present? Or because the provisions of the U.S. Constitution were not applied? (But America had not been discovered. Its Constitution was some hundreds of years in the future.) Or because Conrad mistrusts any judgment that imposes penalties of which he disapproves? Not a word, incidentally, about the extraordinary evenhandedness of Venetian justice. Marin Falier came from one of the oldest noble families in Venice; he had been a member of the "secret" Council of Ten. Yet his fellow noblemen, who had elected him doge only a short while before, unhesitatingly condemned him to death when they found him guilty of treason. And he recovered his dignity by recognizing the justice of his sentence. He was the only doge ever so sentenced.*

---

*Incidentally, Venetian justice was tolerant and humane by contemporary standards. Unlike all other European countries, Venice did not burn a single heretic.

Conrad insists that "the beheading of this old man ... besmirched Venetian justice." I can't see why. Because the man was old? (If not, why mention it?) Would Conrad have approved more if Falier had been young? Professor Conrad does not for a moment consider that any but capital punishment for a doge's treason would have encouraged future doges to betray their trust. As it was, none did. The Venetian Republic, an oligarchy, existed for nearly a thousand years when all around it despotism prevailed. I hope the American Republic will endure that long.

JOHN P. CONRAD

Let me argue these matters a little further.

1. I said that the sacred books of the world religions prohibit killing. It is quite true that in the Old Testament all sorts of bloodthirsty punishments are prescribed, none of which we would accept today as applicable to our criminals, except, of course, the death penalty for murderers. I say now that killing even murderers is wrong, whatever the authors of Leviticus and Deuteronomy may have thought necessary for their times. It is noteworthy that Moslem jurists interpret the Koran as literally as possible so as to avoid infliction of the death penalty wherever they can. Only fundamentalists like the Iranian ayatollahs and the Saudi monarchs choose to adopt a loose interpretation of Mohammed's teaching. Likewise, I am told, the Talmud is full of ways to evade the prescriptions of the Old Testament—long antedating the "liberal" thought that considers the infliction of death an arrogation by the state of a right that belongs only to God.

2. My reading of the Marin Falier episode leads me to believe that the Council of Ten killed an irascible and confused old man, disregarding both his repentance and his great services in former years. I wonder as I read my antiquarian opponent's discussion of this event whether he would like to see our own public officials so treated for high crimes and misdemeanors.

I think Dr. van den Haag believed that the beheading of Marin Falier was an example of how an execution can be carried out with dignity. The historical account that I read relates that there was a crowd outside the palace where the Venetian citizens had gathered. They were not permitted to watch the execution, but when it had been accomplished, the executioner went to the balcony and brandished his sword, dripping with blood, as a token of the justice that had been done. Many allowances can be made under the tolerant maxim *autres temps, autres moeurs,* but I cannot allow this example of Venetian justice the ascription of dignity. I am sure that the American Republic can outlast the Venetian oligarchy without so much blood flowing from the headless corpses of its criminals.

ERNEST VAN DEN HAAG

Professor Conrad asks whether I would like "to see our own public officials" treated as Marin Falier was, if they commit the kind of crimes he committed. The answer is yes.*

---

*Marin Falier's is the only such crime committed in the history of Venice. The only thing remotely similar in our history is the Aaron Burr episode.

Appendix to Chapter 7

ERNEST VAN DEN HAAG

Let me add a note on the number of murders committed in the United States. As indicated, the officially reported number of murders approaches 20,000 per year. However, the actual number of murders is likely to exceed this number by far. Numerous "missing persons" are not recorded as murdered because their bodies were not found or identified, or the cause of death has not been correctly or finally determined. Yet there is no doubt that a high proportion of these "missing persons" were murdered. Other murder victims may not even have been reported as missing at all.*

It must be noted also that far fewer assaults result in murder than in the past, owing to the progress of medicine, which reduced the homicide rate. It is misleading to credit this development to the criminal justice system or to the would-be assassins. That surgeons can save higher proportions of victims, or that wounds get infected less often, is not due to fewer murderers plying their trade.

One must conclude that actual and attempted murders in the United States have increased far more than is shown by the records we can compile. Both death sentences and executions as a proportion of homicides have decreased far more than commonly thought. Even if we were to execute 100 murderers a month (we now execute between zero and five a year), we would be executing in all probability less than 5% of all those who commit murder in any year and are convicted.

JOHN P. CONRAD

According to the Uniform Crime Reports for 1981, there were 22,516 murders and nonnegligent manslaughters committed in the United States

---

*This is the case of vagrants, or often of runaways, who are murdered.

during that year. (That was a decline of 2.3% from 1980; I am not so eager for debating points as to make anything out of that arithmetic during a year in which almost nobody was executed.) Professor van den Haag is sure that there must have been far more murders committed and even more intended but averted by medical and surgical interventions. I am not sure what he would like to do about all these additional killings and averted killings, or how he supposes that the death penalty would have had some effect in reducing their incidence. His implied prescription of 100 executions a month will certainly keep the newspapers full of accounts of life in the death cell, as well as keeping the executioners fully employed. It may be that the American public will be tough enough to stomach all this killing, month after bloody month, but I hope not.

CHAPTER 8

Discrimination and Justice

ERNEST VAN DEN HAAG

Consider now the phrase used in the Eighth Amendment itself. It prohibits cruel *and* unusual punishment, not cruel *or* unusual punishment. Therefore, a punishment must be cruel *and* unusual to be unconstitutional. The framers meant to outlaw unusual punishment, if cruel. But not cruel punishment, if usual. A punishment has to be new (unusual) as well as cruel to be unconstitutional. The death penalty hardly qualifies on that score. For whether cruel or not, the death penalty is not "unusual" in this Eighth Amendment sense.* (There is another sense, of which anon.)

Now, in what sense could the death penalty be cruel? There are two possible legal meanings of *cruel*. First, *cruel* here may mean disproportionate, either to the seriousness of the crime or to other penalties. The death penalty for pickpockets or car thieves may strike us as cruel in this sense. But the death penalty for murder hardly does.

The courts have declared the death penalty for most crimes other than murder, such as rape, to be unconstitutional because cruel.† Whether a crime is serious enough to require so serious a punishment the courts should have left to the legislatures to decide. But although disagreeing with the court's argument, I agree with its conclusion for a reason the court omitted. If we were to threaten the rapist with the death penalty—however much regarded as well deserved or as an effective deterrent from rape—we would

---

*Obviously the Constitution does not mean that judges can first make the death penalty unusual by preventing its imposition and then declare that it has become unusual and now is unconstitutional.

†*Coker v. Georgia* (1977).

unavoidably invite him to kill his victim. By so doing, he would remove a witness without risking additional punishment: If caught he would be put to death anyway. This is a sufficient reason for threatening the death penalty only for murder. (Of some exceptions anon.)

A second sense of *cruel* involves the infliction of gratuitous pain, pain not intended or likely to achieve a rational end that may justify it. Thus, killing an animal for food is not regarded as cruel, but torturing the animal for fun is. Giving a painful medicine is not, but inflicting pain without a justifiable purpose, such as health, is regarded as cruel. Now, punishments are meant to be unpleasant, and the death penalty is certainly the most unpleasant of punishments. But it has rational purposes: to signify that murder is the worst, and therefore the most severely punished, crime; to indicate that murder is different from other crimes punished by prison; to show that there is a discontinuity signified by a different, discontinuous punishment; and, not least, to deter others from committing murder. These purposes seem rational; at least some are, and only one rational purpose is required. The attempt to achieve these purposes by means of the death penalty seems rational too. Our system of criminal punishment metes out more severe punishment the more serious the crime. Death for murder seems quite rational in this light.

It may be objected that we do not know for certain whether the penalty does deter more than other penalties such as life imprisonment would. But this is true for all punishments. We do not know for certain that fifteen years in prison deter more than ten. Yet it seems common sense to presume that the more severe punishment is more deterrent. People certainly are restrained for violating the law more by a $1000 fine than by a $10 fine, more by the threat of 2 years in prison than by the threat of 2 months in prison. Perhaps a point of diminishing, or even zero, returns is reached somewhere. But no one has convincingly shown that that point is reached before the death penalty. Unless this is shown, the death penalty cannot be called irrational from a deterrent viewpoint. From a retributionist viewpoint—Mr. Conrad's viewpoint—even such a showing would be irrelevant. The death penalty would remain morally justified, and not cruel, as long as it is considered to be justly deserved by the crime committed.

At any rate, the Constitution has not been held to require a demonstration of the effectiveness of punishments, without which punishments are regarded as unconstitutional. *Cruel* has meant at most disproportionate, or irrational on the face of it. It never has meant "not of demonstrated effectiveness." (We are not even agreed altogether about what punishments are supposed to effectively achieve.) The Constitution requires evidence beyond a reasonable doubt produced by a "due process of law" to convict anyone of crime. But the Constitution requires no particular evidence to make a law. The lawgivers can—and often do—make laws as foolish as they wish. The laws are valid if they are clear and do not violate specific provisions of the Constitution. It requires neither that laws be effective nor that they be sensible. It leaves that to lawgivers and to the voters.

Let us turn now to the meaning of *unusual* in the "cruel and unusual" phrase of the Eighth Amendment. One meaning, "new," equivalent to "unaccustomed," has already been discussed. Another meaning may be "rare," or infrequent. Both meanings have in common what I think is the principal constitutional bearing of the word, to wit, improperly or irrelevantly discriminatory. For if a punishment is rare, unaccustomed, if it is infrequent, it is applied only to some offenders, who are thus discriminated against, and not to the great majority of others, who may be favored if the "unusual" punishment is more severe than the usual ones.

The "unusual" punishment may discriminate against those to whom it is applied in an entirely capricious or in a systematically biased manner. In both cases, a violation of the Fourteenth Amendment, which guarantees the equal protection of the laws to all, would be involved. The basic meaning of *unusual* thus becomes "unequal"; the infrequency or the unusualness of a punishment becomes constitutionally relevant precisely because it implies discrimination against those who suffer the unusual punishment. It singles out some persons, or groups of persons, who, having committed a crime, are more severely punished by the "unusual" punishment than are others who have committed the same crime. Surely, at least in the past, this happened to blacks who committed crimes against whites.

Owing to the sentencing discretion judges have in our present system, punishments for the same crime often differ, depending on how the judge thinks. Capriciousness is unavoidable if discretion is granted to sentencing judges. And although it could be reduced by reducing sentencing discretion, capriciousness could not be wholly avoided in any system in which the judgment of policemen, of prosecutors, of juries, and of judges must play some role in the arrest, the charging, the indictment, the prosecution, the conviction, and the sentencing of offenders. While unavoidable up to a point, capriciousness is certainly a more serious matter when the death penalty is involved than it is otherwise. Professor Charles Black* has made this the main charge against the death penalty.

---

*See Charles C. Black, Jr., *Capital Punishment* (New York: W. W. Norton and Co., Inc. 1974).

Yet there is no evidence that the death penalty is more capriciously applied than it was when the founding fathers sanctioned it in the Fifth and Fourteenth Amendments. On the contrary, there is every reason to believe that the death penalty is less capriciously applied now than it ever was. Certainly there are more appeals and reconsiderations for each case. In the application of any law some capriciousness is unavoidable. If this were to make laws unconstitutional, we would have to do without laws, indeed, without the Constitution, for it too is unavoidably applied capriciously. God alone is uncapricious in this sense. The founding fathers were aware of the accidents that influence all human actions, including legal ones. But they did not believe that this required us to leave decisions about murderers to God. The Bible certainly supported their view.

Even if one were to grant that they prevail, it does not seem to me that discrimination and capriciousness argue for abolition of the death penalty. Neither is inherent in the death penalty; neither depends on it in any way. Both are characteristics not of the penalty but of its distribution to offenders, or groups of offenders.

Imagine that, instead of the death penalty, we were to distribute, say, work loads, or candy. We could do so in a capricious fashion: One person gets most of the candy, the others little; or one person most of the work, while the others amuse themselves—when neither person, in any sense, has deserved receiving most of the candy or of the work. We could also discriminate more systematically. Whites get all the candy; blacks get all the work. Exactly the same could be done with sentences for equally guilty offenders—we may sentence all the blacks to prison, all whites to death, or vice versa.* Surely this is wrong. But would the remedy be the abolition of candy, or of work, or of prisons? There is nothing in that which is being distributed—candy, work, or the death penalty—that makes maldistribution necessary, or that fosters it in any way. Discrimination is caused by the way the distribution is made and by those who do the distributing, not by what is being distributed. And that is where it must be corrected. So, if the death penalty is imposed in a discriminatory fashion—and it certainly has been so imposed in the past—we must make sure that it is not maldistributed in the future. That is what has been done.

It is true that most of those currently under sentence of death are poor and a disproportionate number are black. But most murderers (indeed, most

---

*There has been a suspicion that prison sentences are meted out more frequently to blacks or that they are more severe. But several articles in the *American Sociological Review* have shown that the suspicions of bias are unfounded.

criminals) are poor and a disproportionate number are black. (So too are a disproportionate number of murder victims.) One must expect therefore that most of our prison population, including those on death row, are poor and a disproportionate number black.*

The temptation to violate the law is lower for those who are well situated in life. A well-to-do merchant or teacher or dentist is not very tempted to rob a store and, in the process, to kill the store owner. A very poor man may be. But only a minority of the poor are criminals. Poverty does not compel crime; it only makes it more tempting. The temptation can and must be resisted. The law is meant to restrain those tempted. It would be redundant to restrain those who are not. Thus, the fact that most convicts come from poor groups and that many are black does not show discrimination. It shows that the poor and black are more tempted to commit crimes, and that a greater proportion of them do.

JOHN P. CONRAD

My opponent continues his attempt to show that capital punishment cannot be cruel or unusual in the "Eighth Amendment sense." We are still debating questions of constitutional law, as we did in the last chapter. Dr. van den Haag argues that there is nothing in the Constitution that bars capital punishment. His position is that the Constitution must be strictly interpreted in the terms of the framers' world; if we discover new limits for permissible legislation, we must amend the Constitution or resort to other legislative remedies.

In my response to Dr. van den Haag in Chapter 7, I drew on Supreme Court decisions that have established for many years the principle that the Constitution stands in continuous need of interpretation in the light of social and economic change. In effect, the Constitution is a body of principles intended to guide the government in its executive, legislative, and judicial actions. Just as such phrases as "due process of law," "freedom of the press," and "interstate commerce" have changed in meaning and emphasis, so we must assume that the prohibition of "cruel and unusual punishment" is a principle for national guidance. It is not a dead prohibition of archaic punishments that no modern legislature would consider inflicting.

---

*A disproportionate number of leading baseball players and boxers also are black. But I do not believe that this shows an antiwhite discrimination. A disproportionate number of prison inmates are male. But I do not think this shows discrimination against males.

If we are to apply the prohibition of cruel and unusual punishment in the context of the customs and values of the late twentieth century, we have to consider what that phrase means to us, rather than what it meant to Patrick Henry, the Virginia firebrand who insisted on its explicit inclusion in the Bill of Rights. Our standards of decency have evolved, as Chief Justice Warren implied in *Trop* v. *Dulles*,[1] and our society has matured, though perhaps not to the extent that some of us would like. There are prohibitions that the Eighth Amendment can provide that would never have occurred to the framers. So long as we accept the guidance that cruel and unusual punishment is prohibited, why should we not rely on the Supreme Court for an interpretation of that phrase, rather than on the encumbrance of the Constitution with further amendments?

Neither the courts nor their critics have been diffident about the application of the Eighth Amendment to outrageous prison conditions. The inhuman treatment of dissidents in Eastern Europe would be banned by the First Amendment, but even if it were not, the Eighth Amendment would proscribe the conditions described in Solzhenitsyn's *The Gulag Archipelago*. At home, the federal courts have held that conditions such as those found in the prisons of Alabama,[2] Rhode Island,[3] Colorado,[4] and Texas[5] are cruel within the meaning of the Eighth Amendment as it has evolved with the momentum of changing standards of decency. Various political primitives protest that overcrowding, vermin, and filth are exactly what jailbirds deserve, but the general view prevails that there is a limit of nastiness that a civilized nation cannot overstep. It is perfectly possible to run a clean and decent prison within acceptable standards of austerity. The courts properly insist that the states must maintain such standards if they are to maintain prisons at all.

Implicit in this position is the construction of the Eighth Amendment to include incarcerative punishment, even though the framers had no experience with prisons as we have used them since the early nineteenth century. They were thinking only of fines and excessive bail and the various forms of physical punishment that prevailed in the eighteenth century. Can we apply the Eighth Amendment to capital punishment as well as to prisons? If not, why not? And if so, how is "cruel and unusual punishment" to be construed so that it does apply? In the next sections of this response I shall tackle these questions.

If Not, Why Not?

Although Dr. van den Haag is a strict constructionist as to the Constitution he seems to insist that capital punishment has rational purposes that never dawned in the world of eighteenth century philosophers. These rational purposes consist of the following aims:

1. *To indicate that murder is the worst crime and therefore to be punished most severely.* Certainly murder is the worst crime (although I am not sure that all eighteenth century legal writers would agree), and I hope never to see the day when it is regarded as less than the worst. But we can signify the primacy of murder by long-term incarceration, perhaps life without possibility of parole.

2. *To indicate that murder is different from other crimes.* So it is. Everybody knows that, and the death penalty will not change the character of that knowledge, especially when it is borne in mind that not all murderers can be executed. Nobody has yet thought of a set of rules that define those murders and those murders only that will be punished by death.

3. *To show that there is a discontinuity signified by a different, discontinuous punishment.* It is not clear how Dr. van den Haag conceives of a continuity among the other crimes that becomes discontinuous with murder. Where is the continuity between an almost lethal assault and, say, the theft of a $50,000 diamond necklace? That in both cases the victim survives the crime hardly seems to establish these two offenses on the same scales for measurement. At best it is a tenuous distinction to maintain that there is a discontinuity between the case of the almost lethal assault in which murder was intended but the victim survived and the case of an assault where murder was not intended but the victim succumbed. If there is a rationale for discontinuous punishment of discontinuous crimes, it is much too subtle for my understanding.

4. *To deter others from committing murder.* It must be clear to my readers that I do not take much stock in this argument. I have dealt with it elsewhere in this debate and will not repeat myself here.

If the Eighth Amendment Should Rule Out Capital Punishment, How Is This Construction Reached?

To begin with, capital punishment is an anachronism, left over from a day when the choices of punishments for serious crimes were limited to various physical sanctions, most of them ugly abuses of the body of the offender. Americans have abandoned all the physical punishments except the death penalty; the invention of the prison made the whip and the branding iron unnecessary and obsolete. Capital punishment was the culmination of a scale that began with the stocks and the pillory, continued with flogging, and proceeded to dragging the criminal through town behind a horse. All these punishments could be scaled proportionately to the seriousness of crimes, and there was a continuity between them and the death penalty. Hours in the pillory could be counted, and so could the number of strokes with a cat-o'-nine-tails, leading up to extremities of pain to be administered. If the maximum number of strokes by the whip seemed to be insufficient for the punishment of the crime committed, the penalty of death had a certain logic. But as the years have gone on, the prison has been accepted as a decent alternative to the archaic floggings, brandings, and mutilations that our ancestors tolerated because they could not think of less repulsive ways to denounce crime and deter potential offenders.

The survival of capital punishment has been accompanied by measures to reduce the cruelty of its imposition and the morbidity of the spectacles that once accompanied its infliction. In most states we have decided that in hanging there is too much risk of a protracted death agony; electrocution or the gas chamber have been seen as less cruel. Even these methods of killing trouble some officials, and recently several states have enacted legislation calling for lethal injections; criminals are to be "put to sleep" in a kind of anesthesia that assures that no one will be pained, either in the process of dying or by the sight of the death.

I do not think that cruelty is so easily to be eradicated. The solicitude that is aroused concerning the pains of death is more for the benefit of the executioners and the witnesses than for the relief of the criminal to be executed. Not much agony is experienced on the gallows or the electric chair, however gruesome the spectacle of such executions may be. The truth is that most people do not like the idea of physical punishment, however easy it is for us to speak in the metaphor of the criminal "paying his debt to society by suffering the supreme penalty."

The real agony is in the long wait for execution by whatever method the state may choose. It is a death like no other in that respect, preceded as it is by an extended period of solitary confinement during which the criminal can make such desperate efforts as he can to gain a reversal of the conviction, a new trial, a commutation from the governor, or a stay of execution. At the end, there is death at a time determined not by fate but by a bureaucrat, and by means that cannot be resisted. It is little wonder that some men in this predicament wish to get it over with as quickly as possible.

At least we have matured beyond the willingness to make an execution a public spectacle, as it once was both in this country and in England. Retentionists are always uneasy when it is suggested that deterrence might be enhanced by public executions, now that such an event might be made accessible to the millions by television. There are strong arguments against such a procedure. At such affairs, in the days when they were frequent events, many of the spectators were inspired to undesirable sympathy for the criminal meeting his fate, while others found in the occasion some spur to boisterous and inappropriate levity. It is hard to decide which response to public executions was the more morbid, but retentionists generally concede that order is best served by killing the criminal in private.

The trouble is that capital punishment is perceived as cruel. Some criminals excite sympathy because of the misery of their lives and the tragic inevitability that can be read into their destiny. Others, like Gary Gilmore, evoke a reluctant admiration for a spurious manliness as they accept their fate. Because we regard the few criminals who are executed with morbid fascination, they become antiheroes, bathed in sentimentality. If they were to be committed to long terms of incarceration, their survival as lifers would assure an appropriate oblivion. When they are executed they have a moment of evil glory, whether they want it or not.

The cruelty of the death penalty is none the less real for being subtle and long. It cannot fail to be unusual; as I argued in Chapter 5, we cannot possibly execute all the murderers, nor can we find a rule whereby the execution of a few can be anything but discriminatory symbolism. For if there are 15,000 murderers to be killed every year but we cannot kill more than 150, or even 1500, we announce to the world that the law does indeed discriminate, using a random decision-making process uncharacteristic of any other judicial process.

Caprice and the Death Penalty

It is impossible to squeeze discretion out of the criminal justice system. Latitude must be allowed for the circumstances that mitigate or aggravate the charge against the defendant and for the degree of personal responsibility that he must bear. Attempts to limit discretion at one point will merely assure that it will be transferred to another point.

Caprice is the misuse of discretion. What is intolerable in the exercise of discretion is favoritism to one defendant irrespective of his guilt or, conversely, undue harshness because of misinformation or prejudice. Up to this point, I assume that Dr. van den Haag will agree with me.

Where we will part company is on my insistence that in death penalty cases there is a special source of caprice that cannot be dealt out of this lethal game. Most criminal cases are now handled by a process of plea-bargaining in which justice is meted out in accordance with the pressures of the docket and the estimates by counsel for both sides as to the prospect for conviction or acquittal in the event of a trial. Not so in murder cases. The trial is much more likely to take place than with ordinary crimes. Even if it does not, the availability of a death sentence results in great pressures on the defendant to accept a lesser charge and a lesser sentence.

Irrespective of whether the case is settled in the district attorney's office or goes to trial, the disadvantage of the defendant is enormous. At the disposal of the prosecutor are the resources of the police and his own office of investigation. Unavoidably, the press has had access to most of the information to be presented in court and sometimes to a good deal more that cannot be presented but that can be widely disseminated, whether true or not. The defendant must ordinarily rely on the public defender or assigned counsel. If more information must be gathered, if additional witnesses are to be identified and traced, it is unlikely that resources can be found to do for the defendant what can so easily be done for the prosecutor. If there is to be a negotiation of the charge, the defendant is at a hopeless disadvantage. If the case is to go to trial, the disadvantage will be even more overwhelming. Even in the exceptional cases where the defendant has the wherewithal to engage a private attorney with courtroom skills, it will be even more exceptional that investigative personnel will be available to match those working for the prosecutor.

The elimination of the death penalty will not eliminate caprice, but with the theatrical elements out of the way, there will no longer be the pressures on the defendant to take the best bargain he can get, regardless of desert. Perfect fairness is an unattainable goal, but that excuses no one from trying to approach it as closely as possible.

Blacks and the Death Penalty

We can agree that blacks commit a disproportionate share of the violent crimes in America, and that they will therefore be overrepresented in prisons and on condemned rows. There is no way out of that state of affairs so long as racial discrimination prevails in our society in such a way that blacks are also overrepresented in the impoverished classes.

In principle, I can even agree with my opponent that if we are to persist with the death penalty, there is no unfairness in the overrepresentation of blacks among the criminals to be executed. But abstract justice, however statistically evenhanded, is not the same as perceived justice. The large numbers of blacks to be executed will be perceived by blacks as the consequence of inherent unfairness in the administration of criminal justice. That perception runs against the support for criminal justice that should be universal. It is difficult to believe that any gain that Professor van den Haag claims for capital punishment can offset the hostile sense of unfairness that its infliction creates among blacks. That sense of unfairness is evident in every opinion poll that attempts to elicit black opinion about capital punishment. The steadfast opposition to the death penalty that has for so long been the established policy of the National Association for the Advancement of Colored People expresses the view of this tragically offended minority that capital punishment is unfairly administered against black defendants.

Professor van den Haag is certain that what unfairness there may be can be forced out of the system. I cannot agree; there will always be enough discretion in criminal justice to make room for injustice. Even where abstract justice has been done to my opponent's satisfaction, injustice will still be perceived by those who share the condemned black's disadvantaged condition. The memory of lynch law is still fresh. The connections between social injustice and criminal injustice are too vivid to suppress under comfortable reassurances about the perfect distribution of penalties by judges so wise and so upright as to be incapable of caprice.

Notes

1. *Trop* v. *Dulles* (1957), 356 U.S. 86.
2. *Pugh* v. *Locke,* 406 F. Supp. 318; see also *Newman* v. *Alabama* (1976), 559 F. Supp. 2d. *Certiorari* denied, 98 U.S. 3057.
3. *Parigiano* v. *Garrihy* (1976), 443 F. Supp. 956.
4. *Ramos* v. *Lamn* (1979), 485 F. Supp. 122. Affirmed in part and remanded in part, 10th Circuit Court of Appeals (1980), 639 F. Supp. 2d. *Certiorari* denied, 101 U.S. 1259.
5. *Ruiz* v. *Estelle* (1981), 503 F. Supp. 1265. Execution stayed, 5th Circuit Court of Appeals, 650 F. Supp. 2d, 555.

ERNEST VAN DEN HAAG

Professor Conrad continues a rather disingenuous fusion, or confusion, between applying the Eighth Amendment prohibition of "cruel and unusual punishment" to new and changing conditions—a legitimate task of the Supreme Court, just as is the application of all constitutional provisions to new conditions—and changing the meaning of the Eighth Amendment so that it appears to prohibit what it never was meant to prohibit. The death penalty is not a new condition, and the Eighth Amendment was not meant to prohibit it. The death penalty is not imposed for new crimes or crimes occurring in new conditions. The only thing that is new, even according to Professor Conrad, is that we (read Professor Conrad and his friends) like the death penalty less than did the framers of the Constitution, or more pompously phrased, that "evolving standards" (his) reject the death penalty.

I don't read the Constitution to mean that the courts can declare invalid any law they don't like passed by a state or by Congress, even if clearly authorized by the Constitution, simply by declaring that it does not conform to "evolving standards of decency" that they, the courts, alone invent and define, even if these standards have not been accepted by legislatures or by the people who are supposed to have evolved them.

Professor Conrad's analogy to prison conditions does not make much sense. He points out that the courts have held prison conditions in some states to be "cruel and unusual" and thus have applied the Eighth Amendment according to "evolving standards of decency." Now, let me grant (although I have some reservations) that the courts acted constitutionally in their intervention into prison administration. There is no parallel to the death penalty. The courts did not abolish prisons. They merely required imprisonment to accord with established constitutional standards. The courts would be right in maintaining that withholding, say, penicillin from a prisoner in need of it is unconstitutional today. Sure, it would not have been so in 1791. Penicillin had not been invented. But the standards of medical care, not of constitutional interpretation, have changed. Prisoners are entitled to be treated according to current medical standards just as they always have been. Standards of nutrition, sanitation, and education too have changed. The court must apply the Eighth Amendment in the new conditions that have been created by these changes. Vermin that might have been tolerable in 1791 are not now, since we have the benefit of inventions that it would be cruel to withhold from prisoners. Prisoners are also entitled to current sanitary standards.

But what has this to do with the death penalty? In what way has death become more "cruel and unusual" since 1791? Have we succeeded in banishing it for the rest of the population? What changes have occurred to make the punishment less acceptable than it was in 1791? As far as I can see, all that has changed is the moral attitude of abolitionists. They are entitled to persuade us to the new standards that have been revealed to them. (Not all that new, incidentally.) But they have to persuade their fellow citizens to change their moral attitude so as to vote against the death penalty. The attempt to put over the change they want by reinterpretation of the

Constitution is both undemocratic and inconsistent with the spirit and letter of the Constitution.

Professor Conrad is right in pointing out that we punish very different crimes—theft, say, and assault—with the same kind of punishment: imprisonment. We have, after all, only three punishments left: fines, imprisonment, and death. But that is no reason for reducing the choice further. The fact that the differences among crimes often cannot be reflected in different kinds of punishments surely does not argue that different kinds of punishment never should reflect the different kinds of crimes. Murder is so different from other crimes, and so much worse, that it deserves a wholly different punishment. Capital crimes deserve capital punishment because they are by far more horrible than any other crimes.

Professor Conrad argues that our ancestors inflicted physical pain on criminals only "because they could not think of less repulsive ways to denounce crime and deter potential offenders," whereas "the invention of prison made the whip and the branding iron . . . obsolete." In short, we are smart and decent, and our ancestors were neither. I don't believe that our ancestors used physical pain "because they could not think of less repulsive ways" of punishment. Rather, they were not as repulsed by physical pain as we are. The change has to do not with our greater smartness or moral superiority but with a new outlook pioneered by the French and American revolutions, and by such mundane things as the invention of anesthetics, which make pain much less of an everyday experience. People in the past lived in rough and uncomfortable conditions that would repel us today. And they used rough and painful punishments.*

Prison, particularly forced labor, has been well known since antiquity. Only our alleged reformatory purpose is new. Our increased productivity—through the Industrial Revolution—made it possible for all of us to live on a far higher scale and to live longer, healthier, less laborious, and less painful lives. Why any of this should persuade us to abolish the death penalty beats me. Actually the abolition—not by constitutional interpretation but by new laws reflecting the generally accepted changed standards of punishment—of punitive physical pain makes the threat of the death penalty for murder more necessary than it was before. We do not need, and, I believe, we could avoid, physical pain in executions. Pain would not make the death penalty more deterrent than it is—death is the ultimate fear of most people. Where-

---

*On the subject of physical pain see my *Punishing Criminals* (New York: Basic Books, (1975), chap. 17.

fore I favor avoiding physical pain. But why should we allow a person to live who deliberately did not allow another to live?

Professor Conrad objects that we can execute only a few of all the criminals who deserve execution. He uses somewhat spurious* figures: "if there are 15,000 murderers to be killed every year but we cannot kill more than 150 or even 1500, we announce to the world that the law does indeed discriminate, using a random decision-making process. . . ." But the law does not use random decision making. Courts, after deciding on guilt according to the law of evidence, decide on sentences according to rather specific criteria stated in the law of homicide. And according to these criteria, only some of all murders are punishable by the death penalty.

In all legal proceedings, factors other than justice play an unavoidable role. No one is executed unless first apprehended—and whether he is depends often on chance factors. No one is executed unless convicted. Whether he is may depend on chance factors too—e.g., the presence of witnesses, or their background (if they too are felons, they may not be believed), the finding or not finding of the victim's body, and, not least, the evaluation of the evidence by the jury. (Different juries may in all conscience come to different judgments.) *Mutatis mutandis*—this is true for all crimes, not just capital crimes. Indeed, of all crimes, only a few lead to actual punishment or imprisonment, let alone the death penalty. Human justice is human and thus subject to all the chance factors human affairs are subject to. This seems no reason to give up our court system or the punishment of criminals, including the death penalty; we may catch only some and punish only some, not all, but to do so is better than to punish none. We may unintentionally discriminate between the guilty people we catch, convict, or punish and those who for one reason or other escape punishment. We must do our best and punish as many as we can. If we waited for perfect justice we would produce only near-perfect injustice. We would have to abolish the criminal justice system and hand over society to its criminal elements. I don't think Professor Conrad really means what he seems to imply.

I do not agree with Professor Conrad's apparent view that in murder

---

*Apropos "spurious": Why does Conrad say that Gary Gilmore accepted his fate with "spurious manliness"? Why defame the dead criminal who had so little to be proud of? What should Gilmore have done to make his manliness not "spurious"? Agree with Professor Conrad? Resist his execution? Break down crying? Show appropriate symptoms of despair? Professor Conrad's phrase seems insensitively insulting and unwarranted. Gilmore was a criminal but he went to this death bravely, even though he made the mistake of approving of his execution when Professor Conrad did not.

cases plea-bargaining is more often avoided in favor of trial than in others. But if it were so, I would not find it objectionable. In general, I find trials preferable to plea-bargains. When there are irreconcilable disagreements between the prosecution and the defense, no bargain can be struck, and the case goes to trial. If there is much publicity, counsel for the defense may like a trial anyway: There is a benefit to him—fame—although not necessarily to his client. Even so, trials decide less than 10% of all cases in most states. When charge-bargaining takes place, the charges are usually reduced to avoid trial. Else the defendant would have no interest in pleading guilty. The defendant is always offered a lesser punishment than he may get if convicted in a trial. The punishment he may avoid through a bargain may be anything—death, life imprisonment, or ten years in prison. The nature of the pressure to make a bargain is the same. Thus, Professor Conrad's objection to plea-bargaining does not apply to capital cases any more than to others. If a bargain is struck, capital punishment is not imposed. But I should not object to trial for all capital cases. Plea-bargaining is often deplored, but whether our system could and should do without it is a controversial question.*

Professor Conrad also feels that in capital cases "the defendant is at a hopeless disadvantage." I don't think so at all. If Professor Conrad were right, more of the 20,000 annual murders would lead to execution or at least to the imposition of the death penalty. The prosecution cannot appeal because of the double jeopardy clause of the Constitution, which prohibits retrial of anyone found not guilty. The defense can, and does indefinitely. I know of no capital case in which, after exhausting all levels of state courts, the defense does not appeal to the federal judiciary, alleging constitutional issues. Evidence such as confessions of the defendant who was not warned that he could have a lawyer, or evidence produced however indirectly by a search without a warrant or with a warrant made out incorrectly, is not submitted to the jury's judgment. It is simply not admitted in court. The prosecution cannot use it—even if it shows the defendant guilty beyond a reasonable doubt. But let that go. What matters is not the advantages or disadvantages of the defense but whether the verdicts are correct and just. Professor Conrad has not argued that the "hopeless disadvantages" of the defendant lead to unwarranted guilty verdicts. If they do not, these disadvantages do not matter.

---

*There is much to be said about plea-bargaining pro and con. But in a different book: It is no more (and no less) relevant to capital crimes and the death penalty than it is to burglary and imprisonment.

JOHN P. CONRAD

Responding to my rebuttal of this chapter, Professor van den Haag has spread a thick coat of misinterpretation and irrelevance, which I must remove. I shall be as brief as I can.

1. The reader may be led to infer that the term *evolving standards of decency* is my coinage. It is not. It belongs to Chief Justice Warren, but the idea goes back to Justice McKenna, who wrote in *Weems* v. *United States* (1909), "The Eighth Amendment is progressive and does not prohibit only the cruel and unusual punishments known in 1689 and 1787, but may acquire wider meaning as public opinion becomes enlightened by human justice."[1]

I am sure that my stern opponent will respond that public opinion has not yet become so enlightened in this country as to reject capital punishment with all its supposed benefits. He would be correct. One of my objectives in this debate is to contribute to the enlightenment that Justice McKenna foresaw.

2. Professor van den Haag observes (with some private reservations that he does not reveal) that the courts are justified in intervening in prison administration under the authority of the Eighth Amendment because standards of medical care, nutrition, sanitation, and education have changed since 1787.

So have standards of penology. As I stressed throughout my first response to this chapter, punishment in eighteenth century America was essentially physical. It allowed for the pillory, the ducking stool, the whip, and, sometimes, the cropping of ears and the slitting of nostrils. The culmination of this variety of punishments was the gallows.

Incarceration became a standard punishment in the nineteenth century. The first American prison was the Walnut Street Jail in Philadelphia, which accepted its first prisoner in 1790. Its example was not generally followed until well into the nineteenth century. Since that time the physical punishments, except for the gallows, have gradually disappeared. They are no longer allowed, even for the discipline of prisoners, and capital punishment has been discarded—with no apparent ill effects—in fourteen states. In those states in which it is still authorized by law, it has certainly become an unusual punishment. The pleas of my opponent to make it more usual do not spring from necessity. I contend that it is an arguable position that capital punishment is cruel and unusual, and that Justice McKenna's dictum requires that the proposition be tested in the federal courts whenever possible. The federal courts are open and require that the adversary process be fully applied to constitutional issues. Let Dr. van den Haag's retentionist lawyers refute the abolitionists if they can.

3. As to our ancestors' heavy-handed use of physical punishment, my opponent offers some unconvincing explanations. They were fine people, he tells us, who just were not repulsed as we would be by the often unpleasant methods of punishment then in use. Further, because of the invention of anesthesia we are far more sensitive to pain than our stoical forefathers. There was also a "new outlook pioneered by the French and American revolutions," although he does not explain what that outlook was.

I have cited Sir James Fitzjames Stephen's explanation that the gallows were necessary in the eighteenth century for crimes that did not warrant hanging in the nineteenth because convict prisons did not exist. Sir James's tendency to oversimplify his arguments does not invalidate this opinion. However, I must agree with Dr. van den Haag that the French and American revolutions did change many outlooks. Perhaps an example from seventeenth century England will illustrate the change.

Sir John Evelyn was an English gentleman who found it convenient to spend as much time as possible abroad during the hostilities between the Cavaliers and the Roundheads. While in Paris, he spent considerable time studying the French culture, including the administration of justice. In the course of his studies he watched the interrogation of a Frenchman suspected of robbery. In his diary he recorded his observation:

> . . . they first bound his wrists with a strong rope or small cable, and one end of it to an iron ring made fast to the wall about four feet from the floor, and then his feet with another cable, fastened about five feet farther from his utmost length to another ring on the floor of the room. Thus suspended, and yet lying but aslant, they slid a horse of wood under the rope which bound his feet, which so exceedingly stiffened it, as severed the fellow's joints in miserable sort, drawing him out at length in an extraordinary manner, he having only a pair of linen drawers upon his naked body.[2]

Sir John concluded his account with the confession that "the spectacle was so uncomfortable that I was unable to stay another." The interrogation had been unsuccessful. The suspect persisted in his denial of the crime for which he had been arrested, and was sent off to the king's galleys, where life expectancy was short and recruits were always needed.

How could a decent and honorable gentleman endure such a spectacle in the first place? I must doubt that the easier acceptance of pain had anything to do with Sir John's willingness to observe, nor will I believe that it was just a case of *autres temps, autres moeurs*. The answer is to be found in Alexis de Tocqueville's reflections in *Democracy in America*.

When all the ranks of a community are nearly equal, as all men think and feel in nearly the same manner, each of them may judge in a moment of the sensations of all the others; he casts a rapid glance upon himself, and that is enough. There is no wretchedness into which he cannot readily enter, and a secret instinct reveals to him its extent. . . . In democratic ages, men rarely sacrifice themselves for one another, but they display general compassion for the members of the human race. They inflict no useless ills, and they are happy to relieve the griefs of others when they can do so without much hurting themselves; they are not disinterested, but they are humane.

The circumstance which conclusively shows that this singular mildness of the Americans arises chiefly from their social condition is the manner in which they treat their slaves . . . [who] still endure frightful misery and are constantly exposed to very cruel punishment. . . . [T]he lot of these unhappy beings inspires their masters with but little compassion. . . . Thus the same man who is full of humanity towards his fellow creatures when they are at the same time his equals becomes insensible to their afflictions as soon as that equality ceases.[3]

However moral progress is achieved, the difference between our attitudes toward torture and that of Sir John Evelyn—or of Argentine military officers in our own time—demonstrates that standards of decency do evolve as a civilization matures.[4] This evolution comes about through the egalitarianism promoted by the French and American revolutions. When we see each other as equals, we can understand each others' sufferings. But just as Americans could not acknowledge the humanity of their slaves, we prefer to deny a full measure of humanity to those who commit crimes, especially those who are poor and black. They are not like us, they are society's failures, and if they suffer, it is not like the suffering we would endure. In any event, they deserve no better from a society from whose opportunities they failed to benefit. We do not torture them, of course, but we are quite ready to execute them if they engage in killing each other, or some of us.

4. Dr. van den Haag supposes that there are some "rather specific criteria stated in the law of homicide" that will settle for the courts which murderers are to be punished by death. The formulation of these criteria has been the struggle in which the federal courts have been engaged, along with Congress and the state legislatures, for the last fifteen years—and the end is not yet in sight. So far, the criteria that have emerged are far from specific.

For example, the death sentence is a jury decision in Texas, where the jury must decide whether "there is a probability that the defendant will commit criminal acts of violence that constitute a threat to society." That requires a prediction of a kind that is peculiarly difficult to make more accurately than mere chance, but Texans are not to be daunted by challenges to undertake the impossible.[5]

Or consider Georgia, where the court must consider whether the offense was outrageously or wantonly vile, horrible, and inhumane," thus calling on the court's subjective judgment of the limits of outrage and horror. I doubt that Dr. van den Haag himself would care to defend the specificity of these laws or of many like them.

5. I thought that the conduct of Gary Gilmore, so much admired by Dr. van den Haag, was repellent to the end. After an ugly eposide in which he tried to induce his paramour to join him in a suicide pact that he would not keep himself, he finally went to the firing squad. Dr. van den Haag thought he was brave, although he concedes by implication that Gilmore had little choice. He did not embarrass the executioners or the witnesses with a futile resistance, nor did he weep in a repentance he did not feel. I think the admiration he received from some was for a spurious manliness, and I will not confuse sentimentality over the fate of a peculiarly callous murderer with sensitivity to a wholly needless killing of that murderer. My opponent's esteem for Gilmore's putatively "manly" qualities is an example of the noxious effect of capital punishment in creating sympathy where none is deserved.

6. I don't know of any recent case in which a murderer was sentenced to death after a guilty plea, but there may have been a few. Defense lawyers will do what they can to negotiate a plea, if only because prosecutors and judges are eager to relieve the docket of a long and expensive trial. In doing so, however, they are handicapped by the prosecutor's power to demand the death penalty. Defense lawyers will advise their clients to take whatever they can get to avoid the risk of a trial culminating in a death sentence.

If the case goes to trial, the defendant's power to rebut the allegations against him depends on the resourcefulness and the skill of his attorneys—and his ability to pay them—to search for witnesses and to conduct the necessary investigations that would lead to favorable testimony. The prosecution has all these resources to the full extent required by the situation.

Dr. van den Haag asks if I know of any cases in which the hopeless disadvantage of the defendant has led to unwarranted guilty verdicts. Of course I don't. I cannot investigate, and even if I could, it is not feasible to second-guess a court's verdict and sentence. But the disadvantage is obvious. It exists in all but the most exceptional criminal trials. It is enhanced by the death penalty, if only because in most cases where death is demanded by the prosecution a full-scale trial will take place. Mistaken identities, lying witnesses, misinterpretations of events, and many other artifacts of human fallibility and duplicity can and do take place. Once the verdict has been rendered, the book is closed. The defense can do little about the facts as accepted by the court. These facts sent the defendant to condemned row, and unless an extraordinary situation develops, the record cannot be reopened. The defense can only argue errors of law and procedure during the trial or, in recent years, the constitutionality of the state laws by which the defendant was sentenced. Professor van den Haag's optimism about the infallibility of our criminal courts is an act of faith in which most observers of our administration of justice would be reluctant to join.

Notes

1. *Weems* v. *U.S.*, 217 U.S. 349.
2. Virgina Woolf, *The Common Reader* (New York: Harcourt, Brace, 1925), p. 83.
3. Alexis de Tocqueville, *Democracy in America*, vol. 2, trans. Phillips Bradley (New York: Knopf, 1945), pp. 165–166.
4. I include the Argentine military in the same select class as the KGB of the Soviet Union and the present regime in South Africa on the authority of Jacobo Timerman, who survived their maltreatment. See his *Prisoner without a Name, Cell without a Number* (New York: Knopf, 1982).
5. For a Texan's account of the vagaries of Texan statutory draftsmanship, see Charles L. Black, Jr., *Capital Punishment: The Inevitability of Caprice and Mistake*, 2nd ed., augmented (New York and London: W. W. Norton, 1981), pp. 114–121.

ERNEST VAN DEN HAAG

Professor Conrad promises to remove the "thick coat of misinterpretation and irrelevance" that, he writes, I've spread. If he doesn't keep his promise he must be excused: There was no such coat to be removed. But unlike Sancho Panza, I won't insist that the windmills are no more than windmills when my friend has so much fun fighting them.

CHAPTER 9

Justice and Equality

ERNEST VAN DEN HAAG

Let me now turn back to a moral aspect of the death penalty that is connected with the constitutional one just discussed. I wish to argue that even if there were discrimination against some groups, and even if discrimination were unavoidably connected with the death penalty rather than with its distribution—both these assumptions are contrary to fact—the death penalty still should not be abolished. Those who argue otherwise confuse justice and equality.

Discrimination means that the penalty is unequally distributed so as to place a group—blacks or the poor—at an undeserved disadvantage: Although no more guilty than others, they are more often or more severely punished.* If and when discrimination occurs it should be corrected. Not, however, by letting the guilty blacks escape the death penalty because guilty whites do, but by making sure that the guilty white offenders suffer it as the guilty black ones do. Discrimination must be abolished by abolishing discrimination—not by abolishing penalties. However, even if one assumes that this cannot be done, I do not see any good reason to let any guilty murderer escape his penalty. It does happen in the administration of criminal justice that one person gets away with murder and another is executed. Yet the fact that one gets away with it is no reason to let another one escape.

One may get away with murder for reasons beyond the control of even the fairest administration of justice. The evidence may simply not be suffi-

---

*We are, of course, all in favor of relevant discrimination, say, between the sick (who need medical treatment) and the healthy (who do not). But not of irrelevant discrimination between, say, whites who receive treatment and blacks who do not.

cient for conviction. Is that a reason for freeing another murderer convicted on sufficient evidence? Even if one whole group gets away with something because of deliberate bias, I cannot see this as a reason for letting a single guilty person belonging to a disfavored group escape his penalty.

I do not see either a moral or a constitutional warrant for preferring equality to justice, although I admit that this has been the practice of our courts. I do not read the Constitution to command us to prefer equality to justice. When we clamor for "equal justice for all" it is justice that is to be equalized and extended. Justice, therefore, is a prior desideratum, not to be forsaken and replaced by equality but rather to be extended by it.

Justice requires punishing the guilty—as many of the guilty as possible, even if actually only some can be punished—and sparing the innocent—as many of the innocent as possible, even if not all are spared. Morally, justice must always be preferred to equality. It would surely be wrong to treat everybody with equal injustice in preference to meting out justice at least to some. *Unequal justice is preferable to equal injustice.* Justice, then, cannot ever permit sparing some guilty persons, or punishing some innocent ones, for the sake of equality—because others have been unjustly spared or punished.

In practice, penalties never could be applied if we insisted that they cannot be inflicted on any guilty person unless we can make sure that they are equally applied to all other guilty persons. Anyone familiar with law enforcement knows that punishments can be inflicted only on an unavoidably capricious, at best a random, selection of the guilty. I see no more merit in the attempt to persuade the courts to let all capital-crime defendants go free of capital punishment because some have wrongly escaped it than I see in an attempt to persuade the courts to let all burglars go because some have wrongly escaped imprisonment.

Although it hardly warrants serious discussion, the argument from capriciousness looms large in briefs and decisions because for the last seventy years courts have tried—unproductively—to prevent errors of procedure, or of evidence collection or of decision making, by the paradoxical method of letting defendants go free as a punishment or warning or deterrent to errant law-enforcers. The strategy admittedly never has prevented the errors it was designed to prevent—although it has released countless guilty persons. But however ineffective it be, the strategy had a rational purpose. The rationality, on the other hand, of arguing that a penalty must be abolished because of allegations that some guilty persons escape it is hard to fathom—even though the argument was accepted by some justices of the Supreme Court.

Just as the abolitionists who argue that the death penalty should be opposed because it has not been shown to be sufficiently deterrent usually engage in a sham argument since they would oppose the death penalty even if it were shown to be deterrent (see Chapter 4), so those who oppose it because of discriminatory application are not quite serious. Not only does the argument make no sense, as I have just tried to show, but they usually will confess, if pressed, that they would continue their opposition even if there were no discrimination whatsoever in the application of the death penalty. Indeed, countries in which the discrimination argument never was taken seriously (such as Sweden) have abolished the death penalty.

From a moral viewpoint, the whole discrimination argument is irrelevant. If the death penalty were distributed quite equally and uncapriciously and with superhuman perfection to all the guilty, but were morally unjust, it would remain unjust in each case. Contrariwise, if the death penalty is morally just, however discriminatorily applied to only some of the guilty, it remains just in each case in which it is applied to a guilty person. Thus, if it were applied exclusively to guilty males and never to guilty females, the death penalty, though unequally applied, would remain just. For justice consists in punishing the guilty and sparing the innocent, and its equal extension, though desirable, is not part of it. It is part of equality, not of justice (or injustice), which is what equality equalizes. The same consideration would apply if some benefit were distributed only to males but not equally to deserving females. The inequality would not argue against the benefit, or against distribution to deserving males, but rather for distribution to equally deserving females. Analogously, the nondistribution of the death penalty to guilty females would argue for applying it to them as well, and not against applying it to guilty males.

The utilitarian (political) effects of unequal justice may well be detrimental to the social fabric because they outrage our passion for equality, particularly for equality before the law. Unequal justice is also morally repellent. Nonetheless, unequal justice is justice still. What is repellent is the incompleteness, the inequality, not the justice. The guilty do not become innocent or less deserving of punishment because others escaped it. Nor does any innocent deserve punishment because others suffer it. Justice remains just, however unequal, while injustice remains unjust, however equal. However much each is desired, justice and equality are not identical. Equality before the law should be extended and enforced then—but not at the expense of justice.

What about persons executed in error? The objection here is not that some of the guilty get away but that some of the innocent do not—a matter far more serious than discrimination among the guilty. Yet when urged by abolitionists, this too is a sham argument, as are all distributional arguments. For abolitionists are opposed to the death penalty for the guilty as much as for the innocent. Hence, the question of guilt, if at all relevant to their position, cannot be decisive for them. Guilt is decisive only to those who urge the death penalty for the guilty. They must worry about distribution—part of the justice they seek.

The execution of innocents believed guilty is a miscarriage of justice that must be opposed whenever detected. But such miscarriages of justice do not warrant abolition of the death penalty. Unless the moral drawbacks of an activity or practice, which include the possible death of innocent bystanders, outweigh the moral advantages, which include the innocent lives that might be saved by it, the activity is warranted. Most human activities— construction, manufacturing, automobile and air traffic, sports, not to speak of wars and revolutions—cause the death of some innocent bystanders. Nevertheless, if the advantages sufficiently outweigh the disadvantages, human activities, including those of the penal system with all its punishments, are morally justified.

JOHN P. CONRAD

Here is my resourceful opponent with an armory of irrefutable arguments. Who will deny that the escape of some guilty men from conviction is no reason for not punishing those guilty men whom we can convict? Not I; I will not link arms with utopians who insist that there must be some better way to deal with crime than to punish criminals. And who will deny that criminal justice, like any institution administered by mortal men, is imperfect and cannot be entirely free of discrimination and caprice? Not I: I have observed it at close hand for too many years to hope for anything more than gradual improvement, never approaching the perfection its critics demand.

What have Dr. van den Haag's propositions to do with the justification of capital punishment? Guilty men must be punished, regardless of the occasional failure of the system to punish some criminals appropriately. Discretion is inherent in the system and may be abused but never eliminated. These are inarguable statements in any realistic discussion of abstract justice. In a bloodless diagramming of the system, they must stand without alternatives. They are posts that establish the boundaries of the thicket we call criminal justice. If we are to retain capital punishment, these points can be cited as unanswerable refutations of any argument that because there is discrimination in its administration it must be abolished.

Logic is at its most persuasive on a blackboard, in a seminar, or in a textbook on jurisprudence. It is the bony structure of the law, but not its life, not its vital principle. We know that we must root out unfair discrimination in the conduct of justice wherever we can find it, and by whatever legislative and appellate controls we can exercise. Injustice weakens democracy, but justice is hard to maintain in the pure form of the logician's design. It is one thing to pay an unfair fine for a traffic offense improperly charged or even to serve an unfair jail sentence for a misdemeanor. It is quite another thing to watch a poor black sent to the executioner, however guilty he may be, when an affluent and well-defended murderer of another race may escape the death penalty and, sometimes, any penalty at all. We can chop all the logic that judges and lawyers have thought of, but unfairness oozes out of the comparison of two such results.

Dr. van den Haag all but concedes that equity on a diagram may not be seen as such on the streets of a plural society when he remarks that "the effects of unequal justice may well be detrimental to the social fabric because they outrage our passion for equality. . . ." Indeed there is outrage, and indeed that outrage damages the social fabric. The damage is done because ordinary people are not logicians, nor are they instructed in the principles of abstract justice. Not even logicians are immune to the passion for equality. That passion has permeated American political thought from the time that the Declaration of Independence was signed. When the Thirteenth and Fourteenth Amendments affirmed the freedom of all Americans, due process of law was written into those additions to our Constitution to assure equal standing of all citizens in our courts: that was seen as critical to the maintenance of freedom. The passion for equality complicates the administration of justice. It has always been hard for an American to say precisely what he means by equality as an objective, or how far he wishes to go in attaining it. What is certain is that inequality before the law is indefensible, and the sight of such inequality will stir up the passions of all who place a value on freedom.

When ordinary people observe a disproportionate number of poor and black people committed to the nation's condemned rows, their conclusion that the law is unfair may be irrational and unfounded, but it seeps into the collective consciousness with many detrimental effects. For the poor, and especially for the black poor, it seems that a poor man cannot expect justice in a rich man's court and that the criminal justice system is an instrument of oppression rather than a protective arm. For those who may not be so immediately affected by the numbers of the destitute and friendless awaiting death, a number of unpleasant rationalizations explain away the apparent injustice. Chief among such rationalizations is the notion that a certain amount of injustice is required for the maintenance of law and order. Only the threat of death will prevent the poor and the shiftless from marauding throughout all quarters of the cities. It is in this way that the social fabric is torn and a potentially lethal opposition of the classes is created.

The poor man going to the gallows has been a fixture in the administration of criminal justice throughout all its recorded history. The poor have submitted, but they have never been reconciled. The belief that they deserve death for their crimes does nothing to strengthen the solidarity of the nation and much to erode confidence in criminal justice.

We now have the spectacle of the occasional execution in a remote electric chair or gas chamber. All the media swoop in to report all the details of the event. The poor and friendless killer, usually a man who has committed a gross and cowardly crime, suddenly becomes a symbol of all that is unfair, not only in the administration of justice but in the social structure of the nation. It was unfair that the killer's victim should die, and it is unfair to suppose that he has been the victim of any impropriety in the processes of adjudication, but he, the killer, is now the center of attention and the undeserving recipient of sympathy. The law deserves better, and the consignment of this man to a long term in prison will prevent him from rising to a spurious martyrdom. "The law must keep its promises." wrote Justice Holmes,[1] but there are promises that it should not have made in the first place.

This is an age when confidence in the integrity and competence of all our institutions is wearing thin. For the courts of the land to be transformed into theaters in which lawyers joust over the fates of sullen killers degrades us all without any commensurate achievement to offset the appearance of injustice. Textbook justice may be done, but in its course the killer becomes a symbol of social injustice rather than a criminal receiving his just desert.

Rather too briskly, Dr. van den Haag disposes of the argument that the death penalty is irreversible not only for the guilty but also for the innocent. That's none of the abolitionist's business, he says; after all, we oppose the death penalty for both the guilty and the innocent. Let the retentionists worry about whether an occasional innocent man is hanged. After all, accidents do happen. Innocent people are killed in traffic, in sports, and in dangerous but necessary occupations, so why should we be disturbed about an occasional innocent falling into the executioner's hands? If the poor fellow had a fair trial and was convicted by a jury of his peers, and the record has been reviewed by an appellate court, the gallows may cheat him of his life, but sooner or later we will all be cheated.

My wily opponent thus asks us to make a plausible comparison between the death of an innocent bystander killed by a runaway truck, or under a collapsing scaffold or by a bolt of lightning, and the fate of an innocent bystander who is sent to his death by an honest mistake of a conscientious court. This parallel may persuade some, but if so, they must resolutely ignore the difference between an act of God and an act of a mortal and fallible judge.

Throughout human history men have found ways to reconcile themselves to sudden and untimely death by events beyond human control. It is generally accepted that when risks are knowingly assumed, as in the case of a racing driver or a trapeze performer, deaths may occur that might have been avoided if the victim had not taken his chances. But in the exceptional case of the innocent man going to an entirely legal death because of some understandable mistakes in the functioning of a man-made system, consciences must be troubled. The inscrutable act of God cannot be avoided, but the actions of a judge can be limited so that in no case can lethal injustice be unwittingly done. The condemned innocent assumed no risk. Once he is killed, he cannot be recalled from his grave. Had he been merely sent to prison, the error of justice could be corrected when it came to light. Not all human errors can be corrected, but forgiveness comes hard when the error is needlessly beyond correction.

Note

1. *The Holmes-Laski Letters* (Cambridge, Massachusetts: Harvard University Press, 1953), p. 806.

ERNEST VAN DEN HAAG

I admire Professor Conrad's spirited rebuttal and am awed by his passion. However, I detect no new argument. The people rest.

JOHN P. CONRAD

I had hoped that Professor van den Haag would expatiate further on the appearance of unfairness in the imposition of the death penalty on the poor. I had also hoped that he would reconsider the irremediable consequences of the death penalty when it is pronounced after an erroneous verdict of guilty. As he has nothing further to say about these matters, the abolitionist must also rest.

ERNEST VAN DEN HAAG

Okay then, since Professor Conrad insists that I "expatiate further on the appearance of unfairness in the imposition of the death penalty on the poor," I will.

It is important for laws and courts not only to be just but also to appear just. Thus, avoidable actions that give the appearance of injustice—whether or not there is any substance to it—should be avoided. The judge should not have cocktails with the prosecution in the absence of the defense or vice versa. However, the substance of justice should never be sacrificed to the appearance of it. Thus, if in a murder case three accused blacks are guilty and two accused whites innocent, the court should not, for the sake of appearances, declare two blacks and two whites guilty. I know Professor Conrad would agree, but his emphasis on racial appearances may lead one to think otherwise.

On miscarriages of justice, Professor Conrad maintains that my analogy to accidents that are statistically likely but do not lead us to give up an important activity such as building, or even a frivolous one such as automobile racing, is misleading. He argues that accidents are acts of God, whereas a miscarriage of justice is a human error.

This argument is faulty for two reasons. First, many accidents are human errors just as miscarriages of justice may be. Second, and more important, what characterizes an accident as accident is that it was not intended but happened despite the wishes of those involved and despite precautions. Statistically such accidents can be predicted. In this sense—and that is the relevant feature of the analogy—accidents that occur, say, in the building industry, in mining, or in automobile racing and that injure or kill innocent bystanders, and miscarriages of justice can be equally due to human error, can be statistically predicted, are unintentional, and are not a sufficient reason to give up the activity that may lead to them. That activity should be given up only if its justification does not outweigh the injury it may lead to. In the case of the death penalty, I have already pointed out why it is useful far beyond the risk of incorrectible miscarriages it involves.

JOHN P. CONRAD

The foolproof precaution against fatal errors in the administration of the death penalty is to legislate its abolition. It is unfortunate that few, if any, of the other accidents that may befall human beings are so completely preventable.

CHAPTER 10

Special Cases

ERNEST VAN DEN HAAG

There are some special cases—special because the threat of the death penalty is the only threat that may deter the crime. We do not know that it will. We do know that in these cases no other threat can.

Unless threatened with the death penalty, prisoners serving life sentences without parole can murder fellow prisoners or guards with impunity. Without the death penalty we give effective immunity, we promise impunity, to just those persons who are most likely to need deterrent threats if they are to be restrained. From a moral viewpoint one may add that if a prisoner already convicted of a crime sufficient to send him to prison for life commits a murder, the death penalty seems likely to be well deserved. At any rate, without the death penalty his fellow prisoners and the correctional officers can and will be victimized with impunity should he decide to murder them. To avoid threatening the convict with the only punishment available to restrain him, their lives are put at risk. This seems hard to justify.

The matter is all too well illustrated by the following:

> Two hard-case inmates apparently wangled their way into the warden's offices and stabbed the warden and his deputy to death with sharpened mess-hall knives.
>
> . . . investigators said that the death mission had been specifically ordered the night before at a meeting of Muslim inmates because Fromhold had resisted their demands "once too often." Fromhold was stabbed thirteen times in the back and chest; Warden Patrick Curran, 47, who dashed into his deputy's first-floor office, was stabbed three times in the back.
>
> Neither inmate had much to lose. Burton was doing life in the cold-

blooded execution of a Philadelphia police sergeant, and Bowen was awaiting trial in another cop-killing and the shooting of an elderly couple.*

I can think of no reason for giving permanent immunity to homicidal life prisoners, thereby victimizing guards and other prisoners.

Outside prison, too, the threat of the death penalty is the only threat that is likely to restrain some criminals. Without the death penalty an offender having committed a crime that leads to imprisonment for life has nothing to lose if he murders the arresting officer. By murdering the officer or, for that matter, witnesses to their crimes, such criminals increase their chances of escape, without increasing the severity of the punishment they will suffer if caught. This is the case for all criminals likely to be given life imprisonment if caught who commit an additional crime such as murdering the arresting officer. Only the death penalty could rationally restrain them.

In some states the death penalty is threatened to those who murder a police officer in the performance of his duties. Thus, special protection is extended to police officers, who, after all, are specially exposed. They deserve that extra protection.† But it seems to me that everyone deserves the protection against murder that the death penalty can provide.

There are still other cases in which the death penalty alone is likely to be perceived as the threat that may deter from the crime. Thus, there is little point in imprisoning a spy in wartime: He expects his side to win, to be liberated by it, and to become a hero. On the other hand, if he had to fear immediate execution, the victory of his side would help the spy little. This may deter some people from becoming spies. It may not deter the man who does not mind becoming a patriotic martyr, but it may deter a man who does his spying for money.

A deserter, too, afraid of the risk of death on the battlefield, afraid enough to desert, is not going to be restrained by the threat of a prison sentence. But he may be afraid of certain death by firing squad. So may be anyone who deserts for any reason whatsoever.

---

*Newsweek, 11 June 1973.

†To be sure, there are studies attempting to show statistically that the threat of the death penalty will not reduce the rate at which policemen are killed. Policemen are quite uncon-vinced. I believe their common sense informs them correctly: The statistical studies I have seen do not demonstrate what their authors believe to have demonstrated. The studies show only that it is difficult to capture the effects of one variable—the threat of the death pen-alty—when there are many other uncontrolled variables present that may reduce or increase the rate at which a crime is committed. It seems unreasonable that criminals should not fear death as we all do.

Even the death penalty cannot restrain certain crimes. Once a man has committed a first murder for which, if convicted, he would be punished by execution, he can commit additional murders without fear of additional punishment. The range of punishments is limited. The range of crimes is not. The death penalty is the most severe punishment we can impose. It is reserved for the most serious crimes. But we can add nothing for still more serious crimes such as multiple murders or torture murders.

Unlike death, which we will all experience, torture is repulsive to us. Thus, we will not apply it even to those who richly deserve it. It is, moreover, most unlikely that anyone not deterred by death would be deterred by torture or that death with torture would be more deterrent than death without. Thus, there is little point in trying to extend the range of punishment upward, beyond death.

Unfortunately, criminals can and sometimes do torture victims. They also can and sometimes do murder more than one person. The law cannot threaten more than death. But at least it should not threaten less. Although the threat of the death penalty may not restrain the second murder, it may restrain the first.

JOHN P. CONRAD

Nobody should apply for work as a police officer or a prison guard under the illusion that these are safe occupations. They are safer than mining or logging or processing asbestos, but in enforcing the laws good men sometimes die at the hands of brutal and cowardly criminals. The safety of our civic protectors is a vital concern of the state, and the punishment of those who harm them should receive our thoughtful attention. But will the death penalty make crimes against police officers and prison guards less frequent? The evidence is unconvincing.

Take, for example, the murders cited by Dr. van den Haag, which occurred in a Pennsylvania prison in 1973. That was during the moratorium on executions, and I suppose that my opponent means to argue that Warden Curran and his deputy might not have been killed had the electric chair been in regular use. I cannot refute that contention, nor can Dr. van den Haag affirm it for sure. But it is at least as likely that under the almost fanatical discipline that prevailed among Muslim prisoners at that time, these killers had a mission in which they dared not fail. Once they had their assignment, there could not be any consideration of official deterrence. The killings had to proceed.

Frank Rizzo, the mayor of Philadelphia at the time, thought the answer was to bring back the rope or the electric chair. In a memorable comment, Warden Curran's widow made it clear that such demands were futile and beside the point: "Two wrongs aren't going to make a right. If I'm bitter, it's going to affect my children. They must learn to understand."[1] There was a lot to understand. The appeal of the simple but strict, exotic but comprehensible doctrines of Mohammed to the disinherited black is difficult for a secular white official to fathom. That it not only authorized but seemed to encourage overt hostility to white power structures required the suppression of this sect in the interest of order. Throughout the 1960s and well into the 1970s, Muslims were often a dangerous element in state prisons, becoming even more dangerous when uncomprehending wardens tried to suppress them. The violence with which they sometimes responded was inexcusable, and certainly inconsistent with their present conduct, which is commendably responsible. To suppose that a certain execution would have deterred Warden Curran's killers is to underestimate the power of the Muslim mystique on those who were in its full sway.

What might have saved the lives of these two officials was not the electric chair at the end of a long proceeding. If routine procedures had been exercised, these killers could not have attacked Warden Curran in his deputy's office, although they might have reached him elsewhere. That two maximum-custody prisoners could have entered the office of the deputy warden armed with knives indicates that they evaded the metal detectors that should have been in place when they left the maximum-security area. Worse, no officer bothered to frisk them before they got to the controlled office area. It strains credulity that either of these men could have been assigned to less than maximum-custody status with the records of extreme violence with which they were credited.

Hindsight at this distance in time is easy to exercise, much easier than seeing to it that routines are followed without exceptions. But as Thorsten Sellin observed in his essay on prison homicides, the only satisfactory way of preventing them is to assure that prisons are efficiently managed. It can be done; I have seen this accomplishment for myself, but it requires exceptional leadership by the warden and thorough training of all staff.

The greatest danger faced by prison guards is not the rare calculating murderer who figures the high risks and proceeds because they are not sufficiently deterrent. What inspires continuous anxiety among staff and prisoners alike is the presence of crazy men and women to whom life, their own or their victims', means too little to enter into their distorted judgments. An example: Some years ago a friend and colleague of mine was killed by such a man in a California prison. It was settled in the killer's mind that my friend was persecuting him: once that idea gained an obsessive state in his consciousness, there was no stopping him. He rushed into my friend's office with a small knife, shouting his accusations, and stabbed his victim in the eye—fatally. He is now in a state hospital, where he was committed after his plea of not guilty by reason of insanity. He will probably spend the rest of his life in psychiatric custody, to which he should have been committed in the first place.

It is indeed reasonable that criminals should "fear death as we all do"—as my unquestionably rational opponent points out. But not all criminals are reasonable. The most unreasonable of them are assembled in maximum-security prisons, where their hold on reality declines and their desperation increases. For such men and women the death penalty is an irrelevance.

Dr. van den Haag dismisses the studies that have been made of the murders of police officers as unconvincing; they contradict the common sense that tells him that the death penalty is a deterrent that will protect the police from fatal attacks while making arrests and performing their other dangerous duties. I am not told what studies he has read and found wanting. There are special problems with research on the deterrent effects of capital punishment. The long moratorium on the death penalty rules out any current comparisons. I must concede that a comparison is meaningless when it is made between murders of police in abolitionist states and in retentionist states that have not executed anyone for over a decade.

So the best we can do is to refer to Sellin's 1963 investigations, in which comparisons were made between abolitionist states and contiguous retentionist states on the numbers of police murdered and the rates of murder per 1000 full-time police. At that time the retentionist states were practicing capital punishment, as their laws intended.

Sellin's study showed that for the period 1961–1963, there were nine police officers killed while on duty in the abolitionist states (Michigan, Minnesota, North Dakota, Wisconsin, Maine, and Rhode Island), which produced a rate of .393 murders per 1000 police employed. In the retentionist states (Connecticut, Massachusetts, Ohio, Indiana, Illinois, Iowa, New Hampshire, South Dakota, and Montana), 21 officers were killed for a rate of .398 murders per 1000 officers employed.[2]

Data of this kind are open to objections, as Dr. van den Haag notes, without specifying what important variables are left out of the comparisons. The numbers are very small, so that a multiple killing of police officers on one year would produce disproportionate changes in the rates. The consolidated data allow for no analysis of the populations at risk to take into consideration age distribution, unemployment patterns, ethnic groups, or the kinds of intervention in which the police were engaged at the time of the murders. Nevertheless, these are the only statistics we have, and they strongly indicate that the death penalty does not significantly influence police killings one way or another. More recent and more technically sensitive statistical analyses must find ways to allow for a long period during which the death penalty has been in virtually complete abeyance.

If we have to discredit studies like those of Thorsten Sellin (and I am by no means adopting this negative opinion of them), we have to rely on the available versions of common sense and prevailing notions about human nature, which are far from unanimity. Professor van den Haag thinks that the dangers the police face in controlling riots, stopping fights and family disturbances, and making arrests of resistant suspects are such that they "deserve that extra protection" of capital punishment. That is plain common sense to my pragmatic opponent and, I am sure, to most police officers as well.

It omits from consideration the loaded pistols that all police officers carry. No one seriously challenges their right to use their handguns when they believe themselves to be in danger of attack. Statistics are not routinely kept on the numbers of persons shot and killed by the police in such situations. In another study, Sellin found that in Chicago during the period 1933–1954 there were 330 homicide suspects killed, of whom the police accounted for 69 and private citizens 261. During that same period, only 45 persons were executed in Cook County.[3] It is reasonable to suppose that this is a fair comparison, made in a city with a high rate of homicide, during a period when the death penalty was frequently exercised. The data indicate that for that period in that city, the police executed more murder suspects than the operator of the electric chair in the Cook County jail. If the threat of death is what deters potential killers from proceeding, the deterrence of the police officer's pistol is a more powerful influence than the remote prospect of the electric chair.

As to the death penalty for spies and deserters in wartime, some obvious objections must be made in addition to my standard insistence that the state must not kill people in cold blood.

Espionage is a two-way street, on which there is always going to be traffic on the American side when hostilities are under way. Some of our spies will be captured. Their best hope of survival is that their opposite numbers who fall into our hands will be spared for eventual exchange. The imposition of the death penalty is particularly obnoxious in the case of American nationals who cooperate with the enemy. The evidence of the substance of their espionage must often be withheld from the court, and the seriousness of the offense—about which opinions will frequently differ—cannot be evaluated.

As to deserters, it must be beyond question that the state has the right to punish those who absent themselves from duty when about to face the enemy. But military forces that must depend on the firing squad to keep soldiers and sailors from deserting are in a precarious condition. Honor and loyalty are more reliable preventatives, and these qualities should not be balanced by the disincentive of an execution. One fights for one's country because one believes in its cause, not because one fears the hangman. A soldier who betrays his comrades by deserting them belongs in a prison cell. There should never be an inference that what kept his fellows in battle was the threat of the executioner.

My opponent's confidence that anyone not deterred by the death penalty would not be deterred by torture is not supported with his customary logical argument. He may be right, but I find it hard to agree with him without more reasons than he offers me. I suspect that if the American people could accept a return of the rack or the wheel or the more contemporary electric shock devices as preludes to the chair or the gallows, there would indeed be an additional deterrent effect.

I differ with Dr. van den Haag on this point, not because I am not equally repelled by the prospect of introducing torture into the armory of criminal justice, but because I want to establish that there must be a limit on the measures that can be taken to deter crime. The squalid methods used by the Soviet state to keep its citizens in line have plenty of historical precedent, going back to the most remote antiquity of which we have any record. To restrain the state from imposing punishments on the body of an offender—as distinguished from his freedom—is the proper limit to place on the administration of justice. Once we permit the state to kill a man on the gallows, or even by lethal injection on a hospital gurney, the barrier against even more repulsive sanctions has been breached, and arguments must be devised to defeat their introduction.

Notes

1. *Newsweek,* 11 June 1973.
2. Thorsten Sellin, *The Penalty of Death* (Beverly Hills and London: Sage, 1980), p. 94.
3. Ibid., p. 100.

ERNEST VAN DEN HAAG

I agree with Professor Conrad that the management of our prisons leaves much to be desired, and that better management might prevent many prison homicides. I do not see why this has anything to do with the death penalty, let alone why it argues against it. Granted, better management might have prevented prisoners getting arms, but if, somehow, they get arms and use them for murder, they still deserve the death penalty.

I cannot give much weight to Thorsten Sellin's comparisons of homicide rates in abolitionist and retributionist states in 1961–1963. The period is too short and the numbers too small to be statistically significant; furthermore, differences between the two sets of states (e.g., age, sex and racial composition of the population, degree of industrialization and urbanization, traditional crime rates, income inequalities) known to be relevant to crime rates are ignored.

Above all, I do not think that murderers look up whether the state in which they may commit a crime has or has not abolished the death penalty. That penalty will be a deterrent over and above life imprisonment, so that there is more deterrence than there would be without it, only if (a) there is a sufficient execution rate (it was much too low in the 1960s—as it is now), (b) it is applied not here and there but, in any given country, over a wide enough area so that would-be murderers generally become convinced that to murder is to risk the death penalty, (c) the death penalty is applied over a long enough period so that this conviction sinks in, (d) it is applied more swiftly and routinely than it is now applied. Sellin's studies ignore these requirements, all of which are quite commonsensical.

CHAPTER 11

Popular Arguments

ERNEST VAN DEN HAAG

Consider now some perpetually popular arguments against the death penalty.

Barbarization

The argument concerning barbarization received its most incisive formulation from Cesare Bonesana, Marchese di Beccaria, in his *Dei Delitti e delle Pene* ("Of Crimes and Punishments," 1764), a short but influential treatise to which, when it was translated into French, Voltaire added a commentary.

Beccaria wrote: "Laws which punish homicide . . . commit murder themselves" by imposing the death penalty. The laws thereby give "an example of barbarity." Beccaria advocated life imprisonment (which meant lifelong imprisonment then) for murder because "the death of a criminal is . . . a less efficacious method of deterring others than the continued example of man . . . as a beast of burden [in] perpetual slavery . . . in chains and fetters, in an iron cage . . ." These conditions of imprisonment would not be tolerated today. It is hard to see wherein Beccaria's life imprisonment would be less barbaric than the death penalty. I should think it more so. At any rate, Beccaria's argument that lifelong imprisonment is more deterrent than execution is ignored today.

However, Beccaria's objection to the death penalty as "murder" still is repeated by abolitionists, who like to refer to execution as "legalized murder." That phrase is oxymoronic (the adjective contradicts the noun it qualifies). Murder is the unlawful taking of an innocent life. Executions, being

241

lawful, are not murders, and they take the life of a person who has been found guilty, not innocent. The victim of murder was murdered. The murderer, found guilty of that crime, is executed. Executions are neither the moral nor the legal equivalent of murder. One can see in the punishment the moral equivalent of a crime (as in "legalized murder") only if one fails to perceive the moral difference between murdering an innocent victim and executing a criminal—or if one willfully is blind to that difference. If not, executions are no more "murder" than arrests are "kidnappings" or taxes "thefts."

To be sure, executions are physically identical to murder: Both kill. But that does not make them morally or legally identical. Many punishments are physically identical to the crimes they punish or to other crimes. The *lex talionis* even demanded that all punishments be similar to the crimes they are meant to punish. Thus, Thomas Jefferson proposed, however reluctantly, that mutilators be mutilated (see Chapter 1, p. 33). A fine, which lawfully takes money from an offender who (e.g.) unlawfully took money from others, is physically identical to the crime punished. Lawful confinement (imprisonment) punishes a kidnapper who unlawfully confined an innocent person. The difference between crimes, such as murder, and lawful acts, such as execution, is moral and legal, not physical: Crimes are legal wrongs; punishments are lawfully imposed to deter others from crime and to retribute against criminals, thereby vindicating the law.

The physical similarity, or identity, of crimes and punishments is just as irrelevant as the physical identity of a crime (e.g., driving a stolen car) and a lawful act (driving a car one is legally entitled to drive). Identical physical acts often have different social and moral meanings. Rape differs from consensual intercourse morally, socially, and legally—but not physically. Physical similarity to crimes does not morally disqualify punishments; they are morally disqualified only if grossly excessive, or if useless and gratuitous.

I feel no need to deal with the more general contention that the death penalty somehow barbarizes social life, since that contention is either definitional or lacks any evidence to support it. Surely it cannot be contended that states without the death penalty, such as New York, are generally less barbarous than states with the death penalty.

Another popular argument is often advanced in connection with "barbarization": Executions, by setting an example of violence, may encourage homicide rather than deter from it. There are some studies purporting to show that the rate of homicide rises temporarily after each execution, presumably because of imitation. Other studies indicate that the rate of homicide falls at least for some weeks after each execution, presumably because of deterrence.* The evidence is inconclusive. It is quite possible that executions encourage some and discourage other prospective murderers. But if either study were to prove correct, it still would tell us little of relevance. Executions may raise or lower the homicide rate temporarily—they may cause some bunching of homicides, as seasonal factors do. But only changes in the annual homicide rate, with which these studies do not deal, would be relevant if we are interested in determining the effects of executions. Although of interest to experts obsessed with statistical manipulations, however inconclusive, these studies do not answer the question we still must ask: Are executions at all likely to increase the annual homicide rate? If they were public, that possibility cannot be ignored. People who, for one reason or another, are on the brink of crime may imitate what they see. If true, this would be an argument not against executions but against *public* executions.

Any public display of violence may mobilize to some degree the violent impulses that most of us harbor consciously or, more often, unconsciously, and that most of us control. Movies that feature violence—war movies, westerns, detective movies—may lead to imitative violent behavior, particularly by the young. So do violent crimes and, perhaps, boxing. No doubt Greek tragedies in their time had the same effect. This hardly is an argument for eliminating all violence in art, on TV, in movies, or in sports. We cannot eliminate it in life either.

Yet there is much to be said for avoiding the display of unnecessarily explicit violence and of gratuitous violence: violence not required for an aesthetically satisfying representation of a subject. Certainly there is an excellent argument for not feeding the young a diet of senseless and repetitive violence.† However, the idea that executions—which have not been public for many years—will make the difference amid all the violence reported in the press and fictionalized in art and entertainment seems rather strained on the face of it, if not altogether absurd.

Still, public executions might serve as a grisly entertainment, as they did in the past, and do more harm than good. Hence, executions should be

---

*For a full discussion of these studies, see David P. Phillips, "The Deterrent Effect of Capital Punishment," *American Journal of Sociology* 86 (July 1980), pp. 139–148, and subsequent discussion by various hands, *American Journal of Sociology* 88 (July 1982), pp. 161–172.
†The National Institute of Mental Health, in its 1982 report *Television & Behavior,* states that there is "overwhelming" evidence that TV violence causes "aggressive behavior" in children. The report's evidence is somewhat questionable, but its conclusion seems common sense: Children learn from TV and are likely to imitate what they see on the screen or elsewhere.

announced as they are now, but they should not become a public spectacle. There are many actions recognized as useful and necessary that, nonetheless, we do not wish to open to public view. Vivisection may be indispensable to medical research, but we do not display it. Nor do we show the painful effects of some useful medications. One may argue against the public showing of sexual activity without therefore opposing sex. Thus, one may argue against public executions without opposing executions. There is no reason to make a spectacle of any punishment, of pain, or, for that matter, of sex.

Now, it is true that the deterrent effect of executions—indeed, of all punishments—rests on their being known. But executions will be known without being shown, just as imprisonment is known without being shown. "Not shown" is not the same as "not known"; not public is not the same as secret. The media certainly should be informed when a convicted murderer is executed. But it does not follow that the event should be televised, or even that it should be described in so much detail as to possibly stimulate imitation.

Abolitionists sometimes challenge retentionists, suggesting that executions would be more deterrent if televised. They imply that retentionists who oppose televised executions do not have the courage of their convictions. The frivolity of this argument has already been indicated. One may add that to see a man at the point of death always inspires pity and terror—however deserved the execution may be. The argument for televising executions might have more merit, although still not sufficient merit, if those favoring it could find a way of televising the murder that led to the execution as well. At least the presentation would be more balanced.

The Pickpocket Anecdote

Debate about public executions brings to mind the pickpocket anecdote. I have not been able to ascertain the source of this anecdote, although it is frequently referred to in the abolitionist literature. Usually—and wrongly—the anecdote is attributed to Dr. Johnson, via Boswell (I have made this mistake myself).

According to the anecdote, numerous pickpockets were seen to be active in a crowd in eighteenth century London that had gathered to see a pickpocket hanged. Those who report the unverifiable anecdote—*se non è vero è ben trovato*—usually conclude that even a hanging taking place before their eyes did not deter pickpockets. How, then, can we expect executions to deter murder? If the death penalty does not deter pickpockets, it won't deter murderers. This plausible conclusion is not legitimate for any and all of the following reasons:

1. More deterrence can be expected only if *ceteris paribus* a penalty has been increased. It was not. Pickpockets had been hanged for centuries. They expected to be hanged if convicted. Those who remained or became pickpockets despite this known threat obviously were not deterred by it. There was no reason to expect them to become deterred by seeing one of their number hanged as they fully expected. Any crime rate will be reduced only when penalties are increased, not when they are unchanged. It is not logical to expect offenders who became offenders aware of the risk and the current penalty to be subsequently deterred by the same risk and the same penalty. More would be deterred only if the penalty were inflicted more often or if it became more severe.

For all we know, the death penalty did reduce the number of pickpockets to an unknown degree. That some remained active does not show that it did not. No penalty is likely to eliminate any crime altogether. Penalties, including the death penalty, can be expected only to reduce the frequency of crime.

2. One may object that the public execution, though it does not change the penalty, makes it more visible, vivid, and impressive. Perhaps. But executions were not unusual in the eighteenth century. They were taken in stride by everybody and regarded as public entertainment. Executions gathered big crowds whose attention was distracted and who offered great opportunities for pickpockets.

3. The facts as presented in the anecdote suffice neither to prove nor to disprove any deterrent effects of the public hanging. Perhaps there were fewer pickpockets active in the execution crowd than in crowds of equal size gathered for some other reason. Perhaps there were more. We will never know unless we learn (a) the number of pickpockets active in the execution crowd, (b) the number of offenses committed by them—and unless we can compare these numbers to (c) the number of pickpockets active in a crowd gathered for a different occasion, and (d) the number of offenses committed by them. Without these data no conclusion can be drawn. Deterrence is always comparative. Nobody maintains that any penalty or any increase of penalties can deter all offenders. Whether dealing with the threat of death or of imprisonment, the theory of deterrence suggests only that penalties reduce (not eliminate) crime and that more severe penalties. including the death penalty, deter more than less severe ones.

4. Even if the harshness of punishments is greatly increased, as well as

the risk of suffering them, the added deterrent effect upon those *habitually* engaged in criminal activities—e.g., pickpockets—usually is slight. Increased penalties have little effect on those already committed to crime. They are effective, rather, by reducing the number of persons who start criminal activities. *Deterrence does not so much influence habits already formed, criminal or legitimate, as it influences habit formation.*

Many deterrence studies fail because they disregard the fact that deterrence affects habit formation rather than habits. Thus, deterrence is effective in the long and not so much in the short run. However, most studies are concerned with short periods. These short-run studies only measure the effect of new or old threats on criminal habits already formed, whereas the effectiveness of deterrence can be determined only by measuring the effects of threats on habit formation.

Criminal habits respond to deterrent threats as economic habits respond to the threats of unemployment and lower wages. These threats have only a slight effect on persons already in a given occupation, be it coal mining or hat making. They have a major effect on the number of new entrants. So with criminal occupations.

Revenge and Retribution

It has frequently been argued that capital punishment is imposed merely to gratify an unworthy desire for revenge—unchristian, uncharitable, and futile. Is it? And is revenge the reason for capital punishment? Obviously capital punishment is imposed not only for revenge or retribution, but also for the sake of deterrence—to spare future victims of murder by carrying out the threat of execution upon convicted murderers. But let me leave this aside for the moment.

Retribution certainly does play a role. It differs from revenge in some respects, though not in all. Revenge is a private matter, a wish to "get even" with a person one feels has injured one, whether or not what that person did was legal. Unlike revenge, retribution is legally threatened beforehand for an act prohibited by law. It is imposed by due process and only for a crime, as threatened by law. Retribution is also limited by law. Retribution may be exacted when there is no personal injury and no wish for revenge; conversely, revenge may be carried out when there was neither a crime nor a real injury. The desire for revenge is a personal feeling. Retribution is a legally imposed social institution.

Nonetheless, the motives socialized by punishment, including the death penalty, may well include the motive of revenge. But motives should not be confused with purposes, and least of all with effects. The motive for, say, capital punishment may well be revenge, at least on the part of the father bereaved by the murder of his daughter. The intention of the law, however, may be to deter other murderers or to strengthen social solidarity by retributive punishment. Either or both or neither of these effects may be achieved.

Consider now the motive of revenge. Is it so contemptible after all? Perhaps forgiveness is better. It does not follow that revenge is bad. It can be, after all, a compensatory and psychologically reparative act. I cannot see wherein revenge must be morally blameworthy if the injury for which vengeance is exacted is. However, revenge may be socially disruptive: Only the avenger determines what to avenge, on whom, to what degree, when, and for what. This leaves far too much room for the arbitrary infliction of harm. Therefore, societies always have tried to limit and regulate revenge by transforming it into legal retribution, by doing justice according to what is deserved in place of the injured party.

Retribution is hard to define. It is harder still to determine the punishments that should be exacted by "just deserts" once the *lex talionis* is abandoned. Yet retribution does give the feeling of justice that is indispensable if the law is to be socially supported. In the case of murder, there is not much doubt about the penalty demanded by our sense of justice. It is hard to see why the law should promise a murderer that what he did to his victim will never be done to him, that he will be supported and protected in prison as long as he lives, at taxpayers' expense.

Although trendy churchmen recently have tended to deny it, historically the main Christian churches, Roman Catholic and Protestant, have staunchly supported the death penalty, often on the basis of numerous biblical passages advocating it for murder and sometimes for transgressions that today we regard as minor. The oft-quoted "vengeance is mine, I will repay, saith the Lord" (Rom. 12:19) is not as opposed to vengeance as it is made to appear. Paul does not quote the Lord as rejecting vengeance but as reserving it to himself: You must not seek vengeance, you must leave it to the Lord. According to Christian tradition, the punishments the Lord will inflict upon those whom he does not forgive are far more terrible and lasting than what any vengeful mortal could inflict on another. What could be worse than hell, the punishment inflicted for violating God's law? God recognizes and does not deprecate the desire for vengeance. He tells us to leave the fulfillment of this desire to Him.

If we return to earth and read on after Romans 12, we find in the next chapter, 13, what the Apostle Paul actually had in mind. "The Ruler," he says in 13:4, "beareth not the sword in vain: for he is the minister of God, a revenger to execute wrath upon him that doeth evil." The meaning is clear. The Ruler, not the injured individual, should "execute wrath." Disruptive private vengeance should be institutionalized and replaced by social retribution, retribution by the ruler. The Gospels, far from opposing it, support retribution in the very passages so often quoted against it.

JOHN P. CONRAD

This chapter deals with three unrelated topics. I have little to say about barbarization, more about pickpockets, and still more about revenge and retribution. Our differences in this exchange are hardly polar, but worth some brief discussion.

On Barbarization

The accounts of public executions to be found in such treatises as Radzinowicz's *History of English Criminal Law*[1] or Foucault's *Discipline and Punish*[2] certainly support my fastidious opponent's aversion for such spectacles. The hangings at Tyburn and Newgate that diverted the eighteenth century London populace—and many of their aristocratic "betters"—were barbaric events. The behavior of the central character—his stoicism or his fright, his last statement of repentance or innocence, his general bearing at the final moment before he swung—was viewed as a theatrical performance as to which comparisons and critical judgments could be made.

Even the most ardent contemporary advocates of capital punishment refuse to recommend public executions. So far as I know, none have accepted the abolitionist challenge to call for the televised presentation of the ceremonies in the electric chair or on the gallows. Dr. van den Haag correctly supposes that the sight of a man facing his final moments in such a situation would excite unwholesome sympathies for him.

In short, our collective squeamishness requires that these dreadful spectacles be kept out of sight. Whatever edification they can offer must be limited to a newspaper account, never graphic enough to match the event itself. We reserve attendance at the executions to the necessary specialists. Impersonality has replaced barbarism. Whether that is an improvement is not for me to judge. I favor abolition of the whole process.

Pickpockets on the Gallows

So far as I can discover, the original version of the pickpocket paradox is to be found in a nineteenth century book of ruminations entitled *Vacation Thoughts on Capital Punishment,* written by one Charles Phillips. I have been unable to obtain a copy of this volume myself, but it was popular enough in its time to go into four editions. Arthur Koestler, to whose *Reflections on Hanging* I am indebted for this discovery, quotes this author as explaining that "the thieves selected the moment when the strangled man was swinging above them as the happiest opportunity, because they knew that everybody's eyes were on that person and all were looking up."[3]

No doubt. That's only a partial answer to my opponent's perplexity. The anomaly of picking pockets while a pickpocket was swinging doesn't respond to his four heavily labored points. I think the explanation of the paradox is simple enough. The pickpockets knew, with good reason, that the chances of their being caught, red-handed or otherwise, were slim. At the time, London had no organized police. Apprehension for crimes such as this depended on the initiative, the persistence, and the good luck of the victim. Occasionally the victim had enough of all these requisites, or the thief was inept, and an arrest could be made, the pickpocket could be tried and sent to the gallows.

But in eighteenth century London, just as in twentieth century New York, the chances of getting away with a minor property crime were excellent. If you can make away with my wallet without getting caught on the spot, you won't get caught. And of what significance is any penalty for picking pockets if pickpockets aren't arrested and brought to justice?

Dr. van den Haag's observation, "Penalties, including the death penalty, can be expected only to reduce the frequency of crime" is meaningless unless the criminals who commit it are apprehended in sufficient numbers to make the penalty a serious prospect for them.

My empirical opponent's econometrics are true enough of coal miners and hat makers, and perhaps more or less true of muggers and burglars, although in these latter occupations the incentives and disincentives are more complex than they are for steady jobs in a mine or a mill. But murder is rarely an occupation. Except for hit men and contract assassins, nobody "enters" the career of murder. The event of murder takes place on impulse, on a real or fancied provocation, or, sometimes, as an unintended but culpable accident in the course of committing another kind of crime. The application of economic analysis to murder is an absurdity that is not fully apparent in a university office or on a seminar blackboard. It is singularly inappropriate in real life.

With all the emphasis that italics can command, Dr. van den Haag proclaims, *"deterrence . . . influences habit formation."* How does he know this? He does not say; he merely deplores the concentration of research on the study of deterrence "in the short run." I have yet to think of a research design that will enable him to test the effectiveness of deterrence in forming habits in the long run, and I predict that my dogmatic opponent is safe from an empirical refutation of his commonsense proposition.

Revenge and Retribution

Dr. van den Haag correctly accounts for retribution as a means of satisfying the desire of victims for revenge without the disorders that would attend personal revenge. Up to that point we are in agreement, but I find it difficult to follow my opponent's perplexities in defining retribution. In my chapter on the subject, I went to considerable trouble to define it and its function in denouncing crime and promoting civic solidarity around norms of conduct. I explained that retribution does not, cannot, and must not depend on the *lex talionis,* which, it seems, Dr. van den Haag has a lingering wish to revive.

Just as neither of us is a lawyer—though we venture intrepidly into discourse on constitutional law when so inclined—neither of us is a theologian. I cannot claim a command of the hermeneutic studies of the Pauline epistles. Nonetheless, the plain intent of Romans 12 is clear enough: Paul was urging forbearance and forgiveness to those who wrong us. In the last verse of this noble chapter, he exhorted his Roman communicants, "Be not overcome of evil, but overcome evil with good," which, theology to one side, seems like an excellent principle to live by. In the thirteenth chapter, on which Dr. van den Haag relies for confirmation of his preference for executioners to deal with evil, I can learn only that a good Christian must subordinate himself to earthly rulers and their power, because that power is ordained by God. The good man has nothing to fear from the ruler, but the evil man must expect the wrath of the ruler as well as his sword. And I suppose that the sword could be expected in first-century Rome, and a good Christian could not plead exemption from the power of the Roman state.

So what is my subtle opponent's point? Neither modern Christianity nor the American Civil Liberties Union contends that the state does not or should not have the power to punish evil in any way that seems suitable to the rulers. As an independent moralist, I say that capital punishment is unwise, unnecessary, and a disfigurement of the criminal law. If religious people and theologians agree with me, I do not see that they are denying the teaching of Saint Paul.

Notes

1. Sir Leon Radzinowicz, *A History of English Criminal Law,* vol. 4 (London: Stevens, 1948, 1956, 1968). See particularly Volume 1, which is replete with the history of capital punishment.
2. Michel Foucault, *Discipline and Punish,* trans. Alan Sheridan (New York: Pantheon, 1977), pp. 3–6.
3. Arthur Koestler, *Reflections on Hanging* (London: Gollancz, 1956), p. 58.

ERNEST VAN DEN HAAG

I rest my case. I do not think my arguments have been refuted. But two remarks are stimulated by Professor Conrad's response.

1. I am not a lawyer or a theologian, as Conrad correctly observes. I am also not a criminal. Nonetheless, I feel competent to write on crime, law, and religion. One does not have to be a participant to form a competent opinion on an experience—else only Nazis could write about Nazism and only ancient Greeks on ancient Greece.

2. St. Paul's epistle is better understood if one distinguishes clearly between justice and mercy. In my opinion, Professor Conrad fails to do so. Justice distributes punishments (or rewards) according to perceived desert. I follow the Bible in believing that murderers deserve death. Mercy is compassionate with the distressed or punished or miserable, regardless of desert. The gospels do stress mercy but do not expect it to replace justice. No society could survive without justice. God himself is represented above all as being just—assigning people to heaven and hell, according to desert. He is, in addition, merciful and asks us to be, to the extent of loving the criminal while hating the crime. The repentant criminal may indeed be redeemed. But Scripture does not say that he will be redeemed in this world, or counsel that we abolish justice, including the death penalty where deserved, in favor of mercy.

CHAPTER 12

Crimes of Passion

ERNEST VAN DEN HAAG

Unlike such crimes as tax evasion or burglary, many murders are "crimes of passion." The classical idea of a *"crime passionel"* conjures up a husband who surprises his wife *in flagrante delicto,* having adulterous relations with another man. In a passionate rage, the wronged husband, or boyfriend, kills her and/or her lover. Such passion has served as a legal excuse in some jurisdictions and is a mitigating circumstance in others, wherefore the "crime of passion" is not punished as severely as the same act would be punished without the motive of passion. I know of no death penalty imposed for crimes of passion in the United States—although the definition of such crimes may vary.

The guileless husband just portrayed seems somewhat unlikely. Did he have no inkling? Why was he armed? Isn't it more likely that he had suspicions and set a trap? If he did, can we still speak of a crime of passion? Although not easily defined, "crimes of passion" undoubtedly occur. If defined with some latitude, they account for about two-thirds of all murders. The friend who in a rage assaults a friend, whether because of money or sex, or in the course of a drunken altercation, perhaps does commit a crime of passion. The outcome may be deadly even if unintended. Rage may lead to recklessness. We may, then, for our purposes, define a crime of passion as an unpremeditated crime, occurring between persons involved with one another or, at the least, acquainted, a crime in which the offender acts irrationally because controlled by a strong emotion and not by rational reflection or calculation. This is by no means a satisfactory definition. It includes passions such as jealousy or rage, but excludes other equally irrational passions that may be addressed to strangers. And it assumes that passions always flare up and do not persist so as to permit calculation. Yet surely Rigoletto, in Verdi's homonymous opera, was motivated by the passion of revenge when he plotted to kill the Duke of Mantua, even though he did calculate. Premeditation and passion are not mutually exclusive.

Still, our definition is helpful by excluding some crimes such as contract murders or, in general, crimes in which the victim and the murderer do not know one another, as is the case in many robberies; all murders committed as part of a felony are excluded, as are murders carefully calculated in advance. These exclusions may be arbitrary but they limit the category in a reasonable way: Usually one does not harbor uncontrollable passions with regard to strangers. And passions do occur with acquaintances. Uncontrollable rages or jealousies (aroused when a putative sexual property right is violated) do occur all too frequently.

This brings up a different question. How uncontrollable is passion? How responsible is the person acting in the grip of passion? How does one distinguish controllable from uncontrollable passion? The law obviously assumes that acts of passion can be controlled to some degree. Otherwise, they could not be deterred, nor should they be punished. Yet if uncontrollable acts of passion were not punishable, they would be implicitly encouraged. Some persons would lose control more readily, knowing that they could do so with impunity.

The whole matter leaves one puzzled. Why is sexual passion regarded as more honorable or mitigating or less controllable than passion for anything else? Does a man who tries to kill a president to impress a girl who is not acquainted with him commit a crime of passion? Did John Hinckley? Did Sirhan Sirhan, who murdered Robert Kennedy, perhaps in a fit of political passion? Are political passions less passionate than sexual ones? May one be overcome by greed when seeing a heap of money? Is jealousy really more gripping than the greed for money—or is it just more popular? Why is the passion for power less mitigating than jealousy when it motivates a crime?* Could a rapist be inspired by passion?

---

*It may be reasonable to make some allowance for provocation or for intense, hard-to-control feelings that may arise between husband and wife. Further, the law is ill equipped to decide who is right in a family fight. Such legal terms as *theft* or *assault* may not capture the essence of family disputes. Still, the policy of many law enforcement agencies, which pay little heed to complaints of assaults by friends and family members, does deprive them of the protection that they may need and to which they are entitled. True, after going to a lot of trouble, the police may be confronted with a complainant who refuses to testify, but this practical reason is hardly sufficient for disregarding all family complaints, as some police departments do, until and unless an actual murder occurs.

The belief that the crime of passion cannot be deterred often rests on the assumption (a) that deterrence requires calculation and (b) that under the influence of passion one does not calculate. Both assumptions seem dubious.

People deterred from stealing usually do not calculate. They just feel that stealing is wrong to begin with or, at the least, that it will be punished. That feeling, not a calculation, deters them—so much so that most people do not seriously consider stealing nor calculate when presented with an opportunity for any crime. But this attitude itself is produced by the knowledge, internalized early on, that stealing is regarded as wrong, reinforced by the knowledge that stealing is punished. Deterrence is not a calculation. It is an emotional attitude dependent on the law to some extent, but not consciously resting on it. In crimes of passion, the passion overcomes the feeling that the crime is wrong and will be punished. But whether or not that feeling will be overcome depends in each instance not only on the force of the passion but also on the fear of punishment. Passions are not a homogenous quantity. They differ in intensity, quality, object, controllability. The possibilities of controlling passions by threats differ accordingly.

Assume, for the sake of argument, that passion is always irrational and never can be restrained. (If this were literally true, the "crime of passion" would not be a crime. A crime is committed only if the person committing it could have omitted it.) If most murders were, in some less radical sense, crimes of passion, if the offender were neither totally uncontrollable nor totally rational, should we abolish the death penalty for murder? I should say not. If, given the death penalty, most murders are crimes of passion, crimes committed by irrational persons or by rational persons in moments of irrationality, this would show that rational persons do not commit murders. Why not? Could it be the effect of the threatened death penalty? The threat of the death penalty may be so deterrent that only irrational persons are not restrained by it. Surely there is no reason for abolishing so effective a penalty.

Unfortunately, the proportion of murders that are not crimes of passion—"stranger-murders," in which the murderer and the victim do not know each other; felony murders, such as murders committed during a robbery—has been increasing.*

The recent increase in stranger-murders as a proportion of homicides may well be related to the absence of the death penalty. Although threatened by law in most states, capital punishment is imposed rarely and carried

*See footnote p. 99.

out only in an infinitesimal number of cases. This may be among the reasons why we have about 20,000 homicides a year in the United States, more than a third of them now stranger-murders.

JOHN P. CONRAD

From the remotest antiquity, cuckoldry has been considered the supreme humiliation that could be inflicted on a husband. It simultaneously violated his property rights in his wife and held up to ridicule his sexual inadequacy. Cuckolds were thought to have lost any claim to virility if they did not act to punish severely their faithless wives and the paramours who intruded on their marital rights. Killing both was deemed appropriate, hence the unwritten law that exculpated the cuckolded husband if he chose to kill one or the other or both. The convergence of many cultural changes, not the greatest of which is the women's movement, has relegated the unwritten law and the attitudes that supported it to the status of an anomaly—increasingly limited to subcultures in which obsolete values survive.

Hence, the *crime passionel,* once committed with such impunity, now becomes an ordinary murder, not properly distinguishable from murders committed for other reasons. The offense would be more accurately designated a *crime culturel,* one that led the killer to decide that his pride and the esteem of his peers were worth more to him than the lives of his victims. There is no reason why leniency should be permitted on this account, but I will not make an exception to my blanket denial that the death penalty is ever a necessary consequence to any crime.

So my opponent and I find ourselves in general agreement on the culpability of those who kill on finding a spouse *in flagrante delicto.* In this chapter he has digressed to discuss—all too fleetingly—the psychological mechanisms underlying deterrence. I don't agree with him, but I will defer until another chapter my own views on this topic.

ERNEST VAN DEN HAAG

This response seems unexceptionable to me.

CHAPTER 13

Death, Rehabilitation, the Bible, and Human Dignity

ERNEST VAN DEN HAAG

The time has come to consider those characteristics of the death penalty that at once make it appropriate for some crimes in the view of retentionists and lead to persistent and passionate opposition to it.

Except for fines, punishments are irreversible. No one can return the years spent in prison to a person who had been wrongly imprisoned. Monetary compensation may compensate for what was lost but cannot return it. The punishment is irreversible. However, the death penalty is not just irreversible, it is also irrevocable—quite unlike a prison sentence, which can be revoked before it is fully served. Once executed, a man is dead. Capital punishment is the most serious punishment we have, and is reserved for the most serious crimes precisely because it cannot be revoked. Irrevocability is at once an objection to, and an argument for, the death penalty, the reason that it is most feared and most opposed.

Death is one of the few irrevocable things in this life. Life imprisonment in practice amounts to some years in prison: currently no less than seven years in federal prison, and anything from no less than six months to no less than twenty years in different states. Even if parole were abolished and one could make sure that a life sentence is intended to last throughout the convict's life, neither he nor prospective offenders need or will believe it. Where there is life there is hope. Death alone is irrevocable. A life sentence can always be revoked; the law can be changed; appeals may be successful; a pardon may be granted. Not least, there is always the hope of escape. When questioned, most life prisoners will tell you that they expect to escape.

Few succeed, but all hope. Thus, the life sentence is actually, and not unrealistically, perceived as a sentence of uncertain duration.

Prison life is grim compared to life outside, but one gets accustomed. Today's prisons have amenities, from baseball to TV, and allow the prisoners many hobbies. Still harsh, prison life is not as harsh as it was. Above all, it still is life and preferred by far to death: The overwhelming majority of those sentenced to death desperately try to get life imprisonment instead.

Why is death so feared? We all have to die. As pointed out before, death is not a new factor in the life of a person sentenced to death: We are all sentenced to death. Prison is a new factor. It deprives the prisoner of a freedom he would otherwise have kept. The death penalty does not deprive the convict of a life he would otherwise have kept. In the words of John Stuart Mill (spoken in the English House of Commons in support of the death penalty), the death penalty "hastens death." Hastening death means a lot. Even murderers who deliberately hastened the deaths of others cling to life as long as they can.

Why do we all cling to life? Do we value it so much? Surely some do. But the great majority simply fears the alternative, death. That fear is hard to explain rationally. Religion aside, we are not worse off dead than we were unborn.* After all, death is simply nonexistence, the ceasing of experience. Therefore, it cannot be painful; it cannot be experienced or felt.

However, death tends to be confused with dying, the process of parting from this life. Physical pain and indignity often are part of dying, but above all, dying is a separation from life, from everything we love, feel, and hope. It is a separation, ultimately, from the experiencing self.

Execution sharpens our separation anxiety because death becomes clearly foreseen and sudden, whereas, absent execution, most people die slowly or, if suddenly, they do not foresee their death. Further, and perhaps most important, when one is to be executed he does not just die, he is put to death, forcibly expelled from life. He is told that he is too depraved, unworthy of living with other humans. Threatened by death, we normally receive all the help and comfort society can give. But the convict is condemned to die. Society, far from helping him to survive, deliberately shortens his life. He is told that his fellow humans do not want him to live among them, or anywhere on earth.

We are all hard put to imagine our own end. Though we know that we will die, we cannot imagine our own nonexistence; we cannot feel what it is

---

*For those who are religious and expect to enter paradise, death should be less feared than it is by the nonreligious.

like not to feel ourselves. The fear of the death penalty is in part the fear of the unknown. It also rests on confusion. Fear is displaced from death itself to the penalty that imposes it, as though that penalty causes something that otherwise could have been avoided. Finally, and not least, the fear of the death penalty is fear of being put to death deliberately, of being ignominiously expelled from among the living by the living.

Capital punishment is the most severe punishment now imposed. Is it too severe? Are there no crimes that deserve it? Is it inhumane? Does capital punishment violate human dignity or the sanctity of life? Here the abolitionist argument becomes most muddy and passionate. Abolitionists will concede that crimes are being committed—torture murders of children, contract killings of innocent persons for money—that deserve the most severe punishment. But abolitionists argue variously (1) that capital punishment does not accomplish much; (2) that murderers are deranged; (3) that they should be rehabilitated, not executed; (4) that however bad their crime, deliberately executing a defenseless convict is worse; (5) that legal execution violates an inalienable human right, even of murderers, to live, and is therefore inhumane; (6) that execution violates the religious or secular command to respect the sanctity of life; (7) that execution violates human dignity and cheapens human life; (8) that there is a trend in favor of abolishing the death penalty in all civilized countries and that we should follow it.

1. Whether capital punishment does or does not accomplish much depends on what it is expected to accomplish. Execution may deter other capital crimes (see discussion in Chapter 3); capital punishment also has symbolic value. It tells wrongdoers that we are serious about punishment. But put these utilitarian arguments aside.

If offenders are to suffer the punishments deserved by their crimes, if punishments are to proclaim the blame the community attaches to their crimes, capital punishment certainly accomplishes as much. It expresses the extreme disapproval of the community by imposing its most extreme punishment. Of the four ends punishment may accomplish—retribution, rehabilitation, incapacitation, and deterrence—capital punishment accomplishes three, more thoroughly than any other punishment can, while making rehabilitation irrelevant.

2. If offenders are found "deranged," so as not to be responsible for their crime, they are not condemned to death. They are found "innocent by reason of insanity." If they are condemned to death, defendants have been found sufficiently sane at the time the crime was committed, and at the time of trial, to be held responsible and to be tried.

Some people feel that anyone who commits a murder must be insane.

That seems to be a definition or a circular proposition. "He is insane. Why? He committed a murder. Why did he commit a murder? Because he is insane." There is no independent (noncircular) evidence to indicate that murderers are necessarily insane. Those who insist on making murderers insane by definition seem to confuse moral categories—murder is bad— with clinical ones—murderers, therefore, must be insane. But the "therefore" is incorrect. Quite sane people often do quite bad things. They should be held responsible for them and not be regarded as insane. Being wicked, or doing wrong, and being insane are different things; otherwise, nobody would be responsible for any wrongdoing.*

3. Nobody knows how to rehabilitate. There seems to be little difference in the behavior of people who have been subjected to rehabilitation programs compared with those who have not been. The recidivism rate is about the same.

Morally, I do not believe that having done something wrong entitles an adult to rehabilitation. It entitles him to punishment. Murder entitles him to execution.

If rehabilitation were our aim, most murderers could be released. Quite often they are "rehabilitated" by the very murder they committed. They are unlikely to commit other crimes. We punish them not for what they may or may not do in the future but for what they have done.

4. We execute a defenseless murderer because he killed a defenseless victim. He could have avoided his act and the consequences. His victim could not avoid being murdered. That he is now defenseless is no reason not to punish the murderer, who knew his act would be punished by execution. Punishment is not a form of fair combat; it is punishment.

5. The "inalienable" human right to live must come from one of three sources: (a) God, (b) nature, or (c) society.

a. Nonreligious people do not recognize God as a rights-granting authority. Religious people believe his will to be revealed in Holy Scripture (the Bible), in tradition, and occasionally in revelation. All these sources indicate divine approval and occasionally advocacy of the death penalty for murder.

Many modern churchmen follow the liberal fashion and favor abolishing the death penalty. They are entitled to their view, whether or not it is consistent with their religion. But it is hard to see how any churchman can

---

*Some people maintain that nobody is responsible for any action, and that therefore nobody can be blamed, since we all are "determined" so that we cannot act other than we do. If so, the criminal could not avoid his crime. But neither could the judge avoid punishing him. Thus, universal determinism is irrelevant to any moral or legal issue.

deny that the Bible and religious tradition have supported the death penalty for the last 2000 years. Since none of these churchmen claim a new revelation, their view cannot claim the sanction of religious dogma.

b. It is not easy to understand what is meant by a natural right. A right granted by nature? How did nature get the authority to grant rights? Why should we accept it? Actually, nature makes it possible to live and to die, to murder, to execute, or to do neither. Far from telling us what to do, nature merely makes it possible for us to choose among the possibilities it makes available. It does not tell us that imprisonment is either better or worse than execution. We should not hold nature responsible for our decisions.*

c. Rights are social rules. They are defined and enforced by society through laws. If people claim moral or natural rights that have not been legislated, they make claims for legislation. But to want a law enacted is not the same as having had it enacted.

If we grant a right to life, we mean that nobody is legally permitted to interfere with anyone else's right to live. Surely, without enforcing such an elementary right societies cannot survive. How is such a right to be enforced? And who will enforce it? It is "to secure these rights [that] governments are instituted among men," our Declaration of Independence states, referring to the right to be secure in one's life, liberty, and pursuit of happiness. As the declaration indicates, governments are needed to secure these rights. They do so by punishing those who unlawfully interfere with the rights of others. Much punishment consists of depriving the criminal of rights he would otherwise enjoy. He is imprisoned, deprived of the liberty he would be entitled to had he not committed the crime. If the crime is great enough, he may be deprived of his right to live. The rights that we grant one another, on whatsoever basis, are forfeited if we commit crimes. That is what is meant by punishment. The degree of forfeiture is specified by law.

To say that the right to life is inalienable amounts to saying that the law ought not to deprive criminals of it. The "argument" from inalienability simply restates what it should prove: Criminals ought not to be deprived of the right to live because it is inalienable, i.e., because they ought not to be deprived of it.

The framers of our basic documents did not prohibit the execution of criminals. Such executions were frequent in their time. Further, as mentioned before (see Chapter 5), the framers provided, in the Fifth and Fourteenth Amendments, that no one should be "deprived of life, liberty, or property without due process of law": They implied that with "due process

---

*See my *Against Natural Rights* in *Policy Review* 23 (Winter 1983).

of law" those who, by means of it, were found guilty of crimes could be "deprived of life, liberty, or property."

6. There is no biblical support for the idea that the "sanctity of life" is inconsistent with the death penalty. Nor is there any support for this idea in church tradition. This "argument" is simply another way of saying, "I am against the death penalty." Restatement of a view does not amount to an argument for it.

7. The Romans thought that *"homo homini res sacra"*—every human being should be sacred to every other human being. To enforce the sacredness of human life, the Romans unflinchingly executed murderers.

One may well argue that human life is cheapened when murderers, instead of being executed, are imprisoned as pickpockets are. It is not enough to proclaim human life inviolable. Innocent life is best secured by telling those who would take it that they will forfeit their own life. A society that allows those who took the innocent life of others to live on—albeit in prison for a time—does not protect the lives of its members or hold them sacred. The discontinuity between murder and other crimes should be underlined by the death penalty, not blurred by punishing murderers as one punishes thieves. Murder is not quite so trifling an offense.

To insist that the murderer has the same right to live as his victim pushes egalitarianism too far. It blurs moral distinctions and seems to recognize only physical equalities. His crime morally sets the murderer apart from his victim. The victim did, and therefore the murderer does not, deserve to live. His life cannot be sacred if that of his victim was.

It is not clear wherein executions violate "human dignity" unless by "dignity" we mean the alleged right not to be executed. This would be a circular argument.

8. There is indeed a widespread trend among Western countries to abolish the death penalty. It has been abolished in much of South America. There the legal abolition of capital punishment has contributed to frequent and haphazard killings. Death squads of guerrillas and of their opponents murder—or, as they would say, "execute"—with great abandon anyone they suspect to be on the wrong side. There is no legal death penalty—and no life is secure.*

The case of Western Europe is different. Although terrorist movements in Germany, Italy, and Spain, let alone the Near East, have murdered many people, the governments of these countries do not impose the death penalty.

---

*On the other hand, the death penalty seems quite effective in preventing terrorism against a government even when it is opposed by the majority of inhabitants. South Africa demonstrates as much.

Yet no nongovernmental death squads have sprung up. There are movements to reintroduce the death penalty. However, abolitionists have prevailed, most recently in France. Nevertheless, it is hard to see why these trends should influence American decisions about the death penalty. Why should we follow the English example? We achieved independence some time ago. We did not follow the German example when the Germans accepted or submitted to Nazism, or the Russian example when Russia became Communist. American domestic decisions should be made regardless of what other nations do in conformity with our own views, not theirs.*

JOHN P. CONRAD

I will forbear comment on my stoical opponent's eloquent threnody on the irreversibility of death, the universal fear that it inspires, and the desire that all of us have to die with some semblance of dignity. With all these reflections I can agree, and, I suppose, few abolitionists will reject Dr. van den Haag's musings on this subject.

Only one quibble: My opponent asserts that "when questioned, most life prisoners will tell you that they expect to escape." During a career that has afforded me many opportunities to talk informally with life prisoners, I do not recall any who have made such a statement. Some do escape, of course, and others make an attempt. Usually these occasions occur during the first years of confinement, when the end seems impossibly distant. As the years go on, most lifers decide that they have too much invested in years of obedient conduct to risk their prospects for release by even seeming to be less than completely trustworthy. I must assume that Dr. van den Haag's lifer-respondents are of a different breed from mine—or that one or the other has been less than candid with him or me.

The substance of this chapter is contained in Dr. van den Haag's eight debating tricks. To defeat my case, he states it in the form of eight assertions, which he then proceeds to demolish with his formidable polemic prowess. It is a daunting project to enter the ruins that he has left behind him and to try to restore the abolitionist redoubt, but that is my task, and I will

---

*Everything said in the text applies as well to the United Nations. This anti-American organization does not have legislative authority. It merely represents the views of the governments of a majority of nations. Many of these governments in Africa and Eastern Europe are beneath contempt.

do the best I can with it. Let me take my shrewd opponent's eight points in the order in which he presents them:

1. *Capital punishment does not accomplish much.* It certainly accomplishes the death of the convict who is executed, and no abolitionist will minimize the importance and the significance of that event. What is less clear is that it accomplishes any purpose sufficiently useful to justify the repellent procedures that are required to carry it out. No one has yet shown that it is more effective as a deterrent than a life term in prison, *pace* Dr. van den Haag and his affirmations drawn from the deep well of his common sense.

If a life term is the ultimate severity that the state is allowed to impose, retributive justice is satisfied. As to incapacitation, the records are abundantly clear that murderers are the least recidivistic of all classes of offenders released from prison. Incapacitation is not a significant consideration with most murderers. Though some are volatile and dangerous in their youth, the advancing years will extinguish the fires of hostility as they reach middle age.

Dr. van den Haag does not convince me—or, I think, any informed observers of American crime—with his claims for the useful accomplishments of the death penalty.

2. *Murderers are deranged.* Not an issue. I agree that most murderers will pass the McNaughtan test with flying colors. Few are psychotic in such a sense that they must not be punished. It is an unacceptable argument to claim that a murderer is insane by virtue of his having committed a murder.

I am not told who is making these claims to the contrary. I concede that there are crackpots on the abolitionist side; I also suspect that there are some to be found on the retentionist side.

3. *Murderers should be rehabilitated, not executed.* So far as this abolitionist is concerned, this is not a supportable argument, either, if by "rehabilitation" Dr. van den Haag means that we seriously believe that programs can be administered to murderers to cure them of their murderousness. I note with some gratification that my perceptive opponent will allow that most murderers could be released if "rehabilitation were our aim." So they could, but I would not release any until they had served a term significantly longer than any other class of felon.

4. *However bad the crime, deliberately executing a defenseless convict is worse.* No argument other than a disguised circularity is offered by my opponent. Dr. van den Haag cannot suppose that it is a justification of an execution to assert that it is done because the defenseless murderer had killed a defenseless victim. However, the proposition that he attempts to refute is correct. It *is* worse to kill a defenseless convict, but not because he

is defenseless. The deliberate nature of the execution is what the abolitionist rejects. We hold that if killing people is wrong—and as to that we are inflexible—then two wrongs cannot make a right. There is no way of prettying up a killing so that it does anything more than add to the overflowing store of social morbidity.

5. *Legal execution violates the inalienable human right, even of murderers, to live, and is therefore inhumane.* I would prefer to leave to the theologians the defense of the general rejection of capital punishment by Catholics, Protestants, and Jews. Just as I argued that the Constitution of the United States must be interpreted and reinterpreted in the light of the needs of our times, so I must suppose that the "modern churchmen" whom my opponent disdains believe that we must consider biblical precepts in the light of a secular world that has changed vastly during the last two thousand years.

It seems to me that the Bible, like the Constitution, contains a set of principles for our guidance, not a prescription of specific rules that must be observed by religious people throughout the ages. For example, the Golden Rule is a virtually universal religious principle, common to all the major faiths. Most religious people accept it as a valid guide to the conduct of their lives, even if it is often difficult to live by. We may suppose that godly men and women found ways of reconciling capital punishment to the Golden Rule in the days when there was no other way to cope with criminals. I insist that such a reconciliation is not acceptable in the twentieth century. If we have no need to kill—and we have none—then we must not kill.

My opponent then brashly dismissed the whole doctrine of natural rights in a fast-paced paragraph. This is not the place to offer a treatise on the history and significance of natural rights philosophy. It should be enough to say that our Declaration of Independence, that foundation stone of American political life, postulated the "self-evident" and "unalienable *(sic)* Rights to . . . Life, Liberty, and the pursuit of Happiness." These rights were not self-evident to utilitarians like Jeremy Bentham, who thought this sort of talk was "nonsense on stilts." He firmly held to his Greatest Happiness Principle—only if the state could proceed without interference in the utilitarian aim of the greatest happiness of the greatest number could happiness be successfully pursued.

Now, here is the most profound cleavage in political philosophy. I believe that any democratic society must be based on a recognition of natural rights to life, liberty, and the individually chosen pursuit of happiness. It is not for the government to make citizens happy. The state's only duty—and it is a formidable task indeed—is to prevent avoidable human misery.

It follows that it is wrong to violate the right of another to life. It is just as wrong for the government to kill as it is wrong for a brutal and nasty criminal to cut short the life of an innocent victim.

Conservative political thought used to rely on the doctrine of natural rights as the basis for justifying the arrangements supporting political and economic stability. I am surprised that my supposedly conservative opponent so incautiously brushes aside a doctrine that has served conservative thought so well. Unless he has become a Benthamite in neoconservative raiment, what choice other than the Greatest Happiness Principle does he have? And to what form of government does he believe that utilitarian doctrine will lead?

Finally, Dr. van den Haag argues that rights have to be legislated. So they do, if the state is to act on them. But if we hold that there is a natural right to life, then the state must not violate that right by killing any class of citizen on any pretext whatsoever. An ugly example: The Nazis claimed the right to kill all Jews and Gypsies and set up the legal and administrative machinery to authorize and arrange for their arrest, imprisonment, and execution. As a natural rights moralist, I flatly reject the right of any state to arrogate to itself the decision to execute millions of people because being a Jew or a Gypsy is legally wrong. Armed with natural rights doctrine, I have no difficulty in maintaining that rejection.

I am sure that Dr. van den Haag rejects the Nazi doctrines as uncompromisingly as I do. I do not know how he reconciles that rejection when he cannot admit the existence of a natural right or allow that there are any rights that are not defined by laws.

True, governments exist to enforce the inalienable rights to life, liberty, and the pursuit of happiness. True, to secure that these rights are enjoyed by every citizen, those who interfere with the life, the liberty, or the pursuit of happiness of any other citizen must be punished. But what is the status of that person who is undergoing punishment? I maintain that he must be considered a citizen who enjoys all the rights of any other citizen, *except* those that must be suspended during the period in which he is punished. No other rights should be curtailed. It follows that life must not be taken when the deprivation of liberty is a sufficient punishment. And Dr. van den Haag has not yet succeeded in showing us that anything is gained by the death penalty beyond the severity of a life term in prison.

6. *Execution violates the religious or secular command to respect the sanctity of life.* I do not know what abolitionist is credited with the phrase "sanctity of life," or why Dr. van den Haag thinks anything can be made of it. I note with unreserved agreement his precept that "restatement of a view does not amount to an argument for it." I have tried to observe this rule as scrupulously as I can throughout this debate.

7. *Execution violates human dignity and cheapens human life.* To defeat this proposition, my learned opponent goes back to the Romans. It was possible for a Roman writer to propose the maxim *homo homini res sacra*, but the administration of Roman law corresponded more closely to Plautus's pessimistic aphorism, *homo homini lupus est*—"man is like a wolf to other men." The state must not be a wolf to its citizens, regardless of the wolfish behavior of murderous criminals.

Two more points made by my opponent under this seventh heading deserve attention.

The notion that it cheapens life to treat murderers like pickpockets is expounded with a labored hand. Pickpocketing these days is not a thriving profession. The skills required are too much trouble to learn when with a pistol under his belt a man can do at least as well for himself. I do not think I have ever encountered an authentic pickpocket in prison; the reason is that there are not many of them and those that are caught are limited to a few months in a county jail. A petty thief has to be unlucky indeed to be hit with a prison sentence.

But a lifer doing fifteen or twenty years before he can even discuss his future with a parole board is not living the same kind of life as an imprisoned pickpocket—or an imprisoned mugger or rapist, either. When a murderer has done a long time in prison, a sufficient discontinuity between his crime and any others, especially pocket-picking, has been established. As my rigorously logical opponent has correctly put it, to restate a view is not to establish an argument in its favor.

The second point for review is the notion that moral distinctions are "blurred" by insisting on the murderer's right to live. I contend that when the state kills anyone, a fundamental moral distinction is not merely blurred; it is ignored. By killing the murderer the state replicates his act as a killer. It validates violence by taking the utmost violent action. To spare the killer is not merely to declare that he has the same right to live as his victim. It is to make plain that *all* human beings, even the least deserving among us, have an equal and inalienable right to live. The state's right to punish does not extend beyond the right to restrict the criminal's liberty by locking him into a prison.

8. *There is a trend in favor of abolishing the death penalty in all civilized countries, and we should follow it.* There is no reason for Americans to follow any trend unless it is right for Americans. Not many South American examples commend themselves for our emulation. I doubt that the abolition of capital punishment in most of these countries accounts for the anarchic violence that prevails in so many of them. Their poverty, the civic discontent engendered by gross contrasts between the privileged and the

"shirtless," and the vulnerability of political life to a violent strain of Marxism must be much more powerful determinants of violence and homicide than the dismantling of the gallows.

Nor can I accept Dr. van den Haag's recommendation of the death penalty as an effective answer to terrorism in such a country as South Africa, where the regime is admittedly "opposed by a majority of inhabitants." Clearly the death penalty has many uses and advantages. Hanging blacks to maintain an oppressive government by a racially elite minority is an abuse of the criminal law that I prefer to believe is now safely behind us as a nation.

We should not follow European examples to be fashionable. We should ask ourselves whether we have anything to learn from the experience of advanced, democratic nations such as England, France, and West Germany. In all these countries, and others in Western Europe, the hangman has been retired, and he is unlikely to be summoned back into service. Are there some peculiar reasons why Americans need the discipline of the executioner whereas Western Europeans do not? Is there some respect in which we resemble more the unfortunate nations in the Communist "camp" that, in other respects, as Dr. van den Haag stresses, are "beneath contempt?" There are not many of Dr. van den Haag's arguments that Communist jurists would not wholeheartedly accept. The executioner is essential to the Eastern European version of socialist order. Western democrats don't need him.

My vehement opponent's strenuous arguments seem to be his most forceful polemic in support of the death penalty. Little significance need be attached to some of them; they are responses to straw arguments that he has stated for the purpose of knocking them down. As to his more plausible arguments, all of them utilitarian in nature, they expose the priorities of that philosophical tradition which holds that the state knows best what contributes to the greatest happiness of its people.

I prefer the absolute priority that is assigned to the right to life, a natural right that is part of the foundation of our political life.

ERNEST VAN DEN HAAG

I note that in his self-confessed "quibble" Professor Conrad admits that at first "lifers" try to escape, and later they don't to avoid risking their "prospects for release." Exactly as I said; either way, no "lifer" ever thinks he'll stay for life.

The Golden Rule states that one should do to others as one would want them to do to oneself, or, negatively, that one should not do to them what one would not want them to do to oneself. What is wrong with this rule is not that it is "difficult to live by" but rather that it may be too easy. The rule does not have much content and does not really tell you whether, say, polygamy or homosexuality or abortion or progressive taxes or killing adulterers or murderers is right or wrong. But unlike Professor Conrad, I see no difficulty in "reconciling" it to capital punishment: Murderers should be executed, and, if I be a murderer, I should be executed.

Jeremy Bentham, contrary to what Professor Conrad thinks, thought natural rights just "nonsense." Only imprescriptible natural rights, in which Professor Conrad appears to believe, are "nonsense on stilts." I share Bentham's opinion, although I'm willing to be more polite. But the opinion does not logically depend on Bentham's Greatest Happiness Principle, which I do not share. One need not be a utilitarian to reject "natural rights."*

I agree with Conrad that it is not the government's duty to make people happy—*ultra posse nemo obligatur* (nobody is obligated beyond his ability). But democracy can do quite well without "natural rights" which can, and do, support many other forms of government and have done so in the past. Anything can be proclaimed a "natural right," as the U.N. has diligently shown.

Democracy is based on the rights society grants the individuals in it, including the right to elect and peacefully oust governments. Whether those who favor these rights believe they come from God, nature, or us, is irrelevant to democracy. (But Professor Conrad is correct. Jefferson and others believed in "natural rights.")

The Nazis based their practice on a biological version of "natural rights." The Communists base theirs on a historical version. Neither faith is inherent in the "natural rights" doctrine. It all depends on what you hear nature telling you. One can reject Nazi or Communist doctrines from a natural rights viewpoint, as Conrad does, or without it, as I do. Unfortunately, it seems to me that history shows quite clearly that nature only tells us what we can, not what we should, do. It is our responsibility to determine what is right—I wish nature did it for us, but this wish is clearly unfulfilled. (However, nature seems to have seen fit to give Professor Conrad information churlishly withheld from me.)

I do not believe, as Professor Conrad does, that "all human beings. . . have an equal and inalienable right to live." I think murderers forfeit that

---

*Readers interested in my views on natural rights, if there be any, will find them argued for at greater length in *Policy Review* 23 (Winter 1983).

right, which they have refused to grant to others. Professor Conrad here
finally explains that this "right" comes, somehow, from nature. Too bad that
nature failed to inform all previous generations, up to the twentieth century,
of the right of murderers to survive their crime and escape execution.
Nature did not inform such natural law and natural rights defenders as Cic-
ero, Thomas Aquinas, Hugo Grotius, or John Locke (who infected America
with the notion of "natural rights"). Not even Thomas Jefferson realized
what Professor Conrad knows, that nature opposes the death penalty. In a
free country Professor Conrad is granted the right to advocate granting
whatever rights he wishes to murderers. But why does he attribute his
wishes to nature? or to natural rights theory? (Whence nature's authority
to command us? Why must we obey, when we could do otherwise? How do
we know what nature wants us to do or not to do? Is nature always right?)

JOHN P. CONRAD

My opponent makes two points in his rejoinder. I will pick up his challenges as best I can. I certainly cannot ignore them.

On the Golden Rule. If any theologian or moral philosopher has claimed
that the Golden Rule is a complete guide to the conduct of life, that claim
has escaped my notice. Ethics and morals are not that easy. The Golden
Rule is silent on the progressive income tax and on the other issues mentioned by Dr. van den Haag in his rejoinder. That the rule cannot be
stretched to cover such matters does not invalidate it, but it does leave plenty
for the moral philosopher to do—much more than I can attend to in my
part of this debate.

Is the Golden Rule easy to live by? In principle, I suppose, it presents
no great difficulties in interpretation. Its very simplicity must have been its
attraction in the mind of Jesus. In daily living there surely are difficulties in
applying it that must be traced to human frailties rather than to any hidden
complexity. Convenience, rationalizations, indifference to the misfortunes of
others, and inability to predict the consequences of one's actions all obstruct
compliance with the Golden Rule.

Nevertheless, on the subject of killing, the application of the rule is
simplicity itself. I would not wish to be deliberately killed by another. Therefore, I do not wish to be a party to deliberately killing anyone else—as I
must when the state inflicts the death penalty—not even the contemptible
and heartless murderers who are now eligible for execution. That Dr. van

den Haag thinks that there are considerations that override the Golden Rule is a forthright assertion that he does not justify.

On Natural Rights. On the one hand, my philosophical opponent has urged on us the strictest fidelity to the framers' understanding of the nature of cruel and unusual punishment, from which we deviate, he thinks, at great risk to the integrity of the Constitution. Now, on the other hand, he denounces the very idea of natural rights, the foundation concept of our Constitution, expressly stated in our Declaration of Independence and in the preamble to our Constitution. He then strays off to an implicit denigration of the Declaration of Human Rights of the United Nations. That need not concern us here.

What does concern us is the continuity in the consensus in this country that natural rights have been stated by the framers and they are the principles that should govern our society and set limits on our laws. It is not some mysterious "nature" that has granted these rights, but rather the framers of our Constitution, who chose to base our system of government and the precepts limiting our laws on the right of everyone to life, liberty, and the pursuit of happiness.

We have had a lot of trouble living up to the expectations of the framers. I doubt that any thinking citizen would wish to abrogate the rights that they laid down. Surely I am not alone in the opinion that because of the acceptance of these rights life in the United States is more free and more satisfying to more people than in any other country in the world. I devoutly hope that these natural rights will continue to be regarded as "imprescriptible," to use Bentham's accurate word or "unalienable," to use the framer's synonym. I will not accept his derision of natural and imprescriptible rights as "nonsense on stilts."

ERNEST VAN DEN HAAG

Properly stated, the Golden Rule is not overridden by executions (nor did I claim it needs to be). I do not wish to be killed by another; therefore, I feel obliged not to kill another. But I do believe that a murderer deserves death; therefore, I would deserve death if I did commit murder. (Imanuel Kant indeed believed that the Golden Rule actually *requires* the execution of murderers.)

CHAPTER 14

The Symbolic Meaning of the Death Penalty

ERNEST VAN DEN HAAG

Fifty-five thousand persons die in traffic accidents every year in the United States. More than 20,000 persons are murdered. Among young blacks, murder is the most frequent cause of death. Nonetheless, the death penalty is imposed on very few murderers, and of those, fewer than five have been executed per year in the last ten years (1973–1983). Given these facts, it is clear that the main significance of the death penalty both to retentionists and to abolitionists is symbolic: The material effects of capital punishment, as far as society is concerned, are negligible. Its symbolic significance is not.* Capital punishment is important as a sign from which one can infer social attitudes and that is meant to express them. Wherefore it is a prominent issue.

Abolitionists feel that the death penalty sends the wrong signal to the public and expresses a barbaric and useless vengefulness. They believe that, by executing criminals, the government sanctions the idea that people have the right to deprive other people of life. They contend that nobody should have that right under any circumstances. Death should never be inflicted as punishment on anyone regardless of what crime he has committed.

Most abolitionists would grant that self-defense and war are occasions that justify killing people. But punishment is not self-defense. If a criminal

---

*To a lesser extent this may be said about criminal justice as a whole: Very few crimes—less than 3%—ever lead to imprisonment.

can be executed by the government, the "sanctity of life"* is not intact. The government itself has failed to respect it. People may fall into the habit of violating it. Yet nobody, abolitionists insist, can be so totally and irremediably evil as to lose the right to live. Sure, the criminal has killed wrongfully; but that should not cause the government to execute him, thereby sanctioning killing. Finally, even if anyone could be evil enough to deserve death in the eyes of heaven, no court, no government would be competent to decide that he does.† No government, no court, no person has been granted the right to deliberately put others to death. This is the basic abolitionist feeling.

Although hardly a Christian dogma, the abolitionist belief is clearly a form of faith—faith in the total "sanctity of life," in the belief that nothing can justify death as a punishment. Many abolitionists repudiate all religion but cling to this remnant of religious faith, which is justifiable only by "the evidence of things not seen," a type of "evidence" that they repudiate when presented in its explicitly religious form. Actually, the major religious traditions never have suggested that the "sanctity of life" excludes the death penalty for murderers. The Holy Scriptures of the Christian, Jewish, and Islamic religions explicitly sanction capital punishment.

Unsupported by religious, let alone secular, evidence, the abolitionist belief that the sanctity, or sometimes the dignity, of life should exclude capital punishment rests on a strong feeling—nothing less and nothing more. Why that feeling has become so strong in our times is a matter, at best, for psychological speculation. It may have something to do, for better or for worse, with the triumph of radical egalitarianism in our life.

In former times people felt that the insane or the criminal were scarcely human. Concern with them was exceptional. No punishment was too harsh. There was little compassion—the criminal was beyond the pale. From this radical unegalitarianism—barely comprehensible to us today—we have veered to an equally excessive egalitarianism: We soft-pedal, even obliterate, all differences, particularly moral differences. We feel guilty about those that cannot be denied. The criminal is not that different—he deserves comfort and "conjugal visits." Nobody can be so different, so evil, as to deserve deliberate execution by others.

---

*Professor Conrad does not use the phrase, "sanctity of life," but many other abolitionists do.
†Some abolitionists add: "Only God can make that judgment." Yet many of them do not believe in God. Even if they did, ours is constitutionally a secular society, which cannot rely on God, or religion, to shirk its obligation to secure the life of its members and to do justice by the best secular means available.

Just as the abolitionist position ultimately rests on the symbolic significance of capital punishment, so does the retentionist position. Retentionists, too, wish to convey an attitude, to send a signal. They, too, wish to defend the "sanctity of life"—but also the sacredness of the moral rules expressed by the law. They believe that the death penalty for murderers is a necessary defense against the desecration of life and of social authority. If there is nothing for the sake of which one may be put to death, can there be anything worth risking one's life for? If there is nothing worth dying for—however involuntarily—is there anything worth living for?

Retentionists deny that there are no actions evil enough to deserve death, or that society has not, or no longer has, the authority, which hitherto it always has claimed, to execute those who have murdered. As do abolitionists, retentionists feel that life should be sacred, and they lament that murderers have always been among us. But they believe that the way to discourage them, as much as is humanly possible, and, above all, to express the vehemence of the social disapproval of murder, to defend innocent life, is to take the life of those who take innocent life, to unequivocally threaten the death penalty, and to unflinchingly carry out the threat against anyone who murders anyone else.

Whether the threat discourages murder more than alternative threats such as life imprisonment has already been discussed. It will be a controversial issue for the foreseeable future. But even if it did, abolitionists would object to the death penalty (see Chapter 4). These gentlemen amaze me. Let me restate the matter briefly.

Professor Conrad (as reasonable an abolitionist as one can get), Ramsey Clark (a former U.S. attorney general), and professors Hugo Adam Bedau and Charles Black, Jr., are prominent abolitionists. So is Henry Schwarzchild of the ACLU. They all oppose the death penalty, not because they believe it has no deterrent effect beyond that of life imprisonment (although they do believe it does not), but because the death penalty would be "wrong" even if it did. Thus, their argument is moral and must be based on their belief that no act, however horrible, justifies the death penalty. I do not share that belief. I never heard any convincing argument in its favor, as distinguished from a reassertion of the belief in some different form. I am genuinely puzzled by a belief implying that, if the death penalty were more deterrent than life imprisonment, the believers would prefer to preserve the life of a convicted murderer rather than the lives of innocent victims, even if it were certain that these victims would be spared if the murderer were executed. Yet I have actually had occasion to question those named above.

They have all insisted that they would continue to oppose the death penalty even if it were shown—as it has not been—that each execution would spare 500 victims of murders that, because of the execution, would not occur. I do find it hard to defend this preference for murderers over victims—indeed, for the life of one murderer over those of 500 innocent victims. I can see no argument—moral or otherwise—for this. I have never heard one. Yet the belief is strongly held and, as is typical for any nonrational faith, it is immune to argument. Even the simplest of arguments: If life is sacred, shouldn't two lives—let alone 500—be more important, more sacred, than one? Aren't innocent lives more valuable than guilty ones?

The abolitionist faith seems a rather odd kind of substitute for religion. It makes existence, life itself, the highest moral value, so high that life should never be taken (or given up?) for the sake of any other value. Worse, and somewhat incoherently, life never should be taken even to preserve other, more numerous lives. Even a guilty life should never be taken to preserve more numerous, innocent lives—even if the life of a murderer is sacred, and, oddly enough, more sacred, in effect, than that of his victims.

All values are devalued if one takes this dogma seriously. If no value is worth sacrificing life for, none can be more important than life, none can transcend it. Ultimately, and contrary to the intentions of abolitionists, abolition, rather than consecrating "the sanctity (or dignity) of life," desecrates it. For what is the value of a life that cannot be dedicated—and if need be, sacrificed—to a value that transcends it? Surely individual life is cheapened if it becomes itself the highest of values and cannot be dedicated to something beyond it. To suggest that the life of the murderer is so important that it cannot be sacrificed to assert the moral value he violated by murdering trivializes innocent life and the rules made to preserve it. To me the proposition implied by abolitionists—that the negative value of no crime can exceed the positive value of the life of the person who committed it—seems bereft of plausibility.

Some German philosophers, including Immanuel Kant and G. F. W. Hegel, went so far as to argue that the criminal not only has the moral duty to submit to punishment—after all, had he designed the laws, he too surely would have punished murder—but has a right to it. It is by means of his punishment, the philosophers felt, that the criminal's human dignity is preserved. He is held responsible for his acts, unlike an animal, a child, or an insane person. Kant, in particular, felt that not to execute a murderer is to deny him his human dignity as a rational and responsible person, and to deny the obligation of society to uphold the moral law.

Few criminals insist on their right to be punished.* Most would prefer to be regarded as not responsible for their crimes. But the right to punish them for their lawbreaking has been accepted by every society and is denied only by anarchists. Unless there are special reasons to the contrary, we all, criminals and noncriminals, should be held responsible for what we do. And if what we do is legally wrong, we should suffer the legal penalties. In the case of murder, the execution of the murderer seems the only penalty appropriate to the crime, the one that is felt to be the deserved retribution and that is most likely to discourage others. If we follow the interpretation of the Eighth Amendment that the United States Supreme Court gave in *Weems*† to the effect that punishments must be proportioned to the gravity of the crime and to other punishments imposed for other crimes, it seems to follow that the death penalty, far from being inconsistent with it, is required by our Constitution.

From a more practical viewpoint, we must remember that the legal process of imposing punishment originated as a socialization of the common impulse to take revenge. In the words of Sir James Fitzjames Stephen, "the criminal law stands to the passion of revenge in much the same relation as marriage to the sexual appetite."‡ Revenge is a major motivation, although not necessarily the intention of punishment (e.g., deterrence or incapacitation, which may be intended, have nothing to do with the motive of revenge). Intention may go beyond, or may differ from, motive. However, just as abolishing marriage would be unlikely to reduce the "sexual appetite," so abolishing punishment would not reduce the appetite for revenge. Reducing punishment too much may indeed leave too much of the "passion of revenge" to be gratified privately. For whenever it was felt that punishment was not imposed justly or frequently or severely enough, people have tended to take the law into their own hands, to seek revenge directly. When due process was thought insufficient in the American West, "lynch justice" developed.

Fortunately, that possibility is still remote in the United States. Except for the criminal underworld, which does not and could not rely on legal processes, few, if any, murders occur because of dissatisfaction by an aggrieved party with the legal punishment meted out to an alleged criminal.

---

*Gary Gilmore did. He was opposed by the ACLU, which insisted that it is a civil liberty for a murderer to be compelled to live against his will, even if he got so tired of the maneuvers of his ACLU lawyers that he preferred being shot.

†Weems v. United States (1909), 217 U.S. 349.

‡J. F. Stephen, *A History of the Criminal Law in England,* vol. 2 (London: Macmillan, 1883), p. 8.

But if the dissatisfaction, already noticeable, with the lenient and uncertain punishments now meted out were to become even more pervasive than it is now, it would be very hard to control. Only by imposing sufficient punishment can we make sure that vengeance murders will not start, as they have in Central and South American countries where the judicial system is deemed to be weak or ineffective. As is shown in every poll, more than two-thirds of the population perceive execution as the only punishment sufficient for murder (see Appendix to this chapter).

JOHN P. CONRAD

Let us make a brief tour of Professor van den Haag's world, the human elements of which are so clearly discernible in this chapter. It is an interesting place to visit, but I do not think I would like to live there. The nastiness and brutishness of the Hobbesian world is suppressed by the law, but if we don't watch out, someone will be at our throats. After all, the police can't be everywhere, and they can't arrest all the murderers so that the courts can have them hanged.

In this world of van den Haag, everyone is born a potential murderer. Only the law, the hard and implacable law, teaches children and reminds adults that every unlawful act will result in severe punishment. This society cannot rely on God or the church for moral guidance. Morality is the law; the law is morality. It is not clear that everything not prohibited by the law is permitted, but our guide does not tell us how moral instruction will be conveyed. We are to understand that the terror of the consequences will prevent us from committing a criminal act.

Anyone who commits a willful murder will be unflinchingly executed after his conviction in court. Three practical aims are thus achieved. First, each execution rids the world of an offender who has forfeited his right to live among the innocent. Second, potential murderers—all members of this society, it must be kept in mind—will be deterred from killing an innocent victim. No one can be sure that this is true, but our sagacious guide considers it not unreasonable to suppose that every execution will save many lives, possibly as many as 500. And third, each execution "sends a signal," a signal expressing the vehemence of the social disapproval of murder.

As mentioned above, this is a society in which everyone is a potential murderer, but, because of the unwavering severity of the law, most people are deterred from committing this, the gravest of crimes. They know, however, that the murderers who have gone to the gallows have not died in vain. They have given their lives, "however involuntarily," to reinforce the necessary defense of social authority. That murderers have died for this cause gives citizens good reason to dedicate their lives for other great causes—perhaps even to die for them—because great causes transcend mere self-preservation. They learn from those hanged men and women that it is worth risking their lives—yes, even losing them—to achieve something greater than themselves.

It can be seen that in the world of van den Haag much depends on the murderer giving up his life on the scaffold *pour encourager les autres.**

Other Worlds. If the van den Haag world is real to my implacable opponent, it must also be real to many other well-meaning retentionists. In the preceding chapters I have done my modest best to show that there are other possible worlds in which standards of behavior depend more on what children learn from their parents and what adults learn from each other in day-to-day living. I have not denied the necessity of the criminal law and the punishments it requires. I have argued that good social behavior depends far more on the incentives by which society rewards decent and productive living than it does on the lessons of punishment. If fines, imprisonment, and the hangman are all that keep us from slitting each other's throats, our condition is desperately dangerous.

In previous chapters I have done what I could to neutralize most of the arguments offered by Professor van den Haag in this chapter. I confess that I am surprised to hear once again that the insincerity of abolitionists is shown by our willingness to spare a murderer even if 500 innocent lives could be saved by hanging him. I had thought that I had silenced that accusation earlier. Let me try again. If I could show Professor van den Haag that the execution of one murderer would stimulate 500 potential murderers to kill 500 innocent victims because these potential murderers would anticipate with relish the notoriety, the experience of "being somebody" in the headlines, would my opponent commute the murderer's sentence to life imprisonment? The absurdity of my proposition does not exceed the absurdity of his. Both are frivolous attempts to embarrass one's opponent, rather than an effort to make a serious point.

---

*See Voltaire, *Candide,* Chapter 23: *Dans ce pays-ci il est bon de tuer de temps en temps un amiral pour encourager les autres* ("In this country it is thought well to kill an admiral from time to time to encourage the others").

On Lynch Law. Professor van den Haag introduces one new argument in the closing paragraphs of this chapter. He ominously suggests that if the people come to believe that the law is too slack they will take justice into their own hands and adopt "lynch justice," as he believes was done in the old American West.

He touches a Californian's sensitive nerve. It is true that in the early years of the California gold rush, criminal justice was poorly organized, and it was seen that desperate men were getting away with murder. Vigilante committees were formed to administer summary justice to desperadoes, and some were strung up on the lampposts of San Francisco. That was a brief episode in California history—not more than a year of two—and it is important to understand that it came about because the police and the courts had yet to be organized at a time when there was a great migration of gold-seekers, many of whom had disreputable antecedents and few scruples. As a lifelong Californian, I have to say that I have never heard of the vigilante committees operating as lynch mobs. Once the police and the courts were in full operation, not much more was heard of the vigilantes.

Lynch law was something else. It prevailed in the southern states from the eighteenth century and was the expression of the will of the dominant white slave-owning classes to maintain the absolute subjugation of black slaves. To assure that the violence of the white population was not opposed by violent resistance from the slaves, acts of murder, assault, and rape committed by slaves were frequently, and in some places, invariably punished by hanging, usually preceded by beatings and other indignities on the slaves' bodies. I do not know of anyone suggesting that lynch law was the consequence of a breakdown of criminal justice in the South. During the years after the Civil War, fear of freed blacks may have intensified the lynchings. Sometimes courageous sheriffs and judges did what they could to prevent these frightful events. Often enough they failed, not because of a failure of criminal justice or because of excessive leniency shown to black men charged with crimes. Southern criminal courts have never displayed any reluctance to punish blacks to the limit of the law if the crimes of which they were convicted involved a white victim. White ruffians in the days of lynch law preferred to get at black offenders, whether guilty or not, with the terror of a lynching party, thereby "sending a signal" of unmistakable import to everyone in the black community.

The vast majority of the American people, despite jeremiads to the contrary, are law-abiding. Sprinkled around the country are outlaws and yahoos who would like nothing better than an occasional lynching. They are unrepresentative of Americans as a whole. There are no visible signs that a general lapse into lynch justice is in the remotest prospect—even when we succeed, as we eventually will, in abolishing the death penalty.

On the Insanity Defense. In his appendix to this chapter, Professor van den Haag has contributed an able attack on the insanity defense. I am in virtually full agreement with everything he has to say about this topic, both as to general principles and as to the desirable procedures for carrying out these principles.

I wish only to add that there is nothing in the training of the psychiatrist or in his clinical practice that enables him to predict anything beyond the probable course of his treatment of a patient—and that without complete certainty. The psychiatrist who fancies his powers of prediction suffers from professional *hubris*. Unfortunately, a great deal of what passes for forensic psychiatry is self-indulgent clairvoyance, vastly more influential with the courts than this offshoot of psychiatry deserves.

ERNEST VAN DEN HAAG

Yes, I agree that we all are potential murderers, just as we all are potential professors. Persons engaging in either activity are not born as a race apart. They are shaped by the interaction of genetic and environmental factors. Among these factors is the law. The threats of the law, including the threat of the death penalty, play a double role.

1. They help shape all other kinds of educational influences that make murder unthinkable to most of us (although, significantly, we enjoy reading about it in detective stories). Murder is unthinkable because condemned and punished by society with death through the ages—for so long that we ascribe the condemnation not to ourselves but to "nature." (But nature is mute and has never been heard to oppose any crime or to advocate it or to punish for it, unnaturally by imprisonment or naturally by death. *We* do all of these things.) Deterrence influences habit formation by influencing education.

2. For those who think of murder, the threats of the law are but one of many considerations. I agree with Conrad—though I am less sure than he is—that by the time the threat is explicitly considered or ignored, i.e., when action is prepared, the threat is not likely to be very effective. Once a person is at that point, society has lost the war, even though it may still win some battles.

Yet if punishment becomes known to be mild, crime becomes rampant.

Si monumentum quaeris, circumspice ("If you want evidence, look around"). If all this makes one a Hobbesian, so be it. I've always thought highly of Thomas Hobbes and feel honored.

JOHN P. CONRAD

We seem to have come to an agreement of sorts. I, too, am an admirer of Hobbes. It is unfortunate that in the popular mind the Hobbesian world has come to be identified as the one that he so eloquently deplored. We are both Hobbesians, I suppose, but neither of us is nasty or brutish.

ERNEST VAN DEN HAAG

I am delighted to agree with Professor Conrad. It is a rare pleasure and greatly enjoyed.

Appendix to Chapter 14

ERNEST VAN DEN HAAG

How Responsible Are Murderers?

We live in a therapeutic age, as many writers, paraphrasing Philip Rieff,* have suggested. We no longer say that someone who displeases us is hard-hearted or wicked. We say he (or she) is sick. No wonder that moral and legal issues about capital punishment are often argued in psychiatric terms. Was the murderer responsible for what he did? Did he appreciate the wrongfulness of his act? Or if the court uses the older (and to my mind better) McNaughtan rule, was he able to tell right from wrong and to understand the effects of his act? Finally, assuming that the murderer was mentally lucid, was he able to conform his conduct to his knowledge? Certainly the criteria of legal responsibility added since the McNaughtan rule are more comprehensive; they recognize that in addition to disturbances affecting the intellect so that a person may not know what he is doing, there are emotional disturbances, which may affect conduct even though not affecting reasoning ability. But it is doubtful whether any psychiatrist is able to distinguish an "irresistible impulse" from one that was not resisted, or an inability to "appreciate the wrongfulness" of an act from a failure to do so, a failure that may be expected to be part of the context of any murder. These psychiatrically useful criteria are legally useless. Worse, they have led to a legal quagmire in which psychiatric experts offer opposing diagnoses to the court, which has no rational criteria for decision. For the evidence from psychiatric hypotheses is conclusive only in a few extreme cases.

It seems indeed quite likely that murderers have peculiarities. We all do. It seems likely too that many murderers, even most murderers, have extraordinary peculiarities such as insufficient socialization, insufficient consideration, or insufficient compassion for others. Perhaps these peculiarities distinguish them from nonmurderers—although no one has as yet shown

---

*The Triumph of the Therapeutic (New York: Harper & Row, 1966).

that murderers share common traits not shared by nonmurderers. Even if they did, peculiarities are not excuses, moral or legal, for murder.* Obviously, laws threatening murder with punishment are addressed most centrally to people who do have peculiarities that make them prone to murder. If the law were addressed only to persons not prone to murder, it would be redundant.

Some people clearly are incapable of telling right from wrong or of knowing the effects of their actions. They may kill without knowing that it is wrong to do so. They may be so detached from reality that they literally do not know what they are doing. They may kill an innocent victim believing that he is a tree. They may not know that they are committing a crime. Retributionists do not wish to punish clearly insane persons, for they are not responsible for their actions. They cannot be blamed any more than an irrational animal can be. Nor, I would add, can they be deterred by threats. Nor, finally, would punishing them deter others: The sane, however prone to crime, do not identify with the insane and will not be deterred by punishing the clearly insane. Thus, the courts, unavoidably, must decide in some cases whether defendants were sane when they committed the act with which they are charged, and if they were not, what to do with them.

In extreme cases the decision is not hard. But there are many persons on whose sanity there is doubt; psychiatrists often disagree in these cases and base their views largely on speculation. What should the courts do? I believe our present practices should be changed. The insanity defense should be dropped from any trial ascertaining guilt or innocence. Insanity should play a role only in a separate sentencing procedure to be required whenever the insanity defense is used.

At present a defendant may be found "not guilty by reason of insanity." I propose that he be found guilty or not guilty depending on whether he did or did not do what he was charged with regardless of whether he knew what he was doing. Whether there was intention *(mens rea),* premeditation, recklessness, negligence—all these questions should be decided without psychiatric testimony on the defendant's state of mind. The court should be guided only by external evidence. A subsequent procedure would establish whether the defendant was sane, with the only questions to be decided those posed by the McNaughtan rule.

Suppose, now, a defendant is found guilty and insane. At present in most state and federal jurisdictions he is sent to an institution for the insane

---

*To be excuses, peculiarities would have to be beyond the control of the murderer, and to have unavoidably compelled him to commit the murder with which he is charged.

and released whenever psychiatrists find him "cured." He may be "cured" and released quite soon—wherefore pleading insanity can be quite helpful. The inmate may even use the prosecution's testimony given to show that he was sane. The court, doubting his sanity, was not persuaded by that testimony. Now the defendant can use it to help persuade psychiatrists that he was sane all along. Unlike the court, the psychiatrists may find no insanity and may release him almost immediately. By training, psychiatrists are interested in the individual—not in the protection of society. And they are not meant to be concerned with crime and punishment. What, then, shall we do with the defendant found insane by the court?

1. Courts should, in the first place, determine whether the defendant did what he was charged with doing. If so, he is guilty.
2. If he claims not to have been able to understand the criminality of his conduct—the only appropriate legal criterion for insanity—he should be sentenced as though sane, but allowed to serve his sentence in an insane asylum if his insanity claim is plausible.
3. After serving his sentence he may be civilly committed if still insane.
4. If psychiatrists find him sane while he is serving his sentence in an insane asylum, a judge should determine whether he is to serve the rest of his sentence in prison or stay in the hospital.
5. Conclusions about the intentionality of criminal acts—e.g., on whether murder or manslaughter was committed—should be based on external evidence and never on the speculations of psychiatrists. Psychiatric testimony should be relevant only to deciding where the defendant is to be confined if found guilty.

Yes, I know, if the defendant was really insane, he was not responsible for what he did and should be neither blamed nor punished. But if he committed a crime he is dangerous enough to be confined, as he would be if sane. If he regains his sanity he also regains his responsibility for what he did when he had lost it.

Although the law must be discontinuous—defendants are either guilty or not—life and people are continuous for the most part. Dr. Jekyll and Mr. Hyde are metaphors. In actuality they are different aspects of the same continuous person, who is responsible for both. Very few defendants had no idea that what they did was a crime—and those who did are not likely to be cured. For others the insanity defense should not be made attractive. How are people to learn "to appreciate the wrongfulness" of crimes—and the law mainly is a teacher—when not appreciating it leads to a "not guilty" verdict?

Defenders of the *status quo* point out that the insanity defense is seldom used even now, for juries are not easily persuaded of insanity, despite (or because of) the vagueness of the law. The Hinckley jury (see below) was exceptional. But the insanity defense has helped to bring the law into disrepute, and it does weaken the prosecution in plea-bargaining—which, after all, decides most cases.

There is a fear of imposing punishment, part of an all too widespread feeling that nobody should be blamed for anything he does, and that criminals are victimized by society and their own mental states no less than their victims are victimized by crimes. That fear should not be favored by letting courts cling to an as yet inchoate science, and by allowing speculative psychiatric diagnoses to take the place of factual judgments of guilt or innocence.

To illustrate. After shooting the president of the United States, John W. Hinckley, Jr., indicated that he did so in order to become a celebrity and gain the attention of a young actress he idolized. He succeeded. Although he was arrested on the spot and his crime was filmed by the cameramen with the president, it took more than a year to bring him to trial. This did not help the reputation the courts are acquiring.

The trial lasted for weeks, devoted to the endless testimony of numerous psychiatric experts for the defense, who swore that Hinckley was insane, and for the prosecution, who swore that he was sane. Actually Hinckley was neither. He clearly was deranged, but not insane by ordinary criteria: He knew what he was doing and that he was committing a crime. Yet the jury found that Hinckley was "not guilty by reason of insanity." He was transferred to an institution for the insane and may be released any time psychiatrists find him sane. The defense, utilizing the prosecution's testimony that he was sane, may now claim he is sane after all, or that he has been cured and should be released. Chances are he will stay a few years in an institution, but no one knows.

If doubt is raised before trial, federal law places the burden of proving a defendant sane on the prosecution, since sanity is a necessary element of guilt and the prosecution has the burden of proving guilt. This seems logical, but it is silly nonetheless: It is almost impossible to prove anyone sane beyond a reasonable doubt. Criminals usually are different enough from noncriminals—which is, after all, how they become criminals—to make it hard to prove them sane. And psychiatric standards of sanity are quite vague and elastic. The law, trying misguidedly to keep up with psychiatry, has made its formerly clear standards vague too, so that almost no defendant who can afford a psychiatrist is sane beyond a reasonable doubt. However, most juries rely on common sense and do not take psychiatric standards and testimony seriously. Unfortunately, the Hinckley jury did. It followed the judge's instructions on the law, which, although not improper, leaned toward the defense. Judicial rulings and instructions usually do, for the defense can appeal when displeased, i.e., when it loses, whereas the prosecution cannot, owing to the double jeopardy clause of the Constitution which prevents the retrial of anyone found not guilty.

This imbalance should be rectified by enabling the prosecution to appeal erroneous rulings and instructions while the trial is going on. This is done now for pretrial proceedings. Thus, judicial errors could be corrected, without double jeopardy, before they affect the outcome. Above all, judges would have an incentive to produce balanced rulings and instructions, whereas now they have an overwhelming incentive to favor the defense.

We also should return to saner standards of insanity. In the past a criminal was legally insane if, and only if, he could not understand that his act was criminal. Since then psychiatrists have found that there are emotional as well as intellectual disorders. Hence, the judge instructed the Hinckley jury that a guilty verdict required the prosecutors to prove beyond a reasonable doubt not only that Hinckley "was not suffering from a mental disease or defect" but also that he had the "capacity to conform his conduct to the requirements of the law" and "to appreciate the wrongfulness of his conduct."

Now, some people indeed cannot "conform their conduct to the requirements of the law" although able to understand it; they cannot resist their criminal impulses. But no one ever has determined whether an impulse that was not resisted could have been. And by making inability to act in accordance with the law a legal excuse we do not encourage law-abiding behavior. If you are on the borderline, your resistance to criminal impulses is not strengthened when you can expect to be found "not guilty" unless the prosecution can prove, beyond a reasonable doubt, that you could have resisted successfully.

The law should restrain those who, because of their weak resistance to temptation, may commit crimes. If the weakness of their resistance to criminal impulses itself becomes a legal excuse, few criminals can ever be found guilty. The law becomes redundant, operative only against people who are not tempted to commit crimes in the first place instead of restraining those who are.

How "mental disease or defect," the absence of which the prosecution must prove, are to be defined is left up in the air by the law, i.e., up to psychiatrists, who do not agree among themselves about the definitions or about the application of their definitions to particular individuals. Most psychiatrists tend to think of all criminals as "sick." To require further that the defendant must be able "to appreciate the wrongfulness of his conduct" is absurd. If he truly had been able to appreciate the wrongfulness of it, the criminal probably would not have committed the crime. Thus, if he did commit the crime it is *prima facie* evidence that he was less than sane and, therefore, not guilty.

In their zeal to find excuses for the criminals they presume never to be evil but always, somehow, sick, legal experts have got lost in a psychiatric wonderland. So have legislators and courts. They should be rescued.

Recently a Yale student, Richard Herrin, killed his fellow student Bonnie Garland, who wished to end an affair with him. He was temporarily sharing her bedroom and killed her with a hammer after she had fallen asleep. He was found guilty of manslaughter, because psychiatrists persuaded the jury that he was temporarily unable to control his acts. Had the definitions proposed above been followed, he would have been convicted of murder. Jean Harris, who killed Dr. Herman Tarnower, whose mistress she had been for many years, because he was about to part with her, also was convicted of manslaughter. Yet she had appeared unannounced at Tarnower's house, equipped with a gun and many bullets. A murder was changed into manslaughter because of the alleged emotional state of the defendant.

On the whole, the insanity plea, as currently used, protects some murderers from incarceration altogether and changes some cases of murder—mostly those in which the defendant can afford psychiatrists—into manslaughter as long as the victim had some emotional relationship with the murderer—or even, as in Hinckley's case, if he did not.

CHAPTER 15

The Abolitionist Rests

JOHN P. CONRAD

Whatever the outcome of this debate in the minds of our readers, it is clear to me—and, of course, to my stern opponent as well—that at this stage of our history, capital punishment is a winning cause in America, if nowhere else in the civilized world. Abolitionists may win some of their cases in the courts, in spite of the retentionists' furious denial that the courts should have jurisdiction over the nature and quality of the punishment that the state may impose on criminals. It is still possible for abolitionists to attain high office from the electorate and subsequently to "sabotage" the executioner's craft by commuting the sentences of condemned murderers. Nevertheless, I must gloomily concede that the public opinion polls, in which the hangman now receives a handsome plurality of the respondents' votes, are corroborated in statewide referendums. If the general public has its way, Dr. van den Haag's cause is won, and without the benefit of his robust arguments.

I construe this predilection for the executioner as the outcome of the common man's yearning for a tough stand, a hard line, a crushing response to the nation's surfeit of criminals. The common man may never have met a criminal, but he knows what will deter him and what he deserves—the gallows, no less, or its local equivalent. In this certainty, the electorate is encouraged by demagogues who tell the world that the return of the executioner will signal to criminals everywhere that they can no longer expect leniency from the courts, and that the state will resume an implacable severity that prevented crimes in the old days and will soon prevent it again.

What humbug! Political candidates and their advisors know that, regardless of the deterrent value of the gallows, the death penalty has nothing to do with the nonhomicidal criminal. The arduous and costly tasks that society must undertake if crime is to be prevented still have to be defined and faced—even if we settle on an unswerving program of killing all murderers and stick to it. The signal that is really conveyed by the noose and the electric chair will be understood by thoughtful criminals and ignored by the reckless. That signal will tell those who receive it that Americans do not understand the crime problem in spite of all the exposure they have had. Whether thoughtful or reckless, criminals know that neither the gallows nor the prison awaits them, whatever their offense may be, if they are not caught, prosecuted, and convicted. They know that the police do not catch them often enough (although there is reason to suppose that most are eventually arrested), that busy prosecutors are only too willing to settle for a guilty plea to crimes less serious than those with which they are charged, and that, if they are convicted in court, the chance of probation is pretty good unless the crime is so heinous as to have become a matter of public notoriety.

Under the circumstances, how can the criminal justice system deter any man or woman desperate enough to gamble on engaging in a criminal career? The police solve a higher percentage of homicides than any other crime reported to them, but, as my well-informed opponent never tires of pointing out, the number of murders increases every year at an unacceptable rate. There are plenty of potential killers who will accept the 70–30 odds against them, perhaps because they calculate that well-planned murders by disinterested and anonymous murderers constitute most of the 30% that are uncleared. Spouse-killers and rapist-murderers are usually brought to justice, homicidal robbers and contract hit men almost never.

We distract public attention from the expensive requirements of more police, more courts, and more prisons in the stentorian advocacy of capital punishment as a panacea for violent crime. The public officals responsible for this clamor know better. They also know that the execution of a contemptible killer comes cheap, compared to all the measures that must be taken to combat crime effectively.

I do not include my profoundly reflective opponent among the disingenuous office-seekers, office-holders, and editorialists who have somehow convinced the majority of the public that killing killers is the solution to the crime problem. Dr. van den Haag has for many years been a sincere believer in the efficacy of the death penalty as a deterrent of homicide, just as he has advocated more severe punishment for those who commit lesser crimes. He has not convinced me, nor has he persuaded many other abolitionists. Nevertheless, he makes what he can of a mixture of commonsense propositions about deterrence, he invokes the *lex talionis,* and he thrusts the indisputable and deplorable facts about the rising murder rate into the attention of anyone who will listen. His case for the resumption of the death penalty is rational and well argued. He is undisturbed by the overwhelming rejection of his argument by psychologists, sociologists, economists, and statisticians—with the lonely and generally discredited exception of Dr. Issac Ehrlich.

What a stark and dismal world my bleak opponent comtemplates! It is not a far cry from the world that Thomas Hobbes defined as a "time of war," when there is "continual fear and danger of violent death; and the life of man, solitary, poor, nasty, brutish, and short."[1] In this van den Haagian world, everyone must be on his guard against every neighbor, for everyone is a potential murderer, prevented from committing the most horrible of crimes only by the tenuous threat of the death penalty. Especially likely to commit such crimes are the poor, who enviously observe the comfortable classes and determine to take by force what they could not gain by merit and industry. The vertiginously rising crime rate must be attributed in very large part to the desperation of the underclasses. It follows that these people must be stringently controlled. The death penalty must be imposed on those of them who carry their crimes to the point of killing.

When pressed for evidence of the superior deterrent effect of capital punishment, as compared with life imprisonment, Dr. van den Haag will first assert that the lack of evidence does not prove that the death penalty does not deter potential killers; it merely means that statisticians and social scientists have yet to discover a methodology to prove what is self-evident to the ordinary citizen with rudimentary common sense. For those who are unimpressed with this reasoning, he invokes the ancient *lex talionis;* it is right that unlawful killers should themselves be killed.

That is a symmetry that cannot be achieved with respect to any other crime. Rapists cannot be raped; robbers cannot be robbed; burglars cannot be burglarized. The state cannot retaliate against these criminals by treating them as they treated their victims. It is nevertheless possible for the state to kill, as it must—in my righteous opponent's opinion—when a man or a woman stands convicted of murder. Only because murder, the crime of crimes, is punishable by death is it regarded with proper horror. Any lesser response would trivialize the death of an innocent victim.

I say that nothing can trivialize murder. Good men and women abhor violence and particularly abhor it when it is homicidal. To suppose that ordinary citizens will accept murder as a matter of course unless the executioner impresses the horror of it upon them is to state a case for which there is not the slightest supporting evidence. It is a misanthropic fallacy that emerges from the most pessimistic misinterpretation of Freudian doctrine—that all human beings are potential killers, restrained from acting on their primitive and destructive urges only by the threat of extreme punishment. The truth is that in this violent country, where the punishment of criminals is more severe than in any other nation except the Soviet Union and South Africa, fewer than 20,000 murderers are found each year—less than .01% of our total population. Even if we adjust the population at risk by discounting the infants and the aged, even if we allow for the murders that take place and are not recognized as such, and even if we allow for the murderous assaults in which the victim survived, our annual crop of killers could not exceed .05% of the population. Perhaps there is another .05% of potential killers who have abstained from murder for one reason or another, and we have 0.1% of the population to worry about. Call for a ten-year cohort of these killers and potential killers and we can elevate the danger level to 1%. But what reason is there to believe that the remaining 99% are restrained only by the threat of the hangman? Is a society imbued with this belief about its members better than a nation of paranoids?

I insist that the murderer is an exceptional person and so is the citizen who can be persuaded only by threats to abstain from acts of violence. Let the reader consider his own experience and his observation of his friends and enemies. How many truly murderous men, women, and children does he know?

The anachronism that is capital punishment originated in an era when physical punishments were all that could be imposed on criminals. In this debate we have both alluded often to the old days when sentences of truly horrifying cruelty were imposed on men and women guilty of crimes far less grave than capital murder. It is a stain on Western civilization that children could be hanged for theft, men could be broken on the rack for robbery, and women burned to death for witchcraft and adultery as recently as the eighteenth and nineteenth centuries, when many of the brightest achievements of European and American culture flowered. It should not have taken so long for a man like Beccaria to emerge with a protest against the evils of punishment as administered in the eighteenth century, or for men like Bentham and Romilly to make their case against the idiocies of nineteenth century criminal justice in England. Not only did it take centuries too long for such men to appear but their opposition was intransigent to the last ditch. The only way to understand the diehards of the times is to remember the dread in the upper classes that upheavals like the French Revolution might take place in their own countries if social controls were eased. Even if a major political convulsion were to be avoided, the security of the comfortable classes required the support of the death penalty. The impassioned arguments in favor of the hangman in both the English Houses of Parliament exposed the transparent apprehensions of the privileged and their trust in the gallows as the best possible prevention of crime. Those were the days when there were over 200 offenses in the statutes that called for execution.

Romilly and his friends prevailed, as did their counterparts elsewhere in Europe. Their success may be partly laid to Yankee ingenuity, which had contributed the penitentiary to the administration of criminal justice. It was adopted with alacrity throughout Europe. The penitentiary is not the brightest gem of American social technology, but it is a feasible alternative to capital punishment. The whip was eliminated for ordinary offenders, and the gallows was reserved for murderers.

The question that I have raised so often in this debate must be confronted again: *Why should we retain capital punishment when a life sentence in prison will serve the deterrent purpose at least as well?*

Implicit in that question is my complete disbelief that there exists a population of potential murderers who would be deterred by the gallows—or the lethal needle—but would proceed with their killings if the worst they could expect was a life sentence in prison. If such extraordinary people exist, a supposition for which there is absolutely no evidence, they would be balanced by an equally extraordinary, and equally hypothetical, few who are tempted to commit murder to achieve the notoriety of public execution. There may be a few in each of these classes, but in the absence of any positive evidence of their existence in significant numbers, no debating points can be claimed for them by either side.

The adequacy of a life sentence in prison as a deterrent to murder—if deterrence is truly our aim—is obvious to those who know what that experience does to the prisoner. The term begins in ignominy. It is lived out in squalor. It ends when youth is long since gone, or, more often than most people know, in the death of the senile in a prison ward for the aged and infirm. Those who fancy that life in prison bears any resemblance to the gaiety of a resort hotel or the luxury of a country club have been beguiled by dishonest demagogues. Commitment to an American prison is a disaster for all but the most vicious human predators, men who discover a false manhood in the abuse of the weak. The unique combination of ennui and chronic dread of one's fellows, of idleness and wasted years, and of lives spent with wicked, vicious, or inane men and women should be—and for most people certainly is—a terrifyingly deterrent prospect. Those who find it tolerable are manifesting the meaninglessness of their lives before commitment.

In his now classic disquisition on punishment, the great Norwegian criminologist, Johannes Andenaes, acknowledged that "it can hardly be denied that any conclusion as to the real nature of general prevention involves a great deal of guess work. Claims based on the 'demands of general prevention,' therefore, can often be used to cloak strictly conservative demands for punishment or mere conservative resistance to change."[2]

Jack Gibbs carries this point a good deal further in his comprehensive survey of thought and rhetoric generated by the deterrence controversy:

> Hypocrisy is not likely to be a question in debates over penal policy when a protagonist either (1) opposes punishment regardless of the deterrence presumably realized or (2) advocates punishment for the sake of retribution alone. However, a party to the debate may endorse punishment, but only *insofar as it deters crime,* meaning that a value judgement at least appears to be contingent on scientific evidence. When that argument is made, hypocrisy does become an issue, and the very notion of scientific evidence becomes disputable. No scientific finding necessarily (i.e., logically) gives rise to a moral conclusion or value judgement, and the compunction to bridge the gap readily leads to personalized evidential criteria. Thus, one may believe that crimes should be punished for the sake of vengeance alone but conceal that belief by arguing that punishment deters crime and dismiss all manner of research findings as irrelevant or insufficient. At the other extreme, if one views punishment as intrinsically wrong, that value judgement can be covertly defended by invoking rigorous criteria for positive evidence of deterrence.[3]

I do not accuse my upright opponent of hypocrisy, but I think the weakness of any case to be made for the superior deterrent effect of the death penalty—as compared to long incarceration—should be apparent to the reader. It is natural in our goal-oriented culture to adopt the deterrent theory. It promises to accomplish steps toward the prevention of the worst of crimes with each cadaver hauled away from the place of execution. Some day, the retentionist hopes, science will justify the killing by showing the effectiveness of capital punishment as measured by the numbers of innocent lives saved. This is the hope that Dr. van den Haag and his friends express so ardently.

It is a hope that will not be realized. The power of the criminal justice system to prevent any category of crimes is very limited. An organized society must administer criminal justice because it cannot ignore crime. Crimes must be punished in the interests of the society's cohesion and solidarity. The methods we have devised to punish criminals will intimidate some of them, will prevent the crimes that imprisoned criminals might commit, and may deter some potential criminals from engaging in violations of the law. To suppose that the criminal justice system can or should prevent crime is to expect too much of it and too little of the larger social system of which criminal justice is only a part.

I contend that the criminal justice system must be process-oriented, not engaged in achieving goals that are beyond its reach. The police should be efficient in apprehending criminals, the courts should be fair in trying them, and the penal system should be humane but secure. The process-oriented hanging of criminals as their just desert for the crime of murder is an archaism surviving from a bygone and primitve age. The assertion that some day it will be shown that it is a necessary deterrent to murder is, at best, a naïve indulgence in wishful thinking.

Throughout this debate I have insisted on the primacy of retributivism in the administration of justice. My utilitarian opponent scorns retributivism as a theory, and in the strict sense in which that word is used by scientists, he may be right.[4] He supposes that deterrence qualifies as a theory because it may be subjected to verification tests. The reader may judge whether Professor van den Haag has cited any tests whatsoever that offer a satisfactory verification of the hypothesis on which his special case of the deterrent "theory" must rest.[5]

I take up my position somewhere between the two extremes defined by Gibbs. I do indeed hold that it is necessary to punish crimes in the interest of retribution.[6] There are enough empirical supports for the notion that punishment will deter in many situations. There are none at all for the notion that the death penalty will deter criminals more effectively than a protracted prison sentence. I do not accept the argument that punishment is intrinsically wrong, but I do hold that punishment must not be inflicted beyond simple necessity. It is not necessary to punish anyone with a sanction more severe than the gravity of the crimes committed and the criminal's record of recidivism for serious crimes. I see no great problem in achieving a consensus on the scale of sanctions, with a life term in prison for the first degree murderer at the apex of the scale.

The rule is that we should punish no more than we must. The death penalty is needless in an age when the maximum-security prison is available. Adherence to the principle of necessity as the limiting factor in determining the nature and quality of punishment will go far toward preventing our nation from ever descending to the horrible depths of degraded justice that are to be seen in Eastern Europe, in South Africa, and in Argentina.

The executioner does what he has to do in behalf of the citizens of the state that employs him. His hand is on the lever that releases the cyanide, switches on the current, or springs the trap. We, as citizens, cannot escape a full share of his responsibility. We voted into office the legislators who make killers of us all. If the deliberate killing of another human being is the most abhorrent of crimes, we are all guilty, even though we shall be scot-free from legal punishment. The pity and terror that an execution inspires in even the most callous is punishment enough for the perceptive citizen. Pity and terror, mixed with the knowledge that what has been done is futile.

As my stoical opponent has repeatedly reminded us, we must all die. Many of us will die in conditions far more painful than sudden oblivion from a whiff of gas or a lethal charge of electricity. None of us has to inflict death on another. The statutes that make such deaths occasionally possible must be repealed in the interest of decency and good conscience. The sooner the better.

Notes

1. Thomas Hobbes, *Leviathan, or the Matter, Forme, and Power of a Commonwealth* (London: Andrew Crooke, 1651; Penguin Books, 1975), p. 186.
2. Johannes Andenaes, *Punishment and Deterrence* (Ann Arbor: University of Michigan Press, 1974), pp. 9–10.
3. Jack Gibbs, *Crime, Punishment and Deterrence* (New York, Oxford, and Amsterdam: Elsevier, 1975), pp. 9–10.
4. On the usage, "theories of punishment," to which Dr. van den Haag has objected, see H. L. A. Hart, *Punishment and Responsibility* (Oxford: Clarendon Press, 1968), p. 70: "theories of punishment are not theories in any normal sense. They are not, as scientific theories are, assertions or contentions as to what is or is not the case. . . . On the contrary, those major positions concerning punishment which are called deterrent or retributive or reformative 'theories' of punishment are *moral* claims as to what justifies the practice of punishment—claims as to why, morally, it should or may be used." Hart goes on to write that if we claim that capital punishment protects society from harm, then we should call "this implicit moral claim 'the utilitarian position.'" I agree with Hart's fastidious use of terms, but the word *theory* is by now too deeply embedded in criminological discourse to be summarily uprooted.
5. By "special case," of course, I mean the deterrence that is ascribed to capital punishment that is beyond the reach of life imprisonment.
6. I readily concede that I am too squeamish to justify punishment for the sake of vengeance. I insist that there is a significant difference between primitive vengeance—the *lex talionis* of Hammurabi, Leviticus, and the Twelve Tables of republican Rome—and the denunciatory, reprobative functions of retribution.

CHAPTER 16

The Advocate Advocates

ERNEST VAN DEN HAAG

There are two basic arguments for the death penalty; they are independent of, yet consistent with, one another.

The first argument is moral: The death penalty is just; it is deserved for certain crimes. One can explain why one feels that certain crimes deserve the death penalty. But as usual with moral arguments, one cannot show this conviction to be *factually* correct (or, for that matter, incorrect) since moral arguments rest not on facts but on our evaluation of them. My evaluation leads me to believe that, e.g., premeditated murder or treason (a fact) is so grave and horrible a crime (an evaluation) as to deserve nothing less than the death penalty, that only the death penalty (a fact) is proportionate to the gravity of the crime (an evaluation).

My widely shared view is opposed by abolitionists, who claim that the death penalty is unjust for any crime, and inconsistent with human dignity. Professor Conrad's arguments in favor of this position seem unconvincing to me. Since most abolitionists believe, as I do, that punishments should be proportionate to the perceived gravity of crimes, the abolitionist claim seems to me logically precarious. It implies either that murder is not so horrible after all—not horrible enough, at any rate, to deserve death—or that the death penalty is too harsh a punishment for it, and indeed for any conceivable crime. I find it hard to believe that one can hold either view seriously, let alone both. But I am wrong: Professor Conrad does, and he is by no means alone in the academic world.

I must confess that I have never understood the assorted arguments claiming that the death penalty is inconsistent with human dignity or that, somehow, society has no right to impose it. One might as well claim that death generally, or at least death from illness, is inconsistent with human dignity, or that birth is, or any suffering or any undesirable social condition. Most of these are unavoidable. At least death by execution can be avoided by not killing someone else, by not committing murder. One can preserve one's dignity in this respect if one values it. Incidentally, execution may be physically less humiliating and painful than death in a hospital. It is, however, morally more humiliating and meant to be: It indicates the extreme blame we attach to the crime of murder by deliberately expelling the murderer from among the living.

As for the dignity of society, it seems to me that by executing murderers it tries to keep its promise to secure the lives of innocents, to vindicate the law, and to impose retribution on those who so horribly violate it. To do anything less would be inconsistent with the dignity of society.

I see no evidence for society somehow not having "the right" to execute murderers. It has always done so. Traditional laws and Scriptures have always supported the death penalty. I know of no reasoning, even in a religious (theocratic) state, that denies the right of secular courts to impose it. We in America have a secular republic, of course, and therefore, the suggestion that the right to punish belongs only to God, or that the right to impose capital punishment does, is clearly out of place. It is not a religious but a secular task to put murderers to death. Our Constitution does provide for it (Amendments V and XIV). However much we believe in divine justice, it is to occur after, not in, this life. As for justice here and now, it is done by the courts, which are authorized in certain cases to impose the death penalty. A secular state cannot leave it to God. And incidentally, no theocratic state ever has. If they make mistakes, one can hope that God will correct the courts hereafter—but this is no ground for depriving courts of their duty to impose the penalties provided by law where required, nor is it a ground for depriving the law of the ability to prescribe the punishments felt to be just, including the death penalty.

The second argument in favor of capital punishment is material, grounded on empirical facts. They are contested, as readers of this book know, but no one would deny that what is contested are facts. The factual question is: Does the death penalty deter murder more than life imprisonment, or does it make no difference?

I do not agree with Professor Conrad's wishful idea that the work of Professor Isaac Ehrlich has been discredited. I believe that Ehrlich's findings—that the death penalty does indeed deter more than any other penalty currently inflicted, so that each execution saves between seven and nine innocent lives, the lives of victims who will not be murdered in the year of execution because of the deterrent effects of executions—have been confirmed by subsequent studies and have stood up sturdily under criticism competent and incompetent, which Ehrlich has convincingly refuted. However, Ehrlich's work is controversial. Anything is, if a sufficient number of people attack it. It is fair, therefore, to say that although the preponderance of evidence is now supporting the hypothesis that capital punishment deters more than any other punishment, the statistical demonstration has not been conclusive enough to convince everybody. Certainly not Professor Conrad and his friends. They have not changed their pre-Ehrlich convictions, and indeed tend to dismiss his work.

But Conrad's fellow abolitionists have admitted that they would want to abolish the death penalty even if it were shown statistically that each execution does reduce the homicide rate by 500 murders per year. Why then worry about statistical proof? And why take seriously people so irrational that they would sacrifice the lives of 500 innocents to preserve the life of one convicted murderer?

Statistics have their place. But here I think they scarcely are needed. Harsher penalties are more deterrent than milder ones. Not only does our whole criminal justice system accept this view; we all do to the extent to which deterrence is aimed at in our everyday life. All other things equal, we penalize our children, our friends, or our business partners the more harshly the more we feel we must deter them and others in the future from a wrong they have done. Social life would not be possible if we did not believe that we can attract people to actions we desire by giving them incentives, and deter them from actions we do not desire by disincentives. The incentives and disincentives are usually proportionate to the felt desirability or undesirability of what we want to attract to or deter from. Why should murder be an exception? Why should we not believe that the greatest disincentive—the threat of death—is most likely to be the greatest deterrent?

Where there is life there is hope. This certainly is one major argument in favor of the death penalty. The murderer who premeditates his crime—and crimes of passion are not subject to capital punishment—if he contemplates the risk of life imprisonment is not likely to believe that, if convicted, he will remain in prison for life. He knows, however inchoately, about parole, pardons, commutations—he believes above all that he, a smart and superior fellow, will find a way to escape. Few prisoners actually do escape. But practically all "lifers" believe that they will, at least when they start their sentence. So believing, they do not greatly fear a sentence of life imprisonment and are not deterred by it. This is why the rate of stranger-murders—murders in which victim and murderer do not know one another and to which the threat of the death penalty should apply—as a proportion of all murders has steadily climbed in the last twenty years. The murderers knew that in practice they would get away with life imprisonment, from which they would be paroled after a few years. Or they hoped they would escape. After all, we executed all of five prisoners in 1981, only one of whom was executed against his wishes. (All of them were white, to the great disappointment of the civil liberties lobby.) At this rate no murderer can foresee execution or be deterred by it.

I find it hard to believe, as Professor Conrad does, that most men are incapable of murder. I admire his optimism. But I find it hard to share. I do not see how he can cling to his faith after Stalin and Hitler, in the presence of assorted tyrants and murderers in power from Albania to Iran to China. But faith obviously is not subject to empirical verification. I am optimistic, however, in my own way, which seems more realistic to me: I believe that most men can be deterred from murder by the threat of the death penalty.

Even if Conrad were right, even if his claim that only a few men would ever become murderers in the absence of the threat of punishment were correct, I should continue to advocate the death penalty to deter these few men. And even if only some of these men need the threat of capital punishment to be deterred, while others would be deterred by the threat of life imprisonment, I should advocate the death penalty to deter the very few who, according to Conrad, do, or even just may, require it to be deterred. The lives of the innocents that will or may be spared because of the death penalty are more valuable to me, and to any civilized society, than the lives of murderers. I do not want to risk their lives for the sake of the lives of murderers.

The reader will have to decide for himself on which side he wants to be.

Index

Aquinas, Saint Thomas, 270
Agnew, Spiro, 168
American Civil Liberties Union, 15, 70,
  161, 177, 183, 189, 275
Andenaes, Johannes, 133, 145, 294
Apprehension, 77, 81, 103, 109, 111, 154,
  216
Arrest, 77, 78, 128
Atonement, 26–27, 34–35, 42

Baldus, David C. (and Cole, James L.),
  149, 154–156
Barbarization, 242–243, 248
Beccaria, Cesare, 21, 24, 46–47, 145, 241,
  292
Bedau, Hugo Adam, viii, ixn, 70, 73,
  275
Bentham, Jeremy, 24, 78
  Greatest Happiness Principle, 265–266,
  269, 292
Beyleveld, Deryck, 140
Bill of Rights, 163
Black, Justice Charles, 70, 73, 205, 222n,
  275
Blackmun, Justice Harry, 174 (dissent in
  Furman v. Georgia)
Blackstone, William, 165–166
Blacks, 174, 206, 212–213, 280
  see also Discrimination
Bowers, William (and Pierce, Glenn L.),
  "Brutalization Hypothesis," 140,
  144
Brennan, Justice William J., Jr. (in
  Furman v. Georgia), 165
Bugliosi, Vincent, 110–111

Camus, vi
Canadian data, 137–139, 143, 147–148, 155
  see also Fattah, Ezzat Abdel
Capital punishment
  appeals, 3, 15
  caprice in, 211–212
  comparisons, contiguous states, 146,
  237–238, 240
  cost, 24–25, 34, 41
  as constitutional question, 157–200
  decline in recent years in U.S., 160–161,
  169–171, 177–178, 201, 273
  discrimination in, 206–207, 223–226
  as deterrent, 11, 63–129, 133–156
  of innocents, 11, 55, 59–60, 221–222,
  225–226, 228
  irrevocability of, 257–258
  as judicial matter, 158–161, 171–175,
  180–181, 185–187
  vs. life imprisonment, 42, 64, 134
  special cases, 233–240
  as suicide, 15, 26, 183, 189–190
  symbolic value, 209, 259, 273–282
  trend in other countries, 34, 262–263,
  267–268
  volunteers for, 34
  see also Execution; Punishment; Public
  opinion
Chessman, Caryl, 2–4, 90–91
Clark, Ramsey, 70, 73, 275
Clearance rates of crimes, 77, 84, 86, 103,
  111, 119, 179
Clemenceau, Georges, 162
Cloward, Richard A. (and Ohlin, Lloyd
  E.), 114, 124

Coker v. Georgia, 433 U.S. 485 (1977), 190, 203

Cole, James W. L. (and Baldus, David C.), 149, 154–155

Comparative statistics, 135–137, 146–147

Consequentialism, 37

Constitution, 182, 204–205, 207–209, 214–215, 271
see also Bill of Rights; Eighth, Fifth, Fourth and Thirteenth Amendments; Double Jeopardy Clause; Supreme Court

Crimes, 63, 78, 89, 97, 106, 172, 235
capital (defined), 64
of passion, 88, 91, 253 (defined), 253–256

Crime statistics, 97–98, 150, 178–179, 201–202

Criminals, career, 63, 85, 99–100, 249
calculation of risks, 72

Criminology, 49, 52

Cruelty, 164–167, 203–204, 211 (defined)
unnecessary, 14–15, 157–158
see also Eighth Amendment

Dean, John, 168

Declaration of Independence, 53, 261

Deserters and spies, 234, 238–239

Deterrence, 11, 29, 33, 53, 56, 60–61, 63–129, 134, 141, 145, 275
empirical support, 65, 67–68, 71, 134, 153, 291–296, 140
argument against deterrence as object of capital punishment, 75
credible threats, *see* Sellin, Thorsten
and habit formation, 120–121, 246, 250, 281
pickpocket anecdote, 244–226, 249–250
as secondary function of punishment, 87
public opinion on, 181–182

Dignity
human, 262–263, 267, 276, 297–298
societal, 9–10, 298

Dike, Sarah, 92

Discretion, 211, 226

Double jeopardy clause, 217, 287

Douglas, William O., 163, 180

Drug addicts, 153, 155

Drunken drivers, 92–93, 102, 108–109, 116, 126–127, 131

Durkheim, Emile, 36, 39–41, 44, 48–49

Eighth Amendment ("Cruel and Unusual Punishment" prohibition), v, 157–158, 164–166, 172–173, 180–187, 103–105, 207–209, 213–215, 218, 277

Egalitarianism, 17–18, 274

Ehrlich, Isaac, 65, 128–129, 139–140, 143–144, 146–150, 154–156, 291, 298–299

Ehrlichman, John, 168

Ellsworth, P. C., and Ross, L. P., 158n

Emerson, Ralph Waldo, 44

Employment and crime, 115, 127

English Bill of Rights, 164–167
see also Eighth Amendment

Equality (vs. Justice), 223–227

Evelyn, Sir John, 219–220

Evolving standards, 166, 180–182, 184–185, 207, 214–215, 218

Execution
methods of, 14–15, 81, 192–196, 210
public, 210–211, 243–246, 240–250
wait for, 210

Fagan, Judge Steny, 120

Falier, Marin, 194–196, 198–200

Fattah, Ezzat Abdel, 148, 154–155

Fear of death, 15–16, 69, 134, 195, 198, 215, 258–259

Fifth Amendment, 53, 157–158, 172, 206, 261

Forst, Brian, 140, 149

Foucault, Michel, 248

Fourteenth Amendment, 53, 157, 172, 205–206, 227, 261

Furman v. Georgia, 408 U.S. 238 (1972), 159, 160–161, 165, 169, 174, 176

Garland, Bonnie, 288

Gibbs, Jack, 145, 194–195

Gilmore, Gary, 177, 183, 189, 211, 221, 227n

Glaser, Daniel, 134

Golden Rule, 19, 39, 265, 269–271

Granucci, Anthony F., 165

Grogan, Steve, 110–111, 120

Grotius, Hugo, 270

Hamilton, Alexander, 162
Harris, Jean, 288
Hart, H. L. A., 11, 21
Hawkins, Gordon (and Zimring, Franklin),
    141, 145
Hegel, G. W. F., 32, 38, 40–41, 43, 46,
    276
Henry, Patrick, 165, 208
Herrin, Richard, 288
Hinckley, John, 286, 288
Hitmen and contract assassins, 92, 249
Hobbes, Thomas, 278, 282, 291
Hollander, Paul, 160n
Holmes, Justice, 165, 228
Honderich, Ted, 21
Hughes, Chief Justice, 163, 180
Hurtado v. California, 110 U.S. 516
    (1883), 163, 173, 180, 182, 189

Inalienable human right to live, 260–263,
    265–266, 269–270
Income (views on capital punishment), 169,
    182
Injections, lethal, 14, 81, 192, 210
Insanity, 237, 259–260, 281, 283
    see also McNaughtan rule
Intellectuals, views on capital punishment,
    175–176

Jefferson, Thomas (and *lex talionis*), 33,
    45–48, 52 (and natural rights), 242,
    269–270
Johnson, Dr. Samuel, 9
Judiciary, 25, 111
    capital punishment as judicial matter,
        171
    sabotage of death penalty, 14, 34, 148,
        160–162, 174, 177–178
    sentencing discretion, 205
    views on capital punishment, 159–162,
        174–175, 188
    see also Supreme Court
Jus talionis, 22–23
Justice, 55, 61, 224–231, 251
    defined, 224
    distributive, 48
    miscarriages of, 55–56, 59–60, 230–231
    perceived vs. actual, 212–213, 216, 223

Kant, Immanuel, 20–24, 32, 38–41, 43, 74–
    76, 78–79, 190–191, 271, 276
Kaufmann, Walter, 46, 48, 52
Kleindienst, Richard, 168
Koestler, Arthur, 249

Leontief, Wassily, 149–150, 154–156
Leopold, Nathan, 26, 35, 42
Lex talionis, 23–24, 33, 38, 247, 250, 290–
    291
    and Thomas Jefferson, 45–47, 52,
        242
Life imprisonment, 25, 72–73, 257, 263,
    267–268, 299
Locke, John, 270

MacIntyre, Alastair
    on identity, 84–85
Madison, James, 47, 162
Malone, Dumas,
    on Thomas Jefferson, 47
Marshall, Chief Justice in *Hurtado v.
    California,* 173–174
McKenna, Justice in *Weems v. U.S.,* 173,
    218
Mill, John Stuart, 52, 190–191, 191n, 195,
    197, 258
Mitchell, John, 168
McNaughtan rule, 1–2, 264, 283–288
Montesquieu, 24
Morality, v, 38–40, 44, 48, 223–267, 278,
    297
Moynihan, Daniel P., 114n
Murder, defined, 241–242
Murphy, Jeffrie, 38

National Academy of Sciences, 140
Natural rights, 261, 265–266, 268–271
Nicholas, Barry, 28
Nietzsche, 46
Nixon, Richard, 168
Norwich, John Julius, 194

Ohlin, Lloyd E. (and Cloward, Richard
    A.), 114, 124
Olmstead v. U.S., 277 U.S. 438 (1928),
    12n
Orwell, George, 12

Pain, 16, 209, 215–216, 219
Passell, 149
Phillips, Charles, 249
Phillips, David P., 144, 150–151, 243n
Pierce, Glenn (and Bowers, William),
  "Brutalization Hypothesis," 140
Plea bargaining, 41, 211–212, 217, 221,
  286
Police officers, death penalty as protection
  of, 233–239
Poverty (and crime), 114–115, 124–125,
  127
Public opinion, v, 158–160, 163, 167–
  169, 181–182, 187–188, 213, 278,
  289
Punishment, defined, 55, 19–42
  aims of, 19, 53–62, 82, 87
  history of, 13–14
  purposes of, 14, 53–62, 252
  physical, 209–210, 218–219
  justification of, 20–21
  social effects, 31, 37
  proportionality, 20, 37–38, 44, 60–62,
    165, 203–204, 209–210, 277, 299
  continuity of, 42, 209
  threatened, 29, 56–57, 63–64, 68, 72
  incentives and disincentives, 96–97, 104,
    113–114, 123, 299
  symmetry to crime, 242, 291
  effectiveness of, 56–57
  see also Capital punishment; Execution;
    Deterrence; Life imprisonment;
    Retribution; Rehabilitation

Quinton, Anthony, 36, 43

Radzinowicz, Sir Leon, 179n, 248
Recidivism, 54
Rehabilitation, 45, 49–50, 53–55, 57359,
  260, 264
Religion, 32, 198–199, 206, 247–248, 251,
  260–262, 265–266, 274
Restitution, 35
Retribution, 17–52, 59, 146, 246–248, 250,
  277, 280–281, 295
Revenge, 246, 250, 277

Rewards, 18
  symmetry between rewards and
    punishment, 18, 31, 39, 96–97
Rieff, Philip, 283
Riley, Leanderess, 6–7, 10
Risk–reward ratio, 97, 101
Romilly, 292–293
Ross, Alf, 20, 29
Ross, L. (and Ellsworth, P. C.), on public
  opinion, 158
Rowe, Alan R. (and Tittle, Charles), 96–
  97, 105, 115, 122, 126

San Quentin Condemned Row, 1–12, 87
Sanctity of life, 274–276
Schwarzchild, Henry, 70, 275
Sellin, Thorsten, 135–137, 140–141, 143,
  146–147, 236–238, 240
Singer, Barry, 113, 122
Skinner, B. F., 104–105, 113, 122–123,
  127n
Solzhenitsyn, Aleksander, 208
de Staël, Mme. Anne Louise, 195, 197
Stephen, Sir James Fitzjames, 23, 30–31,
  50–52, 99, 112, 121–122, 134, 166–
  167, 185, 219, 277
Story, Joseph, 165–166
Stranger-to-stranger murders, 77, 99, 255
Students, and deterrence experiments, 96,
  105, 115, 122, 133
Supreme Court, v, 158–161, 163, 171–175,
  177–178, 180, 183–187, 217
Sutherland, Edwin H., 113

Tarnower, Herman, 288
Temple, Archbishop William, 21, 26–27,
  32, 40–43
Thirteenth Amendment, 227
Thucydides, 93
Tittle, Charles (and Rowe, Alan R.), 96–
  97, 105, 115, 122, 126
de Tocqueville, Alexis, 186, 219–220
Tolstoy, Leo, 100–101
Torture, 13, 76, 80, 235, 239
Trop v. Dulles, 356 U.S. 86 (1957), 166,
  208
Tullock, Gordon, 156n

"Unusual" punishment, defined, 203, 205
    see also Eighth Amendment
Utilitarianism, 19–20, 33, 41, 59, 225

Voltaire, 241, 279n

Waldo, Gordon P., 134
Warren, Chief Justice, 208, 218

Weems v. U.S., 217 U.S. 349 (1909), 166,
    173, 182, 189, 218, 277
Wythe, George, 47

Zeisel, Hans, 151
Zeno, 68, 71–72
Zimring, Franklin E. (and Hawkins,
    Gordon J.), on deterrence, 141, 145

Index to

The Modern Theatre

		Orig. Vol., Page
Anonymous	He's Much To Blame	IV, 163
Anonymous	Matilda	VIII, 1
Anonymous	The School for Wives	IX, 233
Anonymous	What Is She?	X, 217
Cobb, James	Ramah Droog	VI, 139
Cobb, James	The Wife of Two Husbands	VI, 75
Colman, George	The English Merchant	IX, 165
Colman, George	Who Wants a Guinea?	III, 207
Cowley, Mrs.	Which Is The Man?	X, 149
Cumberland, Richard	False Impressions	V, 1
Cumberland, Richard	The Box-Lobby Challenge	V, 137
Cumberland, Richard	The Carmelite	V, 283
Cumberland, Richard	The Imposters	VI, 1
Cumberland, Richard	The Mysterious Husband	V, 69
Cumberland, Richard	The Natural Son	V, 215
Dibdin, Thomas	The School for Prejudice	IV, 331
Holcroft, Thomas	Duplicity	IV, 1
Holcroft, Thomas	Seduction	IV, 253
Holcroft, Thomas	The School for Arrogance	IV, 75
Holman, J. G.	The Votary of Wealth	III, 1
Hull, Thomas	Henry The Second, or The Fall of Rosamond	IX, 337
Inchbald, Mrs.	I'll Tell You What	VII, 1
Inchbald, Mrs.	Next Door Neighbours	VII, 68
Inchbald, Mrs.	The Wise Man of the East	VII, 116
Jephson, Robert	Braganza	VI, 263
Jephson, Robert	The Law of Lombardy	VI, 193
Lee, Miss	The Chapter of Accidents	IX, 81
Macready, William	The Bank Note	IX, 1
Macnally, Leonard	Fashionable Levities	X, 1
More, Hannah	Percy	VII, 181
Morton, Thomas	Secrets Worth Knowing	III, 141
Morton, Thomas	Zorinski	III, 85
O'Keeffe, John	Lie of a Day	X, 299
Philon, Frederic	He Would Be A Soldier	VIII, 225
Reynolds, Frederick	Folly As It Flies	II, 287
Reynolds, Frederick	Fortune's Fool	II, 219
Reynolds, Frederick	How To Grow Rich	I, 217
Reynolds, Frederick	Laugh When You Can	II, 145
Reynolds, Frederick	Life	I, 143
Reynolds, Frederick	Notoriety	I, 279
Reynolds, Frederick	Speculation	II, 1
Reynolds, Frederick	The Delinquent	II, 75
Reynolds, Frederick	The Rage	I, 67
Reynolds, Frederick	Werter	III, 291
Reynolds, Frederick	The Will	I, 1
Reynolds, Frederick	The Fugitive	VIII, 133
Sheridan, Richard B.	A Trip to Scarborough	VII, 237
Siddon, Henry	Time's A Tell-Tale	X, 81
St. John, John	Mary Queen of Scots	VIII, 67
Watson, George	England Preserved	VIII, 309

THE MODERN THEATRE

A collection of plays

selected by

MRS. ELIZABETH INCHBALD

First published London, 1811

in ten volumes

Reissued in 1968
in five volumes
by Benjamin Blom, Inc.

Benjamin Blom, Inc.

New York

THE

MODERN THEATRE;

A COLLECTION OF

SUCCESSFUL MODERN PLAYS,

AS ACTED AT

THE THEATRES ROYAL, LONDON.

PRINTED FROM THE PROMPT BOOKS UNDER THE AU-
THORITY OF THE MANAGERS.

SELECTED BY

MRS INCHBALD.

—

IN TEN VOLUMES.

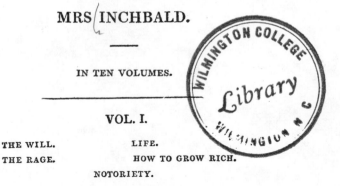

VOL. I.

THE WILL.	LIFE.
THE RAGE.	HOW TO GROW RICH.
	NOTORIETY.

LONDON:

PRINTED FOR LONGMAN, HURST, REES, ORME, AND BROWN,
PATERNOSTER-ROW.

1811.

First published London, 1811
Reissued 1968,
by Benjamin Blom, Inc. Bx 10452

Library of Congress Catalog Card No. 67-13004

THE

WILL;

A

COMEDY,

IN FIVE ACTS.

AS IT IS PERFORMED AT THE

THEATRE-ROYAL, DRURY-LANE.

BY

FREDERICK REYNOLDS.

DRAMATIS PERSONÆ.

SIR SOLOMON CYNIC	*Mr King.*
MANDEVILLE	*Mr Wroughton.*
HOWARD	*Mr Bannister, Jun.*
VERITAS	*Mr R. Palmer.*
REALIZE	*Mr Suett.*
ROBERT	*Mr Russell.*
OLD COPSLEY	*Mr Packer.*
Servants to SIR SOLOMON	{ *Mr Evans.* { *Mr Webb.*
ALBINA MANDEVILLE	*Mrs Jordan.*
MRS RIGID	*Mrs Booth.*
CICELY COPSLEY	*Miss Mellon.*
DEBORAH	*Miss Tidswell.*

SCENE—Devonshire.

WILL.

ACT THE FIRST.

SCENE I.

The Gate of Mandeville Castle, and View of surrounding Country.

Enter MANDEVILLE *and* ROBERT.

Rob. Joy! I give you joy, sir!—Once more welcome to Mandeville Castle!—Look, sir!—there stands the old pile, just as we left it fourteen years ago! Shall I knock at the gate?

Man. Lose not a moment. (Robert *knocks.*) I have travelled far to have the mystery unravelled; and till I know why I have been thus treated—why for three tedious years I have received no letter from my father—no tidings of my child—the interval is insupportable!

Rob. Pretty treatment, indeed, sir!—to bring two gentlemen from India—all the way from the shores of Bengal to the coast of Devonshire—only to get an answer to our letters!

Man. Didn't I write by every packet?—regularly remit half my pay for the support of my daughter?

—And to receive no answer!—to hear nothing from my father, or Mrs Rigid, the governess of my child!—What—what can be the motive of their silence?——In India, I have been guilty of no vices—no extravagance!—and if, before I went, I involved myself in pecuniary embarrassments, was it not to serve a friend?

Rob. It was, sir.—You became security for the ungrateful Mr Howard; and because he took it into his head to die, and leave you responsible for twenty thousand pounds—

Man. We were compelled to fly to India.—Well —well—blame not Howard: if he had lived, he would have proved himself deserving of my friendship. But now, Robert, I am here once more in the centre of my creditors; and if my father has forgotten me—Knock again—the suspence is dreadful.

Rob. (*Knocks.*) Surely, they are all run away, or drowned, or hanged——Hanged!—I beg pardon, sir!—I only allude to the female part of the family —and I dare say many a fair neck has been twisted in consequence of my absence.——Not come yet!— Nay: don't fret so, sir,—the worst come to the worst, we can but make the same exit we did this time fourteen years.

Man. How?

Rob. Can't you remember our stealing out of those gates in disguise?—our being found out by the bailiffs, and dodging them so artfully from place to place, that by the time they had taken out a writ in one county, we were safely perched in another; till at last, after having outwitted half the sheriffs' officers and attorneys in England, we secured our retreat by arriving at Portsmouth late on Saturday night, and sailing for India early on Sunday morning!——Ha, ha, ha!—I shall never forget the captain's smoking us, and after dinner giving for a toast—" Success to the Sunday-men!"

Man. Hush! who comes here?—Old Realize, my father's steward!—Now we shall get information.—Observe!

Enter REALIZE *and* COPSLEY.

Real. Don't talk to me, you old poacher! Hav'n't you been repeatedly warned off Sir Solomon's manor, and didn't he himself see you kill the hare on his ground?—And therefore, at Sir Solomon's request, I dismiss you from being gamekeeper to the Mandeville manors.

Cop. Consider—consider, Mr. Realize!—I am an old servant, and am as innocent of poaching—

Real. You were caught in the fact; and therefore I dismiss you, and appoint in your place—

(ROBERT *comes up to him.*)

Rob. Me, Mr. Steward!—honest Bob Tickwell! —How are you, my old friend?—how are you?— Here we are, you see—hot from Bengal!

Real. Why, it can't be!—Yes: it is!—The long-look'd for come at last!—Huzza!

Man. Realize, I am glad to see you.

Real. So am I to see you; and so will Sir Solomon; and so will all the neighbours.

Rob. There!—I said so!—I knew we should have a joyous welcome!—Come! open wide the castle gates, and prepare the wine—the venison—

Real. Open wide the prison gates, and prepare the bread and water!—Mr. Mandeville, (*To* MANDEVILLE.) sir, I'll trouble you for that two hundred pounds you owe me!

Rob. Psha!—this isn't a proper time—

Real. Where is my money, sir?

Rob. Nonsense! His father will satisfy you.—— Come—we'll all pay the old gentleman a visit together. (*Laying hold of* REALIZE'S *arm.*)

Real. Softly, master Robert—You may both go to

the old gentleman as soon as you like; but, for me,
I don't intend to pay him a visit these twenty years.

Man. No!—Why, where is he?

Real. Where, I can't exactly say—only I fancy
you are about as far from him now as when you were
hot in Bengal.

Man. What, is he gone abroad?

Real. No; he's gone home!—he's dead!—de-
funct!—was b' ried twelve months ago!

Man. Dead!—My father dead!—I didn't expect this. (*Putting his handkerchief to his eyes.*)

Rob. No more did I, sir—Oh! h! h! (*Weeping
violently.*)

Real. Why, what's the milksop crying at?

Rob. I'm crying to think what trouble old Mr
Mandeville's death will occasion to my poor master
—What a fatigue it will be to collect in all the rents
—to pay his debts—to discharge you, and appoint
me steward in your place—Oh! h! h!

Real. Indeed!—If that's all that afflicts you, dry
up your tears, booby—your master is disinherited.

Rob. Disinherited!

Real. Cut off with a shilling!—Mr. Mandeville
has left his whole estate to a woman.

Rob. A woman!—Oh! the old profligate!

Real. To your child, sir, (*To* MANDEVILLE)—to
his own grand daughter!

Man. To Albina!

Rob. Bravo!—Then it comes to the same point:
—my master of course manages the property, and
I'm steward still.

Real. There you're out again! I rather think Mrs
Rigid will manage the property. I rather imagine
the young heiress will be ruled by the old governess;
and as you've been no friend to her, Mr. Mandeville——

Mand. No friend to her!—How?

Real. Nay: perhaps you may call it friendship to
leave her to support your daughter at her own ex-

pence ; perhaps you may call it friendship, not to write any letters, or remit any money, for three years together.

Man. Go on, sir, and let me know all.

Real. Why then you may know, that Mrs Rigid informed the late Mr Mandeville of your unfather-like conduct ; that he invited her and his grand-daughter to his house, and taking a fancy to Miss Albina, he made her his heiress.—There—now you've heard the whole story; and I shall call it friendship if you'll pay me my two hundred pounds.

Man. Not write letters !—Not remit money !— Hear me, sir.

Real. Not now.—The heiress is expected from Dover every moment, and I must go and prepare the Castle for her reception. Come along, poacher ; come and deliver your keys to your successor——I'll take out a writ directly, and he sha'n't slip through my fingers a second time—(*Aside.*) No more dis-guises, Mr Mandeville—No more Sunday-men, Mr Steward.—" Oh ! what trouble will the old gentle-man's death occasion to my poor master !" (*Mimick-ing* ROBERT, *and exit with* COPSLEY *at the Castle Gate.*)

Rob. Now all's out, sir. No wonder at our not receiving answers, when they say we sent no letters. Oh that diabolical governess !—I always said you were to blame, to place your only child under her care, particularly when you knew she was once in love with you, and you refused her, and married her cousin, Miss Herbert.

Man. Oh, name not her !—If my Amelia had survived, I should not have been doomed unheard ! —What ! deserted ! disinherited !—Is this my wel-come home ? Am I to find a father dead, and dying full of resentment against me ? a daughter preju-diced ! nay, perhaps, cursing my very name, and this governess——Speak, sir—justify your injured master.

Rob. I will with my life, sir; but don't be satisfied with Realize's story : let us get information elsewhere.   Yonder is the house of Sir Solomon Cynic. If the old gentleman hasn't fretted away his life by railing at the follies of womankind, perhaps he lives to console and befriend you.   Shall we go to him, sir ?

Man. Take me where you will.   (*Going, stops.*) Robert, how old was Albina when we last saw her ?

Rob. About four years, sir.

Man. And I left her in the fond hope, that I might one day find in her a recompense for the loss of her mother !   And now if I behold her, she will avoid, upbraid me !—That thought is past all bearing.   I'll know the worst, and then my fate's decided.   They may desert, but they shall not despise me !   [*Exeunt.*

SCENE II.

An Apartment in SIR SOLOMON'S *House.*

Enter SIR SOLOMON, *followed by* CICELY.

Sir Sol. I tell you, it's in vain—your application's useless—you are useless—your whole sex is useless.

Cic. Nay, Sir Solomon—

Sir Sol. I tell you women are of no use—none ; but to nurse children, mend linen, make puddings, and beat their husbands.

Cic. But consider, your honour, the hare was killed by accident, not by design ; the dogs chased it into your grounds ; and I hope Mr Realize won't dismiss my poor father——

Sir Sol. Keep off—keep within your magic circle
—I hav'n't been within the reach of a woman these
twenty years ; and you are the very last I'd suffer to
come near me. I have often observed you in my
walks—often noted your mischievous smiles, your
penetrating eyes, and I don't like them—I say I
don't like them—so keep your distance. I won't be
made a fool of a second time

Cic. A second time, Sir Solomon !

Sir Sol. Aye ; I was once as much in love as
Mark Antony, and like him I was deserted by my
Cleopatra. His queen chose a mighty conqueror to
be false with ; but my Susannah, my fantastic Susannah, fixed her affections on a dancing-master—a
caperer ! and ever since I have had such a contempt
for the sex—(CICELY *lays hold of his hand.*)——
Holloa ! you touched me ! I feel the shock—I'm
electrified—I'm——What sweet lips the gipsy has !

Cic. If you would only pay a visit to our cottage, and be eye-witness to the distress you will occasion ! Your nephew, Mr Howard, has often been
there ; and if you would come and imitate his charitable conduct, I and my sisters would be so grateful—(*Still laying hold of his hand.*)

Sir Sol. Your sisters ! Pooh ! nonsense ! what
should I do amongst a parcel of young, giddy, romp-
ing——Hark'ye ! are all your sisters as handsome as
yourself ?

Cic. Handsome !—How you flatter, Sir Solomon !

Sir Sol. I don't—You're the most lovely, most
bewitching—Susannah was a dowdy to you ! Look
here, now—look at the omnipotence of Love !—a
man is never secure from its influence ; and if he
lives independent of the sex till he is so old and de-
crepid that he cannot stir from his bed, yet then,
even then, he may fall a victim to its power.

Cic. 'Tis Mr Howard !—Now I'll ask him to intercede for me.

Sir Sol. Howard?—So it is! and somebody with
him—Go—don't let us be seen together—I'll come
to the cottage soon after sun-set; and if the hare
was really killed by accident———Hush!—begone,
no caressing—we'll reserve all that for by and by—
(CICELY *exit.*)—So—I have once more the true
Mark Antony feel.

Enter MANDEVILLE *and* HOWARD.

Sir Sol. Hark'ye, George! don't let me hear of
your paying any more visits at the game-keeper's
cottage. If I do, a certain young lady shall know of
your inconstancy—-your—(*Sees* MANDEVILLE.)—
Ha! who's that?

How. A stranger, sir, that——

Sir Sol. Stranger!—Why, it's Mandeville!—that
profligate Mandeville!—What brought you from India, sir?—And after what has passed, how dare you
show your face in my house?

Man. How!—You against me too!—what have
I done?

Sir Sol. What have you not done, sir? Hav'n't
you deserted your own child?—Hav'n't you left the
governess to maintain her at her own expense?

Man. 'Tis false; on my life, 'tis false!—I wrote
letter after letter, made repeated remittances; till,
receiving no answer, and unable to endure such torturing suspense, I came at all hazards to England,
to know why I was so harshly treated.

Sir Sol. And now you know that your father has
made Albina his heiress—that she is shortly to be
married to Mr Veritas—to this gentleman's tutor,
sir—and you may also know, that I expect you instantly to discharge the late Mr Howard's debt for
twelve hundred pounds.

How. Mr Howard's debt!—My father's?

Sir Sol. Yes, sir:—Mr Mandeville was his surety.
I have his bond; and, had he behaved as he ought,

I'd have died rather than have asked him for it; but now——

Enter a Servant in Livery.

Ser. Sir, Miss Albina and her governess are this moment arrived at the castle.

Sir Sol. Are they? I'll wait upon them directly. Mr Mandeville, don't expect to see your daughter; for, till she is married to the tutor, Mrs Rigid means to seclude her from all society. And for you, George Howard, you must not associate with a man of his character. Though your father behaved ill to him, remember you are not responsible for his ingratitude. Now for the castle—next for the cottage, and then—All for Love, or the World well lost. [*Exit.*

Man. Then all's confirmed; and I've no hope— no friend!—What's to be done?—Whither shall I go?—where fly?—Who will receive so lost a wretch as I am?—Pursued by enemies—abandoned by a father—forsaken by my child!—who will, who dare befriend me!

How. I will.

Man. You!

How. You have forgot me, Mr Mandeville—I see you have. You don't recollect George Howard, whom, when a boy, you used to take such notice of —I'm strangely altered since you went to India— that is, in person only, I hope; for in mind and disposition I am still the same.

Man. Are you?

How. Oh, Mr Mandeville! I don't know why— Whether it is from the joy at seeing you, or from the grief I feel at the cruel treatment you've received—I don't know which it is—but I'm going to be the same blubbering boy you left me.

Man. Indeed!—'Sdeath! this generosity affects me more than all their cruelty!—Let me go—I heard your uncle's orders,—" You must not asso·

ciate with a man of his character."—Let me begone.
I will not involve you.

How. Not involve me! Didn't my father involve
you? And if I've not the fortune to repay the obligation, I'll prove I have the gratitude to remember
it. From this hour, I am devoted to your service;
and, if the friendship of the son can atone for the injuries of the parent, I shall be far happier in parta-
king your distresses, than in sharing my unfeeling
uncle's riches.

Man. I am most grateful; but I cannot consent.

How. You must—-you shall consent!—-Come,
come—your case is not so lost as you imagine. The
governess isn't the only person who has an influence
over your daughter—there is another——

Man. Who? This tutor?

How. No! his pupil. I flatter myself Albina has
no slight partiality for her father's friend.

Man. For you! How, and where, did you know
her?

How. I'll tell you. When I and my tutor arrived
from the grand tour, we found Albina and the governess at Dover. Mr Veritas and Mrs Rigid being
related, we often paid them visits; and, while the
schoolmaster and schoolmistress moralised on the
miseries of the world, their two scholars as naturally
conversed on its pleasures. In short, we soon laughed ourselves into an attachment; which the governess perceiving, Albina was locked up, I turned out,
and the tutor destined for her husband.

Man. Indeed!—And did she—forgive my weakness, sir—did she once name her father?

How. Often: but the governess has instilled into
her young mind such notions of your barbarity, and
at the same time of her own benevolence, that she
looks on her as a parent; you as an enemy. However, don't despair—if we can once gain an interview—And what say you? Shall we go to the castle
directly?

Man. 'Twill be in vain.   The gates will be shut against us.

How. Never mind: we'll force them open. Come.

Man. Nay; but consider you are dependent on your uncle.

How. No matter.   The hope that the name of Howard may still be dear to him, who now has so much cause to curse it, makes me superior to all selfish thoughts.

Man. Is it possible? You that have had a fashionable education! you that have been schooled in all the arts of modern foppery, and foreign folly! you, to be the only one to pity or befriend me!

How. Why, the fact is, they tried hard to spoil me; but I wouldn't let them—they sent me all over the continent, before I'd been half over England; taught me foreign languages, before I knew my own; instructed me how to pick my teeth all the morning in Bond-street; yawn all night at the Opera.   But I was a bad scholar, Mr Mandeville; and the satisfaction I feel at this moment proves I did right to educate myself.   Now then for Albina!— They may have perverted my head; but, I assure you, they hav'n't corrupted my heart.   [*Exeunt.*

ACT THE SECOND.

SCENE I.

A modern Apartment in the Castle.

Enter VERITAS *and* MRS RIGID.

Mrs Rig. Yes, yes: Albina already thinks me the best of women, and shall soon believe that you are the first of men.

Ver. Granted——But about Howard—Is she as fond of him as ever?

Mrs Rig. No; she don't like him half so well as she did. Ever since he left Dover, I have been undermining him, and extolling you; and, in proof of my argument, Sir Solomon has just told her of Howard's intimacy with a gamekeeper's daughter. This has roused her jealousy—her indignation.

Ver. Indeed!

Mrs Rig. Yes; and as he has now lost her affections—

Ver. I may soon win them!—Bravo, Master Veritas!—You're lord and master of ten thousand a-year!

Mrs Rig. Ten thousand?——Heyday! Have you forgot our agreement? Please to recollect, that on the day of your marriage with Albina, I am to receive half!

Ver. Half?

Mrs Rig. To be sure. What other motive could I have for getting Mandeville disinherited? Did not Albina gain the property through my management? Did not I make a dupe of the grandfather?

Ver. You did.

Mrs Rig. And why do I give you my interest? Why do I select you for her husband?—Why, but because you are to give me a moiety?

Ver. Granted. We'll divide the fortune—and thus I seal the bargain—thus with a righteous kiss.

Mrs Rig. (*Drawing back.*) How! is the man out of his senses?—Don't you recollect—

Ver. I do.—I beg pardon—You're for the Platonic.

Mrs Rig. I *am* for the Platonic system, sir, and hitherto I have not suffered my lips to be profaned by man!—Never, sir!—Not so much from fear of the consequences to myself, as from the danger in which it might involve all mankind.

Ver. That's true philanthropy, Mrs Rigid; and the longer you persevere in your system, the more our sex will be obliged to you.—Ha! Here comes Albina!—Pray, is she also for the Platonic?

Mrs Rig. Sweet little innocent!—She has hardly sense enough to discriminate one passion from another. She is the most artless, lively, tender-hearted creature!—Look at her, cousin—only eighteen!

Enter ALBINA.

Alb. Oh, governess! I have been all over the castle, looking at the rooms—the pictures—the— (*Seeing* VERITAS, *she stops.*)

Mrs Rig. 'Tis Mr Veritas. You saw him at Dover, you know.

Alb. So I did—he was there at the same time Mr Howard was.—Oh, Lord! I'm so happy to see you, sir!—I am, indeed!

Ver. Granted. She loves me!—Poor pupil!— Poor Howard! (*Aside to* MRS RIGID.)

Alb. That I am—because now I shall hear something about Mr Howard. (*To* VERITAS.) Pray, Mr Tutor—first we'll talk of his looks, if you please —Is he as handsome now?—as charming as ever?

Mrs Rig. For shame, Albina!—After what you have just heard from Sir Solomon, how can you condescend to name him? Did not he tell you of his passion for a gamekeeper's daughter?

Alb. He did; but—

Mrs Rig. What, Miss?

Alb. That passion may be only Platonic, you know, governess!

Mrs Rig. Look'ye: let me hear no more of Mr Howard! If you mention his name again, I'll resort to my old mode of punishment—I'll show you I have not forgot the art of locking up, miss.

Alb. There now! I thought it would come to

this! The owner of this immense castle will pass most of her days in one of the closets!

Mrs Rig. No murmuring! but go directly with this worthy man—walk with him to see the park—the plantations.

Alb. Well, since it must be so—come, Mr—Worthy.

Ver. (*Aside to* ALBINA.) Mum! I am not what I seem—When we're alone, I'll communicate—Cousin, we take our leave.

Alb. Madam, good day! (*Going.*)

Enter SIR SOLOMON.

Alb. Oh, Sir Solomon! You're the very person I wanted to see. Do you know, there's an old man in the hall, who says he was servant to my grandfather thirty years; and now, because his dogs killed a hare on your grounds, that he is dismissed from his place, and he and his family must starve!—Dear! —If all your game is purchased at so high a price, I wonder you're not choaked!

Mrs Rig. Go where I ordered you, miss. Sir Solomon and I have business.

Alb. And, sir—Sir Solomon! How came you to trouble yourself about Mr Howard's love-affairs?—I tell you what—I believe you're a great poacher; and, if I catch you snaring any game on my manor——

Mrs Rig. Begone, Miss!—Begone directly.

Alb. Well: I'm going, governess—I'm going. Come, Mr Tutor; and, if we meet that poor old man by the way, I'll tell him he may kill all the game on my estate; and, if that won't keep his family from starving, I'll bid him shoot all Sir Solomon's!—I have plenty of money, and I can't dispose of it better than in protecting an old favourite of him who gave it me!—Come—good b'ye.

[VERITAS *and* ALBINA *exeunt.*

Sir Sol. Um!—There's the sex!—There's true
woman!

Mrs Rig. I must watch her—her disposition al-
ters with her fortune. But, Sir Solomon, now we're
alone, what is the secret you promised to communicate to me?

Sir Sol. I'll tell you—Mandeville is arrived—I've
seen him.

Mrs Rig. Seen Mandeville!

Sir Sol. Not half an hour ago—He is now in
search of his daughter.

Mrs Rig. Mandeville come home!—Mercy!—
What shall we do?—Why, if he once gets hold of
her, he'll persuade her to pay his debts—trick her
out of the whole fortune!

Sir Sol. I know it. He's a sad profligate; and
therefore do you lock up Albina, and I'll lock up
Mandeville.—We'll keep them apart, till she has got
a husband to protect her. I'll go directly, and order
Realize to take out a writ.

Mrs Rig. Will you?

Sir Sol. I will.—Odsheart!—it was the wish of
my life that Howard should marry Albina; but his
attachment to other women shews he is not worthy
her affections; and his now associating with her father, proves he would waste every shilling of the
property.—Therefore, the sooner she marries Mr
Veritas, the better. Adieu!—Go and lock her up.

Mrs Rig. I won't lose a moment.—Ah, Sir Solomon! If Mr Howard had copied the example of
his uncle!—If, like you, he had never associated with
profligate men, or low-bred women!——You would
not have fixed your affections on a gamekeeper's
daughter?

Sir Sol. Me!—Lord help you!—How could you
suppose such a thing? (*Confused.*)

Mrs Rig. I don't suppose it. I know she is too
unpolished—too illiterate—

Sir Sol. Psha! She's too young—too—too every thing!—No, Mrs Rigid, if ever I again become a slave to the tender passions, I should select a woman of your time of life—a woman of experience!—Your young things take no pains to please a man; they rely on their youth and beauty: But your middle-aged woman—she is so industrious!—she dresses at you, talks at you, glances at you.——Oh! Time makes women wonderfully dexterous in the art of love! [*Exeunt* Mrs Rigid, *ogling* Sir Solomon.

SCENE II.

A Garden.

Enter Veritas *and* Albina.

Ver. Ha! ha! ha!—I told you I was not what I seemed. It was very well to put on the mask of learning and gravity before Sir Solomon and Mrs Rigid; but now I'll pull it off—now I'll shew you my real character!—Bless you! I'm an honest fellow!—I'm a choice spirit—a buck of the first water!

Alb. And pray, sir, what made a man of your gaiety become an usher?

Ver. You shall hear:—I finished my fortune before I finished my education. At Westminster School I found I could keep a curricle—At Oxford I found I could keep a pack of hounds—and in London I found——I could not keep myself.—So, not wishing so much talent should remain in obscurity, I set up for tutor, in order to disperse my knowledge amongst the rising generation.

Alb. Upon my word, the rising generation is very much obliged to you.

Ver. Nay: If i have not done much good, I have

done little harm ; for, with all my follies, of this you may be assured—I never did right without rejoicing at it, or wrong without repenting it. This is my history. And now to apply my talents to the right purpose—to Love!—Here's Mrs Rigid.

Enter MRS RIGID.

Mrs Rig. Cousin, a word— (*Takes* VERITAS *aside.*) Mandeville is returned from India : He and Howard are now in search of Albina ; and if an interview takes place, we are undone. Go ; and if you find Mandeville, give notice to Realize, and he'll arrest him instantly.

Ver. Arrest him?

Mrs Rig. To be sure. What does the man stare at ?—Have you any objection ?

Ver. Why, I think, when a gentleman comes a long journey—

Mrs Rig. Well, sir ?

Ver. That a spunging-house is a bad sort of inn to put up at !

Mrs Rig. How! are you only half a sinner ?—Do you repent our bargain ?—Mighty well, sir ! mighty well ! A fine girl and five thousand a-year isn't likely long to want a husband.—Others may be found, sir—

Ver. Granted.—Others may be found ; and five thousand a-year is not to be despised. Besides, I shall make amends by making her a good husband. So I'll swallow my scruples, and go directly.—Cousin, your servant !—Miss Albina, adieu ! [*Exit.*

Mrs Rig. Albina, I beg you will instantly accompany me to the Castle ; and, for reasons which I will hereafter explain to you, I must request you to live in private—neither to pay nor receive visits.

Alb. Lord ! I know your reasons well enough ; you want me not to see Mr Howard.—Well ! I do love him, that's the truth on't ; but if he don't love

me, what can I do, you know?—No! I had rather
not see him—'twill remind me of past happiness;
and if he be shut out from me, the more private I
live the better.—Come; I'll think of him no more.

Mrs Rig. Spoke like a girl of proper pride and
exalted spirit!—Now all's safe! (*As they are going,*
HOWARD *enters*).

How. So! I've found you at last, Albina!—I called at the Castle, and the servants told me they had
orders from Doctor Busby not to admit me—I beg
pardon, Mrs Rigid—I didn't allude to you—I didn't
mean to call you Doctor Busby.

Mrs Rig. None of your insolence, sir!—Albina
is no more willing to be troubled with your company
than I am.

How. Isn't she?

Mrs Rig. No:—You may hear your dismissal
from her own mouth.—Speak, child; repeat to him
what you imparted to me this moment.

Alb. I can't.   Do you speak for me!

Mrs Rig. Repeat it, I tell you: Shew him you
don't care for him: Say you are all gaiety and cheerfulness—Say so, I insist.

Alb. Sir! sir! I am all gaiety and cheerfulness!
I'm so happy that—Oh! Oh! Oh! (*Bursts into tears.*)
I shall break my heart—that's what I shall!

How. So! this is a new mode of being cheerful!

Mrs Rig. Idiot! baby! Call forth your pride: remember your rank—your fortune!

Alb. Fortune! What's the use of it, while another is heiress to his affections? If the gamekeeper's daughter will give me his heart, I'm sure I'll
give her my estate.   Oh! Mr Howard! (*Going up
to him*).

Mrs Rig. (*Laying hold of her.*) This isn't to be
borne! Come with me this moment!—Stand out of
the way, sir! Come, I command you.'

How. Hold! (*Detaining* ALBINA). It isn't on my
5

own account I thus rudely detain you : 'tis on your father's.

Alb. My father's !

How. He is arrived from India, unfortunate man !
—is now in the neighbourhood.

Alb. Is he ? We'll go to him directly. Come, governess.

Mrs Rig. Go to him! Are you mad ? Why he'll ask you to pay all his debts.

Alb. No, he won't ; for I'll offer it long before he can ask me.—Come.

Mrs Rig. Have a care : don't go near him : I know him to be so unprincipled, and so desperate, that if you refuse to give him up your fortune, I shouldn't be surprised if he threatened—nay, actually took away your life.

Alb. Took away my life !—Well ! he gave it me, you know, governess ; and as to the fortune, that certainly ought to have been his. However, as I never did, nor ever will disobey you, I'll tell you how we'll accommodate matters : Mr Howard will be kind enough to say that you won't allow me to see him ; but that, as to money—Lord ! he may have what he likes.

Mrs Rig. What he likes ?

Alb. Ay : Bid him draw for a good round sum at once—fifty thousand to begin with ; and if that won't do—

How. Oh ! fifty thousand will do very well for a beginning : Won't it, Doctor ?

Mrs Rig. Hear me, Albina. Would you undo yourself, and abandon me ? I, who have nursed you, reared you, doted on you ? I, who have been a mother when he proved no father ?—Go, ungrateful girl ! give all to him who forsook you, and leave her who cherished you to starve, and die in a prison.

Alb. Die in a prison !—Leave my kind, good governess to die in a prison ?—Oh, Lord ! I can't bear the thought of it ! (Mrs Rigid *weeps*.) Nay : don't cry so—speak to me—pray speak—Dear ! What was it she said, Mr Howard ?

How. She said you'd better give me the fifty thousand directly.

Mrs Rig. Millions cannot save a man so extravagant as Mr Mandeville—This was your grandfather's opinion ; and he left you the estate solely to prevent his wasting it—And now would you fly in the face of your benefactor ?—And for what ?—Only because a faithless lover takes the part of a selfish parent, who, till you became affluent, never thought or inquired after you.

Alb. That's very true—

How. It's not !—It's false !

Alb. I know better, sir !—But for this good woman, I might have starved ; and I'm bound to fulfil the intentions of my dear grandfather ; and therefore——Don't take on so, my dear governess, and I'll follow your advice in every thing——Don't keep twitching me, Mr Howard !—I shall do whatever she orders me.

How. You will, will you ?

Alb. Yes : I act differently from you, sir—I always obey my tutor, and I won't—

How. And you won't skip a task, or go out of bounds, for fear of being whipped ! hah !—Oh ! the good child ! Oh ! the pretty Miss Albina ! She shall have cakes and toys, and——Look'ye—give over this childish nonsense, and go with me to the gamekeeper's cottage—

Alb. The gamekeeper's cottage ?

How. (*Taking hold of her hand.*) There your father is concealed—I left him under the care of Copsley's daughter—one of the kindest, best-disposed—

Alb. (*Taking away her hand.*) Go, Sir !—I'm satisfied, and I hate you—that's what I do—I hate you more than ever I loved you.—Come, governess.

How. Why, Albina?—Why?

Alb. I have as much pride as yourself, sir;—and, since you treat me with indifference, I shall treat you with scorn—with scorn, sir!—come, madam.

How. 'Sdeath!—What have I said?

Mrs Rig. Quite enough, sir!—Go to your darling rustic—go to your dear Mr Mandeville; and, by way of consolation, tell him that if ever you possess an estate—

How. If ever I do, madam, he shall have it all. And I'll give it him, not so much from motives of benevolence, as of prudence; since I perceive that money can transform the most liberal to the most selfish; and she who, without a fortune, was all innocence, tenderness, and affection, is, in affluence, suspicious, credulous, and unfeeling—Farewell!—Mandeville has a child still; for while you are a slave to your governess, I'll be a son to your father.

Mrs Rig. This is your resolution, is it?

How. It is, most potent, grave, and reverend doctor! [*Exit.*

Mrs Rig. Now, Albina, look at the advantages of a good education.—How contemptible was Howard's conduct! How noble yours!—Continue to behave thus, and you shall be indulged in every thing.

Alb. Ah! I wish you would indulge me, governess —There is a favour—

Mrs Rig. Is there?—Name it!

Alb. Why, you already think me a good girl; but if I could be quite positive about Mr Howard's inconstancy, I should be the very best girl in the whole world.

Mrs Rig. What! do you still doubt?

Alb. How can I help it? How can I think so meanly of him, or myself, as to suppose he would prefer a girl that's like—in short, that I dare say is as unlike me as you are to Doctor Busby—Come now, as he's gone to the cottage, do let me follow him and be convinced.

Mrs Rig. Follow him?

Alb. Why not? Look'ye; you and Sir Solomon say he is guilty. Very well! If I find him so, I'll promise to marry the steward, the parson, or the birch gentleman—any, or all of them, if you like.

Mrs Rig. There's no doubt of his guilt, and this may complete her aversion; therefore I'll let her go. (*Aside.*) Well! on these conditions, I've no objection. But how will you contrive?

Alb. Oh! he sha'n't know me—I'll put on another dress.

Mrs Rig. Another dress?

Alb. Yes: I'll disguise myself as the Little Red Riding-Hood, Little John, Little Pickle, or any other impudent character!—Come—we'll settle that as we go along: and if I find him innocent, why, you shall have one-half the estate; my father the other; and I and Mr Howard will live and die in the cottage, or any other retired spot you choose to point out for us.   [*Exeunt.*

ACT THE THIRD.

SCENE I.

View of an open Country—River—Cottage at a Distance, &c.

Enter MANDEVILLE *and* HOWARD.

Man. Nay, nay: blame not Albina! Blame the governess.

How. Not blame her!—Oh! if I look, or speak, or listen, or—'Sdeath! you don't know half the fatal consequences of her unfilial conduct. Sir Solomon has ordered Realize to arrest you: he and the bailiffs are now in search of you; and, unless you can instantly raise two thousand pounds, you'll be imprisoned!

Man. Well: I am resigned.

How. So am not I. I hate a gaol; and as I must follow you wherever you go, pray let us keep in the open air as long as we can. The fact is, there is no staying here without paying your creditors; therefore let's adjourn to London!—There we may do as we like.

Man. Do as we like?

How. Aye: few people think of paying there. Why, if every man in London were to be arrested for the money he owed!—Mercy on us!—there'd be more prisons than carriages; more bailiffs than horses; and men of fashion and dashing citizens would be the two rarest commodities to be met with! Oh! when a man is in debt, the capital is the place to lie snug in! Therefore let's begone directly. Stop though—Have you any cash?

Man. Not a guinea. Out of my pay as an officer, I could hardly save money enough to land me in my native country.

How. And I have not a shilling!—And here we are two hundred miles from Hyde-Park Corner, without two hundred pence to take us there! What's to be done? Will Sir Solomon advance? Not a half-penny!—Will the tutor? Not a farthing.—Will Realize?

Man. The steward!—He wouldn give half-a-crown to save both our lives.

How. Not half-a-crown to save our lives! Come—come—you wrong him there—I'm sure he'd give more to save mine.

Man. More to save yours!—From what motive?
—From benevolence?

How. No; from self-interest. He has an annuity
on my life. The day I lose my existence, he loses a
hundred a-year; and though he wouldn't give a doit
to save me from perdition, I think he'd pay half-a-
crown to preserve his annuity—Look—here he comes!
—And now I think on't, suppose I try to get our
travelling expenses out of him?—He is always in-
quiring after my health, and—

Man. I understand.—I'll get out of the way.

How. Do.—Retire behind those trees—Mum!—
Observe! (MANDEVILLE *goes behind trees.*)

Enter REALIZE.

Real. So—I've drawn out my forces to the best
advantage—Two of my officers are in ambush near
the castle—two are reconnoitring on the London
road—and two—Ha! Mr Howard! How d'ye do,
Mr Howard?

How. Hem! (*Coughing, and stuffing his handkerchief into his mouth.*)

Real. Have you seen any thing of Mandeville?—
I've two writs out against him—one on my own account, the other on Sir Solomon's; and if you'll tell
me where he is—(HOWARD *coughs loudly.*)—Why,
what's the matter with you?—That's an ugly cough.

How. Ugly!—It's frightful!—it's—Hem!—Oh,
Mr Realize!—I'm very ill.

Real. Ill!—You were very well yesterday, and the
day before, and every day since you came from your
travels.

How. That's it.—I didn't mention it before, Mr
Realize, for fear of distressing you; but, during my
travels—Ough! ou! ou! (*Coughing violently.*) I
slept in the Pontine marshes; and the pestiferous
dews so inflamed my lungs, that ever since—Hoop!
oop! (*Coughing.*) I shall die, that's certain.

Real. Die !—Impossible !—Die !—I've an annuity on his life !—Oh ! curse those Pontine marshes !

How. It's all Sir Solomon's fault.—If he'd let me follow the doctor's advice, I should save my life, and you your annuity.—But avarice, Mr—ava—Oop !—hem !—I'm a dead man !

Real. You're not ! Now, pray live ! I'll take it as a favour if you live !—My dear Mr Howard, what did the doctor prescribe !

How. Change of air, and Bristol waters.

Real. Bristol waters !

How. Yes, sir : and because I can't raise money to take me there—Oop !—because Sir Solomon won't advance a few pounds—

Real. I'm to lose a hundred a-year.   Oh ! the hard-hearted savage ! Why, I'd better give the money myself. I will. Here, Mr Howard, (*Taking out a purse.*) I was always of a humane disposition, and so here's thirty—Hold though : Are you sure the Bristol waters will cure you ?

How. Certain.   The detergency of the atmosphere ; the absorbency of the chalybeate ; the ponderosity of—Hau !—au !—I'm convulsed ! Support me !—Lay hold of me !—(*In his convulsions, he lays hold of the hand in which* REALIZE *has the purse.*)—So—Let me go !—I'm better now— Thank'ye.——— (*Takes away his hand, and the purse with it.*)

Real. Better !—'Gad ! no wonder at it.   The dose you've taken is more likely to do you good, than detergency, absorbency, or all the doctors and apothecaries in Europe ! However, a hundred *per annum* is worth thirty pounds, or the devil's in it ! So keep it, and good bye to you.   Hark'ye, though ; if you see Mandeville, don't say I've placed bailiffs on the London road.

How. I won't.—Good bye.   I hope I shall mend, for your sake, Mr Realize.

Real. I hope you will.   But if you do not, if you

find you grow worse, write me word you are coming home full of health and spirits, and I'll go directly to Sir Solomon, talk of the goodness of your life, and sell him the annuity at a premium! That will be punishing him for his stinginess, and paying me for the dose of physic I've given you. Farewell! Keep yourself warm, and success to the Bristol waters! Oh! curse those Pontine marshes!   [*Exit.*

How. Oh! bless them! I say. Ha! ha! ha! I'm cured of my cough now—Hem! (*Clearing himself.*) Come forth, Mr Mandeville! (MANDEVILLE *re-enters*)—Come and congratulate your friend on the recovery of his health.—Look—Will you go to Bristol?

Man. No: to London.

How. Not yet there are enemies on the road. We must wait till the pursuit is over; and, as I know no safer place than Copsley's cottage, let's return there instantly. Let us go sit and rail at the governess and Albina.

Man. Never.—I must still think she is my daughter, and hope the time may come when she will imitate her mother's virtues. Oh Howard! you should have known Amelia: she had a heart as generous as your own—like you, she gave up all for a distressed —unhappy—

How. Nay; no more melancholy, now, Mr Mandeville. How can a man talk of distress, when he sees he can raise thirty pounds the moment he wants it? A slight cough and a short convulsion will be at any time a bank-note to us. So now for the cottage; and over a jug of old Copsley's October, let us drink " Confusion to our enemies and the Pontine marshes, and success to ourselves and the Bristol waters!"

                [*Holding up a purse, and exeunt.*

SCENE II.

A forward Landscape.

Enter ALBINA *in the Uniform of a Lieutenant of the Navy,* MRS RIGID, *and* REALIZE.

Mrs Rig. We won't detain you a moment, Mr Steward. Only show us the way to Copsley's cottage, and you may return to your pursuit of Mandeville. This young gentleman, Mr Herbert—

Real. Herbert! Pray is this one of the late Mrs Mandeville's nephews?

Alb. I am, sir. I am the first cousin of Miss Albina, sir—of that much wronged and most beautiful creature, sir. I am lately come from sea, and have been in so many fiery engagements, that I don't know whether I am alive or dead, sir!

Real. Po, po! Nonsense! (*Puts on his spectacles, and looks close at* ALBINA.) You have been in fiery engagements! Pooh!

Mrs Rig. Come, come; Mr Realize is too well acquainted with every part of the family to be imposed upon; and therefore we may as well trust him at once. It is Albina! she has put on this disguise, to detect Mr Howard in his love-affair with the game-keeper's daughter.

Alb. Yes, sir; with that little coarse, tann'd—— Show us the way, sir—I know Mr Howard is now at the cottage.

Real. Do you? That's very good.—Love-affair too! —Ha! ha! I wish you could prove your words.

Alb. Why, sir?

Real. Because it would have saved me thirty

pounds. Why, poor gentleman! he is not in a state to make love—

Alb. How, sir?

Real. No—the Pontine marshes have played the devil with his lungs, and he is gone to drink the Bristol waters.

Mrs Rig. Gone to Bristol! When?

Real. Now—this very moment!

Alb. Which way?—How did he go?

Real. How? Why, he went with my money.

Mrs Rig. Psha! This is all an imposition; all a contrivance of Howard's, to avoid detection. Lead on, sir; I'm sure his lungs were sound enough two hours ago.

Real. Well! have it your own way—I only wish I was as sure of keeping my annuity, as that you won't find him at the cottage. No—and what's more to the purpose, that you find somebody else there.

Mrs. Rig Somebody else! Whom, sir?

Real. No less a gentleman than Sir Solomon Cynic! Not ten minutes ago I saw him hovering about the spot, like an old kite over a brood of chickens.

Mrs. Rig. Why, the man's mad!—Sir Solomon make love! Show us the way, I insist, sir. Come, child.

Alb. Dear! If, after all, the old woman-hater should turn out to be the real poacher!—If he should, governess! I'm sure you won't any longer forbid me the sight of Mr. Howard. 'Tis cruel to sport with the affections of a lover; and, in the words of the old song, let me remind you——

SONG—ALBINA.

If 'tis joy to wound a lover,
　　How much more to give him ease!
When his passion we discover,
　　Oh! how pleasing 'tis to please! &c.

[*Exeunt.*

SCENE III.

A Room in COPSLEY's *Cottage—Birds of Prey painted on the Wall—A Recess, with several Trusses of Straw in it—Before Recess, an old green Curtain, partly broken down—A Table and two Chairs—Basket with Apples—Jug of Ale, and small Mug.*

SIR SOLOMON *discovered kneeling to* CICELY.

Sir Sol Oh you loveliest of all creatures! When I railed at the sex I did not know you—You have converted me! your charms have made me a proselyte, and here I swear—here in this low, submissive, suppliant—Wheugh! (*Whistling with pain.*)—This it is to be out of practice! My knees are so unaccustomed to the office, that I believe I'd better get up while I'm able—(*Rises*) So, come, I'll give you a toast, my little cherub—(*Goes to the table, and takes up a jug of ale.*) —Here's Cupid! victorious Cupid!

Cic. Lord!—You're so gallant, Sir Solomon!

Sir Sol. Gallant!—I have more requisites for a lover than any man since the days of Mark Antony. I can write sonnets, throw glances, talk nonsense, tell lies, sing, dance—No, hang it! I can't dance—If I could, I shouldn't be compelled to drink——— "Confusion to all dancing-masters!" (*Drinking.*)

Cic. Well, but your honour! I hope my poor father will be restored to his situation—I am so unhappy——

Sir Sol. I see you are, and I know the cause—Take comfort—I'll give you love for love!—But how shall we meet?—How carry on our amour in a snug, private, pastoral way?—How shall I steal to you un-

noticed and unseen?—And now I think on't—
Zounds! I hope nobody's observing us—if I should
be found out!—if *I* should be detected in an intrigue!

Cic. An intrigue, sir?

Sir Sol. Hark'ye: to make all safe, we'll go to
London. There we may make assignations without
being talked of or interrupted.

Cic. (*With anger.*) Indeed!

Sir Sol. Yes. There half the town are playing at
the same game.—But here in the country, if one gets
a sly kiss, the whole village is sure to hear the smack
of it.—So Marybone is the mark—a new house and
smart liveries! a curricle and a pair of greys; a
piano-forte and a lap-dog—and you shall go by another name.

Cic What! shall I change my name?—Oh, sir!
(*Curtsies very low.*)

Sir Sol. To be sure: you shall no longer be called Cicely Copsley.

Cic. Shall I be your wife?—Oh dear!

(*With great joy.*)

Sir Sol. My wife?

Cic. Shall I be Lady Cynic?

Sir Sol. You Lady Cynic!—You my ——— Ha,
ha, ha!—Why, my dear girl, you misconceive.—I
wish to intrigue myself; I don't want to be the cause
of intriguing in others—Marry you!—Lord help
you—I wouldn't take such a liberty. (*Knocking at
the door.*) Hah! What! Who's here?

Cic. Heaven knows—perhaps my father, perhaps
Mr Howard—perhaps——

Sir Sol. A dancing-master! Oh you sorceress,
you've lured me here to expose me!

How (*Without.*) Holloa! Copsley, Cicely!

Sir Sol. Howard's voice! Mercy on me! If you
don't get me off, I'll have your father hanged—I'll
—Here—I'll go into this room.

Cic. Stop, that's my chamber—Here, sir, go into that place, (*Pointing to the recess.*) and I'll draw
the curtain before you.—Quick, quick!

Sir Sol. This is my first amour this twenty years:
and if ever I come near a petticoat again, may Cupid fly away with me!—(*He enters recess, and sits
on a truss of straw.*) —So—draw the curtain.

Cic. I can't—You see it's broken down, and—
Dear! dear! How shall I fasten it?

Sir Sol. Here—here!—My cane has a sword in
it—(*Draws the sword out of the cane, and gives it to
Cicely.*)—If there's a cranny in the wainscot, run
this through the curtain: if not, run it through my
body.—(*Cicely gets upon a chair and runs the sword
through the curtain, which supports it*)—Oh woman!
woman!—Destructive, damnable, deceitful woman!
—(*Sir Solomon is concealed, and Cicely opens the
door.*)

Enter Mandeville *and* Howard.

How. (*Holding the door open, and looking out*)
Look out—look out, I tell you—'Tis Realize and
the governess; and by their coming this way, I fear
you are discovered—Hush!—observe.

Mand. I do; and see! the young naval officer is
advancing towards the cottage!

How. So he is!—We must avoid him.

Alb. (*Without.*)—" The stormy main, the wind
and rain."—(*Singing.*)

How. Ah, you chirruping scoundrel!—I tell you
what—We had better step into this apartment, and
let Cicely get rid of him—Mind, nobody is here,
Cicely.—That a naval officer!—Pooh!—Don't you
see through his disguise?

Man. Disguise?

How. He's a bailiff!—Can't you discriminate between the navy and the law—between a sea officer
and a sheriff's officer?—I know by the rascal's im-

pudent swagger that he's a bailiff!—Here he comes!
—Mum!—Retire.   [*Exeunt at the opposite door.*

Enter ALBINA *in the Uniform.*

Alb. (*Spying and walking round the room*)—" The
stormy main, the wind and rain!" (*Singing.*) I don't
see Mr Howard—" My ardent passion prove!"—
He's concealed somewhere, I suppose.—" Lash'd to
the helm"—(*Goes up to the curtain.*) He's here!
—" Should seas o'erwhelm"——

Cic. (*Stopping her.*) What do you want, sir?

Alb. " To think of thee, my love!" (*Trying to un-
draw the curtain.*)

Cic. (*Pulling her away*) There's nobody there,
sir.

Alb. Then they're here!—" And think of thee,
my love!" (*Goes towards the door.*) Perhaps, after
all, he is really gone to Bristol; and his lungs are so
much out of order. (*Trying to open the door, and
finding it locked.*) Lock'd! Where's the key?—Oh,
oh! (*Stoops down.*) I see him through the key-hole!
—Oh! you barbarian! (CICELY *tries to pull her
away.*) If you touch me, you little vulgar thing, I'll
cut you into atoms!—I see you, Mr Howard. (*Hol-
laing through the key-hole.*)

Cic. Sir, I beseech you——

Alb. (*Trying to pull the door open.*) Oh! if I could
but get at him!—Come out, sir; or I'll pull the
door—(*Shaking it violently.*)

Enter HOWARD.

How. Well, sir: What do you want, Sir? What
have you to say?

Alb. Say, sir; I'm glad your lungs are better.

How. (*Standing before the door.*) My lungs! Hark
ye, sir! if you want Mr Mandeville—

Alb. I want you, and only you, sir!—My name is

Herbert—I am first cousin to Albina; and if you don't instantly fall on your knees, and ask pardon for the insults you have put upon her, I'll make you a companion for that wild goose—I'll run you through the body, and pin you against the wall——'Slife! now I ook at you, I wonder what she could see in your ugly face to be so fond of you!

How. I'm glad it's not a bailiff, however. (*Aside.*) Sir, if you are that lady's cousin, I must inform you she isn't worth my pity, or your resentment. She is neither faithful to her lover, nor affectionate to her father—In short, sir, I thought her a child of nature, and I found her a Becky.

Alb. A Becky!

How. Yes: a Becky, sir!—And till she reforms her conduct, not all the fighting-men in Europe shall make me alter mine. This is my determination, and so you may tell her, good captain Bobadil.

Alb. Bobadil!

How. Yes: Bobadil may tell Becky—

Alb. Draw, sir. (*Pulls out his sword.*)

Cic. Hold! I entreat you—What is the cause?—

Alb. You.—Come, sir. (*Flourishing her sword.*)

Cic. Me!

Alb. His love for you is the cause. Sir Solomon told me of his falsehood, and now—

Cic. Sir Solomon told you?—Oh! base, slanderous man!—Love never brought Mr Howard to our cottage. No: he came from a far better motive—to bring money to my father—to relieve the distresses of his family : and, with gratitude I speak it, he has already saved us from ruin.

Alb. Indeed!

Cic. Yes; but for him we should have perished; and, as a proof I wasn't the object of his affections, often and often have I heard him say that Miss Albina was the girl of his heart, and that he never would nor could love any other.

Alb. (*Smiling.*) Oh! did you say this, Mr Howard?

How. You have heard my determination. I will not be teased with interrogatories.

Alb. (*Going up to him.*) Nay: don't be so hasty, Mr Howard. Consider, if Sir Solomon has deceived me——

How. 'Tis now too late, sir.—Your visit; her partiality for her perfidious governess; and her neglect of a too liberal parent, are all—all so disgraceful, that, if ever I love again, depend on't Albina won't be the object.

Alb. (*Sharply.*) She won't!—Who will then, sir?

How. Who, sir?

Alb. Ay: who, sir?—Will this little, coarse, insensible peasant?

How. Insensible! Look him in the face, Cicely (*taking her hand,*): tell him you would die to serve your father; and ask him if Albina would shed a tear to save hers.

Alb. He presses her hand!—Let it go, sir!—If you value your life, take away your hand, sir!

How. Why? She deserves it as much as your cousin!

Alb. I can't bear it! Take it away! Then say your prayers, for you hav'n't a moment to live.— (*Poking at him with her sword.*)

How. Keep off, sir—You see I've no arms.

Alb. No arms! That's a poor evasion, coward!

How. Coward! Oh! that I could find a weapon! —Is there no poker—no knife—no—Ha! what do I see?—A sword! now, villain!—

Cic. Hear me, sir—Don't touch it, for Heaven's sake!

Alb. Hear her, sir—Don't touch it, for Heaven's sake!

How. Thus I expose folly and deception! (*Pulls out the sword that supports the curtain—it falls, and*

6

Sir Solomon *is discovered sitting on one truss of straw, with others around him.*)

How. Expose folly and deception, indeed!

Alb. He's innocent! he's innocent!—Oh! Howard!

How. What! the old woman-hater turned poacher! Ha, ha, ha!—Why, uncle!

Alb. Why, man of straw! Ha, ha, ha!—Look—how the old fox squats in the stubble!—Come! (*Handing him out*) What have you to say?

Sir Sol. Nothing.—I'll go home, and read Paradise Lost.

How. And curse Cupid and Mark Antony.—And now, sir! (*To* Albina.) what have you to say?

Alb. That I sincerely ask your pardon: that I see you have been slandered—cruelly slandered!—and if Albina was before partial to you, she shall now esteem you more than ever. Will you forgive me, sir? I'll tell her all that has passed—every thing.—No: I won't tell her you called her Becky. You don't call her Becky now, do you?

Mrs. Rig. (*Without.*) Mr Herbert! Mr Herbert!

Alb. You hear I'm called, sir—Do we part friends?

How. We do: I'm satisfied.

Alb. And I needn't mention Becky?

How. No! No!

Alb. Then, let my governess say what she will, Howard is the husband for Albina! (*Aside*)—Farewell, sir! we shall meet again.—Cicely, there's money for you. And, Sir Solomon—the next time a game-keeper catches one of your hares, don't snare one of his daughters, and make him starve for it into the bargain! And also, to cover your own poaching practices, don't slander an innocent gentleman. If you do, I'll chain you to your bed of straw, depend on't. Adieu! Mr Howard!

" Lash'd to the helm, should seas o'erwhelm,
    I'll think on thee, my love!"   [*Ex*

Sir Sol. Sir, you may smile, and chuckle, and triumph; but I'll be revenged on you and Mr Mandeville yet. I know he is in that room. I saw him sneak in there; and while Realize secures him, Veritas shall secure Albina. I'll overtake Mrs Rigid— The match shall take place this very night; and then, sir—

How. Nay; why should you fret? Upon my soul, I think you're a very lucky fellow—If you had not been in the straw, somebody else might!—You understand?

Sir Sol. I do; and I've plague enough with nephews, without wishing for children to torment me. Let me go—let me follow Mrs Rigid (CICELY *stops him.*) Out of the way, jilt! sorceress! jezabel! or, to sum up all in one emphatic word,—Out of the way, Woman!   [*Exit.*

Mand. (*Peeping.*) Is the coast clear?

HOWARD *opens the door, and enter* MANDEVILLE.

How. Well, have you heard what has passed?

Mand. I have. I perceive this is no longer a place of safety; and what's worse, that Albina's marriage is to take place this very night! Is there no way to break it off?---Consider, for her own sake, for yours, for mine, we should prevent it, if we can.

How. Prevent it! How?

Mand. Have you no influence over the tutor? Has he no sense of honour?

How. Why, if it be true, that " wine draws forth the natural dispositions of the heart," Veritas has still some virtue; for over a bottle I've seen him display most excellent qualities. I'll go to him; I'll try to delay, if not break off, the marriage. In the mean time, you shall take refuge in the uninhabited part of the castle.

Mand. Why there?

How. Because it is supposed to be haunted; and

Realize and his followers won't come there, for fear
of seeing the devil before their time, you know.
Come! While I go to the tutor, Cicely shall shew
you the place. Oh, you little gleaner! If I had
known that straw contained such weighty heads of
corn amongst it, how I would have threshed it! I'd
have laid my flail about its ears till I had beat every
grain of prejudice out of it, and made the old woman-hater acknowledge---

> That, let us rail at women, scorn, and flout them,
> We may live with, but cannot live without them.

[*Exeunt.*

ACT THE FOURTH.

SCENE I.

A modern Apartment in the Castle.

Enter HOWARD *and* VERITAS.

How. What! Veritas turned flincher! Come, one
more bottle, my boy!

Veri. I tell you, I've had enough. I'm going to
be married; and would you have me get drunk before the ceremony's performed?

How. To be sure: would a man marry in his sober senses? Come, though we're rivals, don't let us
be enemies; though you've cut me out with Albina,

I bear you no ill will---Do let us part friends. Come, one more bottle.

Ver. I would; but you know my failing, George: wine makes me so cruelly sentimental; it overflows my heart with sympathy, runs out of my eyes in streams of sensibility; and when I'm no longer myself, I'm so moral, and so honest—

How. So you are. When you're not yourself, you're a damn'd good sort of fellow!

Ver. Granted: I'm never so upright in my conduct, as when I can't stand on my legs! Then wine always makes me speak truth; and if I don't take care, I shall tell you at this moment, that I am a scoundrel---that the governess is another---and that Albina——Good night, George. After the wedding's over, I'll reform, and be a six-bottle man!--- But now, spare and pity me.

How. Pity you! Why?

Ver. Because I'm going to behave like a villain.

How. You're not: I'll prevent you.

Ver. 'Tis too late---The dark deed is on the eve of execution!---Albina's locked up in the old baron's chamber---the lawyer has prepared the settlement--- the parson has got the license, and——Damnation! what am I about? I shall confess every thing---Good night!

How. Here's my uncle and the governess! What can it all mean? Look ye, Veritas, if some new act of villainy is in preparation, do you think I'll suffer my old fellow-traveller to be concerned in it? No: I have too much regard for your honour; and I know you are so apt to repent——

Ver. I am; and the wine converts me already. I'm a fair penitent; and so let's go and drink whole oceans——And yet, George, I don't like to lose Albina: she is the only woman I shall ever love.

How. Nonsense! You've only drunk one bottle,

and therefore there's only one Albina.   Drink another, and there'll be a thousand Albinas! Come
along, my fine fellow: and if wine will make you
moral, damme but you shall drink honesty by hogs-
heads !   [*Exeunt.*

Enter SIR SOLOMON *and* MRS RIGID.

Mrs Rig. Don't tell me, Sir Solomon! Is she
to be my mistress, or am I to be hers? Talk of marrying Howard, and refusing Veritas, only because
you were uncurtain'd at the gamekeeper's cottage!
I wish you had never gone there, with all my heart.

Sir Sol. So do I, with all my soul! But you misconceive: I don't oppose the marriage; I only object to the manner of wooing.   I don't like using
force.

Mrs Rig. Why not, sir? If entreaty fail, why
shouldn't force be employed? Isn't it as much her
interest to marry a man of honour, as it is my duty
to prevent her being united to a profligate?

Sir Sol. That's true.

Mrs Rig. And hasn't Mr Veritas both your promise and mine; and would it be honourable to break
our word with him? No: I say once for all, she shall
be his wife, this very night! She is now locked up
in the baron's chamber; and if she refuses, there she
shall be imprisoned till she complies.   She shall have
no companions but ghosts and spectres---no food but
bread and water---no bed but straw.

Sir Sol. Straw !---There I must intercede for her:
that's so bad a resting-place, that the very thought
of it will spoil my night's sleep, to a certainty!---
However, there is much reason in what you say;
and if she won't select a good husband, we must
choose one for her !---So if the parson, the lawyer,
and the tutor are ready, I'll join the party; and we'll
proceed to the baron's chamber in a body.

Mrs Rig. Spoke like yourself, Sir Solomon!

Stay---wait here a moment, while I go and prepare
them : and if she dare be refractory——

Sir Sol. Refractory !---Why a tutor and a governess would alone terrify a girl of her age ; but backed by a lawyer and a parson---Gad ! I should like to
see any body stand up against so formidable a quar-
tetto ! [*Exit* MRS RIGID.] I am glad of this !---
Now Howard will lose Albina, Mandeville will lose
the estate, and the tutor will be rewarded for his
integrity and sobriety.---(*Noise without.*) Bravo !---
Here they come---and all in high spirits for the enterprise.

Enter HOWARD *and* VERITAS, *arm in arm---drunk.*

How. Come along, Pupil---Come along, Honesty !
---Uncle ! How are you, uncle ?   Give me leave to
introduce to you---a fair penitent.

Sir Sol. Why, how did you get into the castle ?---
Who invited you ?

How. My pupil here.---Speak, suffering saint !

Sir Sol. Out of the way, sir---I'll hold no conversation with drunkards and buffoons---I'll talk to men
of sense and gravity.---Veritas, give me your hand.

Ver. Granted.

Sir Sol. And now let me give it to Albina.---Pup-
py, will you be eye-witness to the marriage ? Will
you behold this worthy man take possession of your
idol and ten thousand a-year ?

Ver. Look'ye, King Solomon——

How. Ay, mind, King Solomon.

Ver. If I thought Albina loved me, I'm so brim-
ful of benevolence, that I'd take her without a guinea ; but to marry her against her inclinations !---to
use force---to---I tell you it's a damned rascally trans-
action.   And if you and the governess would get as
drunk as I am, you'd be as much ashamed of it as I
am !—So drink, drink and reform !

Sir Sol. I drink !

How. Why not, uncle?---There's as much virtue in wine as in women! (SIR SOLOMON *holds up his cane to strike him*—VERITAS *interposes.*)—What! have not you had enough of that cane?—that pinner-up of old curtains! Pooh! I don't value it a straw—not a straw!—So! come, pupil; you've made your speech. And now let's adjourn to the inn, and drink more draughts of morality.

Enter MRS RIGID.

Mrs Rig. All's ready—all's prepared, Sir Solomon!—Howard here!—Why, cousin!

(*Going up to* VERITAS.

How. (*Stopping her.*) Softly, Doctor Busby— You won't let me speak to your pupil, therefore you must not talk to mine. He's a good boy, and you may corrupt him. Keep off.

Mrs Rig. They're both intoxicated!—Heaven defend me!—Why, Veritas, are not you ashamed?

Ver. Not a bit.—There's some apology for drunken honesty—but none for sober villainy. So drink, drink and reform!

How. Stick to your bottle, Doctor. " In vino Veritas!" (*Sings.*)

Ver. Come, George.

Mrs Rig. Come!——Why, would you leave me at this moment? now, when Albina is locked up— when the lawyer and the clergyman are waiting?— What shall I do?

How. Do? Tell the two black gentlemen to strike out the name of Veritas in their papers—substitute mine in its place, and I'll return and marry Albina in half an hour!——No, I won't marry her. Till she's a good daughter, she sha'nt have a good husband!—so come, my boy. Now for the inn!——I say though, isn't it a long way?

Ver. Long! No; when a man's drunk, it isn't the length——

How. True ; it's the width. Farewell, most amiable,
most platonic pair !—" To wine I flew, to ease the
pain !"—(*Both sing.*)

Ver. Farewell, King Solomon !

How. Good by'e, Doctor Busby !—" To wine I
flew, " &c.   [*Exit with* VERITAS.

Mrs Rig. Amazing ! What does it mean, Sir
Solomon ? Has Howard corrupted him ?

Sir Sol. He has ; and now I'm decided : they shall
neither of them enter my doors again ; and as for
Mandeville, I'll make an example of him directly.
I have traced him from the cottage to the back part
of the castle : he is now concealed amongst the
ruins ; and I'll go order Realize to lay hold of him
this very moment. In the interim, do you take care
of Albina.

Mrs Rig. Oh, she's very safe. I have placed Deborah, a steady old servant, as a guard over her ;
and the haunted chamber shall be her abode till we
find a new husband for her. Good night, Sir Solomon !—I could'nt have thought that Mr Veritas
would have turned out such a——But it's a strange
world ; and we have lived so long in it, that nothing
now ought to perplex or surprise us.

Sir Sol. Nothing ever surprises me ; and such are
the changes of this whirl-about life, that, though
your system is platonic love, and mine no love at all,
yet I should'nt be astonished if we were to become
man and wife, and be as happy a couple, Mrs Rigid,
as——No, hang it ! That would surprise me, indeed !

[*Exeunt, severally.*

SCENE II.

*An old Gothic Chamber, with Doors at each Wing—
In the Flat another Door—Over it is the Portrait
of a Man in Armour—a State Bed.*

ALBINA (*still in the Lieutenant's Uniform*) *discovered writing*—DEBORAH *waiting.*

Alb. Deborah!—Do take your hand from the
table, Deborah : you shake it so I can't go on with
my letter.   " Dear Mr Howard,"—(*Writing.*)

Deb. Lord, miss! Is'nt it midnight? and arn't
we alone in a haunted chamber ?

Alb. Haunted! Foolish nonsense; I suppose you've
been prying into those new romances the governess
brought for me—all about abbeys, skeletons, rusty
daggers, fat monks, and fainting nuns.   Pooh! It's
all very well to frighten children; but, for such
grown-up misses as you and I, Deborah—Oh, we're
not afraid of the dead—nothing but the living fright-
ens us.   So sit fast in your chair.———And now for
the letter———" Dear Mr Howard—They have locked me up in an uninhabited part of the castle, and
placed an old mastiff over me."

(*The castle clock strikes* one.)

Deb. There—He's coming !

Alb. Who's coming ?

Deb. The baron !—the baron !

Alb. What baron ?

Deb. Why, in the days of yore, an old Norman
baron was murdered in that bed ; and ever since,
when the castle clock strikes one, that door is sure
to open, (*Pointing to it.*) and in he stalks in black
armour.

Alb. Does he indeed ?—Well ! I shall be very glad to see him ; and, that we may have a full view of him, do snuff the candles.

Deb. Snuff the candles, miss ?

Alb. Ay : let's see what he's made of, Deborah.

Deb. (*In her fright snuffs out one of the candles.*) I saw the picture shake ; and that's a sure sign the baron is approaching.

Alb. So it is. I'll frighten her away if I can.— (*Aside.*) Hark ! Don't you hear the rattling of armour ?

Deb. I do.

Alb. And the clanking of chains, and the screech-owl, and the ravens, and the cats, and the mice ?— and don't you hear me, Deborah ?

Deb. I do. Oh, Lord ! The governess may come and watch you herself. I won't stay to be hacked to pieces !

Alb. Hush ! The door opens ; and there he is, as black as Belzeebub. Oh, dear ! My courage fails me ! Go to him, Deborah ! and while he makes mince-meat of you, I shall have time to run away. Pray do, Deborah.

Deb. Not I ! Heaven protect you !

[*Exit, frightened.*

Alb. Ha ! ha ! ha ! What an old coward it is ! Now nothing ever makes me tremble—nothing ! Oh yes ; the very thought of Howard makes me so nervous—Heigho !—I'll proceed with the letter : (*Sits and writes.*) " and placed an old mastiff over me," —a pretty mastiff indeed !—" because I won't marry the tutor. But I am a girl of such pride, such spirit, such fortitude, Mr Howard,"—(*The report of a pistol is heard.*) What's that ? A pistol at this time of night, and so near me ! Lord ! It's very alarming ! Who can it be ?—Oh, it's the poachers firing at the game ! Psha ! What a fool I was ! Hem ! (*Sits and writes.*) " I am a girl of such pride, such spirit, such forti—" (*Noise of forcing open a door.*)—Well!—(*Noise again.*)   Somebody's forcing the door! He's coming! The baron's coming! (*Noise again.*)   Oh dear! I'll run away! (*Tries to open the door* DEBORAH *went out at, but finds it fastened.*) Oh! she's locked me in! Deborah! Deborah! (*Runs and hides herself behind the bed.*)

(*The door is burst open, and* MANDEVILLE *enters with a pistol in his hand.*)

Mand. Life is'nt worth the struggle! Howard had'nt left me an hour amongst the ruins of the castle, when Realize and his followers came up with me. I remonstrated in vain. They seized me; and seeing no other mode of extricating myself, I fired my pistol in the air, and the cowards vanished.—— Here, perhaps, I may rest in safety. (*Sits down, and puts the pistol on the table.*)—How! A light! I thought this part of the castle had been uninhabited! Sure nobody observes me. Ha! the curtain moves! One of the villains has pursued me! Is there to be no period to their persecution? (*Pulls forth* ALBINA.) Mark me, sir. Return to the agent who employed you. Begone directly, or this pistol——

Alb. Oh Lord! Deborah! Deborah!—

Mand. No noise! Begone this instant! (ALBINA *retires up.*)   Stop. Come back. You may betray me to your curst associates: therefore remain. Sit down. (*Forces her into a chair.*)   Stir not—look not—breathe not!

Alb. I won't. Deborah!——Debo——

Mand. Hush! Or by Heaven!——Stay. Sure I should know that face. Speak—Do you not recollect me?

Alb. No. But I shall never forget you.

Mand. 'Tis the youth who came to the cottage! 'Tis Herbert; and no doubt is on a visit to his cousin. Curst infatuation! I'm doomed to be a tor-

ment. Sir, I've been mistaken; and know too well
the pangs of apprehension, to wish to inflict it on
others. Pray, pray, pardon me! *(Taking her hand.)*

Alb. True flesh and blood, I declare.—I'm better
now. I may breathe again, I suppose.—Ooh—ooh!
(Breathing violently.)—So you're not an apparition
then—you're only a robber?

Mand. Robber!—Sir, I *have* been—Well, well,
it concerns not you; else I could tell you that the
steward of this mansion—this reptile, Realize, who
was about to make a prisoner of me, and to whose
persecution you owe my present intrusion——Oh!
in the lifetime of his master, the late too unsuspi-
cious Mr Mandeville, he would not—no, he dared
not e'en have frowned upon me. But I have done—
I've already been the cause of much uneasiness to
you——Therefore, good night!

Alb. Stay—I must hear more. Did you know
Mr Mandeville, sir?

Mand. Know him!

Alb. Why are you so agitated, sir? If you knew
him, perhaps you also know his unhappy son.

Mand. I do indeed! And if I dare reveal to you—
But I must not trust you—you are a friend of the
governess.

Alb. I am: but I am also a friend of the unfortunate. Come, you had better trust me—I have
great influence over Albina; and, since you are the
friend of Mr Mandeville, I'll persuade her to satisfy
this steward—(MANDEVILLE *shakes his head.*)—
Nay—if you think she has not a compassionate heart,
you don't know her—indeed, you do not!

Mand. She ought to be compassionate. Her mother had a heart o'erflowing with benevolence, and
her father—But he—he is forgotten—deserted.

Alb. Poor man! I often think of him—often shed
tears over his misfortunes. Where is he? Might I
behold him!—(MANDEVILLE *weeps.*)—Nay, if you

7

knew all, perhaps I have more cause to weep than you have.

Mand. You cut me to the soul. I can't support it. Let me begone.

Real. (Without.) This way—The rascal's this way.

Mand. My persecutor again!—What's to be done?

Alb. Stay where you are—It's his turn now.

Enter REALIZE *and two* SERVANTS.

Real. There he is—Seize him—secure him, while I go for officers of justice. You'll pop at us like so many partridges, will you?—(*Servants hold* MAN-DEVILLE.) Keep him tight; and now I may safely say my troubles are at an end.

Alb. (*Meeting him.*) Rather say, your troubles are going to begin. Unhand that gentleman—Let him go, I insist. (*Servants leave* MANDEVILLE.) And now, Mr Steward, a word in private if you please.—(MANDEVILLE *retires up.*)—You recollect me?

Real. To be sure I do.

Alb. Then hear me, sir—I'll pay what he owes.

Real. You pay!

Alb. Yes, I'll pay. Can't you understand me? Go, sir; and for the future don't disgrace your employ-ers by acts of cruelty and oppression—Why ar'n't you gone?

Real. Um!—Before I obey the young lady, I must have orders from the old one. You'll excuse me; but you're not your own mistress, you know, my dear.

Alb. No. But I'm yours, you know, my dear.

Real. You're not. The governess is my mistress. Pooh! You've no will of your own.

Alb. No. But I have a will of my grand-father's; and if you don't instantly release this gentleman, I'll discharge you from being my steward—my steward! Do you hear that, sir?—What does he owe?

Real. Why, he owes me and Sir Solomon above

VOL. I.   E

fourteen hundred pounds; and do you think either
of us will be content with the security of a minor?—
No, no—we'll have the money down.

Alb. So you shall.   Take it.

Real. Take it! Where?

Alb. Out of my grandfather's money.

Real. Psha! he didn't leave so much cash behind
him.

Alb. Didn't he? Then he left houses, lands, and
woods.   So go, sir! Go cut down a wood directly.

Real. Cut down a wood!

Alb. Ay, sir.   And if that won't raise the sum,
cut down another, and another.   It will improve the
prospect, and gratify Albina with the finest view in
the world—that of seeing an unfortunate man made
happy.   (*Turning to* MANDEVILLE, *and taking his
hand.*)

Real. Here's a promising young heiress! Without
the aid of a fashionable husband, she'll lay waste more
wood in an hour than her grandfather planted in his
life-time.

Alb. What! not gone yet? I'm out of all patience.
(*Takes up the Pistol.*)   Go, sir. Begin lopping and
chopping with your own hands, or this pistol—

Real. What a devil it is!—Come, William ; come,
Gregory. We'll go and send the governess.

Alb. What's that you say, sir? Mind me! If you
repeat one syllable of what has passed, this pistol
shall prove more fatal to you than the Pontine marshes.
It shall make as large a hole in your lungs, as the
Bristol waters have in your pocket. Go, dotard.
Quick! quick! (*Follows* REALIZE *and Servants to
the Door with the Pistol, and forces them out.*)   So,
between swords and pistols I've had a pretty hot day
of it.

Mand. How am I to thank you, sir? Till now, I
had but one friend—one only friend ; and he, in poverty, has proved so generous! Oh! if you knew—

5

Alb. I wish I did know him, sir.   Whoever he is, if he has been kind to you, I'm sure I shall esteem him.   Come—though you won't mention your own name, you may trust me with his.   Who is your friend?

Mand. Howard.

Alb. Howard! Has he—has Mr Howard been kind to you?

Mand. He has been my companion, my benefactor! He has displeased his family to assist me ; and, what afflicts me more than all, on my account, I fear, he has offended the lady he most loves.

Alb. Indeed! And pray who—Not that it's any affair of mine—But pray, who is the lady he most loves?

Mand. Who should it be but Albina? His hand, his heart, his life is at her disposal.

Alb. His life! She mustn't let him die then. Tell him so, Mr—Dear! I wish I knew your name. You say you are the friend of Mr Mandeville—the friend of Mr Howard! Can't you confide in me?—(*Noise of unlocking the Door.*)—Somebody's coming! The steward has betrayed us! What shall we do? I'll stand before and hide you. (*Places herself before* MANDEVILLE.)

Enter DEBORAH.

Well, Deborah, what do you want?

Deb. The steward has been with Mrs Rigid: she is suddenly taken ill; and desires I'll bring you to her own room directly.—Why, what's that? somebody is behind you!

Alb. Hush! It's the baron.

Deb. The baron!—

Alb. Don't be frightened!—He speaks highly of you; and though I told him it was impossible, he swears he'll make an angel of you.

Deb. Don't—pray don't let him.

Alb. Well! He sha'n't—he sha'n't make an angel of you. Turn your back, and I'll lay him—(DEBORAH *turns round.*) You see, I must leave you at present. (*To* MANDEVILLE.) But as I cannot rest till I know more of your story, don't leave the castle, I entreat you. Go into that room; and, that nobody may molest you, allow me to lock you in; and, when I return—Will you trust me when I return?

Mand. Most readily.

Alb. Good night!—Nay: what have you to thank me for? Realize meant to make you his prisoner; and now I've made you mine—that's all the difference. Adieu! (MANDEVILLE *shakes hands with her, and exit at the door*—ALBINA *locks it, and puts the Key in her Pocket.*) Deborah! He's gone, Deborah! (*Hitting* DEBORAH *on the back, who trembles violently.*)

Deb. Is he? Which way did he go?

Alb. Through the key-hole; and now we'll go too. —Poor gentleman! I'll return to him as soon as I can; for I feel interested for him beyond description.—Lead on—I'll follow thee! And oh, Mr Howard! My dear Mr Howard! Your friendship for him, and love for me, prove you to be a man of such taste and discrimination, that, if you don't forgive me, and make me your wife—why, I'll live and die—a bachelor!   [*Exeunt.*

ACT THE FIFTH.

SCENE I.

A Garden.

Enter ALBINA *in her own Dress.*

Alb. I can neither sit, stand, nor walk. I can only bite my fingers, beat the devil's tattoo, and sing broken stanzas of despairing songs. " Ah, well-a-day— Ah, lack-a-day!" Dear! Now I only ask if my governess oughtn't to be ashamed of herself? Without giving any reason, she has ordered me to pack up, to set out for Dover, and leave the castle and Mr Howard for ever. I begin to hate her, that's what I do. —Sir Solomon too—I hate him! I hate all old people. I wish they'd go to heaven, and leave us young ones to manage the world by ourselves.

Enter DEBORAH.

Deb. Miss, miss, the carriage is at the door—the postillions are mounting, the horses are prancing, and Mrs Rigid is out of all patience.

Alb. Well, I'm coming!—Deborah, what is the reason——Nay, don't turn your back upon me— don't take me for the baron, Deborah!—Why are we to leave the castle so unexpectedly?

Deb. I don't know: but I believe it's all owing to what the steward told her. Come, be quick—See now!—Here's Sir Solomon come to fetch you.

Enter SIR SOLOMON.—*(A Letter in his hand.)*

Alb. Sir Solomon, I know what you're come for. You mean to force me away from the castle.

Sir Sol. I force you!

Alb. I never disobeyed my governess in all my life—but now——

Sir Sol. 'Tis high time to begin, I think.—Go, madam, *(To* DEBORAH.*)* tell Mrs Rigid, Albina shan't go to Dover.

Alb. Not go to Dover?

Sir Sol. No! You shan't stir from your own house; or, if you do, it shall only be to mine.

Alb. What! Will you stand up for me, Sir Solomon?

Sir Sol. To be sure I will. This letter has opened my eyes: it proves the governess to be the worst of hypocrites; and therefore, from this hour, you shall be your own mistress.

Alb. School's up! School's up!

Sir Sol. Why ar'n't you gone, madam? Do you think I'm not fit to be her champion?—Odsheart! though I am not able to manage young women, I'll show you and your mistress I can be a match for old ones.

Alb. I'm my own governess now!—Go, get along, Deborah!—*(Pushes her out.)*—Oh, Sir Solomon! if you were my grandfather, I couldn't be more grateful.

Sir Sol. Read, read that letter!—I'm sorry to damp your joy, Albina.

Alb. What, does it bring bad news?

Sir Sol. The worst in the world. Read, read! 'Tis written by Veritas.

Alb. (Reads.)

" Sir, I am so thorough a penitent, that I cannot
" be happy till I have made a full confession of my
" bad intentions towards Miss Albina Mandeville.
" The truth is, I bound myself in an agreement with
" the governess to give her half the Mandeville estate
" on the day of my marriage. And here, sir, here
" was the cause of the much-wronged Mr Mandeville's
" ruin. To obtain this property, Mrs Rigid gave out

" that he remitted no money for the support of his
" child, though, to my knowledge, she received a hun-
" dred and fifty pounds half-yearly."—Sir Solomon !

Sir Sol. Go on.

Alb. (Reads.) " This story so convinced the
" late Mr Mandeville of his son's inhumanity, that
" he died disinheriting him, and Albina lives to ne-
" glect the best of parents."—*(Drops the letter.)*—I
can't read any more—Oh, my poor father !

Sir Sol. You have for your excuse youth and in-
experience—But I to be such a dupe !

Alb. Where is he ?—Where is my father ?

Sir Sol. There again—there's another bad business !—He's no where to be found. Even Howard
knows nothing of him ; for I met him just now half
distracted, saying Mandeville had gone from the
place where he left him, and, pursued by his enemies, had fled either to London or the Continent.---
He called me a savage, you another.

Alb. And well he might—Let's go after him !—
We'll search the world over but we'll find him—
Come, we'll hire all the horses, servants, and car-
riages in the country—We'll fly—We'll—Aw !—aw !
Here's the governess ! Do you speak to her, for I
can't.

Enter MRS RIGID.

Mrs Rigid. Sir Solomon, how dare you countenance my pupil in disobeying my orders ?—Come
along, Albina ; be a good child, and go with your
best friend.—Why—What's the matter with you ?—
What does the girl make faces at ?—Speak !—Are
you ill ?

Alb. No.—*(Very loudly.)*

Mrs Rig. Heyday ! Do you know whom you are
talking to ?

Alb. Yes.—*(Loudly.)*

Mrs Rig. Fie, fie, sir !—Teach a girl to insult
her mother ! *(To* SIR SOLOMON.*)*

Alb. Fie, fie, madam!—Teach a girl to desert her father!

Mrs Rig. What?

Sir Sol. (*Turning her towards him.*) Where are the letters Mandeville wrote from India?

Alb. (*Turning her towards her.*) Where is the money he sent for my support?

Mrs Rig. Peace! you little insolent!

Sir Sol. (*Turning her.*) Where is the agreement between you and the tutor?

Alb. (*Turning her.*) Where are a parent's affections—a lover's heart?

Mrs Rig. Silence!—Or I'll so chastise you—

Alb. You chastise me!—The threats of my father or Mr Howard would frighten me, because they're good people, and injured people; and if you had behaved well, I had been still afraid of you. But now—Oh! I wish I had a rod, I'd pay you off old scores, that's what I would!—Come, Sir Solomon, let's leave her.

Sir Sol. Ay: let's seek out the wronged, the honest Mr Mandeville!

Enter REALIZE.

Real. He's not to be found!—Mandeville's not to be found; and I shall not only lose my two hundred pounds, but shall also be tricked out of my annuity—For yonder's Mr Howard running about like a madman; and he swears, if he don't find him, he'll put an end to his existence!—(*Sees* ALBINA.) Oh, ho!—Now we shall get information!—Your servant, Miss—or rather Master, Albina!

Alb. Sir!

Real. Who's governess now?—Did'nt I tell you last night this lady was my mistress?

(*Pointing to* MRS RIGID.)

Alb. You did.

Real. And isn't she—isn't she my mistress?

Alb. If you like it.—If you prefer serving her to me—I'm sure I've no objection. So I give you warning, and appoint the game-keeper your successor. Copsley shall be steward to the young lady—Mr Realize to the old one.

Real. Copsely become steward!—Why, governess—mistress!—

Alb. Have you cut down that wood, sir?—Oh, dear!—That puts me in mind—I declare, Sir Solomon, I had quite forgot—There is a stranger now at the castle, who can very likely give us intelligence about my father. He told me he was his friend; and he is such a kind, tender-hearted creature!—We'll go there first—Come.

Mrs Rig. Albina!

Real. Miss Mandeville!

Sir Sol. There, madam, read that letter; and if you wish to avoid the most exemplary punishment, look out all Mandeville's letters, and bring them to my house directly. You also, sir, bring your keys and papers at the same time!—Go this moment; and while Albina's at the castle, I'll wait your coming.

Real. Sir Solomon!

Sir Sol. No reply, sir!

Real. If I'm to lose my place, I hope I'm not to lose my money!—There's Mr Mandeville's debt, two years' salary, and a trifle due from Mr Howard for the Bristol waters. He coughed me out of a dose of physic worth thirty pounds, sir!

Sir Sol. No trifling!—Be gone, sir!—Mrs Rigid, you know my determination.

Alb. Stay!—This is the last time I shall ever see her; and I can't bear to leave her so unhappy. Governess, though I'm a much greater object of pity than you are, yet if my father will forgive you, I'm sure I will. At all events, while I have money, you shan't want!—Adieu!

Mrs Rig. *(Weeping.)* Farewell!

Real. Psha! what signifies crying? You see I'm not affected!—Nothing ever excites my sensibility but the touch of a guinea; and, thanks to my stewardship and the annuity trade! I've saved enough to retire and live as a gentleman ought to do.—And so, with many thanks for favours past, your servant, young lady and old gentleman!---Come along, governess! I shall want a housekeeper; and since you can't be my mistress, I'll be your master!

[*Exit with* MRS RIGID.

Sir Sol. Ah, you two hypocrites! begone!—Oh, Solomon! Solomon! you ought to have known that a woman was at the bottom of all this mischief—Come! I'll see you to the castle, and then---

Alb. I say, Sir Solomon, if we meet Mr Howard by the way, I hope you won't let him kill me!

Sir Sol. Kill you!—Why?

Alb. I know he'll be monstrous desperate!---In a good cause I've a good heart; but, in a bad one ——Oh, Lord!—Deborah is a lion to me!

Sir Sol. Never fear: I'll stand by you. And to prove I can be a protector, without being a poacher, I'll not ask even a kiss, till I have delivered you into your father's hands!—-No!—-And then I won't trouble you, unless you particularly desire it—— Come---I've given all that up for life; and I shall die as I have lived, a bachelor!

Alb. Don't! I hate bachelors---I wish there was a tax upon them.

Sir Sol. There ought; for 'tis a luxury, I promise you.   [*Exeunt.*

SCENE II.

The Baron's Chamber.---Table remaining,
with Pistol, &c.

Enter HOWARD.

How. Not here, either!---No where to be found!
What can have become of him?—Veritas detained
me longer than I intended; and when I returned
to the ruins, Mandeville was gone, thinking, no
doubt, that, like the rest of his unfeeling friends, I
had forgotten and deserted him! I am the most unhappy fellow living!—*(Sits, his hand accidentally
falls on the pistol)* What's here?---A pistol!---Oh,
Heaven!---He could'nt be so desperate! How! the
initials of his name upon the barrel! It is too evi-
dent---he has destroyed himself; and died, suspect-
ing Howard of ingratitude! I shall not long survive
him!---Oh, Mandeville! Mandeville!

Man. (*Within.*) Howard! Howard!

How. What voice is that? Speak!

Man. 'Tis I—'tis your friend.

How. He is living! (*Tries the door.*) Nay: if
'twere adamant, I'd split it into atoms! (*Forces it
open.*)

Enter MANDEVILLE.

How. (*Embracing him.*) My dear fellow! the
next time you kill yourself, don't leave your instrument of death behind you. The initials on this barrel make the worst *memento mori* I ever read.

Man. Kill myself! How you misconceive, my
friend! I took refuge here to avoid Realize; and

meeting young Herbert, he protected me, and locked me in that apartment.

How. Did he? Did Bobádil protect you?

Man. He was most kind to me; and promised to
make Albina kind to me. I wonder he's not returned: 'tis a long time since he left me.

How. Oh! he has a very slippery memory! The
young coxcomb promised to make Albina kind to
me; and I've never seen nor heard of him since.
However, to shew you how very likely he is to keep
his word with either of us, Albina by this time has
left the Castle, and gone to Dover.

Man. Gone to Dover!

How. I saw the carriage at the door an hour ago.
'Sdeath! it's only lost time to think of her or Herbert!—So, let us go to London—let us escape while
we can.

Man. Well, be it so. 'Tis plain I am forgotten—
and therefore I, like Albina, will bid adieu to the
Castle for ever. And while she hurries to scenes of
gaiety and happiness, her father shall——No: while
I have your friendship, Howard, I ought, and will
defy misfortune. (*Noise of door opening.*) We are
interrupted: let us return to the chamber.

[*Exeunt at the door* MANDEVILLE *came from.*

Enter ALBINA.

Alb. Oh dear! I'm such a coward!—Coming up
stairs, I thought I heard Mr Howard's voice in this
room; and I dread his reproaches, and his triumph,
and his anger so much, that I'd rather see the old
baron himself—Oh!—it's all fancy—He's not here!
—So I may open the door, and venture to talk to
my prisoner—Heigho! the sight of people one has
injured is so dreadful, that, I do believe, if Mr Howard——(*She opens the door.*)

Enter HOWARD.

Oh! h! h! (*Screams, and falls in his arms.*)

   How. Holloa! What's the matter?

   Alb. (*Recovering.*) Nothing: I'm better now: I
thought——

   How. Well: what did you think?

   Alb. I thought you had been the old baron—but,
I see---I see---(*Stealing away from him by degrees.*)
Good bye, Mr Howard.

   How. Your servant.

   Alb. There! I said so. I knew he'd be desperate. Good bye, sir; I'm going——Don't you see
I'm going?

   How. Going!---Why, ar'n't you gone?

   Alb. So I am---I am gone. Nay, you needn't be
quite in such a hurry, sir.

   How. I am in a hurry! I can't waste my time on
dolls and kickshaws. (*Turns his back to her.*)

   Alb. Oh! I was sure this would be the case!---
What shall I do? I've a great mind to take courage,
---to summon up all my resolution, and go boldly
within ten yards of him. (*She advances---*HOWARD
*turns, and frowns at her---She is frightened, and stops
---He turns his back again, and she goes nearer to
him.*) Lord! he takes it very quietly---I'll go closer.
So---I dare say if I were to touch him he wouldn't
bite my head off. Mr Howard! How d'ye do, Mr
Howard? (*Pulls him round gently.*)

   How. Keep off! or---

   Alb. Indeed I'm very sorry---I know I've behaved very ill; but it was the governess's fault, and
not mine. Pray now forgive me——Look---on my
knees I entreat you to forgive me this once, and I'll
be such a good, dear, darling girl!---I'll be your
slave---your doll---your kick---(HOWARD *smiles, and*
ALBINA *jumps up.*) Oh, he smiles!---You're a good-

natured creature, Howard! Ha! ha! (*Smiles, and looks in his face.*)

How. I don't smile.

Alb. You do! you do!

How. I say I don't!---And hark'ye, if I were weak enough to forgive you on my own account, how---how would you apologise for your unnatural conduct to your father?

Alb. I'll shew you——Look---(*Takes a paper out of her pocket.*)

How. What's that paper?

Alb. My grandfather's will!---Look! (*Smiling.*)

How. What!---Do you make a display---Do you boast of your ill-gotten wealth? Hear me! (*Lays hold of her hand with great emotion.*) The tutor has confessed---

Alb. I know it---

How. That Mr Mandeville---that *my* friend---remitted money from India---

Alb. I know it.

How. That the governess---that *your* friend---concealed his letters---

Alb. I know it.

How. Then how dare you insult me with this ill-timed triumph? One word more, and we part for ever!---No chuckling!---Listen! (*Taking her hand with great violence.*) If your grandfather had known these facts, would he have disinherited an affectionate son, only to adopt an unfeeling daughter? Would he not have destroyed that testament?

Alb. To be sure he would! And as he can't do it himself, won't I do it for him? There---and there ---and there---(*Tearing the will.*) I'm my own mistress now; and I think I can't do greater honour to my grandfather's memory, than by destroying an instrument that he would now blush to sign, and I for ever be ashamed to profit by!

How. Are you---How handsome she looks---Are you convinced?

Alb. I am: I hate my governess as much for her unceasing enmity to my father, as I envy you for your exalted friendship towards him!---Oh, Mr Howard! Do you think he'll ever forgive me?--- I'm going in search of him; but if you should be so fortunate as to see him before me, pray tell him that things are now what they ought always to have been ---He is the possessor of the Mandeville estate, and I have nothing but what results from his bounty. Farewell!

How. Stay: it's my turn to kneel now! (*Kneels.*) Oh! you angel! (*Rises.*) Mandeville! Come forth, Mandeville! There is no longer any cause for concealing yourself!

Enter MANDEVILLE.

Look at her! Look at Albina, your much-abused daughter! She has parted from her governess! She has torn her grandfather's will! She has---Damn it! why don't you speak to her? Joy choaks me! I'm dumb!

Mand. (*Embracing her.*) My child! My child!

Alb. My father!

Mand. Have I at length a recompense? Oh, Howard! Did I not say the time would come---

How. Why will you speak to me, when you know I can't answer you?

Alb. Will you forgive me, sir? Can you forget---

Mand. Forget! I never blamed you. And at this moment your mother's virtues shine out so brightly in your conduct, that I could wish that will were still in force. I want not now my father's wealth to make me happy---My child, my long-lost daughter is restored to me, and I am blest, and rich beyond my hopes!

Enter Sir SOLOMON, COPSLEY, *and* CICELY.

Sir Sol. Come, Albina! 'Tis time to proceed on our journey. What, Mandeville! Howard! all together! all reconciled!---Tol de rol lol!

How. So, you're come to play the governor!

Sir Sol. Not I. I've been as great a fool as any of you. I thought Mrs Rigid a divinity: but I've found out she's a woman! Veritas has converted me. I'm a fair penitent now, Howard! Mandeville, you have deserved better treatment; give me your hand ---George, give me yours.---And now, my little fellow-traveller, give me the kiss we talked of---No: hang it! 'twill be only distressing you.

Alb. Nay, Sir Solomon; if it will give you any pleasure, I'm sure it will give me no pain.

Sir Sol. Arch rogue! Now, I'll take it by proxy, on purpose to be revenged. There, George, try how you can bear it. (HOWARD *kisses* ALBINA.) So, does it give you much pain? Well, what say you, Mr Mandeville?---How shall we punish these two culprits? Shall we inflict matrimony, or separation?

How. Oh! matrimony, by all means! Don't you think so, sir? (*To* MANDEVILLE.)

Mand. I do, indeed. The day that gives Albina such a husband, and makes me father of such a son as Howard, must be the proudest and happiest of my life.

Sir Sol. Say you so? Then take her, George; and if the marriage state can afford happiness—— However, we won't talk of impossibilities.

How. Now, Albina, will you ever talk of Cicely again?

Alb. Will you ever call me Becky again?

How. Becky!

Alb. If you do, I'll make you a companion to the wild goose in the cottage. " I hope your lungs are better, sir ?" (*Reminding him by her voice and attitude.*)

How. What! were you Bobadil? Were you the little smart, well-made lieutenant?

Alb. I was young Herbert, sir; and I bless the disguise, not only for convincing me of the sincerity of my lover, but also for introducing me to my father---I hope you don't blame me, sir? (*To* MANDEVILLE.)

Sir Sol. He blame you! No: Howard has most reason. What will your husband say to your strutting about in boy's clothes?

How. Say! that I wish all women would wear the breeches before marriage, instead of afterwards.

Copsley. Oh, madam! how shall I thank you? You have saved me and my family from ruin.

Cicely. You have, madam! and we are all gratitude.

Alb. This is your benefactor! you are to thank my father, not me. If you wish to do me a favour---why, there is one---

Cicely. Oh, name it, madam! name it!

Alb. Why, it rather concerns Sir Solomon than myself. Pray be kind enough to have the old curtain repaired, lest he should again wish to take cover behind it. And likewise, do send me some of the straw---I mean to be married in a straw hat---and I'll have one manufactured out of Sir Solomon's stubble!

How. One! We'll have a dozen! And our children shall wear them, in honour of their great-uncle's gallantry!

Sir Sol. Gallantry! Psha! I've something better to think of than women.

How. Indeed you have not. Come, come, uncle, ---rail at the sex as much as you like, you must confess, that life is a blank without them; and the gaming-table, the bottle, and the sports of the field, are all so many substitutes---shadows !-----Woman is the true substance after all---and, compared to her, all other objects are as the glow-worm to the sun ! It may dazzle the sight---but it can never warm the heart !------Don't you think so, Albina ?

Alb. I do, indeed. Women are certainly most superior creatures, and, if by accident they have any faults, men ought not to see them---at least, I hope that will be my case to-night. I have done and talked a great many foolish things : but having their hands and full pardon, (*Standing between* MANDEVILLE *and* HOWARD.) let me have yours, (*To the Audience.*)---and Albina will be the happiest of wives, and the most grateful of daughters.

[*Exeunt omnes.*

THE

RAGE:

A

COMEDY,

AS IT IS PERFORMED AT THE

THEATRE-ROYAL, COVENT-GARDEN.

BY

FREDERICK REYNOLDS.

DRAMATIS PERSONÆ.

GINGHAM	*Mr Lewis.*
DARNLEY	*Mr Holman.*
SIR GEORGE GAUNTLET	*Mr Middleton.*
The HON. MR SAVAGE	*Mr Fawcett.*
SIR PAUL PERPETUAL	*Mr Quick.*
FLUSH	*Mr Munden.*
READY	*Mr Davenport.*
SIGNOR CYGNET	*Mr Bernard.*
Waiter	*Mr Rees.*
Servant to SIR GEORGE	*Mr Abbot.*
Servants to the HON. MR SAVAGE	$\left\{\begin{array}{l}\textit{Mr Ledger}\\\textit{Mr Wilde.}\end{array}\right.$
Servant to MR FLUSH	*Mr Cross.*
Groom	*Mr Simmons.*
CLARA SEDLEY	*Mrs Mountain.*
LADY SARAH SAVAGE	*Mrs Mattocks.*
MRS DARNLEY	*Mrs Pope.*

THE

RAGE.

ACT THE FIRST.

SCENE I.

DARNLEY'S *Garden, and View of his small Villa.*

Enter DARNLEY *and Sir* GEORGE GAUNTLET.

Sir Geo. AND so, Darnley, you prefer this solitary life to all the joys of London!—To be sure
you've a nice snug villa, and a charming wife here ;
—but it's dull—the scene tires—it wants variety,
Harry.

Darn. No, Sir George.—Since I retired to this
peaceful spot, I have not had a wish beyond it : I've
been so happy in that humble cottage, that when
I'm doom'd to leave it, the world will be a waste,
and life not have a charm !

Sir Geo. How you are altered, Darnley ! When
we were brother officers, you were the greatest rake
in the regiment ; but from the time we were quarter'd at Worcester, where you first beheld Miss
Dormer——

Darn. I saw the folly of my former life ; I own'd

the power of her superior charms; and, leaving a busy and tumultuous world, retired with her to this sequestered scene.—'Tis now three years since I married.

Sir Geo. And from that time to this, have you lived in this out-of-the-way place?

Darn. Yes; and till you yesterday honoured me with a visit, I have not seen a friend within my doors.—But isn't it a happy life, Sir George? Our affections have room to shoot—care and distrust are banished from our cottage; and with such a woman as Mrs Darnley to converse with, what is the world to me? I can defy and scorn its malice.

Sir Geo. She's an angelic creature indeed, Darnley; and at Worcester, I had myself nearly fallen a victim to her charms. But about your future life— do you mean to live for ever in these woods and meadows?

Darn. No—would to heaven I could!—I fear I must forego my present calm, and mix in active life again. When I married, I sold my commission, you remember, to purchase this small farm—Mrs Darnley's portion was but a trifle; and an increasing family has so enlarged my expences, that unless I return to the army——

Sir Geo. Ah!—you want to be raking again?

Darn. No—I want to secure an independence for my family—I want to see my children affluent; and to attain this, I have once more applied to my uncle Sir Paul Perpetual, who was so offended at my selling out, that he has ever since abandoned me.

Sir Geo. What! does the old beau still persevere in his resentment?

Darn. His anger has increased; for he writes me word, he intends marrying Lady Sarah Savage, on purpose to have heirs more worthy his estate.—Oh, my friend!—'tis hard, that fortune should bestow such treasures, and then compel me to desert them!

Sir Geo. So it is : But now I think on't, this Lady
Sarah Savage and her brother are my intimate
friends ; and as you are their neighbours, I'll introduce you and Mrs Darnley to their notice.—When
are they expected from town ?

Darn. To-day.

Sir Geo. Then we'll pay them a visit : Lady Sarah Savage shall interfere with your uncle ; and if
that fails, her brother can easily ensure your promotion in the army—But see ! here's Mrs Darnley.

Darn. Look at her, Sir George—do you, can you
blame me ?—who would not act as I have done ?

Sir Geo. I would, by heavens !—I'd live with her
in a hermitage !—die with her on a pilgrimage !—
I'd——'Sdeath ! if I don't mind, I shall discover
all. (*Aside.*)

Enter MRS DARNLEY.

Darn. (*advancing to her.*) Maria !

Mrs Darn. Oh, Harry !—I have been looking for
you every where—I declare you're grown quite a
truant—Before your friend came, you used to walk
with me over the farm ; or ride with me to see your
children ; or sit and read to me under our favourite
beech tree—but now——Sir George !—I beg your
pardon—I did not see you before.

Sir Geo. Madam ! (*Bowing obsequiously.*)

Darn. My friend is all kindness, Maria : he has
promised to introduce me to the honourable Mr Savage.

Mrs Darn. What ! take you to Savage House ?

Darn. Ay—why not ?—You shall go with me.

Mrs Darn. No—let me stay here—I am not weary
of my present life.

Darn. Nor I—but 'tis a great connexion ; and
though not absolutely distressed, I would improve
my fortune—I would see you and my children have
every comfort.

Mrs Darn. We have, while you are with us---Consider, we never lived a day apart ; and if they lure you into fashionable scenes, you'll be corrupted, Harry---you'll despise the humble roof you once revered, and I perhaps shall be forgotten and neglected.

Darn. Never!---I cannot bear the supposition ; and while we have hearts to endure, and hands to labour, there is sufficient for our cottage !---I will not go--- My friend, who sees my motive, I'm sure, will not condemn me.

Sir Geo. No---always obey the ladies---But, Darnley, I see our horses---you recollect we were to ride to see your children : So, madam, I have the superlative honour------

Enter CLARA SEDLEY---*A basket of flowers is hanging on her arm, and she is eating an apple.*

Sir Geo. What, Clara !---been picking flowers, my angel !---well !---I thought they had all died---all died from envy, egad ! ha ! ha !---excuse me---I never laugh but at my own wit.

Cla. Do you ? then you laugh very seldom, I believe.

Sir Geo. No---very often ; for I take the joke, though nobody else does, ha ! ha !---Come, Darnley---adieu, ladies---I'll not run away with him !

[*Exeunt* DARNLEY *and* SIR GEORGE.

Cla. What a coxcomb it is !---and if he wasn't a duellist into the bargain, I'd tell Mr Darnley all my suspicions---that I would---but he's so fond of fighting, that I heard him say, he once sent a man a challenge for wafering a letter instead of sealing it.---I wish he was gone.

Mrs Darn. Indeed so do I, cousin---Mr Darnley is so changed since he arrived---his ideas so enlarged--- he talks of visiting at Savage House---of improving his fortune.

Cla. Fortune !---ay ; and this morning he gave me

his note for two hundred pounds, begging me to get
one of my guardians to lend money upon it---his excuse was, that his expences exceeded his income,
and by his uncle's marriage with Lady Sarah Savage, all his expectations were ruined---Now, my life
on't, this is all Sir George's doings---he has stole into our cottage like the arch fiend into paradise, and
I won't eat another apple while he stays! (*Throws
away the apple she is eating.*)

Mrs Darn. Is Darnley then distressed?---Oh, Clara!

Cla. Don't be unhappy---I shall apply to both my
guardians, Sir Paul and Mr Flush; they are now at
Bath, and one way or other the Villa shall flourish
still---Lord! I shall have plenty of money when I
come of age, and I'll throw it all into the scale, and
come and plant, sow, and reap with you and your
husband.

Mrs Darn. What! give up the gaieties of London,
cousin?

Cla. London! ay: I hate it---I once passed a
month there; but they hurried me so from sight to
sight, that in the bustle all places appeared alike---
I saw no difference---And, if you'll believe me, one
morning, after seeing Westminster Hall in term-time,
they took me inside Bedlam; and so confused was
I, that I did not know the lawyers and their clients
from the keepers and their patients.

(*Signor* CYGNET, *without.*)

Sig. "Trompite, trompite tra!" (*Singing an Italian air.*)

Mrs Darn. Who can this be?

Enter SIGNOR CYGNET, *spying.*

Sig. "Tra---tra---tra!" (*Singing.*)

Cla. Bless us!---What animal's this?

Mrs Darn. He has mistaken his way, I suppose---

Sir!---(*Signor don't regard her.*) I beg pardon, sir---
but perhaps you don't know that this garden---

Sig. " Beviamo tutta trè !"---Ah, ha!---les de-
moiselles!---Ladies, à votre service.---

Mrs Darn. Sir! (*Curtseying.*)

Sig. I and the honourable Mister Savage arrive
last night---ce matin I take a my little valk---see
your small chateau, and am so enchanté with the
spectâcle, that---me voici!---I honour you with my
first visit---eh bien!---vat is your names?

Cla. Our names!---rather we should ask yours.

Sig. Mine!---Diable!---do you not know me?

Cla. No---how should we?

Sig. Vat! not know I am Signor Cygnet?---de
first violin Europe! de best composer in de whole
world!---de husband of Signora Cygnet---de great
singer at de opera---de professional---de abbey---de
---Morbleau!---and am I not myself?

Cla. No---I don't think you are yourself.

Mrs Darn. And so, sir, you are on a visit at Mr
Savage's?

Sig. Oui---In my vay to Bath I condescend to
pass a few days there---Lady Sarah Savage, she love
music, or pretend to love---vich is de same ting, you
know---they entertain me comme çâ---give me good
dinners, and take tickets for mine and my vife's con-
cert---mais there be two tings I don't like.

Cla. And what are they, sir?

Sig. Vy Mister Savage, he give me cold suppers,
and sleep in the best bed himself---Now, begar!---I
vill have hot suppers and de best bed, or else I take
a my fiddle and promenez---" Malbrouk s'en va, &c."
(*Singing*)---De grand duke---O! de grand duke---he
never use me thus---never---jamais!

Cla. The grand duke!

Sig. Oui---ven I was at Florence, how you tink he
treat me? accoutez---he quarrel with all his minis-
ters---all but one!

Cla. And who was that one?

Sig. Me!---me he shake by de hand, and go to my vife's benefit toût le même---de same as ever!

Cla. (*To* MRS DARNLEY.) Upon my word, music seems so important a science, that I think you had better let your little boy have some lessons---it is necessary for his education---isn't it, Signor?

Sig. Necessarie!---ma foi: 'tis de only education now-a-days---never mind vat you call Latin and Greek---put de fiddle in his little hand, and let him scrape away! den he vill be great man---like me; and call for hot supper and best bed vcrever he go.

Mrs Darn. What! shall I give up making a parson of him, Clara?

Sig. Parson!---pif!---vat is de parson to de musician?---he ride his old white horse---preach away at four or five churches, and vat he get?---forty pounds a-year---Eh bien! I and my vife ride in vis-a-vis--- sing only ven we like, and make five thousand a-year---ah ha! voila la difference!---Parson!---begar! de blind fiddler get more money.

Mrs Darn. More shame for the country then, where foreign arrogance is so rewarded, and gentlemanly merit so insulted---Come, Clara---

Re-enter SIR GEORGE GAUNTLET.

Sir Geo. Don't be alarmed, Mrs Darnley; but I and your husband have just been present at an accident, that——

Mrs Darn. An accident, sir?

Sir Geo. Yes: Lady Sarah Savage, who is one of those ladies called female phaetoneers, was driving four in hand across the heath: the horses took fright, and ran away with her, when Darnley, with more gallantry than prudence, rode a-head of the unruly animals, and stopt them on the edge of a precipice.

Mrs Darn. Heaven be praised!---and where is the lady, sir?

Sir Geo. My friend is conducting her to the villa, where he begs you'll instantly join them.

Mrs Darn. By all means---Come---(*To* CLARA.)

Cla. Signor, won't you assist your friend?

Sig. Non---I am musician, not physician, and my head is so full of de tune---

Cla. So full of de vapour, he means---like the inside of his own violin---Come, cousin---Now isn't it a pity that while we have butterflies and bullfinches in the garden, we should be tormented with coxcombs and fiddlers---insects, adieu!

[*Exeunt* CLARA *and* MRS DARNLEY.

Sir Geo. Signor, I rejoice to see you; you have often assisted me in my amours, and I now want your aid more than ever.

Sig. Eh bien!---my vife has a concert at Bath next week.

Sir Geo. Has she? then I'll give a dinner to some Somersetshire bumpkins, and force off a score or two of tickets---You saw the lady I first spoke to---she has won my heart, and I have won her husband's.

Sig. Dat is good---den if you make de discord between them---

Sir Geo. Ay, Signor: if I excite jealousy! and this accident has sprung the mine---Lady Sarah Savage is already half in love with Darnley---She has invited him to Savage House; and if he takes Mrs Darnley along with him---

Sig. Dey will be both out of tune for ever!---ah ha!---I go to Mr Savage, toutesuite.

Sir Geo. Do---and increase Lady Sarah's love for Darnley---assist in all my schemes; triumph I must and will: for I offered Mrs Darnley my hand long before this husband won her heart.

Sig. I will be first fiddle, rest assurè---tenez; I vill compose two duettos---one between Lady Sarah Savage and de husband---de other between you and

de vife---allôns. You no conceive the power of music, Sir George.

Sir Geo. I do, Signor---for, as Shakespeare says,
" There's nought so stockish, hard, and full of rage,
but music for a time does change its nature."

Sig. Shakespeare! vat is dat Shakespeare! He
never compose a single tune ; and dough at present
he make a little noise, begar, you'll soon find de fiddle and de bravura will lay him on de shelf---now-a-
days, sound always get de better of sense, mon ami---
Alr ha! venez! you no forget my vife's benefit.

                              [*Exeunt.*

                    SCENE II.

A Room inside MR DARNLEY's *Villa,---Prints,
Books, Fowling-pieces, Fishing Tackle, &c.*

            Enter MRS DARNLEY *and* CLARA.

Mrs Darn. Well, Clara : if Lady Sarah Savage be
a picture of town-bred women of fashion, let me remain a plain simple rustic all my life---Did you ever
see any thing so confident---so masculine ?---Her
brother, too! " What you call impudence," says
he, " we call ease."

Cla. Ay : they're a precious pair ; and yet in London they are both the Rage !---quite at the top of
the beau monde---But, cousin, they've ordered their
carriages, and insist on our going to Savage House---
Mercy on us! what's to become of two lambs amongst
such a parcel of wolves ?

Mrs Darn. This is Sir George's scheme : to delude
Mr Darnley from this tranquil spot into fashionable
life, is the first step towards effecting his base de-
signs---He told Mr Savage about your fortune too---

Cla. I know it : and the vulgar man made down-right love to me directly---Faith, coz, I believe Sir George wants to get me married, and you unmar-ried.

(LADY SARAH SAVAGE, *without.*)

Lady Sa. Bring round the phaeton, and, d'ye hear, don't tighten the curbs---I'll whip and gallop them every inch of the road.

Cla. " She'll whip and gallop them!" There now ! ---this is one of the modern breed of fine ladies, who, instead of being feminine and tender, have the Rage for confidence and boldness---Look at her dress---she's more like a man than a woman, and her lan-guage is as masculine as her manners.

Enter LADY SARAH SAVAGE, *dressed in a Great-coat, with a number of Capes; a plain round beaver Hat ; a fur Tippet and Sash. Boot Shoes, a Whip in her hand, and a Riding-habit, under Great-coat. Two Grooms enter with her.*

Lady Sa. John, exercise the pointers and the hounds---I shall shoot to-morrow, and hunt the next day.

Groom. Any thing else, madam ?

Lady Sa. No---nothing---Oh, yes : Call at the tay-lor's and enquire for my fencing jacket---tell him I broke two foils in my last rencontre, and ask him if any body ought to make assaults in a gown and pet-ticoat ?---Ah, my little dears !---here--- (*Seeing* MRS DARNLEY *and* CLARA, *she makes them pull off her great coat, which the groom takes.*) Well ! and how do ye do ?---Oh, William ! tell the recruiting serjeant I must learn the new military manœuvres, and bid him bring the largest fusil in the regiment---there---go along---   [*Exeunt grooms.*

Mrs Darn. I hope you have recovered your fright, ma'am.

Lady Sa. Recovered !---heh !---why, where's my deliverer ?---my dear charming Mr Darnley ?

Mrs Darn. Madam !

Lady Sa. He is certainly the most divine engaging creature---I mean to take him home with me, and the phaeton is waiting---so call him, child--- (*To* CLARA.) call him directly.

Cla. Call !---whom, madam ?

Lady Sa. Why, Mr Darnley, to be sure ; what does the girl stare at ?---did she never see a person of quality before ?

Cla. Never---it's the first time, ma'am ; and if this is the specimen, I hope it will be the last---I'll call Mr Darnley.   [*Exit.*

Lady Sa. I wish I was like you, my dear---I wish I was married---it's so comfortable---so convenient--- heigho !---I shall be so glad when old Sir Paul is my stalking horse---my husband, I mean---shan't you, Mrs ------- ?

Mrs Darn. Excuse me, madam : when I reflect, that Sir Paul is Mr Darnley's uncle, and by your union he is deprived of all his future fortune, you cannot blame me, if-------

Lady Sa. Deprive my dear Darnley of his fortune ! ---so it does---well !---that's vastly droll !---but then it makes mine, which is the same thing, you know--- See !---here's my bear of a brother !---you've no idea what low, vulgar company he keeps !---nothing but buffoons, Bow-street officers, and boxers !---and only conceive, my dear, me and my friends mixing in such horrid society.

Mrs Darn. Surely Mr Savage cannot wish-------

Lady Sa. He does, ma'am : and only conceive, I say, my intimate acquaintance---people of the first consequence---such as Signor Cygnet, the husband of the fine Soprano---Monsieur Puppitini, the inventor of the dear fantoccini ; and Count Spavin, the greatest of horse doctors---only imagine such pick'd company as this, mixing with my brother's low-lived, wretched crew.

Mrs Darn. Indeed, ma'am, people of rank ought to set a better example.

Enter the Honourable MR SAVAGE.

Sav. So, Savage---sister, I mean---I lost ten pounds by your silly accident---The moment I saw the horses off, I said to my friends around me, Ten pounds to five, the driver gets a tumble---" Done !"---" It's a bet," says I---away flew the racers---snap went the reins---five to four in my favour !---when, plague on't ! the 'squire rode across, stopt the carriage---you saved your neck, and I---lost my wager.

Lady Sa. You brute ! did you ever hear your brother, Lord Savage, talk in this manner ?

Sav. My brother !---pough !---he's a gentleman, to be sure---proud, independent, and all in the grandee style---but I !---I'm not like him---I'm a man of fashion---I'm not a gentleman.

Lady Sa. No---that you are not, upon my honour.

Sav. I am the hero of my society---he is the slave of his---He keeps high company, ma'am, (*To* MRS. DARNLEY.) lives with judges, generals, and admirals---but does he ever encourage the arts and sciences ? does he ever shake hands with men of genius ? such as peace-officers, tennis-players, and boxers ?---no, no---that was left for me.

Lady Sa. Yes : and though born to wealth and titles, there you stand, that have been six times bottleholder at a boxing-match !---vulgar science !---I hope Sir Paul don't understand it.

Sav. No---not now---but if he makes you his wife, it may be necessary he should learn---I say, ma'am, that was a straight one---wasn't it ?

Mrs Darn. Indeed I don't know, sir---Would Mr Darnley were here !---I am unequal to their society;

but from the little I have learnt, I think one hour of
domestic life worth all this new unintelligible scene.

Sav. Hark'ye : (*To* LADY SARAH.) here's a letter from the old beau, Sir Paul---he is coming to
Bath, and can only stay one day with us, in his way;
but as people of quality are not always people of
quantity, you know, he sha'n't stir, till the marriage
is effected---mum !---I'll keep him close——

Enter DARNLEY.

Ha ! squire !---Come, Mrs Darnley, (*Takes her by
the hand.*) I'll drive you and your pretty cousin——

Mrs Darn. Sir, I'm unused to visiting ; unfit——

Sav. Nonsense !---I never take an excuse ; when
I ask people to my house, I make them go when I
like---stay while I like, and behave as I like---so come
along---'Squire, mind you don't snap the reins ; and,
d'ye hear, as my sister is rather lame---only just recovered from the gout---

Lady Sa. The gout !---How dare you, sir ?

Sav. What !---do you deny it ?---do you disown
having been cured by a quack doctor, and returning
him thanks in all the papers ?---" Lady Sarah Savage informs Dr Panacea, that his alagaronic anti-
spasmodonic tincture, has entirely removed the gout
from the extremities ; and she now hunts, shoots,
eats, and drinks, more freely than ever !"---Now isn't
it a shame, ma'am ? between them, they plunder
both the patient and the physician.---The quack
cheats the doctor of his fee, and the woman robs the
man of his gout.   [*Exit with* MRS DARNLEY.

Lady Sa. Oh, Mr Darnley !---I am so glad you're
going to Savage House---'twill be such a relief---
Come---I'll appoint you my rural cicisbeo---my
guardian shepherd---you saved my life, and I won't
let you die for me, I am determined.   [*Exeunt.*

ACT THE SECOND.

SCENE I.

The Honourable MR SAVAGE's *Park and Garden---*
A Canal, with a Vessel on it---A Bridge---A Tem-
ple, surrounded with Weeping Willows----At the
Wing, a Portico, and Steps leading to the House.

Enter DARNLEY *and* SIR GEORGE GAUNTLET, *from*
the Portico.

Sir Geo. Why now indeed you are an altered man.

Darn. I am----I am----the wine----the scene---the
company---has so transported me, that I begin to
think I'm not quite sober, Sir George---I do indeed.

Sir Geo. No wonder at it---you've led the life of
a recluse, and every new scene dazzles you---you
are like a nun escaped from a convent.

Darn. No---more like a friar in one---at least if I
may judge by my eating and drinking---But, my
friend---this is a glorious place, and I begin to think
I've lived too long out of the world---coop'd up in a
cottage---buried in a farm---What did I know of life,
and all its pleasures?

Sir Geo. Ay : what indeed?---In town---and Savage House, is the same thing, you see ; for they always bring London into the country with them---but
Lady Sarah, Darnley---I saw you at dinner ;---she
gave you such affectionate looks------

Darn. Fie! fie! Sir George---you forget---I am a married man.

Sir Geo. A married man!---what then?

Darn. Why then I love my wife---I do---I tenderly love her---and when I chuse to play the fool, let me expose myself, but not wound her, for heaven's sake!

Sir Geo. Nonsense!---you don't know Lady Sarah---she is one of those confident females, who won't let a man escape---who mark you for their prey---lure you into their talons; and, if you don't yield, will so claw you——

Darn. What! make me love her whether I will or not?

Sir Geo. Certainly:——But consider the advantages of her friendship: first, she can get you promotion in the army; secondly, by gaining an ascendency over her, you may prevent her marrying your uncle; and, thirdly, you can provide for your family without injuring your honour---There!---there's an opportunity!

Darn. That's true; and if I thought---Hark'ye; as we're alone, and you're my best of friends---I've got a letter from her! the Signor brought it me---here! (*Taking out a letter.*)---She appoints me to meet her in her dressing-room.

Sir Geo. Bravo, Signor!---(*Aside.*)---let's read.---(*Reads the letter.*)---" Lady Sarah Savage, having something particular to communicate to Mr Darnley, begs to see him in her dressing-room in an hour's time."----Go, by all means---go, I insist.

Darn. Why, if I can persuade her not to marry Sir Paul, or even get her to interfere with him---I'll go!---I'm fix'd---I'll write to her this instant. " He that essays no danger, gains no praise!"

Enter the Honourable MR SAVAGE, *hastily.*

Sav. Joy! joy, my lads! Sir Paul is arrived! And how do you think the old boy introduced himself to my porter ?—" Tell your master," says he, " a young gentleman desires to see him."

Sir Geo. Young gentleman !—that's excellent !—He's at least seventy-two.

Sav. No ; you wrong him : he's only seventy.—Sir Paul Perpetual—Old P. I mean ; for that's his nickname, you know—has been the ancient beau of the age these thirty years ; and as his great grief is, that he never had a son, he wants my consent to marry my sister.

Darn. And do you mean to consent, sir ?

Sav. Certainly.—I say, (*Aside to* SIR GEORGE.) —I want his fortune to repair my own, and therefore he shan't leave the house till the marriage is effected—you know my way—I've given the hint to the servants.

Enter a Servant.

Ser. Sir, here's the young gentleman.

Sav. 'Squire, take my place at the table—push the wine about, and tell the jovial crew to prepare for quizzing—quizzing, you rogue !—Go.   (DARNLEY *exit.*)—The license is in my pocket ; a parson's in the house ; and if we can but confuse the young gentleman, we'll marry him in a joke, and afterwards take his fortune in earnest.

Enter SIR PAUL PERPETUAL, *in a Riding-dress.*

Sir Paul. " Be lively, brisk, and jolly !—lively, brisk, and jolly !" (*Singing.*) Ah, my boys !—here I am—as young and hearty—but I can't stay ; I must be at Bath to-morrow.

Sir Geo. At Bath !—what ! to drink the waters ? to renovate before marriage, Sir Paul ?

Sir Paul. No—upon my soul, there's no occasion ; —though, at present, perhaps a little physical advice wouldn't be much amiss ; for, between ourselves, I've just cut a tooth, and suffer'd most violently from the hooping cough! (*They laugh.*)—Why, what do you laugh at?

Sav. Nothing—nothing—only we wonder'd how such a chicken as you could struggle against a pair of such mortal disorders!—But, seriously, what takes you to Bath?

Sir Paul. Such an event!—I have traced a son; a boy above twenty years of age! that's my first reason—my second is, to see my grandfather.

Sav. Your grandfather!

Sir Paul. Hark'ye—he shall make settlements on my first four children.

Sir Geo. Pray, Sir Paul—I beg your pardon, though—what age may your grandfather be?

Sav. Two hundred, if he's an hour! heh! an't I right, Old P.?

Sir Paul. Old P.! there it is, now!—Here I stand, that walk as much as any man—that ride as much as any man—that am every night at a concert, an opera, or a club—that sing, dance, game, or intrigue! and what's more, that have done all this for sixty years!—and yet to be call'd Old P.!——They said I never was a father; but I shall soon prove the great and glorious fact.

Sav. Ay! how will you prove it?

Sir Paul. How! why you've all heard of my little Nelly—poor girl! she was jealous, and she left me to marry a tradesman—a clerk at a lottery-office—and three months after we parted, she was deliver'd of a boy—a fine boy! as like me as one Cupid is to another.—A year after her marriage, she died, and I can hear nothing of her husband; but let him say what he will, I'll swear the boy was mine; I'll swear it, because I'm convinced I'm father to more children than one, Sir George.

Sir Geo. Very likely; but where did you learn all this?

Sir Paul. From Nelly's sister.—A month ago I

accidentally met her at Tunbridge: She had neither seen nor heard of the husband since her sister's death; but she remember'd the child went by his mother's name.—It's mine! I'm sure it's mine!— and (*They laugh again.*) I tell you what—you'd better be careful; for when you and other young sprigs of fashion smile at me, jeer me, and call me the infirm Old P.!—'gad! you little think, you dogs, you are laughing at your own father, perhaps!— However, I've traced my boy to Bath, and whoever discovers him shall have the two best racers in my stud.

Sav. What! Fidget and Fizgig? then I'll seek for young P. myself—I'll find him—I'll——But hold— hold—(*Stopping* SIR PAUL, *who is going.*) don't go yet—your nephew's in the house.

Sir Paul. What, Darnley?—zounds! then I won't stay a moment—no—not even to see my dear Lady Sarah, who I'll marry, if it's only to disappoint that rural reprobate—that——I'm gone.

Sav. No, you're not—I'll tell you a secret; you shall stay a week with me.

Sir Paul. A week!

Sav. Ay! I've my reasons—so don't think of stirring; for your horses are turn'd out to grass—your saddles and bridles snug in a hiding-place, and all the gates double barr'd, inside and out.

Sir Paul. What the devil! make a prisoner of me?

Sav. Nonsense!—I only forestall your wishes:— I'm sure you want some soft discourses with my sister; and don't I know what my visitors like better than they do themselves? don't I know you like getting drunk?—So come; come in and drink! (*Pulling him.*)

Sir Paul. I don't—I hate drinking;—and death and fire! havn't I told you I want to find my son?—

Sir Geo. (*Aside to* SIR PAUL.) Humour him; humour him, Sir Paul; or he'll refuse you his sister.

Sav. Ay : give consent, or else——

Sir Paul. Or else I lose my wife, I suppose. When I'm in the country, don't I like always to live quiet, and keep early hours ; and would you lock me in a house where you never see the sun ? where you go to bed just before it rises, and get up the moment after it sets ?

Sav. Will you give up the marriage, and let Darnley have his wish ?

Sir Paul. No—I'll die first—I'll—

Sav. Then will you join the jolly crew, and prove—

Sir Geo. That you have as much health, youth, and spirits—

Sav. As any choice spirit—

Sir Geo. Or young gentleman—

Sir Paul. In the whole world !—I'm roused ! I'm fired ! and, to shew I'm season'd ! true English heart of oak—allôns !

Sav. (*Singing.*) " Bring the flask ! the music—

Sir Geo. (*Singing.*) " Joy shall quickly find us—

Sir Paul. " Let us dance, and laugh, and sing, and drive old Care behind us !" [*Exeunt at Portico.*

Enter MRS DARNLEY.

Mrs Darn. Can this be the mansion of elegance and taste ? I meet with nothing but rudeness and neglect !—I wish I could find Mr Darnley !—I dare say, by this time, he is sicken'd of the scene, and anxious as myself, to see his home again.

Enter DARNLEY *from the Portico, half drunk, with* LADY SARAH SAVAGE'S *Letter in his hand.*

Darn. (*Speaking as he enters.*) Fill away, my boys ! —fill —fill !—while I like a faithful gallant !—gallant !—hold, hold, friend Darnley. This letter is to benefit your interest, not sacrifice your honour.

Mrs Darn. Heavens !—what do I see ? Mr Darnley !

Darn. (*Not regarding her.*) Yes:—you do ; you
see Mr Darnley.

Mrs Darn. Why—what's the matter with you ?—
what's that letter ?

Darn. This letter ?—this is a love-letter, my angel !
—Ha !—why, it is !—it is my wife !

Mrs Darn. Yes : that wife who in the hour of dissipation you forget—Can I believe it ?—in a little
hour can all our past attachment—But why am I
alarmed ?—fashion may dupe the wicked and the
weak ; but virtue such as his must scorn its empty
power.

Darn. Forget !—no, never !—and now I look at
you, I think I ought to be massacred for having, even
for a moment, neglected you.—Oh, Maria ! I have
such news for you !—Lady Sarah has been so kind—
she has promised to promote me—to befriend you—
and, in short, she has taken a liking to the whole family.

Mrs Darn. And why, Harry ?

Darn. Why ! ay : there's the rub ! but don't be
jealous, Maria—I entreat you, don't be jealous !—for,
by heaven, I love you !—I do, so tenderly, that if it
were not for my promise, I could find in my heart to
return home directly.

Mrs Darn. Do ; let us begone—the place distracts
me ; and I fear this high company will corrupt you.

Darn. High company !—hang it :—if that's all
you're afraid of, there's not much danger in this
house, I fancy.—But, my letter—my word to Sir
George—and consider our interest, Maria.

Mrs Darn. Oh, no—consult our happiness, my
love ; and surely there is none in this tumultuous
scene—we left all joy behind us, in our children and
our cottage, Harry ; and there alone we shall recover it—Come.

Darn. She's right—the pretty prattler has reason
on her side, and who can disobey ?— (*Looks with-*

out.) Ha! Sir George and Lady Sarah in close conversation!—they beckon me!—again!

Mrs Darn. Why do you pause?

Darn. I'm in for it—the die is cast!—Maria!—excuse me. (*Going from her.*)

Mrs Darn. How! will you leave me, Mr Darnley?

Darn. What can I do? 'tis but for a short time.—

Mrs Darn. You must not. (*Laying hold of him.*)

Darn. Nay: only for an hour.

Mrs. Darn. (*Letting him go, and taking out her
handkerchief.*)—This is the first time you ever used
me thus.

Darn. So it is—now what a pretty scoundrel I am!
—and this is fashionable life, is it?—Oh fool! fool!
to quit substantial peace for artificial pleasure!—
don't weep, Maria—I go for our mutual advantage
—I go to make our children happy.

Mrs Darn. Then stay with their mother—they never wished that we should part.

Darn. Nor will we—we've lived so long and happily together, that I would rather lose the little we
have left, than hurt your quiet.—(*Enter* SIR GEORGE
GAUNTLET.) Sir George, stay with her—I'll see
Lady Sarah, entreat her forgiveness, and return instantly; for, oh my friend!—my heart drops blood
for every tear she sheds.

Sir Geo. P'sha!—remember your interest—Lady
Sarah will soon reconcile your scruples, and leave
me to compose Mrs Darnley—nay, take your opportunity—you must keep the appointment—I insist—so begone!—(DARNLEY *exit.*) What a fuss
here is about a man's leaving his wife for an hour,
when so many worthy couple would be happy to part
for ever!

Mrs Darn. Sir George, tell me, where is he gone?
Tell me, that I may fly and overtake him!

Sir Geo. Why! can't you guess?

Mrs Darn. No, indeed, I cannot.

Sir Geo. Not that he is gone to Lady Sarah to keep an assignation with her?

Mrs Darn. An assignation!

Sir Geo. In her dressing-room, at this very hour— the gay scene has so altered him, that you see he has left you to keep the appointment.

Mrs Darn. I'll not believe it—he is above such baseness.

Sir Geo. Won't you?—then I'll prove it.

Mrs Darn. I defy you!—he knows the value of my heart too well to trifle with it; and I've known his so long, that I'll not venture to suspect it—no— though his friend defames it.

Sir Geo. Nay then—you remember his hand-writing—here is his answer to the lady's letter—read.
              [*Giving her the letter.*

Mrs Darn. (*Looks over it.*)   Ha!—it is too plain —I am deceived—deserted.

Sir Geo. I was the bearer of that letter, and preserved it merely to shew it you; I thought it the duty of a friend.

Mrs Darn. And, from the same duty, you advised him to write it. Oh! I have known you long, Sir George—you are one of those who find no happiness but in marring that of others—who seduce the affections of the husband, the better to betray the honour of the wife! and, when you've spoilt all social and domestic peace, the friend you laugh at, and the woman scorn!—I know you well!

Sir Geo. My dear ma'am, how you mistake!—I meant to oblige you.

Mrs Darn. Sir—there is but one way—leave me— nay, I insist—

Sir Geo. I shall obey.

Mrs Darn. I must have stronger proof before I am convinced, and then observe, Sir George, if his truth weakens, I'll add strength to mine! my constancy and honour shall be so exemplary, that I will

shame him from his follies, make him repent, and,
when reclaimed, be proud to say he is my own again!
[*Exeunt.*

SCENE II.

An elegant Apartment leading to LADY SARAH's
Dressing-Room—the Door in the Flat.

Enter CLARA.

Cla. Yes: yes: it's all over the house—Sir George
makes no secret of the assignation; and, I've no
doubt but Darnley is now in that room waiting for
Lady Sarah Savage—she can't come at present—the
servant says, she's gone to the stables to see the
beasts unharnessed—faith! if she'd go to her brother's party, she'd see that business already done!—
however, I'll prevent Darnley's exposing himself;
and, as he is certainly concealed in that room, I'll
talk to him. Dear!—here's my guardian again!

Enter SIR PAUL PERPETUAL, (*hastily.*)

Sir Paul. So far, I'm safe, my dear girl; you
don't know what your poor guardian has suffered in
this high—no—this low-lifed house!—they forced
me into a room full of buffoons, boxers, and black-
legs—made me drink a bowl of punch, and I'd as
soon drink so much poison—then, winking and nodding, they began whispering pretty loudly—" Smoke
the old prig!—damme, quiz him!"

Cla. Quiz him!—what's that, guardy?

Sir Paul. Why, with our young men of quality,
quizzing is a substitute for wit, my dear; so one
man challenged me to play on the violin, and when I
rose up to move my elbows, another whipp'd the chair

from under me; a second put hot coals into my
pocket, so when I felt for my handkerchief, I burnt
my fingers; a third tried to cut off my tail, but that
assassin I pursued, when unluckily in running after
him, they had tied a string across the stairs, and I
pitch'd headforemost into a barrel of water, they had
placed for the purpose.

Cla. Indeed, it's quite terrible, guardy.

Sir Paul. Then they shew'd me a license; brought
me a fat parson, and said, if I'd instantly be married,
they'd let me go to find my son—if not, I should be
lock'd in, and have plenty of it—now here's hospitality!—but they've overshot the mark; and if I get
out of their doors, I'll not only break off the match,
but promise to befriend Darnley.—

Cla. What! disappoint lady Sarah, and relieve my
poor distressed friend—then I'll get you out of the
house—I will, if I'm quizz'd to death for it—You
see that door—if he meets Darnley, he'll at least interrupt the assignation.———

Sir Paul. Secure my escape—only get me out of
this den of savages, and, if I don't befriend Darnley,
may I never live to see old age. Where does the door
lead to?

Cla. I fancy to lady Sarah's dressing-room; for it
is full of half boots, horse great coats, military sashes,
helmet caps, and amazonian jackets! and this is your
only way to escape—enter that room.

Sir Paul. Yes.—

Cla. Put on one of lady Sarah Savage's great coats,
tie one of her sashes round your waist—throw a fur
tippet about your neck, and with a whip in your
hand, and her driving hat on your head——

Sir Paul. I understand—the servants will take me
for their mistress, and open the gates; Oh! you dear
girl! (*Kisses her.*)—I'll about it instantly—(*Opens
the door in flat.*) I say, Clara, the hounds below are
unkennell'd; they have started me for game, and af-

ter keeping them at bay, by sousing in a flood of water, I take to cover; that is, I put on lady Sarah
Savage's cloathes to avoid passing for a wild beast;
mum! (*Enters the room.*)

Cla. If he does but get out of the house, the marriage is broken off, and Darnley made happy.

Lady Sa. (*without.*) I'm at home to nobody but
Mr Darnley.

Cla. (*Going to the door.*) We're undone, ruin'd;
stay where you are; here's lady Sarah.

Sir Paul. (*Putting his head out*)—The devil!

Cla. Hush! lock yourself in, and don't stir till I
tap at the door, or stop—stop—lest she or somebody
else should tap, don't open it till I give you a signal
—let me see; what shall be the watch-word? Oh,
" quizzing," you won't forget " quizzing," guardy?

Sir Paul. No—I shall remember it these fifty
years; so when I hear the word " quizzing," out I
come, and—softly—here she is. (*Shutting himself in.*)

Enter LADY SARAH, *with pocket-book and tickets in
her hand.*

Lady Sa. (*Speaking as she enters.*) Tell my dear
signor, I shall get rid of all these benefit tickets; heh!
(*Taking out her spying-glass.*)—what young creature's this?

Cla. How d'ye do again, ma'am?

Lady Sa. Again! you're vastly forward, child; I
never saw you before.

Cla. No, ma'am! that's very strange; you saw
me this morning at Mr Darnley's, and invited me
to your house.

Lady Sa. Oh, ay: now I recollect; you must
excuse me; we people of rank are so very absent,
we're extremely intimate with a person in the morning, and don't know them at night; well! I'm vastly glad to see you; but you mustn't stay here, I'm
engaged, child.

Cla. I sha'n't intrude, ma'am—good day.

Lady Sa. Adieu! stop—stop—I forgot; give me two guineas.

Cla. Two guineas, ma'am!

Lady Sa. Yes: for these tickets; they're for the signor's wife's benefit at Bath next Monday, the whole town will be there—nay, I shall attend—I'd make you take more, but as you'll have to pay card money by and by, it would be asking you to one's house absolutely to make a bargain of you! (CLARA *gives the two guineas.*) there—you may go.

Cla. A bargain indeed! and a bad one too: for, if I was mean enough to make money by my guests, would I lay it out on foreigners who loll in carriages? no—not while so many of our gallant soldiers and sailors have only wooden limbs to stand on! (*Half aside*) I am gone, ma'am, (*Curtseying.*) and now may Darnley get out of the scrape—Sir Paul get out of the house—and she and her brother knock their stupid heads together.   [*Exit.*

Lady Sa. I suppose this silly creature has interrupted the charming Mr Darnley, and he has stept into my dressing-room—(*Goes to the door, and finds it fastened.*)—lock'd inside—it must be so—(*Listens*) —I declare I hear him moving; (*She listens again.*) —he sighs!—poor man! (*She speaks loudly.*)—don't be dejected, my dear sir; when I'm married to that old tottering beau, Sir Paul, I'll think of nothing but you. So come, Mr Darnley, (*Enter* MRS DARNLEY) come, my sweet Mr Darnley.

Mrs Darn. Can it be possible?—then all's confirm'd, madam, when I am convinced that my husband—that Mr Darnley has been decoyed into that room.

Lady Sa. (*Spying at her.*) Bless me!—it's Mrs Darnley!—this is a little awkward—however I'll soon talk her out of it. (*Aside.*) Don't be uneasy, my dear —these fashionable intrigues are very harmless, I'll assure you, and if you had had my free and liberal education—but, poor thing! I suppose you were sent to school for instruction.

Mrs Darn. To school! as certainly, ma'am—

Lady Sa. There it is then: for what could you learn! only to sing well enough to spoil conversation—to play on the harpsichord, so as to give papa, mamma, and the whole family an afternoon's nap—to dance so awkwardly as to be always out of tune and place; and to speak just French enough, to make you forget English; this is a boarding-school education—But I, my dear——

Mrs Darn. Hear me, madam! when I first saw you, I was the happiest of women—I had a husband who loved and honour'd me—who doated on his children, and knew no pleasure but in his family! and now how severe is the reverse! you have robb'd me of that treasure, seduced it from my heart, and I return to a melancholy home, without a friend for my own distresses, or a father for my children!

Lady Sa. And how can I help it!—did'nt I mean to do you both a service by introducing you to the great world?

Mrs Darn. Great world!—there again, madam! —when I enter'd this house, I expected from the exalted rank of its owner to have been surrounded with kindness, elegance, and hospitality!—but I find that high birth doesn't create high breeding; nor am I, because humbly born, less likely to set a polish'd example than yourself—Oh, Darnley! why will you not come forth and save your once loved wife from agonies too great to bear.

Enter MR SAVAGE.

Sav. So, Savage—here's a pretty story buzz'd about!—they say that Darnley, the country 'squire, is lock'd up in your dressing-room! if this is true, you Jezebel——

11

Lady Sa. Scandalous brute !—but I don't wonder at it, you've had such a low, vulgar education.

Sav. I had an education !—well, that's more than
ever you had !—but look'ye, Miss, no time must be
lost ; for if Sir Paul discovers your intriguing, he'll
break off the marriage, and we are ruined—yes;
ruined, madam ! (*To* MRS DARNLEY.) you and your
infamous husband will make your own plots and mar
mine—so I'll unkennel him.

Mrs Darn. Hold, sir—indeed he is not to blame—
he was betray'd into that room.

Lady Sa. Betray'd !—nay, then I must confess,
brother, that Mr Darnley is there ; I dare say he
conceal'd himself on purpose to expose me to Sir
Paul—nay, I am sure of it now.

Sav. (*Looking thro' the key-hole.*) I see him thro'
the key-hole—the rascal's in disguise ! (*Enter two
servants.*) John, call up the club—unloose the hounds
—tell the whole house to prepare for quizzing—
quizzing, you rogue.——

SIR PAUL, *dressed in* LADY SAVAGE'S *Great Coat,
&c. opens the door, endeavours to escape, but meeting* MR SAVAGE, *retires again directly.*

Sav. John, open the back-door, and shew the disguised gentleman out of the house directly—go—and
as for you, Mrs Darnley——

DARNLEY *enters, and* MRS DARNLEY, LADY SARAH,
and SAVAGE, *stand astonished.*

Sav. Confusion !—Darnley !

Mrs Darn. Is he then innocent ?—Oh Harry !
(*Embracing him.*)

Lady Sa. Amazing ! why, who was that wretch
in my coat, hat, and tippet ?

Darn. No less a gentleman than Sir Paul Perpetual—Clara told me the whole story—he put on that
disguise to avoid the snares that were laid for him,

and he has ere this left the house, determined to
break off a union, that would have undone me and
my family—Lady Sarah, I entreat your pardon; but
here (*Taking* MRS DARNLEY *by the hand.*) here is
my apology.

Re-enter Servant.

Ser. Sir, I have shewn the disguised gentleman
down stairs.

Sav. Go to the devil with you.——

                              [*Kicks the servant off.*

Lady Sa. Brother!

Sa. Sister!

Lady Sa. We are the fools that are outwitted.

Sav. Yes: we've turn'd out the wrong man—but
let's pursue and overtake him instantly; come,—
'squire, I insist you leave my house directly; and as
to you, Miss—if I catch the young gentleman, I'll
have some sport, I'm determined—I'll turn you both
loose amongst the hounds below, and the Club shall
decide, whether old P. isn't the prettiest-looking female of the two!   [*Exit with* LADY SARAH.

Darn. I resolved, Maria, to meet any censure, rather than give a pang to such a heart as yours; but
let us be gone——

Mrs Darn. Ay: let us return to our villa, nor
ever wander more.

Darn. No—not yet, Maria.

Mrs Darn. Not yet!

Darn. No—I have a plan to execute—Sir George,
my best of friends, has invited us both to his aunt's
house at Bath, and is now waiting without to conduct us.

Mrs Darn. Do not go! let me entreat you! do not
—I have a thousand fears.

Darn. Nay, nay: he will introduce us to friends,
who can render us essential service; come—come—

indulge me—the society will be pleasant, and unlike this ill-bred scene—

Mrs Darn. Well! if it must be so—Ah, Harry! I have now pass'd hours in the humble and exalted scenes of life, and I find that good breeding is confined to no rank or situation! it consists in good sense, and good humour; and I believe we may see as large a share of it under the roof of the cottage, as in the splendid mansions of the great!   [*Exeunt.*

ACT THE THIRD.

SCENE I.

A superb Room in FLUSH'S *House; handsome Side-board of Plate—Pictures in elegant Frames—gilded Chairs—two Servants in fine Liveries, putting Silver Coffee-pot, Tea-urn, &c. on the Table for Breakfast, third Servant shewing in* READY.

Enter READY.

Rea. Tell your master, his agent desires to see him.

Ser. Sir, Mr Flush is hardly drest yet.

Rea. Not up!—why it's two o'clock.

Ser. Very likely, sir—my master seldom rises sooner—besides he gave a grand supper last night; all the first people in Bath were present, sir.

Rea. Well! well! tell him Mr Ready is here. (*Servant exit.*) Now isn't it amazing that a man who was only twelve years ago clerk to a lottery-office-keeper in London, should be so rich, and so visited! And how has he done all this? how, but by the modern mystery of money-lending!—by opening a shop

in the city for linens, gauzes, and muslins—by keeping a fine house near Bond-street, and another in
Bath. His son manages in London, and I here;
while he, by not appearing, is every where noticed
and respected.

Flush. (*Without.*) James! Thomas! tell the cook
to send a plan of my dinner.

Rea. He's such an epicure! and he, who formerly
could scarcely get necessaries, is now not satisfied
with luxuries.

FLUSH *enters with two Servants.*

Flush. (*Sits.*) Ha! Ready! how d'ye do, Ready?
Rea. Sir! (*Bowing.*)
Flush. Sit down, Ready—sit down. (READY *sits.*)
well! how go on money matters?

Rea. I have alter'd the advertisement as you desired, and inserted it in the Bath and Bristol papers.

Flush. Read it—read it. (*Takes up a pine-apple
on the breakfast-table.*) You scoundrels! (*To the servants.*) is this a pine apple for a gentleman? buy a
larger; buy one if it costs ten pounds; I can afford
it—read, Ready, read.

Rea. (*Reading a newspaper.*) "Money Matters.
—The nobility, gentry, ladies of fashion, officers of
rank, bankers, &c. may be secretly accommodated
with money to any amount, on personal security
only, by applying to P. O. Holly-street, Bath—No.
93."

Flush. Excellent! well! does the trap fill? have
you caught any birds?

Rea. Plenty; plenty of pigeons already; (*Takes
out his pocket-book.*) here, here's a note for five hundred—left by a dashing young parson—I think it's
good.

Flush. (*Looking at it.*) It is—treat him well; give
him value; I can afford it.

Rea. Value! but in what manner?

Flush. (*Rising.*) Oh! pay him in the old way, Ready; first, give him my draft at a week for thirty guineas, then offer him damaged linen and muslin to the amount of one hundred and twenty, and bid him call again in a fortnight—you have his note all the time you know.

Rea. Certainly, sir; and when he calls———

Flush. Give him a bad bill for one hundred and fifty, and pay him the odd hundred in trifles; such as paste buckles, gilt bracelets, Westphalia hams, painted prints, neats' tongues, and Stilton cheeses— so shake hands, and have done with master Parson.

Rea. But not with the bill, sir.

Flush. No—my bankers discount it, and pay it away; till, passing through different hands, some- body gives value for it at last, and then the glorious work begins—then comes the hero into combat! an attorney is employed! an attorney, my boy! action is brought upon action! declaration filed upon de- claration! till the drawer, acceptor, and indorsers all get into the King's Bench—the King's Bench— no—I beg pardon; the high money-lenders, and low attornies, have so fill'd it with their dupes, that there isn't room there—the house overflows! so Newgate, Newgate is the shop!

Enter a Servant.

Ser. Here's your son just arrived rom London.

Flush. Shew him in.   [*Exit Servant.*

Rea. I'm told, sir, Mr Gingham is quite another man since I saw him.

Flush. Yes, yes, you knew his curst, ingenuous, candid disposition; he learnt it in the country, the dog would speak the truth, and his simplicity so in- jured our trade, that I threatened to turn him out of doors; but he has reform'd, Ready! the boy has the good sense to tell a lie now, and I've sent for him to witness his blessed reformation.

Rea. Ay, sir, your son always spoke his mind too freely—in short, Mr Gingham was too honest for his profession.

Flush. He was; however, he has given me his word, never to speak what comes uppermost; and he is now, what he ought to be, a regular, solemn, jesuitical—in short, he's a very promising young man.

Enter GINGHAM.

Ging. Sir, your hand—Ready, yours. Well! here I am—quite converted—like father, like son—tell a lie without blushing.

Flush. Here—I told you so—ay, ay, I knew the boy would come to something good at last—So, my dear boy, you have left off telling the truth—speaking your mind?

Ging. Mum! close as the cabinet—keep you in my eye—put on your face, and do it so punctually, you wouldn't know young P. O. from yourself— (*Looking about the room.*) Zounds! what a fine house you've got! how it's furnished! what plate! what pictures!

Flush. The result of trade and honest industry, Frank—yes—it's pretty furniture, isn't it?

Ging. Pretty furniture! it's so handsome, that, except yourself, curse me if I see a shabby bit in the room!—nay, nay, upon my soul, I didn't allude to you; I meant Ready.

Rea. He's at his old tricks, I see—as candid as ever.

Ging. Plague on't! I could sooner bite off my tongue, than stop its speaking what I think! Nay, sir, now pray—

Flush. Well, well, I excuse you this once; I, a shabby bit! however, we shall soon see—How goes on the shop in London?

Ging. The shop!

Flush. Ay, the shop in the city that you've the care of—the linens—the——

Ging. Oh, ay; now I recollect: why very well upon the whole, I believe, sir—very well—only, between ourselves, I am afraid it won't last; I think we and our tricks shall be found out—you understand—

Flush. Found out! 'sblood, sirrah——

Ging. Softly, sir—softly—don't put yourself in a passion, and lay the blame on me; don't charge me with our ruin; for every body knew my opinion long ago; didn't they, Ready? I told it to a thousand people—Says I, " Swindling will never thrive, and I and my poor father shall get duck'd at last !"

Flush. You did ! did you ?

Ging. That I did, sir ; and I'll prove I said so— The other night I slept at the west end, and two friends—distress'd old officers in the army—brought their notes to be discounted—says I, " Gentlemen, it won't do—you'll get little cash, but a quantity of trumpery nonsense, such as hams, cheeses, prints, linens, and other vegetables !" Said they, " We know that—we know you and your father are two infernal sharpers; but a guinea now is worth ten a month hence—so give us the money."

Flush. Well, and you took their note, didn't you ?

Ging. No, I didn't—I gave them the cash, shook the two old soldiers by the hand, and said I was tired of such d——d swindling practices.

Rea. This is sad work, Mr Gingham; you'll never be at the top of your profession.

Ging. The top !—Oh ! what, the pillory ? no—I leave that to you, Ready.

Flush. Was there ever such a scoundrel ?—but we'll hear more. (*Aside.*)—So, you sleep at the west end of the town, do you ?

Ging. Always—it's vulgar to be in the city of an evening; besides, I like to walk in Kensington-gar-

dens in the morning—you know Kensington-gardens,
father?—the place where there's such a mixture of
green leaves and brown powder—of blue violets and
yellow shoes; and where there's such a crowd, that,
to get air and exercise, you stand a chance of broken
bones and suffocation! Well!—there I strut away,
my boys——

Flush. You do—do you?—I can hardly keep my
hands off the rascal—So then, I suppose, the moment my back was turn'd, you never thought of business.

Ging. Business!—no, never—did I, Ready? I recollected my father play'd the same game before
me; that when he was clerk at the lottery-office, at
billiards all the morning, and at hazard all the evening—Therefore, says I, where's the difference?—
none, but that he had the policy to conceal his
tricks, and I the folly to shew mine—heh! I'm right,
an't I, Ready?

Flush. You villain!—is this your reformation? not
even conceal your own faults, much more mine!
Expose my character, neglect my trade, and strut
away in Kensington-gardens! I have done with
you; from the country you came, and to the country you shall return.—Speak the truth, indeed!
Zounds! sirrah, what has truth to do with money-
lending?　　　　　　　　　　　[*Here* READY *exit.*

Enter CLARA SEDLEY.

Cla. Oh, guardy!—I'm just come to Bath with
Mr and Mrs Darnley—we are all on a visit at Sir
George Gauntlet's, and——
　　　　　　　　　　(*Seeing* GINGHAM, *she stops.*
Flush. It's only my son, Clara—a simple foolish
young man.

Ging. (*Bowing to her.*) More knave than fool,
upon my honour, ma'am.

Cla. The gentleman don't praise himself, I see, Mr Flush.

Ging. No, ma'am—nor do I know any body that will praise me—unless my father, indeed.

Flush. Silence, sir!—Well; but about the rural pair, my dear ward; do you know I have a great regard for Mr and Mrs Darnley?

Cla. Have you? I'm vastly glad of that; for your joint guardian, Sir Paul, is so employed in seeking for his lost child, that he has forgot his promise to assist Darnley; therefore I want you to do him a favour.

Flush. A favour!—he may command me.

Cla. The case is this:—His increase of family has so enlarged his expences, that he has thoughts of returning to the army.—Sir George has promised to procure him a company; but Mrs Darnley, not chusing he should owe his promotion to him, wishes he should purchase. Now, guardy, if you would lend him two hundred pounds.

Flush. Two hundred pounds, child!

Ging. Ay, two hundred pounds, father.

Flush. Who bid you speak, sir?—Why, Clara, in money-matters there is an etiquette.

Cla. True: but this is your friend.

Ging. So it is, ma'am: the man he has a great regard for.

Cla. And when you consider the charms of Mrs Darnley, and the wants of her children——

Ging. He can't refuse, ma'am—indeed he don't intend it—and therefore, as I see he means to grant the favour, I'll save him the trouble of putting his hand in his pocket.—Here, ma'am, (*Taking out bank notes.*) here are two bank notes of a hundred each— they belong to Mr Flush—now they belong to Mr Darnley—(FLUSH *gets in his way, and prevents* CLARA's *taking them.*)—he begs you'll give them to his

friend—and present his compliments—and say, he'll
double the sum.

Flush. Stand off—stand off—or by heavens I'll—

Ging. (*Offering* CLARA *the notes across his father.*)
Double the sum, whenever call'd upon, ma'am.

Flush. Hold your tongue, or I'll knock it down
your throat, sirrah!—I say, Clara, in the way of business, I've no objection to do Mr Darnley a service;
that is, if I can make a profit by it—first, he should
send me his note.

Cla. Here it is, sir. (*Giving it to* FLUSH.)

Flush. That's right—now we can proceed—Here,
sir—(*Giving the note to* GINGHAM.) take the note
to my agent, and tell him to give Mr Darnley thirty
pounds—I can afford it.

Ging. This is too bad—take in his own friend,
and a man with a family! (*Aside.*) Sir—a word, if
you please—I told you, we were all blown upon—
now here's an opportunity for retrieving our reputation—lend him the two hundred pounds—prove, for
once, we can behave like gentlemen; and, hark'ye—
we sha'n't reach the top of our profession. (*Putting
up his neckcloth.*)

Flush. This is beyond bearing!—Quit the room
directly—'sdeath! leave my house, sir; begone, I
disinherit you—I——

Cla. Lord!—why so angry, guardian? I'm sure
he is a good young man, and as warm in his heart—

Flush. Warm in his heart!—nonsense!—will he
be warm in the funds? no—never—while he is so
candid—so——

Cla. Not while he is candid, sir?

Flush. No—do you think I made my fortune by
candour or openness? answer me, sir—did I ever
get a shilling by speaking the truth?—speak!

Ging. (*In a melancholy voice.*) No, sir, I never
said you did—I know the contrary, sir; madam, I'm

of a communicative disposition, I own; but there are many secrets of my father's I never blabb'd.

Flush. Are there, sir?

Ging. Yes, that there are, sir.

Flush. I don't recollect them.

Ging. Don't you? Why, now, did I ever mention, sir, that you got these pictures by suing out execution? That you got that plate, by its being pawn'd to you for half its value; that you intrigue with a female money-lender; and that the last time you were made a bankrupt, you went to get your certificate signed in a new vis-a-vis? did I, or will I ever mention these things?

Flush. Begone, sir—I'll never see you more— Yet, stay—you have papers in your possession; meet me in an hour's time at my agent's, sir—at Mr Ready's.

Ging. Forgive me this once, father; I'll never let the cat out any more.

Flush. No, sir, I never will forgive you—I am engaged, sir, and you know we great men are select in our company.

Ging. Well, if it must be so—farewell, father! the world is all before me, and what trade to follow, Heaven only knows. Good bye, madam—your sex will never befriend me, because I can't keep a secret, you see.

Cla. I will befriend you, sir; for while there is so much deception and hypocrisy in the world, it would indeed be unjust not to approve such frankness and honesty. Guardy, let me intercede for him; I'll answer for his conduct.

Ging. Ay; and if ever I mention ducking or swindling again—There, you see he's fix'd, ma'am.

Cla. At present he is, and therefore leave him; perhaps by the time you meet him at the agent's, I shall have talk'd him into good humour. Adieu:

depend on't, I shan't forget your generous intentions.

Ging. Nor shall I, yours : and if fortune smiles on me, I'll prove that I deserve your kindness—If ever my father pardons—but I see he's more and more angry, so I take my leave. May every blessing attend you—may you meet with a heart as liberal as your own—May your cousins' distresses vanish— may your guardian once more value a son, who can't help speaking the truth for the soul of him. [*Exit.*

Cla. Upon my word he's a charming man ! and pardon him you must, guardy, if it's only to please me.

Flush. No—I'm determined.

Enter a Servant.

Ser. The dinner's ready.

Flush. Come, Clara, you shall dine with me ; I want to talk to you, and if I could see my joint guardian, Sir Paul——

Cla. I met him at your door—he's only just gone by.

Flush. Just gone by ! that's a mistake; for the old beau has been gone by these thirty years : however, come in—come, and eat and drink what you like. Call for Burgundy, Champagne, or Tokay— Ay, call for Tokay at a guinea a pint ; I can afford it, my dear ward, I can afford it. [*Exeunt.*

SCENE II.

The Crescent and the surrounding Country.

Enter LADY SARAH SAVAGE, *and* SIR GEORGE
GAUNTLET.

Lady Sa. Sir George, I own my weakness; the
proud, the haughty Lady Sarah is humbled: Darnley has ensnared my heart, and, one way or other, I
must ensure his pity—Heigho! you are his friend,
Sir George.

Sir Geo. You see I am; and that he esteems me
more than ever, is evident from his bringing Mrs
Darnley to my house—did you mind his orders to
her?—take an airing, my dear, with Sir George in
his phaeton! it will raise your spirits, my love!——
Ha! ha! he absolutely throws her into my arms.

Lady Sa. Yes; but she absolutely contrives to
get out of them again.

Sir Geo. She does; and therefore, there is no way
but the one I mentioned; we must make Darnley
jealous.

Lady Sa. True: I'll tell him that you love his
wife.

Sir Geo. Nay, nay, not me—fix on somebody else
—we'll soon find an object, and then, by convincing
him of her falsehood, he naturally turns his thoughts
to another woman; which is you, you know—and
she wanting a protector, consequently flies to another man, which is me, you know—we'll add the
signor to the confederacy.

Lady Sa. You're a sad wretch—a sad wretch indeed, Sir George, to impose on a friend, who places
such confidence—such—I won't hear you—positive-

ly I won't hear you—only observe, if I don't win the cruel Darnley's affection, I'll drive my phaeton down a precipice in reality; I will, or with the bayonet of my fusil, pierce my too tender heart, and expire at his feet.

Enter the honourable MR SAVAGE *hastily.*

Sav. So, Sarah—I and Sir Paul have had such an adventure!—though we quarrell'd last night, we made it up to-day; for I never think alike two hours together—Do you, sister?

Lady Sa. Never: but when I think of you, brother, then I think more than I say, I assure you.

Sav. No; you say more than you think, I assure you—but, would you believe it? the old boy has seen his son—we traced him from the stage coach he came in, to the pump-room, from the pump-room to the billiard-room—there Sir Paul saw him playing with the marker, and when he heard the young man's name, he fainted; actually fainted in my arms.

Lady Sa. What, in a fit! poor old man! well! if you'll believe me, Sir George, I never saw a person in a fit in all my life.

Sav. Long before he recover'd, the young man was gone—the bird was flown—for the standers-by, all blacklegs, began laying bets on Sir Paul's recovery, and those who were against him wouldn't let water be thrown in his face.

Lady Sa. Inhuman wretches!—they ought to have sous'd him to death: but pray, brother, who is this child? where does he come from? what's the story?

Sav. Why—about twenty years ago, Sir Paul's lady quarrell'd with him at Tunbridge, and married a citizen—Four months after the marriage she had a son, which the citizen brought up as his own, and Sir Paul now swears the boy was his—'gad! it will be curious; for the child will have two fathers.

VOL. I.   K   †

Lady Sa. Curious! not at all—but why should you meddle?

Sav. Because it secures me the two best racers in the stud—Fidget and Fizgig; and what's better, because it still secures us Sir Paul's fortune; for though he won't marry you himself, he intends his son should; and, if I could but once more see the young man—I know he goes by his mother's name—(*Looking out.*) heh! it's him! there he is again!—get out of the way; don't interrupt—

Lady Sa. No—I have too great a regard for Sir Paul's property to interrupt any plan for securing it; besides, Sir George and I have business—come—I say, brother, tell the old gentleman to be careful, and in his eagerness bid him not claim another man's child instead of his own! [*Exit with* SIR GEORGE.

Sav. Where can Sir Paul be loitering? he said he'd follow me—mum! [*Stands aside.*

Enter GINGHAM.

Ging. Oh! what a whirligig world is this! I that was brought up to lend money, must now try to borrow it: but where? who'll trust a wandering linen-draper? who'll trust the notorious young P. O.? however, I've got my equivalent; I can speak my mind now—no longer need I smother my thoughts, and be ready to burst: no longer have an itching on my tongue, and be ready to bite it in two—no, no, I may open now. The sweet lady sends me word my father is inexorable, but hopes she shall soon see me again; heigho! I hope so too; when I think of her, my heart feels such queer sensations—I have it: she has taken lessons of my father, and swindled me out of my affections; but then my poverty—I can never indulge even a hope.—(*Sees* MR SAVAGE.)—Ha! here's the friend of the queer old gentleman, who fainted in the billiard-room.

Sav. (*Advancing pompously.*) Sir, the honourable
Henry Savage has the pleasure—the felicity——
What are you——

Ging. The honourable ?

Sav. Ay : why didn't you know it ?

Ging. No : nor never should if you hadn't told me
—ha ! ha! ha! ha!

Sav. Ha ! ha! ha! you're a droll dog ! 'gad ! you
shall come to my house, and pass a week with me.

Ging. Faith! a year with all my soul! I've nothing to do with myself; I've left off trade ; haven't
change for sixpence in the world, and so my little
right honourable—I'll honour you with my company.　　　　　　　　[*Shaking him by the hand.*

Sav. Hush! if you want money, don't own it : we
great people are close——

Ging. I know it; economical too !—You live
cheap.

Sav. What ! people of fashion live cheap ?

Ging. To be sure ; you don't pay ; and if that isn't
living cheap, the devil's in't !—ha ! here's the fainting gentleman again !—who the deuce is he ?

Sav. I fancy you'll find him a pretty near relation
of yours—at least if you were born at Tunbridge,
and your mother's name was Gingham.

Ging. It was ; that's the name of her, and of the
town.

Sav. Say you so ?—(*Enter* SIR PAUL PERPETUAL.)
The racers are mine, Sir Paul !

Sir Paul. Ay : my whole stud—any thing, every
thing ! only let me have another peep at my dear
boy !—only let me prove to posterity—

Sav. There he is.

Sir Paul. Where ?

Sav. There! there is your son ! who was born at
Tunbridge—whose mother's name was Gingham,

and who is now without a shilling in his pocket, or a friend in the world—joy! joy! old boy! you've got a young P. at last!

Sir Paul. Stand off! let me come at him; come to thy father's arms!

Ging. My father!

Sir Paul. Ay; thy real father: who has a fortune to bestow on thee, and health, youth, and spirits to share in all thy pleasures—The dog has my right eye to a T.

Ging. (*To* Mr Savage.) Pray does your friend bite in his fits?

Sav. (*Aside to* Gingham.) Hark'ye—it's Sir Paul Perpetual, better known by the name of old P.—he has an immense property.

Ging. Has he?

Sav. Yes; and if it's certain you are his son, he'll give you every farthing of it.

Ging. Oh! if that's the case—if he has an immense property—let me see who dare deny it. Sir, your blessing!—(*Kneeling.*)—I always said I wasn't my father's own child.

Sir Paul. Rise, my boy! my darling! and tell us how the citizen educated you.—The turn of my nose exactly!

Ging. I've done with linens, gauzes, and muslins now!—let the shop and all its swindling go to the bottom—I'm the son of Sir Paul Perpetual, better known by the name of old P. I'm not a tradesman——

Sir Paul. Tradesman! zounds!—my son brought up in a shop! how it freezes my warm blood!—look'ye, my boy—two things I must request of you —never to talk about trade, or mention your former father's name.

Ging. Never—I'll never mention his name, because I despise it: but as to trade, what's bred in the bone, you know, father——

Sir Paul. Well—well—come to Mr Savage's house; there we'll introduce you to your intended wife—Lady Sarah Savage will soon break you of talking about trade or the city—so come along.

Sav. Ay: pray give up the city—the rich rogues have no taste for us men of wit and genius—they estimate every thing by property, and if the great Ben Jonson—nay, if the great Big Ben, were alive, is there one citizen would give the poor dogs a dinner?

Sir Paul. No—you're right there; in the city a man that has no money, has no wit—the smallest bank-note is more entertaining than the wittiest manuscript; and talk of Ben Jonson's name for jokes —damme, Abraham Newland beats him hollow! isn't it true, my boy?

Ging. As true as that you beat any other father hollow—come—henceforth, no money-lending tricks for me. But young P. O. shall stick to gay old P.

[*Exeunt.*

ACT THE FOURTH.

SCENE I.

A Drawing-Room in MR SAVAGE'S *House at Bath.*

Enter SIR GEORGE GAUNTLET *and* SIGNOR CYGNET.

Sir Geo. Bravo! signor, bravissimo!—and so Lady Sarah Savage has actually persuaded Darnley, that his wife loves another man?

Sig. Si—at first he no believe—but Lady Sarah lay it down with such courâge—her oaths were so superbe, and mine so magnifique, that at last he accom-

pany us with tears—pauvre mister Darnley!—Ah, ha!
—you no forget my vife's concert?

Sir Geo. And who did you say Mrs Darnley was
attached to?

Sig. Attendez—Sir Paul—what you call—old P.
—he has found one child—eh bien!—the enfant was
at the comedie, and saw Madame Darnley and her
cousin maltraite by some qu'on appelle bobbies—
villains who fight de duels, and interrupt de music
—Vell! de child relieve de ladies, conduct them
home—sup, and dough all de time he make love to
Mad'moiselle Clara—

Sir Geo. Yet Lady Sarah Savage fixes on him for
Mrs Darnley's gallant—excellent! and if this scheme
fails, I understand she has another—there is Mr Flush
—a sort of money-agent.

Sig. Je connois—je connois—he make a you poor,
by lending you cash.

Sir Geo. This Mr Flush has got Darnley's note
for two hundred pounds—now he can't pay it; and
therefore, if Lady Sarah Savage buys it up——

Sig. Je comprehende—she say, give me my heart,
or pay me my money—ah, ha!—I see you will be
the first fiddle yourself;—(*Looking out.*) le voici!—
here is Mr Flush!

Sir Geo. No—it's Sir Paul and the son you spoke
of—good day, signor—and if you see Darnley, tell
him I'm out of town.

Sig. I vill!—ecoutez—I no like to meet this Sir
Paul—ven he ask me to his house, he always sing
himself—toujours—if he has de cold—de sore throat
—il chante! and begar, he sing as well with the
hoarseness as without—bon-jour, Sir George—bon-
jour—(*Going, recollects and turns back.*) Ah, ha!—
you no forgot my vife's concert?   [*Exit.*

Sir Geo. Darnley, jealous of his wife! and she under my own roof!—now, if I can persuade her to
retaliate—here's her supposed gallant.

Enter SIR PAUL *and* GINGHAM, *elegantly dressed.*

Ging. I tell you, father, Clara Sedley is the girl of my heart!—your ward is the girl for young P.

Sir Paul. Nonsense!—haven't I made you a gentleman—stuck a sword by your side?—haven't I brought you here to address Lady Sarah Savage?—ha! Sir George!—now mind (*To* GINGHAM.) and conceal your low education—not a word about trade or the warehouse; for I mean to put you into the army, and I've told every body you've been on your travels.—Sir George—my son!

Sir Geo. (*Bowing.*) Sir, I'm very proud of the honour.

Ging. Sir,—I'm very proud of—(*Bowing up to him, and spying at his chitterlin.*)—right India muslin, by all that's—mum!

Sir Geo. You've been a great traveller, sir,—much abroad!

Ging. Abroad!—yes, sir—I was seldom at home —generally at the West End ; for, between ourselves, though I was brought up to trade, I always despised the warehouse—always—pshaw!

Sir Paul. (*Taking him aside.*) Zounds!—mind what you're at—consider, if you talk as my son, about linens and the warehouse, they'll take your father for a tradesman; they'll say I'm a haberdasher, knighted on a city address.

Ging. A haberdasher!—that's a good one, a very good one—upon my soul, Sir George, my father isn't such a fool as you take him for—no—that he isn't—are you, father?

LADY SARAH SAVAGE (*without.*)

Lady Sa. When Mr Flush comes, shew him up stairs.

Sir Geo. Here's your intended wife, sir—'gad! I hope it will be a match, for Lady Sarah is so anxious

for a husband, that in the scramble, she might seize
me at last—Come, Sir Paul—let's leave the happy
pair together.

Sir Paul. Now, remember what I told you—Lady
Sarah is the essence of fashion and good breeding;
and if you want to polish, and rub off the city-rust,
imitate her—copy her elegant manners.

Sir Geo. Ay; she's the rage!—and, if he wants
to secure her affections, bid him imitate his father,
Sir Paul—copy you, and he must succeed with the
women.

Sir Paul. Ay, that he must, Sir George—there's
not a girl at Newmarket, not a dancer at the opera,
nor a singer at the ancient concert, but adores me—
they treat me with the same respect they would a
father—they say I'm so quiet—so inoffensive—so
harmless.

Ging. Harmless! do they say you're harmless, father?

Sir Paul. Ay, harmless; and under that idea,
I've done more mischief than any ten dangerous
men in Europe—So, copy her manners, and success
to you, my boy!   [*Exit with* SIR GEORGE.

Ging. Bravo! these are fine times, Master Gingham—but will they last?—is there no trick play'd,
or to be play'd thee?—Sir Paul, I'm told, has a way
of disguising himself in women's clothes—surely this
isn't another masquerading affair——Ah! here's
spouse!—now to imitate her fashionable manners.

Enter LADY SARAH SAVAGE.

Lady Sa. Marry him I will; because, in the first
place, there's a scarcity of husbands; and, in the
next, being his wife secures Sir Paul's fortune, and
makes Darnley for ever in my power—besides, I can
draw the youth into all my schemes—hem!

Ging. Hem! (*Imitating her.*) If this is a woman
of fashion, the breed is grown pretty bold, I think.

Lady Sa. I must shew him my spirit—terrify him before marriage, in order to tame him after. (*Going towards him, wriggling her head.*) Sir!

Ging. (*Going towards her, wriggling his head.*) Ma'am!

Lady Sa. Give me a chair! (*Staring full in his face.*)

Ging. A chair, ma'am?

Lady Sa. Yes, a chair, sir.

Ging. (*Staring full in her face.*) Essence of breeding!—she's the essence of brass! (*Brings her a chair.*) A chair, ma'am.

Lady Sa. (*Staring vacantly.*) He little knows what a life I shall lead him.

Ging. (*Shews alarm.*) Heh!—a chair, ma'am?— here's a chair, I say. (*Loudly.*)

Lady Sa. Oh, I forgot—I am really so absent—. (*Sits down.*) he! he! he! (*Spying in his face.*)

Ging. (*Sitting down.*) Are you really?—he! he! he!—I should like to—(*Mimicking.*) imitate her manners! hang me if I dare—she has set me all in a tremble—pheugh! (*Puffing himself with his hat, and drawing his chair from her.*)

Lady Sa. Look up, my hero! (*Slapping him.*) You can't think how I rejoice at your being design'd for the army. I'm of a military, martial turn myself, and shall serve every campaign with you.

Ging. You serve campaigns!—I wish I was out of the room—pheugh! (*Aside.*)

Lady Sa. I shall make an excellent soldier—a dauntless warrior!—and if you talk of little unfledged fluttering ensigns, look at me—look!—(*Shaking him.*) march!—wheel about!—left!—make ready!—present!—fire!

Ging. (*Looking first at her feet, then at her head.*) It is—it is an impostor!—ugh! (*Whistles.*)

Lady Sa. Sha'n't I make a warlike appearance?

animate one army, and intimidate another ! restore
the name of Amazon—revive the age of chivalry ;
and if there are fools that threaten, and cowards that
dread an invasion ;—oh ! how the thought fires me !
—(*Rises.*)—give me a few champions like myself,
and we'll stand on our white cliffs, and scare away
whole nations.

Ging. Damme, it's another man in woman's
clothes ! Don't agitate yourself—be composed—(*To
her, as she walks about.*) What would I give to be
snug behind the counter !

Lady Sa. I am no timid helpless woman ; I can
shoot—I can fence—flourish a sword, or fire off a
musket !—penetrate your sword-arm at the first
thrust, or lodge a bullet in your forehead at forty
yards.

Ging. Keep cool—my hero, keep cool ! Oh ! it's
a clear case—it's a man, and here am I to rub off
the rust, by being run through the body ! Sit down,
my fine fellow ! sit down.

Lady Sa. Fine fellow !

Ging. Ay, I see how it is—Sir Paul has adopted
me out of joke, and you are to make mince-meat of
me for my vanity !

Lady Sa. Why, what is all this ! (*Smiling.*) mince-
meat !

Ging. He smiles ! then the joke's at an end, and
they don't mean to hurt me ! Give me your hand—
you comical dog, give me your hand.

Lady Sa. Comical dog ! what do you mean ? explain.

Ging. Explain ! nay, that's too bad—Do you think
I don't know you, my jolly boy ?—do you think I
can't see you are a gentleman ?

Lady Sa. What ! I a gentleman ?

Ging. Ay, and a brave one too !—why, I suspected you at first sight !—I saw there was nothing fe-

minine about you ; and then, when I looked you full
in the face, Pooh, says I, this can never be a woman.

Lady Sa. Not a woman !—Have I studied modern fashions—exceeded all the present race of
high-spirited women—only to be mistaken for——
Oh Lord ! I never wept before in all my life—but
this—Oh ! I shall faint !—Oh, Oh ! (*Sits in a chair,*
weeping.)

Enter FLUSH.

Flush. My rascal of a son has gone off with all
my papers—Darnley's note among the number—
and though Lady Sarah would give twice the value
for it, I cannot find him——

Ging. (*Advancing to him.*) Hush !—not so loud,
father—he'll flourish a sword—fire off a musket !

Flush. He !—who ?—but how came you here, sir ?
in this disguise, too !

Ging. Phoo !—it isn't me that's disguised. A
word—(*Whispers to him.*) There ! (*Pointing to* LA-
DY SARAH SAVAGE.)

Flush. What ! that lady ?

Ging. No, that comical dog——I'm sure of it——
Mum !

Flush. Ha, ha, ha !—You blockhead ! why, it's
Lady Sarah Savage ! She's rather masculine, to be
sure ; but, Lord help you—she and I are old friends.

Ging. What ! you know her, do you ?

Flush. Know her !—why, I'll take my oath she's
a woman.

Ging. He'll take his oath !—Oh, then, I see my
error—She's on the pavé, discarded ; and they want
to palm her on me.

Flush. Fool !—would you make more blunders?
Can't you tell a woman of fashion from a —— ?

Ging. No :—There it is, sir—if women of fashion

will talk and dress like women of another description, who the devil can tell one from the other?
and if, likewise, they will hunt, shoot, and fence,
and prefer masculine assurance to feminine diffidence, is it amazing, that a gentleman should con-
found the sexes? However, I'm glad it's not a man.

Flush. Come——come——without further enquiry,
give me Darnley's note; the one Clara brought;
the comical dog there, as you call her, is in love
with Darnley, and wants to hold the bill as a rod
over his head: I shall only ask her one hundred
pounds premium for it.

Ging. (*Taking the note out of his pocket-book.*)
Only a hundred premium! heh!

Flush. No; I can afford it: and she, by arresting
him, can make her own terms—you understand?

Ging. Perfectly; so I'll shew her the note, and
make peace—(*Goes toward* LADY SARAH, *who is
still sitting.*)—madam—lady.

Lady Sa. Pshaw! don't come near me, brute.

Ging. I am convinced of my mistake, ma'am—
this gentleman will take his oath on the subject, and
therefore—in hopes of making amends—here is a
note, my lady; a note of Mr Darnley's for two hundred pounds.

Lady Sa. What did you say, sir?

Ging. A-note of Mr Darnley's, ma'am.

Lady Sa. (*Looking at it.*) So it is; sign'd with
his own dear hand—(*Rises.*)—Well, now I look at
you again, sir, I'm quite ashamed of our silly misunderstanding—I am indeed—he! he! perhaps it was
my fault—nay—I dare say it was—and so, that's
Mr Darnley's note, is it?

Ging. It is; and now I recollect, wasn't the lady
I conducted from the play his wife?

Lady Sa. It was—but *entre nous*—what's the price
of that foolish bit of paper?

Flush. Only three hundred pounds! one hundred for the premium, and two for the principal.

Lady Sa. Here is the money then.

Ging. (*Putting his hand on hers.*) Softly; keep the principal, because you'll both want it; and as to the note, I'll keep that, lest somebody else should want it! (*Putting it in his pocket.*) you brought me up to the trade, and if I haven't learnt a trick or two, Mr Flush, it's no fault of yours.

Flush. What! would you turn swindler, you rascal?

Lady Sa. Ay, this is a new mode of getting money.

Ging. No—not so very new—is it, Mr Flush?— However, as the wife is the only person that ought to have a power over the husband, I'll e'en go instantly to Mrs Darnley, and give it her.——

Enter DARNLEY.

Darn. (*Fiercely.*) What, sir?

Ging. A note for two hundred pounds, sir—have you any objections? never mind the loss of the premium, Mr Flush——you can afford it, you know—— adieu!—Mr Bluff, (*To* DARNLEY, *who is frowning.*) your servant—it wouldn't do—you comical dog, it wouldn't do!—(*Shewing* LADY SARAH SAVAGE *the note, and exit.*)

Darn. (*To* LADY SARAH SAVAGE.) 'Sdeath!— this is the very man you told me of.

Lady Sa. Ay, now can you want further proof of his attachment to your wife?—I'll leave it to any body:—isn't it evident, Mr Flush?

Flush. His giving her two hundred pounds is a strong circumstance, to be sure—but then, when I recollect the money is mine, and not his—

Darn. What then, sir?

Flush. Why then, I think, the lady ought to be
in love with me, and not him, sir.

Darn. I'll set out for London, and never see her
more—yet no—I'll be satisfied—I'll know the worst.
—I'll instantly pursue this new-found idol of her
heart, and if I catch him in her presence——

Lady Sa. Kill him—for a wretch, who can't distinguish the human species, isn't fit to live—come—
I'll go with you.

Flush. So will I—but pray don't kill him, till I've
got my papers.

Lady Sa. Nay, don't fret about it, Mr Darnley—
you shall return with me to Savage House—come—
never think of going to London at this time of year
—it's so thin—all the great houses are lock'd up,
and there's no making a fashionable party; is there,
Mr Flush?

Flush. Your pardon, ma'am—I and my attorney
can always collect a fashionable party; and if the
great houses are lock'd up, why there are great people in lock-up-houses; so don't be afraid of finding
good company, Mr Darnley.   [*Exeunt.*

SCENE II.

A Library in SIR GEORGE GAUNTLET'S *House.*

SIR GEORGE, *and a Servant, meeting.*

Ser. Sir, sir! Mrs Darnley is coming here to look
for some books.

Sir Geo. That's fortunate : did you deliver my
message to her and her husband?

Ser. I did, sir; I told them you were gone out of town, and would not return till to-morrow.

Sir Geo. Very well! then, in case of accident, leave open the private door that leads behind the library. (*Servant opens a door that leads behind the Library.*) A man of intrigue should always have a place to lay snug in; and where is he so little likely to be discover'd as amongst works of study and reflection? Here she is! mind we're not interrupted. (*Servant exit—*Sir George *retires towards the Library.*)

Enter Mrs Darnley.

Mrs Darn. Will Mr Darnley never be convinced of this friend's hypocrisy? he is so credulous, that he even now places more confidence in him than ever: I'm glad Sir George is out of town—I can at least pass another hour in peace, and—(*Going towards the Library,* Sir George *meets her.*)

Sir Geo. Don't be alarm'd, Mrs Darnley; I'm only a living volume, and if you will peruse my thoughts, you'll read of nothing but yourself—you are engraved here in indelible letters, upon my honour.

Mrs Darn. Sir, I was inform'd—but this is no time for parleying—alone and unprotected! (*Going;* Sir George *stands in her way.*)

Sir Geo. Nay, you know I have long profess'd a regard for you; long thought you the finest woman on earth; and, as a proof, didn't I offer you my hand, before my friend——

Mrs Darn. Friend! call him by some other name, Sir George, and don't profane such honourable terms.

Sir Geo. Why, isn't he my friend? haven't I so completely gain'd his affections, that he wishes me to win yours? does he not bring you here—to my house ?—leave me tête-a-tête with you ? and, in every respect, prove so kind, so obliging——

Mrs Darn. Hold, sir—if he has exposed me to insults, I am the person to accuse him—not you. I know his heart, and I know yours—one has my love —my esteem—the other——

Sir Geo. Has what, my sweet creature ?

Mrs Darn. My scorn.

Sir Geo. Nay then—I must tell you, that when I condescend to love a woman, I always insist on making her happy ; and therefore, with opportunity on my side, and the whole world to lay the blame on your husband——

Mrs Darn. On him ! the world is not so easily deceived : but lest it should, I'll vindicate his fame— I'll proclaim the falsehood of his friend—his perfidy——

Sir Geo. Gently—gently—I see I must take advantage now or never ! (*Goes to the door.*)

Mrs Darn. What do you mean, sir ?

Sir Geo. First to fasten the door, and then, my angel—(*As he opens it, to fasten it closely,* GINGHAM *enters, and pushes by him.*)

Ging. And then, my angel—to give you two hundred pounds—this note, ma'am, is Mr Darnley's— it accidentally fell into my hands, and I designedly place it in yours—put it up, ma'am—keep it tight in your pocket ; for what with one having a rage for disguises—another having a rage for swindling—a third—(*Seeing* SIR GEORGE.)—ha ! my judge of good breeding, is it you ?

Sir Geo. This blockhead has ruin'd one scheme already, I see.

Ging. I'll tell you a secret, Sir George ; you *fashionable* people are very *vulgar*—it is your fine clothes, gay equipages, and superb houses, that are well bred, and not yourselves, egad ! now only pull

off that spangled coat—stick yourself behind a counter, and——

Sir Geo. Sir, don't you see I'm busy ?

Ging. To be sure I do.

Sir Geo. Why don't you leave the room, then ?

Ging. Because I've no where else to go.

Sir Geo. Then I command you : this lady and I
are engaged.

Mrs Darn. Engaged, Sir George!——Sir, (*To*
GINGHAM.) if you'll conduct me to Mr Darnley, I
shall think myself a second time indebted to your
gallantry.

Sir Geo. Madam, I insist—(*Crossing* MRS DARN-
LEY, *and taking her by the hand.*)—retire this instant, sir—retire——

Ging. Oh, I perceive—he detains her for base
purposes ! Oh fie, fie !—fie for shame, Sir George—
is this your good breeding——your hand, ma'am——
(*Trying to pass* SIR GEORGE.)

Sir Geo. 'Sdeath—obey me, or this sword, with
which I've so often fought——

Ging. Often fought ! what, in earnest ?

Sir Geo. Rascal ! draw.

Ging. No—I'd rather not.

Sir Geo. What ! you don't like to fight ?

Ging. No—who the devil does ? but you call me
rascal, sir—now I've been long in doubt whether I
am one or not—but if I was half as clear on the subject as you must be, I'd own it publicly—I'd say,
" I, Sir George Gauntlet, am such a rude—ill-bred,
—vulgar——"

Sir Geo. Coward !—come on. (*Drawing his sword.*)

Ging. Come on !—Well ! why shouldn't I ? I may
be alarm'd at masculine women, but I don't care
that—(*Snapping his fingers.*)—for effeminate men !
so, though I never learnt to fence in all my life—

though I don't know whether to hold my sword in
my right hand or my left, have at thee !—ha !—ha !—

SIR GEORGE *and* GINGHAM *make two or three passes,
when loud knocking at the door interrupts them.*

Sir Geo. Zounds !—if this should be Darnley—
(*Looks out.*)—It is ! I'm ruin'd—undone !

Ging. Ay, ay, I must take lessons—I'm touch'd,
—pink'd——(*Shaking his hand, which is slightly
wounded.*)

Sir Geo. If I stir, I meet Darnley—hark'ye, sir,
(*Aside to* GINGHAM.) that lady's husband is now
on the stairs, and your present wound is only a
slight one ; but if you hint or speak one word against
my honour——

Ging. You'll run me through the body, I suppose
—well ! as I can't fence—mum !

Sir Geo. I shall not leave the room—I shall be
conceal'd, and on the slightest insinuation, by heaven ! I'll come forth and cut you into atoms : promise—or you know my way——

Ging. I do—I'll live and fight another day.

SIR GEORGE *goes behind the Library, unperceived by*
GINGHAM *or by* MRS DARNLEY.

Ging. I wish I knew the name of Sir George's
fencing-master—(MRS DARNLEY *comes to him.*)—
My dear ma'am, don't be uneasy—it's only grazed,
and if they don't send doctors and apothecaries to
me, I shall live to pink him, again and again.

Mrs Darn. Let me bind your hand, with my
handkerchief. (DARNLEY *enters behind.*) Indeed—
indeed, I owe you much.

Darn. (*Still behind.*) 'Tis now beyond a doubt—Oh
woman ! woman !

Ging. (*To* MRS DARNLEY.) You haven't got the

rage—no, you are what a woman ought to be; mild, gentle, affectionate—an angel, by all that's sacred.

Darn. How! make love before my face!—(*Advances.*) So, Mrs Darnley——

Mrs Darn. Oh, my dear —I'm so glad you're come—this gallant, generous young man——

Darn. Generous young man!

Mrs Darn. Has been wounded in my cause, and——

Darn. And you bound up his arm with your handkerchief!—nay, don't deny it, madam—with my own eyes I saw it.—Well, sir! what have you to say, sir? to that handkerchief, sir?

Ging. Say, sir!—why, I say, the handkerchief is as fine cambrick as ever was sold—twelve shillings a yard, sir!—at least I used to sell such for a guinea—a guinea, Mr Bluff——as to any thing else, if you are the lady's husband——

Darn. I am her husband, sir!—who has long loved —long adored her! and now comes here to witness her falsehood and his own dishonour.

Mrs Darn. What does he say?—dishonour!

Darn. Yes, madam,—with him! with this gallant, generous young man! Did he not last night accompany you from the play, and now do I not find you praising each other to my very face? observe me, Maria—as you have found me tender in my affections, so you shall find me severe in my resentment.

Mrs Darn. I know not what he means, but I thought they'd make him hate me—I guilty of falsehood! dishonour to my husband! Oh, Harry! if you believe me so debased, take up that weapon, and pierce me to the heart! in pity do!—I cannot live, and know that you condemn me.

Darn. (*Taking her hand.*) Do you not love him?

Mrs Darn. Whom?

Darn. (*Pointing to* GINGHAM.) Him.

Ging. Me!—love me!—I wish she did, for if I

didn't use her better than you do, I'd cut my jealous
head off!—look'ye, great lord and master:—she is
more faithful to you, than you deserve—I know it,
because, just before you enter'd the room, Sir George
Gauntlet, like a vile seducer as he is, was attempting to——(*Here a book falls from the library.*) crau—
au—au! (*Checking himself.*) I shall be a dead man
before I know it.

Darn. Sir George Gauntlet!—paltry evasions!—
he is out of town, and has so often proved himself a
friend——

Mrs Darn. Friend!—Oh, Mr Darnley! at last I
am compell'd to tell you he is your enemy and mine
—it is that very friend who would destroy your domestic peace; who would rob you of a heart that is,
and ever shall be, all your own! and that, even now,
might have triumph'd o'er a helpless woman, had
not his friendly arm been stretch'd to serve me.

Ging. It's true—I'll swear it!—I'll——(*Another
book falls.*) crau—au—au!

Darn. I'll not believe it—he is above such arts,
and I would have you, madam, not increase your
guilt, by daring to abuse my best of friends.

Ging. Best of friends!—upon my soul, you've a
rare set of acquaintance then.—Sir! I always had a
knack of speaking what comes uppermost, and I say,
Sir George wanted to turn me out, in order to lock
her in—I say, he gave me this wound, in trying to
defend her from his insolence—I say he is now conceal'd in this room!

(*Books fall from the Library, and leave an open space.
Gingham looks round, and sees Sir George's
face frowning at him through the aperture.*)

Ging. No—I don't say he is in the room—I don't,
because—because—(*Looking round again.*) it's better to be choak'd than kill'd.

Darn. See how he prevaricates: and therefore,

that my friend may be slander'd and I deceiv'd no
longer, 'tis time I should decide—Maria!—It almost
kills me to pronounce it——(*Aside.*) we meet no
more——   (*Going.*)

Mrs Darn. (*Holding him.*) Stay—spare me but a
moment—I cannot, will not, lose him; Harry, think
of our love—our children.——

Ging. Sir! sir!—let me ask you two questions—
(*Another book falls, and* SIR GEORGE *frowns at him.*)
Ay, grin away you——sir, can you fence, and will
you fight?

Darn. Perhaps, you'll find I can, sir.

Ging. And if I prove that Sir George hid himself
to avoid you, will you stand by, and see a poor fellow cut to atoms?

Darn. No—on the contrary, I shall be so convinced of the truth of your story——

Ging. Say you so? then come out, you black infernal seducer!

(*Runs up to the Library—forces open the front doors,
and amidst the falling of all the books,* SIR GEORGE
GAUNTLET *is discover'd.*)

Ging. There—there he is! and now come on, if
you dare—here's a pair of the best fencers in Europe? (*Snatching up a sword, and placing himself by*
DARNLEY.)

Darn. 'Tis all unravell'd—detested hypocrite!

Sir Geo. Ah, Darnley!—how d'ye do?—this is a
droll circumstance, isn't it?—but I hope you are
convinced—

Darn. Yes, sir, I am convinced.

Ging. We're all convinced, sir.

Darn. That you and Lady Sarah have join'd in a
conspiracy to deceive me and betray my wife; that
you have meanly put on the mask of friendship, to
conceal the blackest artifices, and that if you had

come to my house, and boldly plunder'd me of all
my fortune——

Ging. He'd only have been hang'd!—but now he
shall be cut to atoms.

Sir Geo. Be cautious in your language, Mr Darnley—you know my disposition.

Darn. I do—I know you well: and henceforth, if
you dare, either by action, word, or look; mark me,
sir—raise but a blush in her unsullied cheek, I will
resent it—I'll inflict a punishment great as your arrogance deserves!

Sir Geo. Arrogance!

Ging. Ay, arrogance!—are you deaf?

Sir Geo. Sir, this requires an explanation; you
shall hear from me.

Ging. Pooh!

Darn. Delay not then, for I shall leave your house
this moment. (SIR GEORGE *exit*.)—Come, Maria,
to you and this gentleman I have a thousand apolo-
gies——

Ging. Bless you! I'm amply paid in letting my
tongue wag—and as to any thing else, allow me
once more to speak my mind to your sweet cousin,
Clara.—Come, let's go to her—Oh, you well-bred
ruffian!—to be first pink'd, and then nearly choak'd
by such a ———; on the whole, though, I never
fought better in all my life!   [*Exeunt.*

ACT THE FIFTH.

SCENE I.

*A Room in a Tavern—Dinner under covers—*DARN-
LEY *discover'd sitting at the Table—Waiter attending.*

Darn. Tell Sir George Gauntlet, Mr Darnley is
waiting.—What's o'clock?

Wait. Six, sir.

Darn. The time draws near—I wonder where my
friend can be? put some wine on the table, and leave
me.

Wait. Sir George is below, in close conversation
with a gentleman, who seems anxious to see you,
sir.

Darn. His second, I suppose—tell him, I am here
—(*Waiter exit.*) 'Sdeath!—to what have I reduced
myself—I that had every joy this world can give
—a peaceful home—a wife that loved, and children
that revered me!—I to be now in a tavern, on the
eve of meeting with a profess'd duellist; to be about
to commit murder, or else to live dishonour'd and
disgraced—Oh, Maria!—when thou shalt hear thy
husband is no more, wilt thou forgive me?—wilt
thou—but my fate determines hers, and if I fall she
is for ever lost!

Re-enter the Waiter.

Wait. The gentleman from Sir George Gauntlet,
sir.

Darn. Admit him—now then for the event!

Enter GINGHAM *hastily.*

Ging. I'm so fagg'd—so completely knock'd up:—

(*Sees the dinner.*) ha, ha! what's here!—the very thing to revive me.

Darn. I hope, sir, you haven't been talking to Sir George.

Ging. Yes, but I have though—you employ'd me as second, and if you're shot, it shall be in the way I like best. (*Sitting down.*) Waiter! waiter!

Wait. (*To* GINGHAM, *who is going to pull off a cover of one of the dishes.*) Sir! sir!—Sir George order'd that dish not to be touch'd till he came.

Ging. Did he ?—then it's the pick'd thing, I suppose, so I'll eat it all up directly, (*Uncovers it, and sees a brace of pistols laying 'midst powder and ball.*) here—it's quite at his service, and I wish the whole were in his stomach, with all my soul!—(*Giving the dish to the waiter, and uncovering another.*) Ah! here's something that I can swallow. (*Begins eating.*) Well, after hunting every where for Sir George, I found him below stairs at last—" So," says I, " My little librarian"—alluding to the book-case you know—" when are you and this jealous husband,"—alluding to you, you know—" to fight this foolish duel ?" (*Drinks a glass of wine.*) Clara! my dear Clara Sedley!

Darn. Well, sir.

Ging. Says I, " The fact is this; one will be kill'd, the other be hang'd, and the world get rid of two hot-headed fellows;"· says he, " Will Darnley make me an apology?" says I, " He might as well."

Darn. You did not!

Ging. Ah, but I did though: " It's very well for fashionable husbands to leave their wives with friends, in hopes of getting divorces and damages; but what right," says I, " has a country 'squire to quit his farm, and trust his wife with baronets, fools, and coxcombs—to plant his own horns?" says I. (*Drinks.*) " Success to trade."

Darn. And how did this end, sir ?

5

Ging. How!—why the other second interfered—said Sir George couldn't fire at you, and advised him to apologize—he hesitated—I put my hand on my sword—reminded him of my fine fencing—he sign'd this paper—I've already shewn it to Mrs Darnley, and so—(*Drinks.*) Here's the child that has two fathers!

Darn. (*Reading the paper.*) 'Tis ample, final satisfaction—wasn't my Maria happy?

Ging. She was—but with women, grief soon follows joy, you know—she says, your uncle, whoever he is, has order'd you to quit Bath, and go abroad—that she is to be left behind, and, as your fortune is exhausted, she fears you must consent—I'm sorry I'm pinch'd too—however—(*Drinks.*) Here's confusion to your stingy old uncle!

Darn. Unfeeling, persecuting man!—separate me from all I love!—I know the motive for this barbarous conduct—he has found a son, on whom he means to lavish all his favours, and while he rolls in luxury, I and my family may starve—may—but he comes.

Enter SIR PAUL PERPETUAL.

Sir Paul. So, Mr Darnley: how dare you intrude into the houses of great people, and thus repeatedly disgrace me?—look'ye, sir—I have made up my mind—you must seek your fortune abroad—I'll pay your expences to the continent; and, lest your family should be a burthen to you, I'll provide for your wife at home.

Darn. Oh, sir! do not part us!

Sir Paul. I will!—I'm resolved! (*Seeing* GINGHAM.) hah!—what do I see?—my boy!—my darling!—how came you here, you rogue?

Ging. Father, you're come in time—just in time, to finish the bottle! (*Filling him a bumper, and putting it in his hand.*) drink! drink the last toast!

Sir Paul. Ay, what is it?

Ging. " Confusion to Darnley's"——

Sir Paul. With all my heart—" Confusion to Darnley's——"

Ging. " Stingy old uncle !"

Sir Paul. (*Spitting out the wine.*) Stingy old uncle !—why that's confusion to myself, you dog !

Ging. What ! is it you ?—well ! hang me if I didn't think it was my father—that is, my other father, the money-lender—Cousin—relation—how are you ? (*Shaking* DARNLEY *by the hand.*)

Sir Paul. Nonsense ! never mind him——I've brought you your commission—a company in a regiment serving in Ireland.

Ging. Have you ? (*To* SIR PAUL.) Who'd have thought my father was your miserly uncle, heh ! (*To* DARNLEY.)

Sir Paul. It's three hundred a-year, my boy !— Psha ! don't mind him, I tell you, (*Pulling him away from* DARNLEY.) I reserve every thing for you—I always meant to give all I could to my son.

Ging. Did you !—Oh then it comes to the same point ; why, perhaps, you'll give me two hundred pounds.

Sir Paul. Ah, that I will.

Ging. What ! and the commission too !

Sir Paul. Yes, and the commission too ! here they are both—and some ten years hence, I'll join the regiment, and serve under you ; under my brave son !

Ging. No—under your brave nephew, if you like— I don't understand the exercise, and Darnley does ; and therefore, as we're all relations—all in a family, I'll e'en give him the commission—Nay, don't be shy, cousin—it makes no difference, father, does it ?

Sir Paul. Death and fire ! it does, sir, it makes all the difference, and I swear——

Ging. Softly—you can make me a hero in another way—as I was brought up to trade, pop me into the train-bands—then I can be kill'd in the Ar-

6

tillery Ground in one day, and be alive in the shop
the next! so keep the commission, cousin; keep it—
(*Forcing it into* DARNLEY'S *hand.*) and here—
here's the money to take you, your wife and children, to Ireland—(*Giving the bank notes.*)—there!
now moderate your joy, father; you've done a kind,
generous action, to be sure: but why—why in such
an ecstacy?

Sir Paul. Ecstacy! agony, you puppy!

Ging. Gently, gently; at the public breakfast I
shall sound forth your praises.—Come, cousin—the
best of the joke is, I've another father; and though
he won't lend you a shilling, I'll make him send you
linen enough to shirt your whole regiment.—Farewell, thou liberal man!—-look!—-Self-gratification
has brought tears of joy into his eyes.

[*Exit with* DARNLEY.

Sir Paul. Tears of joy!—if being cheated out of
my money makes me cry for pleasure, what shall I
do if I get it back again?—was there ever such a
fellow?—however, the commission is of no use to
Darnley——but then the two hundred pounds, and
the ease with which he did it.

Enter a Servant.

Ser. A letter from your ward, Sir Paul. It requires an immediate answer.

Sir Paul. (*Reading it.*) " Sir, I am now at the
public breakfast, where Lady Sarah Savage actually
insisted on my coming. I have discovered a deep plot
of Mr Savage's; and, when I tell you I am in danger
of being run away with, without my consent, I'm
sure you will fly to the relief of your—Affectionate
ward,   " CLARA SEDLEY."

Sir Paul. I'll come directly—(*Servant exit.*)—So,
—so—they have heard of her sudden acquisition of
fortune—of the copper mines being discovered on
her estate, and now, like true savages, they mean to

paw the property—but I've a husband for her in my eye. She has formed an affection for this liberal son of mine, and the dog can't take *her* for a man in woman's clothes.

Enter FLUSH.

Flush. You knave!—if I catch you—how! has he left the tavern?—Ah, Sir Paul!—pray, sir, have you seen any thing of my son?

Sir Paul. I know nothing of your son, sir.

Flush. He has been distributing my property—giving away my money, Sir Paul.

Sir Paul. 'Gad! my son has been doing me the same favour.

Flush. Ay, sir; but my son has swindled me out of two hundred pounds.

Sir Paul. That's the exact sum my son has swindled me out of—so let's shake hands, and cry for joy!

Flush. Well, well--I can afford it--but, Sir Paul, there is only one way he can make me retribution—you've heard of our ward's copper mines, and though you have only known me as a private gentleman, and I you as joint guardian, yet I think you will consent to her marrying the man I propose.

Sir Paul. And pray, who may the gentleman be? —not the Honourable Mr Savage, I hope, for he has no property but my two racers.

Flush. No—no—my son—my rogue of a son!—will you agree?

Sir Paul. Why, I would with pleasure, only—

Flush. What, brother-guardian?

Sir Paul. I mean to propose my rogue of a son.

Flush. Your son!—why how came you by a son? —but to the point—my boy has won her heart, Sir Paul.

Sir Paul. So has mine too, Mr Flush.

Flush. Yours too!—'Sdeath, Sir Paul—this racing has turn'd your brain.

Sir Paul. Racing!—I've done with it, sir—I hate it—I'm above the turf now.

Flush. Above the turf! I wish you were under it!—do you pretend she loves both our sons?—two men at the same time, sir?

Sir Paul. To be sure—she's not the first woman that has loved twenty at the same time, sir—but, as she can't marry without our joint consent, and is now in great distress at Lady Sarah Savage's public breakfast, let's adjourn there directly.

Flush. With all my heart—I can afford it—Public breakfast!—why this is later than usual—(*Looking at his watch.*)—Nine o'clock at night!

Sir Paul. Ah, these are late hours! but what need we care, Mr Flush;—we that have health, youth, spirits—do you know there is only one house in England that affects my constitution.

Flush. And what house is that?

Sir Paul. (*Whispers him.*) I never was there but twice—the first time there was a motion about relieving poor insolvent debtors, and the house was so empty I got an ague. The next time, somebody moved to remove the hackney-coaches from Bond-Street, and the benches were so cramm'd, that I was thrown into a fever!—So hey for the breakfast.——Youth's the season made for joy!

Flush. Love is then our duty! &c.

      [*Exeunt, singing together.*

SCENE II.

A Garden at Mr Savage's *on Lansdown Hill—A Marquee at the upper Wing, in which is seen a Table full of Fruits, Wine, Meat, Tea-urns, Coffee-pots, &c. A distant View of Bath—Moon rising—Long Flourish of Clarinets.*

Enter Lady Sarah Savage *and a Servant.*

Lady Sa. Call Miss Clara—— (*Servant enters marquee.*)—I have given this party in order to secure this young creature and her fortune; for my brutish brother has so lessen'd our gold, that only her copper can save us from sinking—if her guardians refuse, we are prepared for bolder schemes.

Enter Clara.

Well, my dear girl, how do you like our breakfast ? —breakfast by moon-light ! isn't it quite charming —so nouvelle ?

Cla. Quite——and in addition to tea and coffee, here are fowls, fruit, and wine; so that you may breakfast, dine, drink tea, and sup, all in the same meal—nouvelle !—surely nobody else is so singular.

Lady Sa. I don't know—I never copy——the world's so very ignorant—that, only act unlike other people, and you're pretty sure of being right.—But didn't you like the music—the singing ?—

Cla. No ; I don't like much these fine singers— it's a long time before you prevail on them to sing, and then when they once begin, faith they never stop. I declare I only saw one person I liked amongst the party.

Lady Sa. And who was that—the dear Signor?

Cla. No—the dear creature, my guardian's son.

Lady Sa. What! that monster? I wonder who invited such a heterogeneous animal, and you to prefer him——

Cla. Even to your brother, ma'am—I know Mr Savage designs me his hand; but, if my guardians will agree—and why they leave me in this scene of danger, when I wrote to Sir Paul——

Lady Sa. Here they are both—I'll go call my brother, and by the time I return, I hope I shall call you sister—adieu!—Gingham, indeed!   [*Exit.*

Enter SIR PAUL *and* FLUSH.

Flush. Here she is—here's the girl to answer for herself—now be cool, Sir Paul—compose yourself, and I'll fairly put the question to her—Clara, haven't you fix'd your affections?

Cla. To confess the truth, I have, sir.

Flush. Very well—softly, Sir Paul!—and now, what is the gentleman's name?

Sir Paul. Ay, what is his name, Clary?

Cla. Gingham, sir.

Flush. There! I told you so—it's my son!

Sir Paul. Why there! I told you so—it's my son!

Flush. Your son!—in the first place, I don't believe you have a son; and, in the next, do you pretend that this Gingham——

Sir Paul. Is my boy! my own darling child!—and I'll prove it.

Flush. Well, well, if this is the case, I'll make you a fair proposition; let's call in both our sons, and let the one she prefers be her husband.

Sir Paul. Agreed—and I'll bet you a hundred pounds she chooses mine.

Flush. Done—I'll bet you a hundred she chooses mine.

Ging. (*Within the marquee.*) My life! my love! my Clara!

Flush. Here he comes! (*Rubbing his hands.*)

Sir Paul. Here he comes! (*Rubbing his hands.*)

Ging. (*Within the marquee.*) I cannot live a moment from thee—I—

GINGHAM *enters from the Marquee, and, seeing his two Fathers together, pauses, and starts.*

Flush. Now, Clara—Silence, Sir Paul!—don't you choose him!—him!—for your husband?

Cla. I do, sir.

Flush. Huzza! I've won my bet!

Sir Paul. Here is a father don't know his own child!

Ging. (*Coming between them.*) And here's a child don't know his own father! upon my soul, gentlemen, I cannot tell which of you had the honour of inventing me; but here I am; and if you have more property to distribute—if either of you has another two hundred pounds, I'll dispose of it so neatly, that tears of joy shall trickle down your cheeks!

Flush. (*After looking some time at* SIR PAUL.) Sir Paul!

Sir Paul. Mr Flush—We were joint guardians just now, and——

Flush. And now we're joint fathers, it seems.

Sir Paul. This must be the tradesman—a word in private, if you please, sir. (*They enter the marquee.*)

Ging. Lay your heads together; settle it as you please; for while Clara smiles on me, I care not whether I'm son to a haberdasher, or heir to the grand Turk.

Cla. I hope they won't quarrel—I fear Mr Flush will insist——

Ging. He insist!—bless you, he'd sell me for half a crown!

Re-enter FLUSH *and* SIR PAUL.

Sir Paul. He's mine! he's mine! the father knows his own child at last—I never suspected Flush was clerk to a Lottery Office, and consequently little thought he was the tradesman who married my Nelly—'gad! I always took him for a gentleman.

Ging. Did you?—that was very good-natured of you——and so you give me up, Mr Flush?

Flush. Yes, I can afford it.—The Tunbridge story is perfectly explain'd, and I have done with you, you rogue—Your wise father here has promised to restore my papers, so now you may speak truth till you're black in the face.

Ging. May I?—then I won't; lest other faces should be of the same complexion—but, gentlemen, since you've found out who I belong to, will you inform me who this lady is to belong to?

Cla. Ay, Mr Flush—I'm sure I shall have your consent—you are a monied man, and have lived with people of rank.

Flush. Your pardon, ma'am, if I had lived with people of rank, I had not been a monied man—the fact is, I touch cash wherever I can, and Sir Paul has bribed me so handsomely, that I have sold my consent—I have sold my ward as well as my son, and for this plain reason—I can afford it.

Sir Paul. Clary, take his hand, my girl. (*Giving her to* GINGHAM.) The dog has an odd way of speaking his mind, but instead of checking him, encourage him; many a man only wants to be told of his errors to correct them, and that is my case——

Ging. Your case, sir?

Sir Paul. Yes, my boy—since you talked of self-gratification bringing tears of pleasure into my eyes, I resolved to try the experiment—I determined to retrench my expences, to sell my hounds, dispose of my stud, and see if I could not lay out my money on rational and solid pleasures ; in bestowing happiness on two as innocent and injured creatures as ever existed !

Enter MR *and* MRS DARNLEY.

Sir Paul. Niece, your hand—Darnley, forgive what's past, and henceforth if I don't prove a friend to you, tell that son of mine to speak his mind to me —tell him to take another two hundred pounds out of my pocket ; nay, disperse my whole property— any thing, so you don't drink " Confusion to a stingy old uncle !"

Mrs Darn. Sir, we owe every thing to your son— he has been our pilot through the storms of fashion, and if he now secures to us independence and our cottage——

Sir Paul. Independence and a cottage ! 'Slife ! you shall have affluence, and a farm as large as Salisbury plain—I'll come and see you every summer ; ay, for sixty years to come !—odsheart ! they say I'm like an old volcano, burnt out ! but it's a mistake—I'm like an Egyptian lamp that flames for ever —A'nt I, my boy ?

Ging. Must I speak truth, father ?—mum !

Darn. (*To* SIR PAUL.) You have made me the happiest of men, Sir Paul ; but you must excuse me when I say, that your son has the first and greatest claim——

Ging. Nay, cousin ; if you knew me half as well as I know myself, you would find I have as many faults as any of you.—But come, let's adjourn from this vulgar fashionable scene, and while they drink one toast, we'll give another—

—May manners masculine no more deface
The charms, that constitute each female grace,
To man be bold and daring schemes confin'd ;
Woman for softer passions was design'd,
And by meek virtue—to subdue mankind !
                                    [*Exeunt.*

LIFE;

A

COMEDY,

AS IT IS PERFORMED AT THE

THEATRE-ROYAL, COVENT-GARDEN.

BY

FREDERICK REYNOLDS.

DRAMATIS PERSONÆ.

Sir Harry Torpid,	*Mr Lewis.*
Gabriel Lackbrain,	*Mr Fawcett.*
Primitive,	*Mr Munden.*
Marchmont,	*Mr Murray.*
Craftly,	*Mr Emery.*
Clifford,	*Mr Farley.*
Waiter,	*Mr Simmons.*
William,	*Mr Curties.*
Jenkins,	*Mr Atkins.*
Jonathan,	*Mr Thompson.*
James	*Mr Abbot.*
Servant,	*Mr Lee.*
Mrs Belford,	*Miss Chapman.*
Rosa Marchmont,	*Miss Murray.*
Mrs Decoy,	*Mrs St Ledger.*
Betty,	*Miss Cox.*

SCENE.—A Sea-port Town, and the Neighbourhood.

LIFE.

ACT THE FIRST.

SCENE I.

Outside of CRAFTLY'S *Library; View of the Town, the Sea,* &c.

Enter MARCHMONT, (*with a Manuscript in his hand,*) *and* ROSA.

Rosa. Cheer up, cheer up, my father! surely this should be a day of joy.

March. It should; but 'twill not be; I have out-toil'd my strength.

Rosa. You have. For ten long years, the pro-duce of your pen has been our sole support; and for these six months past, the labour of the brain has been unceasing; night after night has been devoted to that one composition. (*Pointing to the manuscript in* MARCHMONT'S *hand.*) But now the book is fi-nish'd; and yonder lives the gentleman who, by the purchase of it, will recompence you amply. Look, there's the library; will not that revive you, father?

March. It will; for thence will come forth gold; and, oh! my child, you know too well how much we stand in need of it.

Rosa. I do indeed; and, if I dare advise, out of the little profit that produces, store up a part, my father.

March. No; 'tis already all disposed of—all devoted; and to the best of purposes—to make you happy, Rosa; to place you far above the frowns of fortune. There, (*Giving her a newspaper.*) read; read that advertisement; 'tis of my inserting.

Rosa. (*Reading.*) " Wanted, as teacher to a young person of the age of sixteen, a lady who will instruct her in music and drawing, on moderate terms. Apply at the Priory, near Ashdown."—-How! this for me, my father!

March. Yes; 'tis for you I have encounter'd such unusual toil. Think not that vanity's my motive: but consider, child, my health's precarious; and when I am gone, what will become of thee?

Rosa. O! cease, sir, cease to talk thus!

March. Nay, we are now prepared: for mistress once of these fine arts, you may ensure a livelihood by instructing others: as tutoress, you may procure an honest, ample income; and your father—yes, my Rosa, death will lose half its terrors at the recollection that my child's provided for.

Rosa. Death!—oh! in pity, sir—I can't exist without you—what, what will money yield me?—remember, when I've lost you, I am bereft of all that's dear to me on earth—I have no mother to—

March. Mother!—-have a care!—-have I not charged you, on your life, never to breathe that deadly, harrowing word?

Rosa. You have; but the occasion called it forth; and 'tis indeed most hard that I'm to know no more, than that she's in her grave. Oh! let me once again entreat you to impart her history; give me each circumstance; or, if you will not tell me how she lived, inform me how she died.

March. (*Sternly.*) Well then, she died of a broken heart.

Rosa. What! she was wronged?

March. She was; by a villain, a most abandon'd villain.

Rosa. Oh! may heaven pour down its choicest vengeance—

March. (*Laying hold of her hand.*) Hold! his punishment is equal to his crimes—'tis in his head! his heart!—it gnaws, it maddens, it consumes him! —Fear not, my girl, I—I can answer for his sufferings; hell knows no torments like them.

Rosa. What! you avenged her wtongs?—noble, virtuous man!

March. Virtuous!—death and shame!—Hear me, Rosa; hitherto I have commanded silence on this subject, now I implore it; if you've one spark of pity for your distracted father, never, never name your mother.—Virtuous!—oh! my child! (*Weeps, and lays his head on her neck.*)

Rosa. Well, well, compose yourself: from this hour depend upon my silence.

Enter CRAFTLY *and* JENKINS, *from the Library.*

Craft. Come along, Jenkins; come from the crowd in the library, and I'll tell you such a secret.—Hey! that scribbler Marchmont; what brings him here?

March. Mr Craftly, may I entreat a word with you?—I must inform you, sir, that hitherto I have maintained myself and this unequalled child, by what my publications have produced from men of your profession in the capital.

Craft. Well, sir, and what's this to me?

March. You shall hear, sir. This day I have completed a new work, which, from the nature and locality of the subject, I offer first to you. It is a Satire on Extortioners; and is intended to expose that selfish, ravenous set, who, pirate-like, plunder each stranger that frequents our coast.

Craft. And you want me to buy it!—ha! ha! ha! —Do you hear him, Jenkins? he supposes I deal in books!

March. Why, don't you keep a library, sir?

Craft. To be sure I do; but there's every thing going forward in it but reading. Look, take a peep at them. One half of the company, you see, are making love, or talking scandal; and the other buying trinkets, or shaking the dice-box. Books indeed! why one would be enough for your frequenters of a watering-place; first, because most of them never read at all; secondly, because I doubt whether many of them can read; and thirdly, because those who do, so soon forget every line of the author, that one volume is a library to them.

March. Nay, sir, but when you reflect on the tendency of the production—

Craft. Psha! hang the tendency: write a panegyric on the glorious art of raffling, and then perhaps I'll talk to you. See! see how the flats bite! —all pulling out their cash, all putting down their names:—that's the manuscript, that's the real productive writing: and I'll bet, I get more by my evening raffles than ever bookseller got by Milton or Shakespeare. Besides, you are alive: if you want your book to sell, you should shoot yourself. An author never lives till he dies. So, to London, —send your works back to London.

March. I will; for there, (thank Heaven!) a library is still the seat of study and of learning, and never yet was prostituted to gaming and chicanery. —Come, Rosa, let us return to the Priory.

Craft. Take care, sir; remember that Priory belongs to my ward Gabriel; that the rent is small, in consideration of its ruinous state; recollect there are arrears.

March. I know; but he's too liberal—

Craft. He! what has he to do with it? don't I turn him round my finger? So be on your guard, sir; and instead of satirizing extortioners, extol raffling.

March. Never, sir; for though my toil's incessant, and my gains small, I will not profit by corrupting morals; and I would rather welcome beggary or famine, than pen a line to injure virtue, or degrade myself. Come, my child; we've been perhaps too sanguine; but we will not despair.

　　　　　　　　　　　　　[*Exit with* ROSA.

Craft. Insolent gazetteer!—but I'll humble him; yes, yes, I've already laid a train for him.—And now for the secret; what new master-stroke do you think this clever little octavo (*Pointing to his head.*) has achieved this morning? Mrs Decoy, a widow of family and fashion, first cousin to a baronet of ten thousand a-year, has consented to marry Gabriel.

Jenk. What, your ward?

Craft Aye: Mr Primitive, his rich uncle in Jamaica, desired me to select a wife for him, and I've done it: the widow has consented, and Gabriel is at this moment paying his first addresses to her.

Jenk. Impossible! a woman of family and expectations marry such a rustic!

Craft. That's it—that's the very reason. She says she is tired of town life, and town lovers; and therefore selects Gabriel for his rural simplicity. But I don't care about the motive; she's to give me twelve hundred pounds for my consent, and a third of what Mr Primitive settles on her into the bargain: now that's what I call a good morning's raffle.

Gab. (*Without.*) "Come, let us dance and sing—"

Craft. He comes; the enamoured swain appears. Now we shall hear how the courtship went on.

Enter GABRIEL, *singing*.

Gab. " While all the village bells shall ring."—
It's a match, guardy!—the great lady consents : I'm
a great man, you're another, and you shall be another, Jenkins.

Craft. Bravo! excellent!—What, and you like
the thoughts of matrimony now?

Gab. Hugely.—I thought at first it would lead to
wrangling and quarrelling ; but—he! he! he!—I
find that's all a mistake ; for the moment we are
united, that moment we are divided.

Craft. Divided!

Gab. Yes: a husband mustn't sit next to his wife
at table, nor hand her out of a room, nor dance with
her. In short, he mustn't be seen with her :—" So,"
says she, " we can't quarrel if we don't meet, you
know."—" No," says I ; " and, at that rate, if a man
wishes never to see a woman, ecod! he can't do better than marry her : so, send for the parson, become
Mrs Gabriel Lackbrain, and then, you know, I bid
you good-bye for life."

Craft. Well, and what did she say then?

Gab. Why, she laughed, and talked of her accomplishments ; reminded me of her finished education,
and spoke a good deal of one Meters and one Tasio.

Craft. Psha! it's the same person—Metastasio.
—Dolt! blockhead!

Gab. Blockhead! how could I help it? didn't you
bring me up among the mountains? And so I told
her—says I—" I know nothing of either of these
Roman warriors, and I don't see why I should : Latin won't teach me to sow barley, or Greek to fatten
a pig."—Says I, " I'm no foreigner ; I can write
and read my native language; and I wish, with all
my soul, your great scholars could say the same."

Craft. You did, did you? then she laughed again,
I suppose?

Gab. She did consumedly. But to conclude, she told me, though she preferred the country, I might visit London; and, that her cousin, the rich baronet, would introduce me to all the first circles. This, you may be sure, won my heart; for I had always a buckish turn, you know. So we struck the match; she sent for the clergyman——

Craft. Sent for the clergyman !—We'll go directly, and, by way of settlement, read the letter of Mr Primitive. Odsheart ! she's the very woman he'd select; so disgusted with London ! so devoted to the country !—Oh ! she'll have a thousand charms for him ;—and, what's better, she'll have more than twelve hundred for me (*Aside.*)—So, come, you rogue, come and be married.

Gab. Aye, the sooner the merrier, I say ; for I do so long to see the baronet, and visit London : and when I get there, dang it, how I'll astonish these cocknies ! I know they look upon us countrymen as a parcel of comeys and doeyes, that can only clap our hands upon our hearts and talk of conscience, innocence, and nature ; but they sha'n't wrong us in that manner ; they sha'n't suppose us so much behindhand ; for I'll convince them there's more love-making in our woods than in their squares; more drinking in our alehouses than in their taverns ; and for speculating and shaking a dice-box, you can satisfy them about that you know, guardy.—But now for the great lady.—" Come let us dance and sing, &c." 　　　　　　　　　　　　　　　　[*Exeunt.*

SCENE II.

A Room in the Hotel.

Enter CLIFFORD *and* WAITER.

Clif. You're sure there's no such person just arrived?

Wait. I'm sure there's no lady in the house of that description: but, if such a one should arrive, you may depend on the earliest intelligence from the best of waiters, in the best of hotels, in the best of watering-places.

Clif. That's right; and here's an earnest of my future bounty. (*Giving him money.*) Be wary now, for my existence depends upon recovering her. I came from London in pursuit of her, and she certainly took this very road. But, in the mean time, lay the cloth in the dining-room. (*Opens door in back scene.*) Why, here's company.—(SIR HARRY TORPID *discovered sitting in a chair, with a newspaper in his hand, fast asleep. A table close to him, with wine and glasses on it.*)

Wait. No, sir, the gentleman's just going. He came here about two hours ago, intending to enjoy our sea breezes for a fortnight; but, as usual, he is already tired, and will be off again in a moment.

Clif. Indeed!—Why, 'tis Sir Harry Torpid.

Wait. It is, sir: and, between ourselves, I fancy he is a little tired of himself; for he bribes the post-boys to drive like madmen till he gets to a place; and, when there, behold how it ends! in snoring over a newspaper, whilst the same boys are preparing to drive him equally fast back again.

Clif. Yes, I've known him long; and the cause of all this is, his having nothing to do.—But he wakes; I'll talk to him; leave us.   [*Exit Waiter.*

Sir H. Tor. (*Yawning and stretching out his arms.*)
Aw ! aw !—still in this infernal place ! still alone !
still—(*Rises.*)—Damme ! I'll be off. I'll try Tunbridge again : to be sure I've been there already
twice this summer : however, any where but where
I am. Here, waiter, a chaise and four again.

Clif. What, Sir Harry, have you forgotten—

Sir H. Tor. What, Jack ! Jack Clifford !—my
dear fellow, you're just come in time ; I was reduced to the last extremity ; had taken my after-dinner
snooze, read the advertisements twice over ; and, except paying the bill and wrangling with the waiter,
hadn't a single hope on earth.—But now ! sit down
and finish the bottle, my boy.

Clif. Why, you're a strange creature, Sir Harry !
but yesterday I saw you in Pall Mall.

Sir H. Tor. Yes, and very likely there you may
see me again to-morrow. I'm sick to death of these
sea-port towns. One goes to the libraries, the card-
rooms, and the tea-rooms ; and nothing interests,
nobody seems alive.—Upon my soul, Jack, if these
sea cormorants didn't continually compel me to put
my hands in my pockets, I shouldn't know that I was
alive myself. But you, what is your pursuit here ?

Clif. The most tormenting one in the world—love,
Sir Harry.

Sir H. Tor. Love ! Oh, how I envy you ! what
would I give to be in love !

Clif. Don't, don't think of it ; it has made me
miserable.

Sir H. Tor. So much the better ; that's what I
want ; and if I could but work myself into a most
unhappy passion—no matter with whom—were she
ever so ugly or ill-tempered, it would still answer my
purpose.

Clif. What ! would a scolding wife answer your
purpose ?

Sir H. Tor. To be sure : instead of sitting alone

in a coffee-room, picking my teeth, or yawning over a newspaper, think of having a fine, active, cheerful companion, who will scowl at me, snarl at me, and set my whole soul in a delicious ferment!—then, Jack, after an hour of delightful quarrelling, what say you to the reconciliation, to the kissing and making up again?—And, to complete the charming fire-side, call to mind half a dozen little Sir Harries; think of their noise, their nursing, their expence.— Oh! all this must produce agitation; and, were I as miserable as you are, I should be the happiest dog in England.

Clif. Psha! you know not what you talk of. Do you call it happiness to lose the object you are attached to?

Sir H. Tor. Lose her!

Clif. Yes, that is my case. My aunt, Mrs Clifford, lately brought with her from Switzerland, a lady of the name of Belford. At first sight I loved her; but, on declaring my affection, she treated me with scorn: however, I persisted, and, aided by my aunt's entreaties, hoped for success; when suddenly she left the house, and fled I know not whither.

Sir H. Tor. What, and you pursued her?

Clif. Yes; but hitherto in vain: cursed chance! I can gain no tidings of her.

Sir H. Tor. All the better again: the pursuit, my boy, the pursuit is every thing; and I only wish somebody would run away from me.

Clif. 'Sdeath! this trifling is ridiculous: were I as weary of myself, would I not seek out some employment?

Sir H. Tor. I have—I have tried every thing— devoted half my life, and nearly all my fortune, to racing, hunting, drinking, gaming, volunteering—in short, at the age of thirty, I've so outlived every enjoyment that, if I can't contrive to fall desperately in love, that I may run after somebody—to be sure, there's one other prospect—my creditors grow so pressing, that probably I shall have to run away from somebody; and then, you know, I'm comfortable; for, next to love, certainly debt is most likely to keep a man in hot water.

Enter WILLIAM.

Clif. Well, sir, have you been more fortunate than your master? have you any news of the run-away?

Will. Yes, sir; a lady, answering Mrs Belford's description, was seen this morning at a farm-house about eight miles off.

Clif. Indeed?—my hopes revive, and she shall answer for her haughty conduct. Come, shew me the way.

Sir H. Tor. What, will you leave me alone, Jack?

Clif. You! why I thought you were going to Tunbridge.

Sir H. Tor. Yes—but I'd rather go with you. It will be luxury to the solitude of a post-chaise; and, besides, who knows but this is the very woman I'm to fall in love with?

Clif. Have a care, sir—cross me in my passion, and——

Sir H. Tor. You'll blow my brains out?—There I defy you; for, if I thought I had any, I should have done them that honour many years ago. But, come now, a friend may be useful—you may want his advice, his assistance.

Clif. Well, I don't like to part with you, so allons.

Sir H. Tor. Allons—and now I start fair again.—But hold, hold—all right and honourable, I hope?—One had better do nothing than do badly; and, to fight against time, a man must sleep of nights—aye, and of days too: so remember, Jack, you found me sleeping—and don't, by drawing me into a bad action, deprive me of the best friend I have in the world.   [*Exeunt.*

SCENE III.

A Room at Mrs Decoy's.

Enter Mrs Decoy *and* Betty.

Mrs. Dec. Ha! ha! the day's our own:—they're snared, they're caught; and your ruined mistress will once more roll in wealth and splendour.

Bet. She will, madam—and all owing to your coming to this town on a matrimonial speculation.

Mrs Dec. Matrimonial speculation indeed, Betty! —Yes, when a run of luck had reduced me to the last shilling, didn't I tell you I would go to a watering-place, and save myself by catching a golden calf?—And I've succeeded; and how?—simply, by telling Mr Craftly I was heiress to a rich baronet, devoted to retirement, and would give him twelve hundred pounds, and a third of what's settled on me, merely for his trouble in consenting.

Bet. I know. But are you sure of your husband's wealth?

Mrs Dec. Oh, there you may trust me. His uncle, now in Jamaica, lately changed his name to Primitive, for a fortune of two hundred thousand pounds; and, in consequence of his daughter's death, adopted his nephew Gabriel, and appointed Mr Craftly his guardian—and a rare guardian he is! While he is nightly picking up a few pounds at his library, here have I, at one throw, raffled myself into a provision for life.

Bet. You have, ma'am; and I'm sure Mr Gabriel's a lucky man.

Mrs Dec. That's more than I know: he's but the husband of necessity: my cousin, my dear Sir Har-

2

ry Torpid is the object of my choice.—But silence! here are the two Gabies: I must support my character. [*Exit* BETTY.

Enter CRAFTLY *and* GABRIEL.

Craft. (*Bowing, all respect, &c.*) Madam, my ward has told me of your condescension; and though you laughed at him about Meters and Tasio——

Gab. Laughed at me! Lord help you! why Mrs Decoy isn't singular there; and, if it wouldn't make her jealous, I could tell her that all the women do the same:—yes, other young bucks may boast that the dear creatures smile upon them; but, ecod! I never look them in the face that they aren't in an absolute roar, he! he!

Craft. True; Gaby's an eternal source of good-humour. And now, if you've nothing further to propose——

Mrs Dec. Nothing, sir—only, to prevent the possibility of any misunderstanding, I hope Mr Gabriel has no objections to separate servants, separate incomes,—in short, a separate establishment?

Gab. None at all, ma'am: if you wish it, I'll sign articles of separation first, and marry you afterwards —I will, with all my heart and soul—that is, if guardy approves, for I always obey him.

Craft. Good boy! and this marriage is a reward for your obedience. But now to read Mr Primitive's letter, in lieu of settlement. Listen, for 'tis most important.—(*Reads.*) " Dear cousin Craftly, although I disapprove of early marriages, (having in the person of my unfortunate daughter seen the fatal effects of them,) yet, as I intend shortly to return to England, I beg you will select for Gabriel a wife of a quiet, retired disposition; and if, after residing with them at the Cottage one twelvemonth, I approve of their conduct, I hereby pledge myself to settle on them two thousand a year during my life, and the bulk of my fortune after my decease."

Gab. Bravo, nunky! dang it, we shall be up to our chins in clover, ma'am.

Craft. Stop—here's an awful proviso.—(*Reads.*) " But if, on the contrary, I find them unworthy my esteem, I shall not only revoke this promise, but consider myself at liberty to adopt whoever I think proper.   PAUL PRIMITIVE."

Gab. That's awful! rot it, it's main hard if we cant keep worthy for a twelvemonth. Besides, who else is he to adopt?

Craft. Who! why, the child of this unfortunate daughter he speaks of. Though he deserted her in consequence of her marrying Marchmont, he was still doatingly fond of her—and if Rosa should throw herself in her grandfather's way——

Mrs Dec. True—the sight of her might revive sensations——

Craft. Never fear—I've been aware of all that—and Marchmont and his daughter shall be kept out of the way. There are arrears of rent—and neither of them shall see Mr Primitive.—Mum!

Enter a Servant.

Ser. Madam, the clergyman is this moment arrived.

Mrs Dec. The clergyman! Lord! I'm so embarrassed:—aren't you, Mr Gabriel?

Gab. Why, I do feel somewhat flurried; but it's because I'm not used to it; if I was like you, I should not mind it. Lord bless you, I shall be quite bold and comfortable the next time I marry. But come, first for the ceremony, then for the Cottage.

Mrs Dec. Ay, then for the Cottage—and when we get there, I hope Mr Craftly will recollect that we shall want several new and additional articles of furniture.

Craft. I know; and, as it will give me a consequence in the town, I beg you'll so far indulge me,
that whatever either of you want, I may bespeak of
my own tradesmen in my own name.

Gab. Icod, we'll indulge you—and to begin, bespeak us a set of high horses and low carriages.

Mrs Dec. Ay—a dashing curricle, and a gay sociable.

Gab. No, not that; because, if we've a separate
establishment, any thing sociable will knock all up,
you know.   No, if we must travel together, we'll
have such a carriage as Mr and Mrs Jar have—a
wide postchaise, with a fine thick partition between
us; that's the way to prevent wrangling.   But now
for it—now for the clergyman—and then, Gaby, receive the reward of thy youth, thy beauty, and thy
accomplished manners.   [*Exeunt.*

ACT THE SECOND.

SCENE I.

*Outside of the Priory—distant View of the Sea—Gar-
den-Chair.*

Enter CLIFFORD *and* SIR HARRY TORPID, *hastily.*

Clif. Well, but I insist—listen—hear me, Sir
Harry.

Sir H. Tor. I tell you I'm not Sir Harry—I'm
another person—new born—just come into the world;
and, till this moment, never was alive.

Clif. Nay, but what has occasioned it? is it because you've found the object I'm in search of?

Sir H. Tor. No—'tis because I've found the object I'm in search of—the thing I've been looking for all my life—a woman—a lovely, agitating, tormenting woman. My dear fellow, give me joy; I'm as miserable as yourself.

Clif. Psha! I almost wish you were.

Sir H. Tor. Why I am—I tell you I am. But you shall hear whence my good fortune arose. After we had searched in vain for your runaway, I went to Craftly's library; and, as usual, was sitting in that listless, lifeless state, when yawning fill'd each pause the tooth-pick left; when (lucky chance!) I was awakened from my torpor by the voice of a distressed female: I looked up, and saw the most divine, fascinating, attracting little angel! tears were starting from her eyes; and, with supplicating hands, she was entreating that rascal Craftly not to send her father to prison.

Clif. What! and you became interested for her?

Sir H. Tor. Yes: how could I help it? She told him, he was a poor author—wrote for his bread—and if he arrested him for the rent he owed, in his present infirm state, he must perish. At this, my heart, which had hitherto been a sleeping partner, began bounding about like a tennis ball; and at the same moment, before she could raise her handkerchief to her eyes, one of her tears fell on my hand: I looked at it, and soon saw another—it was my own! the first I had ever shed. I hailed the sight; and only cursed my unlucky stars, I had never before known the luxury of weeping.

Clif. Why, heyday! this is indeed a transformation!—And did you speak to her?

Sir H. Tor. I did—and to that savage Craftly—but he was inexorable. On which, I fairly told her, I had nothing to do—my time was entirely on my

hands; and if she'd give me leave, I'd horse-whip
him through the world. To this she objected; and
not daring to offer her money—and indeed the sum
I had in this little gentleman, (*Producing a pocket-
book.*) being too insignificant to be useful—she went
away hopeless and disconsolate. I instantly enquired all about her; and there she lives; and here I'll
live; and let her treat me with indifference, I shall
still be grateful.

Clif. What! if she don't return your passion?

Sir H. Tor. To be sure. She has made me a
most unhappy, agitated being; and that's conferring
an obligation I never can repay.

Clif. Psha! I'll leave you to indulge your folly.
And now, mark the difference between us: I have
resources within myself; and if I fail in obtaining
the object I'm in search of, I shall fly to solitude
for consolation.

Sir H. Tor. Don't, Jack, don't think of it; I've
tried it.

Clif. You tried solitude!

Sir H. Tor. Yes; it won't do at all. For once,
when I found nothing else would answer, I went
alone to a remote part of the Isle of Wight, hired a
sort of hermitage, let my beard grow, and determined to dig my own grave, and howl if any body came
near me. Well, I couldn't dress my meat, or make
my bed, you know; so I was obliged to hire a kind
of a laundress; and though she was both old and
ugly, so tired was I of myself, that the sound of her
feet was music to me, the sight of her face trans-
porting to me, and her conversation—Oh! I used
to listen to her infernal nonsense with such rapture!
—Ah! Jack, Jack, you may talk of Petrarch and
other anchorets living alone; but it's all an imposition; they never got on without a Laura, or some
other snug thing, in their hermitages, you may depend on't.

Clif. Well, you're incurable; so adieu. When **I**
want you, I shall know where to find you.

Sir H. Tor. You will; for here I sit for life. (*Sitting in garden-chair.*)   [*Exit* CLIFFORD.
And, thank Heaven! now I can sit still a little; for
hitherto I have been so confoundedly fidgetty, that,
except when sleeping, I could never bring myself to
an anchor for two minutes together.—Gad! I wonder whether she's got home: I suppose not; for **I**
made so much haste from the library— (*Rises, and
gets behind a tree.*) No, she comes! the lovely, agonizing angel comes!

Enter ROSA.

Rosa. My poor father! how shall I tell him that
the interview has failed; that the unfeeling man rejects my supplications, and the reward of all his la-
bours is a prison? Alas! I dread to impart it.

Sir H. Tor. (*Advancing, and bowing.*) Then let
me do it for you, ma'am.

Rosa. The gentleman who was so kind to me at
the library!

Sir H. Tor. Yes, ma'am; and who from this hour
begs to be employed by you; who will go to London for letters for you, to India for muslins for you,
to the north pole for furs for you.

Rosa. Sir, you're very good; but I cannot think
of troubling—

Sir H. Tor. I like trouble, ma'am; and if your
father want assistance, if he want an amanuensis—
to be sure I can't give him thoughts or jokes—but
I'll copy for him till I'm as black in the face as his
own ink, ma'am.

Rosa. Sir, this kindness from a stranger, from one
on whom we have no claim—

Sir H. Tor. You have the strongest claim; you
gave me life, ma'am; you found me in a state of
apathy, inanity; but now! think of my enviable si-

tuation; instead of coffee-rooms, club-rooms, and card-rooms, I shall live in the open air, kneel all night under your window, and rend the sky with my despair and rapture!

Rosa. How! what mean you?

Sir H. Tor. Mean! that, doating as I do, I shall love every thing around you, reverence the woods that shade you, worship the winds that blow upon you, and idolize the little lap-dog that barks at you.

Rosa. Sir, I don't exactly understand you :—but my father expects me—good day.

Sir H. Tor. What! you cast me from you ?—Well, no matter, you've done my business, and I'm equally obliged to you.

Rosa. Sir, the obligation is on my part : the interest you have shewn for a most unhappy parent deserves my warmest gratitude ; and though, from our different situations, it is too probable we may never meet again, yet be assured, sir, I shall often think of him, who, in the hour of affliction, mingled his tears with mine.   Farewell, sir.   [*Exit.*

Sir H. Tor. (*Taking out his handkerchief, and weeping.*) Farewell! Farewell!—I'm choaked with grief, and yet never was so happy in all my life.— But what shall I do? how employ myself to serve her?—Suppose I try to pay her father's debts ?— Well, no bad beginning. But how? I've only these few notes, (*Taking out a small pocket-book.*) and if I offer them, it may perhaps offend —Distress—suppose—I have it—she's returning, she's coming this way; I'll drop it purposely that she may find it. My friend, (*To the pocket-book.*) I filled you to lay out in pleasure ; half's already gone in taverns and in travelling, and you've procured me not one atom; but if the other half snatches a needy author from a prison, you will have done your duty nobly—yes, that will indeed give pleasure. But she comes :

(*Drops the book.*) I'll to the woods, and give a loose
to sighs and tears, and happiness unequalled. [*Exit.*

Re-enter ROSA.

Rosa. Not there! my father not in the Priory!
—where, where can he have gone? Surely they
haven't already—(*Treads on pocket-book.*)—What's
this?—a pocket-book, and open, and bank notes!—
Heavens! how came it here?—Oh! no doubt it belongs to the stranger; he has lost it; dropt it by accident; and perhaps already feels distress from wanting it. Where shall I find him? for, after what has
passed, it would be gratifying to make even this
small return. Ha! he comes!—no, 'tis my father—
and in such haste! and looking so disordered!—

Enter MARCHMONT, *hastily.*

Speak, speak, sir!—what has happened?
March. So—I have out-run—escaped them—Oh!
(*Faint and overcome.*)
Rosa. Merciful powers! how pale, how wan you
look!
March. I have cause; for, even now, waiting in
yonder path for your return, two men approached,
and seized me. They said I was their prisoner, and
for rent due from the Priory; and, what is most per-
plexing and mysterious, they offered instant freedom, provided I would sail with you to some far-
distant land. This staggered and enraged me; I
struggled with them, and, in the conflict, I escaped.
But oh! my child, my feeble frame, already worn
with labour and with sorrow—your hand, your hand,
sweet girl.
Rosa. (*Leading him towards the chair.*) Oh! is
there no way to satisfy these most unfeeling men?
the debt is but a trifle.
March. No; but, poor and friendless as I am, 'tis

more than—soft!—assist me—I can go no further.
(*Falls into the garden-chair.*)

Rosa. And must I see you perish!—Oh, my father! live, for my sake live! Consider now our
hopes are vanished, and I left alone, no friend, no
mother—Oh! pardon, pardon! I forgot, I forgot.

March. (*Wildly.*) No mother, said you?—and
why, why, at this moment, is she not here to succour and console you?—But she's revenged; for
could she see me thus reduced, thus on the eve of
being torn from the sole pledge of our affection—

Rosa. (*Flying into his arms*) You shall not; we
will fall together.—(*Turns from him.*) Heavens!
when money could restore him, is there no mode?
—no—Ha! what have I here? (*Looking at the
pocket-book, which has been all the time in her hand.*)
Enough; more than sufficient for the purpose.—
Blessed sight! I—I can save him. (*Going hastily towards* MARCHMONT.)—And yet—(*Pauses, and recollects.*)—what am I doing? this money is another's;
and I must not—Oh! no, I dare not touch it.

March. Hark! they are coming!—Rosa, raise
me; help, help me to avoid them. (*She tries to raise
him; he falls back in the chair.*)—No, it will not be;
I am their victim.

Rosa. (*Kneeling.*) Oh! Thou who watchest over
trembling innocence! instruct, direct me.—There
is a parent perishing from sickness and distress;
here is the remedy to save him. Am I, his child,
to see him suffer on; or am I, by dishonest means,
to snatch him from the grave?— (MARCHMONT
sighs; she flies to him.) My father, speak—speak to
me, my father!

March. I do, I do.—(*Takes her hand.*) Ha! what
agitates you? what makes you tremble thus?

Rosa. Guilt, father, guilt. I have the power to
preserve you—look, here is the money—but it is not
mine, father, it is not mine.

March. Not yours!

Rosa. No; I found it—nay, worse, I know whom it belongs to. Pity me—spare me—I could with joy lay down my life to serve you; but I cannot—no, not e'en to save a father, can I descend to actions robber-like and base.

March. What! this is your resolution? (*Rises.*)

Rosa. It is: and do not blame me, sir; I act but from the lesson you have taught me. You bade me die rather than live dishonoured; and I've to thank you for the precept; for, though the sure result be fatal to us both, something within assures me I am right, and that the father will applaud the child who welcomes death in preference to dishonour.

March. (*Runs and embraces her.*) Come to my arms—you have revived, restored me! Now I can meet imprisonment, or death; my daughter's virtue will atone for all.

Rosa. You can forgive me then?

March. More—I can worship you! and since returning strength invigorates my frame, let us not sink beneath misfortune.—

Enter SIR HARRY TORPID, *behind.*

No; though the agent is our foe, the principal may still befriend us. What say you, Rosa, shall we go instantly and apply to Mr Lackbrain?

Rosa. Most willingly: but, alas! he's guided by his guardian.

March. True; but he oft has served me; I am his debtor for more than rent. Come, come, let us not despond.—(*As they are going,* SIR HARRY *advances.*)

Sir H. Tor. Sir, I beg pardon; I hope I don't intrude; but, as you seem somewhat fatigued and unwell, suppose you let me apply to this Mr What's-his-name: upon my soul, I've nothing better to do.

March. Sir!

Rosa. It is the gentleman who dropt the pocket-book, and I'm most happy to restore it. Sir, on my return I found this—

Sir H. Tor. It's not mine, ma'am; by all that's serious, it's not mine.

Rosa. Nay, I'm convinced that it is yours; and I request—

March. And so do I, sir; my daughter must not profit by any such accident.

Sir H. Tor. Well, as you please, sir:—but it's of no use to me; it gives me no pleasure; and therefore I shall only drop it again, you may depend on it.

March. That concerns not me, sir.—Come, my child, you see how you've restored me. And thus it ever is; let honour triumph; and, like the morning sun, it will dispel the mists of sorrow and despair.

[*Exit with* ROSA.

Sir H. Tor. So! as proud as Lucifer, I see that.—But I'll lay him under an obligation, I'm determined I will—if I set his house on fire, only to put it out again.—Who can he be?—Where can he come from?—I know my old flame, Mrs Decoy, is in the town; and I'll go enquire of her directly.—And here the chace begins; yes, now I perceive why every thing was tedious and uninteresting—I never hunted out the unfortunate—there is the secret. Let a man make virtue his pursuit, and he'll find life a very pleasant sport, I promise him.

Exit.

SCENE II.

An Apartment at MRS DECOY'S.

Enter GABRIEL, *dressed in white.*

Gab. Ha! ha! ha! what a rare jolly thing matrimony is!—If I had known it had been half so comical, to be sure I wouldn't have had a slice of it
many years ago.—And then, to get such a wife!
Oh, I'm the luckiest fellow!—I must remember I'm
married though; for my guardian has so hurried me
into it, and I've so seldom seen my spouse, that, after a glass or two at dinner, I didn't recollect her—
no, icod! and I trod on the toe of another man's
wife instead of my own.—I must also mind on another account; no longer, Gaby, must you be a gay
deceiver; no more with killing glances murder every
heart.

Enter MRS GABRIEL LACKBRAIN, (*late* MRS
DECOY.)

Mrs Lack. Come, my adorable! the curricle's
waiting; and as the Cottage must be our place of
residence, the sooner we get there the better. But
you must invite the baronet; positively Sir Harry
is the friend of all others to pass the honey-moon
with us.

Gab. No doubt; and if so great a man will condescend—I tell you what—suppose you get pen and
ink, and write to him directly?

Mrs Lack. I get pen and ink! I write! do you
imagine a person of my accomplished education ever
devotes a moment to writing?

Gab. Nan!

Mrs Lack. No, sir ; that is your department ; and whilst you are keeping accounts, managing the house, and looking after the servants, I shall be employed in more important matters—in dancing, singing, playing—in short, in gratifying my husband's vanity, by making myself adored by all mankind.

Gab. What ! so when I want my dinner, you'll be making yourself adored by all mankind ! upon my word !—However, you know best ; and if you are so accomplished that you can't write a letter, why I must do it for you. So come to the Cottage, and then—

Enter a Servant with a Letter.

Serv. From Mr Craftly, sir ; he says it is of the utmost consequence.

Gab. Indeed ! (*Opens it, and reads.*)——" Dear Gabriel, Marchmont having escaped from the bailiffs, and being now in search of you to entreat lenity, it is absolutely necessary you should see him, and confirm what I have done : therefore let Mrs Gabriel go alone to the Cottage, and you may follow in a few hours ; for, before Mr Primitive arrives, both Marchmont and his daughter must be disposed of. P. S. I have ordered all the new furniture you and your wife desired."—Go alone ! what ! part already ?

Mrs Lack. Nay, you never disobey your guardian, you know ; and 'tis but for a few hours. So, shew me to the curricle, sir. (*To the Servant.*)— And don't now, pray don't hurry yourself.—Heigho ! I'll support your absence as well as I can.

Gab. And so will I yours.—Heigho ! (*In imitation.*)—Don't be uneasy, I won't be long.

Mrs Lack. Adieu !

Gab. Adieu ! (*Again in imitation, and kissing her hand.*)　　　[*Exeunt* MRS LACKBRAIN *and Servant.*

Gab. Oh ! Gaby, Gaby, if marriage be a lottery,

for certain you've drawn the thirty thousand pound prize. Dang it! how all the neighbouring squires will burst with envy, to know that the " country put," as they please to call me, is heir to a baronet of ten thousand a-year! and to hear him call me cousin, dear cousin!—Oh, how I will strut, and cut them!—I'll speak to nobody but the mayor, and to him only, because he has a chance of being knighted.

Enter SIR HARRY TORPID.

Sir H. Tor. Not here either! why they certainly told me this was her house.

Gab. (*Strutting, and not seeing him.*) Room, room, for Sir Harry's cousin. (*Coming against* SIR HARRY.)

Sir H. Tor. I beg pardon; but pray does Mrs Decoy live in this house?

Gab. (*Pompously.*) Decoy! there's no such person.

Sir H. Tor. No!

Gab. No.—Ask for Mrs Lackbrain—Mrs Gaby Lackbrain.

Sir H. Tor. Ha! ha! ha!

Gab. Why, what do you grin at? have you any objection, sir?

Sir H. Tor. None, none on earth; I am very glad to hear it. I knew she came down here on a fortune-hunting scheme; but I little thought any body would be fool enough to be taken in by her.

Gab. Taken in! why, do you know who you're talking of? do you know she's cousin to a baronet?

Sir H. Tor. I do.

Gab. That he means to leave her ten thousand a-year? that he's soon coming to visit her? and what with hard drinking, keeping him up all night, and making him ride break-neck fox-chaces, it's main

hard if they don't bury him in a fortnight; and
then, you know, Mr Gaby touches every shilling.

Sir H. Tor. No, he don't.

Gab. Why?

Sir H. Tor. Because there's no shilling to touch,
ha! ha!—The baronet's as poor as she is; and Mr
Gaby may bury him; but, egad! he must pay for
the funeral.

Gab. Impossible! Odratten! who told you this?

Sir H. Tor. Himself; and, what's better, now he
tells you so.   Sir Harry Torpid, in person, informs
you, that the late Mrs Decoy's over head and ears
in debt; and that whoever is her husband, instead of
possessing ten thousand a-year, he'll be soon peeping through the iron bars of the county gaol.

Gab. (*Half crying.*) County ga—ol!

Sir H. Tor. Yes, 'tis too true.   But where is he?
where is the poor devil? Before he's caged, I should
like to have a peep at him.

Gab. Sir—Sir Harry—I—I am he. (*Crying.*)

Sir H. Tor. You!

Gab. (*Crying louder.*) Yes, I'm Gaby! I'm the
poor devil that's to peep through the iron bars. Rot
it! only think now; she talked of her family and fortune; said she'd introduce me to fashionable life,
and promised to make a buck of me.

Sir H. Tor. Well, and she will make a buck of
you.   But don't take it so to heart—don't cry so;
there's a little dear—I dare say you won't be arrested these two hours.

Gab. It's all my guardian's fault, all owing to his
precious octavo.—And see, here he is. (*Looking out.*)
Odrabit you! how I should like to be even with you.

Sir H. Tor. So he is—and as I live, the poor author and his daughter with him!—Why, what brings
him here?

Gab. Why, Mr Marchmont owes me for rent, and
money lent, about two hundred pounds; and so, by

my guardian's orders, he's also to peep through the iron bars.—Zounds! if I wasn't afraid—but there it is, sir—he rules me with a rod of iron; and, at the age of twenty-four, here am I, a full-grown baby in leading-strings.

Sir H. Tor. Psha! rouse, exert yourself; and if you wish to be revenged, liberate this poor gentleman, release him from the debt he owes you, and you'll not only be even with your guardian, but feel what I never felt till this morning, the pleasure of being in good-humour with yourself.

Gab. I've a great mind—but will you stand by me?

Sir H. Tor. That I will, and, moreover, go with you to your wife, and accommodate and arrange—

Gab. Say you so? then I'll work myself up, and pay you off old scores, you old—

Craft. (*With ut.*) Gabriel! where are you, Gabriel?

Gab. There, it's all over; his voice plumps me down like a thunderbolt.

Sir H. Tor. Nonsense! I'll be at your elbow. Come, come, I saw wine in the next room; a glass or two may rouse, inspire—come, this way, this way.
          [*Exeunt at door in flat.*

Enter CRAFTLY, MARCHMONT, *and* ROSA.

March. What, what can be the motive for this persecution?

Craft. No matter, sir; you know the terms: instantly go abroad with your daughter, or hope not to escape a second time.

March. Abroad! what can a foreign country yield me?—Without friends, without money, and dependent on the labour of the brain, how can I support myself?

Rosa. Aye; consider, sir, to leave the Priory would be parting with the only friend we have; the garden we have reared with our own hands, the trees we have planted to shade us in old age.

Craft. Psha! stuff! decide instantly, or the bailiffs that are now in the house—

Rosa. Oh, for mercy!—look at him, behold his pallid countenance, his languid form—is that an object of resentment?—(CRAFTLY *turns from her.*)— Nay then, I will appeal for pity to another, the principal shall answer me.

> [SIR HARRY *and* GABRIEL *appear at the door, in flat.*—SIR HARRY *has a bottle of wine in his hand, and is filling a glass for* GABRIEL.

Sir H. Tor. Bravo! capital! another glass, and you'll do wonders.—(GABRIEL *drinks it off.*)

Craft. Ay, ay, ask Gabriel; he'll give you an answer, I warrant.

Rosa. (*To* GABRIEL, *who has now come forward with* SIR HARRY.) Oh! on my knees let me entreat you, sir, have compassion on a most unhappy parent; and if you are not so far ruled by that unfeeling man—

Sir H. Tor. (*The bottle and glass still in his hand.*) He ruled! pooh! he's his own master now—aren't you, Gabriel?

Gab. (*Who has hold of* SIR HARRY's *arm.*)—Yes, I'm no longer a full-grown baby, or in leading-strings, or—(*Leaves* SIR HARRY *and advances,* CRAFTLY *comes up to him and frowns.*)—Yes, I am though.— (*Returns to* SIR HARRY.)—Another bumper, or it's all over again.—(SIR HARRY *fills,* GABRIEL *drinks.*)

Craft. (*Following* GABRIEL.) What do you mean, sir? dare you for a moment dispute my authority?

Sir H. Tor. (*To* GABRIEL, *who finishes the glass.*) —And now, instead of sending Mr Marchmont abroad, or to prison, he bids me say, that he not only releases him from the debt he owes him; but as to his guardian and his authority—Oh! damme, he don't care that for him. (*Snapping his fingers.*)

Gab. (*Snapping his.*) No, I don't care that for you, old octavo.—(CRAFTLY *advancing in a menacing attitude,* GABRIEL *runs behind* SIR HARRY, *and speaks over his shoulder.*)—I don't ; I tell you I don't ; and Mr Marchmont is free ; and now you're raffled in your turn.

Craft. Hear me, hear me, I command. Instantly call up the bailiffs that are below stairs, and order them to seize him, or by heaven—

Sir H. Tor. Bailiffs below stairs !—Come along, friend Gabriel : you lay hold of Mr Marchmont's arm, and conduct him through the myrmidons, and I'll take care of the lady : and, dy'e hear, bring the bottle along with you ; and, once arrived at the Priory, we'll drink success to the sons of genius, and confusion to those who oppress them.

Gab. With all my heart. Here goes. (*Fills a glass, and drinks.*) Success to myself, and confusion to those who oppress me.

Craft. Death and fire ! I'll go directly to Mrs Lackbrain ; I'll—

Enter JENKINS.

Jenk. I'm sorry to be the bearer of unwelcome news ; but several tradesmen are below, who have sent in large lots of furniture to the Cottage, and they insist on receiving their money directly.

Craft. Ay ! I'm glad of that ; now comes my triumph. Pay, husband, pay for your wife's furniture.

Jenk. No, sir : they say Mrs Lackbrain is considerably in debt; that she came down here on a matrimonial speculation ; and therefore, as you ordered in the furniture in your own name, they look to you, and you alone, for payment.

Gab. (*Spitting out wine he had been drinking.*) Icod ! he'll peep through the iron bars before me, ha ! ha !

Sir H. Tor. Yes, and he may call up the bailiffs to arrest himself now, ha! ha! ha!—But lead on, and don't despond, friend Gabriel.

Gab. Not I: if I've got one troublesome companion by the bargain, I'm sure he has got a couple ; and a man may by accident get rid of a wife, but the devil himself can't shake off John Doe and Richard Roe; icod! they'll stick to you.—And so, thank ye kindly for the furniture, guardy.—And now, brother genius, now for freedom and the Priory. [*Exeunt.*

ACT THE THIRD.

SCENE I.

Outside of Hotel and View of the Town.

Enter CRAFTLY *and* JONATHAN.

Craft. Arrived! my cousin Primitive now in the hotel! Why, zounds! we didn't expect him home these six weeks.

Jon. No, sir; but the fleet sailing sooner than was intended, and the wind being peculiarly favourable——

Craft. Well, but how is he? and how are you, Jonathan? I'm heartily sorry—that is, glad—that is—Death and fire! that he should arrive when one's so perplex'd and embarrassed!

Jon. My master is all joy and expectation, sir—

so anxious to behold the new-married couple, and
the cottage, and the farm—he has talked of nothing
else all the voyage—but you'll excuse me, sir, I have
a message to Mr Clifford.

Craft. Clifford! why, what has your master to do
with Clifford?

Jon. Why, sir, his father, who resides in Jamaica,
has appointed Mr Primitive his guardian—the young
gentleman is already apprized of the circumstance
by letter, and I'm now going to request an interview—but see—there is my master, after an absence
of thirty years! you behold him come home to share
his fortune with the young couple.

Craft. So I do. (*Exit* JONATHAN.) And as I mean
to touch a third of his fortune, I must keep him in
the dark about the young couple—yes; much as I
detest, I must not expose them—for, as the joke goes,
if we don't hang together, by Heavens we shall hang
separately.

Enter PRIMITIVE *from the Hotel.*

Welcome, my dear cousin--once more welcome to
your native town! Why, you made haste to get
here. You did not stay long in London.

Prim. London! plague on the place, it's worse
than ever.—In point of heat, Jamaica's cool to it—
in point of noise, a hurricane is silence to it—and
for company and conversation, certainly the crew of
the ship I came in runs it very hard indeed, cousin.

Craft. Ha! ha! ha! still devoted to a country
life, I see.

Prim. Oh, yes—I think of nothing else—for there's
the seat of purity and peace; and now for it, coz—
now for the darling theme—Gabriel's married, I find.

Craft. Yes, he's married.   (*Sighs aside.*)

Prim. And to a woman of your chusing—to a
sweet innocent soul, that's as much attached to rural life as her husband is.

13

Craft. Yes, as much as he is.

Prim. And they're now at the cottage—and I am come in time for the honey-moon.—Oh, my dear cousin, this is all your doing!—you gave him a country education—you taught him to manage the farm I purchased—and now if I can but get rid of my old malady—if I can but forget my poor, poor daughter —

Craft. What! grieve for her, when she has been dead these twelve years? and consider, you scarcely recollect her, for she was but a child—only eight years old, when you sent her from Jamaica to a London boarding school.

Prim. That's it—sending her to London was the cause of all—There Marchmont saw her, eloped with her! Oh! if I had but brought her up in the country! But come—I'll do my best—only, in the midst of my happiness, if now and then you see a tear trickle down my cheek, you'll know it is for my lost, my wronged Louisa.

Enter JONATHAN *and* CLIFFORD.

Jon. Here's Mr Clifford, sir.

Prim. Well, sir, have you read your good father's letter?

Clif. I have, sir, and I find my income is not only to pass through your hands, but, in case of my neglecting my studies, you have the power to with-hold it altogether.

Prim. Even so, sir—your father has heard a bad account of you; he has been informed, that, instead of studying law in your chambers, you are always idling and raking. And here—here's a proof of it —what brings you to this gay, dissipated place, sir?

Clif. My physicians prescribed it, sir.

Prim. Your physicians, sir?

Clif. Yes, sir,—fatigue from study, and the bad air of London, produced such a pain in my chest.

Prim. Pain in—Well, come, that's not unlikely; for by the advertisements in the newspapers, the bad air of London affects every body's health. Faith, there is nothing going forward but lumbagos, nervosities, catarrhs, and imbecilities.

Craft. Psha, that's all an imposition—a trick of the quack doctors.

Prim. Nay, don't tell me, cousin; for, passing through the west end of the town, every young man I met was debilitated, or short-sighted, or ricketty, or had a defect in his voice. Poor fellows, you can't think how sincerely I pitied them! I did indeed; and, if I had not reserved all my fortune for Gabriel, I'd build an hospital for the benefit of the infirm and decayed beaux of Bond-street.—But come, the more I talk on't, the more I sigh for the Cottage—so we'll just go visit a few old friends and relations, return and rest in the hotel, and betimes in the morning set off, and surprise the innocent, the Arcadian couple.

Craft. So we will; and as to the settlement, cousin—

Prim. Oh! if they behave as I expect—I sha'n't wait till the year's out—and d'ye hear, Mr Clifford, do nothing dishonourable, and I shall neither controul you in your pleasures, nor your expences; and, if you delight in rural scenery and innocent mirth, come and pass a few weeks at the Cottage—I'll warrant 'twill cure your pain in the chest.—Now, cousin! odsheart! I'm so pleased and so gratified, that, if it were not for some secret gnawings about my poor daughter—but s'life! why do I think of her? as you say, she was but a child when I last saw her, and she's gone, and I'm the happiest (*Half crying,*) merriest old fellow living.

[*Exit with* JONATHAN *and* CRAFTLY.

Clif. 'Sdeath! what can my father mean by making me dependent on the caprice of an old dotard!

—However, I see I can easily dupe him, and in the end, I shall not only get my own income, but part of his into the bargain; and now once more for the object of my search, the disdainful Mrs Belford—zounds! shall I never recover her?

Enter WILLIAM.

Will. Joy, sir! she's found—the runaway's found! —not half an hour ago I saw her enter the Priory.

Clif. What, Mrs Belford?

Will. Yes, sir; she's gone there as a teacher of music and drawing to Mr Marchmont's daughter, —and, knowing he was a strange character, and might prevent your gaining possession of her, I have already seen him, and secured him in our interest.

Clif. That's well, then she's for ever mine; but now—how did you contrive to deceive Marchmont?

Will. Why, sir, I met him on the road, and told him a person of very suspicious character was now with his daughter—and if he'd wait on you, you'd give him information and advice; and see, here he is, sir.

Enter MARCHMONT *hastily.*

March. Mr Clifford, am I to believe—

Clif. 'Tis too true, sir; the person now with your daughter may not only corrupt her young and inexperienced mind, but absolutely decoy her from your protection.

March. Astonishing! who is she?

Clif. To speak the truth, a lady who has eloped from a most affectionate husband; and as she is a distant relation of mine, I'm pursuing her to restore her to her family.

March. And being lost to herself—she would reduce all others to her level—Oh! she is the agent of some villain! and now I recollect—the pocket-book my daughter found, no doubt was dropped by her, to aid their dark intentions.

Clif. Pocket-book! ha! that must have been Sir Harry's—I'll work on this, and turn it to account, (*Aside.*) Now you mention it—I saw in her possession a pocket-book of curious workmanship;—silver'd—blue.

March. The same—the same—Oh! that is ample confirmation; and this is the result of my too sanguine folly; for, on a false and most precarious prospect, I advertised for a teacher for my child; and now, she who has nursed me, toil'd for me—nay, whose very thoughts have saved me hours of labour, she's to be corrupted and taken from me! Come, let us lose no time in hastening to her—

Clif. No, but I hope you will not trust her story—we've been too long acquainted, I presume—

March. We have, and you've no motive for deceiving me—No—no—she is employed by some seducer—and I would rather trust my daughter with an host of men, than with one woman of suspicious fame. But she's in danger, and let me fly to save her.   [*Exeunt.*

SCENE II.

A Gothic Apartment in the Priory.

Enter ROSA *and Mrs* BELFORD—*Mrs B. in a Hat and Veil.*

Rosa. Oh! you do not know how deeply you have interested me. Pray proceed with your story——you lately came from Switzerland, you say?

Mrs Bel. I did: under the protection of a most kind and liberal lady—but on my arrival, being per-

secuted by the artful addresses of her nephew; and
she, innocently becoming his advocate, I was compelled to leave her.

Rosa. And have you n oother friend?

Mrs Bel. None, none on earth; and am reduced
to such an abject state of poverty, that, reading your
advertisement for a teacher in music, I thought I
would apply for the situation, as the last hope of saving me from want.

Rosa. And I'm so glad you read it! My father
will soon return, and then I hope he will persuade
you to live with us for ever.—He is most tender and
affectionate; but, as he tells me, I want a female
monitor, for, alas! I never had a mother to instruct
me.

Mrs Bel. No!—

Rosa. No! she died when I was yet an infant;
poor woman! I often shed tears to her memory. I'd
give the world were she alive—

Mrs Bel. Would you? good girl! I have been—
nay, perhaps, am still, a mother; and could I even
hope my child e'er thought or talked of me as you
do—but no more of this—let us to the theme on
which we meet—and, before I venture to instruct
you, give me a specimen of my scholar's talents.

Rosa. Most willingly: I'll sing my favourite bal-
lad.

SONG.

> Sweetly in Life's jocund morning,
>   Beam'd on me a father's smile;
> Joy with livelier charms adorning,
>   Cheering grave instruction's toil.
> Cruel memory, too severely,
>   Tells me those blest hours are gone,
> Which with him I prized so dearly,
>   He has frown'd, and they are flown!

Love, which drew these sorrows on me,
  Love alone can yield relief;
The pitying power that has undone me,
  Pours the balm that heals my grief.
What though memory so severely
  Tells me that my joys are gone ;
Let but him I love so dearly
  Smile, and all my cares are flown.

Mrs Bel. Merciful powers !——Who taught you this ?

Rosa. My father.

Mrs Bel. Your father !—speak—his name ?

Rosa. Marchmont.

Mrs Bel. And you!—Oh, yes : I see it now—'tis she !—'tis she herself ! (*Weeps, and kisses* ROSA's *hand violently.*)

Rosa. Bless me, what agitates you ?

Mrs Bel. Nothing ! pardon me—it is your likeness to your mother that distracts me !—then these words---they were your mother's, Rosa.

Rosa. Did you know her ? Oh ! speak of her---inform me quick, tell me every thing about her---I would walk barefoot through the world, and think each pang that wrung my weary feet were joy, were ecstacy, could I but learn some tidings of my mother !

Mrs Bel. What ! has your father never told you ?

Rosa. Never : the subject is forbidden me ; and if, perchance, I name her, he shews such anger and such secret horror !—

Mrs Bel. Oh ! If I dared to reveal—but no, still —I must still be mute. (*Aside.*)

March. (*Without.*) Rosa ! Rosa Marchmont !

Mrs Bel. (*Trembling*) Heavens ! that voice. (*Aside.*)

Rosa. It is my father.

Mrs Bel. I know---I recollect the sound---and like the knell of death it strikes upon my heart ! what can I do? where go? I'll fly---and---alas! my limbs will not support me.

Rosa. Nay, stay. Why---why be afraid to see him?

Mrs Bel. True; why should innocence descend to fear---and yet 'tis most awful to encounter--- (*Trembling, and looking towards the door.*) Ha! he comes---hide, hide me from his sight! (*Pulls down her veil, and gets behind* ROSA.)

Enter MARCHMONT *and* CLIFFORD.

March. Look! look where she stands, infusing poison into the breast of innocence!

Clif. Ay, that's she; and, if you value your own or your daughter's honour, part them this instant.

March. Rosa, shame on you, girl, to countenance and be corrupted by a stranger.

Mrs Bel. Corrupted! I corrupt her! (*Aside.*)

March. (*To* MRS BELFORD, *who is still behind* ROSA, *with her veil down.*) Mark me, madam—You see before you one who, though oppressed by fortune, scorns to infringe the laws of hospitality, and willingly would share his last sad pittance with the poor:—but when he's told by him whom he respects, that you have stolen to his house, to spoil and rob him of his only treasure, he must and will be answered. I am above condemning you unheard, therefore explain—(MRS BELFORD *shews great agitation.*) What! not a word? (*Pauses.*) Again I do entreat you---still silent! Nay, then we part--- this is no fit asylum for you.

Mrs Bel. Oh, mercy! mercy!　　　　　[*Exit.*

Clif. I'll follow her, and take this opportunity to bear her quietly to her home.

March. Be it so,—but observe me, Clifford—as I have done my duty, you do yours:—though guilty, she is still an object of compassion; and therefore,

rather pity than reproach her. (*Exit* CLIFFORD.) My
daughter! (*Resting his head on her shoulder.*)

Rosa. My father! what have you done?

March. What I ought to do—saved my Rosa
from disgrace;—and yet I know not why—poor woman! I feel as if I'd acted harshly towards her.

Rosa. And well you may, sir; for, if I dare impart
it, she was my mother's friend.

March. How?

Rosa. She knew her, loved her, and expressed
such admiration——

March. Peace, I command you:—vile impostress!
this was an artifice so base, that I no longer pity,
but despise her. Nay: not a word—Attend me to
my study.—She your mother's friend! Oh, she was
all innocence and truth! And at this moment I see
her in those eyes—that form—that—but what am I
conversing on? where wandering?—to my study—
lead to my study.   [*Exeunt.*

SCENE III.

A Room in the Hotel.

Enter PRIMITIVE, JONATHAN, *and Waiter.*

Prim. There, there—this room will do, waiter,
this room will do.

Wait. But I tell you, sir, it is bespoken—and the
hotel is so cramm'd with company, I can't offer you
another.

Prim. Call the landlord then—he'll find room for
an old acquaintance, I warrant.

Wait. Sir, my master's not at home—just gone to
the sailing match, in his own yacht, with Miss Laura
Maria and Miss Anna Matilda.

Prim. Miss Laura Maria and Miss Anna Matilda! and pray who the deuce are they?

Wait. My master's own daughters, sir—as accomplished young ladies as any in the county,—just come down from Rantipole-house Academy, near London, sir.—But, sir, this room belongs to Mr Clifford.

Prim. Mr Clifford—Oh, then you may go—he is my most intimate friend, and I'll answer for the consequences. (*Exit Waiter.*) Why, Jonathan, this town is Londonized, quite turned upside down;—when I left England, this hotel was an alehouse, and the landlord here a post-boy—and now he goes to sailing matches in his own yacht—sends his daughters to Rantipole-house, and calls them Miss Laura Maria and Miss Anna Matilda! mercy on me! mercy on me!

Jon. Strange alterations, indeed, sir :—but about your cousins. After so long an absence, I warrant they were all glad to see you.

Prim. Why, there again we are all metamorphosed, Jonathan. I found the alderman, who is now in his sixtieth year, learning to dance; and on my expressing my astonishment, he told me the dancing master owed him thirty pounds for soap and candles—and the debt being a bad one, his wife insisted he should take it out in lessons—and there he was—sa, sa, (*Mimicking*) ha! ha!

Jon. Ha! ha!

Prim. Then young Shiftly, whom I left a plodding lawyer, is now a snug apothecary :—he says physic is by far the finest trade going; for the women, blessings on them! wear such thin dresses, that, what with friendly showers and propitious east winds, the whole medical tribe get cloathed by their nakedness! And I'm sure he speaks truth; for, when we landed, dont you remember, I was ashamed to look about me? Says I, " Fie, Jonathan, don't you

see the ladies are all in their bathing dresses, and if
you peep at them, you'll"——But, however, 'tis a
cursed delicate subject; and, upon my soul, shocks
my modesty only to talk on it.—Oh! would I were
safely perched at the fire-side of the cottage.

Jon. Aye, that will make you amends—there you
will witness no folly nor dissipation.—And what say
you, sir? Suppose I go and prepare for the morning?

Prim. Do, Jonathan—and, d'ye hear, be stirring
as early as five—but don't trouble yourself to call
me. Joy and expectation will keep me awake—
(*Exit* JONATHAN.) Yes, there I shall sit down content for life, and with the two unsophisticated cottagers, looking up to me as a father—Father! Psha!
I can't bear the word—it reminds me of my poor
dead—s'life! I can't bear that word either—Plague
on't, why did she die? What right had she to leave
me, who never wrong'd her—didn't I tho'? Because she married the man of her heart, didn't I,
like an old worldly savage, desert, abandon—I'll tell
you what—dont you talk of the vices of mankind,
Mr Primitive; by Heaven, you're as great a profligate as any of them. (*Stamping of feet is heard without.*) Heh! what's that noise? (*Looks out.*) As I
live, a man bearing a woman in his arms! another
cousin, I suppose.—I'll observe. (*Retires up stage.*)

Enter CLIFFORD *with* MRS BELFORD.

Clif. There—rest there awhile. (*Placing her in a
chair.*) Nay, nay—resistance is in vain, the landlord
and all his servants are at my disposal; (*Locks door,
and puts the key into his pocket*) and in the morning
we'll take a pleasant sail to Lisbon.

Mrs Bel. Oh! for mercy! you know not whom
you force me from!

Clif Nay, nay, 'tis all for your advantage—but as
'tis necessary to make instant preparations for our
voyage, I must to my chamber, and get money and

other articles—now don't be uneasy, 'tis all for your
happiness, I assure you.   [*Exit.*

Prim. (*Advances, not seen by* MRS BELFORD.) So,
this is one way of curing the pain in the chest!

Mrs Bel. Heavens! but a few short minutes past
I was in sight of all that's dear to me on earth—
of Rosa, and—yes, I am weak enough to own it—
of Rosa and her father. Where am I now?—imprisoned by a villain! on the point of being forced
to a foreign country! without hope, without friends!

Prim. No, not without friends—you see one before
you.

Mrs Bel. Away—you're a confederate with this
vile seducer.

Prim. I a confederate! I a seducer! Bless you,
only look at these wrinkles; (*Pointing to his face.*)
and if that does not satisfy you, feel if a seducer ever
possessed this, a heart that beats and sympathizes
for the distresses of a woman.

Mrs Bel. It does.—And now I look again, I think,
oh, yes! I'm sure, you will not add to my afflictions.

Prim. No—and to prove it, without asking, or
knowing who this Rosa is, I'll instantly conduct you
to her.

Mrs Bel. No, not to her—for kingdoms not to
her.

Prim. Why? has she too been unkind to you?

Mrs Bel. No, she never could—but her father! he
who should protect me with his life—he banished
me his house—he—Oh! my brain cannot support
the recollection! But I will shew him—Yes, if I
deign to think of him again, 'twill be with scorn—
with fixed determined scorn.

Prim. That's right, I applaud your spirit—let him
and Clifford cut each other's throats, and do you go
with me.—Harkye! are you fond of retirement? do
you love a pastoral life?

Mrs Bel Oh, yes! that is what I sigh for—retirement's all that's left me.

Prim. Say you so—then I'll conduct you to such an Arcadian scene! You must know, my nephew and niece have a cottage about four miles off, and I'm going to live with them, and you shall be of the party—and we'll plant, sow, and feed the pigs and poultry together—and then—for society! to be sure, our live stock can't be so witty as the pleasant Mr Clifford and his friend. However, there is this consolation—sheep can't betray us, nor cows tell lies of us—so, come, let us be gone (*Trying to open the door, finds it locked.*) S'life! I forgot we are prisoners here.

Mrs Bel. We are—and so surrounded by enemies, that tho' you have the wish, alas! you've not the power to serve me; and look, here he comes again.

Re-enter CLIFFORD.

Clif. My mind is alter'd.—There may be danger in remaining here to-night—therefore we'll to the ship directly—and for old Primitive——

Prim. Well, sir—and what of old Primitive? Your servant, Mr Studious—I'm glad your pain in the chest is better.

Clif. (*Much confused.*) Better—sir! I don't understand—I assure you, at this moment I don't feel very well, sir.

Prim. No? How should you, sir? I never heard that ill treating a woman was for the good of a man's health—but, come, sir—favour me with the key of that room.

Clif. Certainly, sir.—You may depart when you please: but for this lady (*Taking hold of her.*) she must stay with me.

Prim. Must, sir!

Clif. Aye, must, sir: we never part again.

Prim. So, you'd detain her? (CLIFFORD *nods assent.*) Pray, sir, give me leave to ask you—What is your income?

Clif. My income, sir?

Prim. Aye—Have you any thing in houses, lands, or the funds? or, simply nothing more than what your father allows you?

Clif. Nothing, sir.

Prim. Then I give you joy—persist in your gentlemanly intentions, and your father will disinherit you; or, if that will not content you, I will annihilate you. Yes, sir, tho' I never betrayed innocence —I know too well what it is to desert it! And the goadings I feel at this instant for having abandoned my own child——I'll tell you what—rather than undergo the agony of forsaking another female, I'd march up to the mouth of a cannon, be shot at by a whole regiment, or, what's more, submit to be hanged, for ridding the world of the decayed, the honourable Mr Clifford.

Mrs Bel. Nay, consider, sir, we are in his power.

Prim. Psha! what should I be afraid of! Tho' older than he is by forty years—I'm still the youngest of the two. My stamina is not undermined by dissipation—I've got no pain in the chest—and, if exchanging shots isn't the modern mode of fighting, I'll go a step lower, and condescend to box him.— Yes, I will; I'll box him.

Clif. Well, sir, I acknowledge my dependence; and if you will but listen——

Prim. Not a word, sir—first open the door—and next, in person, conduct us safely out of this house. Nay, no demurring—do it: I insist.

Clif. And if I do, I hope——

Prim. Sir, I shall make no promises. (CLIFFORD *opens door and exit.*) Come, madam—in my time gallantry was a very different sort of business. Tho' we were cowardly enough to avoid the dangers of seduction, we were still bold enough, and I hope ever will be, to protect innocence and punish villainy.

[*Exeunt.*

ACT THE FOURTH.

SCENE I.

A small Room in the Cottage, folding Doors thrown open in the back Scene, and variegated Lamps hung round the···; also, Festoons of Flowers—a short Dance—Voices are heard singing,

> " Come, come, one and all,
> " Attend to my call,
> " And revel in pleasures that never can cloy;
> " Come see rural felicity,
> " Which love and innocence ever enjoy."

Enter SIR HARRY TORPID *from Ball Room.*

Sir H. Tor. This retirement! this pastoral life!—Gad, instead of being inside of my friend Gabriel's cottage, one might fancy one's-self in the purlieus of Covent Garden; for, not an hour ago, talking with Mrs Lackbrain at the paddock gate, I suddenly received a blow on my head, which I as suddenly returned, and, I fancy, laid my adversary low ; but it being quite dark, and the lady wishing to be gone, I haven't the honour of knowing to whom I am indebted.—However, it was a glorious bang! it roused me! 'tis life! agitation! And whoever the gentleman is, I've to thank him for bringing me into a fine whirligig state.

Enter BETTY.

Ha! Betty, what brings you here?

Bet. My mistress, sir, desired me to give you this note the moment I found you alone.

Sir H. Tor. Indeed ! (*Taking letter, opening it, and reading.*) " Dear coz, I haven't yet been able to find out who the savage was that interrupted our little *téte a téte* at the paddock gate : but, if you wish to renew the conversation relative to providing for Marchmont, meet me in my dressing-room in half an hour, and I'll do all in my power to serve him.

　　　　　　　　　　LYDIA LACKBRAIN."

So, more cottage diversion ! However, if, without injuring my honour, I can restore Marchmont and the lovely Rosa to independence, my time cannot be passed better.—Tell your mistress I'll be punctual !

Bet. Yes, sir.

Sir H. Tor. And for this affair at the paddock gate, bid her hush it up, if she can.　As I could not distinguish my antagonist, I hope he wont know me —for fighting to a man in love is—but, go, for here's my friend Gabriel.　　　　　　　[*Exit* BETTY.

Enter GABRIEL, *half drunk from Ball Room.*

Gab. Oh ! my dear, dear friend—you're the very man I have been looking for.—Come—come with me this moment.

Sir H. Tor. With you ! Where ?

Gab. Where ! Why, in search of the most obstropulous, infernal—Dang it, would you believe it, cousin baronet ? Mrs Gaby's faithless ; and now, in the very middle of our honey-moon—I do actually think that real downright *nem. con.* is going forward.

Sir H. Tor. Fie ! impossible !

Gab. Harkee ! You know Miss Sally Sasafras, the apothecary's heart-breaking daughter—who, if possible, kills more people than her father :—well, I had pierced her to the soul with one of my murdering glances—and, after putting on her hat and cloak, had persuaded her to walk with me, when, as the devil would would have it, I overheard my wife whispering with a man—Ay, and though it was too dark to see him, ecod, I felt him.   For, thinks I, if you'll plant lumps on my head, I'd better plant bumps on yours; so I gave him such a douce——

Sir H. Tor. (*Eagerly.*) My dear fellow, where—where did this happen?

Gab. Where! Why, at the paddock gate, now, not an hour ago. (SIR HARRY *looks confused.*) Good soul! I knew you'd feel for me consumedly.

Sir H. Tor. I do!—and for myself too consumedly. (*Aside.*)

Gab. I said he would take on as much as if the case were his own:—but don't you, now,—don't be down-hearted.—You'll see that I'll serve him just as I served Jemmy Swagger.

Sir H. Tor. And, pray, how did you serve Jemmy Swagger?

Gab. Why, I behaved very ill to Jemmy Swagger, and he sent me a challenge—so I took my friend with me—this young gentleman (*Pulling his stick from under his coat;*) and so I thumpt him till he ask'd pardon: and in like manner I'll serve this paddock hero, and you shall be by all the time. Ha! ha! you like fun—you like life, you know.

Sir H. Tor. Yes! but I don't like death, you know—give it up, for your own sake—These sort of rencontres always get into the public prints. People just catch the names of the parties, huddle the innocent with the guilty, and coolly remark, a blackguard business, and a damned set of scoundrels altogether—give it up therefore.

Gab. No, I wont—you have been very kind to me, and I'll break his bones, if it is only to amuse you, cousin.—(*Loud knocking at the door.*)—What's that?—(*More knocking.*)—Again! and so early in the morning!

Enter BETTY.

Bet. Oh, sir, my mistress is terrified out of her senses! Mr Craftly is below, telling her that Mr Primitive is unexpectedly arrived from Jamaica, and will be here in half an hour.

Gab. My uncle here in half an hour! Od dang it —I'm sorry to disappoint you—but you see I must postpone the operation.

Sir H. Tor. My dear sir, don't mention it; if you postpone it for ever, it will be no disappointment to me, I promise you. Adieu! Now for the dressing-room, and, having served Marchmont. then for the Priory! Gad, this is bustle! this is life, while it lasts, or the devil's in it!　　　　　　　　　[*Exit.*

Gab. My uncle so near—so—

Enter CRAFTLY *and* MRS LACKBRAIN.

Mrs Lack. So, so! here's a pretty business—Mr Primitive not half a mile off, and you're in a fine state to receive him—with a head full of wine at this time in the morning.

Gab. And what are you? with a house full of dancers and whisperers at this time in the morning.

Craft. Psha! wrangling won't help us. I fancy we are none of us over fond of each other.—Indeed, for my part, I candidly acknowledge, I'd rather do you both a mischief than a—service.

Mrs Lack. I am sure you're very kind, sir!

Craft. But as the old pigeon is arrived, we must combine to pluck him; and, first, we must undermine this favourite he has brought with him.

Mrs Lack. What favourite?

Craft. Why, a lady he met with last night at the hotel. He has already conceived a great regard for her; but, as he acknowledges he knows nothing of her, and Clifford assures me she is a woman of suspicious character, you'll give hints on her introduction.

Mrs Lack. Never fear, leave me alone—I'll say I know her.

Gab. That's enough—if she says she is one of her acquaintances, 'tis all over with her—or, if that fails, I'll say she is one of mine.

Craft. Good! and now, while Mrs Lackbrain disposes of the company, and puts on a more plain and appropriate dress, you and I will go and receive the old gentleman.—And remember, from this hour, you are plain simple cottagers—and, hard and irksome as it is, you must henceforth appear a fond, loving couple.

Mrs Lack. (*Sighing.*) 'Tis very irksome! but we must do it: but, go, go, and impose on your credulous uncle.

Gab. I'll do what my head will let me, for at this moment there's more dancing in it than in your ball-room. However, if there's any danger, guardy here will lend me his little octavo; and, now I think on't, we must take pains on his account, because he paid for all this pretty furniture, you know. Ha! ha! ha!—

Craft. Psha! nonsense—come along and try, try to disguise your situation.

Gab. Pooh! don't my situation disguise me? Besides, what are you afraid of—remember the sons of genius. Didn't I, by drinking a few generous bumpers, make a fool of him who has made a fool of thousands?—but now for it—now let me recollect— I am a fond, steady—u—u—h! (*Hiccuping.*) That's it, I'm the exact thing already. (*Exit with* CRAFTLY,—MRS LACKBRAIN *at folding doors.*)

SCENE II.

Outside of a Cottage, standing in a romantic Vale surrounded by Mountains.

Enter PRIMITIVE *and* MRS BELFORD.

Prim. Huzza, there! there it is, the end of all my hopes and all my wishes! Delightful, innocent, romantic sight!

Mrs Bel. This is, indeed, a spot more lovely than e'en my fancy pictured.

Prim. Oh! 'tis Arcadia! Paradise! And, to make my joys unbearable, think that Nature does not alone confine herself to the outside; no, she also dwells within. And the young cottagers—the dear, the darling pair! but represent the spot around them.

Mrs Bel. No doubt: for here is no temptation to be guilty. (*Singing in cottage*—" *Come, come one and all,*" &c.) Listen, what singing's that?

Prim. Dont you know? It is the ploughman as he trudges to his morning's work, carolling his simple ditty! Sweet fascinating sound! (*Music in cottage.*) And, hark again! Do you hear that music?

Mrs Bel. I do—to me it sounded like a flute.

Prim. Flute! bless you—it is the shepherd's pipe —it is the music of Arcadia! Oh! if this lasts, I sha'n't live to see the inside.

Enter JAMES *from the Cottage.*

Heh! who comes here? One of the servants—mum! He won't know me, so I'll be cunning, and sift him —now mind—Good morning, sir.

James. The same to you, sir.

Prim. I wish to speak with Mr or Mrs Lackbrain;

but 'tis too early ; I suppose they are neither of them
out of bed yet.

James. Yes, sir, they are both up.

Prim. Up ! what, at five in the morning ?

James. Yes ; and, what's more extraordinary, they
are up every morning at the same hour.

Prim. There now ; in London, who ever hears of
such early rising ? One question more, if you please,
—Pray where may you be going ?

James. Why, if you must know, sir, I am going
to leave these cards of invitation at some great
houses about twelve miles off. (*Produces them.*)

Prim. Cards of invitation ! I dont like that ; it
smacks of the squares----the city----the----give me
leave---(*Takes one, and reads.*) " Mrs Gabriel Lackbrain at home every evening this week." You may
go---I'm satisfied !---never---never was such an instance of domestic and connubial happiness !----at
home every evening ! Come, let us enter and behold.   [*Exit* JAMES.

Enter CRAFTLY *and* GABRIEL, *still drunk.*

Craft. (*Speaking as he enters.*) This way, Ga-
briel---this way---

Gab. Softly ; the air makes me worse---your arm ;
lend me your arm---(*Lays hold of* CRAFTLY'S *arm.*)

Prim. There he is ! there's the true, genuine, and
unadulterated child of nature—Come to thy uncle's
arms. (GABRIEL *is afraid to leave* CRAFTLY'S *arm.*)
S'life, what are you afraid of, Gabriel ? come to thy
uncle's arms, I say ! (GABRIEL *leaves* CRAFTLY'S
*arm, but, finding he can't support himself, staggers,
and reels back to* CRAFTLY.) Look ! now, look at that
rural embarrassment ! don't be ashamed, boy ; it is
worth all the ease and impudence of town-bred puppies.

Gab. I'm quite overcome, I assure you, uncle.

Prim. Delightful diffidence ! you rogue, I've heard

of your pranks, of your early rising every morning, and of your being at home every evening; and if I hadn't, your countenance would have betrayed you: —Look at that flush of health! (GABRIEL *smiles.*) —look at that rosy hue! (GABRIEL *bursts out laughing.*)——ha, ha! there again! now that's the true broad laugh of innocence and nature.

Gab. (*Aside to* CRAFTLY.) I say, guardy, there's no fear of his finding me out; for, ecod! he's as drunk as Chloe.

Prim. But come, where is your other half? If she prove as uncorrupted as yourself, I sha'n't wait till the year's out; no—I'll sign the settlement to-morrow.

Enter MRS LACKBRAIN, *in a plain Chip-Hat, Cloak, &c.*

Craft. That's well, that's a neat cottage dress.

Gab. Ah! here she is, uncle, here's the sweet source of connubial joy.

Mrs Lack. Dear Gabriel!

Gab. Divine Lydia! (*Taking her hand and kissing it.*)

Prim. Fond pair! the golden age is returned, and I see—(*Taking out his handkerchief, and half crying.*)—I see they were born to make me the happiest of middle-aged gentlemen.—But now for it; now for the inside.—Odsheart! I forgot though—I must particularly recommend this lady to the attention of you both; she is an object of compassion; (*Taking* MRS BELFORD *by the hand.*) and, as such, I'm sure must be welcome. (GABRIEL *and* MRS LACKBRAIN *both draw back.*)—Why, what d'ye stare at?—She deserves it, believe me, she deserves it.

Mrs Lack. No doubt: but pray, sir; have you known the lady long?

Prim. Till yesterday I never saw her.

Mrs Lack. So I thought:——but this is not a proper place for explanation; pray walk in, and we'll talk further.—This way, ma'am, this way.

Prim. Aye, this way.—And now, as the song says,

> Henceforth I'll lead a village life,
> In cottage most obscure-a;
> For, with this loving man and wife,
> My joys are quite secure-a.

[*Exeunt* PRIMITIVE, MRS BELFORD, *and* MRS LACKBRAIN.]

Craft. Well, Gabriel, what do you think?

Gab. Think! that he beats me hollow:—I'm only a child of nature; but, damme, he's a natural. And now, if spouse undermines the stranger—

Craft. Aye; once get her out of the house, and Clifford will instantly take her abroad. You see that vessel yonder—he's waiting for me to bring him information.

Gab. Indeed!

Craft. Yes; and Marchmont and his daughter are for ever cut out of their chance. So now all's safe; and while I go to Clifford, do you send for a lawyer to prepare the settlement; and then we'll say the golden age is returned.

Gab. We will; and I'll go send for a lawyer directly.—[*Exit* CRAFTLY.] But now, first for my paddock gentleman: by this time I hope my servants have found him out, and—dang it! nothing shall make me forget my promise to cousin baronet; —and then, let nunky once sign the settlement, and I'll also say, as the song says,—

> The scene is changed, 'tis alter'd quite,
> No more I'm simple Gaby;
> I'll learn to dance, to sing, and fight,
> And ogle every lady.   [*Exit.*

SCENE III.

*A small Room in the Cottage; a Door in the Flat,
a Chair placed near it.*

Enter SIR HARRY TORPID, *from Door in Flat.*

Sir H. Tor. 'Sdeath! this will never do: I have
been alone in that dressing-room these two hours;
and though I'm in love, I still can't support solitude;
—no, I shall certainly relapse, if somebody don't
come and rattle me into an agreeable state of vexation. I feel all the symptoms, the doze, the stupor,
the numbness.—Egad! I almost long for my friend
Gabriel, and his lumps and bumps; any thing in preference to this dying style of living.—Ha! a reprieve! I see the thing of all others likely to produce agitation—a petticoat! and, no doubt, Mrs
Gabriel. I'll return to the dressing-room.—[*Re-enters.*]

Enter PRIMITIVE *and* MRS BELFORD.

Prim. Now do, for my sake, pray, pray justify
yourself.

Mrs Bel. Sir, I have told you I am slandered.

Prim. Well, but consider, what Mrs Gabriel says
is perfectly true; I know nothing of your history,
she does; and if I should defile this innocent abode,
by introducing to it a person of suspicious character——

Mrs Bel. Suspicious!

Prim. Pardon me; these were my niece's words,
not mine: and when she added, her husband's constancy might be corrupted——

Mrs Bel. Corrupted! and by me!—Sir, I can

only answer, I am innocent; and if this be doubted, let me be gone. I know, by losing you, I've lost my best, my only friend; but if you think I'd be indebted for my safety to those who say I would disgrace my benefactor, and mar connubial and domestic love, you know but little of me. I cannot guess the motive for their cruelty; nor should I, by accusing others, vindicate myself; but let me tell you, sir, slander is a rank and poisonous weed, and never yet took root in pure unsullied ground.

Prim. Well then, why dont you explain yourself? —Plague on't! why not tell me your name, your family, your history?—Come now, do, do be good-natured.

Mrs Bel. Alas! I dare not.

Prim. Dare not!

Mrs Bel. No; my pride won't suffer me; and my story would but expose one, whom, spite of all my wrongs, I still am weak enough to——(*Pulls out her handkerchief, and weeps.*)—Ask me no more—pity me, and let me be gone.

Prim. (*Half crying.*) 'Tis all over—I see 'tis all over.—Farewell.

Mrs Bel. Farewell! and, for the service you have rendered me, my gratitude shall only die with me. —(*Going, she returns, and kisses his hand.*)—Oh! I did hope you would have proved a father to me.

Prim. Did you? (*Weeps.*) My poor daughter hoped the same—but I deserted her. I—Go; since you wont communicate, I entreat you go: for pity's sake, dont let us be bidding farewell all night.—— (*Takes out a purse, and puts it in her hand.*) There, you know where to apply when you want more; you understand me? whilst I have a guinea, you shall never want a part of it.

Mrs Bel. Bless you! bless you, sir!—But I forgot; I have left some drawings and manuscripts in the next room; may I venture to return for them?

Prim. You may : but, if you see me when you come back, dont speak to me ; we've had enough of leave-taking—damn it ! another farewell would choak me.—[*Exit* MRS BELFORD.]—Poor soul ! I hope 'tis no crime to pity her.—And, spite of the chaste society of the Cottage, I've a great mind to call her back, and—no, no, I mustn't risk defiling so spotless and immaculate a scene.—Heigho ! I'll sit down and compose myself.—(*Looks round.*)—Ay, ay, in that chair I may rest, unseen by her, while she passes.—(*Pointing to the chair near the flat.*)—Yes, here I may be quiet.— (*Sits in it.*)—And if I can but sleep and forget her—-Poor soul ! she hoped I might have proved a father to her.—Poor soul !— (*Falls back, and dozes.*)

(SIR HARRY *opens door, which is exactly behind the chair, but dont push it far enough to hit the chair.*)

Sir H. Tor. (*Peeping out.*) No Mrs Gabriel yet ! —Surely I heard somebody—soft, I'll peep further. (*Pushes the door further open, and hits against the back of the chair.*)—Not a soul.   Damme ! I'll bear it no longer.—(*Bangs open the door, and it hits violently against chair.—*PRIMITIVE *jumps out, and, unseen by* SIR HARRY, *gets behind the door to watch.*) —Rather than be left alone, and endure this tedium, this inanity, I'll plunge into any society.—(*As he is going*)—

Enter MRS LACKBRAIN, *hastily.*

Mrs Lack. O, my dear Sir Harry ! I've run myself out of breath ; and I'm so frightened, and so faint—so—I shall be able to speak in a moment—there.

Sir H. Tor. What's the matter ?

Mrs Lack. Why, Gabriel was the person at the paddock-gate ; knows I've an assignation in that dressing-room : he's coming here to search ; and if

you're discovered, he'll find out that you were his
assailant, and instantly fight you.

(PRIMITIVE *watching all the time.*)

Sir H. Tor. Well, let him: damme! employment
is the very thing I wanted.

Mrs Lack. Nay, think of my reputation——my
hopes with Mr Primitive.—And, look! see what a
tremendous cudgel he wields over his head.

Sir H. Tor. Gad! so he does; and that may produce more employment than is necessary: and since
I am unarmed, and your reputation is in danger, I
tell you what—I was before going; and if you'll
promise to befriend Marchmont, I'll fly so fast, that
time itself sha'n't overtake me.   [*Exit.*

GABRIEL, *singing, and shaking Cudgel.*

Mrs Lack. So, sir, you think I've a lover here?
but it's all a falsehood, sir: and I should like to
know if this is a return for securing Mr Primitive's
fortune, by my scandalizing this Mrs Belford?

Prim. (*Looking over door.*) Scandalize her!

Gab. You secured! why, 'twas I—'twas the sweet
child of nature that——

Mrs Lack. Don't tell me, sir; I say it was my
doing.

Gab. And I say it was mine: wasn't it my servant that made him believe cards of invitation signs
of domestic comfort? being up all night, a proof of
early rising? And didn't I convince old Hurlo-
Thumbo that reeling was rural awkwardness; and
the flush of claret, the rosy hue of health?—But
enough of old Hurlo-Thumbo.

Prim. Hurlo-Thumbo!

Gab. Now for the dressing-room.

Mrs Lack. O, pray do, sir, pray search the dressing-room.

Gab. I will; and Jemmy Swagger shall be no-

thing to it.—But first I'll lock the door, and then
go bring cousin baronet to see me perform such an
operation.——(*Locks the door, leaving* PRIMITIVE
standing up in the chair; who taps him on the head.
—GABRIEL *turns round, and they meet face to face.*)

Enter MRS BELFORD.

Prim. Your servant, rural innocence!—your most.
obedient, connubial love!

Gab. What! is it you, uncle?

Prim. Yes, it's old Hurlo-Thumbo.—For you,
wronged, injured lady, (*To* MRS BELFORD.) without prying further into your history, henceforth accept those favours I designed for them; henceforth
let me be a father to you.—And, d'ye hear, sir?
(*To* GABRIEL.) if you expect to profit by my future bounty, retire—retire, and repent.

Gab. Well, we'll go, uncle.—And I begin to think
I shall repent; for I'm still so much a child of nature as to feel sorry for my behaviour to that lady:
I am indeed; for though my education has made me
a fool, I think I'm not quite a knave:—though my
head is wrong, my heart is right; and I dare say,
when we're all sober, we shall still be friends.

                    [*Exeunt* GABRIEL *and* MRS LACKBRAIN.

Prim. Psha! away with you!—Odsheart! town
manners are to me unbearable, even in their proper
sphere: but brought into the country; introduced
into the calm, sequestered vale!—Though I hope
and trust the case is singular; and that the English
cottage is, and ever will be, the seat of peace, industry, and virtue.   [*Exit with* MRS BELFORD.

ACT THE FIFTH.

SCENE I.

The Inside of CRAFTLY'S *Library, filled with Toys,*
Jewellery, &c., as Libraries are at Watering-Places.
—A Raffling-Table in the Centre.

Enter SIR HARRY, *from Door in Flat.*

Sir H. Tor. So—'tis as poor Rosa expected. Craftly has the appointment of the new steward, and her
father is again at his mercy. What's to be done?
There is no way but to expose him to Mr Primitive.
Gad, I'll try hard for it---I dont mind trouble. That,
(*Snapping his fingers.*) for content, and the placid
streams of life; give me love, and a little agreeable
hot water.

Enter PRIMITIVE *and* MRS BELFORD.

Mrs Bel. Alas! that is his situation---a distressed
author. By his pen he earns a scanty pittance for
himself and daughter; and for her sake I thus presume to recommend him to the stewardship.

Sir H. Tor. (*Advancing to* PRIMITIVE.) And I
presume to back that recommendation. The gentleman at the Priory is a worthy man.

Prim. Why, that's true---and I certainly am much
indebted to you for bumping me out of that chair;
and I can't bear to deny my dear adopted any thing.
But you should consider, my worthy friend, Craftly
is the only person who, from his experience, can
select a proper steward for me; and, therefore, he

must have the nomination.----Nay, I am peremptory,
sir.---And now (*To* MRS BELFORD.) let me congratulate you on your arrival, from the dens of Arcadia, at the seat of learning and rationality.

Sir H. Tor. Learning and rationality !

Prim. To be sure, sir. What with the works of
deceased authors, and the society of living ones, I
know no place more amusing and instructing than
the house of a respectable bookseller---and such a
one is Craftly ! But let me look about me. (*Puts
on his spectacles.*) I'm told he has made great improvements since I went abroad. Bless me, what a
noble room ! And here, (*Going towards the coun-
ters.*) what's here ? Children's riding-horses, crick-
et-bats, powder, pomatum, candlesticks, and tea-
pots ! Psha ! we've made a mistake. Come along---
this is a toy-shop---this can't be a library.

Sir H. Tor. Not a library ! ha ! ha ! that's good !
---What ! I suppose you thought Craftly dealt in
books ?

Prim. To be sure. What else should he deal in ?

Sir H. Tor. What ? why, in raffling.

Prim. Now, what the devil is raffling ?

Sir H. Tor. Ha ! ha ! ha ! he dont know what
raffling is ! (*Goes up to the table.*) Look, look at this
gaming-table. Behold this dice-box. Here ! here's
the seat of learning and rationality ! (*Throws dice.*)

Prim. Heaven defend me ! And you call this raffling, do you ?

Sir H. Tor. Yes ; and trifling and insignificant as
the sport may appear, I know no species of gaming
more fatal or pernicious. Mrs Lackbrain is at once
an instance. She told me herself, that when only
nine years old, Mr Craftly persuaded her mother to
let pretty Miss throw for a pocket-book.------She
grasped the dice-box in her little hand, and being
successful, her passion for play became so uncontroul-

able, that she was never easy till she lost every shilling of her fortune.

Prim. I wont believe a word on't---he is too ho-
nourable---too prudent.

Sir H. Tor. Wont you? then bet me a hundred
pounds, and he shall confess it to your face.

Prim. I bet!---I commit the very crime---!

Sir H. Tor. Nay, then humour me so far as to
say 'tis a bet. See! here he comes---and, to secure
his confession, say you have betted that raffling is a
more productive trade than bookselling. Come now
---do---do indulge me.

Prim. Well, in order to convince you of your error, I will humour you.

Enter CRAFTLY.

Cousin, I rejoice to see you; but, before I say a
word on other subjects, you must decide a wager
between me and this gentleman. Ha! ha! What
do you think? I have laid a hundred pounds that
you get more money by raffling than bookselling.

Craft. Indeed! and has he taken the bet?

Sir H. Tor. I have---and be cautious---a hundred
pounds is an object to a poor baronet; and remember, I am on the side of bookselling.

Prim. And I on raffling; and I'm most anxious
to win.

Sir H. Tor. And so am I.

Craft. You are, are you? Then, in addition to
gratifying the old gentleman, I'll work you for the
furniture, (*Aside.*) Joy, cousin! the wager's yours!
I know no more of books than he or any other man
of fashion does. So, I say, (*Aside to* SIR HARRY.)
who'll peep through the iron bars first now?

Sir H. Tor. Psha! I'll have stronger demonstra-
tion---Prove it---prove it, sir.

Prim. Aye, prove it, sir.

Craft. (*Elbowing* PRIMITIVE, *and winking.*) Don't

be afraid----I'll satisfy him. (*Takes out a paper.*)
Look here now---here are twelve names to raffle for
that silver tea-cadee, at half-a-guinea a piece.

Sir H. Tor. Well, where's your profit? It costs
you six guineas.

Craft. No, it dont----it only costs me three----so
there, you see. (*Elbowing* PRIMITIVE *again.*)---'Tis
two to one in our favour already; ha! ha!

(PRIMITIVE *tries to laugh with him, but cannot.*)

Sir H. Tor. Ay: but another thing----All the
names are not paid for.

Craft. I know----Mr Wilkins isn't paid for----and
why? Because I'm Mr Wilkins.

Prim. You Mr Wilkins?

Craft. To be sure. The highest throw, you see,
wins the prize; and the filling a raffle is the work of
time.----Then one comes---throws " thirty-five," and
goes to town----another " forty," and follows----ano-
ther " forty-five," and he goes too. Very well!
Then, I'm to inform them by letter who's the win-
ner---then, of course, you know, I'm the winner;
for I throw " forty-seven," and write word, Mr Wilkins has won the tea-cadee There----now----now
are you satisfied? or will you hear more, simpleton?
ha! ha! ha! (*Laughing, and still elbowing* PRIMI-
TIVE.)

Sir H. Tor. No---I'm quite satisfied---aren't you,
Mr Primitive?

Prim. Quite----I never was more satisfied in all
my life; ha! ha! ha! And, as I dont wish to be
raffled out of my property, take notice, that, instead
of accepting a person of your nomination, I appoint
the gentleman at the Priory sole steward to all my
estates.

Craft. Hem! appoint him steward?

Sir H. Tor. Ay; would you have him appoint
Mr Wilkins?

Prim. Yes; would you have me appoint Mr Wilkins?

Sir H. Tor. I say, who'll peep through the iron bars first now?

Prim. But come---let us go instantly, and acquaint your friend with his appointment.

Craft. Nay, cousin, but hear me, upon my word I meant no harm---I thought all was fair in gaming.

Prim. More shame for you—and, thank Heaven, I'm too old-fashioned to countenance such practices! so, preferring the distressed author to the raffling bookseller, I take my leave of you and Mr Wilkins for ever.   [*Exit with* MRS BELFORD.

Sir H. Tor. And pray, sir, make my best respects to Mrs Wilkins; and take my advice, improve young minds by the sale of good moral publications, instead of corrupting them in the worst manner—by initiating them into all the horrors of the gaming-table.

[*Exeunt.*

SCENE II.

A Wood.

Enter ROSA.

Rosa. Where, where can my father have wandered? I tremble every moment for his safety---for alas! we are again in the power of the persecutor; and already, perhaps, he has fallen a victim to his malice---and yet there is one hope; the kind, the generous Sir Harry Torpid promised he would see Mr Primitive.

Enter SIR HARRY TORPID.

Sir H. Tor. And he has seen him, and it's all sett-

led---no more fagging, copying, and composing now:
—No---instead of daughter to a poor poet, you are
heiress to a gentleman of three hundred a year.

Rosa. Nay, no tantalizing---But tell me, who is
the new steward?

Sir H. Tor. Who? Why your father! Aye, things
are as they ought to be.   Mr Marchmont is steward
to Mr Primitive's estates, and Craftly and his dice-
boxes will be sent to the round-house---But dont
suppose you have to thank me---Here comes your
benefactress.

Enter MRS BELFORD.

Rosa. Heavens! to her!---The very person I so
longed to see.---Welcome, welcome!

Mrs Bel. (*Taking her hand and kissing it.*)   Do I
again behold you?---Pardon me; but I have thought
of nothing else since first I saw you.

Sir H. Tor. No more have I---that's my case ex-
actly---and for the service you have rendered---

Mrs Bel. What I have done has been for your
sake, Rosa.   We are compelled by strong and cruel
circumstances (ay, Heaven has so decreed it) to live
for ever separate.---And, had I left you in distress---
but now the dread of poverty is past---and that
thought, perhaps, will cheer me in my hours of ab-
sence---perhaps may make the loss of you supportable.

Rosa. The loss of me!---what, now, when you've
so served, and so attached me, will you leave me?

Mrs Bel. Ay, for ever.---Ask me not why, sweet
girl! tempt me not to unfold a history that will plant
thorns in your breast, and expose---no, never, never
can the mystery be solved.

Rosa. Nay, but we will not separate.---And, look!
yonder's my father; I'll call him to thank you, (*Going.*)

Mrs Bel. (*Holding her.*) Not for your life! not for your life!

Rosa. Nay, do not deny me; let me administer relief to one who stands so much in need of it.

Mrs Bel. Mark! what picture's that he so intently gazes on?

Rosa. I know not: but 'tis connected with his secret grief; for oft, when he conceived himself unseen, I have observed him press it to his lips, till he dissolved in tears.---And look again!---see now how he devours it with his kisses!

Mrs Bel. Maddening sight!---I know too well who it resembles.---Oh, villain! villain!

Rosa. Villain!

Mrs Bel. Yes; I have too long spared him; too long in pity smother'd the dark tale.---But now 'tis open enmity---avowed defiance---and he shall feel an injured woman's vengeance.

Sir H. Tor. How!

Rosa. Amazement!

Mrs Bel. Instantly conduct me to him; and tell him, she who conferred an accidental service, entreats no recompence but this: tell him, last night I whiled away my hours in composition of an artless tale; and, as an author of superior fame, I come to him for censure or for praise.---(*Producing the manuscript.*) Give it---'twill interest---'twill instruct--- oh! yes, 'twill strike him to the heart.

Sir H. Tor. Gad I'm frightened out of my senses. I hope you'll let me join the party; for, upon my soul ! there's no staying alone under such mysterious circumstances.

Mrs Bel. No, sir; these meetings must be private.---Come, Rosa.---Poor girl! I tremble for you: I see I have alarmed you; and on your account I could again be silent and discreet: but the picture ---you saw him press it to his lips---you saw him hide it in his breast---that rouses---fires me !---while I have strength and life, conduct me to him.

[Exit with Rosa.

Sir H. Tor. And what is to become of me ?— Whilst I have life and strength, I'll conduct myself to Mr Primitive, and we'll return and overhear all that passes. And now I ought to be on the pinnacle of happiness, for I am so choaked with agitation--- but, however, I see a man may have too much of a good thing.　　*[Exit.*

SCENE III.

An Apartment in the Priory ; painted Windows ; a Gothic Table, and Three Chairs.

Enter Marchmont *and* Rosa.—(Rosa *has the manuscript in her hand.*)

March. Astonishing !---Raised to prosperity by one I so neglected, and ask no recompence but the revision of a manuscript !—'Slife, 'tis incredible : and remember, Rosa, we have already had reason to suspect her ; and therefore, till I know the motive for her generosity, I shall not condescend to profit by it.

Rosa. What! wont you see her ? will you again dismiss her?

March. Unthinking girl ! why, wherefore should she serve me ?---You are yourself, perhaps, the bribe : and shall I owe preferment to my daughter's shame ? —No, she shall not enter.---And yet, if, after all, her motive should be good ; if, to the only one who has stept forth to serve me, I prove suspicious and ungrateful---that must not be——give me the manuscript, and conduct her in.

Rosa. Here, here it is, sir, (*Giving it.*)---And recollect, these are but the heads, the outlines of the book ; and you are to decide whether the materials are sufficient to ground a work upon.---And now look, sir, (*Goes to the wing, and leads on* MRS BELFORD, *with her veil down,*) here is our benefactress.

March. Madam, after what past when last I saw you, I scarce know how to address you.---Pray be seated.---

ROSA *draws a chair ;* MRS BELFORD *sits.*

I'm told you have conferred an everlasting favour on me ; and, as a recompense, you only ask what is most flattering to an author's pride.---I shall not trouble you with thanks, but will proceed.---(*Seats himself ;* ROSA *sits by* MRS BELFORD.---*Reads.*) " Sketch of a Romance, to be called Henry and Eliza.---Eliza, against the consent of a parent, as fond as affluent, married Henry.---Two years soon passed in harmony and joy, and Heaven blessed them with a pledge of mutual love.---The third began with *poverty* and *sorrow ;* and, to preserve her child and husband from distress, Eliza appealed to the feelings of her enraged father ; who, in compassion to her sufferings, supplied her with a remittance, as the last token of parental love."--- (*Pauses and weeps.*)

Rosa. (*Rises.*) Go on, sir : I feel as much interested as yourself: pray go on.

March. (*Reading.*) " Henry, though possessed of honour and of talent, could not resist temptation : and, allured to the gaming-table, by the arts of a female seducer, lost the remittance, sacrificed the sole maintenance of his family, and left Eliza to the mercy of his creditors."—(*Rises and goes forward.*)--- " The house, and poor remains of their effects, were taken from her ; and, when she sought the husband of her heart, he was not to be found.---Lost in the vortex of dissipation, he had forgot the wife he once

adored; and, revelling in luxury and guilt, thought
not that Eliza was destitute and forsaken."——Oh,
horror! horror!—(*Drops the book.*)---Speak! who
are you? whence came you?

> [MARCHMONT, *whilst reading the above, is much
> agitated, pauses often, and trembles violently.*
> MRS BELFORD *also is much agitated; appa-
> rently gazing intently on* MARCHMONT, *half
> rising from her chair,* &c. ROSA *observes
> them both with astonishment, and occasionally
> bursts into tears.*]

Rosa. (*Taking up the book, and presenting it to*
MARCHMONT.) Proceed; for pity's sake, proceed
—nay, you must, you shall.

March. Oh! I cannot.

Rosa. (*Reads.*) " Eliza, thus reduced, thus deserted both by parent and husband, no longer could
maintain the only comfort that was left her.---Dis-
tress soon tore her from her child: she placed it under the protection of a relation of its father; and,
to support herself, she changed her name; and, in a
state of menial service, went to Switzerland.--- There,
woe-worn and forlorn, robbed of all hope, a prey to
anguish and despair"—

March. Distraction! madness!—I know the rest
—(*Snatching the book from* ROSA, *and advancing towards Mrs B.*)—she died—died of a broken heart.

Mrs Bel. (*Who has before risen from her seat,
throws up her veil.*) No, she lives.—Behold me,
Marchmont, after an absence of twelve cheerless
years—behold that once loved wife, who would have
begged, starved, perished with you.—(MARCHMONT
staggers, and faints in a chair.)

Rosa. My mother! (*Runs and embraces her.*)

Mrs Bel. The story of my death was but an artifice to save me from inquiry; and now I came, in-
censed with wrongs, to goad you to the soul with my
reproaches; but the remembrance of our former

love, that altered look, that worn, exhausted frame—
Poor Marchmont! I may avoid, but I cannot upbraid him.—Farewell!—(*Going,* ROSA *holds her.*)

March. O my torn heart!—(*In turning in the
chair, the picture is discovered hanging from his
neck.*)

Rosa. Look, look, my mother!—Is he not now
an object of compassion?

Mrs Bel. He is.—But see! he wears a basilisk to
strike me dead—the picture, Rosa.

Rosa. Nay, but for my sake, mother: though as
a husband guilty, he has been the best of fathers:
and since this hated object is the bar, I will remove
—(*Takes the picture.*)—How!—that look—those
eyes—merciful powers! it is the portrait of my mother!

Mrs Bel. Can it—(*Trembling, and looking at it*)—
yes, mine is the picture he devours with kisses—mine
the resemblance that he bathes with tears!

[MARCHMONT, *suddenly recovering, and pulling*
ROSA *forward, without seeing* MRS MARCH-
MONT.]

March. (*Rises.*) She's gone!---fly---follow---call
her back: tell her, I am not so guilty as she thinks
me; for, as I hope for happiness to come, my heart
was ever only hers: and though involved in blackest
dissipation, my truth and constancy were yet untainted: tell her besides---

Rosa. Look, father!

March. Ah! do I once more—my child, fall pro-
strate at her feet; entreat, implore forgiveness.—
(*They both kneel.*)—My wife!

Rosa. My mother! can you pronounce a pardon?

Mrs March. I would, but tears prevent me.—
(*Gets between them, and embraces them both.*)—Merciful heaven! receive a suppliant's thanks; for thus
encircled by my child and husband, what now is
wanting?

Enter PRIMITIVE *and* SIR HARRY TORPID.

Prim. What? why a father—and here he is.—
That father who deserted you—who adopted you—
who—hang it! why dont you speak, Sir Harry?
you see my tongue sticks to my mouth.

Sir H. Tor. Who took the name of Primitive for
an estate of two hundred thousand pounds—who
will share it with you; raise you from poverty and
sorrow, to joy and affluence, to—damn it! I copy
your example; my tongue sticks to my mouth too.

Mrs March. Heavens! in my benefactor do I behold a parent?

Prim. You do; and but for the cursed circumstance
of changing names, we should have known each
other long ago.—But now I hold you to my heart.
—You also, my little grand-daughter—zooks! I must
give you a kiss for your likeness to your mother,
(*Kisses her.*)

Sir H. Tor. So must I, (*Kisses her.*)—I beg pardon, but I always copy Mr Primitive.

Prim. For you, Mr Marchmont, I was once coming forward to throttle you; but, when I recollected
I deserved the same punishment, I pitied and forgave you. Henceforth I'll be a friend to you, a father to your wife, a grandfather to your daughter,
and what's more, with your leave, I'll be a grandfather to Sir Harry.

Sir H. Tor. Ay, do; pray let me be one of the
family: I've long had a predilection for matrimony;
and, from what we've just witnessed, I'm sure it will
produce agitation in abundance.

March. Then, sir, if I'm to be consulted, I can
only say, you saved me once from ruin, and I know
no man that so well deserves my daughter.

Prim. So he did me; and I know no man that so
well deserves my grand-daughter.—And now, what
does she say?

13

Rosa. That to deserve him, who has so served you and my dearest father, will be the future study of my life.

Sir H. Tor. (*Taking her hand and kissing it.*) Then, thus I seal the bargain—and now, I only beg one thing—after marriage don't let us be too happy —you must now and then differ with me to keep me alive, for there is only one place in which I dread a difference,—and that is here.

You who can save, or kill us with a breath,
Stamp our existence, dont put Life to death;
Impatient now, we wait your dread commands;
So let us live, for *Life* is in your hands.

[*Exeunt.*

HOW TO GROW RICH;

A

COMEDY,

AS IT IS PERFORMED AT THE

THEATRE-ROYAL, COVENT-GARDEN.

BY

FREDERICK REYNOLDS.

DRAMATIS PERSONÆ.

PAVE,	Mr Lewis.
SMALLTRADE,	Mr Emery.
SIR THOMAS ROUNDHEAD,	Mr Munden.
LATITAT,	Mr Fawcett.
HIPPY,	Mr Townsend.
WARFORD,	Mr Pope.
SIR CHARLES DAZZLE,	Mr Betterton.
PLAINLY,	Mr Powell.
NAB,	Mr Farley.
FORMAL,	Mr Thompson.
Servant,	Mr Rees.
SIR CHARLES'S *Servant,*	Mr Ledger.
SIR THOMAS'S *Servant,*	Mr Simmons.
SMALLTRADE'S *Servant,*	Mr Blurton.
LADY HENRIETTA,	Mrs Glover.
ROSA,	Miss Murray.
MISS DAZZLE,	Miss Chapman.

SCENE.—A Sea-port Town in England.

HOW TO GROW RICH.

ACT THE FIRST.

SCENE I.

An Apartment in SMALLTRADE'S *Banking House—
Doors open in the Hall, and Clerks seen writing.*

Enter WARFORD *and* PLAINLY.

Plain. NAY, do not think me curious or impertinent, Mr Warford---I have lived so long with you
and your uncle, that I cannot see you unhappy without enquiring the cause.

War. My uncle is himself the cause---his weakness
and credulity will undo us all.

Plain. Excuse me, sir ; but I'm afraid the young
lady now on a visit at our banking house---the charming Lady Henrietta !-- has she not made a very deep
impression ?

War. To confess the truth, she has ; and though,
from my inferior situation in life, I can never aspire
to the gaining of her affections, she may still have
to thank me for saving her from ruin.

Plain. From ruin, sir !

War. Ay ; she is now on the very brink of it—
When her father, Lord Orville, went abroad for his
health, he gave her a fortune of eight thousand pounds,
and left her to the care of her uncle, Sir Thomas
Roundhead—At his country seat, Mr Smalltrade
met with her, and, being banker to her father, he
thought it his duty to invite her to his house.

Plain. And she had no sooner enter'd it, than she
became acquainted with Sir Charles and Miss Dazzle—I suspect their infamous designs.

War. Yes, Plainly ;—when Miss Dazzle has robb'd
her of her fortune at the gaming-table, Sir Charles
is to attempt to deprive her of her honour—but if I
don't shame and expose them !---Oh ! think of the
heartfelt satisfaction, in saving such a woman as Lady
Henrietta ! 'Tis true, most of her fortune is already
lost, and Sir Thomas is so offended at her conduct,
that (wanting an heir to his estate) he has adopted
his god-daughter, Rosa.

Plain. 'Sdeath ! I wish Sir Charles and his sister
were driven back to London—They are a disgrace
to this our fashionable sea-bathing town.

War. What most I fear is, lest my uncle should
join their confederacy—I know it is their plan to
lure him into partnership, and he is so anxious to increase his fortune, that, under the idea of growing
rich, he may be deluded into any scheme. (SMALL-
TRADE *appears at the doors, reading a ledger.*) Here
he is—Be secret and discreet, Plainly, and perhaps,
the next time we converse, I may be proud to tell
you, I have saved an innocent lady from treachery
and ruin !   [*Exit.*

Small. (*Coming forward.*) " Smalltrade debtor to
Sir Harry Hockley, two thousand pounds in specie
—Creditor two hundred in paper."—Ah ! that's very
well ! I don't know how it is—My little nice bank is
not the thing it was—People of real property have

become country bankers now, and play'd the devil with us petty, dashing traders. (*Knocking at door.*) Plainly, see who's there.

Plain. Give me leave, sir, (*Taking ledger, &c.*)

[*Exit.*

Small. There's nothing like a snug country bank —ready money received—paper notes paid—and though I make fifteen per cent. and pay their drafts in my own bills, what of that? A five guinea note is so convenient for carriage or posting—lays so close in a letter, or slips so neatly in the sleeve of a coat —Oh! it's of great use to the country, and a vast benefit to myself.

Re-enter PLAINLY, *followed by a Servant.*

Serv. Is this your country bank, as you call it?

Plain. It is.

Serv. I want change for this draft of Sir Harry Hockley's.

Plain. Very well—How much is it for?

Serv. A hundred pounds.

Small. What?

Serv. A hundred pounds.

Small. Mercy on me! You've set me all in a tremble! Draw on a country bank for a hundred pounds!—Why, does your master suppose himself drawing on the bank of Amsterdam?

Plain. True, sir; and, if you recollect, we had a large run upon us yesterday.

Small. So we had—a very large run! Sir Thomas Roundhead drew in one draft, for the enormous sum of twenty-five pounds; and here's your master draws for a hundred.—Talk of a country bank! the bank of England couldn't stand this.

Serv. I can't tell, sir—Sir Harry said he had ten times the money in your hands.

Small. So he has, and what then? Doesn't he place money in my hands, that it may be safe? and if he

is to draw it out in large sums, that is, if he is to get
it when he wants it, where would be the use of a
banker? Plainly, pay the draft in my own notes;
and, d'ye mind, let them be all at thirty and forty
days' sight—Young man, go with my clerk. [*Exeunt*
PLAINLY *and Servant.*) 'Tis near the time my accomplished cousin, Miss Dazzle, is to wait upon me
—She writes me word she has to communicate a
new mode of growing rich—Dear! how I long to
hear it! It's my way always to catch at every thing
—Here she is.

Enter MISS DAZZLE.

Miss Daz. Good morning, Mr Smalltrade—I'm
sorry we hadn't the pleasure of seeing you at our
gala last night.

Small. Pray be seated, cousin. (*They sit.*) Ah!
I'm told it was the most grand, expensive entertainment.

Miss Daz. Expensive! your pardon, sir—It didn't
cost me and my brother a shilling.

Small. No!

Miss Daz. No—and what will surprise you more,
it is our sumptuous house, our brilliant rooms, and
extravagant entertainments, that pay all our expences
—In short, Mr Smalltrade, we've found out a new
mode of growing rich.

Small. Have you? (*Rubbing his hands.*) That's
what I want to hear about.

Miss Daz. And that's what I came to impart to
you—In a word, sir, we keep a bank.

Small. Do you? Well, that's one way.

Miss Daz. Yes, such a bank! so opposite to yours!
We know nothing of notes, checks, clerks, or cur-
rency—We don't rise early in the morning to settle
our accounts, or shut up before evening, to prevent
our customers from settling theirs—No, all our business is done in the dark, my dear cousin.

Small. In the dark! so is mine too, my dear cousin.

Miss Daz. Then, while you are satisfied with a hundred pounds profit in a week, we are not content with a thousand in a night; and if ever we stop payment, which fortune avert! we have nothing to surrender, but mahogany tables, wax-lights, cards, and dice-boxes.

Small. (*Rising.*) I understand—you keep a Faro-table—Oh! take me!—take me as groom-porter, and I'll make my fortune, if it's only by picking up the droppings.

Miss Daz. There's the point—if you would but consent to become a partner with myself and my brother, our profits would be trebled.

Small. Would they? That's nice!

Miss Daz. The case is this—Occasionally, though it seldom happens, we want ready money to carry on the campaign.

Small. Ready money! Ah! there's the devil—I've nothing but paper.

Miss Daz. Nonsense! Your notes can be changed into cash, and Sir Charles and I will pay the discount.

Small. What! pay the discount out of your own pockets, and give me a third of the profits besides?

Miss Daz. Certainly.

Small. Then I'll be a partner, and—Yet, hold, hold—I'd better not determine too hastily. (*Aside.*) Miss Dazzle, here's my visitor, Lady Henrietta, so, as we're disturbed you see, I'll wait on you in an hour, and talk further.

Miss Daz. By that time Sir Charles will arrive from London—Good day.

Small. Adieu! Zounds! I always had a turn for gaiety, and I don't think I need fear being imposed upon; for I've so long managed a trading bank, that I must understand a gambling one!—I say, cousin,

not a word to her, about the new mode of growing
rich—Good day !   [*Exit.*

Miss Daz. So, the old gentleman is caught in the
snare ; and, aided by his bank, what will not ours at-
chieve ? Lady Henrietta, who has refused my brother's hand and title, will now be his on other terms;
and Warford, who is our enemy, will be involved in
his uncle's ruin.

Enter WARFORD *and* LADY HENRIETTA.

Lady Hen. Why so grave, Mr Warford ? You
really can be very pleasant if you please ; but those
gloomy looks !---I declare you are quite an alter'd
man ; isn't he, Miss Dazzle ?

Miss Daz. Every thing changes, Lady Henrietta.

Lady Hen. Why, that's very true ;—now, to look
at the alterations in this town since last summer—
Friends have become enemies, and enemies, friends
—You shall hear—The other night, I went to Lady
Changewell's, where I used to meet all my old ac-
quaintance—To my astonishment, I didn't see a soul
I knew.

Miss Daz. Really !

Lady Hen. No—an entire new set of faces—So,
I asked her ladyship after her friend, the little Colonel—She said, " they didn't speak now." " Where
is your companion and favourite, Lady Brilliant,"
said I—" Oh! the creature is in debt," said she, " and
wants me to lend her money."—" And where is
your dear, darling, loving husband," said I.—" My
dear, darling, loving husband lives with an Italian
Countess," says she—" We're divorced, and I am
to be married to-morrow to my old bitter enemy,
Sir Francis Fickle—I now think him a most delightful, charming fellow, and believe he's the only real
friend I ever had, ha! ha! ha!"

Miss Daz. Excellent !

Lady Hen. Yes—it's seldom a friendship lasts above a year—Is it, Mr Warford?

War. I hope there are instances, madam.

Lady Hen. So do I, sir—but I am afraid they are so rare—Heigho! if I don't mind, I shall catch your spleen, and be as grave and sentimental as yourself.

War. And why not, madam? Why be ashamed of sentiment? 'Tis true, it is the mode to ridicule and laugh at it; but I doubt, if fashion, and all its fopperies, can find a pleasure to supply its loss.

Lady Hen. Vastly well! Didn't I tell you, Miss Dazzle, he could be very pleasant? You really have talents, Mr Warford; but the worst of them is, they go more to instruction than amusement.

War. Then I am satisfied, Lady Henrietta; and, if I could convince you, that happiness is not to be found, either in the fever of dissipation, or the delusions of a gaming table—

Lady Hen. Fie! don't abuse gaming,—the thing I doat on—

War. Excuse me, madam;—but, if I might advise, you had better never play again.

Lady Hen. Oh! monstrous! Why, you tyrant, would you shut me from the world, and cloister me in an old castle? If you did, I'd still game—I would, if I betted on the ivy, and took odds on the ravens and rooks—Wouldn't you, Miss Dazzle?

Miss Daz. Me! I'd keep a rookery on purpose.

Lady Hen. Ay, that you would—But come—I'm going to meet my uncle, Sir Thomas, at the library —would you believe it? He, too, is so offended at my turning gamester, that he has forbid me his house, and adopted his little god-daughter for his heiress; —but—let's walk.

Miss Daz. With pleasure——we shall see you at Faro in the evening.

Lady Hen. Oh certainly—Nay, how you frown

now, Mr Warford. Come, I'll make a bargain with
you—if I lose a thousand pounds to-night, I'll promise never to game again—never! because, having
nothing left to lose, I must e'en make a virtue of necessity, and reform, in spite of myself—Come.

[Exeunt.

SCENE II.

Outside of Sir Charles Dazzle's *House—View of
the Sea.*

Enter Sir Charles, (*followed by a Servant with a
Portmanteau.*)

Sir Char. So, once more I'm escaped from the
fever of London, and got safe back to my favourite
sea-port—Take the things in.

[Exit Servant into house.

I suppose my sister has so plucked the pigeons in
my absence, that there's scarcely a feather left in
the town.

Enter Miss Dazzle.

Miss Daz. Welcome from London, brother——I
have just left the idol of your heart, the charming
Henrietta!—As usual, the banker's nephew was attending her.

Sir Char. Ay, ay; it's all pretty plain——but I
won't be scandalous.

Miss Daz. Well, if she's his to-day, she'll be
yours to-morrow—I have seen Mr Smalltrade—he
talks of becoming a partner; and if you play your
cards well, Lady Henrietta will be completely in
your power.

Sir Char. Yes; for when I've won all her money

—I can be generous enough to become her protector! (*Aside.*) Well, sister, we shall ruin them all; and now-a-days, you know, you can't do your friend a greater service.

Miss Daz. What! than to ruin him?

Sir Char. To be sure—Where is the ruined man that doesn't spend twice the income of the richest citizen in London? Don't many of them have executions in their house in the morning, and give galas at night? An't the very bailiffs turned into servants, and don't they still stake five thousand on a card? Nay, I know a man that has done it all his life.

Miss Daz. Do you? who?

Sir Char. Myself!—I never had a shilling, and I've always lived like a Nabob—And how have I done all this? How, but by hospitality! By entertaining my friends elegantly at one table, and genteelly picking their pockets at another.

Miss Daz. Very true; and when we've ruined the banker, his nephew, and his visitor, they'll think themselves much obliged to us—But mind and humour Smalltrade; for, without ready money, we can't go on—Who's here?

Sir Char. (*Looking out.*) Where?——Oh! it's a hanger-on of mine—a mere jackall, who dangles after me in hopes of preferment—I brought him from London, thinking he might be useful.

Miss Daz. What, is it Pavè?

Sir Char. The same—The dog has a good heart; —great good humour, and is descended from a respectable family; but, in running after people of rank and high company, he has so reduced his fortune, that he now depends on me to get him promoted.

Miss Daz. Ay; I've heard of him——introduce him to a lord, or promise him an appointment, and he'll do any thing to serve you.

Sir Char. Aye; so great is his furor, that an in-

terview with a prince, or an audience of a minister,
would turn his brain—but, I believe, were he once
provided for, he would neither betray his benefactor nor disgrace his country.

Enter PAVE. (*A long roll of paper sticking out of his
pocket.*)

Pav. (*Running up to* SIR CHARLES.) Sir Charles!
—hark ye. (*Whispers.*)

Sir Char. Lord Orville coming home! What then?

Pav. Then, Lord Orville is your acquaintance,
and I am your friend, and—you understand—I'm
always ready.

Sir Char. Pray, sister, have you any interest? If
you have, this gentleman, Mr Pavé—

Miss Daz. I should be very happy; but I fancy
there is nothing more difficult than to get a place.

Pav. Yes, there is, ma'am,—to deserve it! And
that I deserve it, is evident from my long list of promises—(*Takes out roll of paper.*) here it is, ma'am.
—My four first promises depend on Lord Orville,
you see—my next is from you, baronet.

Miss Daz. Pray, Mr Pavè, do you find that, when
these great people make you promises, they always
keep their words?

Pav. Oh! Sir Charles will answer you that question, ma'am—Heh!—Mum! Baronet!

Sir Char. Nay, Pavè, you know the other day I
referred you to a man in power.

Pav. You did;—and he referred me to another,
who kindly sent me to a third, that politely hurried
me to a fourth, till at last I got kicked down stairs
by a person who said he knew none of us—You see
the scheme is this, ma'am—Nobody will speak first
in your favour, but all promise to second any body
who will, because, judging by themselves, they know
nobody'll speak at all.

Miss Daz. Well, if I was you, Mr Pavè, I'd try
13

some more public mode of getting preferred—For
instance now, suppose you advertised.

Pav. Don't mention it—I did advertise once, and
what do you think happened? A gentleman waited
upon me, calling himself Lord Sulwin—superb equipage—elegant appearance—free in his promises—
secure in his interest—I bowed, smiled, gave his
lordship a thousand guineas—and he proved to be
an attorney! a money-lending rascal! and I've
never seen or heard of him since!

Sir Char. An attorney! ha, ha, ha! Should you
know him again?

Pav. Know him! I shall never forget him, because he did the thing so genteelly, as he expressed
it—Oh! if I catch him!—

Enter SMALLTRADE.

Small. How d'ye do, Sir Charles? Cousin, a word
—(*Taking* MISS DAZZLE *aside.*) Well, I've made
up my mind—I'll enter into your scheme—I'm determined to grow rich.

Miss Daz. Ay, I thought you'd see your interest,
Mr Smalltrade.

Small. I do—I see we shall make fools of them
all——At night I'll come and be a looker-on; and
now, if you'll step into the house, we'll arrange articles of partnership.

Miss Daz. With all my heart—Come, sir.

Small. A third of the profits, remember; and,
hark ye, as your visitors are so fashionable, I suppose I must make an appearance—look like a gentleman! I can do it, I assure you—but then, how to
understand the technicals—to talk like the rest of
you—Oh! evil communication will corrupt my good
manners—So, come along.

Miss Daz. Brother, will you follow? Mr Pavè,
we shall see you in the evening.

[*Exit into house with* SMALLTRADE.

Pav. (*Stopping* SIR CHARLES, *who is following.*)
Gad! this must be some great man—Baronet, who
is that little fellow?

Sir Char. A man of very great power—If you'll
remind me, I'll introduce you at night.

Pav. Introduce me! Oh! don't trouble yourself,
—I can do that myself.

Sir Char. I believe it—Mind you are useful now
—recollect I brought you down to assist in all our
schemes—Speak highly of your patron.

Pav. Ay, and of myself too, Sir Charles: for, in
this unthinking age, say you're a clever fellow, and
every body believes it—They remember they heard
you praised, and forgot where—I know my duty—
Success to you, my ever dear, kind patron! [*Exit*
SIR CHARLES.] Dirty, shuffling rascal! I've been
his dangler these five years, and never got any thing
but promises—Oh! if Lord Orville, or even that
great little man, would befriend me!—I'll get a new
patron—I will! Sir Charles's contemptible tricks
are beneath a man of my consequence—I'll about it
instantly; and though necessity may make me dependent, it shall never make me mean; for if I can't
be promoted so as to be of service to my country,
hang me if I'll be promoted at all.   [*Exit.*

ACT THE SECOND.

SCENE I.

An elegant Saloon at SIR CHARLES'S----*One door leading to Faro-Room---the other to Supper-Room.*

Flourish of Clarinets.

Enter WARFORD *and Servant.*

War. Tell Mr Smalltrade I desire to speak with him.

Serv. Mr Smalltrade is engaged, sir---looking on at the gaming-table.

War. Tell him his nephew is come, according to his orders.   [*Exit Servant in Faro-Room.*
'Sdeath! 'tis as I suspected---he has sent for me to bring articles of partnership between himself and these impostors---What is to be done? He is convinced he shall make his fortune by the undertaking; and so great is his credulity, that, till he is completely ruined, he will not detect the imposition---Can I believe it? Yonder he comes. (*Stands aside.*)

Flourish of Clarinets.

Enter from Faro-Room, SMALLTRADE, *full dressed, handing in* MISS DAZZLE.

Miss Daz. Well, Mr Smalltrade, how do you like Faro? Don't you see it's the way to get money?

Small. I do----I see my fortune's made. (*Turns about.*) Heh! What do you think? Shan't I do? Don't I look like one of us? (*Struts about.*)

Miss Daz. You do indeed.

Small. I've learnt all your cant words too—I'm not a greenhorn or a flat—I'm an old rook and a black-legs!—Just like you and your brother.

Miss Daz. Well, but Mr Smalltrade!—the music—gaming—the company——altogether, isn't it a most enchanting amusement?

Small. It is indeed——and Faro's a monstrous pretty game. Cousin, do you know I'd a great mind to have had a touch myself.

Miss Daz. How! you play, sir?

Small. I don't know how it was—I felt an odd, ticklish sensation—a sort of itching at the end of my fingers, and presently I caught myself putting a guinea on a card.

Miss Daz. Well, but you took it up again?

Small. No, I didn't—I let it lay, and somebody else took it up for me.

Miss Daz. What, you lost it?

Small. I did—I lost my guinea! Oh! it's a sweet game! I don't wonder at the money rolling in—But where's the supper?

Miss Daz. Yonder.

Small. So it is.—What a feast for the senses! Eyes, ears, taste, feeling, all gratified!—But hold, hold—By the law of the land, don't we come under the vagrant act? Mayn't a justice of the peace send you, I, and all the noble host of Faro, to be whipt at the cart's tail?

Miss Daz. You forget—Gold makes justice blind.

Small. True—that's another way of growing rich —But where's Warford? I wish Warford would bring the articles.

Miss Daz. There he is, sir—I'll leave you to talk to him—for in the next room, they can do no more without me than I can without them. Adieu! call me when you want me.   [*Exit.*

WARFORD *advances.*

Small. Well, sir, what do you stare at? Does the splendour of my dress surprise you, or are you angry because I want to grow rich? Where are the articles, sir?

War. They are not yet finished, sir.

Small. Look ye, sir—you think this bank isn't so good as mine; but I'd have you know they have ten times our customers. People will game, sir.

War. Will they, sir?

Small. Yes; there's a curst, ticklish sensation, makes a man game whether he will or not; then, when I give turtle and venison at home, I'm obliged to pay for it myself; but here egad! they make other people pay for it: and a couple of lemons, squeezed into a quart of water, will fetch twenty guineas a tumbler!—But, George, now, isn't this a most delicious scene? The supper! Look at the supper, you dog! Doesn't the very smell make you happy?

War. Sir, I am sorry to see you so imposed upon.

Small. Imposed upon!

War. Yes, sir—If you have any feeling for yourself, regard for me, or affection for Lady Henrietta, who is placed under your protection, you will refuse to countenance such infamous designs—They will draw you into the partnership, rob you of your fortune, and laugh at you for your folly.

Small. Indeed!

War. Yes, sir; and without your assistance they must fall to the ground; for, though they make large sums every night, they contrive to spend 'em every day.

Small. Oh! then they do make large sums, do they?

War. Certainly—But how is it done? By perverting the laws of hospitality—by annihilating the bonds of society, and, under the specious mask of rank and character, perpetrating crimes that common sharpers are excluded from.

Small. What's that to you or me? If the money's made, it's quite enough to satisfy my conscience! So, go, sir—finish the articles of partnership, and bring them instantly.

War. Oh, sir, consider—Even now perhaps Lady Henrietta is falling a victim to their artifices, and if you join the confederacy, all—all will be undone!

Small. Go, sir—no reply—I must and will be obeyed. (*Exit* WARFORD.) Senseless flat! While I can fill my stomach in one room, and my pockets in the other, what do I care for him or Henrietta? But now to take a peep, just to see who's losing. (*Looks in Faro-Room.*)

Enter PAVE.

Pav. Really, this is a most shocking business— I'm told they've drawn in their relation, a silly country banker—Sir Charles brought me down to be useful, but no prospect of advantage to myself shall ever induce me to take part in a bad administration.—— Ha! yonder's that little great man—Now, if I can but coax him into my list of promises!—Sir, your most obedient.

Small. Sir, your most devoted.

Pav. I see, sir, you're a friend of my patron, Sir Charles—And, next to being a man of rank ones self, I know nothing like living amongst them— Where does your interest lay, sir?

Small. My interest! Who the deuce is this?

Pav. I wish I knew his title. (*Aside.*) Pray be seated, sir. (*They sit.*) Now, sir, (*Taking out his roll of promises.*) look at that list of promises! Many of your noble friends, you see, sir—but nothing done! nothing!

Small. Many of my noble friends! Oh! what, you

want promotion, do you?—My dear sir, I've no influence.

Pav. Excuse me, sir—I know better—Do you think I can't tell a great man when I see him? (SMALLTRADE *looks pleased.*) Besides, when was it that such manners, such an appearance, and such a style of dress, couldn't command every thing. (SMALLTRADE *looks more pleased.*) My dear sir, you remind me of the old court, you do indeed— Of an old bedchamber lord.

Small. (*Greatly pleased.*) Bedchamber lord! Ay; I'm very upright. (*Holds up his head.*)

Pav. Perhaps you are diffident, sir—never applied?

Small. Why, that's very true—I never did ask a man in power, a favour, never—I've a great mind to try.

Pav. Do—make the experiment, and, by way of sounding, get a small snug appointment for me, before you ask a grand one for yourself.

Small. I will—I'll get a little one for you, and a great one for myself—Was there ever such a delicious scene? How riches do pour in upon me!

Pav. Riches! Why, did the scheme never strike you before?

Small. Never—And I'm amazed I could be such a greenhorn. (*Rises.*) Oh! I'll go and ask Sir Charles directly.

Pav. Ask Sir Charles! Pooh! he's only one hope himself.

Small. One hope! What's that?

Pav. Why, don't you know? As we're alone, I'll tell you—There's a country banker—They've drawn in the old greenhorn to be a partner!

Small. What!

Pav. He'll stop payment of course, and as he's not a man of character—only a little sneaking, shuffling shopman—Formy part I'm glad on't,—an't you, sir?

Small. Indeed I am not, sir.—So he's to be a bankrupt, is he?

Pav. Certainly—I shall, perhaps, be one of his creditors—But, between you and I, I sha'n't sign his certificate.

Small. You won't sign his certificate!

Pav. No—what business has a tradesman to turn black-legs? To be sure he won't sneak into the Gazette, like a tailor or a tallow-chandler, for a paltry hundred or so; No—he'll preserve his dignity; fail like a gentleman for thirty or forty thousand pounds —You take the joke, don't you?

Small. No, dam'me if I do! And they mean to ruin him, do they?

Pav. Ruin him! Oh! it's all settled! Sir Charles told me he saw him lose a guinea just now—" Poor devil," says he, " he little thinks how near it is his last." Ha, ha, ha! (*Walks up the stage.*)

Re-enter WARFORD (*with the Articles.*)

War. According to your commands, sir, I have brought you the articles.

Small. Have you? then thus I tear them. (*Taking and tearing them.*) George, I ask your pardon —I'm so ashamed, yet so gratified, that, though that impudent dog has insulted me, I can't help liking him for having open'd my eyes.

Pav. (*Coming down stage.*) Well!—have you thought—Oh, mum—applying to a friend!—That's right—stick close to every body.

Small. Did you ever hear such a fellow? But come, let's return home, and, instead of this new-fangled mode of getting money, we'll grow rich the old way—by honesty and industry, my boy.

War. Stay, sir—think that Lady Henrietta is still in danger, and sure you will not leave the house till she is released.

Small. What can I do, George? Neither you nor
I can persuade her; and, unless her father, Lord Orville, were here——

Pav. Lord Orville! That's the man! He can settle us all—Oh! I wish I knew how to oblige him.

War. Do you, sir? Then, his daughter, Lady Henrietta, is now at the gaming-table, and if you will but
save her as you have this gentleman, I'll answer for
it, her father will reward you.

Pav. Reward me! my dear sir, when a lady's in
distress, do you think I care who or what her father
is? Lord Orville's daughter! Whugh! Here's an
opportunity! Oh! I'll go find her out directly.

War. Be cautious, sir—for, if Sir Charles discovers
your intentions——

Pav. What then, sir? Do you suppose I'm influenced by any but people of merit and distinction?
Such as Lord Orville, and your elegant friend, my
graceful bedchamber lord, who, I know, will not forget the snug appointment—Where shall I conduct
the lady?

Small. We'll wait below—And, d'ye hear—tell
Miss Dazzle not to forget to fleece the country
banker.

Pav. I will—and shew Sir Charles I'm a man of
real consequence. Adieu! wait here a moment,
and you'll see the little tradesman come out howling!
But it won't do—I sha'n't sign his certificate! Ha,
ha, ha!

Small. By this time he's lost his last guinea, ha, ha,
ha! (*Exit* PAVE.) Come, George, let's go wait below, and depend on't, that fellow will extricate Henrietta—What an odd dog! He seems so anxious for
preferment, that I've a great mind to turn away my
under clerk on purpose to give him a place.

[*Exeunt.*

SCENE II.

Another Apartment at SIR CHARLES'S.

SIR CHARLES *and* LADY HENRIETTA, *discovered at Cards.*

Sir Char. Point—sixty.

Lady Hen. Good.

Sir Char. Sixieme major.

Lady Hen. Good.

Sir Char. Quatorze.

Lady Hen. Good—(*Rises.*) I'll play no more— Never was such a series of ill luck—Well, Sir Charles, what have I lost?

Sir Char. Oh, a trifle! Never think of it, Lady Henrietta.

Lady Hen. Nay, you may as well seal my doom at once—Come!

Sir Char. Well, if you insist—Here are your notes for money lent at Faro, one thousand pounds, and what I have now won is five hundred, making in the whole fifteen hundred pounds.

Lady Hen. A very pleasant trifle! But don't imagine I can't pay you, sir, don't——

Sir Char. Nay, allow me to relieve you at once— Take back the notes, forget the debt, and think me amply paid, if but a smile the return.

Lady Hen. No, Sir Charles—I cannot consent to be so obliged—'Tis true, my imprudence has involved me beyond all hope of being extricated, and my father is abroad, and my uncle won't protect me!— yet, sir!——

Sir Char. Lady Henrietta, I know your situation, and feel for you—therefore let me entreat you to ac

cept the notes ; and, when you want a protector, you
know where to find one.

Lady Hen. A protector, sir !—

Sir Char. Be not alarm'd—you know my intentions are honourable; and, since you have no other
friend to protect you——

Lady Hen. Sir, I deserve this, amply deserve it—
I might have known, when a woman turns gamester,
her fortune is the least she loses.   The society vili-
fies her feelings—the fatigue ruins her health and
understanding, and, when she has nothing left to
stake, her pride is insulted, and even her honour
made a sport of !

Sir Char. How you mistake me ! Because I profess to be your friend, you suppose me your enemy
—My sister is in the next room waiting to receive
you—You will not leave my house ?

Lady Hen. Am I made a prisoner then ? Heavens ! how have I sunk myself!

Sir Char. Pray be composed—I will place you
under my sister's care—She shall decide whether I
deserve your affections—Come, come, be calm—
(*Taking her hand.*) Consider, where would you go?

Lady Hen. Any where, so I leave your house—
Don't imagine I have no friends, sir.

Sir Char. I am your friend, and feel your interest
too much to part with you—Nay, you must, you
shall be persuaded—(*Holds and detains her.*)

Enter PAVE.

Pav. So, heaven be praised, I have found you at
last, phugh! (*Puffing himself.*)

Sir Char. What brings you here?

Pav. To be useful—Ma'am, your most obedient
—What! at your old tricks, my boy ? (*Smacks* SIR
CHARLES *on the back, and points to cards.*)

Sir Char. Hush ! don't you see I'm busy !

Pav. Mum ! don't expose yourself—Lady Henrietta, I rejoice—Oh! what a likeness of her father !

Sir Char. 'Sdeath! What do you mean, sir?

Pavè. Mean! that we were born to protect women, not insult them, and while I wear a sword, they shall never want a champion!—I tell you what, sir—your behaviour has been lately very offensive, and if the lady will give me leave, I'll conduct her to a little great man who is waiting to receive her.

Lady Hen. As I live it's Mr Smalltrade! Yonder I see him.

Sir Char. Come here, sir—Answer me, is this your gratitude?

Pav. Gratitude! Now, observe, ma'am—I have been his dangler these five years—I've waited whole hours in the streets, only to catch a smile from him —dined at his side-table, and got nothing to eat but scraps and offals—talk'd of his gallantries, confirm'd his gasconades, and laugh'd at his jokes, though he knows he never cut one in his life—But now, come, my sweet lady.

Sir Char. Lady Henrietta, will you trust yourself with that reptile?

Lady Hen. With any body rather than Sir Charles Dazzle.

Pav. You hear, baronet, you hear! the reptile's not so contemptible—And, to shew my condescension—hark ye—I'll speak to Lord Orville for you— make out a list of promises—put his lordship at the head, and in the course of five years, if he don't provide for you, I will! I will, if it's only to shew you that one man of rank can be more useful than another, you see—Come, madam.

Sir Char. Confusion! am I outwitted? made a laughing-stock of?

Enter MISS DAZZLE.

Miss Daz. So, Sir Charles, have you seen that blockhead, Pavè?

Sir Char. Blockhead! villain.

Miss Daz. He has undone all my schemes on the banker.

Sir Char. And mine on Lady Henrietta.

Miss Daz. You brought him to be useful, didn't you?

Sir Char. I did; and he has completely answered my expectations! Well, sister, if ruin is the road to happiness, we are the merriest couple—Lady Henrietta shall not escape, however—William!

Enter a Servant.

Go to Mr Latitat's—tell him to come to me directly.

Miss Daz. To your attorney's, brother?

Sir Char. Yes; I'll leave her to the law now—In the mean time, let's to Mr Smalltrade—There's a vacancy in the borough, and if I can secure his interest and gain the election, I'll sell my tables, leave off hospitality, reform, and live like a gentleman!

[*Exeunt.*

ACT THE THIRD.

SCENE I.

An Apartment at SMALLTRADE'S.

LADY HENRIETTA *discovered sitting at a Toilette.*

Lady Hen. So, the day of reckoning is at last arrived; and here I sit, forgotten by my father, ne-

glected by my uncle Sir Thomas, and unpitied by
every body—Even Mr Pavè has avoided me—finding Lord Orville was offended with me, he retired,
saying he would give me no further trouble—Alas!
how, how have I involved myself?

Enter BETTY.

Bet. Lord, ma'am, I'm frighten'd out of my senses—What do you think Sir Charles has done?

Lady Hen. What, Betty?

Bet. He has employ'd a gentleman, who, he says,
will get the money from you directly—An attorney,
ma'am.

Lady Hen. An attorney!

Bet. Yes, your ladyship—Sir Charles insists he
lent you a thousand pound.

Lady Hen. So he did, Betty—He lent it first, and
won it afterwards—Have you seen Mr Warford?

Bet. I have, ma'am, and—(*Hesitating.*)

Lady Hen. And what, Betty?

Bet. When I told him your distress, my lady, and
said you would thank him to lend you a hundred
pounds to convey you abroad, he made no reply.

Lady Hen. No!

Bet. No, ma'am—but left the room instantly.

Lady Hen. This wounds me more than all! that
Warford should desert me! Yet why do I upbraid
him! He warn'd me of my danger, and now, too
justly, shuns me for my folly.

Bet. Lord, don't fret about it, my lady—who
knows but this lawyer may prove a very gentleman-
like man—Talk of old friends—give me a new acquaintance, I say! (*Loud knocking.*) Here he is,
ma'am! here's the attorney—(*Looks out.*) Upon my
word! what an elegant equipage! see, ma'am! a
handsome phaeton, and two servants on horseback.

Enter a Servant.

Serv. Ma'am, here's a gentleman in a phaeton, who says his name is Latitat.

Lady Hen. Shew him in. [*Exeunt* BETTY *and Servant.*] Really this must be a strange kind of an attorney; but in these days, nothing surprises!

Enter LATITAT *in an elegant Morning Dress.*

Lat. Let my carriage wait—Ma'am, your most obedient.

Lady Hen. Pray be seated, sir—(*They sit.*) I'm told, sir, you have some law business.

Lat. I have, ma'am—but no hurry about that—I always do the thing genteelly—Pray, ma'am, were you at the last grand meeting of archers?

Lady Hen. No, sir, I was not.

Lat. That's unlucky—I got the verdict—that is, I won the prize—hit the bull's eye—carried off the bugle-horn—here it is—(*Puts his hand in wrong pocket, and takes out papers.*) No—that's a bill in Chancery—Here, ma'am—(*Pulls out bugle-horn.*) received it from the lady patroness—kiss'd her hand —proclaim'd victor—march'd in procession— colours flying—music playing—clients huzzaing! Did the thing genteelly, ma'am!

Lady Hen. Indeed, sir, you were very fortunate.

Lat. Oh, I'm a nice fellow, ma'am!—Then at cricket—last grand match—got sixty notches—the Peer run out—the Baron stumpt, and the General knock'd down his own wicket—I was long-stop—famous at a long-stop, ma'am—cricket or law! ball or debtor! let neither slip through my fingers! heh, ma'am! do the thing genteelly.

Lady Hen. So it seems—But, pray, sir, how can you follow the law amidst such a confusion of professions?

Lat. Law and confusion are the same thing, ma'am.

—Then I write my own songs, draw my own pleadings, ride my own races—To be sure I never won
one in my life—but then I always rode like a gentleman ! Heh, ma'am ! do the thing genteelly.

Lady Hen. Certainly—but now, may we talk about
my business ?

Lat. Don't alarm yourself—that's all settled—my
friend will be here presently—he'll shew you every
accommodation.

Enter Servant.

Serv. A gentleman in a curricle, ma'am.

Lat. In a curricle ! Oh ! that's my friend—Shew
him in. (*Exit Servant.*) Now here ! here's another
proof of my talents ! When I came to this town,
ma'am, little Nab hadn't a shilling ! I learnt him the
practice—Now he lives in style, drives his carriage,
and will lend you a thousand pounds.

Lady Hen. Will he, sir ? I'm very much obliged
to him.

Enter NAB, (*smartly dress'd.*)

Nab. (*Speaks as he enters.*) Put clothes on the
horses, and raise the top of the curricle, that the lady mayn't catch cold.

Lat. Mr Nab, Lady Henrietta—Lady Henrietta,
Mr Nab—There ! make your bow—(NAB *bows affectedly.*) And now shake hands.

Lady Hen. Shake hands, sir !

Lat. Yes—Let him do the thing genteelly—(NAB
gently touches her hand.) There ! the business is settled ! You're arrested at the suit of Sir Charles Dazzle, and little Nab will drive you away in his curricle.

Lady Hen. Arrested !

Lat. Lord, don't be uneasy—his house is a palace—full of the best furniture, the best wines : and,
I give you my honour, the best company ! You'll

find some very fashionable people there—some of your intimate friends—heh, Nab?

Nab. Yes, ma'am; and I entertain my company so superbly, that when they leave my house, it's always in good humour, I assure you—Besides, we can make up a Faro bank—every thing in style.

Lady Hen. This it is to be deluded into the vortex of dissipation—May it be a lesson to my sex, and prove how short the distance is from the gay associates of high life to the low companions of my present hour—But since it must be so—since I have no friend to succour or protect me, I must, perforce, submit—Come, sirs, conduct me.

Enter WARFORD.

War. Where are you going, gentlemen?

Lat. To take the lady an airing, sir—Will you join the party?

Lady Hen. Mr Warford, I little expected to see you here—The gentleman who reproved me in prosperity, is at least consistent in shunning me in adversity.

War. What is your demand, sir? (*To* LATITAT.)

Lat. Nab, shew the writ.

Nab. The debt and costs are one thousand and twenty pounds.

War. Here is the money then. (*Gives* LATITAT *bank notes.*)

Lat. The what!

War. There are bank notes for the sum.

Lat. (*Counting them.*) So there are—Why, this is doing the thing genteelly, Nab!

Nab. Amazing!

War. What do you stare at, sir?

Lat. Excuse us, sir, we are a little surprised to be sure; for, when my friend and I do shake hands with people of fashion, we generally pass some time with them.

War. No matter, sir, the debt is discharged, so
begone.

Lat. Begone!

War. Yes; leave the room instantly.

Lat. Leave the room! Is this language to a gentleman?

War. Gentleman! away! 'tis such pettifoggers
as you that disgrace the profession—that live on
the miseries of the unfortunate, and, in a land of
freedom, mutilate laws that are the guardians of liberty—Harkye, sir, were I a barrister or judge——

Lat. Barrister or judge! Pooh! they can't do the
thing so genteelly as we can.

Nab. No! I'll give a dinner with any judge in
England.

Lat. I'd rather be an attorney than chief justice.

Nab. And I a bailiff than high chancellor.

War. Very likely: but I insist——

Lat. Certainly——we're going, sir——Good day,
ma'am——We live in hopes! Here! where's my
phaeton and servants?

Nab. Call up my curricle and followers!—Good
day, ma'am!

Lat. If any future accident should happen either
to you or that gentleman, we shall be always happy
to give you an airing. Come along, Nab—Barrister
or judge! Pooh!——(*Looks at notes.*) Oh what a
pleasure it is to do the thing genteelly!

[*Exit with* NAB.

War. Now, Lady Henrietta, I hope your fears are
at an end.

Lady Hen. No, Mr Warford, they are rather increased; for if I am to be relieved at another's expence——To whom, sir, am I thus indebted?

War. You'll know hereafter—at present be satisfied with being told, that the instant I heard of
your distress, I flew to your uncle, Sir Thomas
Roundhead——he forgave you all that had passed,

found a friend thàt advanced the money, and now
waits with open arms to receive you.

Lady Hen. Is he my benefactor? Does the old
lord of the manor for once forget his game to relieve
a gamester?

War. I found him in close conversation with his
god-daughter Rosa, whose father is parson of the
parish.

Lady Hen. Mr Medium?

War. The same—The late minister being dead,
Sir Thomas had just got the living for Mr Medium,
and was in such high joy, that he begged I'd bring
you instantly—He said he was just going to sit as
magistrate, but by the time he got there, the justice
business would be over.

Lady Hen. And if he has no poacher to try for
snaring his game, we will find him in the same good
humour you left him—Come, Mr Warford—Oh!
you are indeed a friend; and, had I earlier listened
to your kind advice—but it's all over—The recollection of these two genteel men so terrifies me,
that, if I game again, I hope I shall be compelled to
take an airing with the one, and shake hands with
the other.   [*Exeunt.*

SCENE II.

*An old Hall, hung with Stags' Horns, Family
Pictures, &c.*

Clerk discovered sitting at a Table—A Chair above it.

*Two Constables—A young Woman, a young Man,
and* HIPPY, *discovered.*

Clerk. Stand back—stand back—his worship the
justice approaches.

Enter Sir Thomas Roundhead.

Sir Tho. Od, I'm so happy! Old Medium has got
the living, and I've given Rosa a holiday—I know
she can't kill a bird; so I've put a gun in her hand,
and sent her out with the gamekeeper, to beat the
outskirts, and drive the game in—Well, Formal,
(*To Clerk.*) what complaints? (*Ascends his chair.*)
Any thing about the manor?

Clerk. Please your worship, (*Woman advances.*)
this poor woman is deserted by her husband, and left
on the parish—The man is a footman, and has been
detected in open nem. con. with an old widow.

Sir Tho. Don't talk to me about nem. con.——
Haven't I told you not to let my delicacy be shocked
with any improper charges? Take her away—Any
body else?

Clerk. Please your worship, (*Man advances.*) this
poor man is a labourer, and has five children to maintain——but he has been so beaten and bruised by
'Squire Sturdy, that he can't work for his family.

Sir Tho. Serve him right—why didn't he get out
of his way, when he knew the 'squire was so fond of
boxing, that he must have practice to keep his hand
in—Dismiss him—Any thing more?

Clerk. Nothing of any consequence, your worship,
—only young Hippy, the miller's son, here—an honest, industrious young man—was found by the
gamekeeper with a hare under his arm.

Sir Tho. With what?

Clerk. With a hare, on your manor.

Sir Tho. On my manor! (*Comes from his seat.*)
Oh, you assassin! Nothing of any consequence indeed! Why, what's nem. con., crim. con., or pro
and con, to the shedding innocent blood? You dog!
speak—answer me—What have you to say for yourself?

Clerk. (*To* Hippy.) Speak to the magistrate.

Hip. Please your majesty——

Sir Tho. Please my what?

Hip. Please your majesty, I'll tell you all about it—The other morning, as I was crossing the wheat stubble, along with old Nicholas——You know old Nick, your honour?——

Sir Tho. Curse old Nick—Go on.

Hip. Na—don't you hurry me—I seed something in the corn going a-tittup, a-tittup, a-tittup—So, says I,—" Say nothing, Nicky, and we'll see what it is."

And presently there came within my legs as fine a large banging hare as ever you clapt your two most gracious eyes upon.

Sir Tho. Well, sirrah!

Hip. So, knowing as how such great beasts only devoured the corn and barley off your majesty's manor, I kept him tight between my legs, and squeezing him in this way—Look'ee! (*Puts his hat between his legs.*) I pinched him by little and little, 'till at last a got the staggers; and then says I, " Now, old Nick, knock his brains out."

Sir Tho. You did, did you?

Hip. Yes, that I did; and Nicky kept his word— for there a lay as dead and lifeless—Icod, it would have done your heart good to see Nicky and I laughing; he, he, he!

Sir Tho. And it will do my heart good to see Nicky and you hanging; he, he, he! (*Mimicking.*) —Seize him—take him to jail.

[Constables seize him.

Hip. To jail!

Sir Tho. Ay; I'll learn you to poach on my manor.

Hip. Oh Lord! why, your honour was just now pleased to pardon 'Squire Sturdy for almost killing a man; and here I'm to be tucked up for only squeezing a hare! Odraten! this can't be justice.

Rosa *sings, without,* " Hark away," *&c.*

Sir Tho. Ah ! here's my little god-daughter !—
she never killed any game ; and if she had been out
that day, she'd have scared the hare away.

Enter Rosa, *singing, and followed by two Gamekeepers, with quantities of Hares, Pheasants, and Partridges.*

Rosa. Come along, William—shew my god-papa
what sport we've had !—There ! (*Gamekeepers throw
down game.*) An't I a nice little sportsman ?

Hip. Icod, if my neck's to be twisted, what's to
become of hers ?

Rosa. Why, you don't look pleased, Sir Thomas
—perhaps you don't think I've killed half enough ?

Sir Tho. Yes, I do—Oh ! h ! h ! (*Looking at the
game.*)

Rosa. Nay, consider, Sir Thomas, it's very well
for a young beginner ; but I tell you what, I'll soon
make you happy——let me go out again to-morrow,
and I won't leave a single hare, pheasant, or par-
tridge, on the manor.

Hip. Doey—doey, your majesty, and let me go
wi' her.

Sir Tho. Come—I'll soon settle this business—
Constable, take that poacher to the county jail—
No words—take him directly.

Hip. Dang it, if ever I squeeze a hare again——
Good day, Miss—Odraten ! I suppose you and old
Nick will soon come after me.

                [*Constables force him off.*

Sir Tho. And now, William, do you take the
other poacher to the parsonage-house.

Rosa. To the parsonage-house, sir ?

Sir Tho. Ay, to your father's——You jade ! I'm
tired of your follies—You know I took you from the
parson's, that you might get well married—but you
couldn't hit the mark.

Rosa. No: but I hit the birds; ay, and marked 'em too—However, I know why you're angry with me—you've made it up with your niece, Lady Henrietta; and, because I couldn't marry some great man, who might have got you new manors, and all that, you mean to try what she can do.

Sir Tho. Yes, she shall be my heiress now—so go home, Miss.

Rosa. Well, I don't care—I know where the game lies; and while there's a feather on the manor, I won't want a day's sport, depend on't.

SONG.

Ah, cruel Sir Thomas! to abandon your promise,
   And leave Rosa, poor girl, to lament;
But take honour and gold, and your favour withhold,
   You cannot take health and content.
      While my dogs, at the dawn,
      Brush the dew from the lawn,
      Sniff the scent of the game,
      And our spirits inflame,
      Through thickets or stubbles,
      Their courage redoubles;
Then checking their speed---" Hey, Basto, take heed!"
Oh! Sir Thomas Roundhead! Pop, your game it is dead!
I can hit well my man, and a lover trepan;
   Yet Amazon-like I will be;
   As sure as a gun, from each suitor I'll run,
   But the hero who overcomes me.
      While my dogs, &c.
            [*Exit with Gamekeepers.*

Enter LADY HENRIETTA.

Lady Hen. My dear uncle!

Sir Tho. My dear niece! I rejoice to see you—Mr Warford told you, I suppose.

Lady Hen. He did indeed, Sir Thomas; and the thousand pounds you sent me was the most critical, fortunate——

Sir T. Round. The thousand pounds !

Lady Hen. Yes—but for that I had been living in a palace, viewing the best furniture, tasting the best wines, and keeping the best company, in the world.

Sir T. Round. My dear girl, I sent you no thousand pounds.

Lady Hen. No!

Sir T. Round. No—The young gentleman, indeed, told me you wanted money, but I had none by me—Mine's all in the country bank—all lock'd up—Smalltrade never pays in specie—and as to his five pound notes, they're like French assignats ! Dam'me, a good old English guinea's worth a thousand of 'em ! This I told Mr Warford, and he said he himself could find a friend to advance it.

Lady Hen. Generous, disinterested man ! But how, how am I to repay him ?

Sir T. Round. I'll tell you—I have quarrell'd with that hussey, Rosa, and as I wish to have a senator for my heir, I mean to get you well married—Nay, I have a husband already in my eye.

Lady Hen. Have you, sir ?

Sir T. Round. Yes ; there is a vacancy in the borough, and the new member shall have your hand and my estate.

Lady Hen. And pray, sir, who is likely to be my representative ?

Sir T. Round. There is only one candidate at present, and he is an old admirer of your's, and an old friend of mine—Sir Charles Dazzle.

Lady Hen. Sir Charles Dazzle !

Sir T. Round. Yes ; he's a man of rank and talents ; and, if we may judge by his style of living, he's the richest baronet in England—But now, let's in to dinner, and talk further—Oh ! when Sir Charles has married you, he shall do me three such favours —all relating to my own estate.

Lady Hen. And what are they, sir ?

Sir T. Round. You shall hear—The first is, to turn the road, and send my neighbours half a mile round—The second is, to enclose the common, and keep it all to myself—The third is, to cut a canal right through the town, and build powder-mills on the banks! This, my dear girl, will double my rental, and this is my way of growing rich!   [*Exeunt.*

ACT THE FOURTH.

SCENE I.

SIR THOMAS'S *Park.—View of his House, Garden, Ponds, &c.*

Enter SIR CHARLES DAZZLE, *and two Servants.*

Sir Char. Knock at the gate, and announce my arrival.   [*Exit Servant.*
So, Lady Henrietta has not escaped me yet—Hearing Sir Thomas meant to provide for her, I instantly wrote to him, and offer'd her marriage—this he agreed to, supposing my fortune will ensure the election:—As to that wretch Pavè—I just now met the mad rascal, running full speed after a nobleman's carriage.

2d Serv. Yonder is Mr Pavè, sir.

Sir Char. Ay, meditating on the drawing-rooms of princes, and the levees of ministers.

Re-enter Servant.

Serv. Sir Thomas is waiting to receive you, sir.

Sir Char. Shew me the way—Now here, here's another proof that ruin is the road to riches; for, without having an acre of my own, I am going to take possession of the largest estate in the county—Poor Sir Thomas! poor Henrietta! I'll soon convince them that now-a-days people live better without money than with it.   [*Exit.*

Enter WARFORD *and* LADY HENRIETTA.

Lady Hen. How can I thank you, sir? Nay, don't deny your generosity—I have learnt all from Sir Thomas—And tell me honestly, Mr Warford, have you not, by extricating me, involved yourself?

War. No, Lady Henrietta; I gain'd this money by easy, honourable means; out of an annuity of two hundred pounds, allowed me these ten years past by my uncle, I have, by frugality and prudence, annually saved a moiety—saved it to befriend me in the hour of danger. And if it has assisted you, how great and ample is my recompence! But think not of that— think of Sir Charles Dazzle—What brings him to Sir Thomas's?

Lady Hen. The worst of purposes—he comes to be my husband! Sir Thomas has accepted his proposals, and in my father's absence I have no friend to protect me but you—Oh, Mr Warford! little did I think, when I entered my uncle's house, I should again be in the power of such an enemy.

War. Nor shall you be—I'll see Sir Thomas instantly—expose Sir Charles's villanies.

Lady Hen. That would be useless—Alas! there is but one way—and that is so difficult—so uncertain! You know, in consequence of my imprudence, Sir Thomas had adopted Rosa for his heiress.

War. He had.

Lady Hen. Previous to my arrival, he quarrell'd with her, and sent her back to the parsonage house —Now, as I know the old gentleman only wants a man of rank to inherit his estate, the way to save me, would be to restore Rosa to his favour.

War. I understand—But how—how is that to be accomplished?

Lady Hen. By seeing her father, the minister of the parish, by persuading him to interfere for his daughter—if he succeeds—

Enter a Servant.

Serv. Your uncle and Sir Charles Dazzle request your ladyship's company.

Lady Hen. Is it possible? Am I forced to meet the man who has so insulted me? To be under the same roof with him, and at last be doom'd to marry him?

War. Talk not of it—I'll endeavour to restore Rosa to your uncle's favour. Tell me, sir, (*To Servant.*) where does the clergyman live?

Serv. What! the new minister, Mr Medium, sir?

War. Yes.

Serv. He lives across the field, at the white house, sir.

War. Then I'll wait on him, and return to you instantly.

Lady Hen. Adieu, Mr Warford! Oh! now, more than ever, I feel the effect of my follies! Had I, like him, grown rich by prudence and economy, I might ere this have fixed my own choice; and, instead of being united to a man I detest, I might have found one who would have loved and honoured me! But as it is,—farewell, sir,—we shall soon meet again.

[*Exit.*

War. Farewell, Lady Henrietta.—Distraction! Must that villain triumph over her! No, I'll not lose a moment—I'll see this minister. (*Going.*)

Enter PAVE, *who stops him.*

Pav. See the minister! What, in that dress?
Pooh! you can't get an audience.

War. Excuse me, sir—I've the most important
business—

Pav. Why, he's in town I tell you.

War. He's in the neighbourhood I tell you, and
where I must and will see him. So, stand back, and
don't detain me from an interview, that makes or
mars my peace for ever.

[*Pushes* PAVE *aside, and exit.*

Pav. In the neighbourhood! The minister in the
neighbourhood! Impossible! This is not his county
—And yet—he's on a visit perhaps, or on a secret
expedition! If he should, and I can catch his eye!
get a squeeze, a nod, or a smile, and at last wheedle
him into my list of promises! whugh!—

Enter HIPPY.

Hip. Odraten! I've made my escape—Miss Rosa
spoke to her father, who spoke to Sir Thomas, and
now, if I can find Mr Medium, and thank him—Pray,
sir, have you seen the minister?

Pav. There! Have I seen the minister? They're
all after him.

Hip. He has saved me and Nicky—But here's
his daughter, Miss Rosa.

Pav. His daughter! the minister's daughter!
My dear fellow, take this—(*Gives him money.*) and,
d'ye hear? speak to her in my favour—speak highly
of me—hint I'm of the old Norman blood.

Hip. What blood?

Pav. The old Norman blood!—You understand,
mum! you understand——

Enter ROSA.

Rosa. It's a shame to turn me out of the house,

and adopt Lady Henrietta, and all because I couldn't marry a great man! Faith, I've a good mind to run away with the churchwarden—I have, and—Bless me! what pretty-looking gentleman's this?

Hip. Miss, he wishes to say a word to you—(*Whispers her.*) he's an old Norman blood.　　[*Exit.*

Pav. (*Aside.*) To use her father's language, I wish the budget was open'd.—Ma'am! (*Bowing.*)

Rosa. (*Curtsying.*) Lord, what a charming man!

Pav. She smiles upon me—now then for the ways and means.—Oh you paragon! till I throw myself at your father's feet, allow me to fall at yours! (*Kneeling.*) and thus, and thus—(*Kissing her hand*) to swear allegiance to you, your sire, and your whole august family.

Rosa. Was there ever such an elegant creature!

Pav. Here let me swear to ratify the treaty of alliance, to cement the family compact, and preserve the balance of power as long as I live.

Rosa. Dear, how he must adore me! I can't stand it much longer.

Pav. Never will I rise till you sign preliminary articles, till you swear you believe me your faithful ally, your leagued confederate, and ever loyal vassal.

Rosa. (*Kneeling by him.*) I do! I do! And moreover, I swear that I honour the Norman race more than my own! and sooner than such a sweet-looking gentleman should break his heart for me, faith I'll run away with him directly.

Pav. What! Let me taste that treasury of charms!

Rosa. Yes.

Pav. And carry off that exchequer of excellence?

Rosa. I would! I would! this very hour I would!

Pav. Huzza! huzza! I'm the Prime Minister's son.

Rosa. What! (*Rising.*)

Pav. I'm the minister's son! Now let Lord Or-

ville bow to the ground—let Sir Charles Dazzle
wipe my shoes—let those that kept me dangling in
their halls, stand shivering in mine ! and they who
spurn'd me, pitied me, and call'd me " poor Pavè"
—let 'em now pull off their hats, and cry, " Room
for the minister's son."—Dam'me, while it lasts, I'll
make the most of it !

Rosa. Lord, I knew he was a great man by his
talking so unintelligibly. Let's to Sir Thomas Round-
hea 's directly.

Pav. To a Baronet's ! pooh !

Rosa. Nay ; he's a great friend of my father's, and
will rejoice at our marriage.

Pav. Well then—But your father, my angel !
how I long to see him, to help him in his orations !

Rosa. Oh ! he wants no help in them—His discourses are excellent, only rather too short : for my
mother always confines him to twenty minutes.

Pav. Does she ? then your mother is a true lover of her country.—Come.

Re-enter WARFORD.

War. Miss Rosa, a word if you please,—I want to
see your father.

Pav. I dare say you do—but excuse us !—we have
important business. (*Mimicks* WARFORD's *manner.*)

War. Nay, I won't detain you a moment.

Pav. Stand back, sir, and don't detain me—I've
the most important business—an interview that makes
or mars my peace for ever. I say, my little clerk,
he is in the neighbourhood, and if you want an audience—I have it—Snug—all under my thumb—mum !
You understand—Come, my sweet angel ! ask for the
minister's son !

Rosa. Ay ; ask for the minister's son. [*Exeunt.*

War. Was there ever such an extraordinary fel-

13

low! But, as I cannot find Mr Medium, I must to Sir Thomas's, and see Lady Henrietta instantly. [*Exit.*

SCENE II.

A modern Apartment at Sir Thomas's—The Room hung with Pictures—In the centre a large Picture, with a Curtain before it.

Enter Sir Thomas Roundhead *and* Sir Charles Dazzle.

Sir Char. Sir Thomas, you have made me the happiest of men!

Sir T. Round. No thanks—She shall be yours—Read that agreement. (*Gives him a paper.*)

Sir Char. (*Reads.*) " On condition that Sir Charles Dazzle marries Lady Henrietta, Sir Thomas Roundhead agrees to settle on her one thousand a-year during his life, and the whole of his estate at his death."—Shall we sign directly?

Sir T. Round. No, we can't till we've got her consent—and I assure you, it will require all my eloquence to persuade her—Here she comes—leave us together.

Enter Lady Henrietta.

Sir Char. When you are ready, Sir Thomas, I'll wait upon you—Lady Henrietta, your most obedient. [*Bows, and exit.*

Lady Hen. Impudent sycophant! How his looks betray his triumph! Well, uncle, do you really persist in marrying me to that gentleman?

Sir T. Round. Certainly—I will have a man of rank for my heir; for the read must be turn'd,—the common enclosed,—and the canal and powder-mills accomplished.

Lady Hen. And I would rather work on the road, graze on the common, or be drown'd in the canal, than marry Sir Charles Dazzle—Besides, I am inheriting another's right—Rosa ought to be your heiress.

Sir T. Round. Ay, that is, if I could have married her to a great man—But now, read that agreement.

Lady Hen. (*Reading.*) " Sir Charles marries Lady Henrietta—Sir Thomas settles one thousand a-year—and the whole of his estate at his death."

Sir T. Round. Well! will you sign it ? Look ye, no demurring; for if you refuse, neither I nor your father will give you a shilling.

Lady Hen. Ungenerous!

Sir T. Round. Consider too—how are you to repay Mr Warford ?

Lady Hen. How indeed! And sooner than he should suffer for his liberality—Yet, to be the wife of my avow'd enemy—I cannot—will not, be so wretched !

Sir T. Round. Won't you? We'll see—Sir Charles Dazzle ! (*Calling him in.*)

Lady Hen. Hold, sir—give me but a moment—Wait till my father arrives.

Sir T. Round. No—you shall sign instantly—Sir Charles !—

As he is going, enter ROSA *hastily, and runs against him.*

Rosa. Oh, Sir Thomas!—Oh, my lady !—I'm—— out of breath.

Sir T. Round. What's the matter, Jezabel ?

Rosa. I've done it ! I've hit the mark ! Such a gentleman has run away with me ! No less than the Prime Minister's son !

Sir T. Round. The minister's son !

Rosa. Yes; he's of the Norman race, the second person in the world; I'm the third, and you shall be the fourth—Here he is!

Lady Hen. (*Looking out.*) As I live, it's my old friend, Pavè—If I humour this, I may restore Rosa to favour, and save myself—Lucky, lucky thought!

Sir T. Round. Pooh! this can't be the minister's son—And yet, by his appearance—He has certainly a very important, formidable air.

Lady Hen. Sir Thomas, I can affirm it as a fact —This is the very person—I know him intimately.

Sir T. Round. Do you? 'Sdeath! what an awful sight! My respect's so great, I don't know where to stand, or how to look.

Enter PAVE.

Lady Hen. How d'ye do? (*Nods to him.*)

Pav. How d'ye do? (*Nods to her.*)

Sir T. Round. He knows her—it is him! Lord, I wish I had paid my obedience.

Lady Hen. Mr Pavè, this is Sir Thomas Roundhead. (SIR THOMAS *draws back.*) Nay, don't be frighten'd, uncle—the gentleman is very condescending.

Pav. Condescending! Lord! I'm the most familiar creature—Your hand, Tommy, give me your hand.

Sir T. Round. Tommy! why, he's familiar indeed! Gad, I feel bold enough to talk to him—— Pray, sir—Hem!—is there any news?

Pav. What! (*Staring at him.*)

Sir T. Round. (*Alarmed*) I only ask'd, sir, if there was any news.

Pav. Fie, Tommy, fie! Never pump a minister— Mum! or any of his family—fie!

Lady Hen. (*Aside to* SIR THOMAS.) Now's your opportunity—fix him at once—Offer him Rosa with your estate.

Sir T. Round. I will—For this is indeed a man of rank! Sir! dread sir! if I don't presume too much —I have a small estate—not indeed adequate to your situation—but, if you will accept it with this young lady————

Pav. How much is it?

Sir T. Round. Scarce worth mentioning—only a thousand a year at present, but, at my death, it will be five thousand—Will you have the condescension?————

Pav. Well, I'll indulge you, Tommy, I'll indulge you—Five thousand a year, no bad certainty in case of accident. (*Aside.*) In return—if there are any favours, I or my father————

Sir T. Round. Oh, sir! (*Bows very low.*) there are, to be sure, sir, one or two trifles—First, you see (*Counts with his finger on his left hand*) I want to turn a road—secondly, to enclose a common—thirdly, to cut a canal—fourthly, to build powder-mills— fifthly————(*Beginning to count on his right-hand.*)

Pav. Stick to one hand, my dear Tommy! stick to one hand, and don't agitate yourself—the trifles shall be accomplished, so draw up an agreement.

Lady Hen. I believe this will do, sir—It's only to scratch out my name and Sir Charles's, and insert Miss Rosa's and Mr Pavè's—I'll do it, and you may sign directly. (*Goes to table, and writes.*)

Rosa. (*To* PAVE) I say, while they're settling the agreement, I'll shew you my father's picture.

Pav. Your father's picture! Ha! where is it?

Rosa. There—behind the curtain!—He's in his gown.

Pav. Gown!—robes you mean————Let's see.——

Lady Hen. Stop————sign the contract first.

Sir T. Round. Ay; sign first—There—there's my signature. (*Signing.*)

Pav. And mine! (*Signing.*)

Rosa. And now, there's my dear father in his gown and cassock.

> [*Undraws curtains of pictures, and discovers a painting of* MR MEDIUM, *the clergyman, in his gown and cassock—*PAVE *sees it, and stands stupified.*]

Sir T. Round. Yes; there's old Medium—What surprises you, sir ?

Lady Hen. Ay; there's another minister—What makes you so dumb, Mr Pavè ?

Pav. Respect and reverence at that awful sight —Oh, Sir Thomas ! that parson's picture has so deeply affected me, that only this contract can console me. (*Taking it.*) Nothing like a certainty in case of accidents—Come, Miss Medium !

Sir T. Round. Why, where are you going ?

Pav. To my father's, Tommy, to my father's— to take care of the road—the common—the canal —the—in short, to secure your whole property.

Enter SIR CHARLES DAZZLE.

Pav. Ah, Sir Charles, have you made out a list of promises ? In the course of five years—that is, when I come to my estate, I'll think of you—Farewell, old What's-his-Name—Tommy, adieu ! I retire with a handsome provision however. (*Looks at contract, &c.*)   [*Exit with* ROSA.

Sir Char. Sir Thomas, what does that impudent fellow do here ?

Sir T. Round. Impudent ! why, do you know who he is ?

Sir Char. Yes; I know him to be an impostor, a rascal—and, if he has got any thing from you——

Sir T. Round. Got any thing ! he's got my whole estate—Oh Lord !

Sir Char. Pursue him directly—I'll go with you.

Sir T. Round. Oh dear ! come along—As for you, madam, depend on't, you shall still be Sir

Charles's, and for that fellow—Oh the villain! I believe he's a poacher, and, because he couldn't snare the game, he has stole the whole manor! Come!

[*Exit with* SIR CHARLES.

Lady Hen. Ha! ha! he's a delightful man; and, as he has twice saved me from Sir Charles, I hope he'll do me the favour a third time—But now to Warford, and make his generous heart partake my joy.   [*Exit.*

ACT THE FIFTH.

SCENE I.

A modern Apartment at SIR THOMAS's, *a Window open, and Balcony behind.*

Enter ROSA.

Rosa. How unfortunate! To be retaken and separated from my dear Mr Pavè.—(*Goes to window, and looks out.*) Surely Hippy can't have forgot me—I dropt him a letter out of this window, to carry to Mr Pavè, in which I told him I was lock'd up, that he mightn't get the estate, but I was ready to elope with him this very night—Dear! where can Hippy be?

Enter HIPPY, *at the Window.*

Hip. Hush! is nobody here?

Rosa. Nobody.

Hip. Odraten! this is poaching with a vengeance
—Well! I've seen Mr Pavè, and he'll carry you off
—he will! here's his answer.   [*Gives her a letter.*

Rosa. (*Reads.*) " My dear girl—that the contract
may be fulfilled, I'll be near the ladder in an hour,
and the signal shall be a noise at the window—Your's
ever---Pavè."——Oh charming! charming! What!
you came in at the balcony by a ladder?

Hip. To be sure I did---Leave old Nick and I
alone for fixing one—But I must return to the gen-
tleman---So, do you go and get ready, and when you
hear the noise at the window, trip down the ladder,
a tittup, a tittup, a tittup, as we said of the hare, you
know.

Rosa. I will! I will! But pray let the noise be
loud enough.

Hip. Loud! Odraten! I'll smash every pane sooner
than you sha'n't hear us—Depend on Nicky and I's
doing our best—Good bye, Miss, and remember the
noise.

Rosa. Ay, I won't forget—Good bye.

[*Exit* HIPPY *at window.*
And now I'll go and get my hat and cloak—Sir
Thomas is below with Mr Latitat, and the electors
of the borough—In the hurry of business, nobody'll
think of our elopement—Oh! how I long for the
noise at the window!   [*Exit.*

Enter LATITAT.

Lat. So—stole off unobserved—A fine quarrelling
below—The old justice wants Sir Charles to be the new
member—The electors want a better man, and I, as
returning officer, insist upon the same—But all depends upon Smalltrade—he's at the head of the corporation—and, as Sir Thomas has sent for him—I must
overhear their conversation--- The fact is, the justice

wants to outshoot the banker---the banker wants to
out-run the justice---and the attorney wants to out-
bowl them both! Here they come!---That I may be
evidence of all that passes, I'll e'en let down this cur-
tain---(*Lets down the window-curtain, and gets behind
it.*) So! this is doing the thing genteelly!

Enter SMALLTRADE *and* SIR THOMAS.

Sir T. Round. Don't---don't talk of that impostor
—I have secured Rosa as a hostage, and if he don't
marry her, the contract's void—So, as we're alone---
(*Fastening door.*) Sit down—sit down, and let's talk
about the election. (*They sit.*)

Small. I should like to have seen you counting
your fingers, securing the common, the canal, and
the powder-mills—and then to have seen the blow-
up! Oh! you've a fine round head! And what
would you do with the canal?

Sir T. Round. What! I'd secure the borough by
it: for, if the electors didn't do as I wished, I'd open
the sluices, and inundate the whole town—You can
only lay them under contribution, but, dam'me, I can
lay them under water.—You see, old friend, if Sir
Charles is the new member, I have promised to marry
him to Lady Henrietta—Now, the first thing he
wants, is to get your interest.

Small. And the next thing is to take my principal,
I suppose—Oh, I know him of old—The fellow hasn t
a guinea—unless indeed, he's kept the one I lost at
Faro—No, no; I want some good citizen, and I told
Latitat, our returning officer, to find one.

Sir T. Round. Yes; but Sir Charles is the only
candidate, and therefore—

    [*Loud rattling at the window,* LATITAT *pops
        his head out from behind curtain, and on*
        SMALLTRADE's *looking round, puts it back.*]

Small. What's that noise?

Sir Tho. Nothing but the wind shaking the win-

dows—Therefore I say, as Sir Charles and the electors are below, let's go and talk to them. (*Rising.*)

Small. Softly—mind you're not tricked again—for
that Latitat is such a dirty, shuffling rascal—

[*Loud rattling again;* LATITAT *pops his head out;
on* SMALLTRADE'S *looking round, puts it back
again.*]

Small. Now what the devil's that noise?

Sir Tho. 'Tis the wind I tell you—it's always so
when it's easterly—Do, let's go directly to the electors.

Small. Ay, there's no talking business in this
room—So, leave me to manage Latitat—I'm a match
for a lawyer.

Sir Tho. Are you? then you're a match for any
thing—I hate 'em all.

Small. So do I—And I'll tell you what, Sir Thomas, instead of giving me a day's sport on your manor, only get me a day's shooting in Westminster-
Hall, and if I don't wing and pepper the whole
breed, say I'm no marksman, and Latitat's no rascal.
[*Exeunt.*

Lat. (*Puts his head out.*) Upon my soul I'm very
much obliged to you—(*Comes from behind.*) A very
pleasant situation! Abused before my face, and peit-
ed behind my back!

Enter ROSA *in her Hat and Cloak.*

Rosa. I've just heard the noise at the window, and
now—ha!

Lat. Oho! the mystery's out—an intrigue, heh?
This is the best part of the election; and, as they
can't make the return without me, I may as well be
a party in this cause—Here I am, my dear.

Rosa. Sir! Heavens! who are you?

Lat. Me! the prettiest fellow living! I'm a member of ten clubs, and wear twenty different uniforms.

Initials on one button—arrows on another—brushes on a third—feathers on a fourth—Then I won the bugle-horn, got sixty notches, rode five races, owed ten thousand pounds—lived within the Rules—did the thing genteelly!

Rosa. And has Mr Pavè sent you, sir?

Lat. Pavè!

[*Here* PAVE *puts his head out from behind curtain.*

Rosa. I think it's very hard he didn't come himself.

Lat. Pavè! That's the man I pass'd on as Lord Sulwin! Zounds! if it should be him—However, I won't lose the girl.—Come, my angel! (*Taking her hand.*)

Rosa. Lord, sir, how am I to know Mr Pavè is your friend?

Lat. How? I'll tell you—Every body knows my way of growing rich, is by never paying what I borrow, and, notwithstanding this, Pavè lent me a thousand pounds! Now, wasn't that friendly? So, I'll peep at this door to see if any body's watching, and then——(*Goes to stage door.*)

PAVE *comes forward.*

Pav. (*To* ROSA.) My dear girl, descend the ladder—Your friends will protect you till I come.

[*Exit* ROSA *at window.*

Lat. (*Looking round.*) Nobody's near us, my sweet angel!—

Pav. Isn't there, my dear lord? So, still doing the thing genteelly, my boy!

Lat. Ah, Mr Pavè, I assure you, I am most happy to pay my respects to you. (*Bows.*)

Pav. (*Bowing.*) And I assure you I shall be more happy, if you'll pay me my thousand pounds—(*Collaring him.*) Give me my money, or get me preferr'd.

Lat. Now don't—pray don't expose me—here in the country I haven't pass'd for a lord.

Pav. For what then, sir? (*Shaking him.*)

Lat. For a gentleman. (PAVE *shakes him more.*) I'm returning officer of the borough.

Pav. What! (*Letting him go.*)

Lat. I'm returning officer I say; and, as the election takes place in a few hours—

Pav. My dear fellow, I ask you a thousand pardons—In the first place, I didn't know there was an election, and in the next, I little thought you could so essentially assist—Excuse me, Mr Latitat—Lord Sulwin I mean.

Lat. Oh, sir, you are too kind.

Pav. Not at all—How has your health been since I saw you? I recollect you had a superb equipage— four fine bays—I hope they're all well—And so, there's an election, my lord?

Lat. There is, sir; and, if any friend of your's is a candidate—

Pav. There's the point, my lord—I do know a gentleman, a very clever gentleman!—Don't think of that little debt you owe me! And as we're alone —harkye—(*Whispers him.*)

Lat. You a candidate!

Pav. Why not? I'm heir to an estate of six thousand a year, was near being son to Mr What's-his-name, and have a list of promises as long as the borough.—So do, pray do, the thing genteelly.

Lat. I've a great mind—it would be serving those two old blockheads as they deserve—Gad I will! Give me your hand.

Pav. Will you?

Lat. Hush! here's Smalltrade.

Pav. What, old Certificate?

Lat. Stand aside—For, as his interest turns the scale, we must dupe him into our scheme—Mum! Not a word.

PAVE, *being in a travelling great coat, muffles himself,*
   and draws his hat over his face; he stands aside,
   and SMALLTRADE *enters.*

Lat. So, Mr Smalltrade—Sir Charles is to be our
new member.

Small. Yes, Lati, for want of a better—Ah! I wish
we could have found another candidate!

Lat. Another candidate, sir!

                    [*Looks round at* PAVE, *who bows to him.*

Small. Ay; some good citizen—that would have
given us grand corporation dinners, built a new
town-hall—thrown a bridge over the river, and put
all his money in my bank.

Lat. Come here—Look behind you.

Small. Look behind me!

Lat. You see that gentleman—He's the son of
———— Alderman Double.

Small. Alderman Double! What, the great London brewer?

Lat. The same—He wishes to become a candidate.

Small. Does he? That's the very thing—I'll go
and talk to him.

Lat. Softly—He has been travelling all night, and
has got a violent pain in his face—I tell you what,
I'll settle terms with him, and if you've a mind, we'll
chouse Sir Thomas.

Small. Chouse Sir Thomas! Ay do, you've my
consent.

Lat. Have I? Then I'll take him and return him
at once—Come, Mr Double, Mr Smalltrade will excuse you're not speaking.

Small. You'll settle it with Mr Latitat. Ay; I
wish the pain in your face better with all my soul—
(PAVE *nods, and makes signs of paying handsomely
with his hands.*) Sensible soul! how well he understands the business—Take him, Lati, and I'll go and

detain the two baronets till the return's over—Good day, Mr Double.

Lat. If this isn't doing the thing genteelly, the devil's in't.   [*Exit with* PAVE.

Small. There goes the young alderman—Poor Sir Charles! poor old Roundhead! Oh! if I was such a stupid blockhead! But I don't know how it is—we country bankers are never imposed upon.   [*Exit.*

SCENE II.

Inside of SIR THOMAS'S *Garden.—Garden Gate in the back Scene.*

Enter LADY HENRIETTA.

LADY HENRIETTA.   (*Reading.*)

" The tender pair, whom mutual favours bind,
Love keeps united, though by Alps disjoin'd;
To passion ill returned short bounds are set,
The lover that's forgotten will forget."

And what have I to do with that? As I was never in love, I can never forget—And yet it's very odd I should just hit on that passage—Heigho! I wonder where Mr Warford is.

Enter WARFORD.

Bless me, sir! you take one so by surprise—I thought I should never see you again.

War. And now, madam, you see me for the last time.

Lady Hen. The last time!

War. Yes; Sir Charles has crush'd all my hopes of happiness, and I have prevail'd on my uncle to let me leave England for ever.

Lady Hen. Leave England! Oh, I beg your pardon, sir—You can't do that.

War. No, madam!

Lady Hen. No, sir—you recollect you and I must settle accounts first, for you don't suppose I'll let you be out of my sight while I owe you an obligation! A pretty thing indeed! to lend a lady a thousand pounds, and then go abroad and compel her to come after you to repay you.

War. Lady Henrietta, I am miserable—I have lived under the same roof with a treasure I now see given to another! But I alone am to blame—It was presumption, in my humble situation, to aspire to such excellence; and I now meet the reward my arrogance deserves. (*Going.*)

Lady Hen. Stay, Mr Warford—Just let me set you right about one thing. There are people, sir, that can distinguish merit in obscurity—nay, can admire it too—I, for instance, now, can perceive, that, while I possess nothing from rank and birth, you gain every thing from virtue and honour.

War. This language overpowers me—And if I thought I was even pitied——

Lady Hen. Pitied!——Oh, Mr Warford! doesn't the man who shunned me in the hours of dissipation, and returned to me in the day of distress, deserve something more than pity?——Yes——and, as this is the last time we shall ever meet, let me avow my gratitude—my esteem! Let me be proud to tell you, that, had I my own choice, I would give my hand where my heart has been long disposed of.

War. Is it possible? Can the humble, deserted Warford be so blest?

Lady Hen. You deserve every thing, sir—But go, go, and be happy—Find out some fair who may return your love, nor ever think of one so lost, so wretched as myself!

10

War. I cannot leave you thus! I'll see your un-cle, appeal to his humanity! Nay, you are not Sir Charles Dazzle's yet.

Enter MISS DAZZLE.

Miss Daz. No—but she will be presently—This is your last tête-à-tête, I assure you.

Lady Hen. Is Sir Charles elected then?

Miss Daz. He is—What, you thought, if he lost the election, you would lose him?

Lady Hen. Certainly, madam—I knew Sir Tho-mas designed me for the successful candidate, and you'll pardon me, if I could have chosen a dearer representative than your brother.

[*Huzza without, and music.*

Miss Daz. There! do you hear those acclama-tions? Now, Mr Warford, you may take leave of the charming Henrietta, and make your bow to my sister, Lady Dazzle.

War. Ungenerous woman! Is it not enough to triumph—   [*More huzzaing without.*

Enter SIR THOMAS ROUNDHEAD.

Sir Tho. There! it's all over——Sir Charles is elected, and I've at last got a senator for my heir! Miss Dazzle, I give you joy.

Miss Daz. And I give you joy, Sir Thomas—and you, Lady Henrietta——and you, Mr Warford—— Come, shall we go and see the procession?

Sir Tho. Certainly—(*Exit* MISS DAZZLE.) Niece, do you wait here to receive your husband, Sir Charles Dazzle.

War. This is beyond bearing—Sir Thomas, hear me.

Sir Tho. I'll hear nothing—Henrietta, wait to re-ceive the new member.

Enter SMALLTRADE.

Small. Now, where are you going?

Sir Tho. To congratulate Sir Charles on his election, to be sure.

Small. Are you? then you may as well stay where you are.

Sir Tho. Why so, old Smalltrade?

Small. I'll tell you, old Roundhead—he has lost the election.

Omnes. Lost the election!

Small. Yes; the young alderman has it—Double's the man.

Sir Tho. Double's the man!

Small. Yes; it's all my doing—Now how foolish you look—I say, your worship, doesn't this remind you of counting your fingers? Oh, you old flat!

Sir Tho. Why, what is all this? And who the devil's Double?

Small. A great brewer, and the son of an alderman! Latitat found him out, and has managed the whole business himself. Now, an't you prettily outwitted? And won't you allow that a banker's head is twice as deep as a justice's?

Sir Tho. Hold your tongue, or——

Small. Curse me, but if I thought I should ever be such an old flat as you, if I wouldn't build powder-mills on purpose to blow myself up in!—(*Music without.*)——Here he is! here's the new member! I ordered Latitat to bring him here, that you might see, with your own eyes, what a stupid fool we have made of you.

Sir Tho. Did you? I'm very much obliged to you—But no brewer or alderman enters my garden. —Here, William! Thomas! (*Going.*)

Small. (*Holding him.*) Now do—Stay and see how much you've exposed yourself.

Sir Tho. I won't—Let me go.

Small. You shan't—Here they come.
[*Long flourish of Clarinets, Trumpets, &c.*

Enter PAVE, *chaired, with Electors,* ROSA, *and*
LATITAT.

Pav. (*As he enters.*) Gentlemen, you have re-
tur ed me as your representative, for which I return
you my most hearty thanks; and, to shew my gratitude, I invite all the country—men, women, and
children—to dine with Sir Thomas to-day, and to
sup with little Certificate in the evening. (*Turning
round.*) Huzza! I've done it at last.

Sir Tho. Smalltrade, who's an old flat now?

Small. I am *doubled*, by all that's ridiculous.

Sir Tho. Doesn't this give you a ticklish sensation? Isn't a banker's head twice as deep as a justice's——And won't you build powder-mills to blow
yourself up in?

Small. So, Mr Pain-in-the-face, (*To* LATITAT.)
you and the young alderman here have done it.

Lat. Yes: we've done the thing genteelly! But
don't be angry——the new member means to be liberal.

Pav. Certainly—— if either of the honourable
gentlemen in my eye want franks——

Sir Tho. Franks!—Sirrah——

Pave. Order, Tommy—order—Harkye, old Certificate! (*Whispers* SMALLTRADE.)

Small. How! You'll move to abolish country
banks?

Sir Tho. Ay, do—I'll second that motion.

Pav. Come here, Tommy. (*Whispers him.*)

Sir Tho. How! Move to stop canal-cutting?

Small. Ay, do—I'll second that motion.

Lat. And encourage attornies: for they do the
thing genteelly.

Pav. Now I'm promoted, I can be a better patron than Sir Charles—I'll prefer you all.

Rosa. Will you ?—that's charming.

Pav. To you, Latitat, I give up your debt—To you, Tommy, I restore your contract—To you, old Certificate, I give my list of promises—To you, Lady Henrietta, I give the man you love—And, lastly, to you, Rosa, I give the best present of all, for I give you myself, my dear girl; and, next to Mr What's-his-name, damme, if I know a finer fellow.

Lady Hen. Nor I—Will you consent, Mr Smalltrade ?

Rosa. Will you, Sir Thomas ?

Lady Hen. We'll put all our money in the country bank.

Rosa. And I'll never poach on the manor as long as I live.

Sir Tho. Smalltrade !

Small. Roundhead !

Sir Tho. Shall we ?

Small. Ay ; we have shewn ourselves such a couple of old flats, that we can't expose ourselves any further—Here, Warford, take Lady Henrietta ; and, depend on't, my settlement shall be equal to the justice's.

Sir Tho. And you, sir, (*To* PAVE.) since you are become a senator, take old Medium's daughter—— One half of my estate goes to Henrietta—the other to you——that is, on condition you secure me the road—the common—the—(*Counting again.*)

Pav. Softly, sir, softly——counting may be ominous——

Lady Hen. And now, as most of us have tried different ways of growing rich, let us acknowledge, that, while Sir Charles's plan has been the worst, Warford's has proved the best ; for, had the time the former wasted in dissipation and deception been employed, like the latter, in honesty and industry, Sir Charles had now, like Warford, been rich and happy.

Small. Aye; application and economy is the surest road to riches.

Pav. No—I'll shew you a better way—by gaining patronage and promotion here!

Here let our friends around support our cause,
And we'll grow rich indeed—by their applause.

[Exeunt omnes.

NOTORIETY;

A

COMEDY,

AS IT IS PERFORMED AT THE

THEATRE-ROYAL, COVENT-GARDEN.

BY

FREDERICK REYNOLDS.

DRAMATIS PERSONÆ.

NOMINAL,	Mr Lewis.
COL. HUBBUB, (*his Guardian*)	Mr Quick.
SIR ANDREW ACID,	Mr Wilson.
LORD JARGON,	Mr Munden.
CLAIRVILLE, (*his Brother*)	Mr Farren.
SAUNTER,	Mr Davies.
JAMES,	Mr Farley.
O'WHACK,	Mr Johnstone.
LADY ACID,	Mrs Webb.
SOPHIA STRANGEWAYS, (*Ward to Sir Andrew*)	Mrs Wells.
HONORIA, (*Niece to Col. Hubbub*)	Mrs Esten.

NOTORIETY.

ACT THE FIRST.

SCENE I.

An Apartment at SIR ANDREW'S.—*Two Doors open in Flat.—Bells ringing.*

Enter JAMES *from Door, and another Servant.*

James. Run—fly—scamper—Don't you hear the company are breaking up?—Call Lord Jargon's carriage.

LADY ACID *appears at door, curtsying, as if taking leave of somebody.*

Lady Acid. Good night, my Lord—Delightful man! I am determined he shall be in possession of Honoria—if it's only in return for his attachment to me.—James, call up the carriages, and see the compnay disposed of—I'm so fatigued!—Heigho!—Se-

ven o'clock again! I haven't been to bed any sooner
this fortnight.

SIR ANDREW (*without.*)

Sir And. Where are all the servants? (*Without.*)
Lady Acid. Here's my fretful husband just got up!
He's so old fashioned, and so sour—he's never pleased but when others are vexed—and never unhappy
but when his friends are happy.

Enter SIR ANDREW, *in Night-Gown and Cap.*

So, mf—esutylgij ot up, I suppose?
Sir And. So, my soul—just going to bed, I suppose?—What! at the old work—Rout, ball, or concert, heh! Making fools happy with my money?
Lady Acid. Psha! you've no idea of life.
Sir And. No; but I have of death—It would kill
me in a fortnight—Besides, every body laughs at
you—Not one of your acquaintance, who, by the
by, have loved and hated each other all around, but,
on leaving the room, exclaims—" Well! it's very
fine! mighty grand! But will it last? Won't there
be a crush by and by?"
Lady Acid. Ridiculous, Sir Andrew! An't I visited by every body? Don't all the beau-monde attend
Lady Acid's parties?
Sir And. The beau-monde! why, they'll visit any
body that is fool enough to invite them.—Let who
will give an expensive entertainment, they'll flock to
it, like rooks to a ruin.—But this won't do—it's seven
o'clock, and I must be eating.—Here—you sir, (*Enter* JAMES.) bring my breakfast.
James. Breakfast!—What, here, sir?   [*Exit.*
Sir And. Yes;—here, sir.—I am sure the beau-
monde (as your ladyship calls them) will have no
objection to something substantial. Poor devils! at
these sort of parties they get nothing to feed on but
scandal and faro.

Lady Acid. Provoking, Sir Andrew!—You're always teasing and vexing me; and I insist on knowing what part of my conduct——

Sir And. Hold—don't suppose I suspect your character.---No---'midst all your gaieties, I still believe you to be so constant and honourable, that there's no indulging one's self in finding fault with you.

Lady Acid. If you don't think so, your cousin, Colonel Hubbub, does, or he would never have trusted me with the care of his niece Honoria. But I leave you to your ill-nature.

Sir And. Ay; go to bed---You to your pillow, I to my coffee.

Lady Acid. Mind me, sir---If you see Honoria, give her the advice I desired you.---Tell her the colonel has written for his ward, Mr Nominal, to challenge that wretch Clairville, and that I shall do all in my power to give her to Lord Jargon---And so, good night, most good-humour'd husband!

Sir And. And so, good morning, most sweet-temper'd wife! [*Exit* LADY ACID.] I've made her unhappy, however.—'Gad, I don't know how it is, I like to see every body's face as long as my own.—(*Breakfast brought in,*) Here it comes—And here's the paper. (*Sits down, and takes up newspaper.*) Now for it !---now for bad news! " Theatre-Royal, New Comedy."---Psha! making people grin and distort their faces.---Give me a deep, horrible, agreeable tragedy---" Bankrupts."---Ay, here they are---" One ---two---three---thirteen."---Come, very well!---that's very well!---" Promotions."---There they are with their curst joy again!---" Stocks fallen one and a half." ---Some lame ducks, however---" Marriages---ten." Well! long life to you, for you'll be as miserable—

Enter HONORIA (*from Doors.*)

Hon. Dear sir, ten thousand pardons---I thought to have found your ward Miss Strangeways here.

Sir And. Sit down, Honoria, sit down---I want to talk to you---Come, take some breakfast.

Hon. Breakfast!---I haven't been to rest yet--- You forget the joys of high life, sir!

Sir And. Joys!---She's happy too!---Um!---Silly, ignorant girl, to take pleasure in such unmeaning scenes!

Hon. Pleasure! they give me pain, sir——mi-sery.

Sir And. Do they? Take some breakfast. (*Offers her some.*)

Hon. What have I been doing to-night, sir?--- Talking to men I detest, and listening to women I despise---mixing with people who have neither feel-ing, amity, nor sense.---This I have done for years, and this I must still persevere in; for my education has taught me to smile when I was miserable, and to be fashionable at the expence of my peace.

Sir And. Sweet creature! How prettily she prat-tles! Go on.

Hon. Yes, sir; with a mind naturally attached to domestic happiness, I am compelled to deride all peaceful scenes, because my uncle, the colonel, who has cruelly delivered me to the care of your wife, sir---But I interrupt you—I see I do—I'll keep my sorrows to myself.

Sir And. Don't---don't keep them to yourself--- I like to hear you talk about sorrow and misery; and if you know of any more elsewhere, you'll not offend me by imparting it! But now I think on't, tell me that unlucky story of the fellow ascending your win-dow by a rope ladder.

Hon. Fellow! Sir Andrew! When you are more respectful, I'll talk to you---till when---(*Going.*)

Sir And. (*Stops her.*) Stay---be not offended--- I'll sympathize with you, Honoria,—I'll give you sigh for sigh, and tear for tear. Come; make me

your confidant, and you sha'n't repent it.---Nay, you
must---you shall---I do love to hear a tale of woe!

Hon. (*Sitting.*) Oh, sir! how have I been slandered and defamed! I never knew Mr Clairville but
as a friend—as a protector: that we had secret meetings I cannot deny; but I was never alone---your
ward Sophia was always present---and she will witness to the world that he was too honourable to
make base proposals, and I too unfashionable to accept them.

Sir And. Go on—I like to hear you, Honoria. If
I remember, your acquaintance began at the colonel's villa in the Isle of Wight, when you were sailing, and fell from the vessel.

Hon. Yes, sir; and while his brother, Lord Jargon, and other foplings of the party, who before had
offered up their lives to serve me, while they stood
idly on the deck, and saw me just expiring, Clairville, then a stranger, leaped from another vessel,
and, plunging 'midst the waves, caught me in his
arms, and brought me safe to land.---Then came the
conflict---The colonel's boat, by adverse winds, was
blown from shore; and I and my deliverer remained
part of that day alone.---I saw, compared, and loved
---his heart beat in unison with mine; and, now, sir,
do you pity or condemn me?

Sir And. I pity you, pity you sincerely, and curse
the colonel for placing you under the care of my
wife, because I know she designs you for Lord Jargon—But Nominal, whom your uncle intends for
your husband, is hourly expected from France.

Hon. Talk not of that, sir; for I dread the consequences of his arrival.---The night Clairville was discovered in my apartment, the colonel told him he
would send for his ward, Nominal, to avenge the injured honour of his family! Oh, sir, if a duel should
ensue!---Yet, if Clairville receives my letter, that

and other ills may be prevented (*Aside*)---But somebody is coming, sir---allow me to retire.

Sir And. Do, and depend on my protection, Ho-
noria---I am always a friend to the unhappy.---Good
morning. [*Exit* HONORIA.] So, there goes another long face!---Here's my ward, the celebrated
Miss Strangeways---She's an authoress, an actress,
a musician, a painter, and, in short, every thing.---
I know she's in love with me, and I'll have the satisfaction of teazing her soul out.

Enter MISS STRANGEWAYS (*with a paper in her
hand.*)

Soph. Positively I will be revenged.---The colonel does nothing but make love to me ---Heigho!
I'm so fatigued, guardy---and it's in vain going to
bed, I've so many places to call at.

Sir And. What! all over the town, as usual?

Soph. Yes: first I'm going to Lady Bustle's, to
finish my picture of her little French lap-dog---then
to call at the bookseller's, and correct the press---
then to leave this farewell ode to my dear Juggla-
mintha, at the newspaper office. (*Reading.*)

" Oh! thou, whose amaranthine feelings know
" The iron agonies of copper woe."

Sir And. Iron agonies of copper woe! That's a
fine line, and charmingly distressing.

Soph. Yes; and then I'm going to rehearse a
new tragedy at the private theatre; and, if you'll
believe me, my dying scene is yet unsettled.

Sir And. That's a great pity, Sophia---for I think
the dying scene the best part of the play.

Soph. Yes; but one insists on my dying on one
side of the stage, another on the other.---Now, what
am I to do?

Sir And. Why, what many great politicians have

done before you---die between both sides.---But, my angel, when am I to be honoured with an assignation ---a *téte a-téte*, heh?

Soph. Fie, guardy!---You know I told you I loved you better than the colonel, and——that I'd make fools of you both before I'd done with you. (*Aside.*)

O'WHACK (*without.*)

O'Whack. (*Without.*) Arrah! stand by now! I am the valet de chambre to Mr Nominal.

Sir And. As I live, Nominal is arrived! This is his Irish servant, who, to his brogue, has joined a smattering of French---Do stay and hear him.

Soph. What! mix Irish with French!

Sir And. So it seems; and he so confounds the two languages, he is scarcely intelligible---But here he comes.

Enter O'WHACK, *followed by* JAMES.

O'Whack. Mon Dieu! you dirty blackguard! don't you know me by my politesse? Jontleman and lady, your most obedient---By the red nose of Saint Patrick, I am toute nouveau; and, d'ye see, I would be after spaking to my master's guardian, Colonel Hubbub.

Sir And. How is your master? Is he as singular as his guardian describes him?

Soph. Singular! What, is he like the colonel, Sir Andrew?

Sir And. The image of him---While at college his love of notoriety first displayed itself; but, by living entirely with English abroad, he is become as eccentric and absurd as the colonel wishes him.

O'Whack. By the powers! you've hit it---Ma foi! he is toujours wanting to get into notice; and, between our three selves, he keeps me as his valet, frizeur, and all that, only becase I perplex, and make

a noise, and am quite au fait at botheration where-
ever I go.

Soph. Pray, what brings Mr Nominal so suddenly from France ? Isn't it something about an affair of honour ?

O'Whack. Oui ; you may say that—He is come
to challenge one Clairville, for getting into the window of Mademoiselle Honoria: and to be sure he
won't give the young seducer a little snug dejeuné
of cold lead.

Soph. 'Tis so then—Poor Clairville !

Sir And. Tell us now, had you a pleasant journey ?

O'Whack. Pleasant ! Oh ! by the eternal powers,
tout au contraire, my dear : we were stopped, and
robbed, and murdered : that is, we should have been,
but for a fine young haroe, who came and rescued
us ! Marbleu ! he made them skip like frogs.

Sir And. A robbery and a duel ! This journey
may produce much pleasing distress---Pray, who was
this young haroe ?

O'Whack. Je ne sçai pas, honey---But you may
talk of your Cæsars, Cleopatras, and Paddy-Whacks
---he beats all your champions of posterity.---Oh !
had you seen, when my master and I were sprawling,
how he laid about him with his piece of timber——
Depend on't, as our fille de chambre said, the shillaly is the true je ne sçai quoi, after all.

Soph. A very entertaining fellow, Sir Andrew.—
What's your name, friend ?

O'Whack. Blunder O'Whack, Jontleman ! The
Blunders are the oldest family in Ireland---We were
planted there like so many potatys, by a great gene-
ral, who was afterwards Lord Lieutenant to King—
What d'ye call the old monarque ?—Oh ! King Lear
—Ay, that's it—King Lear.

Soph. King Lear !

O'Whack. C'est vrai, Miss— and after that, the

family got a curst tumble about the reign of Jack
Cade—Pardonnez moi, though—I' forget my business—I must be after informing the colonel of his
ward's arrival.

Sir And. Spare yourself the trouble, Mr O'Whack
—Colonel Hubbub is not here—but I'll take care to
inform him.

O'Whack. Je vous remercie, my dear—But do
you mind now—depêchez-vous, and tell him, my
master's so particular in his person and manners, that
you may hear of him any where—Monsieur, good
luck to you!—My lady, j'ai l'honneur d'être très-
humble serviteur!—Oh! by my soul! the true comme il faut's better than whisky.   [*Exit.*

Soph. If the servant is a picture of the master,
Nominal will have too much good humour to quarrel
with Clairville.—Faith! I almost love him by description—But I must leave you, guardy—adieu!

Sir And. Nay, don't hurry, my angel—it's too
soon for the dying scene.

Soph. I know it;—but first I'm going to see a
friend.

Sir And. See a friend! Then pray let me go with
you; for that's a thing I never saw in my life.
                                        [*Exeunt.*

SCENE II.

The Park.

Enter O'WHACK, *with Books under his Arm.*

O'Whack. By Saint Dennis! these law gentlemen
are as heavy---I wonder what my master would be
after with them.   Ce ne fait rien, I must take them
home as he ordered me.

Enter SAUNTER (*spying, and looking out at* No-
MINAL.)

Saun. Astonishing! I never saw a man so dressed
walk the streets before. Who can it be? (*Turning round, sees* O'WHACK, *who bows to him*)—Ha!
O'Whack! how came you here? What, is your
master, my old college friend, returned from his
travels?

O'Whack. Oui, your honour—et la voilà! there
he is!

Saun. What, is that Nominal? Well, this is excellent!—I knew Nominal always loved singularity;
but I never thought he'd make himself so particular,
that his friends shouldn't know him.

O'Whack. C'est extraordinaire, my dear—but,
with all his oddities, you can't help loving him.—
Oh! his heart is as warm as l'eau de vie, and his
soul—by St Patrick, the rest of the world's all blar-
ney to him!

Enter NOMINAL.

Nom. Ah, Saunter, my dear fellow! Well, what
do you think? Won't it do? Sha'n't I take, heh?
—Harkye, I have them already.

Saun. Have! Whom?

Nom. Every body, you dog, every body!—I've got
a name—they stare at me—point at me—laugh at
me every where. An't I a happy fellow, heh?

Saun. If happiness consists in being laughed at,
you are—But, Nominal, wouldn't it be as well to be
known for being rational, as being ridiculous?

Nom. Rational! Pshoo! a plain sensible man is
never thought on now. Who the devil ever thinks
or cares about such a sober, honest fellow as you,
who pay every body, and offend nobody?—But I
now—such a rogue as I, who pay nobody, and offend every body—why, they all like me. They court

me as a new acquaintance, not cut me as an old friend, my boy.

Saun. Well, every man in his way—for my part, I detest singularity.

Nom. Then you're an undone man ; for, by being singular in nothing, you'll be despised in every thing. For instance, now, George—when you go into company, and inquisitive people say—-" Who is he? What Mr Saunter?" nobody can describe you—you have been guilty of no absurdities—no improprieties. But when I condescend to enter a room, there's a general buzz of applause, and the women all whisper, " That's he, the famous Ned Nominal, who games, who drinks, who fights, who intrigues. Oh! the sprightly, vicious fellow !" In short, George, I'm a public character.

Saun. A public character ! What then?

Nom. Why, then, I make a damned noise without any meaning.

Saun. Believe me, Nominal, you are deceived—A character so useless can neither excite admiration nor attention.

Nom. Useless ! Oh, George, George !—how little dost thou know of modern life !—Useless !—that's the very thing that makes me. Now, let me put a plain and simple question to you—Isn't a cat that walks on four legs a useful animal ?

Saun. A cat on four legs useful !—-'tis an odd question—Certainly.

Nom. Very well. And what do you think of a cat with only two legs ? Why, it's useless ; and yet you and the rest of the world shall give it twice the admiration and attention. And there's the difference between us, George—You are a very useful, worthy fellow, and, consequently, are despised—I am a very useless, mischievous fellow, and, of course, am admired—Therefore, my dear boy, take my advice—expose yourself, and get into notice.

Saun. Why, you are the counterpart of your guardian, the colonel; and when he finds you thus bitten with the love of notoriety, he'll be delighted—transported.

Nom. Yes; but I mean to disappoint him.

Saun. Disappoint him!

Nom. Ay; and for three reasons, George.—First, because he wants me to marry Honoria, a girl I don't care for—Secondly, because he has brought me to fight one Clairville, a poor devil I never saw;—And, thirdly, because being in opposition makes more noise than being under government.—You understand me—I mean to quarrel with him.

Saun. And how will you contrive it?

Nom. His greatest antipathy is to law and lawyers. I'll pass on him as a student.

Saun. Student! Why, you don't understand the practice.

Nom. No; who the devil does? But a little goes a great way, George—so never fear.

Saun. Well, I must leave you for the present, for I have business elsewhere.—I'll see you to-morrow; and, in the mean time, success to your studies, your sports, and singularities! [*Exit.*

Nom. (*Looking after him.*) What an old-fashioned appearance! I wish I had him a little—I'd soon teach him how to expose himself.—O'Whack!

O'Whack. Toujours pret, your honour.

Nom. Take these law-books home—put them on the table, and give the room a studious appearance, for the reception of my guardian.—You know what I intend.

O'Whack. Oh! leave me alone for catching the old fox—I'll do it sans ceremonie.—Your honour, —see who's coming this way—By my salvation, it's the sweet young haro that saved us and our chapeaus from the robbers!

Nom. That's lucky. I want to thank him.—Besides, if the robbery is well introduced in the papers, it may give an eclat to my arrival ; and, some way or other, I must be before the public every day.

Enter CLAIRVILLE, *with a Letter in his hand.*

Clair. Joy ! Give me joy, sir !—Excuse this freedom from a stranger : but bliss so unexpected—so exquisite, was never known before.

Nom. What ! it's all in print, is it ? the whole robbery ! Well, what do they say of me ?

Clair. Oh, sir ! when we parted last night, I was miserable—I fancied I had lost the loveliest creature the world e'er wondered at——But picture the reverse !

Nom. Curse the reverse ! So, I'm to be robbed, and get nothing by it !

Clair. In this letter she tells me, that, to-night, she will give me a private interview !—Yes ; though my father left, with his title, his estate to my brother, and that brother has cruelly deserted me—yet, at this moment, I'm the happiest man alive. But excuse me—I am all haste, all anxiety, to prepare for the appointment.   [*Going.*

Nom. Hold, sir, hold ! 'Gad, who knows but this private interview may lead to a public uproar ; and as he did me a service——(*Aside.*) Sir, I am much indebted to you—and if I can be of any use——

Clair. None in the least ; I thank you.——Yet, now I think on't, Honoria is so narrowly watched, that a friend may be necessary——He seems a gentleman, though an odd one——I'll accept his offer. (*Aside.*) Sir, you may assist me.

Nom. How, how ?

Clair. The lady, sir, whose name, as well as my own, I must beg leave to conceal, is so much suspected by her family, that, alone, I may be interrupted in the interview—If, therefore, you will meet

me at Grosvenor-Gate, at ten o'clock, I will conduct
you to the house, which is a short way from town—
But if we are discovered, and the business becomes
public——

Nom. Why, then, I shall be doubly obliged to
you.

Clair. Well ; but if your name is brought forward
and abused ?

Nom. Why, then, the obligation will be trebled.
I like abuse ; and I'll tell you why—It brings one
into notice ; and if somebody doesn't cut me up, I
mean to do it myself.

Clair. How ! abuse yourself ?

Nom. Certainly—for if I don't let people know
what a singular, absurd, useless sort of fellow I am,
how will they find it out ? Silence sinks you into obscurity, my boy ; and, for my part, I'd rather be
laughed at for standing in the pillory, than not noticed at all.

Clair. Well, this is the strangest system ! What,
you want to get a name, I suppose ?

Nom. I do ; and, heaven be praised, 'tis easier
now to be obtained than in days of yore. Then,
conquest, patriotism, and virtue, were the only paths
to fame ; but now-a-days, eccentricity, impudence,
and dissipation, settle the business——And if I don't
cut out Cæsar or Mark Antony to-morrow———But
come along——I have some law-business with my
guardian ; and, after that, for you and your interview.

Clair. Ten thousand thanks—But may I ask how
you intend getting a name to-morrow ?

Nom. I'll tell you—I mean to fight a duel, commence an intrigue, and complete an elopement—but
where are the ladies, or who is the gentleman, I neither know nor can inform you—only be assured, I'll
accomplish it ; and then, my boy ! when I lack wit,

I'll boast of my exploits; and when I want money,
—why, I'll shew myself as a curiosity! So, allons!

[Exeunt.

ACT THE SECOND.

SCENE I.

NOMINAL'S *Lodgings—Table with Books on it—*
O'WHACK *discovered placing the Books.*

O'Whack. The colonel will be here dans une moment—if my master hadn't l'argent enough of his
own, he wouldn't be after teazing his old guardian
in this manner—Voila! tout est arrangé, and now to
receive him a la mode de François, as we say in Ireland.

Enter COLONEL HUBBUB *and* SIR ANDREW ACID.

Col. (*Dancing and singing.*) Ti, di, di, di!

Sir And. Keep quiet, I tell you—Oh, curse your
joy!

Col. Ti, di, di, di! The lad of spirit! The boy
after his guardian's own heart '—Here, here's a contract to marry my niece Honoria.

Sir And. Be serious, I tell you; grinning don't
become you.

Col. Here, this gives him my niece, with thirty
thousand pounds; and if he had returned a solid,
studious, good-for-nothing sort of young man, do
you think I'd have signed it? No! but to have him
come home a dashing dog!——a choice spirit!——

Ods heart; if his uncle, the old general, was alive, he'd die with joy!

Sir And. Old general, indeed! A pretty uncle he was, to leave his nephew to the care of such a guardian as you—But I remember him; he loved dissipation, and despised prudence as much as yourself.

Col. He did; and he appointed me guardian to the dear boy, that I might see the glorious breed preserved; and now he is a choice spirit.

Sir And. A choice devil! What, you want him to be a fellow who can fight a duel in one field, and be second in another; who drinks hard, and rides harder; who talks much, thinks little, and reads less; who carries off young women, and runs away from old ones!—In short, who loves notoriety, and makes noise and confusion wherever he goes?

Col. That's it! You've hit it exactly—only with this difference, that, though I despise prudence, I detest knavery; and if ever he behaves like a villain, if ever he does a dishonourable action, I'll cut him off with a shilling, and I know the old general would have done the same—But where is he? Ti, di, di, di! Od, I'm so happy——(*Offers to take snuff out of* Sir Andrew's *box, who refuses it.*) Why, what's the matter with you, cousin? you don't seem to partake my joy.

Sir And. Yes, I do—nothing so pleasant as to see every body on the broad grin. I hope it will last, that's all! But I know you mean to ruin him, as you have your niece Honoria, instead of improving her mind, teaching her the languages——

Col. Her the languages! Why, old boy, haven't you found out that one tongue is enough for a woman?—No, no; I have brought her into high life— sent her to concerts—operas——

Sir And. Operas! Now that's a pretty business— to pay a piece of gold to sit five or six hours in a house, where you fall asleep to save hearing what you don't understand.

Col. Five or six hours! Psha! that's nothing to what I do—I pay some thousand pieces of gold, to sit seven years in another house, where I must fall asleep; for, hang me, if ever I heard a word I understood!

O'Whack. Bon! Ha, ha, ha!

Sir And. So here's another merry rascal! Ay, do look at each other, and smile—I never saw one fool look at another in the face without grinning. (*Exit* O'WHACK.)—And give me leave to tell you, colonel——

Col. Well! don't be angry—Isn't it strange you can't bear to see every body happy? But come, where's the boy, the heart of oak? (*Looking over books on table.*) Why, what's here? A law dictionary!

Sir And. A law dictionary! Something serious at last! (*Reads.*) " Acto Quinto Jacobi primi!"—No hazard table!

Col. Hazard! Ay, that's right—making himself master of that fine art, law! 'Sblood! if he had the least inclination for that solemn, sable profession, I'd break his bones! I'd——But he comes! the dear profligate comes! Ti, di, di, di! My boy, my life!

Enter NOMINAL, *in a Dressing-Gown, reading a Book.*

Nom. C cuts off the remainder, and D loses his tail.

Col. Come, my darling, let's hear of your frolics, —mine and the general's old tricks!

Nom. (*Still reading.*) That infernal tail!——Ha, guardian! Sir Andrew! both welcome! Been at the hall lately? (*To Colonel.*)

Col. Been at the devil!—Come, let's hear of your pranks!

Sir And. Gad, if he should turn out studious after all!

Nom. Curious cause this morning—friend Paul
Prig for plaintiff—tell you his speech.

Col. Why, what are you at?

Nom. He rose, twirled his band—began—" My
lord—Hem!—Gemmen of the jury—hem!—I'm for
plaintiff—I think—I know—I've read my brief—
hem!"—nodding, and cocking his eye to the jury.

Sir And. Cocking his eye to jury?

Nom. Yes, better than any talking—" My lord—
hem!—I see—I see, I know I'm right"—cocking
again—I've done—hem!—Foreman winks—judge
sums up—verdict for Paul—client ruined—all the
young Prigs laugh—any thing makes them laugh—
hem!

Col. Zounds! what is all this? let's hear.

Nom. Hear! never without fee—name your case
—joint trustees, perhaps—if not, why not?—what
are your ages?

Col. What are our ages?

Nom. Infants, very like.

Sir And. I an infant! why, I was never more deceived in my life. Colonel, this is the most studious,
choice spirit I ever saw—I give you joy! (*Offering
him snuff.*)——Young man, this capering, grinning
gentleman described you as a perfect rake—I expected to see you reading Hoyle—Do you mean to
pursue the profession?

Nom. Certainly—student now—hereafter counsel—Been at the Old Bailey lately? (*To Col.*)

Col. Old Bailey! Look ye, you dog! leave off this
foolery, or——

Sir And. I'm delighted, cousin! now, why don't
you partake my joy?—Faith, I must go and tell my
wife and ward of this—Mr Nominal, I'm sorry I'm
obliged to leave you—

Col. Leave him! why don't you go then?

Sir And. Give me your hand; (*To* NOMINAL.) persevere in your studies, and I and Lady Acid shall be always happy in your company---Good day---Colonel, don't make long faces; he'll make full as much noise and confusion in this present profession------ Though he won't fire a pistol, he can file a bill in Chancery; and which is the least mischievous, I leave you to determine---hem!

[*Offers snuff again, and exit.*

Col. Rat you! I'm glad you're gone----Now, my dear boy, it's all very well to appear prudent and studious before that stupid old fool: but since he's gone, lay aside this trifling---Come, leave off talking about such low, dull nonsense as counsellors and Westminster-Hall, and let's hear you speak like a man of sense, about fighting, drinking, racing---

Nom. Racing! as I hope for the seals, here's the case---Look! (*Shews a book.*)

Col. What! do you persist in your ignorance?

Nom. Never read Puffendorff! Heh! fine book--- better than army list.

Col. Look ye, I have done with you for ever---- Oh, you senseless blockhead! to be making money instead of spending it----to be following a prudent, stale, old-fashioned profession, instead of being ruined and getting into high life, you dog!---*You* avenge Honoria's honour! 'Sdeath, I'll beat Clairville myself; and, before I hear of you, Puffendorff, or Paul Prig again, I'll marry her to a drummer, or a common trooper---I will, you stupid, inflexible, upright rascal!

Nom. Now I am satisfied. (*Aside.*)

Enter O'WHACK.

O'Whack. Ecoutez, your honour ---- the strange young haro is waiting for you at Grosvenor Gate.

Nom. I'll come directly---leave my travelling-coat in the hall---Guardy, adieu---brother Prig waiting.

Col. Stay ; one rational word before you go----
Would you——

Nom. Hush ! can't stay ; reply another day----
mean time find me in the Hall---Adieu ! law's a fine
profession----puts an end to grinning, transports, ec-
stacies---Adieu ! leave you with Puffendorff---hem !

[*Exit.*

Col. Here's treatment ! leave a colonel in the
army alone with Puffendorff ! Ignorant puppy ! to
give up fashionable life for a profession in which the
greatness of his reputation is chiefly known by the
size of his wig !---where---(*Seeing* O'WHACK.) You
too, you Irish, French, pyebald rascal ! you helped
this pretty reformation, I suppose.

O'Whack. Point de tout, your honour---your own
self couldn't have set him a more dissipated example
than I did---Oh ! à Paris, mon colonel ! to be sure I
didn't lead him into any mischief at all at all !

Col. What do you mean ?

O'Whack. Tacez vous, jewel !---when I slept out
all night, got drunk with usquebaugh, intrigued with
the Marchioness Tipperary, and beat her poor husband, it was only to oblige your honour, that I
might stand before you, and say---" Voila ! Monsieur O'Whack, who kept it up to the last !"

Col. Why, you impertinent——do you mean to
laugh at me ? Marchioness Tipperary, indeed !

Enter JAMES.

James. Sir, sir ! a word with you---Miss Honoria's window is open, and she and Miss Sophia are
waiting for Mr Clairville.

Col. Sophia with her ! that's lucky----Harkye, is
Lady Acid at home ?

James. No, sir ; she and Sir Andrew are just gone
out together----But Miss Sophia asked me, whether
you were expected there to-night.

Col. Sho did, did she?—Oh! it's plain she can't
live without me—Poor love-sick creature! I'll go and
comfort her—I'll lock up Honoria, kick Clairville
out of the house, and thus have her all to myself—
Shew me down, sirrah! and, d'ye hear, tell your
studious master I'm gone to chastise the man I desired him to challenge—Yes, I'll so shame him, by
beating this Clairville——

O'Whack. Ay, by St Patrick, beat him, your honour, as I did the Marquis de Tipperary—Par ici—
this way!—   [*Exeunt.*

SCENE II.

The Outside of SIR ANDREW'S *House in the
Country---Stage darkened.*

Enter CLAIRVILLE.

Clair. Where is this friend who was to have assisted in the enterprise?—I have sent my servant to
look for him; for, alone, I can undertake nothing.
—Oh, Honoria! let me but once more see you, and
know you are my friend, and I will ask no more—
No, never while I live, will I think of deluding her
from her family: with them, she has all that wealth
and splendour can afford; and with me, how severe
will be the reverse! I know the colonel has brought
his ward Nominal from France, to call me to account for my presumption—but of that I think not,
—let me but gain this last interview—Ha! here's
the stranger!

Enter NOMINAL.

Nom. A thousand pardons——I've been talking

law ; so no wonder at delay—Well !—here we are !
and, do you know, this business puts me in mind of
what I came to England for.

Clair. What was that ?

Nom. Oh ! only to beat a gentleman for scaling a
rope-ladder—-that's all—-some poor, stupid fellow !
But we won't talk of that—-Where's the girl ? heh !

Clair. 'Tis past the time she promised to appear
at the window—-But, understand me, sir—all I wish
to obtain is an interview ; to know she approves my
past conduct, and takes an interest in my future—-
Therefore, what I request of you is this—-while I
guard the house within, you watch the door without :
don't let a soul enter.

Nom. Me ! I'll beat the watch, kick the constable, and cane all the trading justices in town, before
you shall lose one tender moment.

HONORIA, *at the Window.*

Hon. Sir ! sir !

Clair. Ha ! she comes ! like a new world she
breaks upon me ! Oh, let me fly to welcome her !

Nom. Oh ! let me fly to welcome her ! (*Mimicking.*) Now, who she is, or who the house belongs to,
or what it all means, hang me if I know or care !
Only this, that if there was a noise, there might be
a discovery !—if a discovery, a pursuit !—if a pursuit, a rescue !—-and then, oh ! what a figure I
should cut !

Hon. Come in instantly, or you may be discovered.

Nom. (*To* CLAIRVILLE.) Harkye, if you are discovered, and are afraid to mention your own name,
make use of mine—I'm not ashamed of this, or any
business !

Clair. I have no fears. (*Opening the door.*) Now,
now, sir, envy me !   [*Exit into house.*

Nom. Envy you ! that I do—He'll have all the

fame to himself; and here I stand, as melancholy as
a mile-stone—How provokingly quiet every thing is !
—'Sdeath ! is there no noise to wake the old guardian ? is there no noise ? Oh for the squeaking of a
child, the smashing of a lamp, or the howling of a
husband being thumpt by his wife ! No uproar ?

SOPHIA, *at the Window.*

Soph. Sir, as you are anxious to assist your
friend, will you be kind enough to tell my servant,
who is somewhere near, to come home—for if he is
observed——

Nom. I will, madam—Who the devil's she, now ?

Soph. And, sir, when you return, I'll speak to
you from the window ; and, on your answering me,
I'll come down, and let the servant in myself.

Nom. Ay, and me along with him—I'll take care,
ma'am—I'll take care—Stand by, raggamuffin !——
(*Runs against* COLONEL HUBBUB, *who is entering,
and exit.*)

Enter COLONEL HUBBUB.

Col. Stand by, raggamuffin ! What noisy fellow's
that ? Ay, there it is, there's the window open sure
enough ; and I dare say Sophia has promoted the
scheme, in hopes of assisting her amour with me !
Sweet, tender soul ! I shall never forget her telling
me, that, if I'd one more hair on my left eye-brow, I
should be the handsomest man in the army ! and
another time, when she fainted away on only touching the tip of my epaulette—

SOPHIA, *from the Window.*

Soph. Is it you, sir ?
Col. Yes, here I am ! Oh, 'tis too much !
Soph. I'll come down and open the door.
                                    [*Exit from window.*
Col. Open the door ! There ! She wants to be

touching the tip of the epaulette again! poor fond
creature! Yes, I must, I will!

SOPHIA *opens the Door.*

Soph. Come in! (*Sees Colonel.*) Heavens! the
colonel!

Col. Excess of joy dissolves her! Don't give way
to your raptures, most angelic!—I come to give you
love for love.   [*Lays hold of her.*

Soph. Unhand me, colonel!

Col. Let's enter the house—I'll lock up Honoria,
turn Clairville out of doors—and then——

Soph. Let me go this instant. (*Struggling with
him.*)

Re-enter NOMINAL.

Nom. Ha! what are you at? Retire, madam.
                    [*Exit* SOPHIA *into house.*
Now answer me, seducer! Would you delude the
innocent?

Col. I delude! Who the deuce are you?

Nom. A justice of peace, come to promote tran-
quillity—But your name? your profession? speak
this instant. (*Shaking him.*) Zounds! do you suspect my office?

Col. No, not in the least—I know you're a peace-
officer by the curst noise you make. (NOMINAL
shakes him again.) Gently; and, to satisfy you, I'll
tell you who I am—my name's Hubbub——

Nom. Hubbub!

Col. Yes; I'm here doing duty.

Nom. My guardian! faith, this is better than Paul
Prig!

CLAIRVILLE, *at the Window.*

Clair. (*Aside to* NOMINAL.) Detain him—keep
him where he is, or all's ruined!

Nom. I will.   [*Exit* CLAIRVILLE *from window.*

Sir, (*Bowing.*) if your name be Hubbub, I have to entreat your pardon—I've the honour of being acquainted with part of your worthy family.

Col. Ay, ay, I knew you'd perceive your mistake—But let me enter the house, and play the devil.

Nom. (*Holding him.*) Yes, colonel; I have the pleasure of being intimate with your very learned ward, Mr Nominal.—Times are strangely alter'd, sir —I remember when he was the most noisy, extravagant young man in town.

Col. Ay, those were happy days! But they're all over now! the dog thinks of nothing but Puffendorff and the Old Bailey.

Nom. Yes; I used to have a warrant against him once a-week, and he generally slept in the watchhouse every other night! But now—alas, colonel! I'm afraid we shall never catch him in a riot again!
(*In a melancholy voice.*)

Col. (*Sighing.*) No—he has lost all that good sense and genius now! And after the pains I had taken in instructing and improving him! it's hard— very hard, sir!

Nom. (*Sighing with him.*) Ay, sir; to have him turn out studious, sober, and prudent!

Col. Ah! to disgrace the honour of the Hubbubs! —to vilify the glorious breed!—Stupid, senseless dog! But let me go into the house, for I'm all eagerness to chastise this Clairville.

Nom. Clairville! What's he now in the house?

Col. Yes; and I brought my ward Nominal to fight him;—but he daren't, sir,—he's grown a coward—poor paultry priggish coward; and, if you see him, you may tell him I say so.

Nom. So! I may tell Nominal he's a coward, may I?

Col. Yes! or he'd have beat somebody before this

time—Od rat him! I would rather he'd have caned
me than nobody.

Nom. You'd not dislike to be caned by him, would
you?

Col. No; I should have liked the dear rogue the
better for it—But now I know him to be such a
mean, studious, pitiful puppy, that, hang me if I
think he has the courage to beat a jack-ass!—(NOMI-
NAL *canes him.*) Holloa! what are you about?

Nom. (*Caning him*) He'll beat a jack-ass 'with
any man in the army.

CLARVILLE *comes from House.*

Col. You're a ruffian—a common bravo, employ'd
by Clairville to detain and assault me, and you take
advantage of my not having a sword on—but I'll be
reveng'd!—

Nom. Do, and I'll tell you how! Bring an action
of battery, and Paul Prig and your studious nephew
shall defend it.—Hem!

Col. I don't care—you're beneath my contempt—
but for your employer, I'll enter the house, and have
satisfaction; and for that sneaking dog Nominal—
Oh, the curst puppy! I sent for him to beat Clairville, and here have I been beat myself. (*Exit.*

Clair. My dear sir, once more let me thank you—
I have seen the lady, and all is as I wished—she has
given me this picture as a proof of her affection, and
promised never to marry another man—but, come—
why, what are you thinking of?

Nom. I was thinking when the business is found
out, what a noise it will make—But, hold, hold.—
You and I must have some conversation.—

Clair. The lady told me what I never heard before, that her uncle's ward is design'd for her husband.

Nom. What Nominal? I know him intimately;
nor is there a finer fellow alive—he pricks the blad-

ders of vanity, pulls down arrogance, and chastises
folly; and what's more, he gives his guardian sound
law in the morning, and a sound thrashing at night
—then he's a man of notoriety! has the general shout
—the popular huzza, my boy!

Clair. Popular huzza! he'd have that if he was
going to be hang'd.

Nom. Well, and when I die, give me a public
exit, give me the Tower, state trial, axe, scaffold, and
decapitation! Then my life or history will be written with a thousand extraordinary anecdotes! how
I slept at night, and woke in the morning! walk'd
and rode! eat and drank! and, what was very remarkable and important, wore my own hair till thirty,
and a wig ever after— But come along—I'll introduce you to Nominal; and over the bottle he shall
convince you, that he's as popular as life, spirit, and
eccentricity can make him!   [*Exeunt.*

ACT THE THIRD.

SCENE I.

An Apartment in SIR ANDREW'S *House.*

Enter SAUNTER.

Saun. Never was vanity so insufferable as that of
Sir Andrew and the colonel; and unless my cousin
Sophia puts my scheme in execution, they will tor-
ment her for ever—Here comes Sir Andrew, just as

I left him, teazing and fatiguing her with his tiresome protestations of love.

Enter SOPHIA, *followed by* SIR ANDREW.

Soph. Do leave me, Sir Andrew.

Sir And. Well; but hear me, my little angel—I see your passion for me, and your aversion to the colonel—and I pity you, and will relieve you—Hark ye, make an assignation—nay, don't be afraid—I'll not disappoint you, upon my soul.

Soph. Sir Andrew, this is beyond bearing, and if you would attend Lady Acid's concert, where your company is wanted, it would be more agreeable—Assignation indeed!

Sir And. Ay; you know I've won your tender little heart, and that I could make you miserable if I pleased; but I forego it; I chuse to vex the colonel, and—

Enter JAMES.

James. Sir, the concert is waiting.

Sir And. Concert! Psha! Curse all harmony, say I!—But I must go to please my wife—I say—don't forget, Sophia—when and where you like—I'll be punctual—till when, farewell.   [*Exit.*

Soph. Provoking! to suppose me in love with him! I that am admired by the literati, the cognoscenti, and all the out-of-the-way creatures in town! Here—(*Giving* SAUNTER *a letter.*) look at this, and then say if I oughtn't to be wretched?

SAUNTER *reading.*

Saun. " Lady Acid informs Miss Strangeways, that her extraordinary attachment to the colonel and Sir Andrew is the talk of the whole town—that she has lost her character, and, unless she discontinues her advances, she shall be sent to the country, and lock'd up for life."—Lock'd up for life!

Soph. (*Mournfully.*) Ay, lock'd up for life!
Think of that, cousin—I, that have painted my own
picture, and had it in the exhibition! That can read
a Latin Virgil, or a French Voltaire! And, what's
more, that have written a novel, which has been
translated into several languages!

Saun. Has it been translated into English?

Soph. Ay; into English.—It was so beautifully
obscure, that it took a commentator twelve large
volumes to explain the meaning of it. I too, who
have written and composed a song, which I have
sung in every company, without being asked or desired.

Saun. Why, you have an universal genius, indeed.

Soph. Universal! I dare say my death will increase the national debt; for, after being under
ground with my ancestors, I shall be pull'd up, and
re-buried at the expence of my country! And, after
all this, to have my reputation slandered by two old
coxcombs; and what's worse, to be sent to the
country, and lock'd up for life! Oh, cousin!—what
can I—shall I do?

Saun. Don't be unhappy, Sophia; I have thought
of a scheme by which you may expose the vanity of
these two dotards, and extricate yourself. *(Giving
her two letters.)* Read these two letters, and if you
approve, copy them.

Soph. (*Reading.*) " To Sir Andrew Acid.—
Thou gay deceiver—I adore—ten o'clock—your
own garden—Sophia Strangeways."—Fie, cousin!
—would you have me send him an assignation in
reality?

Saun. Read the other.

Soph. (*Reads.*) " To Colonel Hubbub.—Thou
dear perfidious—I idolize—ten o'clock—the garden
—Sophia Strangeways." Charming! I understand

—both in the same language, and both at the same
time and place. I'll write them directly.

Saun. Yes! a double assignation—Then they'll
meet—Their exposition will be complete, and Lady
Acid will be convinced of your innocence.

Soph. Ten thousand thanks—*(Goes to table, sits
and writes.)* " To Colonel Hubbub"—so—" To Sir
Andrew Acid," *(Rises.)* There, cousin—*(Giving
him letters.)* see them delivered, and meet me in
the garden.—At present, adieu!

Saun. Nay, where are you hurrying to?

Soph. First, to the concert, and after that to—
But now I recollect, don't forget your promise of
introducing me to your friend Nominal—Heigho!
I'm in love with him only for his dress.

Saun. How, Sophia! judge a man by his dress?

Soph. Certainly. If I see a man plainly dress'd,
I guess him to be just such a good-for-nothing thing
as yourself; but if I see a man dress'd unlike all
others, then I know him to be the same unaccount-
able creature that I am myself. So save me from
rural imprisonment, and then introduce me to your
singular friend as soon as you please.   [*Exit.*

Enter O'WHACK *behind.*

Saun. How can I deliver the letters? To avoid
suspicion, the best way would be, to give them to
Sophia's own maid, and if I can find her——

O'Whack. (*Advancing.*) What, Fanny, your honour?---Arrah, I am just going to her. Donnez
moi le billet-deaux, and if I don't put them into her
own ruby hands, say this is not No. 37, that's all!
(*Taking snuff.*)

Saun. Are you sure you know her?

O'Whack. Know her! ecoutez, my dear—she
loves me so tinderly, that she'll go to Kilkenny for
a fricassee for me.

Saun. Well; I believe I may trust you—Here,

this is for Sir Andrew, and this for Colonel Hubbub
—They are both at the concert; and desire her to
deliver them directly.

O' Whack. Si vous plait, honey.

Saun And, d'ye hear? tell her to bring me the
answers—You understand me——

O' Whack. Bon soir, your honour.

[*Exit* SAUNTER.

By the powers! some people know no more of good
breeding, than others do of politesse! Eh bien! I
suppose it answers—For I've observed, none jog so
snugly through life, as your complately rude and
vulgar—Every body gets out of the way for them—
the same as a gentleman with a white coat would for
a chimney-sweeper. Oh, by the powers! the only
place for true etiquette is Ireland; sweet, elegant,
accomplish'd Ireland.

SONG—*O' Whack.*

You may talk of a brogue, and of Ireland (sweet nation!)
 Of bulls and of howls, and palavre, comme ça;
But, mon Dieu, it's no more to the French boderation,
 Than vin de Bourdeaux, like to sweet Usquebaugh.
If I go back again, blood and ouns! how I'll wriggle,
 And congé, and caper, and make the folks stare;
And instead of potatoes, how Shelagh will giggle,
  When I cries, Mam'selle, hand me that sweet pomme
  de terre.
With their petit chansons, ça ira, ça ira, Malbrook, Mi-
  ronton, and their dans votre lit;
By the pow'rs they're all nonsense and bodder, agrah! to
  our diddero, bubbero, whack, langolee.

Oh, mon jolly tight Sheelagh, ah, how could I scorn her,
 When I loved her so dearly, ma foi, hubbaboo!
And go round the globe, ay, from corner to corner,
 For soup maigre, la dance, and for frogs and virtu.
And then to forsake magnifique Tipperary,
 For pauvre Versailles, and its capering throng,

And eat fricassees, only fit for a fairy,
  Instead of substantial beef roti de mutton.
                 With their petit chanson, &c.

Oh, I kiss'd a grisette, who halloo'd out, " Ah, fi d'on ;"
  And yet, I consoled her all night and all day ;
To be sure, and I was not her sweet Irish Cupidon,
  Her petit mignon, and mi Lor Anglois.
But when she found out, sans six sous was poor Pat, sir,
  It was " allez miserable diable John Bull ;"
So I e'en gave this blarneying frenchified cat, sir,
  Of good wholesome shillaly, a compleat stomach full.
                 With their petit chanson, &c.

SCENE II.

A Saloon, Chandeliers.

JAMES, *and the other Servants, waiting.*

James. Yaw! (*Yawning.*) These parties will be
the death of me !—What, none of the musical nobility come yet ? Stand by, here's Lord Jargon! Gad,
I like his plan—he makes love to Lady Acid to secure Miss Honoria—The old lady for the young one
—but mum !

Enter LORD JARGON.

Lord Jar. Am I the first, James ?—I thought
your concert began at eight.

James. No, my lord—this is our Sunday concert,
and it is generally nine before their Lordships begin
playing.

Lord Jar. Lordships! Ah ! true—At these Sunday concerts, lords become fiddlers, and fiddlers
greater men —For my part, I cannot play or sing—
" Donne ! donne !" (*Humming a tune.*)

James. Thus it ever is with his lordship, one word contradicting the other.

Enter HONORIA.

Hon. James, where's Lady Acid?—Ha! my Lord Jargon here!

Lord Jar. Honoria, my angel!—I never say a civil thing—but you look divinely this evening—Nay, why avoid me? Am I so very disagreeable?

Hon. Not in the least, my lord.—Where can be Lady Acid?

Lord Jar. (*Taking her hand*) You know, Honoria, I hate to hear people talk of themselves—of their titles—their fortunes, their talents—Nothing can be so shocking!---Now I---I have an ancient title, great fortune, and not inferior talents---but I never mention these things—you never hear me talk of myself.

Hon. No, your lordship has too much sense to talk on a subject you so little understand.

Lord Jar. True, Honoria, and I have reformed— left off all my old vices, the better to deserve your affection—Gaming now---I haven't thrown a die, or made a bet, these six months.

Hon. Not gam'd, my lord!

Lord Jar. No; I'll bet any gentleman two hundred to one I haven't.

Hon. I fancy your lordship is one of those, who think it better to lose than not play at all.

Lord Jar. No; I have given it up, Honoria.--- But, talking of gaming, allow me to apologize for breaking your bracelet last night.

Hon. It was of no consequence, my lord.

Lord Jar. Your pardon, Honoria—and, though I am above making presents, yet you must allow me to make this poor return—these jewels—(*Giving her a casket, open.*)

Hon. How! jewels! and of such value, my lord!

Lord Jar. Oh, a trifle! for my own part, I never
wear diamonds (LADY ACID *enters*)—for while other
people wear them for me to look at, it's just the same
as if they were my own—but think not of them, but
love, my angel!

Hon. Excuse me, my lord—I cannot accept them
—you may employ them to a better purpose. (*Offering to return them.*)

Lady Acid. Is this your gratitude for his lordship's politeness? Ill-bred, insolent girl! What, you
are still hankering after that wretch, Clairville?

Hon. Call him by some other name, madam—
Wretch! What is his brother, then?

Lady Acid. How! have you the impudence to defend the outcast?

Hon. Outcast! Shame, shame, madam! I know
I talk a language you and your modish friends de-
spise---but here I tell you, that this outcast is the
man of my heart—that it loves him---tenderly loves
him---and would rather share his griefs in a prison,
than his lordship's pleasure in a palace---therefore,
once more, let me offer back this present.

Lady Acid. Look ye, in a word, let me have no
more of your ill breeding. Accept his lordship's
jewels directly, and retire to your chamber---Take
them, I say, and begone this instant.

Hon. What can I do? The colonel's high opinion
of her compels me to obey her in every thing—Oh,
Clairville! why did you save a life that's doom'd, for
ever doom'd, to mix thy ruin with its own? [*Exit.*

Lady Acid. So far, so well, my lord! For when
the colonel hears she was mercenary enough to receive jewels, he'll own you were warranted in your
designs upon her---and now---since we are alone---
I'll open a great and glorious scheme---a scheme
that shall convince you of my unalter'd affection.

Lord Jar. Sweetest of women! you know my determination.---Whoever has my hand, you shall still have my heart.

Lady Acid. I believe it, my lord---and, therefore, I shall risk the dangerous enterprise---Sophia and I were at the exhibition of wax figures this morning--- She was struck with, and purchased, a great theatrical likeness, which is to be brought here in a chair this evening—Now, if you contrive to come home instead of the figure—

Lord Jar. I a wax figure! a peer of the realm a wax figure!

Lady Acid. Dear! it happens every day—But, mind me, the chair will be brought to my dressing-room, which adjoins Honoria's chamber—and where you know you can't be admitted on account of Sir Andrew's jealousy—therefore wait for the chair, bribe the man, and here is a false key, (*Gives one*) which locks and unlocks Honoria's door.

Lord Jar. Loveliest of creatures! (*Kisses her hand*) Where shall I find the chair?

Lady Acid. I'll give you the particulars by and by—In the mean time, remember you get Clairville disposed of——

Lord Jar. What, my brother! Oh, I've so great a friendship for him, that I'll have him arrested, to prevent his being distressed——

[*Flourish of clarionets.*

Lady Acid. Hark! their lordships, the musicians, are arrived.

Enter COLONEL HUBBUB.

Col. There they are! never was Sunday concert so sanctified with nobility.

Lady Acid. What! they're all come?

Col. Yes; and faith there's so many great people turned fiddlers now-a-days, that I should not be surprised, if the House of Lords should be turned into

a concert room ! that glees were sung from the Wool-
sack, and catches from the Cabinet.

Lord Jar. Who have we amongst us, colonel ?

Col. I'll tell you.—First, there's Duke Duett playing on the violin---then there's General Grig blowing the trumpet, Judge Jerk blowing the bassoon,
and Bishop Bravo banging the kettle-drums !—But
what's better, there's Signor Uniquo, who pats them
all familiarly on the back, and says, " bravissimo, my
Lord Judge ! Encora, Signor Bishop !" Then, the
one looks as pleased as if he'd got the chancellorship,
and the other, as if he was preferred to an archbi-
shoprick !—Pray is your lordship fond of music ?

Lord Jar. Me ! I hate, I detest it !

Lady Acid. Hate music ! my lord ! Dear ! I always
thought it was one of your favourite amusements.

Lord Jar. What, music ! Oh, certainly—I love it
of all things.

Col. Well ; for my part I shall not listen to their
lordships, till Uniquo gets them engaged at the opera
—As to you, Lady Acid, I know your sense and virtue despises this trifling folly, and you only promote
it to amuse your friends.

Lady Acid. I do indeed, colonel—(*Strumming of
instruments within.*) I must go and look at them—
Come, my lord.

Lord Jar. (*Taking her hand.*) With pleasure !—
Colonel, is my friend Nominal amongst them ?

Col. My ward ! Zounds ! don't talk of him—but
go, and if you wish for fiddling preferment, pay your
respects to the Grand Signor.

[*Exeunt Lord and Lady.*
My ward, indeed ! Oh that stupid, studious puppy !
I know what it will end in—He'll go sneaking on in
his profession, tell he gets into the Upper House, then
he'll be laid on the shelf, and go out like the snuff of
a candle.—As to that ruffian and the assault, I'll be

revenged on Clairville still—For Sophia, the dear
creature seems fonder of me than ever, since last
night's riot—The women do love a little rudeness
now and then.

Enter JAMES.

James. Sir, Miss Sophia's maid is below, and desires to see you.

Col. There! I said so—Oh, I and my epaulette
play the devil with the women!

James. She has a letter for you, sir.

Col. A letter! Ah! I must—poor Sir Andrew!
he wouldn't believe I was her darling hope.

James. That she will deliver to nobody but yourself, sir.

Col. Well; if it must be so—it's very strange what
can make the sex adore me so passionately!—It must
be my manners, my tender, graceful, insinuating
manners! Shew me to her, James; and, while their
lordships are fiddling for the good of the nation, I'll
amuse myself for the benefit of Sophia, poor Sophia!
—Oh, colonel! colonel! what fools do you make of
the women!   [*Exit, followed by* JAMES.

SCENE III.

SIR ANDREW ACID'S *Garden.*

Enter SAUNTER.

Saun. Where can my cousin Sophia be loitering!
This is the place of assignation, and I see neither
her, nor the colonel, nor Sir Andrew—I hope there's
no mistake, for on their exposition depends her future happiness.

Enter SOPHIA, *hastily.*

Soph. Oh, cousin! my dear cousin, I'm undone! —as much ruined as if I'd never been an authoress, or an actress, or a painter, or a——

Saun. Why, what has happened?

Soph. Lady Acid, unknown to Sir Andrew, has read the assignation you made me send him—she is now convinced the love is on my part, and is pursuing me here to be revenged—Dear me, I wish I had not written to him.

Saun. Not written to him! unless you'd put a stop to his and the colonel's vanity, you know you'd have been sent into the country—nay, lost your character, and never shewn your face in fashionable life again.

Soph. Never shewn my face! Lord! it rather helps one ; and, in fashionable life, loss of character makes one's reputation. But what is to become of me? If I'm sent to the country, I shall die, I know I shall, and so suddenly, I shan't have time to write my own life, and run down half my acquaintance.

LADY ACID, (*without.*)

Lady Acid. Where is the Jezebel? I'll make an example of her.

Soph. Here she comes! and I shall be locked up in an old country castle, where there's a constant knocking at the gates to see the apartments, but not a person to enquire after poor I, the prisoner.

Enter LADY ACID.

Lady Acid. So, Miss, notwithstanding the warning I gave you, you have been writing an assignation to my husband---and this is the place---Look at me---answer me---do you deny it?

Soph. No, madam ; I own that I wrote such assignations to both the colonel and Sir Andrew.

Lady Acid. The colonel too! mercy on me! wouldn't one content you?

Soph. Yes, madam; but I did it to bring them together, and laugh at them; for indeed they have so teased me——

Lady Acid. They teased you? here's effrontery! look ye, I know they hate and despise you, and they have both told me, a thousand times, that your love was troublesome and disgusting.

Saun. Your ladyship, I can contradict that---for I have now in my pocket both their answers to Sophia's assignation---each accepts her invitation, and will be here at the time appointed----besides, you must be sensible that her loving them is a joke.

Lady Acid. Joke! don't talk to me of jokes, sir--- I never made one in my life; and I know she loves them as much as they detest her---and it's all owing to her romantic turn of mind, her acting, her writing——

Soph. Nay, my lady, don't abuse my talents---- didn't my last production go through four editions?

Lady Acid. Yes; and why did it? because it was patronized. And, now-a-days, it is not the book itself, but the name of the person who writes it. While the woman of fashion shall write a bad work, and have a thousand subscribers, a poor neglected man of genius shall write a good one, and not have a single patron! If, indeed, you had followed my advice---written sentimentally and morally---

Soph. I did, madam----I did write morally: and what was the consequence? I had made a sum of money by a novel called " Seduction," and lost it all by writing an " Essay on Charity;" but, indeed, Sir Andrew and the colonel are to blame; and if you'll wait a moment, you'll see them come to the assignation.

Lady Acid. They come! they know better---besides despising you, they value my good opinion too

highly, to trifle with it in this manner---so, retire to
the country.   [*Laying hold of her.*
Saun. Pray hear reason, madam.
Lady Acid. I'll hear nothing ; she shall be punished ! she shall ! (*Sees* SIR ANDREW, *without.*) Bless
me ! what do I see ? my husband, capering and smiling !
Soph. Ay ; there's one of them----and see, madam, yonder's the other.
Lady Acid. The colonel, as I live ! this is amazing ! stand back, and let's observe them.

Enter SIR ANDREW, *with a Letter in his hand.*

Enter COLONEL HUBBUB, *with a Letter in his hand.*

Col. " Thou dear perfidious !"
Sir And. " Thou gay deceiver !"
Col. " I idolize you as much as I despise Sir An-
drew."
Sir And. " I adore you as much as I abhor the
colonel."
Soph. (*Coming between them, close to the Colo-
nel.*) My pretty colonel !
Col. There ! (*Turning from her in great joy, and
putting up his letter.*)
Soph. My charming baronet ! (*Coming up to* SIR
ANDREW.)
Sir And. My angel !

SIR ANDREW *turns to embrace her---the Colonel embraces her on the other side----they see one another.*
SOPHIA *stands laughing between them.*

Lady Acid. For shame ! for shame ! is this your
boasted honour ? at your time of life !---" thou dear
perfidious !" [*Exit Colonel.*] and you, what have
you to say for yourself, " thou gay deceiver ?"
Sir And. Say ! (*Tearing the letter.*) why, when
one's completely miserable, nothing is so pleasant as
18

to see a friend in the same situation----Halloa, colonel!   [*Exit*.

Lady Acid. Sophia, I am now convinced of your innocence, and ask your pardon, and will make you amends, by reading your manuscripts, praising your acting, and saying you're so good a letter-writer, that I believe you're the author of Junius. [*Exeunt*.

ACT THE FOURTH.

SCENE I.

The Park.

Enter CLAIRVILLE.

Clair. My distresses crowd on me so fast, that I will endeavour to see my brother once more ; and if he still avoids me, I must banish Honoria from my thoughts, and seek that place abroad my enemies deny me here.

Enter O'WHACK, *hastily.*

O'Whack. Run—fly ! make your escape, your honour—Arrah ! be off before the coquins lay hold of you—By my salvation ! when I think of your misfortunes, I can't help taking out my mouchoir--(*Taking out his handkerchief, and crying.*)

Clair. What is the matter, O'Whack ?

O'Whack. The matter ! why, if you don't scamper, you'll be bastiled before you can say " Killarney !"

Clair. What can this mean ? explain.

O'Whack. Doucement !—I'll tell you—As I pass-ed yonder promenade, an old friend of mine, who is an officer, or bailiff, d'ye see, told me he was co-ming to carry your honour to prison—What, Mon-sieur Clairville ? says I—The same, says he—Then, says I, be asy now ; for, by St Patrick, if you touch a hair of his head, I'll soup-maigre you this instant. —Says he, I must do my duty——And I mine, says I : and remember, my honey, it is as asy to have pity in your heart, as it is to speak French without the brogue, ma foi !   This softened him, your ho-nour, and he promised to be a cher ami to you till to-morrow.

Clair. Thanks, my good fellow ! thanks !

O'Whack. C'est ne pas tout, though ; Fanny, Miss Sophia's maid, as pretty a fille de chambre as ever made a faux pas, gave me a bit of a hint that there was a curst black business in the wind between your brother, Lord Jargon, and Lady Acid—She thinks they mean to put you in limbo, because Mademoi-selle Honoria loves you ; and, by my soul, if they do, I'll make the old cat cry " Misericorde" till she's black in the face !

Clair. I won't believe it—I know Lord Jargon loves Honoria ; but I can never think, that, on that account, he'd make a prisoner of his brother——But he's coming this way—I'll talk to him—leave us to-gether.

O'Whack. That I will, with all my heart and soul ; for I can't bear to put my eyes upon him——Bon re-pos to your honour—I'll give you a call in the morn-ing ; and, in the mean time, be debonaire, d'ye see ; —I'll carry you through, depend on't.

Clair. My kind fellow—how shall I repay you ?

O'Whack. Oh, your honour, I never forget an ob-ligation, though I may an injury—You saved me in danger ; and if I don't do mon possible to bother all

your enemies, say I'm not the bonne bouch of the
O'Whacks, that's all!   [*Exit.*

Clair. I cannot, will not, suspect him of such
treachery—Though he has been long dead to bro-
therly affection, he never can be capable of such inhumanity.

Enter LORD JARGON.

Lord Jar. (*Aside.*) This poor wretch here! I was
in hopes he was disposed of.

Clair. Brother, a word; I have a favour to entreat of you ; for necessity, extreme necessity, compels me—in short, if you do not assist me, I shall be
arrested in an hour, and in jail, perhaps the remainder of my life.

Lord Jar. Arrested! who can be so hard-hearted,
Harry? You know my friendship and liberality ; but,
as to lending you money, that's a thing I can't make
up my mind to.

Clair. The sum I require is small, my lord—a few
hundreds will convey me far from the persecution of
my creditors ; and, by retirement and economy, in
a few years, perhaps, I shall be able to repay you
with honour, and once more appear in the world as
your lordship's brother.

Lord Jar. I hope you may, Harry—but petitions
are so numerous——

Clair. Petition! 'tis my demand, sir. When the
old lord died, you know, he left his fortune to you,
in the full conviction you would provide for me—
and this is the return! while you are affluent enough
to squander thousands in the whirlpool of fashion,
you are cruel enough to see a brother waste his life
in poverty! But go on, my lord—exult and riot in
my father's riches—I will be prouder of his virtues!

Lord Jar. Oh, the old cant! You never heard me
utter a sentiment in your life—never! for the man
who boasts of virtue and feeling, seldom practises

either the one or the other——But you detain me,
Harry—I am going to sigh away an hour with Honoria.

Clair. (*Eagerly.*) With Honoria, brother?

Lord Jar. Yes, with Honoria, brother! don't you
envy me my triumph?

Clair. Ungenerous man! is it not enough to a-
bandon me to the world, a beggar and a wanderer,
but you must wound me in the tenderest point—distract me with such thoughts? But I have done——
farewell, my lord! perhaps we shall never meet a-
gain!——I now suspect him, and will warn Honoria
of her danger. (*Aside.*)

Lord Jar. Adieu, Harry!—shall I tell the charming girl any thing about you?

Clair. Yes, sir—tell her, pursued by enemies, and
deserted by my friends, I know not where to fly for
safety! Tell her, not so much on my own account,
I lament my misfortunes, as on hers; since, abject
and forsaken as I am, I cannot shelter or protect
her! Tell her, I once hoped—forgive my weakness.
(*Weeping.*)——But if you have one spark of pity for
the lost Clairville, bestow it on Honoria——be her
friend, and you shall still be mine—Farewell!

[*Exit.*

Lord Jar. Ay; go your ways; you'll never see
her again——for here comes the chair that gives me
possession of her for ever.

Enter Chairmen with Chair.

Set it down, and wait till I return—I must step over
to my house, to order servants to be near at hand;
for though I'm determined not to be violent, yet, if
she demurs, I'll force her—I'll——

Enter NOMINAL, *half drunk, singing.*

Nom. Ha! peer! my boy, how are you?—I hate
wine; but I've been drinking to keep up my cha-

racter; and I'm the most unlucky dog alive——I've been searching every where for an adventure, and can't find one—I can't get into notice.

Lord Jar. Can't you?

Nom. No; I can't make myself conspicuous! and yet I've been absurd, particular, and noisy——but what signifies? every body else is the same! The whole town's so ridiculous, that to be stared at, a man should be as quiet and as dull as—a simile! Hey! peer! (*Taking snuff, and offering* LORD JAR-GON *some.*)

Lord Jar. How can you drink? I hate it——If I indulged myself in such odious customs, do you think I should be a favourite with the women? (*Taking a pinch.*)

Nom. Favourite with the women! ay, there's the rub! If I could get the fame of an intrigue, or an elopement, or any other sweet impropriety, oh!—

Lord Jar. Intrigue or elopement!—Um!

Nom. Um! why, what's the matter with you?

Lord Jar. Look ye, Nominal—nothing is so shocking as to impart secrets, or boast of a lady's favours; —it's what I never do, sir—else I could tell you—

Nom. Tell me!—what?

Lord Jar. That I am this moment going on both an intrigue and an elopement!

Nom. The devil you are! who? when? where? open, unfold, you amiable—you surprising senator!

Lord Jar. Fie! do you think I'd betray the confidence of the fair? No; if I was only to hint to you that that chair—that very chair—was to take me to a certain baronet's house, instead of a wax figure—

Nom. Wax figure! go on—dispatch! I'm all on fire! wheugh! (*Rubbing his hands, and shewing signs of great joy.*)

Lord Jar. I say, I should be the greatest rascal living, if I was only to hint that I intrigued with the baronet's wife, that she was to conduct me to the

chamber of a young lady, and that their names
were——

Nom. Hang their names! only let me understand.
—That chair, you say, takes you to the lady with
whom you intrigue, and she conducts you to the girl
with whom you elope? (LORD JARGON *nods assent.*)
Bravo, my boy! bravo! give me your hand; and
now, curse me if I can help laughing, to think how
they'll all be surprised! ha, ha, ha!

Lord Jar. No, nor I—the old husband little thinks
who's coming to make a fool of him! ha, ha, ha!
But, excuse me a moment—I must step over the
way to order servants to be near the house—Stay till
I return, and you'll see what a figure I'll make in
the chair.

Nom. Yes, yes—I'll stay—But go over the way—
get along with you, wheugh!

Lord Jar. I say, Nominal, I fancy you'd like to
go in the chair instead of me? Ha, ha, ha!

Nom. Yes, that I would, ha, ha, ha!

                                      [*Exit* LORD JARGON.
And if I don't!—if I don't perch myself in the center of it—damme if I know any thing of fame or notoriety! Gad, this is the luckiest hit—I might have
been whole years luring one woman into an intrigue,
or another into an elopement——but here's the business ready cut out to my hands; and, therefore, that
no time may be lost—you two coronet-supporters,
(*Laying hold of Chairmen.*) open the chair, and let
me be the peer's proxy!—take me to the baronet's
directly, or, by all that's singular——

First Chair. Blood and oons! is the man beside
himself?

Nom. (*Shaking them.*) No trifling!—Here's a
purse and a pistol! Money or murder! take your
choice this moment!

Second Chair. Take the money, Pat, take the money.

Nom. Here, you rogues, here! (*Giving purse.*) And now I swear, whatever were his lordship's designs, mine shall be harmless and honourable! All I want is the fame of the thing, and if I can get that, hang me if I'll fatigue myself or the ladies! So, open the chair, and away, my boys! (*Gets in, and looks from window.*) When you see his lordship tell him the next time he is going on an amour, not to mention it before hand—Lead on to notoriety! Drink and drive care away!   [*Exit in chair.*

Re-enter LORD JARGON.

Lord Jar. Now, Nominal, now you shall see what a figure I'll cut in the chair!—How! what! gone! the chair too! 'Sdeath! I cut a very pretty figure indeed!—But, I'll be revenged—I'll follow him, and have satisfaction directly; and for Clairville and Honoria, I'll betray one, and imprison the other! I will, as I'm a gentleman and a man of honour.

[*Exit.*

SCENE II.

LADY ACID's *Dressing-room.*—*Toilette.*—*Doors open in Flat—and part of a Bed seen—Chairs and Candles.*

Enter HONORIA *with a letter.*

Hon. Can it be possible? Can she who should protect me, thus betray me? I will not, dare not, believe it! and yet would Clairville terrify me with false suspicions? Let me read the letter once more —(*Reads.*) " I have been just informed, that Lord Jargon and Lady Acid have designs against you, and that, to-night, they mean to put their villainy in ex-

ecution—I hope they cannot be so treacherous; but
as you love my peace or your own, be on your guard
—beware, Honoria! and remember the unhappy
Clairville!" If it be true, how shall I extricate myself? The colonel is so convinced of Lady Acid's
honour, that all supplication to him would be in
vain—Alas! I have no friend to succour or defend
me, and helpless as I am—Ha! she comes! I dread
to meet her.

Enter Lady Acid.

Lady Acid. How! not gone to your chamber, Honoria?

Hon. I'm going, madam—Her very look alarms
me. (*Aside.*)

Lady Acid. What is the girl muttering! I declare
you grow more and more forward and impertinent
every hour—but I'll humble you—I'll make an example of you!

Hon. (*Kneeling.*) Oh! on my knees let me entreat
your pity! do not desert me, do not abandon me—
promise me I shall not be in the power of Lord Jargon, and I'll be your slave for ever.

Lady Acid. Lord Jargon! why, what's the fool
thinking of? Have you lost your senses?

Hon. No—not yet, madam—but if I retain them,
it must be by your humanity—you have often said
that you would be a mother to me—be so now—save
me from this hour of danger, and——

Lady Acid. Danger! let me hear no more of this
insolence, but be gone!——

Enter Betty, *followed by Chairmen with Chair.*

Bet. The chair, with the figure, your ladyship.

Lady Acid. Put it down and leave it. (*Exeunt* Betty *and Chairmen.*) Now comes my triumph! (*Aside.*)
How! not gone yet, Miss? Retire this instant, or—

Hon. I obey, madam—Oh! what, what will become of me?   [*Exit.*

Lady Acid. There she goes! and now for my dear, dear lord! (*Taps at chair window.*) Lord Jargon! Lord Jargon! come forth, and, my dear lord, ensure your prize—-(NOMINAL *lets down the front glass, looks at her, and nods.*) Heavens! what do I see?

Nom. No lord, or wax figure, but as lively a fellow as ever you intrigued with—(*Spying.*) Fine jolly woman.

Lady Acid. Who are you? has his lordship sent you to insult me?

Nom. No; he has sent me not to disappoint you. (*Spying again.*) Rather fat though—(*Knock.*)

Lady Acid. Mercy! there's my husband!

Nom. (*Eagerly.*) Your husband? Tell me, my darling, tell me, is he jealous?

Lady Acid. Jealous!—to an extreme!

Nom. What! he'll bring an action, and sue for a divorce?

Lady Acid. Yes.

Nom. Paragraph and caricature me?

Lady Acid. Certainly.

Nom. Challenge and fight me?

Lady Acid. Undoubtedly.

Nom. Huzza! bravo! I'm made! I'm immortalized! let me out, and let him in directly.

COLONEL HUBBUB, *without.*

Col. In her dressing-room, is she? never mind— I have the privilege of going into it.

Lady Acid. The colonel! worse and worse!

Nom. My guardian! zounds! he mustn't discover me here.

Lady Acid. Sir, if you have any gallantry, or—

Nom. Say no more, my dove, I'm snug; (*Putting up window.*) good b'ye, I'll make you comfortable—(*Nodding, and shutting himself in.*)

Enter COLONEL HUBBUB.

Lady Acid. Colonel, I rejoice to see you.

Col. I beg pardon, madam, for this intrusion ; but when you know my business, I think you'll forgive me—I come to give Honoria to Lord Jargon.

Lady Acid. Is't possible, colonel ?

Col. Yes ; I have made up my mind at last—the high opinion I have of your honour, and the great respect I entertain for his lordship, as your friend, has tempted me to sign this deed of settlement— (*Producing one.*) which gives him Honoria, with a fortune of £30,000.

Lady Acid. My dear colonel, you delight me.

Col. Ay ; she will be then safe from the artifices of Clairville, and your virtuous wishes will be satisfied——you know I once designed her for my ward Nominal.

Lady Acid. Yes ; but he is too dissipated and profligate.

Col. He profligate ! why, he's the most studious, stupid blockhead alive ; I dare say he is now in his library, poring over Puffendorf, or hemming (*Mimicking.*) with Paul Prig.

Lady Acid. Well ! I never saw him, colonel ; but I've heard he's the most noisy, riotous young man in town—has his amours—his——

Col. Amours ! I should as soon suspect your ladyship of an intrigue as he—-Noisy and riotous too ! Oh that he was ! I'd give him a borough to-morrow. (NOMINAL *here raises the top of chair, and pops his head out.*)

Nom. Hem ! (*Retires directly.*)

Col. Zounds ! what's that ? (*Going towards chair.*) The devil ! here's somebody in the chair !

Lady Acid. Ha, ha ! you'll laugh when I tell you what it is—it's a purchase of Sophia's.

Col. Purchase ! I swear I saw a man's head.

Lady Acid. A man! ha, ha! that's very good!—
it's a wax figure.

Col. A wax figure!

Lady Acid. Yes; and, as Sir Andrew knows nothing of it, I entreat you not to tell him.

Col. Oh, I understand——what, it's to supply his
place when he's out of the way?—Well, well! (*Trying to look at it.*)

Lady Acid. Fie, colonel! an't you ashamed to
look at a lady's curiosities? Positively, if you don't
come away, I'll have it removed. (*Pulling him away.*)
But how could you suppose it to be a man? suspect
me of an intrigue?

Col. I don't suspect you—I believe you to be all
virtue, tenderness, and truth.

Sir Andrew Acid, *without*.

Sir And. Ay, ay; I'll tell her myself—(*Speaking
as he enters.*) My dear, Lord Jargon is below, and
desires to see you directly.

Lady Acid. I'm busy, Sir Andrew; let him wait.

Col. (*Aside, to* Lady Acid.) No, no—softly—I
have a thought—is Honoria at home?

Lady Acid. Yes; she's in the next room.

Col. Then, hark ye, as his lordship is below, go
to him, and tell him my intentions; and if he approves, he shall have Honoria this very moment.

Lady Acid. I will, colonel—Oh Lord! here is Sir
Andrew!——As you regard me, don't mention the
figure——If that fellow is discovered, my character's
lost for ever. (*Aside.*)   [*Exit.*

Enter Sir Andrew.

Sir And. So, dear perfidious!

Col. So, gay deceiver! Ah, Sir Andrew, you
ought to blush for your inconstancy——so good, so
faithful a wife as Lady Acid——

Sir And. It's very true, colonel; and if I didn't

think it would make her too happy, I'd own my errors——she is indeed all virtue——I'll tell you what—
she has all your gaieties, with your ward Nominal's
prudence.

Col. Plague take you! am I never to hear of any
thing but that stupid dog's prudence? But your
wife, Sir Andrew—all her amusements are so innocent—wax now—she prefers wax to real life. (*Looking round at chair.*)

Sir And. Wax!

Col. Yes; though she'd die before she'd have a
young man in her room, I don't think she has much
objection to a wax-figure.

Sir And. Wax figure! why, what the devil are
you at?

Col. I didn't say there was one in a sedan chair,
did I?

Nom. No; but I do, though—Zounds! would you
keep me in obscurity?

> [NOMINAL *walks solemnly out between him and
> the Colonel. They stand astonished.*]

LADY ACID *re-enters.*

Sir And. Zounds! the wax figure is a live gallant!

Col. Yes; and my studious ward is a dashing dog
at last!

Nom. Yes; it's I, guardy, who was a student in
the morning, who caned you at night—who will fight
that gentleman, who intrigues with this lady, (*Embracing* LADY ACID.) and will elope with any body!
and what's more, who rejoices to discover himself,
because he exposes hypocrisy, and saves an innocent
girl from misery.

Col. (*Dancing and singing.*) Ti, di, di, di! he has
it! he has it! he has it! the rogue's the true thing
after all!—Come to thy old guardian's arms! let me
gaze on thy dear face!—There it is! the real tumul-

tuous, dashing look! You dog, you shall come into parliament to-morrow.

Lady Acid. Are you mad, colonel?

Sir And. Ay; dam'me, are you mad, colonel?

Col. (*To* Lady Acid.) Out of the way, dissembler! I know you now, and despise you—But is he a real man of sense at last? Will he give up Westminster Hall, Puffendorf, and Paul Prig, to intrigue, elope, fight a baronet, and cane a colonel in the guards? Oh, 'tis too much! Give me joy, old boy!

Sir And. Good night. (*Going.*)

Lady Acid. Sir Andrew, I insist on a hearing.

Nom. Stay, baronet—I hope you're satisfied?

Sir And. Satisfied of what?

Nom. That it's I, and not any body else, who intrigues with this all-virtuous woman—upon my soul, it's me—and do mention it every where, do, there's a sweet, smiling, pleasant fellow; say it's me, and we'll all get into print together.

Sir And. Damnation!   [*Exit.*

Lady Acid. Hear me, Sir Andrew——I'll follow him, and explain the business directly—For you, colonel, I leave you to your delusion; and for your prudent ward—oh! was there ever any thing so unlucky!

Col. Go your ways, hypocrite!——And now, my boy, my darling, let's to supper, and crown the night with mirth and merriment—Odsheart! what a likeness of me, and his old uncle! Come; for I do so long to hear the history of your pranks——

Nom. Ay; you shall hear them all, from Paul Prig to the justice—from the peer to the wax-figure; and then if you don't say I'm as eccentric and ridiculous as you wish me—why, I'll never beat a jack-ass again as long as I live.   [*Exeunt.*

ACT THE FIFTH.

SCENE I.

Outside of SIR ANDREW'S *House.*

Enter O'WHACK.

O'Whack. Oh! my poor master!—he's dead! but-
chered! murdered! shot in a duel, by that Burgeois
peer, Lord Jargon! Misericordie! misericordie!
what shall I do to bring him to life again? I'll go
home—I'll——

Enter SAUNTER.

Saun. So, O'Whack, Lord Jargon has called out
my friend Nominal, in consequence of the affair at
Lady Acid's?

O'Whack. C'est vrai, your honour—and he'll never go out again—Il est mort—(*Weeping.*)

Saun. How?

O'Whack. He's dead—dead as King Lear.

Saun. Astonishing! Who told you this?

O'Whack. Myself! my own sad self! I always
said, when Mr Nominal went out to fight a rencontre——

Saun. What?

O'Whack. That he was too much of a gentleman
to come home alive again—Oh! he and Blunder
O'Whack are one for that——But, your honour, is
there no way of putting a little breath into him?

Saun. Ridiculous! you know nothing of the matter, I see—and I'm all anxiety to hear the issue of this unhappy duel.

O'Whack. Et moi aussi——and I'll go home and wait for his relief—Oh, he's dead! he's dead! and here am I, a solitaire, in the wide world by myself!

[*Exit.*

Saun. Where can I gain intelligence? I have a thousand fears for my friend—Lord Jargon, I know, is full of animosity, and Nominal is too fond of fame to make him an apology—Poor fellow! if he should be killed, or even wounded——

Enter NOMINAL.

Nom. Wounded! why, here I am, George, as sound and as merry——Wounded!—Oh, you dull dog!

Saun. Dull! why, from your servant's account, I might suppose you were dead.

Nom. Dead! Pshoo! do you think I don't know better? Hark ye, since we're alone, I'll let you into a secret—Lord Jargon wanted to challenge me, but couldn't summon up courage: so, sooner than lose the glory of a combat with so great a man, I consented to—— (*Whispering him.*) you understand me; we fought to satisfy the town, not ourselves.

Saun. Satisfy the town! how do you mean?

Nom. How do I mean? why, do you think we fought to please ourselves? Nonsense! that's been gone by long ago—No, no; the case was this—He was compelled to fight to save his reputation, and I chose to fight to get a name! So we kept up appearances, measured ground, exchanged shots—seconds interfered, applauded our spirit, signed the report—and now we're both men of honour as long as we live!—There, you rogue—shot ourselves into notice!

Saun. Bravo! and while the world is sanguinary enough to compel those to bleed like heroes, who

wish to live like men, why, you and his lordship
may glory in having tricked them. But, since my
cares on your account are over, allow me to enquire
at this house after my cousin Sophia—Poor girl! Sir
Andrew has behaved to her in a manner so cruel
and inhuman——

SOPHIA opens the Window.

Soph. Cousin! cousin! I'm locked up——I can't
get out—Sir Andrew has confined me in this room,
till he sends me to the country for life!

Nom. Here's a pretty business!

Saun. What! he was offended at the sham assignation, was he?

Soph. So he says-—But I know it's all owing to
his wife—he is so out of humour with her, that he
must be revenged on somebody. Cousin, won't you
assist me? Will you let me be buried in woods, and
waste my youth with fat calves and sucking pigs?

Nom. No; before you shall waste an hour, I'll kill
all the fat calves and sucking pigs in England—Fair
lady, if your cousin don't release you, I will——Gad,
I was only thinking of an elopement, and pop she
comes to my purpose!

Saun. Be patient, Sophia—I'll go directly to the
colonel, and request his interference with Sir Andrew—But hush! the old tyrant's coming this way;
—shut down the window, and depend on my protection.

Nom. And on mine, sweet excellence! (SOPHIA
disappears.) Faith, that is the luckiest house-—last
night I helped a gentleman into it, and to-day, perhaps, I may hand a lady out of it——I'll have her,
whoever she is——My dear Saunter, tell me what's
her name?

Saun. Don't you know her? It's Sir Andrew's
ward, Sophia; a great authoress and private actress.

Nom. A private actress! that's a public character! Then there's a pair of us; and if we elope, we shall alarm all Europe!

Saun. She has heard of you, Nominal, and, between ourselves, has a great prepossession in your favour—she loves singularity, and is consequently so fond of your character——

Nom. There! I said it would happen——the moment I got the fame of a duel and an intrigue, I knew no woman could stand me! But, George, my boy! how can I see her? speak to her? is there no way?

Saun. None, unless you can prevail on her guardian—Here he is! try him—for my part, I'll to the colonel.

Nom. I will——I'll try him, George; and if I can coax him into an interview, (*Exit* SAUNTER.) I'll humour him, give him a touch in his own way.

Enter SIR ANDREW ACID.

Sir And. Plague on them all, I say; but chiefly that devil incarnate, that Nominal!

Nom. Sir Andrew, I want to ask a favour of you.

Sir And. Do you? I never grant any, sir.

Nom. Nay, you don't know me, Sir Andrew——if you did, you'd grant me any thing—I am a man after your own heart, (*In a melancholy voice.*) I am indeed; so out of humour with the world, that, like you, I wish to see every body in it as miserable as myself.

Sir And. You do, do you?

Nom. Yes, indeed, sir—and if you knew how misanthropically I spent my time—Oh! I once passed such a happy day, Sir Andrew! entirely in your own way—I'll tell you——

Sir And. Exactly in my way!

Nom. Yes, sir; I awoke at five, and saw a neighbour's house on fire! was second in a duel at six, and my man lost the tip of his ear! dined at four, and something in the wine that made six of my acquaintance sick—drank tea, and intrigued with my friend's wife till eight—a fat lady!—went to the new comedy, saw it completely damned—supped with the poor devil of an author; and, to conclude, lodged six of the actors in the round-house! there! wasn't that a happy day! And now, let me see your ward.

Sir And. See Sophia! zounds! neither you nor any body else shall ever see her again! That chaise —(*Points to one without*) is waiting to take her to the country directly, and she shall live and die in an old castle on a brown moor.

Nom. Shall she?

Sir And. Yes; I'll be revenged on her for you all! And so your servant——

[*Knocking at his own door.*

Nom. Stay, thou dear connoisseur in wax-figures, and tell me, how's your wife?

Sir And. Out of the way, sir!—I'll punish her too, —and for you and the rest——

Nom. Ay; you'd play the devil with all mankind if you could.

Sir And. If they were like you, I would; for then the world would be so wicked, that an honest man couldn't make too much mischief! But, because my wife has deceived me, don't think my ward shall— No, no; I have her safe, I'll teach her to make assignations—(*Servant opens door.*) And so, once more your servant, prudent Mr Student! [*Enters house.*

Nom. I shall lose her! here'll be no elopement! no being pursued by her relations—hunted by the court of Chancery—advertised by government, or, what's best of all, carried to the Fleet or King's Bench, 'midst the shouts of old maids, and groans of boarding-school misses!

Enter SOPHIA *from the house, with her cloak on.*

Soph. So—Heaven be praised, I have made my escape—and now, if I knew where to fly for protection—

Nom. (*Having observed her.*) Fly into my arms, my angel—I'll put you into that chaise in a moment, out of town in an instant, at Gretna Green in a second, and in all the newspapers and print-shops before to-morrow morning!

Soph. Upon my word, sir, I'm very much obliged to you! (*Curtsies.*) Pray, may I ask who you are?

Nom. Who I am? Why, if you don't know me, you know nothing—I'm Nominal.

Soph. Nominal! Is it possible? What! the gentleman who so generously released me from the colonel, and has since made so much noise and confusion?

Nom. Yes; I'm the man! I've made a noise! and, if you love notoriety, you must prefer me to all heroes, past, present, or to come! My angel! (*Takes her hand*) where shall I conduct you? As far or as near as you please—(*Aside.*) I shall get as much fame by two miles as two hundred; for, though I mean to be honourable, I know the world is too scandalous to think me so!

Soph. Ah! I wish I could depend on you—You see I've no resource—I must either return to the tyranny of my guardian, or trust to your honour and generosity.

Nom. Trust! Look ye, my charming girl! I've had an intrigue without an intimacy—a duel without enmity, and I meant to have had an elopement without matrimony! But, by Heaven! there's something in your person and manner has so won upon me, that, let me have the fame of carrying you off, and hereafter you shall dispose of me as you please!

Soph. I believe you; and if you will conduct me to a relation's house, a few miles from town—

Nom. Come along, Sophia!—Faith I've been so long looking for a creature so eccentric as myself, that now I've found one, I'll not easily part with it!

SIR ANDREW *within.*

Sir And. Where are you all, James?

Soph. My guardian's voice—make haste, sir.

Nom. Farewell, old misery, and once more for notoriety—   [*Exit with* SOPHIA.

Re-enter SIR ANDREW *from house.*

Sir And. There they go! that devil of a fellow has carried her off! I'll pursue them—I'll—

Enter COLONEL HUBBUB.

Col.(*Speaking to* NOMINAL.) Huzza! that's right —away with her.—Look, old boy! look there!— First he intrigues with your wife, and then he elopes with your ward! Isn't he a fine fellow? Isn't he like me?

Sir And. Yes; he's as like you as one madman is like another—but I'll overtake him! I'll make him studious again, or beat him as soundly as he beat you! I'll be revenged!   [*Exit.*

Col. I knew I should bring him up to some purpose! Instead of practising law, he'll promote it now, and then for a general election—Oh! what a scene will he make at a general election!

Enter O'WHACK.

O'Whack. And has your honour found him out at last? by my soul, I always said he was as full of mischief as yourself, ma foi.

Col. Yes; that he is! he's me in every thing; and here, thou dear tutor, here's something for the pains you have taken in finishing his education, (*Giving him money.*)

O'Whack. Bien obligé, your honour! I never wanted the dear craters more in my life; for there's a fine young jontleman just thrown into prison, who hasn't a sous to save him from starvation—So, d'ye see, as he once did me a bit of a service, I'll do him another; and then there'll be no mauvaise honte betwixt us, you know—

Col. What is his name, O'Whack?

O'Whack. Monsieur Clairville! Poor lad, I believe he was just going to the Eastern Indies, to bring home a large fortune in his pocket, and a little hole in his liver.

Col. Clairville in prison!

O'Whack. C'est vrais, jewel—his brother, who is a lord, and not a gentleman, d'ye see, had him tapp'd on the shoulder, and thrown into jail for a thousand louis d'ors.

Col. I know his brother's treachery well; and now rejoice that Nominal befriended Clairville instead of injuring him—But go to him, O'Whack, tell him, I'll see Lord Jargon, and do all in my power to assist him—Go, and comfort him.

O'Whack. I'll go directly, and ten thousand blessings on your honour in the bargain—Bon jour! Oh! by the eternal powers! I wish we had his lordship in Ireland—I'd lay my best chapeau to a thirteen, he'd never make a speech about the good of his country again!　　　　　　　　　　　　　　　　[*Exit.*

Col. Poor Clairville! I'll enquire into the matter instantly, and then to hear what Nominal has done with Sophia—Oh! the dear fellow! Now

The breed will be preserved from sire to sire,

And future Hubbubs keep the world on fire.

　　　　　　　　　　　　　　　　　　[*Exeunt.*

SCENE II.

An Apartment with Glass Doors.

Enter HONORIA *from doors, and seeing* LADY ACID
entering, shuts them in great agitation.

Hon. Heavens! Lady Acid!

Lady Acid. What's the matter with you now?
What makes you look so pale?

Hon. Nothing, ma'am! nothing—

Lady Acid. I come to tell you, that that wretch
Clairville is in prison, and will remain there for ever,
unless you have discretion enough to accept Lord
Jargon's offers—then he'll be released—Nay, none
of your airs—his lordship is honourable; he means
marriage.

Hon. Marriage! can his lordship have the condescension?

Lady Acid. Yes; and see where he comes to make
his own proposals.

Enter LORD JARGON.

I've been telling Honoria, my lord, that you'll have
the humanity to release your profligate brother from
prison, if she'll consent to share your title and fortune.

Lord Jar. Am I to be the happy man?

Hon. Never, my lord!

Lord Jar. How! never!

Hon. No.—Let me be the simple Honoria, and
enjoy self-approbation, rather than be the wife of
your lordship, and lose the congratulations of my own
heart.

Lady Acid. Hear me, Honoria—think of the title, the fashion !

Hon. Fashion ! contemptible ! I'm weary of the very word What has it ever done, that there should be such magic in the sound ? 'Tis true, it has thrown a veil over vice, exalted the undeserving, and given a sanction to dissipation ; but has it ever relieved poverty, lessened oppression. or wiped away the tear of suffering virtue ? Name it not then—nor name his lordship as a husband—I shall treat both with equal disdain.

Lord Jar. More sentiments ! and where they came from, Heaven only knows !

Lady Acid. Mighty fine, madam ; but since you're so arrogant, the colonel shall be told of your behaviour—he shall hear of your mean mercenary disposition—What ! though you pretend to despise his lordship, you can receive jewels from him.

Hon. Jewels ! Heavens ! was I not compell'd, madam ?

Lady Acid. No matter—the proof is against you —they are in your possession, and when your uncle hears of it, I'm sure he won't refuse his lordship's offers.

Enter COLONEL HUBBUB.

Col. Won't he ? but he will though! Though I love a lad of spirit, I detest premeditated villainy as much as any man—Your brother Clairville is in prison, my lord ; and I'm told by your means.

Hon. Yes, sir——'tis so——by his, his brother's means.

Lady Acid. Peace ! and let me speak—Colonel, notwithstanding your prejudices against me and Lord Jargon, I know, when you hear the conduct of this mean, avaricious girl, you'll confess, that his lordship has a greater claim to her than any other man— You'll allow fine diamonds are rare things !

Col. Yes; next to modesty and good sense, the rarest things now-a-days to be met with.

Lady Acid. Then, sir, with shame I mention it, she has received a necklace from his lordship, worth a thousand pounds.

Col. How! Is this true, my lord?

Lord Jar. I can't answer you—but I won't deny it.

Lady Acid. She will tell you, that I compell'd her to accept the necklace; but, even if that were the case, she might have returned it to his lordship long ere this time.

Col. 'Tis too plain! I see it by her blushes—Base, sordid girl! where are the diamonds? Produce and give them back to his lordship, or I swear—Go fetch them instantly—What! do you hesitate?

Hon. I have not the necklace by me, sir—I—

Col. What have you done with it then?

Hon. To confess the truth, sir—I have sold it!

Col. and Lady. Sold it!

Hon. Yes, sir; to redeem a picture—to—

Col. A picture! give a thousand pounds for a picture—Let's see that!

Lady Acid. See! she hesitates again! Oh! it's all an imposition, and my lord has been defrauded out of his diamonds.

Hon. Wait but a moment, and I'll shew you how he has been defrauded.

Opens glass doors, and leads out CLAIRVILLE.

Here is the jewel the necklace has redeemed—Here is a treasure worth ten times its value! and here is the man I shall adore as long as I live—(*Embracing him.*)

Col. Clairville!

Clair. Yes; that Clairville, who must have sunk a victim to your's (*To Lady.*) and his lordship's ar-

tifices, had not this lovely angel stretched out her
hand, and saved me from destruction.

Col. Well! this is the prettiest picture I ever saw!
Look, my lord; look, Lady Acid.

Lord Jar. I never was better pleased in my life—
ha, ha!—Damnation!

Col. Nay, pray look—you'll not see such a picture again, and what's better, you'll never see your
diamonds again—Clairville, I give you joy, and almost wish you Honoria's husband; but I've left all
that to my ward—the dear boy has the sole disposal
of her.

Lady Acid. Has he? then I hope he'll marry her
himself—Any thing rather then she should be thrown
away on a pitiful younger brother.

Enter NOMINAL *with* SOPHIA.

Nom. Here we are!—the two wonders of the age
—The elopement's all over the town already—And
now what do you think is the next piece of mischief
we're resolved on?

Col. What?

Nom. Marriage.

Col. Marriage!

Nom. Ay; so it is—I never thought of it—but
two such eccentric creatures are fit for nothing but
each other—We've hurried ourselves into it, and
what's more, we've hurried Sir Andrew into it—And
now, if you'll consent—but dispatch—entreat you be
quick—for the lady's on fire, and I'm—ugh!

Col. Why, Sophia, is this true?

Soph. Even so, colonel! You were so inconstant,
that I was obliged to accept another gay deceiver.

Col. Well, well; take her, with all my heart; so
the glorious breed is preserved, I don't care who
it's by—But, you rogue, you must give up singularity now.

Nom. Must I! no—I'll be more singular than
ever—I'll be so true, so faithful, and so constant a

husband, that the whole fashionable world shall laugh
at me!

Lady Acid. (*Aside to Lord.*) This is misfortune!
—Now he's married himself, perhaps he may give
you Honoria—ask him.

Lord Jar. I will. (*Aside.*) Nominal, a word.

Nom. What, my little antagonist!

Lord Jar. I know you are as much above receiving a bribe as I am of offering one; but if you'll
make Honoria mine, I'll give you half her fortune.

Nom. If you'd give me your own into the bargain, I wouldn't dispose of her so dishonourably—
No, no; your brother is my friend, and, if I have any
interest in Honoria, I hope she may be his for ever
—And now, all I recommend to you, and my old
acquaintance here (*To* LADY ACID.) is, to leave the
world, and take the wax-figure along with you!

[*Exit Lady.*

Col. That's right, my boy!—Every thing shall be
joined to-night—Hands, hearts, and estates! I'll
give Clairville property, and if his lordship has any
more presents, another diamond necklace—why, he
may settle it on the first child.

Nom. Won't you follow her, my lord?

Lord Jar. I follow her! not for a thousand worlds!
—Lady Acid!   [*Exit, calling* LADY ACID.

Enter SIR ANDREW.

Soph. Sir Andrew, I hope you've forgiven me
every thing.

Sir And. Yes, yes; you, and your kindred genius have tormented me so much, that I could not
be better revenged than by marrying you together
—I've lost a wife, and the student has found one,
that's all.

Col. "Which has the better bargain."—Ods
life! old boy, an't you delighted to see us all so
merry?

Sir And. Faith I think I am—but don't be too hard upon me—don't be too merry—lest the devil that's within me should tempt me to make long faces again.

Nom. If he does, it must be at another time, and in another place.

Good humour reigns so absolutely here,
That, when there's cause for censure, none we fear.
So great their candour, they so seldom blame, ⎫
That even Nominal may get a name,   ⎬
And Notoriety—be crown'd with fame.   ⎭

END OF THE FIRST VOLUME.

THE MODERN THEATRE

THE

MODERN THEATRE;

THE MODERN THEATRE

A collection of plays

selected by

MRS. ELIZABETH INCHBALD

First published London, 1811

in ten volumes

Reissued in 1968
in five volumes
by Benjamin Blom, Inc.

Benjamin Blom, Inc.

New York

THE

MODERN THEATRE;

A COLLECTION OF

SUCCESSFUL MODERN PLAYS,

AS ACTED AT

THE THEATRES ROYAL, LONDON.

PRINTED FROM THE PROMPT BOOKS UNDER THE AU-
THORITY OF THE MANAGERS.

SELECTED BY

MRS INCHBALD.

———

IN TEN VOLUMES.

———————————

VOL. II.

SPECULATION.   LAUGH WHEN YOU CAN.
THE DELINQUENT.   FORTUNE'S FOOL.
              FOLLY AS IT FLIES.

———————————

LONDON:

PRINTED FOR LONGMAN, HURST, REES, ORME, AND BROWN,
PATERNOSTER-ROW.

1811.

First published London, 1811
Reissued 1968,
by Benjamin Blom, Inc. Bx 10452

Library of Congress Catalog Card No. 67-13004

Manufactured in the United States of America

SPECULATION;

A

COMEDY,

AS IT IS PERFORMED AT THE

THEATRE-ROYAL, COVENT-GARDEN.

BY

FREDERICK REYNOLDS.

A

DRAMATIS PERSONÆ.

TANJORE,	*Mr Lewis.*
PROJECT,	*Mr Munden.*
ALDERMAN ARABLE,	*Mr Quick.*
CAPTAIN ARABLE,	*Mr Middleton.*
JACK ARABLE,	*Mr Fawcett.*
SIR FREDERICK FAINTLY,	*Mr Claremont.*
VICKERY,	*Mr Farley.*
LADY PROJECT,	*Mrs Mattocks.*
EMMELINE,	*Miss Wallis.*
CECILIA,	*Mrs Mountain.*

SPECULATION.

ACT THE FIRST.

SCENE I.

An Apartment in PROJECT'S *Country House.—A Door in Flat.*

CECILIA *discovered, trying to unlock the door.*

Cec. So, nobody being near, I'll make use of the attendant's key, and, for the second time, converse with my dear Emmeline. We were yesterday interrupted by Sir Frederick, and I had only time to say a few words to my old friend and school-fellow, but now—How ! Sir Frederick again !

Enter SIR FREDERICK FAINTLY.

Cec. Sir, I beg I may not be thus constantly disturb'd.

Sir Fred. Disturb'd ! I would request the same favour, Miss Cecilia, but that nothing on earth ever

disturbs me; and indeed nothing ever pleases me—
I'm in a perfect state of happy *nonchalance*—I fancy
though we're both on the same errand—That door,
heh?

Cec. I told you yesterday, sir, I know nothing
about that door.

Sir Fred. Oh, for shame!—What! do you pretend
not to know that it leads to that part of the house
where Emmeline is lock'd up? Come, come, Miss,
you remember I caught you bribing the attendant
to lend you the key—(CECILIA *walks about in agitation*) now why be affronted? nothing ever affronts
me—no, if you were a man, and chose to say I had
caused all Emmeline's sufferings—that I had behaved like a rascal to her—then send me a challenge
—then cane me—then kick me—why, I shouldn't
be affronted—no, I've too much good breeding and
good temper.

Cec. Very likely, sir; but as a visitor at Mr Project's house here in the country, I pry into no family
secrets—if I did, I believe the story of this young
lady——

Sir Fred. Ah, poor girl! she and all her large fortune had been mine if she hadn't—you understand—
love touch'd her brain.

Cec. How do you mean, sir?

Sir Fred. Why, that's the cause of her present
confinement: to be sure she has lately recovered her
senses—indeed is quite restored; but her guardian
and physician think her entering too suddenly on
the world again might occasion a relapse—therefore
she is kept quiet and close in that part of the house
—Would you believe it, ma'am, she preferr'd another man to me?

Cec. Indeed! and who could be so accomplish'd
as to out-rival a lover like Sir Frederick?

Sir Fred. A cousin of her's, one Captain Arable,

whose father, being averse to the match, sent him to
Gibraltar, where ever since—

Enter a Servant.

Serv. Sir, Lady Project desires to see you immediately.

Cec. There now—you need not be mortified—
there's your equivalent: I'm sure her ladyship prefers you to another man, even to her husband.

Sir Fred. She does, so shew me to her. Miss, if
you should get a peep at Emmeline, tell her, as I'm
always in love in the country——

Cec. In the country! Why not in London?

Sir Fred. Oh, that depends on the part of the
town I'm in—I constantly adapt myself, and in every
street I'm a different man—for instance now: in the
Temple, I'm a lawyer; in St James's-street, a loun-
ger; in St George's church, I'm a married man; in
Doctors' Commons, a bachelor; Guildhall gives me
an appetite; the Alley makes me waddle; in the
Squares I'm not worth a farthing; and in Lombard-
street I've as many plumbs as a banker—So tell Emmeline I still love her, and will still be her husband.
                                        [*Exit.*

Cec. Now then for my charming recluse—(*Opens
a door in flat.*) Emmeline, it is your friend Cecilia!
                          [*She leads in* EMMELINE.

Emm. Oh, forgive me, 'tis so long since I have
seen a friend.

Cec. Come, as we were interrupted yesterday, pray
sit down, and proceed with your story: the little I
have heard makes me anxious to hear more—(*They
sit*)—now, my sweet friend, proceed.

Emm. I will when I am able—First then, did you
ever hear the name of Edward Ara—— you see my
weakness; I have not power to proceed.

Cec. Nay, nay; unbosom your feelings: pray go
on.

Emm. I will, I will—the name of Edward Arable —it is enough to say we loved, and were divided— My father chose Sir Frederick for my husband, and, on the morn of our intended marriage, they falsely told me Edward was no more. What was to be done? my lover dead! about to be united to his rival! my health long worn by grief and disappointment! Oh my friend! I had not strength to combat against such complicated misery: a fever seized me; my harass'd brain was heated to delirium, and merciful forgetfulness gave me that comfort, my friends and father had denied me!

Cec. Poor Emmeline! and during your malady, your father died.

Emm. He did, bequeathing me his whole fortune in case of recovery, and appointing Mr Project my guardian. Now mark what follows: two months ago, the physician, who had the care of me, proclaim'd my health restored, and I came to this house in the full hope of taking possession of my fortune, and sharing it with the man who best deserves it— but what is the reverse? I am confined to those rooms; not suffer'd to be seen or spoken to; my letters intercepted and destroy'd, and when I ask the reason for all this, they say, " Your health's precarious, it requires peace and quiet, and if you mix too suddenly with the world, the joy may occasion a relapse" —The joy! What joy, my friend? What pleasure can there be in mixing with that world, that hitherto has only robbed me of my senses, and thwarted me in my affections?

Cec. True, Emmeline; and now I see the motive for your guardian's conduct—He is an enterprising man—has involved your fortune in his schemes; and at present, not being able to give you a fair account, he keeps you close, till, by some lucky speculation, he is enabled to repay you—But is there no way to extricate you? on means of escaping?

Emm. None; impossible.

Cec. I have contrived to unlock one door in your room, you see; why can't I get the key of the other?

Emm. Because it leads to a pagoda that adjoins the house, and which has not been opened since my confinement. Oh, Cecilia! is it not hard to wake as from a long and frightful dream, and find all true? no cheering friend to dissipate your terrors? nay, even he whose very smiles would clear the clouds around me! he to be absent! he not near to sooth me!

Cec. He knows not of your recovery—your letters have not reach'd him, else—Hush! somebody's coming! (*Looks out.*) It is your guardian! I cannot leave you so unsatisfied—let me go with you—we'll plan some letters that may recall his sensibility—His heart was once humane; and had he not ruin'd himself by living beyond his income—

Emm. Ah! there's the fountain of all modern evil! when once a man exceeds the limits of his fortune, the barrier of honour, as well as prudence, is thrown down—money is borrowed never to be repaid—friends are duped, and become enemies—the gaming-table is flown to as a last effort—till, imperceptibly, step by step, the mind, originally virtuous, becomes desperate, harden'd, and unprincipled! and for these errors I am doom'd to suffer!—But he's here—Oh my father! why was I left to be the sacrifice of another's dissipation and extravagance!

[EMMELINE *and* CECILIA *exeunt at door in flat.*

Enter PROJECT, *followed by a Servant.*

Pro. I tell you, go directly to Portsmouth; take my own carriage and horses, and, when the packet arrives from the East Indies, ask for Mr. Tanjore, and give him this letter—Stop, let me read it once more.———

" My dear Cousin,

" My house in town is magnificently fitted up to receive you—to my house in the country I have added two wings, built in the eastern style, to make it more worthy your acceptance; my carriage, horses, and servants, are waiting to conduct you to London; and I have got a bride for you, young, beautiful and rich."

There, that will please the young nabob;—to be sure it was unlucky my shutting my doors against him before he went to India, but these attentions, and bringing his sister Cecilia to my house, will remove former prejudices, and make it a most successful speculation—There, dispatch.

[Giving letter to the Servant.

Serv. I will, sir.   *[Exit.*

Pro. Then, by marrying him to my ward, Emmeline, I shall prevent any overhawling of accounts, and if I keep her close till he arrives——Here comes my wife in a rage at my refusing her money this morning—the miserly spendthrift! to be saving farthings in the comforts and necessaries of life, and wasting hundreds in luxuries and superfluities.

Enter LADY KATHARINE PROJECT.

Lady Pro. So, Mr Project, how dare you refuse me money when I condescend to send for it?

Pro. Because 'tis time to grow prudent, madam. Wait the event of my speculations before you let folly and extravagance again undo us.

Lady Pro. Extravagance!—Sir, 'tis your speculations that have undone us—haven't they all fail'd? —did'nt the first wise bubble burst into air?—

Pro. The first, madam!

Lady Pro. Yes: didn't you give two thousand pounds for a picture gallery? think the pictures all originals? call it the Asiatic Asiphusicon, and say

you should make a fortune by its exhibition?—Very
well, sir, and didn't the famous picture that you advertised, as the " celebrated champion of England,
by Rembrant," turn out to be nothing more than an
old sign of St George and the Dragon, blown down
from an alehouse in Leadenhall Market? was'nt the
boasted beech tree, by Claude Lorraine, daub'd
out a week before by a glazier's boy in Cheapside?——

Pro. No, no, madam. Besides, if it was, didn't
the speculation on bark make me ample amends?—
didn't I, by the monopoly of that medicine, dispose
of it at my own price?

Lady Pro. No : for the doctors and apothecaries,
finding they could get no profit by it, swore bark
was unwholesome physic, and nobody took it.—
Then didn't you run up so many new houses at Pad-
dington, that many of them were built without stair-
cases ; and by the time one part was finish'd, didn't
another fall all to pieces?—wasn't——

Pro. Zounds! have you done, ma'am?—I say it
is your false œconomy that has hurt my fortune :
saving trifles and squandering thousands.

Lady Pro. Squandering !—What, sir, do you pretend I don't consult cheapness?

Pro. Yes ; but how, madam? you will lame my
best horses by sending them to a cheap blacksmith,
and then give a hundred pounds for a hammercloth
—you will quarrel with your maid for burning two
candles instead of one, and the same night lose a
thousand pounds at faro—and, answer me fairly,
that you might use otto of roses instead of lavender,
haven't you sent me to bed supperless for a whole
month?

Lady Pro. Well ; and what then, sir?

Pro. Then you stint the servants in meat and
drink, only to dress them with bags and nosegays—
and once, when you gave one hundred and fifty

pounds for a curricle, didn't you want me to drive
two miles over impassable roads, only to avoid paying
a turnpike ?—another time, when you and your favourite Sir Frederick———

Lady Pro. There he always strikes me dumb—
Oh! if I could recriminate! (*Aside.*) Well, sir:
what of Sir Frederick? I'm sure there's no impropriety in our intimacy: we are never tête a tête—
At the theatre, the opera, all public places, my
grandmother is always present; and if ever Sir Frederick kist the tip of my finger, the old lady saw it.

Pro. That's impossible; for the old lady's as blind
as Cupid.—However, it isn't our interest to quarrel;
and, if my schemes on the alderman and the nabob
turn out as I expect, you shall have what money
vou desire—Come, shake hands,—and now walk with
me towards Aldgate farm, and I'll explain to you all
my plans.

Lady Pro. Aldgate farm! there again! pray, sir,
to whom do you owe the power you have over the
alderman? By whose means is that lump of agriculture become an annuity to you ?—Have not my
charms lured him?

Pro. To be sure: he too has a blindness; and, by
his own affectation of intrigue, and your flattering
his vanity———

Lady Pro. He is become so attach'd to the wife,
that the husband may speculate him out of all his
property. Well, sir, since you confess the obligation, I'll walk with you, and see how this curious
gentleman farmer goes on. Saturday is the day, I
think, the rustic comes from London.

Pro. It is: and, as usual, he only comes to paint
his outhouses and neglect his land.—The farm is
mine, and he thinks I shall give him a long lease;
but, when I find he has finish'd his improvements, I'll
let it over his head.———Oh, Kitty! this is the age
for speculation—People love delusion—ay, so much,

that the more you dupe them, the better they like you; and while a rich citizen shall propose a fair scheme which nobody adopts, a dashing west-end-of-the-town gentleman shall start a visionary one, and, hey! presto!—every body meets him in full cry— This is my plan, and so the nabob and the gentleman farmer shall find it.   [*Exeunt.*

SCENE II.

A view of the Alderman's Farm—Barn with painted doors—Carts, waggons, &c. of different colours— Hay-stack cover'd with an elegant awning—White rails, &c.

VICKERY *discovered with a basket in his hand.*

Vic. Here are alterations!—The vulgar clod who kept this farm before my master, said he built every thing for use; he minded the value, not the look, of a thing:—now I think the alderman has shewn him the difference.—Here he comes, and I must be off to his dear Lady Project with this basket full of choice garden-stuff, and haunches of Nova Scotia mutton. I wish the alderman may succeed better as a lover than as a farmer; though, between you and I, master Vickery, I believe he knows as much of the one as of the other.   [*Exit.*

Enter PROJECT *and* ALDERMAN ARABLE.

Ald. Ar. There, there are improvements!—Welcome to Aldgate farm, my friend.

Pro. Thank'ye, alderman; thank'ye—Any news in London?

Ald. Ar. That for London—that for trade! (*Snap-*

ping his fingers.) here's the spot to make a fortune in. Look, my dear friend : isn't every thing so tasty? so neat? so clean? you see at once this is none of your rough, dirty farms; it belongs to a gentleman, not to a farmer.

Pro. True : all the out-houses so new, so neat! ay, common farmers never think of these things.

Ald. Ar. No : plodding blockheads! they think of nothing but ploughing, sowing, and reaping : they look to the inside of their barns, I to the out! That pretty team now, (*Pointing to one.*) it carries all the ashes and other manure to a neighbouring farmer's; for, you must know, I'm too cleanly to have any dust or dirt thrown on my land; a little chalk makes it look light and pretty——Then the piggery! what do you think of the piggery? there! why there it is.

Pro. Mercy on me! in high varnish! why, it's very elegant. But pray, alderman, haven't you found that the pigs spoil the paint?

Ald. Ar. Yes, and that the paint spoils the pigs; so I've got an excellent remedy—I keep none.

Pro. That's one way, to be sure——But, with regard to the more essential parts of farming, how goes on your cabbage plantation? your speculation on butter? what have been your profits?

Ald. Ar. Profit! ask my bailiff about that. The fact is, Project, I have had a curst unlucky year : the seasons have been against me : a hot winter——a frosty summer——flies, blights, and grubs, in all the corn——sheep, calves, and horses, all with the staggers——-foxes eating up my chickens——-cockneys shooting my geese——-and as for the speculation you mention, why, the cows eat me forty load of hay, and I only made thirty pounds of butter——
" Debtor for hay, one hundred forty-five pounds twelve shillings and eight-pence. Per contra, cre-

ditor for butter, one pound, seventeen shillings, and
ten-pence halfpenny-farthing!"

Pro. Ah! I see it don't answer so well as I expected But about the plantation?

Ald. Ar. Oh! the cabbages—ay; there I've been
fortunate—-I tell you what—that plantation and my
Nova Scotia sheep will make up for all my losses.

JACK ARABLE, (*without.*)

Father—where are you, father?

Pro. Here's your son. I'm told since he left Oxford, and went to study under a special pleader,
that he's much improved—Why his education must
have cost you a great sum of money, alderman?

Ald. Ar. Thousands, thousands! but he'll repay
me.—Hark'ye; he is now a Batchelor of Arts—by
and by king's counsel—hereafter member for the
county—then great orator—the seals—the cabinet!
Oh! there's no doubt but Jack will make his own
fortune and mine too.

Pro. How do you mean?—why don't you allow
him an income?

Ald. Ar. Not a shilling.—I have given him a most
glorious education, and that's fortune enough now-
a-days.—Now he starts fair, and he's like my field of
cabbages; so well cultivated, that there's no doubt of
a fine crop.

Enter JACK ARABLE,

Jack Ar. O father, I've been hunting for you
every where. The Novia Scotia sheep,——pheugh!
                                        [*Puffing himself.*
Ald. Ar. Well, what of the dear animals?

Jack Ar. Why, they have broken into the plantation, and are eating up the cabbages as fast as they
can—I dare say I saw them devour one-third before
I came away.

Ald. Ar. You did, did you?—Where's the bailiff?

—oh! this is an old manœuvre—the farmers are in
a combination against me, and whenever their cattle
want food, they send them to breakfast, dine, and
sup on my crops—they're not my sheep, so I'll go
and pound them—in the mean time, Jack, do you
give my friend, Mr Project, a specimen of your talents.   [*Exit.*

Jack Ar. My talents!—Lord! they speak for themselves I'm sure—don't they, Mr——

Pro. How long is it since you left college, sir?—
and pray what was your chief study there?

Jack Ar. Study, heh?—come—that's fair, very
fair. Why, my study was to shoot without missing;
leap five-barr'd gates full speed—get drunk—make
love to my laundress—break lamps with my mathematical instruments, and knock down the proctors
with the classics—famous, heh?—oh! I finished my
education in a most capital style.

Pro. So I perceive, sir—but how do you like the
Temple, sir?—how does special pleading agree with
you?

Jack Ar. Special pleading!—I'm above that—
mum:—don't tell father, and I'll let you into a secret—I've been two years with a special pleader, and
never saw his fat face in all my life—fair, heh!—
very fair!—no, no:—I know——

Pro. What do you know, sir?

Jack Ar. That Westminster Hall won't do for
Jack Arable—the market's over-stocked—there's
such a crowd of black cattle, and so few buyers, that
one half must be returned on the owner's hand, at
prime cost.—O!—besides, if one did get a brief, the
King's Bench is like other courts, so crowded, that
there's no getting a place in it—and there's the case
—I must come back to father—and what then?—
he won't give me the Spanish.

Pro. The Spanish!—now what the devil's that?

Jack Ar. Why, ready money, not credit or paper.

When I ask him for a few guineas, he reminds me
of my education—refers me to Westminster Hall—
says I shall be call'd next term, and make thousands.
—Thousands! plague on't!—after being three years
a barrister, attending the courts, and going the cir-
cuits, I dare say, I shan't fetch the price of my
gown and wig!—so you see, Mr Project, here am I
with a finish'd education in the high road to a jail.

Pro. No, no—your marriage with Cecilia will
prevent that.

Jack Ar. Ay, I shall be glad to have her.

Pro. What! you love her, do you?

Jack Ar. No, but I love her fortune, and if I
could marry her to-morrow, I'd touch the Spanish,
and be off to London directly—to Epsom races—
the grand cricket match—zounds!—in making me
a special pleader, they'd spoil one of the most dashing dogs in Europe.

Re-enter ALDERMAN ARABLE.

Ald. Ar. I've secured the gormandizers, and
there's an end of that business.—Well, my friend,
how have you found him?—isn't his head like my
land?

Pro. Exactly—so barren that no cultivation can
improve it—(*Aside.*) but since you agree to the
match with Cecilia, the sooner he pays his addresses
the better. What say you? will you go and have
the first interview now?

Ald. Ar. With all my heart; her brother is a nabob, so let's go directly——

Jack Ar. Stop, stop—when we get to Mr Project's house, you must both of you grant me a favour,—you must let me see my brother Edward's
friend.

Pro. Who is that, sir?

Jack Ar. Why, the lady that's lock'd up—my

cousin Emmeline—nay, don't be angry; I only want
her to pay me twenty pounds she owes me.

Ald. Ar. My niece Emmeline owe you twenty
pounds!—how do you make out that?

Jack Ar. I'll tell you: two years ago I ask'd her
to lend me fifty pounds, she had only thirty in her
pocket, which she generously gave me—now you
know she owes me the odd twenty—fair, very fair,
isn't it?

Ald. Ar. Nonsense!—she is under the care of my
best friend here, who don't chuse she should be disturb'd in her seclusion: he does every thing that is
right with regard to that unhappy girl.

Pro. I thank you for your approbation—but come;
let's to Cecilia.

Ald. Ar. Ay, come, my boy; odsheart! strike her
with your talents at once, and if she asks about a
marriage settlement, put your hand to your head;
hit it hard; it won't hurt it, Jack—say, Here it is,
here's the place, like the alderman's granary—so
full——

Jack Ar. Full, father!

Ald. Ar. Faith I forgot—it's empty. However,
don't despair, for three such lads as we are will
make a match, or be a match for any woman in the
world.   [*Exeunt.*

ACT THE SECOND

SCENE I.

An Apartment in Mr Project's *House.*

Enter Project *and* Cecilia.

Cec. I tell you, it's all settled—I've seen young
Arable : he proposed marriage, and I gave him as
warm a reception as you could wish.   Bu Lady
Katharine Project, sir ; she tires me with her insinuations—she says, I come here to seduce her husband's
affections, when you know, Mr Project, he's the last
man on earth I should fix on for a gallant.

Pro. Mr Project's very much obliged to you :
but the truth is this, Cecilia—she knows I see her
partiality for Sir Frederick : this makes her all obedience—but if she could once recriminate ; only
prove I have my gallantries (and I have had them
beyond a doubt) why then snap goes the rod I hold
over her, and all the money I spent in patching up
her reputation——

Cec. Money, in patching up reputation !—how do
you mean, coz ?

Pro. Mean ! that when certain people lose their
character, they spend half their fortune in attempt·
ing to retrieve it—keep open house, give public entertainments—suppers, balls, concerts, galas—then
every body comes ; for if Belzebub himself gave a
dinner, there are people who would go to it !—every
body comes, I say—eat, drink, dance, and retire ;

and while the host and hostess fancy they are sounding their praises, egad! they're only cutting up their reputation, and laughing at them more and more for their folly.

Cec. Are they? then I wish Lady Project would recriminate, for I'm very fond of balls, concerts, and galas; and if you're exposed, you must give them to patch up your own reputation, you know—so adieu!——Oh, I forgot, though—lend me the key of the Pagoda, will you?

Pro. The Pagoda!

Cec. Ay, there's an eclipse to-night, and it will be a charming place to see it from—come give it me—foolish man!—I dare say, now, you're thinking this may lead to some plot about Emmeline; but you forget there are other doors and other keys, Mr Cerberus, and as I've given the bridegroom such a warm reception——

Pro. Well—your kindness to young Arable deserves a reward, and as I've no reason to suppose you mean to make a bad use of the key, take it——heh!—here's the gentleman himself! and, I declare, looking as melancholy as if the honey-moon was over—Nay—don't leave us.

Cec. If I don't, I shall be too late for the eclipse—so good evening—spouse will describe our interview to you—he'll tell you what pretty things I said of him and his father: upon my word they're a charming pair, and though a namesake of mine had long since won my affections, yet, when I saw young Arable—Oh! who can resist a man of his education!   [*Exit.*

Enter JACK ARABLE.

Pro. Joy! I give you joy, sir,—she has consented!—you'll be brother-in-law to a nabob, and I, bringing about the match, shall touch a thousand pounds from the alderman. Come, sit down, my boy,

and tell me all about it—(*They sit.*)—Who had the
first word? you or Cecilia?

Jack Ar. I had the first: she the last.

Pro. Ah! that's one of the sex's privileges; but
how did she conclude? with recommending you to
go to a parson, and finish the marriage?

Jack Ar. No: she concluded with recommending
me to go to school again, and finish my education:
—Mr Project, you'll hardly believe it, but she call'd
me Master Jacky: laugh'd at my learning; ridiculed
my manners; and, when I reminded her that I had
been made a scholar and a gentleman, she said I
might as well say one of my father's cows had been
made to translate Greek, or dance the minuet de la
Cour.

Pro. Why this is a warm reception indeed!—Well,
what was your answer?

Jack Ar. Says I, ma'am!—ma'am! I'm a bachelor of arts, and a student at law; I can solve a problem, draw a demurrer, and read a Latin Ovid.

Pro. A Latin Ovid!—what, not a translation?

Jack Ar. No; a real Latin Ovid, says I, ma'am,—
that was fair, was'nt it! had her there—famous,
heh?

Pro. Was ever time and money so wasted on a
blockhead's education? (*Aside.*)—You should have
told her you were shortly to be call'd to the bar;
that you were now at a special pleader's: if I mistake not, she is a great admirer of the profession.

Jack Ar. No, no; she's not so bad as that either;
for when, by way of a joke, I said that Westminster
Hall would be a knowing place to give a masquerade in—" A masquerade!" says she—" there's one
there every day in the term time!"—famous, heh?
had me there: but there's father just awoke from
his after-dinner nap—'gad, he shall have his share—

Enter ALDERMAN ARABLE.

Jack Ar. Father, I'm come from my intended wife : she speaks so highly of you—

Ald. Ar. Does she? that makes out my dream then : I dreamt she gave you her hand, because she said your father understood farming better than any man in England. Oh! the dear creature!—how was it?

Jack Ar. She said, that, while you were planting shrubberies, building out-houses, and painting the pig-stye, your bailiff was cheating you of the small crops your neglected fields produced; that in a month you would spend more money in fattening a single wether, than would supply the court of aldermen with turtle and venison for a year; that your garden is as expensive as your farm, for that every Monday morning, when your coach is cramm'd with hampers of garden stuff, there isn't a turnip-top within them but costs more than all the pine-apples in Covent-Garden market—that was fair, wasn't it? —very fair.

Ald. Ar. I'll hear no more—it's a libel, and if she wasn't sister to a nabob——a wether cost me more than venison; and turnip-tops more than pine-apples! —I'll be reveng'd.

Jack Ar. So will I—but how, father?

Ald. Ar. How! by making her your wife, whether she will or no—I'm determined to have a power over her; and, Mr Project, I will give you all my crops in and out of the ground—all my live and dead stock—ay, an additional thousand pounds, only to make me father to this jezabel, and then—leave me to manage her education.

Pro. If she won't consent, alderman, what can I do?

Jack Ar. What! a college for that; we classics know a trick or two, and give me an opportunity,

and five to four but I make her Mrs Jack Arable
before to-morrow morning. Zounds! I'll carry her
off, then touch the Spanish, and away to Epsom and
cricket—(*Aside.*)—Come, what say you to the two
thousand pounds?

Pro. That it's a nice speculation; and, as there
can be no harm in getting a girl a good husband, I
will give you an opportunity—Hark ye, she is now
in my garden, in the Pagoda; come with me directly, and———but hold, hold, where will you carry
her to?

Jack Ar. To Aldgate farm to be sure, where
we've a parson waiting, and where we'll convince
her, that we can make a match, or be a match for
any woman in the world: come—

Ald. Ar. Ay, away with you; and when she's my
daughter, instead of being fashionable and impertinent, she shall be humble and industrious: she shall
give up the harpsichord for the spinning wheel; faro
and archery for the hen-house and the dairy; and,
instead of parading *a la militaire* on a high-bred hun-
ter, she shall carry eggs to market on broken-kneed
Dobbin, and be a pattern for all the farmers' wives
and daughters in the land!—Away, my boys!

[*Exeunt.*

SCENE II.

Another Apartment in PROJECT'S *Country House—
A Door in Flat.*

Enter CECILIA.

Cec. So, I've tricked him out of the key, and now
for my dear Emmeline.   [*Opens the door in flat.*

Enter EMMELINE.

Emm. Oh my friend! you come most opportunely—at the very moment when most I needed
consolation and support.   Look there (*Giving a
letter.*) 'tis my guardian's answer to the letter we
plann'd together.

Cec. (*Reads.*) " You are kept here to recruit
your health——your fortune shall be paid you on
the day of your marriage—in the mean time don't
trouble me any more with unreasonable requests,
lest I should imagine you have relapsed—you understand"—
This is beyond all bearing—I cannot endure such—

Emm. How then can I? Oh, Cecilia! when dissipation and ruin deprive the thoughtless profligate
of his senses, there is little cause for lamenting a
disorder that bereaves him of all memory of his
vices: but when a poor sufferer, like myself, whose
only error has been virtuous love, who has done no
wrong but that of cherishing an honest passion, and
that passion for a time deprived her of her reason,
what is to be her fate? is she to be pitied, or thus
for ever punished?

Cec. Don't be unhappy, Emmeline; I feel for you
—pity you sincerely.

Emm. I need it, for if I were, as they insinuate,
I should not have the sense to feel my sorrows so
acutely.   My heart has long been breaking, and but
for your humanity, the struggle had been past—
would it were! and yet, Cecilia—

Cec. What, my friend?

Emm. If I could see and bless the lovely cause
of all————

Cec. Be comforted, you shall see him; come,
cheer up, for sunshine breaks in upon you, Emmeline; look, this key will secure your escape—ay, 'tis
the Pagoda key, your guardian gave it me, and in

my lodgings in London, you may be safely concealed, till Edward comes to punish him, and to reward
your sufferings.

Emm. Is there a hope then for our meeting?
Oh! joy will now distract me,—but think what difficulties—

Cec. None but what we can surmount: the servant who brings a chaise near the garden, will unlock the gate outside; I'll go give him orders directly, and, that no time may be lost, do you retire
instantly into the Pagoda (*Gives* EMMELINE *the key.*)
wait till I come, or you hear the gate unbarred—
Nay, no more melancholy looks; henceforth you must
smile and be cheerful, and some years hence, you,
I, and Edward will sit over a winter fire, and laugh
at our cunning, in outwitting that first of schemers,
my cousin Project.

Emm. Kind, generous girl! I will do all that you
desire—till we meet, farewell! how I tremble for the
event! yet why? if I'm brought back, they cannot
persecute me more, and if I 'scape their snares, the
sight of Edward————Oh! the thought revives me!
and since my guardian is so bold in guilt, wherefore
should innocence be fearful? no, I've a virtuous
cause, and I will nobly fall or triumph in the conflict!　　　　　　　　　　　　　　[*Exeunt separately.*

SCENE III.

PROJECT'S *Garden : a Pagoda at the Wing—moon-
light.*

Enter PROJECT *and* JACK ARABLE.

Jack Ar. So was she caught in her own snare,
heh? Well, this is the place with the foreign name,

the Pagoda, as you call it; pray what put it into your head to build such on out-of-the-way thing?

Pro. Speculation, sir, speculation : the house stood on my hands, so, by running up a pair of wings after the eastern fashion, I thought to catch some thoughtless nabob, but it wouldn't do, they were obstinate ; however, my rich cousin is coming home—

Jack Ar. And he pays for their obstinacy—fair, that's very fair ;—but about this Miss Cecilia—she is coming here to see an eclipse, you say.

Pro. Yes, she has herself given you a fair opportunity, and if you don't carry her to your father's, where a parson and a licence is ready—Stop, I think I saw a light—perhaps she's there already (*Looks through the key-hole.*) she is ! I see her petticoat.

Jack Ar. Do you? that's famous—an eclipse, heh ? gad ! she shall see a constellation. Go, squire, go, tell the alderman to look out for me and my wife—

Pro. No, I must go and look out for my own wife, for if she finds me and Cecilia out of the house at this time of night, she'll talk of recrimination for ever ; so success to you, and remember, she's an angel, my young lawyer.

Jack Ar. Why, as I'm a lawyer, I'd better forget it, for we and angels don't exactly suit each other. You manage your wife, I'll take care of mine. (PROJECT *exit.*) Now for it—now to coax her into the garden—(*Opens the door of the Pagoda.*)—Ma'am ! hadn't you better come out, ma'am—don't be frightened, there's nobody here but me—She's coming, by all that's tender, classical, and famous !

Enter EMMELINE *from the Pagoda.*

Emm. This is my friend's servant, I suppose, with the carriage—where can she be herself ? she promised to follow me instantly ; however, I'll ask him— Heavens ! what do I see ? my cousin Arable ! then I'm deceived, and am undone for ever,

Jack Ar. (*Not knowing her.*) Yes, it's master Jacky! he's not gone to school you see; however, I'll first secure the gate, that nobody may come from the house and disturb us—(*He bars the gate of the Pagoda.*)—Come, Miss Cecilia, come to Aldgate-farm, and teach the cows to translate Greek and dance minuets. What, sulky, heh? let's look in your face —how! why, it is not you, is it? no, egad! 'tis cousin Emmeline.

Emm. Yes, that Emmeline who was once your friend and favourite, who, being deserted by her family, and persecuted by her guardian, meant to escape from confinement, but is disappointed; you have discovered my intentions, sir, and I confess myself completely in your power.

Jack Ar. What! it's a trick, is it?—You stole out instead of the other—come, that's fair, very fair. Well! and how d'ye do, coz? do you know I have finished my education since I saw you—I have famously: but you've been very ill, Emmeline? however, we won't talk about that; you're recover'd, and I'm glad on't with all my heart! yet, you used me most unkindly, coz.

Emm. It seems I have used every body so, else I think I should not have been so hardly treated. I have been amply punished, sir.

Jack Ar. You have, you have, Emmeline; but you should have kept your promise about the Spanish— I always kept my word with you, and once, you know, when we were boys and girls, and you and my brother Edward quarrelled about your little tame fawn, did not you cry, and ask me to make it up between you! and didn't I bid him kiss the fawn and kiss you, and ever after wasn't he so fond of you——

Emm. Let me beseech you, sir, name not your brother: lead not my mind to thoughts that, whilst they charm, distract me. I'm sorry I forgot my promise, but you should remember, I also forgot myself;—remind me, and perhaps——

Jack Ar. I've a great mind——I will!—why the fact is, Emmeline, you offered to lend me fifty pounds, and you only gave me thirty: now you know you owe me the odd twenty.—I'm the last person on earth to dun people for money, but really when it has been owing so long—upon my soul I beg your pardon, but the alderman cuts so close; he has educated me so like a gentleman, and keeps me so like a beggar, that here I am with a head full of the notions of life and dissipation, and a pocket as empty as Oxford in the vacation.

Emm. I regret that my guardian has not left me the means of fulfilling my promise, but when I see my friend Cecilia, I've no doubt but she'll procure what you desire.—And now, sir, let me know my fate: am I to go back to my prison?

Jack Ar. Go to prison! what! when we've Spanish to keep us out of it? no, that's not fair.—We'll go to London, to Epsom, to the grand match; or if, as is most likely, you prefer Miss Cecilia's company to mine, I'll call her to take care of you; for if I leave you till you're safe out of your guardian's clutches, may I lose the long odds, and be flogg'd round the race-course like a blacklegs.

Emm. Now, indeed, you are the brother of my Edward:—then call Cecilia: I dare say by this time she is arrived in the Pagoda; and yonder is a carriage waiting to conduct us to London: there I shall remain till your brother arrives, and then make an appeal to the laws of my country.

Jack Ar. Never, never go to law; leave the whole business to arbitration, for if you don't at first, the lawyers, after emptying your pockets, will only do it at last.—However, I'll unbar the gate, (*Goes to Pagoda.*) gad! this is famous!—how Project and the alderman will be bother'd?—Zounds! what do I

see?—your guardian!—(*Runs to* EMMELINE.) don't,
don't agitate yourself: pull down your veil, and I'll—

EMMELINE *pulls down her veil, and* PROJECT *enters.*

Pro. As I thought.—My wife suspects an assignation between me and Cecilia, and is now coming
to detect me.   Mr Arable, a word if you please.
(JACK *leaves* EMMELINE, *and comes to* PROJECT.)
If you don't get her off,—and I see how it is—you
can't persuade her——

Jack Ar. Can't I? um! *ecce signum*, as we great
scholars say. (*Goes to* EMMELINE.) Come, miss, will
you go with master Jacky, and be made daughter-
in-law to an alderman? (EMMELINE *gives him her
hand, and nods assent.*) There! haven't I a rare granary? Why, I'll back my head at a scheme against
yours, little Project.

Pro. No, you mustn't do that; for this lucky
scheme was all my planning, you know.

Jack Ar, So it was.; and you shall have the full
credit of it, my boy!—The chaise will take us to the
nearest inn, and I'll return for Cecilia. (*Aside to*
EMMELINE.) Bid her good by; give her your sanction. (PROJECT *bows, and kisses his hand.*) There;
now you do as he orders you.—You see, squire, you
see,—this is both famous and fair, isn't it?

[*Exit, handing off* EMMELINE.

Pro. It is! it is! (*Looks out.*) He hands her into
the carriage! the postillion shuts the door!—mounts
his horses!—away they go!—Huzza! huzza!

Enter ALDERMAN ARABLE, *running against him.*

Ald. Ar. Huzza! huzza! he has her! he has her!
—Joy! I give you joy, my friend.

Pro. This is reaping the harvest, farmer.

Ald. Ar. Ay; we're in clover now!—But, Project,
I met that good and sweet woman your wife, in such
a jealous rage——

Pro. That's a better joke than t'other.—She thinks
to detect me in an assignation with Cecilia; but the
bird is flown, you see.

Enter LADY KATHARINE PROJECT.

Lady Pro. So, Mr Project; where have you concealed Cecilia?—Mr Arable, he brings this young
lady to my house,—entertains her in the most expensive style,—gives her the most extravagant suppers,
and, having decoyed her into an assignation, he now
comes here to carry her off.

Ald. Ar. That's impossible, your ladyship, because
Jack has carried her off already.—She is by this
time as safe at Aldgate farm, as Emmeline is in your
house, and I dare say they and the parson are sitting down to a haunch of my Novia Scotia mutton.
—Do you know, my lady, I always kill my own mutton, and milk my own cows?

Lady Pro. At Aldgate farm indeed!—more like
she's in that Pagoda.—Arn't I right, my life?

Pro. You are, my soul.—Hark'ye, did Sir Frederick teach you this?

Lady Pro. There now! I'm always to be choak'd
at the moment of recrimination! I believe Cecilia's
innocent, but to know my husband's falsehood, and
never be able to prove it—I can't bear his triumph
—I (*Taking out her handkerchief.*) am the most unhappy, ill-treated wife—   [*Crying.*

CECILIA *taps at the door within side the Pagoda.*

Ald. Ar. What the devil's that?

Pro. What, indeed!—hush!

Cec. (*Within.*) Why don't you open the door?
'tis I! 'tis Cecilia!

Lady Pro. Oh! it is, is it?—then come out, and,
(*Opens the door of the Pagoda, and leads out* CECILIA.)
I say, Mr Alderman, they're sitting down to a haunch
of Novia Scotia mutton, are they?

Ald Ar. Project, this is reaping the harvest indeed.

Pro. Ay: we're in clover now with a vengeance. Cecilia, what does this mean?

Cec. Why, as all concealment will now be useless, I may venture to inform you that by some accident Emmeline has escaped, I find; and I came here in search of her, and not to meet your husband, ma'am, upon my honour.

Pro. Emmeline escaped!—that was her then that the well-educated blockhead was handing off, saying, " you see! this is both famous and fair!" 'Sdeath! I've out-schemed myself.—I'll pursue her instantly. Alderman, will you go with me?

Ald. Ar. Ay; that I will; my son, Captain Edward, is arrived, and if he and Emmeline should meet,—I tell you what,—as Jack has made two fools of us, I'll persuade the East Indian to let Edward marry his sister, Cecilia. Come along.—Odsheart! I won't wait to order my carriage or have garden stuff—(CECILIA *laughs.*) Now there again! I only wish I had you at the farm.—I'd——

Pro. Come—I know what you're going to say.

Ald. Ar. Do you? then you know more than I do myself; for, plague on the girls! they'll drive me out of my senses!   [*Exit with* PROJECT.

Lady Pro. My dear Cecilia, I never doubted your innocence.—Come, let's go and prepare for London. I long to see your brother, the young nabob. I dare say, he'll bring over the most charming presents.

Cec. Very likely: but my mind is all on Emmeline. Poor girl! may she escape the persecution of her enemies, and be rewarded as her virtue and her sufferings deserve!   [*Exeunt.*

ACT THE THIRD.

SCENE I.

An elegant Apartment at PROJECT'S *House in London.*

Enter PROJECT *and* SIR FREDERICK.

Pro. Not find her! Emmeline not to be found! tell me, Sir Frederick, have you been at young Arable's chambers?

Sir Fred. I have—and he is out of town, at Epsom: positively, I can hear nothing of Emmeline—but what then? fretting won't find her; and if it did, I dare say you'd find something else to fret you—I'm her lover, and you see I'm not uı easy.

Pro. No: you haven't the reason I have—she may fall into the hands of some enemy, who may say, I have entangled her fortune; confined her after her health was restored; and at last convince her uncle, the alderman, that I have wrong'd her—then her friend, Captain Arable, is in town, you say?

Sir Fred. Yes, he arrived last night from Gibraltar—receiving a letter that inform'd him of Emmeline's recovery, he quitted the regiment at the risk of offending his father—Leave me to manage him : Let me see—(*Looking at his watch.*) I am now going to meet him.

Pro. Are you? then tell him of her escape, the necessity of restoring her to my power—hint at a relapse, and persuade him to join in searching for her: I would go with you; but I'm waiting here to receive my cousin Tanjore.

Flourish of Clarinets, without.

Pro. That's him! that's the young nabob——I ordered the band to strike up as he passed through the hall; and, as he's been accustomed to be surrounded with slaves, I've hired those blacks, and other attendants, to give him a sort of pompous entrée.

Sir Fred. Ay, there's the East Indian. I wonder whether Mr Tanjore's as easy and familiar as ever: I remember, when he had neither cash nor credit, he used to call the greatest men by their Christian names; and, though he hadn't a coat to his own back, he was always remarking on the dress of other people.

Pro. Ah! he was no nabob then: now I fear he's as haughty and reserved as he was before free and familiar. Good day, Sir Frederick: I shall rely on your making Captain Arable my friend. (SIR FREDERICK *exit.*) Now for it! now for my best scheme! To be sure, my tricking him, and turning my back on him, before he went to Madras, was rather unlucky; but his coming to my house proves he don't think the worse of me—no, no: I have him: and when I've fairly stripped him, I'll send him to India again, there to make another fortune, for the benefit of me and my speculations!

Another Flourish——Enter Blacks with Music, Servants in superb Liveries, preceding TANJORE *and* CECILIA——*Other Attendants following.*

Tan. Billy, your hand——Where's Betsy? Well, here we are, you see, hot from Madras——warm as Lucifer—rich as Crœsus, my boy!

Pro. 'Tis as I thought! (*Aside.*) I hope you found my carriages and horses all ready: I should have been miserable if you had not condescended to make use of them.

Tan. Should you? then be happy, coz; for I'll make use of them for ever : the carriages and horses are mine, Billy.

Pro. They are : you do me great honour in accepting them——He has forgot our old quarrel——and I shall finger every farthing ! (*Aside.*)——Well; but about India, cousin——you made your fortune very rapidly.

Tan. Yes; the Princess Nundomoree took a fancy to my person and dress——introduced me to the Nabob of Begumboree ; he to the Rajah of Seringapatoree ; and so amongst them you see——But, Billy, what makes you so civil? before I sailed, you wouldn't pay the fare of a hackney-coach for me, and now you give me all your carriages and horses : well, well, I take it very kind of you; and so, hark-ye—a few westerly winds will bring round the homeward-bound fleet, and then hire all the strongest waggons you can get——bullion ! pearls ! diamonds ! —oh, damme, coz, this house will never hold them !

Pro. I hope this house will hold them though—— Oh, for a westerly wind !—In return, my dear friend, the wife I design for you has five thousand a-year— to be sure it's very little ; but——

Tan. A little's better than nothing, you know ; and, if I like her person and manners, why, five thousand a-year will be very pretty pin-money—But what's here, Billy? (*Looking at his coat.*) is this a dress for a cousin of a nabob ?

Pro. What! at the old work ?—Psha ! what signifies dress ?

Tan. Every thing, now-a-days —— a good coat is tantamount to a good character ; and, if the world be a stage, it's as necessary to dress as to act your part well : then consider the effect—Why, when I landed from the packet in my old blue coat, shab-

by red waistcoat, and decayed kerseymeres, I cut
through the alleys, and was pushed and smoaked by
every apprentice and shopkeeper I met ; but, the moment I put on these smart clothes that you sent, I
swaggered through the most public streets—-jostled
all the men of fashion—-cocked my eye at all the
lords, and received the homage and bows of the
very shopkeepers and apprentices that had before
sneered at me. Oh ! in this age of false appearances, there's nothing like a showy outside ; and a
tailor is a man of more consequence than you imagine.

Pro. Well ; but, after the fatigue of travelling,
don't you want some refreshment ? Pray do here as
if you were at home.

Tan. That I do every where : I never stood on
ceremony in my life ; but as to refreshment, that depends on our hostess, who, if I recollect, is rather
close—short commons—heh, Billy ?

Pro. Worse and worse : she has almost starved
me since you went : you haven't yet seen her
though—John, call Lady Project.

Tan. No, no ; call her yourself : in India, I was
always waited upon by the master of the house ; and
therefore go, Billy—go—besides, I wish to speak to
my sister—--Stop though ; I shall want some ready
money.

Pro. What, the Spanish ?

Tan. Oh, nothing else—Go, send your wife, and
pray——

Pro. For a westerly wind ! You shall have what
money you require : so—here's speculation !—Oh,
for a westerly wind !

[*Exit. The Servants follow him.*

Cec. My dear brother, let me once more congratulate you : why, who'd have thought of your coming home so rich ?

Tan. Ay, who indeed ?—you didn't expect it ; did you, Cecily ?

Cec. No ; I expected you'd return as you went. I thought you'd come and say, " Here's a nabob without a shilling, Cecily."

Tan. Did you ? then you thought exactly right ; for—" here's a nabob without a shilling, Cecily !"

Cec. Nonsense !——Mr Project says you have brought over money enough to buy him new houses, new——

Tan. Not enough to buy him a new coat.

Cec. Nay, now you're joking : I know you must be rich, by the style you kept up in India : you lived in a palace, my dear brother.

Tan. I lived in a jail, my dear sister.

Cec. Come, come ; haven't I heard that your furniture was embossed with gold ? that your dinners were more expensive than the governor's ?

Tan. My furniture was the bare walls, and my dinner bread and water. The fact is, a man may starve in India as well as in England ; and, instead of finding gold like dirt, or diamonds like pebbles, I found a sort of gentlemen that must be attended to in all countries ; I mean——bailiffs ! 'Tis true, they didn't visit me on my arrival ; but, in the course of a twelvemonth, they whipped me into one of their hospitable mansions ; and there I should have been at this moment, had not the captain of the packet assisted me in my escape, and landed me generously in old England : I say generously, for curse me if I am nabob enough to pay for my passage !

Cec. Amazing ! if Mr Project knew this, he wouldn't be so friendly.

Tan. He friendly ! no : when he and the club had schemed me out of all the money I had left, they shut the doors against me ; while Sir Charles Stanley—I shall never forget his liberality !—befriended me, and sent me to India. I guess how the mistake

has happened——there is a man of my name at Madras—an old lover of yours—

Cec. Mr Henry Tanjore !—my friend, as well as
lover.

Tan. Well ; he's now as rich as I'm poor—is coming home in the next ships——and scheming Billy,
with his usual perspicuity, takes me for him, and determines to make the most of me—and he shall make
the most of me : there's no favour he can offer but
I'll have the condescension to accept ; and, to begin, I'll marry this five thousand pound lady.

Cec. Don't—don't think of her ; there are a thousand reasons against it.

Tan. Ay ; but there are five thousand for it—no
more bare walls, and bread and water.

Cec. Poor Emmeline ! then I must conceal from
him where she is. (*Aside.*)

Tan. See ! our hostess, Lady Stingy ! To poor
Tanjore she has often refused a dinner ; but to the
rich nabob, I suppose—Mum !—mark how I'll——

Enter LADY PROJECT.

Lady Pro. Joy ! joy on your success, my ever
dear cousin !

Tan. Thanks, thanks, my ever dear Kitty !

Lady Pro. Kitty ! familiar as ever, I see——Well,
coz ! aren't you glad to set foot in old England a-
gain ? once more to see London and the fashions ?

Tan. Why, as to the fashions, coz, they fly so
fast, one can't be quick enough to catch them—nothing lasts above a day. Before I went to India, the
whole town was running after the Goddess of Health :
she died, I'm told, and the Learned Pig came to life :
he went the grand tour, and the balloon came into
power : that bubble burst, and boxing bore down all
before it : then came the varieties of dress, such as
short skirts, short hair, short sticks, and short great-
coats ! in short, if the world did not turn round of

its own accord, people of fashion would make it ; for
the moon, whose votaries they are, isn't half so fickle,
or so changeable !

Lady Pro. Very true : then don't you observe the
alterations in buildings ? My husband and other spe-
culatists have built so many new streets, and London
is so absolutely gone into the country, that a citizen
coming to a route at Marybone, must be at the expence of changing horses, and paying turnpikes !——
But, I understand, you want some little refreshment.

Tan. Little refreshment ! now mind, Cecily—Yes,
any thing will do ; some turtle and venison, a great
deal of game, a quantity of pine-apples, and plenty
of burgundy and champagne. Then about my bed ;
at the rajah of Seringapatoree's, I always slept under a canopy empanelled with looking-glass, and covered with gold and silver tissue—didn't I, Cecily ?
You'll get such a bed, Kitty—So now for dinner.

Lady Pro. Turtle, venison, canopies, and gold
and silver tissue ! Mr Tanjore, you don't intend to
live here in the same style you did in India ?

Tan. No, that I don't ; I hope neither my furniture nor my dinners will be the same—heh, Cecily ?
Then my wedding-day, coz ! I shall celebrate my
nuptials at your house ; and we'll have such a ball
and supper !——between ourselves, it shan't be over-
crowded though ; I'll only ask about three hundred
people.

Lady Pro. Three hundred people ! Sir, I must tell
you, no fortune can support this extravagance ; and
if you give us every farthing you've brought over—

Tan. Why, I shall ; every farthing is yours, upon
my honour ; and, by way of specimen, to-morrow
I'll send you a large chest of shawls, pearls, china,
chintzes——

Lady Pro. Will you ? can you be so obliging ?
Oh ! I doat on pearls and shawls ; and then for china

and chintzes——my dear, dear cousin, come to dinner, and order whatever you like.

Tan. (*Aside to* CECILIA.) There now! and I
haven't brought over a rag, or an empty trunk!—
However, Kitty shall have the presents: there are
Indian goods in England, and I'll buy them with
Billy's own money! Come, sister; come, hostess.

[*Exeunt.*

SCENE II.

Lincolns Inn.

Enter CAPTAIN ARABLE *and* SIR FREDERICK.

Sir Fred. Nay; but reflect, Captain Arable; reflect.

Capt. Ar. I do reflect; and there's my cause for
grief. Have I not quitted my regiment, and offended my father? Is he not now in search of me, to
send me abroad again? and when I expected to meet
Emmeline in happiness and health, do you not tell
me that her malady has returned? that she has
escaped from her guardian, and is not to be found?

Sir Fred. I do; but I hope you don't blame me
or Project?

Capt. Ar. No, far from it; I believe he has been
more a parent than a guardian to her; and you have
sunk the name of rival in that of friend——But my
brother to aid in her escape, and now not to be heard
of! What is to be done? I dare not meet my father;
and if I leave England till I see Emmeline restored
to her asylum, I shall well merit the anguish that
awaits me.

Sir Fred. Psha! you're talking about anguish too;
—now nothing gives me pain; and why? because

I'm so cool and placid, that not even death—death!
no, that pain must be over, for hang me if I think
I've been alive these last ten years—But where are
we to find her, captain?

Capt. Ar. Ah! where indeed? Poor Emmeline!
without friends, without assistance, and with the loss
of that fine sense which now might best support thee,
where—where art thou wandering? Let us be gone,
—let us search every where——

Enter TANJORE.

Tan. My cousin to say he has a wife for me, and
then not tell me her name or residence! however,
I've found out she's at Cecily's lodgings; and so,
while dinner's getting ready——

Sir Fred. Mr Tanjore! I am happy to see you—
What! don't you know me? have you forgot Sir
Frederick Faintly, a member of Bubble's club?

Tan. Sir Frederick! my old acquaintance! How
d'ye do, Fred.? how are you, Fred.? Never saw Fred.
before in all my life. (*Aside.*)

Sir Fred. This is a particular friend of mine, Mr
Edward Arable.

Tan. Psha! hang ceremony: Ned! your hand,
Ned——By the bye, Fred., is your friend a riding-
master?

Sir Fred. Why?

Tan. Cock'd hat and boots! curst vulgar——you
too! never wear a cravat with a full-dressed coat;
it's like a tooth-drawer! Well, what's the news, my
boys?

Sir Fred. I know of none, but that you were last
night re-elected a member of Bubble's.

Tan. Was I? Only observe, Ned—my cousin Billy brought me into this club; and when they had
fleeced me of all my cash, they kicked me out as
a pigeon quite bare——now I return from India,
with my feathers fresh moulted, they re-elect me, in

13

the hopes of having another pluck—ay, it's the way
at all your fashionable gaming-houses—" Mr President, who is the new member proposed ?" " A great
fool, but very rich." Pop, in goes a white ball——
" Who is the next, Mr President ?" " A great genius, but very poor." " Here, waiter, drop in a black
ball."——Your servant though—I can't stay ; I must
go take a peep at my wife.

Sir Fred. Your wife !

Tan. Yes, gad ! it's a most curious business : my
cousin says I'm to be married to a lady worth five
thousand a-year ; but he either won't or can't tell
me who or where she is ! however, I overlooked a
letter my sister was just now writing, and I suspect
spouse is concealed in her lodgings—Mum ! shan't
I delight and astonish her ? in India I was such a
favourite with the women, that one day six prin-
cesses came to prison to see me—Prison did I say ?
Oh, ay, that was when I fought against Tippoo, had
six horses shot under me, and was at last taken prisoner by——

Capt. Ar. Pray, sir, what is this lady's name ?

Tan. Emmeline is her christian name ; as to sir-
names, I never knew but two in my life—Sir Charles
Stanmore, and your humble servant Tom Tanjore—
two as fine fellows as ever handled rupees and pagodas. Fare you well. I shall marry this Emmeline to-morrow.

Capt. Ar. You marry Emmeline, sir !

Tan. Yes, I, Ned ; and, what's more, I invite you
to our wedding dinner, and you also, Fred., and all
your friends, and your friends' friends !—Lady Project desired me to ask the whole town, and I'll take
care the nuptials shall be celebrated in the true eastern style of magnificence——here's my card ; and, if
you wish to be asked again, come well dressed—nothing like a good coat——and so farewell, Fred. and
Ned !　　　　　　　　　　　　　　　　[*Exit.*

Capt. Ar. It must be her; let's follow him directly.

Sir Fred. Stay—suppose you should meet the alderman there; and I know he has business with this Mr Tanjore——

Capt. Ar. Why then, and not till then, let's think what's to be done—Come; lose not a moment—— In his sister's lodgings, and he about to marry her! 'tis dark—mysterious! Mark me, Sir Frederick; I'd traverse half the world to thank the man that has befriended Emmeline! but, if I find she has been wronged; if there should live a villain that has added to her sorrows; I pledge my honour to avenge her cause—my life or his must answer the event.

[*Exeunt.*

SCENE III.

CECILIA'S *Lodgings.*

Enter TANJORE *and* ALDERMAN ARABLE.

Tan. Walk in, sir; walk in; your christian name is Obadiah, you say, and your business is concerning a marriage between your son and my sister——Did I never see you before?

Ald. Ar. Only once: if you remember, sir, it was in Mr Project's park, when the dear Lady Project had fainted away, and you caught her in your arms. I'm not censorious, Mr Tanjore; but if her grandmother hadn't come up at the instant—

Tan. You'd have been jealous, heh?——Well, but about your son—

Ald Ar. Why, sir; I wish your sister to become the wife of my son, Captain Arable: the reprobate has quitted his regiment, to pursue an unhappy

young lady, that I'm determined he shall never be
united to. Now, sir, by the recommendation of that
worthy man, Mr Project—

Tan. Pray, Obadiah, where did you get that curious waistcoat? positively, it's only fit for an alderman.

Ald. Ar. Then it's fit for me, Mr Tanjore; for I
am an alderman—ay, and a farmer too; and if I
could find my son, and Cecilia would consent, we'd
whisk down to Aldgate farm to-night, tack them together to-morrow, and, in the course of a month, you
can get them out to India; and there, you know,
they are snug and comfortable for life. To a man of
your interest, I suppose eight thousand a-year will
be——

Tan. Nothing—a mere trifle.

Ald. Ar. So I thought——Oh! when the captain
gets to Madras, I only wish he may be provided for
as you were, Mr Tanjore.

Tan. Provided for as I was! that's what I wish
myself; for curse me if I know or care about you or
the captain. (*Half aside.*) Yonder's Emmeline, I
fancy——I must get rid of this rustic——Good b'ye,
Obadiah; go look for the captain, and, if you find
him, bring him to my wedding dinner. Lady Project keeps open house while I stay; so bring all your
city and rural friends—carters and common-council-
men——

Ald. Ar. Sir, you delight me; and Aldgate farm,
and all its produce, is at your service. Are you fond
of Nova Scotia mutton, sir?

Enter a Servant.

Serv. Sir, here's a Captain Arable below.

Ald. Ar. Oh, there is, is there? now then I'll go
and detain him till we meet at the charming Lady
Project's. Shew me to him, sirrah. Once more I
thank you, Mr Tanjore; and if you think eight thou-

sand a-year too much, you may reduce it to half;
that is, to the exact profits I clear, or mean to clear,
by Aldgate farm!   [*Exit.*

Tan. Good day, Obadiah.   Now this it is to be a
nabob! I'm as much sought after here as in India,
and exactly from the same motive—friends want money here, and the bailiffs there.   Here she is! An
angel, by the Ganges! I'll marry her before I leave
the house——Soft! what letter is she reading? no
doubt, the one my sister wrote to her—I'll observe.
                                    [*Stands back.*

Enter EMMELINE, *with a Letter in her hand.*

Emm. What has my escape availed me? this letter renews my sufferings with tenfold force!—Married! to whom? (*Reads.*)

" My brother Tanjore agrees to your guardian's
proposals, and determines to marry you.   I must regret this, while I know there is one who so much
better deserves you."

Tan. (*Behind.*) Indeed! he must be a very clever fellow then.

Emm. (*Reading.*) " I have concealed from Tanjore your present residence; yet, I think, if he knew
that you had escaped from your guardian, because
he made a prisoner of you, and embarrass'd your fortune"——What then?—he is weak enough to think
him honest.

Tan. (*Behind.*) No; he's not such a fool as that
either.

Emm. (*Reading.*) " If he knew that Edward
Arable has won your heart—that your uncle the alderman deserts you—that a marriage, under these
circumstances, will be death to you and misery to
him"——

Tan. (*Behind.*) Misery indeed!——this is more
like a funeral than a wedding.

Emm. (*Reading.*) " And, lastly, if you were to

inform him that your father, Sir Charles Stanmore, was the man who befriended him in the hour of misfortune, I think he is not so void of gratitude and humanity, but he would assist rather than distress you."

Tan. (*Coming forward.*) That he would—-Well said, sister! you have done your part; now let your brother do his—Ma'am, my name is Tanjore : your father got me out to India when I hadn't a house to pop my head in; and though the habitation I popp'd my head into there wasn't altogether so comfortable, that was no fault of Sir Charles's—He was my benefactor—I am your friend.

Emm. Is it possible? Will you not force me to accept your hand?

Tan. Accept my hand! I'll cut it off first. I wouldn't marry you for all the bullion in Bengal! Not but what I could love you, Emmeline ; and but for Ned—ah! but for Ned, we might have been a very happy, handsome couple.

Emm. Can this be the man I was taught to expect? Can this be the haughty East Indian, whose riches——

Tan. Riches! that's your guardian's story : he insists upon it I've brought home millions ; and, as he must know better than I do, it would be rude to contradict him, you know—But enough of myself— Tell me how I can serve you? My poverty shall not prevent me going instantly to this speculatist, and commanding him to do you justice. Zounds! I wish I had him in Calcutta! I'd march an army against him as black as his own heart—cram him into the hot hole, and smother him, if he didn't give you your fortune, and the man that deserves you.

Emm. Sir, I insist you run no hazard on my account. I have formed a determination, which I shall now execute : it is, to go instantly and make one more appeal to my uncle—to Alderman Arable.

Tan. What! Obadiah? he was here just now, and seems so fond of your guardian——

Emm. I know it; he has the highest opinion of his honour and veracity; but, as the alderman is the nearest relation I have left, he is the most proper person to protect me; and therefore I shall make this last effort to undeceive him. Yonder is your sister, I see; she will conduct me.

Tan. Allow me time to attend you——Heigho! —I don't know what's the matter with me: I feel such new emotions, and there's such a warm glow about my heart, that, gad, it fancies itself in India! Can you tell me what it means, ma'am?

Emm. Indeed I cannot, sir; but very likely it results from the satisfaction of having done a generous action; and the emotion is new, because, like too many others, you have perhaps sacrificed your time and happiness at the shrine of fashion.

Tan. That's it, ma'am—you have hit it exactly. Oh, what I have suffered by keeping up the appearance of a fine gentleman!—Horses I never rode—carriages I never saw—houses I never entered—frequenting clubs, routs, operas; and, in short, doing every thing I disliked; because I was told it was what I ought to like——But now I've done with it—henceforth I'll live to please myself; and while I don't suffer in my own opinion, what need I care for that of other people?—Come, sweet Emmeline! you shall be happy still.   [*Exeunt.*

ACT THE FOURTH.

SCENE I.

An Apartment in the Alderman's House.

Enter PROJECT *and* CAPTAIN ARABLE.

Capt. Ar. Yes, sir, I am most happy in the opportunity of thanking you for the care you have taken of this unfortunate girl—her escape proves she has relapsed.

Pro. It does ; for, had she been herself, she would have scorned to elope from the care of her guardian. —You say she has left Cecilia's lodgings.

Capt. Ar. Not an hour ago, she and Cecilia went away together ; but where I know not.

Pro. Well, well—I'll go send the young nabob after them ; and I'll likewise consult with her old physician about the best mode of securing her for the future——Good day, captain ; and, remember, who ever first discovers her, gives information to the other.

Capt. Ar. Agreed.

Pro. Oh ! I forgot——if you should see her first, don't let your wishes get the better of your judgment——she may perhaps have a lucid interval, and talk with apparent rationality—but be on your guard, —be convinced she has relapsed, and don't leave her till you see her safe in my custody.

Capt. Ar. Rest assured I shall do every thing her

unhappy situation demands——Good evening——(*Exit*
PROJECT.)——Oh, my lost Emmeline!—three tedious
years are past since last I saw thee; and in that
time we've both endured so much, that I did hope
our meeting might be happy——but 'tis denied——if
we should meet—'tis but to divide with added grief.
——Well, I'm prepared——let me restore the hapless
wanderer to her friends, and then once more abroad
—In the heat of war, I may forget the treasure I
have lost; or, in a glorious death, bury at once my
love and misery! (*Sits down in great agitation.*)

Enter EMMELINE *and* VICKERY.

Vic. The alderman is in the next room, ma'am.

Emm. Then tell him that a relation, who was once
dear to him, requests an interview. (*Exit* VICKERY.)
Is every moment to bring new affliction?—but now
I heard, that he who charmed my heart, and stole
away my senses—that he was coming home to wed
Cecilia—can falsehood be so—I'll not suspect him—
in this very room Edward first proffer'd me his love,
and no tongue but Edward's shall make me think
him faithless.

Capt. Ar. (*Having observed her, rises.*) Sure I'm
not mistaken—it is herself!——Emmeline!

Emm. I am discover'd—who can it be?—perhaps
some agent of my guardian's sent to secure me—
[*As she is going, he stands before her.*

Capt. Ar. What, avoid me, Emmeline!—have you
forgot—

Emm. Edward! my long-lost only friend!—(*Puts
her handkerchief to her eyes.*)—pardon me—my
prospects have so long been darken'd, that the least
flash of light quite blinds me.

Capt. Ar. You must not weep—I came not to increase your sorrow.

Emm. What I have suffer'd since we parted last
—a heated brain—painful confinement—merciless

keepers—and if an interval of reason came, to bring
your form before me, and then remember that our
love was hopeless—Oh ! but now I've found you, and
we'll ne'er part again—(EDWARD *turns away from
her.*)—why that averted look?—why those tears?—
speak !—you are not changed?—I have not forfeited
your love?

Capt. Ar. No—it is not that; but I could wish—

Emm. Name it, and I will fly——

Capt. Ar. That, during those lucid moments, I
could persuade you to accompany me to your guardian's—to return to an asylum form'd to relieve, to
succour, and restore you.

Emm. What ! does he conspire against me?—he
that hath caused all this?—Sir, I was told the motive for this conduct, but I disdain'd suspicion !—
nay—ask not an explanation—I shall not condescend
to answer you.

Capt. Ar. You cut me to the soul—what motives
can I have but those of pity and humanity?

Emm. Humanity !—is it humanity to harass a
mind already shatter'd and impair'd?—to increase
rather than remove the fever you have occasion'd?
—to combine with enemies in cloistering me in a
shameful seclusion, while, false and unfeeling as you
are, you *humanely* give your hand to another !—Oh !
my poor brain !—why did your sense return, only to
make you feel increasing injuries?

Capt. Ar. To another !—hear me, Emmeline—

Emm. No, sir,—'tis now too late—I shall go instantly to your father, and throw myself under his
protection—Farewell, sir !

Capt. Ar. (*Holding her.*) Stay—you know not
what you do—by heaven you shall not leave me thus
—think of our past love—

Emm. I do, sir : I remember, in the hours of happiness and prosperity, we exchanged hearts, and you
have now set me an example which I scorn to imi-

tate—my heart is still your own! I shall banish this last conversation from my memory, and think of Edward, only as he was—the friend of Emmeline—the foe to those who wrong'd her—this will be my best solace in retirement, and cheer a mind that has not long to struggle.

Capt. Ar. I cannot part with you; and, to prove no other for a moment can engross my thoughts, I'll henceforth watch you in your malady—weep as you weep, and nurse each smile that waits you—and if, but one day in the year, returning reason should adorn your mind, I will forego all other women's charms to pass that day with Emmeline—Oh! I have suffer'd in my turn, and were you always thus—

Emm. Why still so credulous?—why now believe——

Capt. Ar. I do not! will not! or, if you are the sufferer they describe, there is a charm about your malady so far exceeding all their boasted sense, that t enhances, doubles my affection! (*Embraces her.*) In losing you I knew what I had lost, and I have caused a wound which it shall be the business of my life to heal.

Emm. Shall we be happy then?—I am most grateful—my guardian has deceived you—he has involved my fortune.

Capt. Ar. This I heard, and that, by marriage with his East Indian cousin, the debt was to be cancell'd —but I'll know all hereafter—at present I am lost in joy.

Re-enter VICKERY.

Vic. Madam, the alderman desires to see you in the next room.

Emm. What shall we do?—to separate so soon!—

Capt. Ar. 'Tis hard, my Emmeline, but, to secure our union, you must persuade your uncle to befriend you—

Emm. I know it, and he is so bigotted to my guardian—but since you desire it, shew me the way —(*To* VICKERY.)—-Adieu, my generous friend! Should but the father imitate the son, my sufferings will be recompenced at last—Adieu!   [*Exit.*

Capt. Ar. Fool that I was to credit what they told me ; but they shall answer sorely for their guilt— Here comes the fop who was to be her husband— How the empty coxcomb kisses his hand to her !—I'll humble him—I'll——

Enter TANJORE.

Tan. (*Speaking as he enters.*) Success, sweet Emmeline, and if Obadiah don't take pity on you, Tom Tanjore will !—if she succeeds, I'll give her such a kiss—Ah, Ned !—how's Fred. ?

Capt. Ar. Be more respectful I insist, sir.

Tan. Respectful !—what makes you so proud, Neddy ?—Oh, oh ! I see—better dressed '—and you think that new coat and waistcoat make you look like a gentleman !—heh ?

Capt. Ar. Answer me, sir—what brings you here ?

Tan. To see your sweetheart, Ned, and if the Princess Nuncomoree was to know that she preferr'd your tragic scowl to my comic grin——

Capt. Ar. Hear me, sir—I'll tell you a secret— your friend Mr Project is a villain !

Tan. What that's a secret ?—why I've known it these ten years.

Capt. Ar. Tell him I say it—but 'tis of no avail— I'll answer for it, he is so void of courage, that he can't persuade himself to fight any man living.

Tan. Now, there you're wrong ; for he is so void of character, that he can't persuade any man living to fight him—therefore have the goodness to tell him he's a villain, and retrieve his reputation—my friendship and his depends on the weathercock, and

the moment that points westerly, up blows a breeze
that oversets it for ever.

Re-enter VICKERY, *crossing the stage with his hat on.*

Capt. Ar. Vickery, where are you going in such
haste?

Vic. I can hardly tell, sir—my master was in such
agitation when he gave me his orders, and he particularly desired me not to inform you.

Capt. Ar. Not inform me!—speak this instant,
sirrah.　　　　　　　　　　　[*Laying hold of him.*

Tan. Ay, speak this instant, sirrah.
　　　　　　　　　　　　　　　[*Laying hold of him.*

Vic. Then the truth is, the alderman has lock'd up
Miss Emmeline, and sent me for her guardian, to
whom she is to be deliver'd and confined for life—
there, now you know the fact, and I take my leave.
　　　　　　　　　　　　　　　　　　　[*Exit.*

Capt Ar. Send for her guardian, and confine her
for life!—What's to be done?—While my father is
attach'd to this hypocrite, there is no way to extricate or save her.

Tan. Yes, there is one—you seem a fine fighting
fellow—Tom Tanjore's another, and as her father
once saved me from being confined, while I can
cock a pistol, or brandish a cane, I won't see his
daughter exposed to a similar predicament—Come
along, Ned—we'll trip up Obadiah, and carry her
off.

Capt. Ar. What! are you the friend of Emmeline?

Tan. Yes, and your's, because you are hers—come
let's have at them—what! do you shirk?

Capt. Ar. I dare not go.

Tan. Dare not!—now this is always the way with
your fighting gentlemen—but perhaps it's constitutional, and the poor fellow's conscience is a little

tender—ay, ay, some of us nabobs have very weak nerves.

Capt. Ar. You misconceive—her uncle is my father—he has forbid me his presence, and would you have me lift my arm against a parent?

Tan. No, Ned: but as he is no father of mine, and Emmeline is in danger, there can be no harm in my trying trick, stratagem, or force, to protect her; therefore I'll start alone; and may I go to India or to prison—and one will of course follow the other—if I don't snatch her from Obadiah, and restore her to my dear Ned!

Capt. Ar. The attempt is hopeless; but, be it as it may, I insist on knowing how I can return your kindness?

Tan. Why, there are two ways—the first is, that you patch up your quarrel with Project, in order that you may celebrate your nuptials at his house; and the next is, that, as Emmeline will like you the better for resembling me, you marry her in the fellow coat to that I now wear—it's a pretty Hymeneal colour, isn't it?—so huzza!—now for the onset!——

[*Exeunt.*

SCENE II.

An Apartment in the Alderman's House hung with Pictures, a Portrait of the Alderman in his Gown and full dressed Wig—leaning on a Plough—a round Table—two Chairs, and Wine on the Table.

The Alderman discovered asleep.

Ald. Ar. So there you are, my dear niece, till your guardian comes for you—(*Locks the door, and takes out the key.*)—I'll place the key by me, and—(*Puts*

the key on the round table, and sits down.)—plague
take the girl —to wake me out of my afternoon's
nap, and the sweetest agricultural dreams—however,
she is now as safe as the rats in my granary, and
Edward shall marry Cecilia directly—that being settled, I'll renew my pastoral and delicious dreams!
[*Dozes in his chair.*

Enter TANJORE *hastily.*

Tan. Where is she?—I don't see her—she's in
this room perhaps—(*Trying to open the stage door.*)
the door lock'd!—ha, Obadiah!—how are you, Obadiah?—(*Waking him.*)—what, still in the same dress?
—damme, that waistcoat will be the ruin of you.

Ald. Ar. What the devil do you want, sir?

Tan. I want Emmeline, Obadiah—cousin Billy
has sent me to conduct her to his house——where is
she?—dispatch, and tell your servant to get a coach,
for it rains as hard as it can pour. [*Rain heard here.*

Ald. Ar. So it does!—oh! my cabbages will
grow as tall and thick as a wilderness——as to Emmeline, Mr Tanjore, I shall deliver her to no person but her guardian himself.

Tan. Won't you?—then I'll give you a toast—
come, fill—nay, do exactly as if you were at home,
Obadiah—Here's success to the next harvest!

Ald. Ar. I rise to drink that—" Success to the
next harvest."—Ah, Mr Tanjore, if all farmers were
so easily satisfied as I am—but they are always grumbling, railing at the weather—(*Rain stopt.*)—Zounds,
the rain stopt!—the cabbages will be burnt to a cinder.

Tan. (*Aside, taking up the key.*) What's here? no
doubt the key of the prison house—'sdeath! why
did I wake him? however, if I get him off his favourite topic, he'll soon go to sleep again—Come, Obadiah! one more bumper, Obadiah!—and now I'll
tell you a long story.

Ald. Ar. Will you?—au! au!   [*Yawning.*

Tan. A very long story, Obadiah——In the East
or West Indies, or somewhere thereabouts, there was
a fine young fellow drinking wine with a grunting
old alderman—alderman, I beg pardon—I mean Bramin—well! after a glass or two, the Bramin yawn'd
—then dozed—then closed his eyes, and at last fell
fast asleep, (*Alderman sleeps, and* TANJORE *rises.*)
then this fine young fellow took a key off the table,
and stealing to the prison door, unlock'd it, and led
forth one of the loveliest——

[*As he is opening the door,* VICKERY *enters hastily.*
Tan. What's the matter, sir?
Vic. Mr Project is below, sir.
[VICKERY *takes up the bottle and glasses, and pro-
ceeds to wake the Alderman.*

Tan. Then let him stay there—Zounds! what are
you at?

Vic. Going to wake my master, sir—There is a physician in Mr Project's carriage, to whom Miss Emmeline is to be deliver'd, and as he is in a hurry——

Tan. Don't touch him—I'll wake him, or the devil or his own conscience will wake him——begone,
sirrah, or—(*Exit* VICKERY *with bottle and glasses.*)
—pheugh!—what's to be done now?—if I can't get
this guardian out of the house without seeing the alderman, murder will be the consequence; for, sooner
than give her up, curse me if I don't shoot Billy,
choak Obadiah, and poison the doctor!—pheugh!—
(*Walking about in agitation.*)

Pro. (*Without.*) He's in this room, is he?—very
well, I shall see him——

Tan. See him! no you shan't—if I can prevent
their meeting at this moment, I may secure Emmeline's escape, and—how can I hide the old farmer?—
I'll stand before him, and spread my coat—no—curse
these short skirts—what can I devise?—Project at
the door! the poor girl's fate depending on the
event—I have it.—(*Turns up the round table, which*

completely covers the Alderman.)—There—now he's
as snug as if he was at Aldgate-farm.

Enter PROJECT *with his hat on.*

Pro. What, cousin! how came you here?—well!
how's the wind?

Tan. Southerly, Billy—by the heat, southerly—
don't wear your hat in the room though—(*Pulls it
off.*)—it's like a citizen left off business—pheugh!—

Pro. Why, where's the alderman?—he has sent
for me about Emmeline.

Tan. The Alderman's not at home—he's just
gone to his farm, to sow turnips, plant potatoes, and
cut cabbages—if you want him, follow him—go—go,
Billy.

Pro. Pooh!—I dare say he's in the next room—
(*Alderman snores.*)—I hear him—at the old work!
—asleep and snoring.

Tan. No, it's not him—it's some of his live stock.

Pro. Not him!—I'll swear to both the tune and
the instrument, so come out, alderman—nay; stand
by—I must see him—so wake and come out, alderman—(*Opens stage door, and leads on* EMMELINE.)
Emmeline! ha! have I at last recover'd you? Come,
madam—without wasting time by recapitulating your
past misconduct, answer me this question—Will you
return to your asylum, or accept the hand of this
gentleman?

Tan. Accept the hand of the gentleman, to be
sure—take it, Emmeline, and we'll go get a parson
directly—there—now you can escape.   [*Aside.*

Emm. No, sir: I will no longer fly to artifice and
subterfuge for safety—I have too long been passive
and submissive, and my cause is not so weak but I
may boldly bring it to decision—Call in my uncle,
and when he hears our charges face to face, then
let him say who is most fit to be confined!—Emme-

line for the errors of the head, or her guardian for
the vices of the heart!

Tan. Well spoken, my heroine—I'll give him a
volley myself presently.

Pro. Call in your uncle!—he will not believe you
—besides where is your evidence—who will stand
up?

Tan. I will—I'm always ready to shew a good
face in a good cause; and the cause and the face
are the two best that ever came before a court—I
love your ward, and may I double the Cape only to
get once more doubled in a jail—jail did I say?—
oh ay:—that was a nickname for one of my palaces
—it was a castle so surrounded with walls, bastions
—in short, it was so superb, Billy, that I wish you
were in it at this moment with all my heart.

Pro. You love her, do you?—then the business is
settled at once—there—I join your hands.

Emm. No, sir; I insist my uncle may be call'd—
he thinks you honest, me deranged, and I'd convince him—(PROJECT *smiles.*)—what! is't a cause
for triumph?—is malady to be derided, not lamented?—weak, thoughtless man!—be thankful that your
own poor reason is not lost, and pray that it may
sooth, and not insult misfortune.

Pro. You mistake, Emmeline—I smiled to think
you could convince your uncle, when I and my wife
can turn him round our fingers just as we please—
Hark'ye, coz—come here—nearer the table—if you
take part against me at this moment, I'm ruin'd.

Tan. Are you?—I've a great mind to twitch
Obadiah, and wake him.　　　　　　　　[*Aside.*

Pro. The fact is, I've embezzled her fortune, and
if you marry her, there'll be no overhauling of accounts—I'll make you amends by assigning over to
you the alderman's farm.

Tan. Oh! that Obadiah heard this! (*Here the
Alderman puts his head over the table,* TANJORE *nods*

to him—Alderman remains conceal'd.) Oh, ho!——
So Billy, you confined Emmeline because you had
involved her fortune! (*Very loudly.*)

Pro. Softly—if you speak so loud, the alderman
will hear you—it is as you say, her health is quite
restored, but I have so embark'd her fortune in my
schemes——

Tan. Say no more, make me over Aldgate-farm,
and she shall be a nabob's wife to-morrow. Yonder's pen and ink, we'll sign directly; and now, Billy, I think I shall repay you for all your kindness.

[*Goes up the stage.*

Pro. You will! you will! oh my dear, dear coz!
you've secured me my best speculation—so, madam,
the tables are turn'd, you see.

Emm. He too desert me! my firmness then forsakes me! my uncle still prejudiced; Edward about
to be lost for ever, what hope have I but in my
guardian's humanity?—Oh, sir! behold me once
again imploring your protection.

Tan. (*Coming down the stage with pen, ink, and
paper.*) Here coz, let's sign—why, Obadiah thinks
he has a long lease, don't he?

Pro. Oh the poor clodpole!—he knows as much
about security as he does about a farm! and, as he
is wasting hundreds on rotten sheep and blighted
cabbages, I'll kindly give you the means of turning
him out at a moment's warning: here—now for my
best speculation! (*Pulls down the table to write
upon it. Alderman leans across the table, and stares
*Project *full in the face.* Project *pushes down the
chair he was going to sit upon, and stands aghast.*)

Ald. Ar. (*With his arms on the table.*) Oh you
consummate scoundrel!—this is your speculation,
is it?

Tan. Why, Billy, the tables are turn'd indeed!

Pro. They are—did the alderman hear?

Ald. Ar. He did; the alderman heard that the

farm was to be let over his head, that he was wasting hundreds on rotten sheep and blighted cabbages; and what's more, the alderman heard of this poor girl's persecution.   Niece, give me your hand; henceforth I'll be a friend, a comforter, a father to you.

Pro. Cousin, I wish I was in your Indian palace.

Tan. Don't be afraid, you'll be there sooner than you expect.

Ald. Ar. Sir, I desire you'll quit my house directly—stop though—(*Takes* PROJECT *aside*)—in three hours time repay me and this lady all the money you have schemed us out of, or——You think I don't understand farming, Mr Project; but this I know, that when stray cattle are found eating up other people's property, they are secured; and the King's Bench shall be your pound, you interloper.

Pro. Cousin, stay and try to compose him,—then follow me, and—ah!—now my only hope is a westerly wind !   [*Exit.*

Emm. Generous young man! I perceive why you took part against me—Uncle, you know not half his kindness.

Ald. Ar. I do though—the sly rogue cock'd his eye to me behind the table, and I suppose whisk'd it up on purpose—well!—come with me to my lawyer's—Oh the scheming scoundrel! he has made such dupes of us, Emmeline, that I'd give up farming to find any body that has trick'd him.—I tell you what, Mr Tanjore, don't give him any of the treasures of the East.

Tan. No, that I won't; for, so far from having the treasures of the East to give, I expect my tailor will send me to the King's Bench every moment :—you take the joke, Obadiah, don't you?

Ald. Ar. I do! Oh the poor clodpole !—come— I'm glad you've outschemed him.

Tan. So am I: and when speculators and mono-

polists, from sordid, selfish motives, distress their fellow creatures, and bring odium on their country,
may they be caught in their own snare, and, like
Project, have the tables turn'd upon them !

[*Exeunt.*

ACT THE FIFTH.

SCENE I.

An elegant Room in the King's Bench.

Enter PROJECT *and* PROMPTLY.

Pro. Ay, ay: this room will do very well for the
little time I shall stay : get it ready, and in the mean
time I'll return, and finish my conversation with Sir
George.   Why, you have very good company here
in the King's Bench.   Oh ! I beg pardon—College,
I think you call it.

Prom. Yes, college is the polite name for prison,
sir : pray, won't you pull off your boots ?

Pro. No, as I shall soon get my discharge, I remain booted and spurr'd ready to ride away, you
see—though Sir George has been telling me, that a
fox-hunter, who has been a prisoner here these ten
years, has been so sure of getting out every moment,
that he has been booted and spurr'd the whole time:
however, I've written to my cousin Tanjore, told
him the alderman has arrested me ; and there's no
doubt but he'll come instantly and pay the debt—
so get the room ready.

Prom. Yes, sir : but about the chum.

Pro. The chum !—what's that ?

Prom. Your companion, sir : every room in the King's Bench has two tenants; and unless you buy the other gentleman——

Pro. (*Giving him money.*) There then, I buy the other gentleman : there's for the chum ; and now, when Mr Tanjore comes, call me—(*Looks round the room.*) um ! hah ! handsome room, good furniture ; and, if all fails, perhaps this is as good a place for speculation as any other.   [*Exit.*

Enter MEANWELL, *shewing in* TANJORE.

Mean. Nay, look up, sir : Mr Promptly, here's a prisoner just arrived, who is so melancholy, that I've brought him to your gay apartments to raise his spirits.   Were you never in jail before, sir ?

Tan. Yes ; in India, sir—heigho !

Prom. Come, look around you, and be cheerful : why, what are you ? and who arrested you ?

Tan. I'm a nabob, and my tailor arrested me for thirty pounds, (*Looks up*) heh ! how ? egad ! this is not like the Indian palace : pray, sir, inform me, are all the rooms like this ?

Mean. No ; I wish they were ; mine is a wretched one ; but, having been all my life at sea, I know nothing about the town : the last tenant of this room was a blacklegs.

Prom. And the present one is a swindler, I fancy, for he came here in a coach and four.

Tan. Came to jail in a coach and four ! ah ! I see how it is : 'tis here as elsewhere—the fraudulent debtor rolls in luxury, the unfortunate one starves; and while a gallant seaman is in one room freezing without fire or food, a dashing money-lender is in the next, quaffing champagne, and drinking " confusion to his creditors !"—but no matter : they hang

5

themselves, or the law hangs them; for the devil will
have his own.

Prom. Ay, ay, we have but three or four of them.

Tan. So much the better: but, as I shall certainly be out in a few minutes——what do you smile at?
—I've sent to my cousin Project; and I'm sure he
won't suffer me to be confined for the paltry sum of
thirty pounds—no, no: my getting out is a certainty; and, as I wish to see this coach-and-four gentleman, before I go, I'll, with your leave, sit down here
till he comes.

Prom. With all my heart—I'm glad we leave you
in better spirits.   [*Exit with* MEANWELL.

Tan. (*Solus.*) Being alone, I get nervous again.
This, now, is the end of dissipation! of losing large
sums at Bubble's club, and wasting others on houses,
horses, carriages—and where was the gratification?—
when I used to dash through the streets in my phaeton, every body was envying, sneering——nobody
seemed pleased—Nobody! yes, hang it, the bailiffs
used to smile; they used to think it a fine sight, and
nod, and wink, as much as to say——" Ah, master!
those horses' heads will be turned towards our lockup houses at last."—Oh! I hope Billy won't forsake
me!

Re-enter PROJECT. TANJORE *is sitting with his back
to him.*

Pro. I'm quite uneasy at Tanjore's not coming—
What are a few thousands to a man of his fortune?
(*Sits down, with his back turned to* TANJORE.)——I
hope he won't desert me—Heigho!

Tan. Heigho!

Pro. This is the chum, I suppose—he don't know
I've bought him. (*Aside.*)

Tan. Here's the swindler, I imagine; he seems
as miserable as myself; I'll condole with him. (*Aside.*)

—Pray, sir, what first induced you to keep a coach and four?

Pro. Zounds! what's that to you, sir? I have bought you, and——(*Here they both look round, and meet face to face.*) What do I see? my dear, dear cousin!——

Tan. Is't possible? Oh, my kind, kind, kind Billy!—(*They embrace, and then rise.*)

Pro. I thought he wouldn't forsake me at this moment.

Tan. I said I should be out to a certainty.

Pro. Well, here we are, coz.

Tan. Yes, here we are, coz.

Pro. I knew I should have the pleasure of seeing you here to-day.

Tan. Did you? it was a pleasure I didn't know of myself: but I shan't stay now ; the sooner we get out the better, I say. Come along, Billy

Pro. Ay; come along, nabob——(*They go to the stage door, and stop.*) Have you paid the debt and costs though?

Tan. No; but you have, and that's the same thing, you know—Come.

Pro. Come! You forget, coz: how can a man that's in limbo, as they call it, come, and——

Tan. What!

Pro. How can I, that am a prisoner in the college here——

Tan. Are you a prisoner?

Pro. To be sure I am: I'm not like you: I can't walk in and out.

Tan. Ha! ha! ha!

Pro. What's the matter with you?

Tan. Ha! ha! ha!

Pro. What the devil do you laugh at? Why don't you go and discharge the debt?

Tan. I can't, I can't; (*Still laughing.*) because I'm in limbo too! I'm a prisoner myself! so give

me your hand—Here we are to a certainty !—Lord!
it's nothing when you're used to it; and if you'd
been in an Indian college as long as I was—Zounds!
what have I said?

Pro. How's that? what did you say? imprisoned
in India!

Tan. Well; it's in vain to conceal it; the truth
must come out at last. So, the fact is, cousin, the
ships are arrived; they have brought over the rich
Mr Tanjore, with bullion, pearls, and diamonds; but,
I'm sorry to say, in their hurry, they left all my treasure behind.

Pro. Then curse me if one of my speculations
have succeeded. I'll give up scheming; I'll——Answer me, sir: How dare you waste a gentleman's
fortune, when you knew you could never repay
him?

Tan. And how came you to waste a lady's fortune, when you knew you could never repay her?

Pro. But you talked of your riches, sir—said my
house could never hold them—

Tan. Well; and haven't I kept my word? Look
ye, sir: when I left this country, ruined by you and
the club, you refused even to shake hands with me
at parting. I'm indebted to you for your hospitality; and for that I thank you—down to the very
ground. You made me welcome in your apartments;
I beg you'll be at no ceremony in mine : Sit down,
Billy.

Pro. If I could only get free, and leave him——
What do I see? the alderman! no doubt, his regard
for my wife has induced him to come and settle my
affairs.—

Enter ALDERMAN ARABLE.

Ah! my old generous friend! I thought you'd forgive me; I knew you'd procure a discharge.

Ald Ar. You thought right; I have procured the discharge.

Tan. Why, Obadiah, are you too in limbo? What the devil brings you here?—(*Looks at his dress.*)—Ah, ah! didn't I say that waistcoat would be the ruin of you?

Pro. Mr Nabob, I leave you to the misery you deserve—Never mind though; while you stay in the college here, you needn't pay your debts; and nothing is so comfortable as to have a good warm house over your head—So good b'ye, chum.

Tan. What! have you brought his discharge, Obadiah, and——

Ald. Ar. No; but I've brought yours; here it is, my boy: I heard you were pounded, and I came as eagerly to get you out as if you'd been part of my own live stock. Come along though; I want you to go directly and find my son Jack: he's either at his own chambers or Bubble's club: you must find him, and tell him I want Emmeline's marriage-settlement drawn directly.

Tan. Emmeline's marriage-settlement! with whom, sir?

Ald Ar. Hark'ye; come here. (*Takes* TANJORE *aside.*) Lady Project has at last consented to an assignation; her passion for the pastoral virtues of her sweet shepherd, as she calls me, has induced her to meet me tête-a-tête in her dressing-room; now, in an hour's time—Oh! I knew my person and the Nova Scotia mutton would make an impression at last! therefore, at her intercession, (*Turning to* PROJECT.) I've determined that Emmeline shall marry her old suitor, Sir Frederick; he was her father's choice, and, as Edward has offended me, he shall be mine.

Pro. Say you so? then I've an iron in the fire yet. (*Aside.*)

Tan. What are you at, Obadiah? Lady Stingy will make as great a dupe of you as her husband has

she is a woman of design ; one of those half-and-half
ladies whose reputation depends on keeping open
house ; and entertainment, or no entertainment,
makes or mars her reputation—Don't you remember
her fainting in my arms?

Ald. Ar. I do ; but her grandmother was close at
hand. Yes, I am the idol of her heart; and she is to
receive me in her dressing-room, that sacred temple
that not even her husband ever entered—Good day,
Mr Project ; I've already quitted Aldgate farm, and
taken a snug, profitable one near Islington, where
you'll always be welcome to——the rotten sheep and
blighted cabbages !—Come, nabob.

Tan. We'll talk further about this Lady Project.
—Chum, good b'ye ! while you stay in the college,
you needn't pay your debts, you know ; and nothing
is so comfortable as to have a good warm house over
your head, particularly when the wind is high and
westerly—hem !—Come along, Obadiah.

                        [*Exit with Alderman.*

Pro. (*Rubbing his hands.*) Bravo ! if Sir Frederick marries Emmeline, he takes her with the fortune in its entangled state, and, consequently, I shall
be discharged——(*Enter a Servant, who gives him a
Letter.*)—From my wife ! (*Reads.*)

" My dear husband,
" I've only time to say, that if you hear of an assignation between me and the alderman, be convinced it is to secure the marriage between Emmeline
and Sir Frederick, and thus restore you to

                        Your affectionate wife,
                        KATHARINE PROJECT."

Kind wife, and kind Sir Frederick ! I'll go and communicate the good news to Sir George——Oh ! this
is a safe speculation, and not like the Indian one !—
Fool ! blockhead that I was, to take that broken-
down prodigal for the rich Mr Tanjore ! However,

this is a different scheme—yes, yes; it depends on my wife's prudence, and, heaven be praised! not on ships, water, nabobs, or westerly winds! [*Exit.*

SCENE II.

BUBBLE'S *Club.* *A Flat with two Doors.*

Enter, from one door, JACK ARABLE *and a Servant.*

Jack Ar. Curse my bad luck, or rather curse my bad management, to be at Epsom only ten minutes, and lose all the Spanish!—I thought to make an excellent hedge; when, plague on't, I found I had betted the long odds both ways!—then to borrow thirty of the man at the coffee-house, and take a dash here at Bubble's; to lose that too! and then be bothered by one's clerk about law-business—Well, sir, what—

Serv. The special pleader has sent you these declarations, sir.

Jack Ar. Why, is it term-time?

Serv. Term began four days ago, sir.

Jack Ar. And I on a race-ground the whole time! come, that's fair, very fair. (*Sits.*) I don't think my education so finished as I thought; for, if it was, I never could be so ignorant as to bet the long odds both ways. I wonder who wins; for, when I complain of my losses, every body else says they have lost too! hang me if ever I saw a man that had won in my life.

Enter TANJORE, *from the other Door.*

Tan. Done it at last! Huzza! here's retribution, Jack, retribution!

Jack Ar. Why, what is this? Who are you, sir?

Tan. The luckiest dog in Europe, Jack! Your
father Obadiah sent me to look after you here at
Bubble's; and, not seeing you, I put my hand in
my pocket, where I found five guineas my sister had
lent me! " I'll have a touch," says I; " this faro
bank dished me formerly, now I'll try to dish them."
—Down went the five guineas on your namesake, the
knave of clubs, Jack——the knave in my favour! I
cocked it——once more in my favour!——cocked it
again, till it had won so often, that I thought the
ships were arrived, and I was a nabob in reality!

Jack Ar. And what's all this to me? what do I
care for your luck?

Tan. (*Putting rouleaus, guineas, and bank-notes,
on the table.*) Here they are! look, you rogue, look!
How I feel for the poor devil that lost them! I always pity the unlucky ones; don't you, Jack?

Jack Ar. Zounds, sir! I am an unlucky one; that
was my poney, and that was my bank note.

Tan. Was it? then take it again, and go and put
it on the knave; I'm serious, Jack; take it, and——
By the Ganges! that's a neat nisi prius dress. What!
you prefer a scarlet coat to a black one?

Jack Ar. Ay, and cards to briefs; so give me the
Spanish, and let me be off.

Enter CAPTAIN ARABLE, *hastily.*

Capt. Ar. Stay, and grant a brother's last request:
nay, I must and will be heard: By my father's orders, are you not going to draw a settlement between Emmeline and Sir Frederick?

Jack Ar. Me going to draw a settlement! no;
I'm going to cock the knave; and, as to father, he
can't blame me, because he once play'd himself, you
know.   I'll tell you how it was, sir: (*To* TANJORE.)
He was sent for, as magistrate, to put down a ha-
zard-table—in he came with the constables—pushed
down the groom-porter—seized the caster—laid hold

of the dice-box—when, lo ! as if there was magic in
the wood, he cast his eyes at the guineas on the table, and avarice so completely got the better of justice, that he halloed out, " Seven's the main—at all
in the ring, my jolly boys !"

Tan. Well ! and they cheated him, gave him loaded dice ?

Jack Ar. No ; that wasn't worth while ; they saw
what a flat he was, so picked his pocket at once !—
famous, heh ?——Adieu, brother ; farewell, benefactor !—Here's the Spanish once more !

[*Exit, looking at the bank note.*

Tan. (*To Captain.*) Don't stop him, Ned ; let
him go, I say ; if he's out of the way, the settlement
can't be drawn : I gave him the money on purpose.

Capt. Ar. This is but temporary consolation : while
the alderman's absurd vanity attaches him to Lady
Project, there is no hope of saving Emmeline—and
to lose her, after all the conflicts we have suffered !
to see her given to another, at the moment when I
thought her mine for ever ! then perhaps to see her
mind, but late restored, again involved——by heaven ! that thought will madden mine !

Tan. So it ought, if you will talk of your own
sufferings and forget her's—Poor girl ! did you tell
her ?

Capt. Ar. I did, and when she heard she was to
wed Sir Frederick, there was a wild emotion in her
countenance portending that her fever would return—she said, " they'd rob her of all hope, and
once more steal her senses ; yet they should not, I
would not let them, would I ?" then with a sigh
she left me—Oh, my friend ! I am not used to sink
beneath misfortune, but this last scene has quite un-
mann'd me.

Tan. More shame for you ; it only animates me ;
misfortunes always rouse me ; and if ever you should
be in prison at Madras, the gaolers there will tell

you so. I've already exposed the husband; now I'll
try to manage the wife; she loves money; here's
plenty, so I'll go directly and bribe her.

Capt. Ar. That will be hopeless, nothing but exciting the alderman's jealousy.

Tan. I'll try that too—Obadiah half suspects me
at present, so wait for your brother, and come together to Lady Project's, and, by the time you arrive,
if all isn't to your wishes, may the monsoon deluge
me! may Tippoo torture me! may the Marattas
——but this is no time for fine speeches——follow me to Lady Project's,—(*Going, returns.*)——
D'ye hear, Ned, bring your wedding coat along with
you, for damme, but you shall be Emmeline's husband this very night!   [*Exeunt separately.*

SCENE III.

Enter LADY PROJECT *with a Paper in her Hand,*
follow'd by a Servant.

Lady Pro. When the alderman comes, shew him
up stairs. (*Exit Servant.*) I have honoured him with
this tête-a-tête in my dressing room, to secure the marriage; and he sha'n't leave the room, till he signs
this agreement, which binds him in a penalty of ten
thousand pounds to give Emmeline to Sir Frederick.
Thus, by œconomy——

Serv. (*Without.*) Sir, you mustn't pass.—This is
my lady's dressing room.

Tan. (*Without.*) I tell you, I will come up. Stand
by, sirrah. (TANJORE *enters.*) So, Kitty! here's the
nabob.

Lady Pro. Heavens! where do you come from,
sir?

Tan. From the college, coz; where I left Billy

so certain of getting out, that he was ready booted and spurr'd.

Lady Pro. Sir, I insist you leave the room—I'm engaged—besides I should be sorry to use hard words ; but your conduct has been so little short of that of a swindler——

Tan. Coz, why so ? though I didn't get money in India, I've got it in England—look here!

[*Shewing bank notes.*

Lady Pro. Hundreds, I declare! Who gave you these notes ? some swindling knave, I suppose.

Tan. It was a knave, but not a swindling one, upon my honour. Look here, and here! enough to give ten wedding dinners, and buy all the shawls, china, and chintzes in Europe.—Don't the sight charm you?

Lady Pro. It does ; and when a man has money, it don't signify whether he got it in India or England. My dear cousin, my house and table were always open to you ; and if I knew how to oblige you——

Tan. There is a way, Kitty—as you still govern the alderman, persuade him to let Edward marry Emmeline—do, and half these are yours. (*Putting rouleaus in her hand.*) There,—and I wish from my soul that all who have luck at the gaming table may dispose of their winnings in so benevolent a manner.

Lady Pro. Impossible!—The only mode of settling my husband's affairs, is by Sir Frederick's marrying Emmeline ; and therefore, as my pride will not suffer him to remain in prison, and the living there is too expensive, I shall make the alderman sign this agreement, which binds him in a penalty of ten thousand pounds——

Tan. Make him sign this agreement—make him renew Emmeline's malady—break his son's heart—separate—curse it! what's the use of winning, when

money will not purchase even momentary gratification? Now do, Kitty: there's a dear, liberal, generous girl.   Think how they love each other: think——
here are more rouleaus, here————

[*A knocking at the door.*

Lady Pro. Bless me! if this should be the alderman? (*Looks out.*) It is! come to keep an assignation, and find another man in my dressing room! Go,
sir, get out of the way directly—step into the next
room—hide yourself——

Tan. I say, Kitty, don't you remember when
Obadiah caught you fainting in my arms?

Lady Pro. I do; and that's an additional motive
for concealing yourself.—Now pray retire. (Tanjore *nods assent.*) Thanks, my kind cousin. (Tanjore *pauses.*) Why, what's the matter with you?
What makes you put your hand to your head? Are
you ill?——

Tan. Softly: it's my old complaint— a giddiness
—a vertigo—I'm going—hold me, or I shall tumble
—Oh, I'm sick, I'm——

Lady Project *holds out her arm to support him.*
Tanjore *rests himself upon it, and the Alderman
enters.*

Ald. Ar. Where is my life, my love?——Holloa!
what the devil's all this?

Tan. Only the tables turn'd again, you see, Obadiah, you see—(*Comes away from* Lady Project.)
Cousin, I m better.

Ald. Ar. Why, where's her grandmother? Oh!
this is beyond her husband's speculation!

Tan. (*Aside to Alderman.*) If you want further
proof, look at those rouleaus which she took as a
bribe; then read that agreement; then—

Ald. Ar. My eyes are open'd: I was partly convinced before I came; but now I give all my love
to the wind—pheugh!—there, it's gone! and the

alderman's himself again! (*Enter a Servant.*) Step
over the way to Sir Frederick's, and tell him to
come here directly, and bring Emmeline and Cecilia along with him. (*Servant exit.*) I left them there
in company with the real nabob, the rich Mr Tanjore, who seems as fond of your sister as I am of my
new farm; and takes as much notice of her person
as you have done of my waistcoat.——It's a match,
isn't it?

Tan. I hope so. It's an old attachment. He's a
worthy fellow, and next to being a nabob myself, I
should like to be brother to one.

Enter SIR FREDERICK, EMMELINE, *and* CECILIA.

Lady Pro. Ay; now, alderman, you can give Emmeline to her husband.

Ald. Ar. So I can, and so I will. Emmeline, give
me your hand—nay, don't think to avoid me. I insist you marry the man I have in my eye.

Sir Fred. (*Advancing to take* EMMELINE's *hand.*)
Alderman, you are all kindness.

Emm. Let me entreat you, sir, hear me—

Ald. Ar. I'll hear nobody. I wouldn't hear the
Board of Agriculture if they were going to adjudge
me a prize. I tell you, take the man I chuse for
your husband—(*Enter Captain and* JACK ARABLE.)
there; (*Giving* EMMELINE *to* EDWARD.) now don't
interrupt me, for the clouds are chuck full of water,
and there's been lately so much bad weather, that
sunshine will be welcome to us all.

Tan. Emmeline, I give you joy. Ned, your hand.
Fred., yours. Obadiah, I shall like you and your
waistcoat as long as I live. Kitty, yours. And now
let me advise you to order your coach and four,
drive to the college, and try to raise the wind—a
westerly one if possible.

Lady Pro. Come, Sir Frederick; I believe we'd
better retire: only I beg leave to observe, that, if any

body defames my character, I shall prosecute them,
notwithstanding the expences of the law. I'll have
my reputation justified if it costs me five pounds.
Come, sir.

Tan. Ay ; that's about the value of it. Go, Fred.,
go—go. (*Lady and* SIR FREDERICK *exeunt.*) I say,
Kitty, my love to your grandmother.

Ald. Ar. Edward, forget and forgive, my boy.
Though Project has hurt Emmeline's fortune, there's
enough left to make you live happy—if not, take a
landed estate near mine, and I'll shew you how to
make a fortune by farming, you rogue.

Jack. (*To* TANJORE.) Yes ; I cock'd the knave,
but I lost all the Spanish—Hang it ! I'm half tired of
gambling, and if I won ten thousand a year, I don't
think I could tell how to spend it.

Tan. Couldn't you ? then take a wife, Jack, and
she'll tell you how to spend it—enter into the school
of matrimony, Mr Bachelor of Arts, and there finish
your education.—Cecily here has set you an example : haven't you ?

Cec. I have, from two motives ; first, because Mr
Henry Tanjore has long won my affections; and, secondly, because he means to give affluence to his
namesake. My dear brother, you may now return
to India, and live in a palace in reality ; for a third
of my husband's rupees and pagodas are at your disposal.

Jack Ar. Are they ? that's fair, very fair.

Emm. (*To* TANJORE.) And is there none to share
your treasures ?—is there no fair one worthy a heart
so warm and so benevolent ?

Tan. (*Shaking his head.*) Hereafter perhaps it
may find one like Emmeline's.—Till then, I shall
pursue a plan, which, had Project follow'd, he had
now been happy—that is, not to waste a fortune in
dissipation, and try to retrieve it by false and unjust
speculation.

If we must scheme, let us try Projects here,
When they have merit, where's our cause for fear ?
If they have not, good humour props our cause ;
So make us Nabobs by your kind applause.

[Exeunt omnes.

THE

DELINQUENT;

OR,

SEEING COMPANY.

A

COMEDY,

AS IT IS PERFORMED AT THE

THEATRE-ROYAL, COVENT-GARDEN.

BY

FREDERICK REYNOLDS.

DRAMATIS PERSONÆ.

THE DELINQUENT,	*Mr Kemble.*
SIR EDWARD SPECIOUS,	*Mr Brunton.*
MAJOR TORNADO,	*Mr Munden.*
OLD DORIC,	*Mr Fawcett.*
YOUNG DORIC,	*Mr Lewis.*
DORVILLE,	*Mr Claremont.*
TRADELOVE,	*Mr Atkins.*
WINE MERCHANT,	*Mr King.*
UPHOLSTERER,	*Mr Beverly.*
LANDLORD,	*Mr Waddy.*
OLD NICHOLAS,	*Mr Liston.*
TOM TACKLE,	*Mr Emery.*
Waiter,	*Mr Harley.*
Servant to SIR EDWARD,	*Mr Field.*
Servant to YOUNG DORIC,	*Mr Abbot.*
OLIVIA,	*Mrs H. Johnstone.*
MISS STOIC,	*Mrs Dibdin.*
MRS AUBREY,	*Mrs Gibbs.*

SCENE.—*A Sea-port Town.*

THE

DELINQUENT.

ACT THE FIRST.

Outside of Hermitage—Spikes, &c.

Enter Sir Edward Specious.

Sir Edw. So; this is the house; and, that no time may be lost—*(Rings the bell.)* Faith! 'tis a strange awful sort of habitation; but no matter; were it a town impregnable, in such a cause, I would assault it.

Enter Nicholas, *an old tottering Gardener.*

Come, shew me to Miss Stoic.

Nich. My mistress! mercy on me! do you know who she is?

Sir Edw. To be sure; she's a woman.

Nich. And you are—

Sir Edw. A man.

Nich. The more the pity! Good day!

Sir Edw. What the devil! am I pitied for being a man?

Nich. Certainly—my mistress pities all mankind; that is, they are so hateful to her, that she has forsworn the world, and lives alone in that hermitage.

Sir Edw. Alone! why, what are you?

Nich. Me! pooh! I'm nothing!

Sir Edw. No! but nothing as you are, I fancy there never was a female hermitage without something like you—But, don't be alarm'd—I visit the old lady for the sake of a young one, the lovely Miss Olivia.

Nich. Miss Olivia!

Sir Edw. Ay: I met her last night at a friend's house,—and, hearing she was the adopted child of your mistress, Miss Stoic's brother—

Nich. She is;—of the gallant Major Tornado, who, blessings on him! arrived here two days ago.

Sir Edw. Major Tornado! tell me—was he lately at Naples?

Nich. I can't say: but it is not unlikely, for he came over land from India.

Sir Edw. From India! 'tis the same—I met him there, on my travels, three months ago; and a more active, animated—But a hermitage! Major Tornado two whole days in a hermitage; with no companion but this Petrarch in petticoats—Zounds! is he alive?

Nich. Hardly! the quiet of a country life is almost death to him; and whilst his sister is constantly praising the charms of retirement, he is secretly cursing them. But here he comes, to describe, in person, his dislike to rural felicity.

[*Exit into the House.*

Enter MAJOR TORNADO.

Sir Edw. Major Tornado! I rejoice to see you.

Major. Sir Edward! my dear fellow! how long have you been in England? the sight of a civilized being is pleasant any where; but in the country, amidst trees that never move, prospects that never alter, and brutes that never utter—Where do you live? Where are you going? don't shirk—for, like a drowning man, I'll cling to you, till we both sink together.

Sir Edw. You are very good; but I don't mean to sink. The country has, for me, a thousand charms; and, for civilized society—answer me—can cows speak scandal, or sheep tell lies of us?

Major. No; I wish they could—any conversation's better than none; for, is it to be expected, that an old soldier, who, for forty years, has been listening to the glorious rattle of the cannon, can now sit down contented with the baaing of lambs and the squeaking of little pigs? No, give me noise, battle, occupation! And, sooner than pass another two days of still life in that hermitage, curse me, but I'll do good to the community by sending challenges to all the apothecaries, and bringing actions against all the attornies.

Sir Edw. 'Tis very strange! Pray, have you tried rural sports?—shooting—fishing—

Major. Shooting! that's very well! as if a man, that has been accustomed to wing game six feet high, can take interest in popping at partridges! and for fishing, I tried that yesterday; and falling fast asleep with the line round my hand, the first bite from a large jack plumped me souse into the water. But, I'll tell you what—I've one resource —I mean to build a neat cottage, on the modern plan.

Sir Edw. On the modern plan?

7

Major. Ay; that is, a house with dining rooms, drawing rooms, ball-rooms, and stabling for about fifty horses : and, if the workmen will be so merciful, as to take two years to finish it, I shall have all the pleasure, without any of the fatigue ; for, at that time, my leave of absence expires, and I'll return to India without once setting foot in it.

Sir Edw. Why, you are in a bad way indeed! Have you no mental resources ? Nothing to excite love or friendship, or—

Major. Don't talk of it :—I have an adopted child ; but—

Sir Edw. But what ?

Major. She's undutiful to me, ungrateful to my sister here, Miss Stoic, and I'm sorry for it. Her story interested me, it cut me to the heart; and though I adopted Olivia without seeing her, yet I pictured to myself a lovely, helpless orphan, bidding me welcome by the name of father—benefactor—But, now, look ye, Sir Edward, if Time don't make his clocks strike months instead of hours, my leave of absence will extend much beyond this world ; for I can find no peace or comfort but in war, battle, and general uproar.

Sir Edw. Undutiful and ungrateful, do you say ? How ? in what manner ?

Major. How ! why, when her best friend there, my sister, (*Pointing to Hermitage.*) finding her mind untutored, and her manners awkward, wished her to remove from her present negligent governess, Miss Olivia refused to comply forsooth—But I've done with her—As soon as I can find a house to place her in, she shall bid adieu to this neighbourhood for ever ; and to me, and my friendship, and—No, hang it, after all, perhaps, if I must have employment, I can't pass time much better than in, now and then, sending a bank note to a poor, abandoned orphan.

Sir Edw. Right, major ! do not quite forsake her ;

—and, as you're such a stranger here, if I can be of service—My aunt, for instance, has a house a few miles off, and will, I'm sure, be ready to receive her.

Major. Indeed! that's the very thing; for I promised my sister she should be sent away to-night, and I'll go tell her directly. But, I say, who is to conduct her? For, though I've the highest opinion of your character, Sir Edward——

Sir Edw. 'Sdeath, sir! if you doubt that I'm a man of honour—

Major. Oh! no; not at all.—But, begging your pardon, it is possible now-a-days to be a man of very great honour, and yet be a very sad rascal: for seducing the wife or daughter of your friend, and afterwards shooting him in a duel, don't in the least deprive you of the fashionable appellation. Yet, seriously, Sir Edward, you rank so high in every good man's praise, that I safely may trust you.

Sir Edw. You may depend on't.—I see you would avoid Olivia.—I will inform her of your wishes.

Major. Do;—directly—while I prepare an attendant (*Going towards the Hermitage.*) Look! what a miserable hole am I going into! My sister has a strong, enlighten'd mind, and can support solitude; but I'm so little of the hermit—Hark ye! come back as fast as you can, and I'll take a peep with you, at all the pretty faces in the public walks; for, though Miss Stoic hates our sex, I'm very fond of hers; and if I find I can't manage time any other way, i'cod I'll take a wife.

Sir Edw. Do.

Major. I will; for, next to war, I know nothing more likely to give a gentleman ample employment.

[*Exit into Hermitage.*

Sir Edw. Bravo, Sir Edward! you have won the prize—and yet shan't lose each good man's praise; for here's the stalking-horse to cloak my guilt; here is the desperate and convenient friend, that is to answer for his patron's crimes.

Enter the DELINQUENT.

Why what's the matter? what agitates you?

Delin. That which gives joy to you, the sight of England, of your native land—No friendly, kindred smile hails my return; and I, who once was welcomed and loved like you, now, if I'm known, I'm known to be destroyed.

Sir Edw. Be patient, and remember well—'Tis but a year ago since, in a poor Italian inn, I found you almost perishing for want.

Delin. You did; at Lucca—and I repeat what then I told you, much as my life is worth, so much I owe you. (*With sullen pride.*)

Sir Edw. Remember, too, I knew you at first sight; knew you were the man who had so wrong'd and so deceived my father; but, burying in oblivion all past injuries, offer'd to protect you.

Delin. You have; and what are your commands? I see you have in view some daring, desperate service; and I am bound and pledged to undertake it.

Sir Edw. Why, then, in brief: Here, at the neighbouring school, there is a lovely girl; and none can thwart me in my plans but her suspicious governess. You understand—she must be some way silenced, and yet my name kept secret.

Delin. And mine proclaimed——Well, be it so; yet——

Sir Edw. No remonstrance: be it yours—be it yours to execute my wishes. No hesitation, or——

Delin. And do I hesitate? No—Yet think a little, Sir Edward. You can, as yet, look into yourself—can see a spotless and untainted heart: and if, expanding with its pangs, hereafter it would burst its bonds, as mine would now, how will you curse the selfishness of him who joined to screen you from the

world's reproaches, but left you tortured by your
own!

Sir Edw. Farewell! I have not leisure for this
busy, dull advice. You'll wait for me at home—and
mind, though I've the power to overwhelm you, it
is my wish to serve and to befriend you.   [*Exit.*

Delin. Still, still must I smother in my proud
breast all feeling of a man?—Must I, who once was
equal to this worldly youth, in pówer, and wealth,
and fame—still must I submit to be menaced and
commanded? Better the penalty of my delinquency
were death at once, than to endure this daily respite
from perdition. (*Going.*) Yet, no; death robs me of
the hope of finding that, for which alone I ventured
to revisit England: and, could I clasp the long-lost
treasure to my heart!——Oh! that tender thought
recalls me to my former self; and, when I think of
what I was——Distraction! when, when will merciful forgetfulness yield that repose which cruel men,
and too severe a destiny, deny me?   [*Exit.*

SCENE II.

A Room at MRS AUBREY'S.

Enter MRS AUBREY.

Mrs Aub. 'Tis very strange! Olivia not returned!
Oh! she little thinks each minute seems an age!
And much I wish her generous benefactor would arrive; for I suspect I am her only friend; and friendship such as mine, alas! is but of poor avail.

Enter OLIVIA.

Oliv. Oh, my dear madam! what do you think?

I'm afraid you'll be so angry; for I've lost something; indeed I have—something you've had possession of ever since I first saw you.

Mrs Aub. Speak! what is it, Olivia?

Oliv. My heart—nothing less than my heart. I took it out with me; but, somehow, I dropt it on the sea-shore; and who should pick it up, but such a sweet, rude, delightful——Do you know, when I asked him for it again, he downright refused me; and so I told him to give me another——and he did, very civilly; he gave me his own; and they beat in such unison, that I don't think either of us will be sorry for the change as long as we exist.

Mrs Aub. Heavens! who is it? Not Sir Edward Specious?

Oliv. Oh! no—the confident creature only arrived just time enough to see me insulted by two intoxicated coxcombs: So, flying to my assistance, and forcing them to acknowledge they had both got drunk and forgot themselves; " Get drunk again," says he; " for you can't do better than forget what's so little worth remembering." —— Lord! ma'am, though you don't like Sir Edward, I do verily believe we shall quite quarrel, and pull caps about this gentleman.

Mrs Aub. Olivia, yours is the age of danger; and, judging by your own of others' merits, man has with you no art, the world no vice: but, after seven long years of tenderness and care—now, when I hoped to reap the harvest of my toils—think, should I see it blighted and despoiled by insects, venomous as vile?——

Oliv. I thought, as 'twas holiday-time, and all my young friends were gone to their respective homes, that I might amuse myself in my turn; and, I'm sure, losing one's heart is very pretty amusement: but, if you think otherwise, I had rather it had broken into a thousand atoms, than that the best of monitors and friends should, for one instant, think Olivia thoughtless and ungrateful.

Mrs Aub. Oh! but for you——(*Embracing her, and weeping.*) You see my weakness——Should you forsake me——

Oliv. Forsake you! you, who have so watched, and——

Mrs Aub. Have I?

Oliv. And sure I needed it; for all but me, alas! have homes, have parents.

Mrs Aub. Hold, I implore you! 'tis the subject upon which he who adopted you has commanded a fixed and eternal silence.

Enter Sir Edward Specious.

Sir Edw. Ladies, your most obedient—I have the honour to inform you that Major Tornado is arrived from India.

Mrs Aub. Arrived! Where? Oh! let us fly to meet him.

Sir Edw. Nay; I'm sorry to add, that Miss Olivia has offended his sister, and, at her request, she is instantly to be removed.

Mrs Aub. Removed! Oh! slanderous, sordid woman! 'Tis to monopolize her brother's wealth she thus defames the rival that she dreads. I'll confront her with the best of proofs—(*Taking* Olivia's *hand.*) That look of artlessness and truth, opposed to hers of treachery and guile, shall flash conviction on his mind, and innocence shall triumph!—Come.

Sir Edw. You are wrong—leave it to me—I have settled with the major, and she will be sent this very night to a friend's house of mine.

Mrs Aub. Sir, you are very kind; but let 'em banish her to distant climes, I'm also banished; for but with life I'll leave her.

Sir Edw. Stop—one word——(*Taking her aside.*) Are you aware that, of my large estate, this house forms part? And, as my steward tells me there are arrears of rent——

Mrs Aub. Ha! do you menace?

Sir Edw. Not at all—Between ourselves, I would accommodate——Befriend my suit——be a complying, civil governess, and——

Mrs Aub. Begone! at present, I am mistress of this house—and, not me alone, you mistake your country, if you think there lives one guardian o an English seminary that would unite with libertines, like you, to blast the hopes of parent and of child— Begone! or I'll proclaim you, sir.

Sir Edw And who'll believe you? he who, for years, has courted popularity, by public acts of spirit and humanity, can laugh at private malice; and therefore, be prepared for a most powerful and deadly foe. (*Going.*)

Oliv. Detain him! make friends with him! I tremble at his threats!—Sir——

Mrs Aub. There is the door, sir.

Sir Edw. Madam, I comprehend you. (*To* OLIVIA.) And if the major fail to influence this busy friend, still I'll not despair; for the aspiring mind yields not to common obstacles; but, in a contest glorious as the present, is most determined where 'tis most opposed. Farewell, and trust to those who are your real friends.

[*Exit, looking at* MRS AUBREY.

Oliv. Dear madam, why were you so rash?—My heart forebodes——

Mrs Aub. Fear not, but away—Though weakest armed, we have the strongest cause; and the proud courage of the virtuous few can vanquish hosts of braggards such as these. [*Exeunt.*

SCENE III.

Outside of Hotel—Sea-Shore—A Yacht.

Enter Landlord and Waiter, from the Hotel.

Land. Come, bustle, bustle! for see what crowds of carriages are pouring down the hill—Look! isn't it a noble sight? chaises, sociables, phaetons, curricles, gigs, whiskies, tandems, taxed carts, and dog-carts!—and all—all flocking from the races at the next town, to make sport for Paul Pigeon and the Pelican.

Wait. Ay; but have they cash to pay for it? for of many that went from this town with full pockets, I'm sure most will come home with empty ones.

Land. And see! here's one already——here's honest Tom Tackle——I warrant they've stript him of the last feather, and——

Enter TOM TACKLE.

Well, Tom, racing is a bad business, isn't it? (*Tom crosses.*) Why, what's the matter? Are you going to buy a rope to hang yourself?

Tom. No; I'm going to buy one of those smart koind of dog-carts yonder; because, now I've got the poney, why, like other pups of fashion, I'll turn coachy, you see.

Land. Got the poney! How?

Tom. Why, by jockeyship, to be sure——Look! (*Shewing a purse full of guineas.*) He! he! he! mother only made me a sort of a simple sailor, to be sure; but then, good soul, she also made me a north-countryman—and I don't think she could have done more for me if she'd made me great Cream of Tartary——And so, you see, though Miss Fidget were

the favourite, and all hollow the best horse, yet
somehow I found the blacklegs, as they call 'em,
were all for taking the long odds on Master Jacky ;
so, thinks I, I'd better be for Master Jacky and
blacklegs too ; and, of course, you know, we won ;
and accordingly I went up to your lords and baronets, to touch my winnings, when, would you believe
it ? they talked of settling with me two hundred
miles off—at one Tattersal's, at Hyde-Park-Corner.
—" But," says I, " gentlemen, I hope ye be joking,
for I hate to seem awkward or unfashionable ; but, if
you're serious, I must really horsewhip you all round
the race-course ;"—and I just gave a smack or two,
and here's the prize-money. He ! he ! he ! I might
have known it all along ; for we Jack Tars are sure
to win it, ay, though the odds be a million to one
agains us.

Land. So you are ; but then, Tom, to be so rude
to your superiors———

Tom. Superiors ! bless ye, there be no such thing
at races, or any kind of gambling. (*Landlord stares.*)
No ; betting do bring on such a sweet familiarity,
and we sporting gentlemen be somehow so all on a
footing, that, at the ordinary, when Lord Tiffany
proposed a maggot-race, " Done, Tiffy !" cried I—
And when Sir William swore he'd win all the hearts
in the ball-room, " I'll tell you what, Billy," says
I, " I'll make love, for a hundred pounds, to any
beauty in the room ; and make it play and pay, and
crossing and jostling, just as you like ;" and then
they all laughed, and I laughed too—And, icod ! I
only wish they had tried me ; for, at making love,
making punch, and dancing a horn-pipe, Tom a-
gainst the field, boy !——But now for my carriage !
(*Whipping.*)

Land. Stop—you forgot that that's Sir Edward's
yacht ; and that you, as master of it——

Tom. No—and if Ned, that is, Sir Edward, do

choose a race upon the water, mind if I don't jockey sea-sharks as neatly as I have done land ones.

Voices without. Here—stop—draw up!

Tom. There they are! and here I go! And, I say, should any of the most genteel and tip-toppest o' your customers like a game at Put, or Scratch, or Sneezums, or Pope Joan, why, you'll send for me to mother's cottage——As it's the best way to make a fortune, so I'll push it, while fortune be in the humour——I say, (*Holding up his purse.*) Jack Tar, North Country, and Master Jacky, against the field! He! he! he!

Land. There they are indeed! and, foremost in the rank, two such wealthy-looking gentlemen, stepping out of their own post-chaise and four——Why, during race-time, fortune seems in humour with every body, I think.

Enter YOUNG DORIC, DORVILLE, *and Post-Boy.*

Young Dor. Go, mind the horses, sir. [*Exit Boy.* And mind, I say again, 'tis fortune has undone me.

Dorv. And I say again, you're ruined by seeing company.

Land. Oh! ruined, are they? Now I look at 'em again, I think I never saw two more vulgar, sharper-like—Tom, we've no beds, no—Mum!

[*Exit* TOM *into the Hotel.*

Dorv. There—you see——

Young Dor. Be quiet—I'll bring you through—— Landlord, my friend here will want tea and supper, and all that—but, for myself, my food is love—And if you know the dear, divine, Miss Olivia Tornado, whom I saw just now, and sought for on the sea-shore——Where does she live? Who does she visit? At what parties can I meet her?

Dorv. You meet her! here's assurance again!—— Why, who'll invite you?

Young Dor. Who? why, the greatest person in

the town—myself—I'll invite myself—and I'm right,
—am I not, old Pelican?

Land. Certainly; for perhaps nobody else will invite you.

Young Dor. How!

Land. Why, look ye, when gentlemen of fortune and respectability visit this town, the town visits them; but when people bring with them neither money nor manners, why, even old Pelican turns his back upon them.

Young Dor. Stop—In your inn is there a handsome ball-room?

Land. To be sure there is.

Young Dor. Then, observe——write a hundred cards in my name—in the name of Jack Doric, of Piccadilly, London—and invite a hundred of your first neighbours to a splendid ball and supper——and look, here are a hundred respectable gentlemen to answer for it. (*Shews a note-case.*)

Land. So there are! Oh, your honour, a thousand pardons.

Young Dor. One for each pound—a hundred will do.

Dorv. 'Sdeath! what madness and effrontery!—Nobody knows you, and, of course, nobody will accept your invitation.

Young Dor. Won't they? My dear fellow, people think so much more of the supper than they do of the person who gives it, that if, by mistake, instead of " Jack Doric's," he were to write " Jack Ketch's compliments," my life on't, there wouldn't be three excuses——And now I'll tell you both a secret—Spunging is a sneaking, hacknied art; and, instead of toiling to get dinners, always try to give them.

Land. Give dinners!

Young Dor. To be sure. Let every body suppose you don't want money, and any body is so ready to lend it to you, that, whilst the poor and crin-

ging spunge borrows half-crowns with difficulty, he
who gives sumptuous entertainments confers a favour by accepting hundreds—and, as a proof, (*To
Landlord.*) George talked of ruin, and you turned
your back—I give a supper, and it's " Oh, your honour, and a thousand pardons !"

Land. Gad ! so it is : and I can't help laughing
at the world and myself too.

Young Dor. No ; and were my motives sordid,
each bottle of your wine, to-night, should yield me
twenty times your profit : but 'tis from love I act—
I would be known and noticed by Olivia's friends—
So, come, I'll help you to make out the cards ; (*To
Landlord.*) and for my friend, you, George, prepare
the paragraphs and puffs : for balls are nothing now,
till stampt by newspaper report ; and every giver of
a fete must, like quack doctors, publish lists of
names, to shew they've equal custom and repute.

Dorv. Stay—are you aware that, out of £15,000,
earned by your late good father, as an architect,
this hundred is the last ?

Young Dor. I am ; and also that my uncle will
dissolve our partnership : but, if I fail, I only wrong
myself; and, if my plan succeeds, you know my
friend shall share in my success. 'Tis my last stake,
and, by heaven, I'll make the most of it. So, here !
house ! waiter ! rooms, wine, and supper, for a hundred !   [*Exeunt into the Inn.*

ACT THE SECOND.

*A Room inside of the Hermitage.   Door in the back
Scene.*

Miss Stoic *discovered sitting with a Book in her
Hand, reading.*

Miss Stoic. Oh, world, world! but that thy strange
mutations make us hate thee, life would not yield to
age! Well, well! So long misanthropy has chill'd
my soul, so long I've shunn'd life's miserable scenes,
that sometimes I prefer to read those bards that
point its blessings out.   Sterne, Congreve, or a modern German play—oh, had I met with social minds
like these—but here's my brother; and for a time
I must assume the love of solitude and rural peace.

Enter Major Tornado.

Well, sir, I hope the hour of reason has arrived, and
that you own your error.

Major. I do: you were right, Dorothy, you are
always right; but when I abused a country life, I
little thought it could afford such pleasures.

Miss Stoic. (*With triumph.*) Oh, the country can
afford pleasures then?

Major. Plenty; 'tis the place of all others for an
old soldier to retire to; for, I'll tell you—Sir Edward took me to their club, to their Arcadian meeting, and, upon my honour—that is, for the time it

lasted—I don't think I ever saw a more general engagement, or much sharper fighting.

Miss Stoic. Fighting!

Major. Aye: it seems there are three parties in this vale of peace and innocence; 'Squire Dobson's party, Vicar Robson's party, and Apothecary Hobson's party; and, like good quiet neighbours, they have been all in Chancery these twelve years, about the right of fishing in a gudgeon stream; which stream proving to be the same I tumbled into yesterday, one said I might at any time fish and drown myself there with his leave, and another said I should not drown myself there without his leave, till, from words, these rural Yorks and Lancasters got to blows, and then—oh, I was wrong, sister; for I see now there's no difference between camps and country towns, except that, by combating for kingdoms, you sometimes gain promotion; but, by fighting for gudgeons, you don't even get half-pay for your services.

Miss Stoic. For shame! for shame! this is the sex; this is your boasted male society! Had you kept company with such as me——

Major. What, with the ladies! Oh Lord, their parties run ten times higher; for we drank tea with the sheriff's wife, an old red-rose dowager; and her opposite neighbour, a white rose, having lately built a new bow-window to improve her prospect, curse me if Mrs Sheriff didn't order her husband to erect a gallows, and hang a tall highwayman plump in the front of it. It will do, it will do! I am already chuck-full of rural ardour, and to-morrow I shall have more of it: for Sir Edward Specious gives a grand concert to both armies, and has appointed me generalissimo.

Miss Stoic. You!

Major. Aye: I am to marshal out the music, reconnoitre for the singers, and manœuvre the band: and I know what I'm about; for, instead of the rustic carol, and the shepherd's pipe, they shall have nothing but war's alarms, and wind instruments. And, see, I'm not to spare expence ; no, he has given me these two hundred pounds. (*Shewing bank-notes.*)

Miss Stoic. Two hundred pounds!

Mrs Aub. (*Without.*) Let me pass! I must and will see him!

Miss Stoic. Heavens! here's insolence! Mr Aubrey!

Major. What, the bad governess! The—now we shall hear—

Enter Mrs AUBREY.

Mrs Aub. Oh, sir, admit Olivia! She is without, imploring to behold, for the first time, her friend, her sole protector.

Miss Stoic. Then there let her stay: I wholly influence my brother's mind, and—

Major. You do, sister; and think you, madam, (*To* Mrs AUBREY.) I can wish to see one so untutored and ungrateful?

Mrs Aub. Ungrateful! Oh, your pardon, sir; but the inventor of a slanderous tale is scarce more criminal than he who wantonly believes it; for calumny would perish in its birth, but that a credulous, misjudging world, rush forth to hail and to mature it.

Major. Why, that's very true, indeed.

Mrs Aub. Judge for yourself then, sir, and oft you'll find that from some random and unmeaning cause, vice gains that credit which virtue would for ever lose, but for its own superior triumph.

Major. True again: for whilst our old colonel was never accused of inebriety, though his face was the herald of three bottles a day; yet, because I once in my life quaffed too much port, the whole regiment raised the cry of " mad-dog," and I was nick-named

Major Blackstrap, ever after. So let me investigate——

Mrs Aub. Oh, I will fly—

Miss Stoic. Hold! she treads not on this hallow'd
ground! And for you, brother! dare to dispute my
word, and on such poor, suspicious evidence as
her's!

Mrs Aub. (*With pride.*) Madam!

Miss Stoic. Aye: whence came you? What's
your mysterious story? Why conceal——

Mrs Aub. Conceal! 'Tis known that years ago I
came as governess to Mrs Lorimer, and on her death
was her successor. What more should I reveal?

Miss Stoic. Only why, in frantic grief, you have
so often proclaimed yourself a guilty wretch; aye,
and at Olivia's sight, have bid her shun you as a pes-
tilence, a fiend—(Mrs AUBREY *shews great agitation.*)
—Deny it not.

Major. How! Is this true?

Mrs Aub. No—yes: pity me, spare me; but, for
protecting her—thus let me kneel and bless you!

Major. What!

Mrs Aub. She has no faults, nor have I one to
her. Oh yes, I have—but not as monitress; for,
school'd myself in error, I would have rather died a
thousand deaths than not have profited by such example, and taught Olivia gratitude and truth.

Major. Enough—you have confirmed my sister's
story; guilty yourself, you have corrupted her, and
I've for ever lost—Go, leave me!

Miss Stoic. Stay—I insist Olivia is removed to-
night.

Major. She shall.

Mrs Aub Where? not to Sir Edward's! You
cannot—will not—(*Major points towards the door.*)
What! you persist! Well, let me go:—But, till Olivia shall herself consent to be the sacrifice of art and
falsehood, I will, alone, be surety for her honour—

Farewell! once more my blessings wait you; (*Kissing his hand.*) and, did you know the secret motives that direct me—

Major. Relate them now.

Mrs Aub. Never; they would complete Olivia's ruin. And yet I hope the eventful hour will come, when a poor orphan, long from its kindred branches torn, shall, in defiance of the withering storm, still grow and flourish in its native soil. [*Exit.*

Major. Now this I call a very odd woman—a very odd woman indeed! and what with one kind of rural felicity and another, I'm all over in a sort of charming conflagration. Poor girl! poor Olivia! I say, sister, 'tis lucky I never saw her.

Miss Stoic. It is: nor had you seen this artful governess, but for my senseless servant—He knows that none of human form gain entrance in this calm abode.

Enter OLD NICHOLAS, *hastily.*

Nich. Lord, ma'am! I'm so flurried! Here's a servant from one Mr Jack Doric, of Piccadilly, London; and he insists on your company this evening to a ball at the hotel.

Miss Stoic. My company!

Nich. Ay: and yours also, Major—here are the cards.

Miss Stoic. I shall run wild. Brother, go forth yourself, and silence these invaders, whilst I seclude myself in my recess.

Major. Do; retire to your sanctum sanctorum.

[*Exit* MISS STOIC *at a door in back scene.*
I'll lecture them! I'll teach them to disturb this sacred, solitary——Shew me to this servant, sir.

Nich. What for, sir? Sure you don't mean to go?

Major. Go!—any where—every where—and tho' I don't know this Mr Doric, of course he knows me; or, if he don't, 'tis the more civil of him to ask me—

and with his ball, Sir Edward's concert, and the
Yorks and Lancasters, I may forget Olivia——No,
never—my memory, that helps me where I owe a
favour, so fails me at an injury, that I forgive, and
can't help glorying in my weakness.   *[Exeunt.*

SCENE II.

A Road.

Enter DORVILLE.

Dorv. So—as I thought—none yet have noticed
Jack's mad cards of invitation; and I've no hope but
one—the letter which, unknown to him, I sent his
uncle yesterday, stating his love of study and improvement. Should this regain his worthy partner's
friendship, mine will be well rewarded.

Enter YOUNG DORIC.

Young Dor. Joy, joy, my boy! I have again held
converse with Olivia, met her this moment with her
governess—and, what do you think? they come—
both come——

Dorv. What! to the ball?

Young Dor. Ay: they refused at first; but when
they saw, amongst my list of visitors, Major Tornado's name, they told me such a long affecting tale of
him, his sister, and Sir Edward Specious, that 'twas
resolved to meet him at my ball; and if it saves Olivia from the snares of villains, this, my last hundred,
shall afford me more pure, substantial joy than all
my former thousands yielded.

Dorv. Granted: but suppose the Major don't
come, or, what is worse, suppose nobody comes?

Young Dor. Ay : there's the rub.

[Holds down his head.

Dorv. What ! you begin to be alarmed ?

Young Dor. Not for myself, but for Olivia and her friend—their fate depends on my success, and not one answer yet—-none nibbling at the bate !— Zounds ! is credulity confined to cities ! and here, where air increases appetite, shall suppers go un- eaten ?

Dorv. Pooh ! nonsense ! in London, you are known.

Young Dor. So I am every where. A common swindler might expect no guests—but, famed Jack Doric ! on whose gala nights, all Bond-street, and all Bow-street, are let loose, and who so occupies both town and country talk, that even scandal must give way to my chalked floors, hot suppers, and hot rooms—and, shall not bumpkins bite ? Now, when two helpless women rest their hopes——

Enter Servant.

Well, sir, what news ? What has detained you ?

Serv. Lord, sir, consider—I've had to deliver a hundred cards of invitation, and wait for almost as many answers.

Young Dor. Where are they then ? (*Snatches them out of his hand.*) Now be propitious for Olivia's sake : (*Reads the cards.*) " Mrs Squeeze's compli- ments, comes—Rev. Tim Tantrum's compliments, comes—Doctor and Mrs Tarradiddle's compliments —bring with them their town visitors, Alderman Cram, a Dutch Commissioner, and two gentlemen from the Victualling-Office." Bravo ! they bite— and if they come in crowds, why, 'tis the London mode ; for, when the gala season once sets in, they flock like geese, and cackle for their supper ! Ah, but the Major--What says Olivia's benefactor !

7

Serv. Oh, sir, he is so eager, and so pleased, that he has gone to the ball-room already.

[*Exit Servant.*

Young Dor. There, George! what say you to my system now? Had I gone cringing to the Major's door, would it have served Olivia?—But, back'd by balls, and such a host of guests, may I not hope to ask him to a wedding supper next! And then, no longer will I send out cards of invitation, with the words " at home ;"—but, grown domestic, I shall advertise, that I am " out," the whole year round.

Enter the DELINQUENT.

Delin. Your pardon, sir; but, if your name be Doric—(*To* DORVILLE.)

Young Dor. I, sir—I am that happy gentleman.

Delin. One word in private, then.

[YOUNG DORIC *beckons* DORVILLE *to retire.*
Your name's familiar to my memory,—and, when I read it on the card you sent Sir Edward Specious—

Young Dor. My card! what, you're left out! My dear sir, if I had room, I'd ask all Europe; but at this rate, I shan't get in myself.

Delin. Sir, you mistake—seeing your name, I merely came to ask if you ever heard of one Sir Arthur Courcy,

Young Dor. Oh! is that all?—Courcy?

Delin. Ay; of Rowland Castle, in Northumberland; he who fled for debt.

Young Dor. Debt! no—(*Considering.*)—Yes—didn't my uncle, Mr Doric, rebuild the castle by his orders?

Delin. He did: speak quickly—do you know Sir Arthur's person?

Young Dor. No——

Delin. Sure! are you quite sure?

Young Dor. Quite; or if I did, and his distress proceeded from misfortune, do you suspect that I'd

betray him? No; rather I'd invite him to my ball,
and, scorning modern ostentatious shew, revive that
ancient English hospitality, that cheer'd the wretched, and upheld the poor.

Delin. Would you? I knew him well. (*Shaking*
YOUNG DORIC's *hand violently.*)

Young Dor. Indeed!

Delin. And on some future day perhaps——where,
where can he repay those thanks I offer now?

Young Dor. There—(*Taking a card out of his
pocket.*) And, for yourself, pray join us at the ball—
You'll see, at least, one object worth the seeking—
the lovely Miss Tornado.

Delin. Miss Tornado! What! (*Having the pocket-book in his hand, to place the card in it.*)

Young Dor. Ay: attended by her kind, her worthy governess.

Delin. Worthy! (*Trembling, and in his agitation,
letting a letter drop from his pocket-book, unseen by
him.*) You're deceived—she is most guilty—and, not
to part her from her lovely charge, by any means
however desperate—(YOUNG DORIC *appeals.*) yet, if
she's innocent, the deed will drive me mad.—Oh!
that I were already so—then might I plead i nsanity
for pardon: for none but madmen would forsake that
peace, which virtue yields—preserve it—cling to it
—fortified with that, you boast a bulwark may defy
the world!   [*Exit.*

Young Dor. Now, is this an old complaint, or
suddenly brought on from my not asking him to supper? I'll go, and—(*Treads on letter.*) Oh ho! this
may explain, perhaps—listen, (*Reads.*) " Where
have you been loitering? I have kept Major Tornado out of the way, by employing him to provide
singers at a great expence for my concert: and, by
the inclosed assignment to you, of Mrs Aubray's
house, you may keep her out of the way, by arresting her directly in your own name, for the 40*l.* due

for rent.—Proceed in this, whilst I proceed to bear
away her pupil—Edward Specious."—So! a most
lively town—and I shall have a good company.
What's to be done?

Dor. What indeed!

Young Dor. You've not a guinea to discharge
the debt, and my last shilling must discharge the
bill—But come—ere this, the ball's begun, and
should it cross Sir Edward in his plots, and this poor
tenant be released from bondage, let the floor crack
with crowds of company—His is the genuine social
plan, who cheers the men and makes the women
happy.   [*Exeunt.*

SCENE III.

Ball —Anti-Chamber.—Music.

Enter MAJOR TORNADO.

Major. So!—hard at it again.—The Yorks and
Lancasters have been drawn out in regular line of
battle, and to decide!—Who should lead down first
couple!—They all called for the court calendar, but
that not having the honour of knowing any of them,
" Molly put the kettle on," cried I, and looking
fierce, and handing out a sweet, interesting partner,
they all grounded their arms, and tript after me, like
so many prisoners of war. But where's Mr Doric,
and, who the deuce is he? Nobody seems to know
him; but, they say, that's nothing; and, for my
part, I like this new-acquaintance system as well as
any of them; for if a man only visits friends, egad !
he won't be ask'd out twice a year. (*Music repeated.*)

   [YOUNG DORIC *is seen receiving the salutations of
   the company in the recess.*

That's him! ahem! (*Pulling out his chitterlin, &c.*)
I mustn't be behind hand, for I'll consult him on Sir
Edward's concert—ask him for singers and musicians.

Young Dor. (*Advancing.*) Major Tornado, I'm
inform'd. (*Taking his hand.*)

Major. Nothing unpleasant, I hope, has so long
detained you?

Young Dor. Detain'd! Oh! no—I staid away on
purpose. We never arrive now, 'till an hour after our company, and generally go to another party,
and leave them; for you don't come to see me, you
know, nor I to see you—-but you come—you—
pray, why do you come?

Major. Why, be——upon my soul, I can hardly
tell you.

Young Dor. No! and therefore, to relieve both
host and visitor, why not the plan that I propose?
Why not these great confectioners and cooks prepare the company as well as the provisions.

Major. Prepare the company!

Young Dor. Ay; isn't it as easy to make a little
lord as a large trifle? a woman of fashion, as a whipt
syllabub? or a purse-proud citizen, as calf's-foot
jelly? And then, Major, we should have the best of
parties on the best of terms; for they'd eat no supper, talk no nonsense, and be taken off with the frag-
ments.

Major. You are the very man I want. Sir, can
you help me to conduct a concert?

Young Dor. To be sure I can.

Major. To-morrow, at Sir Edward Specious's
house, and, between ourselves, we've not one singer
yet: but, as director, I'm empowered to use all
these bank-notes, look! to the best advantage. (*Shewing them.*)

Young Dor. And Sir Edward wants singers?

Major. He does indeed.

Young Dor. And that's to pay for them? (*Major nods assent.*) Then, in the next room, there is a lady with the clearest and divinest tones! but, by this letter, which I found, a savage landlord, for a debt of forty pounds, now waits to cage the warbling bird. But pay the rascal with Sir Edward's money, and he himself shall, late or early, own that you have used it to the best advantage.

Major. So he will.—Here, ask the lady to give her notes, and thus I give Sir Edward's—Yet, hold! this savage landlord should not gain his point.

Young Dor. No, he won't: for, hark ye! he arrests her to—(*Whispering and laughing.*)—He! he! and, better still—her name is Aubrey.

Major. Aubrey! what Aubrey?

Young Dor. Oh! he has heard her voice before, but not to such a tune as this—So, whilst you live, see company, Major; for, at the rate of forty pounds a head, you'll soon grow rich by hospitality—and, for Sir Edward, tell him, the next time the school is in arrears, he had best make it help his education, by taking it in lessons,—ha! ha!— You've used his money to the best advantage! (*Smacks him on the back.*)   [*Exit.*

Major. What! what Mrs Aubrey? Surely, not Olivia's governess! Yet, now I recollect, my sister said——Bless my soul! there's no end to rural diversion! and, haply, whilst pursuing that, I have forgot the best diversion life affords—that of assisting the unfortunate.—Poor, poor Olivia! Zounds! if I'm duped—(*Going.*)

OLIVIA appears.

Oh! here's my partner!—the unknown lady that I danced with.—Psha! I've no spirits now.

Enter OLIVIA.

Oliv. So! I've found you, sir, at last—Upon my

word, a very truant gentleman! to leave your partner staring round the room—Pray, sir, do you mean
to dance again?

Major. No, madam; I—

Oliv. No! I wish you had told me so an hour ago;
for I've refused a dozen gay, young—but then, perhaps, they'll never think of me again—and, somehow, you—Come,—come,—go with me.

Major. (*Turning away.*) I cannot.

Oliv. Dear! (*Looking in his face.*) How you're altered!—You looked as cheerful and as pleased——

Major. (*Taking her hand.*) Farewell! and, unlike
her who occupies my thoughts, may you ne'er meet
a parent's or protector's cold neglect!

Oliv. (*Bursting into tears.*) Parents! alas! you've
touched upon the string—

Major. In tears! what! they're no more?

Oliv. I know not; but he, who for years supplied
to me their loss,—he, who engrossed my blessing
and my prayers, has listened to a base, calumnious
tale, and cast me on the world, the wretched orphan
that he found me.

Major. Orphan!

Oliv. He has! he has;—but his past kindness still
rushes on Olivia's memory, and her overflowing
heart, (*Falling at his feet.*) thus, thus pours forth its
gratitude and love.

Major. (*Trying to raise her.*) Olivia!—come to
your protector's arms! (*Embracing her.*)

Oliv. My more than parent—my benefactor!

Major. My blessings on thee!

Enter immediately from the back scene, YOUNG DO
RIC *and* MRS AUBREY.

Young Dor. And mine! and this wrong'd lady's
on you both—and, henceforth, if I can but raise one
guinea in the world, I'll give a little party to some
friends, just for the chance of a desert like this.

Oliv. (*Flying to* MRS AUBREY.) Oh! Mrs. Aubrey! you, who have shared, and oft outsmiled my sorrows, does this, (*Kissing the Major's hand.*) does this repay you?

Mrs Aub. Most amply; and now, if we are doom'd to part——

Major. Part! shew me who dare propose it. Shew me another villain like Sir Edward——

Young Dor. And I'll pay him with his own banknotes—Major, the debt's discharged.

Major. Well, well, of him I think not—let us this instant to the Hermitage; for I am sure my sister is as much imposed on as myself; and her secluded life pleads some excuse; but I—I to quarrel, and offend—'tis the air, 'tis the country air—I've caught the breezes of the Yorks and Lancasters, and they have blown me top-side down—But here's my haven and my hope—come, come!

Mrs Aub. (*Curtsying to* YOUNG DORIC.) Sir, I've to thank you for your kindness.

Oliv. (*Curtsying.*) And I once more, sir—

Young Dor. And I'm sure I've to thank you, ladies; for never felt I rapture like the present; (*Ladies and gentlemen cross the stage.*) and since the trade's so pleasant and productive, should I again turn dealer in such merchandize—(*Points to ballroom.*)

Major. Oh! we'll, we'll be your customers.

Young Dor. Indeed! then I'll this moment to my guests, and boldly ask them to a concert next.—To-morrow, Major, we'll oppose Sir Edward; and if you'll join in the direction, his shall conclude in a discordant solo.

Major. Ours in full chorus of harmonious joy.

[*Exeunt.*

ACT THE THIRD.

SCENE I.

Outside of the Hermitage.

Enter MISS STOIC *and* NICHOLAS *from Hermitage.*

Miss Stoic. Dolt! dotard! to send away Sir Edward Specious' servant—Go—call him back directly.

Nich. Lord, ma'am, what can I do? You abuse me for admitting Mrs Aubrey in the morning, and then the Major brings her home at night.

Miss Stoic. Ay; and Olivia with her; and therefore Sir Edward is the very person I would hear from. Away!   [*Exit* NICHOLAS.
Olivia's innocence confirm'd, I cannot turn her from my door, but, like my brother, must confess I've been imposed on by a slanderous world!

Re-enter NICHOLAS, *with* SIR EDWARD'S *Servant.*

Serv. From Sir Edward Specious, madam. (*Giving her a letter.*)

Miss Stoic. Now, then! (*Reads.*) " As I must not have the pleasure of seeing you, owing to your solitary life, I write to say, I have been deprived of Miss Olivia's hand and heart by the malignity of her artful governess; but with your kind assistance, I still hope to call her Lady Specious."—With my assistance! Oh! I understand—and he shan't want an opportunity—I'll send an answer in an hour, and,

till then, let calm philosophy compose his mind;
(*Exit Servant.*) for, as the antient bard expresses
it, " Man's but a vapour, and full of woes—just cuts
a caper, and down he goes."

Enter, hastily, from the House, MAJOR TORNADO.

Major. Help, sister! help to relieve the garrison,
or it will surrender at discretion; for there's Olivia
has been storming it with such a volley of interrogatories.

Miss Stoic. What interrogatories?

Major. Why, poor girl! such as, Why I adopted
her without seeing her—why I concealed from her
her parents' names—and I can't stand it—I can
march up, like a hero, to the mouth of a lighted
cannon, but the voice of a supplicating woman!—
Do you know, because I named Lord Danvers with
unusual feeling, she snatched his picture from me.

Miss Stoic. Lord Danvers' picture!

Major. Ay: and I can't get it back again; but I
hope—Zounds! I don't know what I hope.—Sister,
befriend me, tell her at once my sacred promise to
Lord Danvers.

Miss Stoic. Your sacred promise!

Major. Ay: to her former benefactor—to that
gallant friend, who, wounded in his country's cause,
and dying upon India's plains, implored me to protect his infant charge—" Take her," he cried,
" and, to secure her from her parents' power, swear
never to reveal their names, but call her by your
own!" I pressed his hand in token of compliance;
he told me more of the disastrous tale, and, blessing
me, expired—Impart thus much, and pity for us both
will teach her to be silent.

Miss Stoic. And if pity don't, philosophy will; for
she shall copy my superior mind, and smile at this
world's vain pursuits.—Brother, 'tis done. (*Going.*)

Major. Thanks, thanks!—Be careful though, hint

not Lord Danvers was her grandfather, but say that
he adopted her, like me, from motives of humanity.

Miss Stoic. Think you I'll help her to unfold the
names of parents who so wrong'd her? No; I have
hitherto myself neglected her, and therefore shall
atone by tender, sisterly, and philanthropic care.

Major. What a pair of treasures! (*Kissing her
hand.*)   [*Exit* MISS STOIC.
Bless my soul! I'm so agitated, and so happy—I'll
build my cottage this moment—I'll turn country
gentleman for life, and, with dear Olivia, a husband
for her like Mr Doric, a young family, a pack of
hounds—Yorks, Lancasters, and a large farm in my
own hands, I'll bring rural tactics to such perfection,
that retired brother-officers shall say, Gibraltar be-
sieged is dull to my modern cottage.

Old Dor. (*Without.*) Very glad to see you indeed, old boy—and that's the house of the old hermitess, is it?

Major. How now! old hermitess! More agitation!
ho! ho! (*Retires.*)

Enter OLD DORIC *and* TRADELOVE.

Trad. Your hand again, old school-fellow! What,
so you came here for amusement, I suppose?

Old Dor. Quite the contrary—came on business
—call'd suddenly from London to Somersetshire—
met Bob Smalltalk at Bristol—know Bob Smalltalk
of your town?—Got into gossip—told me of all your
new building-jobs—new town-hall, bridge, family-
seats—so, being only forty miles off, rode post-haste
on speculation; and, except horse bolting after fox-
chase, and pitching me from one county to another——

Trad. Indeed!—why, 'slife! were you much hurt?

Old Dor. No; quite the contrary. And, now I'm
here, mean to take one George Dorville by sur-

prise ; and, over a bottle, thank him for the account of Jack's reformation. (*Producing a letter.*) Hark ye, another Inigo Jones—going to town to turn active partner—and would sooner—but bad company—— mistook, and went to west end of town ; when, no-torious now, fashionable people all come into the city.

Trad. What! to pay money into their bankers' hands?

Old Dor. Quite the contrary; to borrow money of their bankers—and where one smart equipage jogs down St James's-street, twenty rattle up Lud-gate-hill—But time's precious ; must make interest 'gainst my rival architects—so, mum !—first canvass Nick's old sweetheart here.

Major. (*Behind.*) Nick's old sweetheart !

Old Dor. And mine also, ha ! ha ! We were the honest men long searched for in the dark by old Diogenes the second.

Major. (*Advancing.*) Sir, answer me—Who the devil do you call old Diogenes the second ?

Old Dor. What's that to you, sir ?

Major. Every thing, sir : and I insist you own this lady's hatred to the world proceeded solely from her hatred to its vices. (*Pointing to the Hermit-age.*)

Old Dor. No : quite the contrary.

Major. What !

Old Dor. Why, don't I know ? Didn't she write red-hot love-verses in the newspapers, under the signature of Laura Seraphina; and didn't my friend, Ned Nick, the attorney, answer them by the name of Rolando Furioso ? And didn't the press groan for months with " Feelings amaranthine ! chains ada-mantine ! and bleeding hearts panting ?"

Major. What then, sir ?

Old Dor. Why, then didn't Furioso, that is, Nick the lawyer, work himself into such a real pas-

sion for his unknown Seraphina, that is, Dorothy, the
spinster,—that, after chasing the incognita through
sylvan vallies, and through flowery meads, he at last
found her in the dark alcoves of Crutched Friars;
and, alas! instead of the roseate youth, and dazzling
smiles the glowing poet fancied, he saw such wrinkles,
and such wizen looks, that, to console his heart's
despair, he——

Major. He what, sir?

Old Dor. Why. he charged her six shillings and
eight-pence for every stanza, and sent Seraphina a
bill of costs as long as his own face! and then I
went between 'em, as their modern, mutual friend—
and being, as you see, a sort of lady's man, she forced me to reject her too, and then, like all philosophers, she left the world, because the world left her;
but I can make her think it still a paradise—and the
reward I ask—hark ye! (*Pulling Major towards
him.*) is to be architect to her old fiery, bully-loving
brother.

Major. What old fiery, bully-loving——

Old Dor. Why, he from India; and he must
comply; for the poor nabob's Seraphina's pigeon.

Major. Very likely. (*Putting on his hat fiercely.*)
But he's not your's—a fiery, bully-loving——dare
you, to my face, repeat that?

Old Dor. No; quite the contrary. (*In great
alarm.*)

Major. 'Tis well; and I'll this moment to my sister; not to distress, but to amuse her with your vanity; for if she ever deign'd even to look—pooh!
stick to your trade—raise houses upon terra firma,
and don't build castles in the air; for, though not
bullying, as you suppose, I prize my sister's honour
as my own, and carry arms for you and Furioso.

[*Exit into Hermitage.*

Old Dor. What! reflect on my profession! stop
—come back!

Trad. Nay, now, 'tis but a paltry cottage, and you are losing better jobs. Come, I have one in view for you myself.

Old Dor. Indeed!

Trad. Ay; with a man of real consequence. I cannot exactly recollect his name,—he gave a sumptuous ball last night, and all are pushing for his custom. I've got it for myself already, and now, I'll kindly speak a word for you.

Old Dor. Will you? that's noble! lead on—and, for you swaggerer's base reflections—zounds! let him be told, 'tisn't the occupation makes the man, it is the man makes the occupation. And, in this great commercial land, an honest tradesman, who can pay his way, may strut with any nabob in the world. So, if you think I am afraid—pooh! quite the contrary. (*Putting on his hat.*) [*Exeunt.*

SCENE II.

A Room in SIR EDWARD SPECIOUS'S *House.*

Enter *the* DELINQUENT.

Delin. 'Sdeath! I grow weary of his villainy; it is not further to be borne; for, whilst thus constantly employed in covering his detested crimes, perhaps the object that I seek calls loudly for protection; and, desperate as I am, would I not rather succour than oppress, even my deadliest foe? but one, who's twined around my heart—Oh! let me burst my ignominious chains, and fly from this disgraceful——

Enter SIR EDWARD SPECIOUS *hastily.*

Sir Edw. So ;—this is fortunate !—partake, partake my triumph ! for, spite of all their paltry arts, the faithless fair is in my power.

Delin. Indeed ! (*Surlily.*)

Sir Edw. Ay : the lady she resides with means to·night to take her to a concert,—and, mark— not only on the road, will leave her to your care—

Delin. Mine !

Sir Edw Ay : but so confine this hated governess by stratagem and art, that bear her pupil but on board my yacht,—

Delin. Never !

Sir Edw. How ! dare you ?—

Delin. I dare—when first, abroad, I answered for your faults, they were the offspring of gay, giddy youth ; and still the noble name of gentleman was not quite lost in your pursuits ; but when, to gratify licentious passion, you'd doom one virtuous woman to confinement, and force another to despair and infamy, you wrong, without redress, that sex, which man but lives to love and to protect.

Sir Edw. Wretch ! traitor ! must I remind you who you are ?

Delin. No ; tell me who I was.

Sir Edw. I will; for it will gall you to reflect, that you, the proud Sir Arthur Courcy, of Northumberland, famed for his landed and commercial rank, implored my father to become his bail, and meanly left him to discharge the debt.

Delin. Ha !

Sir Edw. [*Holding* DELIN.] And after that, when this Sir Arthur's bankruptcy ensued, dared he appear to his commission ? no; he fled the kingdom— and now, as outlaw—ay, as outlaw, may be tried for crimes most flagrant and felonious.

Delin. Peace ! or, by heaven !——

Sir Edw. Nay, more,—this outlaw spread such desolation round, that many a peasant's cheerful home was changed to drear imprisonment; and his own family beside.———

Delin. [*Breaking from him.*] Nay take my life, for every word's a dagger to that heart, that still could prove its motives were not evil; but that it boldly has involved itself, not skulked, like you, beneath another's name.

Sir Edw. 'Tis well, sir; but there was a time when you'd have owned yourself obliged—

Delin. Knelt! proud Sir Arthur would have knelt, and risen prouder from the grateful posture; but when you trample on a worm, remember it has feelings—haply tender as your own.

Sir Edw. Well, well, perhaps I was too warm; forget what's past, and some more desperate agent shall be found.

Delin. What! you're resolved!

Sir Edw. I am! and, had you granted this my last request, it might have led e'en to reversing of your outlawry; for all those bonds my father purchased, from revenge, had been returned into your hands, and, freedom thus restored, you might indeed regain the noble height from whence you fell.

Delin. What! freedom?

Sir Edw. Ay: and expect, besides, another bright reward: the lovely prize but once on board the vessel, we'll sail directly for Northumberland.

Delin. Northumberland!

Sir Edw. Yes; to that very spot, where, beyond doubt, the tender treasure that you seek now claims the pity you so wish to prove.

Delin. [*Having shewn much joy during the preceding speech.*] Will you? I am no longer master of myself—nature, resistless nature, mounts within my soul, and, like a whirlwind, hurries me to action.—The time,—the place—

Sir Edw. There—this letter will explain (*Giving him letter.*) no more—away!

Delin. Ah: to my native shore,—to liberty, to life! (*Rushes out.*)

Sir Edw. Within there!

Enter Servant.

Where is the master of my yacht?

Serv. Tom Tackle, sir? Oh! he's below in the hall, sir.

Sir Edw. I'll come to him.   [*Exit Servant.*

Pride—love—revenge!—all, all will triumph now!

[*Exit.*

SCENE III.

Outside of the Hotel.

Enter DORVILLE *from the Hotel.*

Dorv. Not yet returned! Surely no creditor has come from town and suddenly arrested him. Plague on't! if there has—now, at the moment when this letter from his uncle gives hopes of lasting happiness and wealth. Well, well, I'll seek and shew him— Oh, he's here; and, as I feared—by heaven! two bailiffs with him!

Enter YOUNG DORIC, *followed by two Persons.*

So, you're at last rewarded as you ought.

Young Dor. Yes, I am, exactly; for this gentleman, an active, enterprising upholsterer, (*Upholsterer bows very low.*) has almost forced me to take a ready-furnished villa of his about a mile off. And this gentleman, a smart advertising wine-merchant, (*Wine-merchant bows also.*) actually insists on stocking it' with his own best Port and Madeira; and 'tis no fault of mine, for, as I said before, upon my honour, gentlemen, I doubt very much whether I can pay you.

Winc Merch. Oh, we know who we're trusting! One who is visited by all the town.

Uphol. So noticed, so respected—and by such solid and substantial—Do, pray indulge us; say 'tis a bargain, and we'll fly to execute your orders.

Young Dor. Well: since I must indulge you—fly, fly, my fine fellows!

Uphol. Enough:—And we shall ever feel so much indebted to your kindness. (*Bowing both very low.*)

Young Dor. (*Returning the bow.*) Not more than I shall feel indebted to you, gentlemen.

[*Exeunt Wine-Merchant and Upholsterer.*

And for the fair, industrious tradesman's sake, I am glad that you are match'd; for 'tis such pushing and high-priced extortioners that injure credit, and make swindling flourish.

Dorv. It is; but they are right in their surmises now; for, by this friendly letter from your partner—

Young Dor. My uncle! What, from honest old Toby! and to you! Oh, let me read!—" Dear Mr Dorville, in answer to your pleasing account of Jack's reformation, close study of architecture, and being now on the road to London, to take part as active partner"—Oh, you dear, friendly, lying, correspondent!—" I heartily thank you, and as I cou'dn't say more, if I were to write volumes, Your's, Toby Doric. P. S. Hope Jack will be in town to-night, being suddenly called on a building job to Bristol." So, by this letter, I am now in London—and I am here, surrounded by a whole town, all dressing for my concert.

Dorv. I know; but if I write that you're detained, from over study and fatigue—

Young Dor. Do: write this instant; for, backed by

him, Olivia may be mine ! And then commence your
book of travels—you'll knock up old Munchausen.

[*Exit* DORVILLE *into Inn.*

Oh ! ever credulous and complying uncle ! let me
but coax you to a trifling settlement, only a paltry
twenty thousand to begin with—Oh ! [*Kissing the
letter.*

Enter OLD DORIC *and* TRADELOVE.

YOUNG DORIC'S *back is towards them.*

Trad. That's the great man—and, at the concert
that he gives to-night—this famed Von Rapidotz,
so puffed for months in all the London papers—

Old Dor. What ! that great Russian fiddler ! he in
England ! Go, and if no building job, get him to ask
me to his concert.

Trad. Mum !—(*Going up to* YOUNG DORIC.)
Sir, my friend here is an architect.

Young Dor. (*Not turning round.)* Pooh ! Pooh ! I
haven't time. (*Turning up towards the Hotel.*)

Old Dor. Stop——let me try. Sir, my name is
Doric, of the Minories.

Young Dor. What ! (*Much agitated, but not turning.*)

Old Dor. Doric and nephew, that's the firm—
and if you want a Blenheim, Wooburn, or a Castle
Howard, Jack is quite capable, quite. (*With difficulty moves* YOUNG DORIC *round, who is trying to get
away, and they meet face to face.*) Death and fury !
quite the contrary.

Young Dor. What, nunky ! my dear sir !—(*Going
to embrace him.*)

Old Dor. Keep off, and answer me. Is this your
style of studying architecture ? And will these balls
and concerts, and Von Rapidotz, get you one customer or friend, you profligate ?

Young Dor. To be sure ; for don't great parties lead to great connections ?

Old Dor. No ; for when, at your request, I gave my gala in the Minories, those I left out all quizzed me, as " Beau Bricklayer ;" and for my guests—— some laughed at, none knew me, and many swore I was a damned bad waiter.

Young Dor. And where's the wonder ? when, instead of chalking the floor, you painted it ; and so late in the afternoon, that the wet oil tript up all the dancers ; and, when songs commenced, didn't you claim your privilege, as master of the house, and roar " Lullaby," and the " Beautiful Maid," till you were left clapping and encoring yourself ?

Old Dor. And if I did, wasn't I, for a whole week after, almost poisoned and starved ; for my old house-keeper wouldn't allow me a bit of fresh meat, till I had fairly eat up every scrap and fragment——But we're no longer partners——no ; a lawyer shall this instant draw up articles of dissolution ; and I'll not only never quit you till you sign them, but so expose you in the town——

Young Dor. Expose me, sir ! Expose a gentleman !

Old Dor. Ay, there it is—Though born to trade, your father bred you as a gentleman : and, to my mind, we are all gentlemen and ladies now ; for, whilst each maid *out-grecians* and *out attitudes* her mistress, my milkman's daughter, Miss Gloriana Georgiana Chalky, daily rubs out her father's scores, by learning scores from Monsieur Kickpailini——And so, expect me with the articles.

Young Dor. Stay, sir—one word. You used to love me as a son ; and if I should gain trade by these assemblies——

Old Dor. Why, then——Pooh ! 'tis impossible !

Young Dor. Nay ; join the concert—hear but this

famous Russian play——and if he don't tickle them
like trout——

Old Dor. What, he'll——(*Smiling.*)

Re-enter DORVILLE *from the Hotel, with the Letter.*

Dorv. Here—here's another batch of lies !—here's
another tickler for old Toby !

Old Dor. Hem !—(*Putting on his hat.*) Quite the
contrary.   [*Exit.*

Dorv. Why, zounds ! what brought him here ?

Young Dor. And, zounds ! what brought you here,
just at the moment ?—But I'll be after him, and——
No, dam'me ! I am wanted at the concert—so, follow him, and make amends—Speak of my villa, and
my stock of wines—prove that the town quite likes
to be deceived—say I am in love—say——

Dorv. Fear not—I know the prize that you contend for.

Young Dor. Aye ; I say 'tis not rank, or riches,
or renown ; but more than all combined ; for 'tis fair
woman, and connubial bliss :

And if it ends but in a valued wife—
Say I'm at home, and architect for life.

                                     [*Exeunt.*

ACT THE FOURTH.

SCENE I.

An Anti-Chamber leading to Concert-Room.

Enter YOUNG DORIC, *meeting the Major.*

Major. Where's this Von Rapidotz, so long ex-
tolled in every public print? Why, he has so cut up
Sir Edward's concert, that there's more fiddlers than
company.

Young Dor. And I'm overflowing—But Miss Olivia, major——

Major. Oh, the dear girl! my sister's grown so
fond of her society, that she can't bear her from her
sight, and therefore brings her in a chaise herself—
and now, if you would know, beside, the person that
Olivia's fond of, come here——I'll whisper in your
ear.

Young Dor. 'Slife! whom, sir?

Major. Doric—Jack Doric—I told her you should
know the secret, and I am glad, with all my heart;
for you've so true a taste for rural sports, that poets
well may paint the blessings of a country life, if all,
like you, thus made the welkin ring with song, with
dancing, and with revelry.

Young Dor. Sir, you amaze—transport—

Major. I know; and therefore I will tell you more.
—Prove you are no adventurous, fortune-hunting—
Your pardon—but as we're total strangers, and as
Olivia has suffered by man's perfidy so long, pray,

(*Taking his hand.*) pray excuse me; but were you guardian of so sweet a flower, you would do much to shelter it from danger.

Young Dor. And, as her lover, I could kiss the hand that raised, that nourished, and would thus defend it. Be satisfied—I will not think of an alliance, till you're convinced that I deserve it.

Major. Enough—and now, once more advance we to the rural warriors. Mind though, my sister must consent; for 'tis my pride to follow her advice, in spite of Rollo Furioso. (*Going, returns.*) I hope— I trust you'll be Olivia's husband,—you were her friend when I forgot that name; and if your motives be not worthy——

Young Dor. Look, sir, is this the countenance—

Major. No; you've those open, fascinating smiles, that would enliven e'en recruiting officers; ay, or make lawyers chuckle in vacation.——And so, I charge you, let me quickly give the two best parties an old man can witness—a wedding and a christening dinner, boy.   [*Exit.*

Young Dor. Ay; or a young man's either—for they're substantial food—Oh! rapturous thought! Olivia may be mine! But how? unless my uncle will relent, I'm the adventurous fortune-hunting——

Enter DORVILLE.

Well, George, what luck? Did you o'ertake—

Dorv. I did: I found him at the lawyer's, and he's so anxious to dissolve the partnership, that they are actually preparing the articles.

Young Dor. What! there's no hope!

Dorv. None—but the chance of this night's concert. He can do nothing till to-morrow.

Young Dor. Right—and if Olivia would arrive—

Old Dor. (*Without.*) I will—I will come up, I tell you.

Young Dor. So, there ends the battle, at a knock-down blow— Try, try again—I'll stand apart.

[*Retires up stage.*

Enter OLD DORIC, *with paper in his hand.*

Old Dor. So—all in grand style, I see—friends, fiddlers, footmen,—crowds, coronets, constables, pick-pockets, peace-officers—and, tell me, sir, was I insulted by my nephew's orders?

Dorv. Insulted, sir! by whom?

Old Dor. By his constables---his staff-officers from London; for, taking me for an Old Bailey acquaintance, they cock'd their eyes, and bawl'd aloud, " Vy, Dicky, you ben't expected."—" No," says I, " nor Toby either; but I warrant we're both of us as good as many of the company"—and so I forced my way,—and so, sir, show me to the concert-room, for Jack shall sign these articles directly.

Dorv. Nay, sir, consider—you will be his ruin.

Old Dor. Well, let him thank himself—he knows he was my favourite, and, now, when building is the first profession,——aye, you may stare, sir—but, are not all men measured by their houses? Stand they not long or short in public estimation, according to the size of their apartments? And don't great rooms make painters, dentists, and e'en surgeons great? for who will follow genius to a garret? None—so, lead the way, and quick! dispatch! for if, as partner, I pay half the piper—i'cod! I'll hear some piping for my money. [*Exit with* DORVILLE.

Young Dor. Wheugh! beat! beat for ever! and, at the very crisis, when, with his friendly aid, I might have shouted victory! Well, well, I cannot blame him—(*Music within.*) Ah! there's Von Rapidotz ---Pooh! his famed flourishes are useless now. (*More music, and cries of* " Bravo! Bravissimo!" *within.*) Hark! with what shouts they hail his first attempt

I'll rouse! I'll profit by the sound; for music, that can bend the knotted oak, may soften e'en old Toby's heart.

Re-enter OLD DORIC, *with the Articles.*

Old Dor. Sign, sign directly, or we smash together —Oh! you're indeed an active partner. I thought at most it would have cost five pounds; but here to have the first appearance of a player, whose price, in Russia, is two hundred ducats——

Young Dor. Who says so, sir?

Old Dor. Who? every public print: and 'tis no wonder, for the whole room was in an ecstacy, almost before he moved his elbows—Ay, and when, by chance, he dropt his diamond pin, young, old, lame, splenetic, all tumbled, neck and heels, to have the glory of replacing it.

Young Dor. (*With exultation.*) Indeed!

Old Dor. And one, a travelling gentleman, who often had been charmed with him abroad, swore instinct was his music-master, for that his father was a poor Cossack.

Young Dor. That's capital! for I'm his father!

Old Dor. You!

Young Dor. I made, I named—I praised—him, as you heard: and famed Von Rapidotz is Jack's own child.

Old Dor. What! (*With astonishment.*)

Young Dor. Mum! he's a poor emigrant from Switserland, who, having nothing to support himself, his children, and his wife, but some wild talent in the art of music, applied, in vain, to get employment —in vain, because he wanted name and reputation —I gave him every thing—I puff'd him as a prodigy, and all good-naturedly, so, take my word, that, —ha! ha! ha! whilst one hears him, where he never played, others huzza before they hear at all.

Old Dor. (*Smiling.*) Zounds! you most impudent——

Young Dor. Why, where's the harm, when thus they're in such ecstacy? (*Pointing to the room.*) He came here, express, to tell me, he had glorious offers now, and speak his own and his loved partner's joy—And, should it aid my partner—should it but lead to trade and to connection, I may regain an old friend's love, which, on my life, I covet from my heart; for, while yon senseless shouts afford no bliss, his approbation will secure my own.

Old Dor. It will—it will—(*Tearing the articles.*)

Young Dor. What! you are jesting.

Old Dor. No; quite (*Tearing on*) quite the contrary. (*Embracing* YOUNG DORIC.) Dam'me! I'll give another gala myself, and at this villa Dorville spoke of; and ask a certain person, called Olivia—and, name what settlement you please; don't stand upon a thousand pounds or two—a concert and a supper will soon settle that.

Young Dor. Thanks—thanks! and for my villa, consider it, at least, as half your own.

Old Dor. Half! we're partners, Jack—and, as I long to see it, and there's that old fiery, bully-loving Major, now brandishing his cane about the concert-room—come, I'll be off.

Young Dor. Do; and my chariot, which now waits to take home visitors, shall instantly convey you—and, when the concert's over, we'll have a quiet supper by ourselves, and drink success to harmony, Von Rapidotz, and trade—Come!——

Enter DORVILLE, *with a Servant, from Concert-Room.*

Dorv. Stay, sir—one word.

Young Dor. I can't—I must attend my uncle.

Dorv. What! to sign articles of dissolution?

Young Dor. No: quite the contrary.

[*Exit arm in arm with* OLD DORIC.

Dorv. Bravo! that's excellent—and, William,

since the Major cannot guess why Miss Tornado is
detained so long, go see if she be coming.

Will. Lord, sir, there are such crowds of carriages and people, that 'tis impossible to see, or hear,
or——

Dorv. No matter; he is so vexed at her delay,
that 1 desire you'll obey him.   [*Exit* WILLIAM.

Re-enter YOUNG DORIC, *laughing.*

What! what adventure now?

Young Dor. Oh! the best yet—the night's so dark,
and there is such confusion 'mongst the carriages,
that my stunn'd uncle, in his fright and bustle, seeing the door of a brown chariot open, coolly whips
in, and, thinking it is mine, orders the coachman to
drive home directly.

Dorv. 'Slife! and whose chariot was it?

Young Dor. I know no more than he does; but
this I know, the servants were so drunk, that they
mistook him for their master; for they all bow'd,
and drove him off in style—and, let them land him
where they will, be it a palace, or a private gentleman's, he'll swear it is his partner's villa, and call
for half of every thing he likes.   But come—ere this
Olivia is arrived.

Dorv. No; and I guess the cause—she is detained
by this Miss Stoic;—and, now I recollect—what
colour is the Major's chariot?—don't it resemble
your's?

Young Dor. It does; and, should they drive him
to the Hermitage?—Mum! we'll ask directly—and,
as 'tis clear she'd part me from Olivia, may honest
Toby take her house for mine! for he's so hasty,
and so obstinate, that, should they charge him to de-
camp, I shou'dn't wonder if he charged her too, and
boldly march'd the hermit to the round-house.

[*Exeunt.*

SCENE II.

Inside of the Hermitage.

Enter NICHOLAS, *drunk, with a Tankard.*

Nich. So! success to solitude! for the Major's
gone to the concert, and Mistress and Miss Olivia
are gone—and Mrs Aubrey;—no, she's not gone,
because she's locked up in that sanctum sanctorum
there. I believe somehow, I'm gone. (*Loud knocking.*) Now, for a guinea, that's the Major in his chariot. (*Going towards door.*) They say that too much
ale, (*Pointing towards tankard,*) makes one see double; but, faith, for my part, I can't see at all—yes,
I can; (*Looking out,*) I see, 'tis the Major.

Enter OLD DORIC.

Oh! your honour! (*Bowing and reeling.*)
Old Dor. What! you're as sober as the rest. Why,
zounds! they reel'd Jack's chariot thro' the air: but,
pheugh! (*Puffing himself.*) I'm safe at home at last
—and, as I live, (*Looking round,*) our villa is a pretty
partnership concern—so snug—so tasty. Supper,
sirrah! (*Very loud and authoritatively.*)
Nich. Supper! Why, Major!——
Old Dor. Major! begone!   [*Exit* NICHOLAS.
—The coachman call'd me Major too: but 'tis their
drunken folly.—And, now as senior Co. to pop on
the best chamber, and best bed. (*Going to the door,*)
Why this door's lock'd—and, as it seems, inside.
(*Looks through the key-hole,*) What! a white petticoat!   Oh, Jack! now, is this fair and equal by
your partner?   But I'll be quits with you, for, as

I'm first, and this, perchance, may prove the key,
(*Taking it from the wall*,) I'll have my share. (*Opens
the door.*)

Enter MRS AUBREY.

Madam, (*Bowing*,) you're welcome to our villa.
(*Smiling, and putting up his chitterlin.*)

Mrs Aub. Your villa! no poor evasion, sir—Where
is the owner of this miscalled Hermitage? who lured
me to that secret room, and then, unknown to me,
secured the door.

Old Dor. Hermitage! (*Alarmed, and looking
about.*)

Mrs Aub. Aye, where is the artful Miss Stoic?
But, to my joy, Major Tornado comes—and in so
right a cause——

Old Dor. Major! what, that old fiery, bully-loving
—(*Looks out*) Oh! oh! talk of the right cause,
dam'me, I'm in the wrong box, and that rascal, Jack,
has shoved me in the lion's den, without a partner
to share half the mauling.

Miss Stoic. (*Without.*) Nay, brother, 'twas your
sottish servant's fault.

Major. (*Without.*) S'blood! sister, I'll play the
devil.

Old Dor. There! he'll play the devil! Not that
I am afraid of a whole troop of Majors.

Major. (*Without.*) Granted.

Old Dor. Oh, Lord; he's here!
[*Exit hastily into door in back scene.*

Enter MAJOR TORNADO *and* MISS STOIC.

Major. Granted—'tis no fault of your's, sister;
and Olivia is by this time safe at the concert; but,
much as I'm prepared for rural sports, to miss her,
and to miss my chariot; and, after walking home
thro' rain and dirt, to find my servants all laid flat
with that Arcadian leveller called ale——

Mrs Aub. Where is Olivia, sir ?

Miss Stoic. (*Aside, and much agitated.*) How !

Major. Why, more rustic bliss ! Mrs Aubrey ! the chaise was fractured in a crystal stream——

Mrs Aub. I'll not believe it—no; why was I made a prisoner, madam? why thus confined ?—

Miss Stoic. Confined ! brother, 'tis well philosophy has steel'd my mind.

Mrs Aub. Philosophy ! oh ! when its source is virtue and strong sense, no system is more noble ; but made the veil for worldly and ambitious views, 'tis a perverted term, and tho' it preach in saint-like language, it means, or leads to danger and destruction.

Major. Nay, when the world's so guilty, is there no merit in avoiding it ?

Mrs Aub. No ; for if it be as misanthropes describe, let them remain, and help to correct its guilt, nor cowardly forsake what true philosophy might vanquish ; but 'tis in vain—I see she triumphs, where I hoped to please ; and since my heart forebodes new danger to Olivia, alone, once more I'l lsuccour and protect her.

Miss Stoic. Protect ! brother, they're leagued to rob me of your friendship ; and this false story of confinement well corresponds with their associate's tale of love, respect, and Seraphina.

Major. Associate ! he ! that old builder, who shall find I am the real Rollo Furioso. (*Shaking his stick.*) Madam, my sister's honour—(*Noise within of something falling*)—Why, what's that noise, and in your sanctum sanctorum? Oh, ho ! (*Going hastily towards the door.*)

Miss Stoic. Hold ! dare not approach that hallowed ground. (*Holding Major.*)

Major. Zounds ! I will murder—(*Breaking from her, and getting near the door ;* OLD DORIC *rushes out.*)

Old Dor. Don't—I ask pardon—and if you think I can defend that lady—(*Pointing to* MISS STOIC.) Quite the contrary.   [*Exit.*

Miss Stoic. Sir, I insist——(*Going.*)

Major. Sister, one word—confess—impart where I can find Olivia; and if I can forget——

Miss Stoic. Go, ask the real culprits—ask of Sir Edward and his vile dependant, and for forgetting— I shall remember and resent for ever.   [*Exit.*

Mrs Aub. Ask of Sir Edward! Oh! mercy!

Major. Come, best of friends; and, ruled by you, we will preserve Olivia still.   [*Exeunt.*

SCENE III.

A Cavern—an opening in the back Scene, and Yacht seen.

Enter TOM TACKLE, *with three Sailors.*

Tom. Come along, my lads; for though this Mr Delinquent has brought the young lady safe into this cavern here, whilst we get the boat ready to receive her, yet, why shou'd she sigh, and hang upon him, and entreat him to take her away again? Look ye! I'll bet a seventy-four to a Thames wherry, he means foul play to Sir Edward—so, come, boys! first for the boat, then for our prize; and then we've done our duty by a noble, gallant master.   [*Exeunt.*

Enter OLIVIA, *following* DELINQUENT *from Cavern.*

Delin. Away! your eyes are basilisks.

Oliv. Oh! think—think how I was lured into your power—by apt contrivance, when the carriage broke,

you flew to my relief, and I, believing you'd befriend and pity——

Delin. Pity! for you! I need it for myself: for
prove that reason holds, and the whole earth contains no bosom so unfeeling.

Oliv. 'Tis this that gives me hope—I'm sure you
are no willing agent—(*Falls at his feet.*) and see—
see at your feet one who, an hour ago, cherished the
fond hope of being united to him she loved—now,
sad reverse! alone, and guarded by a desperate
crew, waiting to meet a worse than pirate's fury——

Delin. Forbear! it strikes me to my brain—my
heart!

Oliv. (*Clinging to him.*) And if she calls for those
who mourn her loss, none, none shall answer her but
winds and waves, and thus cut off—thus torn from
every friend—

Delin. Friend! who are your friends? my curses
on 'em! for, had they watch'd you as they ought,
you had been safe, and I——that's comfort still—
I'm not more criminal than he, who, trusting to this
fiend-like sister's power——

Oliv. How! Major Tornado!

Delin. Ay; your own father—who first forsakes
you on a slanderous tale, and then conceding to Sir
Edward's plots, unites, like me, with villains to destroy you.

Oliv. What! class the virtuous with such infamy!

Delin. No; link the author of such evil——

Oliv. Hear me! though direst vengeance be the
sure result, I will not have his name, who gave me
more than life, compared one instant with a wretched
hireling, whom, much as I contemn, I more despise
myself for having stoop'd to parley with such baseness.

Delin. Hireling! live I to—take my defiance then.
(*Seizes her hand, and suddenly draws back.*) Gracious powers! does my sight fail, or—it is—(*Read-*

ing.) Lord Danvers' picture! (*Pointing to the picture hanging round* OLIVIA'S *neck.*)

Oliv. Ay: and know, the man that you call villain, is but my father by adoption; for when the brave Lord Danvers fell, he charged him to protect his loved Olivia, and named her as his own; because, forsaken by her natural parents, they lost that right her generous benefactor claim'd.

Delin. (*Looking at her closely, and raising the hair over her forehead.*) Nearer—still nearer! Oh heaven! that strong, resembling look! your hand— (*Nearly fainting.*)

Oliv. Mercy! this strange, mysterious—

Delin. Soft! not a word—steal gently, or they'll hear—now, swift as lightening.—(*Trying to force her off with rapidity.*)

Enter TOM TACKLE, *and Sailors meeting them.*

Tom. So—we have caught you, sir—and you, false lady—part them this instant. (*Forces* OLIVIA *from* DELINQUENT, *and, with another sailor, stands between her and* DELINQUENT.)

Delin. Never! for wild and savage as I'm proved, e'en the tiger springs to guard its young; and nature arms a parent with such nerves, that if one moment she'll forget past wrongs, I'm gifted with a giant's strength, and thus rush on, to clasp my long-lost daughter to my heart. (*Forcing past* TOM *and Sailors, and embracing her.*)

Oliv. Father! forget! Oh! let me bend—(*Going to kneel.*)

Delin. To heaven! you had a father there. (*Pointing to heaven.*)

Tom. What!—she—you!—speak!——your own daughter?

Delin. Ay: and for her I sought my native land; for her I sunk to slavery and shame—and you, who boast an English sailor's name, and often conquer

by humanity, will you still fight in a seducer's cause?
or, struggling for a father's rights, give him the
means to recompence his child for crimes that make
her shudder at his sight.

Tom. Oh! now I do understand, force has been
used—and since Sir Edward is so main fond of public praise, we sailors will instruct him how to gain it
--not by betraying, but protecting women—and for
this paltry vessel, and the command,—that for 'em
both!—better to serve before the mast, and die, as
our brave comrades have, abroad, than sink a name
which they have raised to such immortal glory.—
Come, you've no time to lose—come to my mother's
cottage, and I'll tell Sir Edward.

Delin. Do; tell him to imitate your bright example.—Oh! my Olivia! hereafter you shall know
all that I dare reveal—but much as I've endured,
this—(*Kissing her hand.*) this repays me!

[*Exeunt.*

ACT THE FIFTH.

SCENE I.

*A Cottage and Villa outside.   Practicable Window
in Cottage.*

Enter TOM TACKLE, *from the Cottage.*

Tom. Mess! I can't stand it—for, fond as I am of
sea, yet, what with mother's sobbing, and this poor

5

father and daughter sobbing, I've had such doses of
saltwater—and then this master I so loved, this false
Sir Edward!—dang it! I know not how to steer,
but this I know, he's waiting to be told she's safe on
board, and should he find them in that cottage—
Well, well, I'll do my best, and if I've luck enough
to make this poor Delinquent swim, and bring my
master to the port of honour, I shall bless fortune
more than if I'd won Newmarket losings through the
year.

Enter SIR EDWARD, *hastily.*

Sir Edw. So—I have found you, sir;—and by
your long delay, I fear to ask—speak! is Olivia safe?

Tom. Quite—quite safe, your honour.

Sir Edw. What, my friend bore her to the ship?

Tom. He did—she's the nicest, the loveliest—
but, begging your pardon, sir, the North's a long
way off, and 'tis so much more real and genteel to
marry in one's parish church, that, with your leave,
I'll step to Parson Poppit's house—

Sir Edw. Hold, sir—instant conduct me to my
prize.

Tom. What, to the vessel?

Sir Edw. Ay, to partake and glory in my triumph
—Come.

Tom. To be sure, sir—I know my duty to a noble, tender-hearted master. (*Sarcastically.*) But
since your friend has kindly kept his word, those
bonds you promised in return (*With anxiety,*) are
they about you, sir?

Sir Edw. No—they are not, sir.

Tom. That's lucky, very lucky; for, as I never
had the means to free a messmate on my own account, let me on yours: give me your keys, I'll follow you on board: and, talk of glory and of triumph,
I'd rather save one drowning friend, than sink a

hundred foes—though I can do that too whenever they insist on such a movement.

Sir Edw. Freedom to him!—who more than ever must conceal—never; but the reward I promised *you,* the purse that was to save ycur honour—here, take it.

Tom. What! save my honour at the loss of honesty! Come, come, sir, I'm not penny wise and pound foolish either; and for the sake o' justice (*Throwing the purse down.*) let it cast anchor there; for it will do more good in any hands than his who thus misuses what his friend so needs: I'll seek reward elsewhere. (*Going towards the Cottage.*)

Sir Edw. Stay, sir—you stir not. (*Following him, and stopping short on looking through the Cottage window.*) Heavens! that form! it is—Olivia in the arms of this detested wretch! and you to shelter—Confusion! let me pass, and since his fate is in my hands, thus I'll baffle and o'erwhelm them.

Tom, You cannot—will not!—he is—

Sir Edw. Her lover, villain!

Tom. No—her father!

Sir Edw. Father!

Tom. Aye, there's the treasure he so long'd to find; and think on how and where they met—think who reduced him to ensnare his own lost, doating daughter, and look, behold—(SIR EDWARD *turns away.*) what! I thought, I knew it, and I can feel for you as much as them; for I had rather fight the navy of the world, than face a friend so shipwreck'd and forlorn.

Sir Edw. (*After a pause.*) On what—on what have they resolved?

Tom. To sail to Italy, or share imprisonment. (SIR EDWARD *crosses hastily.*) Where, where be'st going, sir?

Sir Edw. Distract not, torture not with questions; follow me.

Tom. What, to atone?

Sir Edw. Atone! a common tale would not have check'd my design; but to persist in plunging in despair parent and child, long parted and thus found, demands that daring and ferocious spirit, which still, thank heaven, your coward master needs. Come, and receive the promised deeds.

Tom. Ay, and the purse too; for 'tis the present of a noble master now, and I am flatter'd by accepting it.

Enter MAJOR TORNADO, *behind.*

But, I say, hint not Sir Arthur Courcy is in England, or that 'twas he who forced away his daughter, because this Major and his hermit sister, these two field officers, ye see—

Sir Edw. I know, but let me hasten to repair my own heart-rending wrongs.

Tom. Do; and Sir Arthur will repair this old hero in his leading-strings; and so, sir, here go two men of honour!   [*Exeunt.*

Major. (*Advancing.*) Arrived in England! he! her father prove to be the wretch!—Well, after this I have no hope of agitation, an earthquake couldn't move me; and I who pledged my sacred honour to Lord Danvers, ever to guard her from this worst of foes—I—they're right—quite right—I am indeed in leading-strings; but I will burst at once to manhood, and shew this base Sir Arthur Courcy —(*As he is going.*)—

Enter OLD DORIC.

Old Dor. Sir Arthur Courcy! what, of Rowland castle?

Major. Ay, once owner of that stately pile.

Old Dor. Stately indeed! for I was architect: I built, I alter'd, I improved; and while each town and road-book pay me compliments, icod, they little think that's all I'm paid.

Major. What, not paid?

Old Dor. No: and when Sir Edward Specious wish'd to buy up my debt, says I, " the art of dunning, like the art of trade, consists in sticking close ; and whilst a polish'd creditor, like you, might wait and wait, till doomsday, even attornies say, pay that old pestering Toby first, or we shall have no peace : and then you're call'd a gentleman, and get their thanks ; I'm dubb'd a savage, but I get my money."

Major. You are the creditor I want: hark ye, he is in England now, somewhere in the neighbourhood.

Old Dor. The neighbourhood ?

Major. And his wrong'd child, Olivia, whom I sought, she, she is in his power; but you can save her by confining him, and for the debt, I'll pay it ten times o'er ; but I will part her from a wretch, whom pity, honour, and revenge—Come, this will do, I have the old heroic feel.

Old Dor. So have I : and whilst you are seeking him, I'll get the proper real officer, and, betwixt law and war—Say, shall I find you at the hermitage ?

Major. No! I've had enough of hermitages ; you'll find me yonder at the inn, where, worn with terror and anxiety, poor Mrs Aubrey now must hear, that 'tis this outlaw has ensnared Olivia, and by my credulous and restless—Look ye, if time should ever hang heavy upon your hands, find out some honest mode to fill it up, and not like me—Zounds! even now I'm wasting it—dispatch, restore her to my power, and the whole world combined—yes, Tornado is himself again.   [*Exit strutting.*

Old Dor. Yourself! that's against you ; for, in my mind, you'd better be any body else, and so perhaps had I, for I came here to see Jack yonder in his real villa, and hear the rogue's excuses, and now I'm go-

ing to confine the father of the girl he'd marry:
Come, come, before I cross him in his love, let me
first see I'm not made a fool; let me be sure my
partner's gain'd no customers, for if he has, that for
Tornado and his bouncing; I'll take Sir Arthur by
the hand, and, as the father of my nephew's wife,
tap all who tap him on the shoulder, ha! ha!—This
is no hermitage I ope—no, no, this augurs property
and trade.

(*As he is going to knock at the door of Villa, enter
from it Upholsterer and Wine Merchant hastily.*)

Uphol. Come along, we've told him he's found
out, and now we'll take another way to match this
swindling profligate: come, quick, quick.

Old Dor. Swindling! what swindling?

Uphol. Why, this young fashionable Mr Doric;
and if, like us, you are a creditor, 'tis fair to give
you notice, he hasn't change for sixpence!

Old Dor. No!

Uphol. No: but his partner has, one Toby Doric,
who expects great building contracts from his influence; he, he shall pay the piper, and we are upon
the search: mum! he is not far off.

[*Exit with Wine Merchant.*

Old Dor. No, but he will be in a twinkling, for
when he works upon his own account, 'tis by the job,
and not the day, as quick as he can do it.

Enter from the house YOUNG DORIC, *with papers in
his hand.*

Young Dor. (*In a melancholy tone.*) Partner!
Partner! won't you take your share?

Old Dor. No, you are welcome to the whole concern.

Young Dor. What! not go halves in these small
memorandums, partner! And 'tis no fault of mine;
the mayor, a sculptor by profession, so wish'd to
make Von Rapidotz's bust; and the two wives of

leading aldermen so struggled for my company and his, that here's a contract for the new town-hall, another for the bridge; and, since the profit's all my own, I will go sum up my account: debtor for parties, a few paltry pounds: per contra creditor, for trade, enough to make me partner to Olivia.

Old Dor. May I believe you, Jack?

Young Dor. Why, if you don't you're very singular, for with all else I'm quite Sir Oracle, except when I confess that I am poor; then they would rather trust me than my word; and even there they're safe; for, bless the corporation! here's a receipt in full of all demands; and for the building part, (*Taking his arm.*) we are the two main pillars of the art: I the Corinthian, you the Gothic order.

Old Dor. I Gothic—I—(*Smiling.*) Jack, you're no fool, and, start quack doctor, orator, or conjuror, I'll back your tricks, and be your partner still; but now for your betroth'd, of whom I've much to tell you as we walk.

Young Dor. Have you? away then; and I long to hear of the wrong carriage, and wrong house; ha! ha! it is a merry world; and there are fools that love it for its folly: we are the wise, who, revelling in its sports, get trade, get laugh——

Old Dor. Good cheer——

Young Dor. And social love!   [*Exeunt.*

SCENE II.

A Forest, and distant View of the Sea.

Enter OLIVIA *and the* DELINQUENT.

Oliv. Nay, father, I'm resolved.

Delin. 'Tis well: to part were more than nature

sure could bear; but still to share an exile and an outlaw's fate, and, galling thought! to sacrifice at least one valued friend, the kind Mrs Aubrey—and for him who aggravates his guilt, by thus ensnaring and involving you!

Oliv. No, no, the friends I leave are prosperous and free; and what if guilty? you are still my father; and I, your daughter, should more guilty prove, if in affliction I'd another thought but that of aiding and consoling you—Come.—Oh, if hereafter I should claim a recompence, 'tis to be told more of my mother than that Lord Danvers——

Delin. What more, Olivia! Have a care! the fever'd brain has ever one peculiar chord, which, touch'd, convulses it to madness.

Oliv. Well, well, 'tis past—lead on—(*Noise without.*) Hark! we're prevented.

Delin. (*Looking out.*) We are, and by Lord Danvers' friend; by him, no matter what his motive, who has so wrong'd and so neglected (OLIVIA *appeals.*) Nay, since at all hazards I have gain'd my treasure, I'm not so void of fortitude and pride, but, at all hazards, to maintain it.

Enter MAJOR TORNADO *hastily.*

Oliv. (*Flying to him.*) Oh! if you ever prized Olivia's peace. let me pass free.

Major. Rash girl! (*Taking hold of her.*) Thus, thus, I part you from a man, who, beggar'd by extravagance, sought safety for himself abroad, and left a virtuous, a lovely wife, to——

Delin. Hear me : was this Lord Danvers' story?

Major. It was, and, had he survived his wounds : few moments more, I should have known——

Delin. That 'twas my fate to marry with his daugh ter : I, who, in wealth, in honour, and fair fame 'ank' high enough e'en to gratify his ambition.—I maᵈ her mine, and in a few short years this virtuous, lovely, (for she was both) yet young, unthinking wife, ruin'd an easy husband's ample fortune, and overwhelmed him with bankruptcy, with beggary— but I forget—there is her daughter, and though you dare to criminate her father, he scorns to shock her with her mother's errors.

Major. Paltry evasion! when ruin and when bankruptcy ensued, did she suggest to you degrading flight?

Delin. No—stung with shame and with remorse, wild with my own and other's wrongs, and past prosperity still nursing pride, I had not courage to oppose the charge, but fled an outlaw, and commenced a slave. To the horror of my state, I soon learn'd that my unhappy wife, still plunged in fashion's vortex, had so gall'd her father's pride, he took Olivia from her care, and whilst Lord Danvers sought in India for repose, your mother pined and died.

Oliv. Died!

Delin. Ay, and with her all the recollection of her faults; for though Lord Danvers and his friend have deem'd it manly to resent, I felt it nobler to forgive. And love for her, who still was faithful in her love, is all, Olivia, all that now survives. (*Embracing* OLIVIA.)

Oliv. Forgive her! oh, bless you! bless you! (*Embracing him.*)

Major. I can't stand this, I am again at my credulity; but I will rouse: so, sir, hear me. Are you the feeling father you profess?

Delin. Ah! sir——

Major. Is exile a loved daughter's reward? or will her sharing lessen your affliction?

Delin. (*Shewing compunction*) Oh, my child! my child!

Major. And, since your doom is lasting exile or

bondage, prove, prove you have no narrow, selfish
thought, and welcome it alone; be great, (DELIN-
QUENT *shews more compunction.*) be——what! you
submit, you'll yield her to her friends?

Delin. Yield! (*Looking at* OLIVIA, *and struggling
with himself.*) The torturing thought long struggled
in my mind, but now it bursts, and I can proudly
say, I am a feeling father: where is that friend who
watch'd, who cherished, and has stored her mind
with such transcendent charms, that 'tis past bearing
to resign them: but 'tis decreed, she the best merits such a bright reward, and to her only will I yield
it.

Major. What! what! Mrs Aubrey! look, she
approaches, (DELINQUENT *trembles, and turns towards* OLIVIA.) and with joy I see her, for when
she heard you were Sir Edward's agent, she shewed
such agony, such——but this repays her.   [*Exit.*

Oliv. Father! for pity—

Delin. Olivia! I am firm; farewell, and in a happier world—(*Weeping and falling on her shoulder.*)

Enter MAJOR *with* MRS AUBREY.

(*She is much agitated, and tries in vain to look towards* DELINQUENT—*the Major takes her hand.*)

Delin. Now then (*Advancing rapidly with* OLIVIA
—MRS AUBREY *is turned from him.*) Madam, accept
a grateful father's thanks, and, as the best return for
all your tender and maternal love——

Mrs Aub. (*Turning round, and throwing herself
at his feet.*) Plead, plead for me, Olivia: tell him
that, struck with penitence and shame, I hoped the
virtues of a duteous daughter might best atone the
errors of his wife: and, to instill into her mind precepts my parents taught me to despise, I spread the
report of my death, and as your monitor enjoyed
those rights which as a mother I so justly lost: but

now my task's performed, and grieve not at our parting, child, for, blessed with such a father's love, you may defy adversity and exile.

Oliv. Mother!—Speak, father! speak!

Delin. I would, but tears prevent me. (*Embracing her.*)

Major. Now what a pretty figure do I cut! and, what with believing false evidence, and disbelieving true, I hope I shall never sit on a court martial; if I do, it won't be over in a hurry: but this I'm fix'd upon, you never quit your native land, while Indian gold or English valour can defend you.

Delin. Sir, 'tis in vain; besides Sir Edward, I've such mortal foes——

Major. So you have; there's that old architect.

Enter YOUNG DORIC *hastily.*

Young Dor. Pheugh! I'm out of breath, I've run so fast to be beforehand and forestall my partner and this sailor——Sir Arthur, you're restored to liberty; Sir Edward has released his debt, Doric and Co. have done the same, and, should there still remain one who'd enforce the outlawry, I and the Major here will give a ball, will pay the savage with his own bank notes, or, if that fails, hark'ye, (*Taking the* MAJOR *aside*) 'tis but to open the wrong chariot door, and Rollo-like, we'll shove him in a hermitage.

Mrs Aub. Restored to freedom! Olivia, unite with me again in thanking him.

Oliv. I do,—with heartfelt gratitude and joy.

Delin. Sir, you remember, that when last we met——

Young Dor. I do, Sir Arthur (*In a melancholy tone.*) I remember I left you out of my party, but if I luckily should get a wife, and a more roomy mansion, speak—(*Aside to* MAJOR *again.*) and I'll ask you to the wedding supper.

Major. He'll ask me to the wedding supper ! What say you, Olivia ? But here's the man.

Enter OLD DORIC *and* TOM TACKLE.

So, sir, are you quite hostile still ?

Old Dor. No, quite the contrary : I come with this brave tar to offer freedom to Sir Arthur, and chains to that dear tricking rogue. Sir, (*Advancing and bowing to* SIR ARTHUR) we are only builders to be sure ; but fashion being stamp'd more by long purses than long pedigrees, we from the city are the true beau-monde ; and if you would but mix your noble house with mine—(SIR ARTHUR *smiles.*) You will ? Jack, sign and seal, (YOUNG DORIC *kisses* OLIVIA'S *hand.*) and by your zeal, mind that the new firm prospers like the old one !—mind you're no sleeping partner, boy !

Major. (*Shaking* OLD DORIC *by the hand.*) I'll build another Rowland Castle, on purpose to employ this same unrivall'd architect ; and in Northumberland, on purpose to restore Sir Arthur to his native rank ; and all I ask is to be joined as partner in the firm ; for draw for life on my benevolence, I'll pay your drafts, and thank you for accepting them.

Old Dor. (*Bowing*) Oh, gallant, penetrating Major—but you (*To* TOM TACKLE,) why don't you speak ?

Tom. Because you won't let me : one walks before me, and t'other talks before me ; but this I will say, here be the promised bonds, Sir Arthur, and I do hope that my unhappy master——

Delin. Shall be forgiven for his servant's sake. Major, henceforth we're brothers—and you, the chosen husband of Olivia, make home the haven of your hopes, nor at the loss of fortune, time, and fame, seek peace in crowds, or friends in fashion's blaze.

Young Dor. Right :—for 'tis in fashion as in galvanism, there may be now and then some twitches of feeling, but 'tis always cold at the heart—and in one place alone will I give galas more—here !

Doric and Company, if you unite,
Hope to see company to-morrow night.
                              [*Exeunt omnes.*

LAUGH WHEN YOU CAN,

A

COMEDY,

AS IT IS PERFORMED AT THE

THEATRE-ROYAL, COVENT-GARDEN.

BY

FREDERICK REYNOLDS.

DRAMATIS PERSONÆ.

GOSSAMER,	Mr Lewis.
BONUS,	Mr Munden.
MORTIMER,	Mr Holman.
SAMBO,	Mr Fawcett.
DELVILLE,	Mr Whitfield.
COSTLY,	Mr Townsend.
CHARLES MORTIMER (a Child)	Miss Gilbert.
FARMER BLACKBROOK,	Mr Thompson.
GREGORY,	Mr Abbott.
WAITER,	Mr Simmons.
MRS MORTIMER,	Mrs Pope.
EMILY,	Miss Mansel.
DOROTHY,	Mrs Gibbs.
MISS GLOOMLY,	Mrs Mattocks.

SCENE—Richmond and the Neighbourhood.

LAUGH WHEN YOU CAN.

ACT THE FIRST.

SCENE I.

A modern Inn on a grand Scale—Porticos, &c.

Enter COSTLY *from the Wing, and* WAITER *from the Inn.*

Wait. Welcome home, sir—welcome from Barnet races.

Cost. Thank'ye, Tom, thank'ye : look !—here they are, you rogue—(*Shewing money.*)—five hundred by the sweepstakes !

Wait. What, the favourite won I suppose, sir ?

Cost. No—lost !—lost on purpose :—hark'ye, Tom —as there are false dice at hazard, so there are false jockies on the turf—we knowing ones can load both when we like—heh, you take, Tom ?

Wait. I do, sir ; and I wonder who'd take you for

a landlord:—instead of being master of the new hotel, one would suppose you one of the first men in the county.

Cost. And so I am one of the first men in the county—isn't that the largest house, and don't it contain the best card-rooms, billiard-rooms, and ball-room in the county?—and, if you come to that, who in the county keeps so many servants and carriages, or gives such dinners and suppers, as I do?

Wait. True, sir; and if they talk of hospitality—

Cost. Ay; if they talk of hospitality—do any of them make so much of their visitors as I do?

Wait. No; that they don't, I swear, and that's what puzzles me—whilst our house is always crammed with customers, the Red Lion over the way is deserted!—and yet old Boniface only charges half the price that you do.

Cost. That's it—that's the very reason—your best customer is your rich cockney; and he always stops at the dearest inn—always—for he fancies nothing good that's not expensive, and judges of the quality of an article by the quantity he pays for it.—For instance now; turtle!—do you imagine half the citizens who eat turtle like it?—no; but it must be good, because it is so d——d expensive!—(*Mimicking Aldermen.*)—therefore, let Boniface charge as high as I do——

Wait. I understand, sir:—but that would be very difficult.

Cost. Difficult!—impossible—but it can't be helpt —in towns like Richmond, where the season is short, the bills must be long, so—hush, here's company— now to business—(*Putting himself in order.*)

Enter DELVILLE, MRS MORTIMER, *and* CHARLES.

Cost. This way, madam, this way!—Tom, shew the Golden Fleece.

Mrs Mort. No, no; there's no occasion—this

young gentleman has been prescribed change of air by his physicians, and if you could recommend us lodgings, sir——

Del. My dearest cousin, leave every thing to me —walk into the hotel—take some refreshment, and Sambo shall look through the town, and find lodgings for you.—Come, come—you can trust the black, I'm sure.

Mrs Mort. Trust him! ay, with my life!—Poor Sambo! how amply has he profited by the education you have given him!

Del. He has indeed:——brought from his own country at six years old, and train'd up 'midst all the follies and dissipation of London, though his head has been enlighten'd, his heart remains uncorrupted.

Enter SAMBO. *His Dress—a white Jacket, Silver Shoulder-knot, white Waistcoat, glazed round Hat, Gold Band, Cockade, Boots, and Leather Breeches.*

Del. Sambo.

Sam. Sir!

Del. See what lodgings there are in Richmond, and bring word to me and Mrs Mortimer at the hotel.

Sam. (*Alarmed.*) Lodgings, sir!

Del. Ay, sir; we want some directly.

Sam. We want some!

Del. Yes; don't you comprehend, sir?—Now, cousin, pray, pray be persuaded.

Mrs Mort. Well, since you will have it so—Come, Charles—oh, Mr Delville! when, when shall I repay you for all your kindness and attention?—(*Exit with* CHARLES, COSTLY, *and* WAITER, *at the Hotel.* DELVILLE *is following;* SAMBO *stops him.*)

Sam. Sir, I hope you'll forgive me—I hope you won't be angry with me, sir—but—but—

Del. But what, sir?

Sam. Perhaps you don't recollect that Mrs Mortimer is a married woman, sir?

Del. A married woman!—and what then?

Sam. Then she has a husband, sir—a husband who once saved my life!—saved me when drowning; and you were pleased to thank him, and say he had conferr'd so great an obligation——

Del. I know I did, sir :—and still—what then?

Sam. Then, with submission, sir, is this the way to repay it?

Del. Silence!—how often have I told you not to touch on this subject?—if a beautiful woman will throw herself in my way; if, as soon as her husband goes to Gibraltar, she will continually invite me to her house—consult me in all her affairs—accept money from me——

Sam. Accept money from you, sir!

Del. Ay: at this moment, don't Mrs Mortimer owe me above five hundred pounds? and, after all these proofs, do you suppose she has no other motive for coming out of town with me, than her child's health?—Oh, I see it all—and, as it's impossible to persuade her not to love me, I'll e'en be kind, and give her love for love.

Sam. Don't—don't be rash, sir : and as to persuading her not to love you—leave that to me—I'll do it directly.

Del. You do it, sir!

Sam. Yes, sir; I'll tell her how you pursue your studies in the Temple!—that you leave me to do all the law business, and while I'm copying out pleadings in one room, you're writing love verses in another. —I'll tell her of a certain opera dancer, and remind her, though your good qualities are beyond naming, yet, where women are concerned, you're so thoughtless, and so desperate, that—Oh, I'm often rude enough to wish there was'nt a gown or petticoat in the world!

Del. Psha!—go where I ordered you, sir; and for the future no impertinence, Sambo:—cease to interfere in matters that don't concern you.

Sam. Nay, but this, sir——

Del. How! do you demur?—recollect who you are.

Sam. I do—I am your slave.

Del. No—not my slave—I gave you liberty.

Sam. You did, sir; and that made me your slave. —Gratitude has bound me faster to you than all the chains of Africa! 'Tis now fifteen years since you brought me to England; during which time you have fostered me, educated me, and treated me more as a brother than a servant!—and now, when I warn you of your danger, you call it impertinence!—Ah, sir!—rather say 'tis selfishness; for my fate is so involved with yours, that if your heart bleeds, Sambo's will break, I'm sure.

Re-enter WAITER.

Wait. Sir; the lady—Mrs Mortimer is asking for you.

Del. There! I've been neglecting her, and listening to your African philosophy:—go, sir—begone directly—nay—no reply—go see for the lodgings directly.—(SAMBO *exit.*)—Plague on the fellow's conscientious language!—he has made me half a coward, and I begin to feel——

Wait. Sir—won't you go to the lady?

Del. True, true:—I am too far embark'd—shew me to her; and as the man says in the play—" Let me run into the danger to avoid the apprehension!"

[*Exeunt.*

SCENE II.

A Street in Richmond.

Enter MISS GLOOMLY *and* DOROTHY.

Miss Gloom. How! it can't be, Dorothy—Mrs
Mortimer and Mr Delville eloped together?

Dor. Even so, ma'am :—as sure as you're the first
of sentimental writers, an elopement!—I saw them
stop at Costly's inn, and get out of the same post-
chaise ; and here!—here ll be fine work when Mr
Mortimer comes home :—first there'll be a duel—
then there'll be a divorce—then he'll be single again :
and then—ah, ma'am! I see you can't help smiling
at the thought of Mr Mortimer's being once more a
bachelor.

Miss Gloom. I smile! fie! for shame, Dorothy.

Dor. Nay; say what you please, ma'am; but
though the faithless man rejected you, and married
your niece, yet, as your own Artemesia says, " his
name is never utter'd, but you feel the most tumultuous animation!"

Miss Gloom. Animation!—agitation, child—will
you for ever misquote me?—but I own my virgin
weakness, Dorothy, and acknowledge I shouldn't
break my heart if Mr Mortimer were once more an
insulated being.

Dor. Then why not write and inform him?—

Miss Gloom. To confess the truth, I have written
to him—two months ago I sent him a letter to Gibraltar, acquainting him with his wife's conduct toward Mr Delville, and, as he was soon to return to
England, advising him to hasten his departure—To be
sure I was rather early in my intelligence, but I

knew nothing would so soon bring him to my presence as a little harmless scandal about his wife.

Dor. Scandal indeed !—it's no longer scandal now I am sure : and Mr Mortimer will be all gratitude and love, and——

Miss Gloom. I hope he may: but if he a second time disappoint me, I know how to be amply revenged: —I can marry his uncle, the rich stock-broker, whenever I please :—but of that another time—now how to bring about the divorce ? how to get evidence ?

Dor. Evidence !—Oh, if you want a witness, suppose I sift Sambo—Mr Delville's black ?

Miss Gloom. Do—find him out directly, and in case he's not communicative—here—bribe him—— (*Gives* DOROTHY *a purse.*)—I'll wait for you at home ; and mind you're attentive.

Dor. Attentive ! ah, ma'am !—I only wish Mrs Mortimer had minded your advice as I have done ! —if she, like me, had passed whole days in reading your moral and entertaining productions—

Miss Gloom. Entertaining !—why the girl's mad ! I never wrote any thing entertaining in my life.

Dor. Didn't you, ma'am ?

Miss Gloom. No—all my works are calculated to excite sighs, and tears, and terror, and distress—in short, to make people unhappy—and I hold laughter to be of so low and immoral a tendency, that, in the thirty-six volumes I have published, I defy you to produce a single joke.

Dor. Well ! that's true enough : and they certainly do make one unhappy.

Miss Gloom. Oh, they do, do they ?—then that's the real fine writing—but see !—the black's coming this way—I'll leave you together ; and if you succeed in your cross-examination, you shall not only be handsomely fee'd, but I'll read you a manuscript of so distressing a nature, that your features shall never be vulgarized by a smile again ! [*Exit.*

Enter SAMBO (*Looking about.*)

Dor. Ah, Sambo—how d'ye do, Sambo !—why, what are you looking for ?

Sam. I was looking for lodgings, Mrs Dorothy.

Dor. Lodgings !—um—what, for your master and Mrs Mortimer, I suppose—(SAMBO *looks astonished :*) nay, I know all about it—I know they've eloped together—and, hark'ye, Sambo—my mistress is so anxious about a divorce——

Sam. A divorce !—oh, oh ; what, that's her object?

Dor. Her object, sir ?

Sam. Ay : is it for that she persuaded Mrs Mortimer's father to disinherit her, and Mr Mortimer's uncle to desert him ?—and when poverty drove him abroad, and separated him from his wife, was it for that she shut her doors against her ?

Dor. No matter—serve her right, sir—how dare she marry Mr Mortimer, when she knew my mistress was in love with him ? But the divorce, Sambo— let's talk about the divorce—In the first place, Miss Gloomly wants your evidence——

Sam. My evidence !

Dor. Ay ;' and in the second, to unlock the secret pleasantly, she has sent you these golden keys— (*Shewing purse full of guineas*)—here—take them ; and now, Sambo.—(*Forces it into his hand.*)

Sam. (*Throwing the purse down.*) S'life !—does she think I'll betray my master ?

Dor. Hey-day !—why not, sir ?—when was your master so liberal ?—did he ever make you a present of any thing so valuable ?

Sam. I don't know—he made me a present of myself !—and, poor as you may think the gift, I'll not sell it for all the gold in the universe.

Dor. Not sell it !—if you come to that, it isn't the first time, I'll answer for it—no, Mr Negro—let me remind you, that people of your complexion are often bought and sold.

Sam. And so are people of yours. Black men are not the only men that are bought and sold. Every body has their price; particularly chamber-maids: they are always knock'd down to the best bidder. But I didn't come to quarrel—so good day, Mrs Dorothy.

Dor. What! and you won't take the purse?——(SAMBO *shakes his head.*)—Dolt! blockhead!—I see you know nothing of the value of money.

Sam. Faith! not much—I spent my whole fortune one morning; for, though my ancestors all came from the gold coast, my patrimony could only purchase me a French-horn—so once more good day, Mrs Dorothy.

Dor. Mighty well, sir: but remember your evidence may be forced from you—take care a lawyer's not employed.

Sam. Do you take care a lawyer's not employ'd —I have studied the practice—in fact, I'm a sort of student of the Temple, and let me advise your mistress not to waste her money that way—bid her lay it out in French-horns, or any other instruments of harmony—but never let her buy discord, or corrupt fidelity with it, I entreat you.   [*Exeunt.*

SCENE III.

View of Richmond, the River, Bridge, Hill, &c.

Enter EMILY.

Emi. Lord! Lord! who'd have thought of being laugh'd out of one's affection?—Had Mr Gossamer

been a serious, melancholy swain, I should have been
on my guard ; but he made love to me in joke, and
I couldn't help returning it in earnest !—and here !
—my guardian has sent me to his country-house, to
keep me out of his way—but I don't care—Mr Gossamer is a man after my own heart, and he has promised to write to me !—and I've sent Gregory to the
post-office ; and if there be but a letter——

Enter GREGORY.

Emi. Well : what news, Gregory ?—has my dear
Mr Gossamer kept his word ?—Come now—quick,
Gregory—quick.—(*Laying hold of him.*)

Greg. Lord ! what a madcap you are, miss !—no
wonder at your loving such a Merry-Andrew gentleman as Mr Gossamer—but here it is !—here's the
letter.

Emi. (*Snatching it from him.*) So it is !—in his
own dear facetious hand—now for it : (*Reads.*)

" My dear Emily,

" Since you were sent into the country, I ventured
to make one more application to your guardian, and
he actually order'd his servants to turn me out of
doors——consequently, I determined to have some
sport with him ; and I've the pleasure to inform
you, I began hoaxing him yesterday."—
I'm glad of that !—a'n't you, Gregory ?

Greg. Yes : that I be, miss—though, hang me if
I know what hoaxing means ?

Emi. Don't you ?—why it's all the fashion !—-to
hoax a person is to make a butt, a fool, a laughing-
stock of them—and Mr Gossamer is so celebrated in
the art, that—but Lord ! where was I ? (*Reads
on.*) " I shall soon follow this letter ; and in the
meantime, recollect the world is full of vexation and
disappointment, and therefore copy my motto, and
Laugh when you can !

GEORGE GOSSAMER."

There now! only think of my guardian's refusing
his consent! and if I marry without it, I lose all my
fortune ; and Mr Gossamer is a lord's younger brother, and they've never any money, and—heigho!
—come, Gregory, I may as well return to my prison.

Enter DELVILLE.

Del. Miss Emily, an old friend and school-fellow
of yours—Mrs Mortimer—

Emi. Mrs Mortimer, sir?

Del. Is now at the hotel, and seeing you from the
window, sent me to——

Emi. I'll wait upon her directly—Come, Gregory,
now I may consult her about my love affair ; and,
indeed, I hope Mr Gossamer will make haste and
get my guardian's consent—for I wish to be married
—that I do :—nobody knows how I wish to be married—dear me! nobody knows how much I long to
be married !—Sir, good day.

(*Curtsies to* DEL ILLE, *and exit with* GREGORY.)

Del. So, whilst she and Mrs Mortimer converse
together, I will myself see for apartments, and come
what will we never part again—heh! who's here—
as I live, my old college friend—the laughter-loving
Gossamer!

Enter GOSSAMER.

Del. What, George!

Goss. What, Ned!—Ned Delville!

(*Shaking hands.*)

Del. Why, I haven't seen you these hundred years
—but I've heard of you—ah, George! George!—
I'm told you're as great a boy, and play as many
monkey tricks as ever!

Goss. Then you're told right, Ned—I leave you
and other wiseacres to follow serious, grave pursuits
—for me, I'm fool enough to study mirth and mer-

riment; and as long as I'm a man I hope I shall be a boy!

Del. Well, well!—I see there's no reforming you —so tell me what brings you to Richmond, George?

Goss. A fine girl and thirty thousand pounds! I love them both with all my heart and soul.

Del. And do they love you?

Goss. To distraction!—both ready to jump into my arms!—only the guardian, he's a little trouble-some—but you know the old way—play with him like a trout—tickle him into consent.

Del. Take care, George; for how often at West-minster and at Oxford, whilst planning to trick others, have I seen you trick'd yourself?

Goss. Never: since I took to the glorious profes-sion, never had the worst of it.

Del. No? why, don't you remember the boyish trick I play'd you at the Sun Inn? Didn't I lure you into the attorney's bed-chamber, and coax you to let off squibs and crackers, in order to get you into a law-suit?

Goss. You did—you did—and when the ceremony was perform'd, didn't I run out of the room, lock you in, and leave you to pay all the costs and damages? —I say, there I hoax'd you, Ned!—Then again, the bet about the hogshead of claret?

Del. Psha!—nonsense—that was many years ago: I defy you to suceeed now.

Goss. Don't—don't defy me, Ned.

Del. Why, s'life! have you the impudence to sup-pose you could make a butt of me now?

Goss. Of you or any man living: and if you chuse to bet me another hogshead of claret!—but you won't—you've bought experience—the burnt child, you know—heh! Ned.

Del. Zounds! I've a great mind to accept your offer, on purpose to make you pay for your presump-tion.

1

Goss. Do: I'd take it as a favour, Ned—Do let me once more make a laughing-stock of you? Do bet me a hogshead of claret, that before to-morrow morning I don't play you as fair a trick—

Del Before to-morrow morning? Well—since you provoke me—it's a bet.

Goss. (*Embracing him.*) My dear fellow, thus and thus let me return you thanks!—I'll go to work directly—I'll go drink one bottle of Costly's claret, the better to secure whole dozens of yours!—I'll—but hold—hold—where am I to find you?

Del. At the hotel.

Goss. That's enough!—and remember now—no quibbling—if it's as fair a trick as the others, you'll acknowledge the wager s mine.

Del. Agreed! and by making you smart for your folly, I hope I shall shame you out of a conduct devoid of all feeling, sense, and morality!

Goss. Morality!—nay, now—what system is more moral than mine?

Del. What! why that of rationality—of sentiment.

Goss. Sentiment! psha!—where one rascal is preach'd or lectured out of his vices, thousands are laugh'd and ridiculed out of them: and because I'm cheerful, don't fancy I want feeling!—No; I've as much sensibility as graver men; but the world is full enough of misery, and rather than add to it, I often dress sorrow in smiles, I promise you—so be on your guard—remember the attorney—and laugh—laugh when you can, my boy!   [*Exeunt.*

ACT THE SECOND.

SCENE I.

Another View of COSTLY's *Inn.*

Enter COSTLY *and Waiter.*

Wait. (*Meeting* COSTLY.) Oh, sir! you're wanted, sir!--Alderman Plethora has been calling for you this half hour.

Cost. Alderman Plethora!

Wait. Yes, sir: he complains of bad treatment---he says his physicians ordered him to sleep in the country, and accordingly he came to your house to be snug and quiet——

Cost. Well! and was'nt he snug and quiet?

Wait. No, sir: he says the maid put him in a chamber over the billiard-room, and under the ball-room, so that he slept between two fires. Then you are wanted by the club---by the Sons of Friendship, sir---they complain of their wine---they say it's execrable.

Cost. My wine execrable?

Wait. Ay, they wonder such stuff can be sold by a landlord of your consequence---and they desire you'll taste this bottle of port yourself.

(*Waiter has a bottle in his hand.*)

Cost. I taste it!---do they want to poison me?----Damn me if I'd drink a glass of it for the profit of the whole pipe: no, no---give my compliments to

the Alderman and the Sons of Friendship---but,
hush! somebody's coming---this way.   (*Retires.*)

Enter DELVILLE, *from the Wing.*

Del. S'death! that he should arrive at such a
time as this? (*Looks out*)---'Tis he! 'tis Mortimer
himself!---and should he meet his wife, all, all will
be undone----perhaps he'll force her from me----per-
haps persuade her to relent, and lure her to his arms
---Distraction! that must never be---she's now in my
possession, and shall I risk the loss of her?---Land-
lord---a word with you---you don't wish to interrupt
an amour, do you?

Cost. An amour, sir?

Del. Ay: if a lady and gentleman had eloped together, and were pursued by a brother or a husband,
you wouldn't stop their progress, would you?

Cost. Not I, sir: always send them forward for
the good of the road: and none pay better than
your runaway lovers---that is, going down ---coming
back they lose their appetites, and call for nothing
to eat or drink.

Del. Understand me then: the lady is in that detached part of your inn; and, in the first place, I wish
nobody to come near the room; and, in the next, to
have a chaise and four ready at the gate.

Cost. I take! it shall be done.

Del. Then, Mortimer, I defy you!---(*Aside*) and
now, how am I to repay?

Cost. Repay!---Oh, don't you trouble yourself about
that; I'll put it in the bill---whenever I oblige a customer, or a customer disobliges me, I always put it
in the bill!---so mum---you go to the lady.

Del. I will: and mind now---reward yourself handsomely, I charge you.

Cost. Never fear---you shall have charge for charge
I warrant. (DELVILLE *exit into inn.*) Now observe, Tom; observe---(*Taking Waiter aside.*)

Enter MORTIMER.

Mort. So! I can walk no further; bodily fatigue
I can encounter cheerfully, but not the ceaseless labour of the heart—'tis here! 'tis here! I am exhausted ' and though so near my journey's end, I fear I
have not strength to reach it!---This inn may afford
me a conveyance: I'll enquire.—Sir, (*To* COSTLY,
who takes no notice of him)---sir, may I ask----

Cost. Keep off: don't you see I'm busy?

Mort. I beg pardon: I thought you belong'd to
this house.

Cost. I belong to this house! that's a very good
joke---this house belongs to me---but, like other great
people, i don't give dinners and suppers without expecting to get something by them;---and (*Putting
his hand to his pocket*)—you take, don't you?

Mort. I do: I understand you well: but, when I
tell you these feet have borne me a long and tedious
journey of two hundred miles, and that I only ask
a resting-place in some stage coach or return'd
chaise——

Cost. Return'd chaise!—psha! (*Turns from him
with contempt*)--Now mind, Tom, what I've told you,
and I'll go give orders to the other servants. (*As he
is going into inn,* SAMBO *comes out*)---Ah, Blacky,
how d'ye do, Blacky?

Sam. Thank ye, Mr Landlord—thank ye.—(*Sees*
MORTIMER.) Bless me! who is that gentleman?

Cost Gentleman indeed! it's some poor devil who
wants a return'd chaise.

Sam. And won't you let him have one?

Cost. No; he has no money.

Sam. Hasn't he! then I have—Oh! Mr Mortimer, don't you recollect me?

Mort. Sambo! faithfu Sambo!

Sam. You once saved my life, sir, and may I lose it
if ever I'm ungrateful—A return'd chaise!—Go---get

him all the chaises and horses in the inn; and though he has no money, Mr Landlord, I think, with submission, your profits might, once in a way, allow you to find a resting-place for a poor and weary soldier. —(COSTLY *and Waiter exeunt.*)—Well, and how have you been, sir?---and what brings you so unexpectedly from Gibraltar?

Mort. (*Producing a letter.*) This letter:---hear me—it calls your master villain—it charges him with such accomplish'd infamy—— but since you know the truth or falsehood of the charge, read, and at once confirm or dissipate my fears.

Sam. This letter!—pray who is it from, sir?

Mort. From Miss Gloomly: and though I know her to be artful and censorious, yet would she dare commit her name——but read, and if you can, good fellow, relieve a doating husband from agonies too great to be endur'd.

Sam. (*Reading.*) " Sir, I think it my duty once more to apprize you of the growing impropriety of your wife's conduct towards Mr Delville.—They are become the talk of the town; and as you are soon to leave Gibraltar, let me advise you to hasten your departure; and if on your arrival you will call at my house, you shall hear more from your

Constant friend,
DIANA GLOOMLY."

Mort. There!—What say you, Sambo?--- Is Delville the most deprav'd, and I the most accurs'd—— (SAMBO, *who has been trembling all the time, lets the letter fall.*)—Ha! what alarms you?—why do you tremble thus?

Sam. I—I tremble, sir!—bless you!—I—I don't tremble, sir.

Mort. No?—why, you shake, man.

Sam. It's an ague—nothing but an ague!—I brought it with me from the West Indies, and—and hadn't I better go order the chaise?

Mort. How! do you prevaricate?—then your master shall himself inform me!—Where is he?—in that inn, sir?

Sam. No—yes—but, but——

Mort. But what, sir?

Sam. Why—why, there's somebody with him——

Mort. (*Laying hold of him.*) Who is it?—speak directly, sir——

Sam. Not Mrs Mortimer, sir—upon my honour, not Mrs Mortimer, sir—and he's innocent, and she's innocent, and we're all innocent!—besides, if he were with her, 'twould be solely out of friendship for you—only to keep off other lovers—to——

Mort. Stand by—I will be satisfied—I'll see Mr Delville.

Enter GOSSAMER, *drunk, and meeting* MORTIMER.

Goss. You see Mr Delville!—save yourself the trouble—my business is much more important than yours, and even I can't see him.—(*Hiccups*)—D—n this landlord and his wine—I'm poison'd—poison'd, to a certainty.

Mort. (*Breaking from* SAMBO, *who holds him.*) Away! I'll know the worst.

Goss. (*Stopping him.*) Stop—I'll tell you a secret. Delville—our friend, Delville, has betted me a hogshead of claret I don't make a laughing-stock of him —now the business is half done—I've found out such a hoax for him—hark ye—(*Whispers* MORTIMER) he has elop'd with a married woman.

Mort. What?

Goss. He has carried off Mrs Mortimer—they are now in the hotel: and, in my mind, our friend's a d——d rascal for his pains—What right has he to make a gentleman unhappy?—to bring tears into the eyes of an honourable husband?—that's not my plan, I assure you—I always make people laugh——

(*Observes* MORTIMER's *agitation*)—no—not always
—for my jokes don't seem to take now, I perceive.

Sam. (*Pulling* GOSSAMER's *coat.*)   No; for a
good reason, sir : because——

Goss. Because you're the tragic muse—Avaunt,
thou sable goddess!—and, sir, if you chuse to join
with me, we'll—(MORTIMER *weeps, and takes out his
handkerchief*)—Oh, oh!—some intimate friend, I suppose—What, you know Mr Mortimer?—pray, sir—
no offence, I presume—was he very fond of his wife?

Mort. Fond! oh, he had no hope beyond her.

Goss. Poor gentleman!—I wish I was near him, to
comfort him!—but courage! take courage, sir : perhaps it's not yet too late to save her—and I've a
cursed comical head of my own, I can tell you—I
have! and if, by one of my facetious stratagems, I
can make a butt of Delville, win a hogshead of claret, and restore Mrs Mortimer to her husband, why
then——come, I'm sure you'll laugh at my jokes
then, won't you, sir?

Mort. Nay, nay, 'tis all in vain.

Goss. Not a bit—I'm now going to Emily, but I'll
return instantly, and hoax him certainly!—and in
the mean time keep clear of the tragic muse, and
laugh—laugh when you can!

Mort. Stay, sir—but one question more, and the
die is cast for ever—Did you see them together?

Goss. To be sure I did—not half an hour ago, I
saw him on his knees to her; and now, because
they're *téte-à-téte,* nobody must come near him—but
courage, I say!—I'll save her—I'll restore her to
her husband!—and if I do not, blame my head----
(*Putting his hand to his heart*)----not my heart!----
(*Putting his hand to his head*)----damn this wine----
(*Hiccups*)—poison'd, poison'd, to a certainty!
[*Exit.*

Mort. (*After a pause.*)   Well, well---I'll resent it
like a man.

Sam. Resent it!—don't, sir, for my sake—if my master must suffer, let the law punish him.

Mort. What will the law afford me?---a pecuniary atonement!—and when I've lost the only treasure that I covet, will millions purchase me a moment's peace?—no—though he sees I couldn't guard her honour, he'll find I've courage to assert my own--- I'll go and——yet, hold—let me consider——

Sam. Ay, do, sir: consider for ever, rather than hurt my dear master.

Mort. My boy!---my only child!---should it be my lot to fall, what will become of him?---his mother is no longer fit to educate him, and therefore let me claim Miss Gloomly's promise, made to her brother on his death-bed---yes: that shall be my first employment, then expect me, Delville!---Sambo, you'll find me at yonder inn.

Sam. Nay, sir: but suppose you were just to see Mrs Mortimer——

Mort. See her! what! to be despis'd, insulted, triumphed over?---no---no---I will not condescend to let her know my sufferings.

Sam. Well; but if I see her, mayn't I mention—

Mort. No, sir, do not name me-—and yet---- (*Pulling her picture from his breast*)---since she's another's, and I'm no longer privileged to wear it, give her back her picture---Ah! 'twas my companion in many a cheerless hour—I passed whole days in gazing on its charms; and even now, I tremble as I look, and tears of pity and of love fall as I part with it!---(*Weeping, and kissing the picture.*)

Sam. Do—pray, sir, let me tell her all this.

Mort. No:--- but you may say in memory of our past affections, I'll keep the bitter secret to myself —I'll not proclaim her errors to the world:—tell her, I may condemn, but I will not expose her! [*Exeunt.*

SCENE II.

A Room in the Hotel—Folding Doors in the back Scene.

Enter MRS MORTIMER *hastily.*

Mrs Mort. Can this be Mr Delville ?—can he believe what he affirms ?—I encourage his addresses !
I give proof of love !---Oh ! he knows as little of my
heart as I have known of his---but I begin to understand him now—the friend breaks forth into the lover ! and amongst the various hardships of our sex,
I might have known men cannot be our friends---
they talk of friendship, but their thoughts are love !

Enter SAMBO.

Speak, Sambo---you---you can vindicate my inno-
cence---have I, even in the slightest degree, once
taught you to believe I loved your master ?

Sam. Don't—don't ask me, ma'am---I'm no judge.

Mrs Mort. How ! do you conspire against me ?---
Oh Heavens ! on what grounds am I accused ?—is it
because, at his own request, I suffered him to accompany me and my son to this place---surely, as my
relation and friend from early life, there was no
great impropriety or proof of love in that ?---is it,
then, because he persuaded me to accept money
from him ?---alas ! imperious necessity compell'd me,
and but for his timely assistance, I and my poor child
must have been reduced to misery and want !

Sam. Indeed, madam !

Mrs Mort. Yes : Mr Mortimer, out of his small
pay as lieutenant, could remit nothing for our sup-

port; and his family and my own had driven me to distress---to despair---but, thank Heaven!---not to dishonour!---(*Kneels.*)----No, Mortimer!---if, since the day we parted, I've been untrue to you, in action, word, or thought, may I meet the greatest punishment on earth—your anger, your disdain!

Sam. " Dear Yanko say, and true he say!"—- (*Singing and dancing.*)---Then it's all a mistake---all a big, odious, scandalous lie---Bless my soul!—how could the report have originated?

Mrs Mort. No doubt in the conceit of a coxcomb —in your master's vanity.

Sam. And in Miss Gloomly's slander; and, begging your pardon, madam, in your own thoughtlessness—don't be angry—but the world judges by appearances, and when I'm married, I shall request of Mrs Sambo——

Mrs Mort. Then the world judges falsely—Virtue is artless, free, and unsuspicious---'tis only vice that glosses o'er its crimes; and to the truly innocent, the censure or applause of gossip tongues is equally indifferent!---But I will go and——

Sam. Go!---I say---where will you go to?

Mrs Mort. Alas! I know not.

Sam. Don't you?---then I'll tell you---you'll go to your husband.

Mrs Mort. My husband!---oh, the very thought revives me---the sight of him is all I hope and pray for---but ah!---he is far off.

Sam. Far off, is he?---hem!---look---who gave me this picture?

Mrs Mort. That! why, 'tis the same I gave Mortimer——

Sam. I know it: and it's the same he gave me— now, not five minutes ago—and he press'd it to his heart, and kissed it! and now, if you'll go with me, he'll press and kiss something else.

Mrs Mort. How! what mean you?

13

Sam. Mean!—that you don't suppose he'll prefer paint and ivory to the pure flesh and blood of the original?—Come along—he's over the way—at the opposite inn; and if my master could feel as I do— if, like me, he knew the pleasure of bringing a fond couple together, I'm sure he'd never have the heart to part them.

Enter DELVILLE.

Del. Heh!—where are you going, sir?

Sam. Going, sir!—I was going to deliver this lady to her husband; and I was saying, sir, that if a man knew the pleasure of bringing a fond pair to-gether——

Del. (*Pulling* SAMBO *from her.*) Be gone—leave the room this instant, sir—and, d'ye hear, for your life, don't let us be interrupted.

Sam. Not interrupted, sir!

Del. No—she has made a dupe of me, and I'm resolv'd to be reveng'd.

Sam. Reveng'd!

Del. Ay: cann't you guess my meaning?—Hark ye!—she and Mortimer shall never meet again.

Sam. Not meet!—what! you'd detain her?— you'd—(*Catches hold of* DELVILLE *by one hand, and points to* MRS MORTIMER *with the other.*)—Look at her, sir—she is now innocent!—her husband, after a year's absence, is waiting to embrace her!—her and his only child!—look, I say, sir; and then tell me, if, even in my uncivilized country, a being can be found savage enough to part them?

Del. How! again this insolence!—have a care, or I may find means to send you back to that unculti-vated country.

Sam. Do:—send me where you like—let me toil, fret, and be treated like a slave—only don't let me see the master of my heart descend to actions which will embitter his life and my own for ever!

Del. Look ye, sirrah—you but increase my desperation ; and if you do not instantly leave the room,
force—force shall be employed.

Sam. Well, I'll save you the trouble, sir—since my
remonstrances have fail'd, I am not the proper person to contend further—What shall I do ?—suppose
I apply to Mr Mortimer—no—no—murder will be
the consequence—suppose—gad ! I have it—lucky,
lucky thought. I'll go—I'll go.

Mrs Mort. Stay—don't leave me, Sambo.

Sam. Don't be afraid, ma'am—my master will soon
be put in good humour :—at all events, I'll wait within hearing ; for though I know my obedience as a
servant, I'll shew him I hav'n't forgot my duty as a
man !   [*Exit.*

(DELVILLE *locks the door.*)

Mrs Mort. Heav'ns ! what do you mean ?

Del. (*Much agitated, and laying hold of her hand.*)
Hear me, madam :—you've rais'd a flame I cannot
now extinguish, and should it prove most fatal to us
both, you have to answer for the consequences—
better than life I love you, and but with life I'll part
with you.

Mrs Mort. How ! not part with me ?

Del. No—Love, uncontroulable love, urges me
to the glorious enterprise ! and let Mortimer call me
to the field, or make me pay the forfeit of the law,
in either case my life and fortune shall answer the
event.

Mrs Mort. Your fortune ! ay, thus it ever is : the
poor wretch who steals a purse the law condemns to
death ; but the exalted robber, who purloins a wife,
and cowardly assassinates a husband's peace, pays a
small penalty, which, in the modish circle of his
friends, adds to his fashion, and establishes his fame !
—but mine's a different case.

Del. Of that I think not ; and be the penalty or

beggary or death, I'll think my happiness too cheaply bought!—(*Here he lays hold of her, and she breaks from him*)—Nay; hope not to escape—the doors are all secured.

Mrs Mort. Secured! unlock them then, or I'll expose you, sir!—I'll call for help.

Del. That too is useless: the whole house is in my interest; and thus in my power—thus deserted by the world——

Mrs Mort. (*Kneeling to him.*) Oh! for mercy, Mr Delville—you once called yourself my friend!

Del. That time is past: at present I'm not quite master of my reason; and, if you wish to save me or yourself, accompany me abroad—leave Mortimer for ever.

Mrs Mort. (*Rising.*) No: I'd rather die a thousand deaths than raise one blush in a lov'd husband's cheek.

Del. (*Laying hold of her forcibly.*) Then I will force you——

Goss. (*Without.*) Help! murder! thieves!

Del. S'death! what interruption's this?

Goss. (*Without.*) Murder! the door! open the door, Delville.—(GOSSAMER *kicks open the door in back scene and enters; his hair is disordered, his waistcoat open, and he holds a handkerchief to his side, spotted with blood; in his other hand a pistol.*)—Support me! lead me to a chair! oh! oh! oh!—(DELVILLE *and* MRS MORTIMER *place him in a chair.*)

Mrs Mort. Mercy! what's the matter, sir?

Goss. Ask no questions. A surgeon—get a surgeon directly. I'm wounded, and in your cause, Delville—look—I'm not joking now, Ned. (*Tries to shew his wound, but, feeling pain, suddenly puts his handkerchief to his side again.*)

Del. Poor fellow!—how he bleeds!—Why, where did this happen, George?

Goss. Down stairs—with the club—with the Sons

of Friendship, Ned—I thought to pass a quiet day
in their harmonious society ; but dinner was hardly
on table, when one amicable gentleman knocked
another down—on which—ugh!—*(Feels pain, and
puts his hand to his side.)*

Del. S'life! and did you take part in their dispute?

Goss. What could I do? one must be sociable,
you know; and I kept cool, till I heard you call'd a
scoundrel and a seducer!—then, Ned, I gave the
lie : and then the president, who, out of pure friendship, carries loaded pistols in his pocket, forc'd one
into my hand—another into my antagonist's; and we
fir'd, till—ugh! stop this red sea—some lint—some
styptic—or I faint—I die!

Mrs Mort. In my room there's a medicine-chest
—I'll get it directly.

Del. Hold, madam : you must not stir!

Goss. Not stir! what, you are one of the Sons of
Friendship, are you, Ned?—However, I won't die
for any of you—so—I'll get it—I'll—*(Raises himself up, but, exhausted by the effort, falls back in the
chair.)*

Del. Zounds! was there ever any thing so unfortunate? well, well—compose yourself, George—I'll
get what you require, and return instantly—instantly,
madam :—*(Looking and frowning at* Mrs Mortimer*)*—so hope nothing from my absence.

[*Exit at stage door.*

Goss. Is he gone, ma'am?

Mrs Mort. He is, and will soon bring you assistance : and you won't—you won't die, sir.

Goss. Yes : I shall—I shall die, ma'am; but—
(Changing his voice and countenance)—it will be
with laughing—ha! ha!—There I had you, Mr Delville.

Mrs Mort. What! don't you bleed, sir?

Goss. Yes, freely of claret, but not a drop of

blood! and I can afford it; for I've won a whole hogshead by the frolic!—But we're losing time—go to that door—Sambo, who told me of your situation, is waiting to conduct you to your husband—go, and for the fright I've occasion'd you, pray pardon me: I wish to laugh, but never at the expence of distress like yours.

Mrs Mort. Sir, I'm all gratitude.

Goss. Nay, nay: I'm amply paid, and—Zounds! here's the butt again—here's Delville!—I must let the red sea flow on—*(Sits in the chair as before.)*—Mum! look out for Sambo.

Re-enter DELVILLE, *with a phial and lint.*

Del. So—now I think on't, this may be one of his tricks.—Come, shew me your wound, George?

Goss. Softly—kneel down, and you'll have a better view.—*(*DELVILLE *kneels.)*—Now's your time—*(Aside to* MRS MORTIMER.—*Here* GOSSAMER *covers* DELVILLE'S *face with his waistcoat;* SAMBO *appears at a door in back scene, beckoning to* MRS MORTIMER, *and she walks tremblingly towards him.)*—Do you see any thing now?—*(Still covering his face, and* MRS MORTIMER *getting nearer door.)*

Del. No; nothing, sir.

(Here MRS MORTIMER *exit with* SAMBO, *clasping her hands, all gratitude to* GOSSAMER *; who, seeing she is gone, jumps up, puts his handkerchief in his pocket, and buttons his waistcoat.)*

Goss. Then do you see any thing now?—huzza! —there's a hoax for you!

Del. Confusion! where's Mrs Mortimer?

Goss. Where's my hogshead of claret?—Why, Ned! this beats the attorney!

Del. S'death and shame! I'll pursue her—I'll overtake and bring her back again.

Goss. *(Holding him.)* What! and trouble me to make you a butt again?—She is by this time safe with her husband!—and now, Ned—now isn't mine a moral system?—A sentimental fellow would have shot you for your bad conduct—but I laugh you out of it: I let you live and reform! and if you will but copy the example of your honest negro, you'll enjoy that cheerfulness a good conscience can alone secure you.

Del. Psha! I have done with you—from this moment, farewell!—and, were you not beneath my resentment, you should hear from me.

Goss. And sha'n't I hear from you?—won't you send me the claret, Ned? won't you act like a man of honour?

Del. You talk of honour! you! a needy, fashionable——

Goss. There! there's more of the old cant again: because I'm fashionable, I cann't be honourable?— Oh, Ned! Ned! get rid of all your vulgar prejudices, and wherever you find virtue and merit, whether in the rich or the poor, the peer or the peasant, learn to respect and admire them: so, good night; and if you pursue Mrs Mortimer again, be sure I'll let the red sea flow again——" Oh! I'm dying! dying!— there—don't you see any thing now?"—(*Mimicking.*) —ha! ha! dam'me, there's a hoax for you!

[Exeunt separately.

ACT THE THIRD.

SCENE I.

A Street in RICHMOND.

Enter MISS GLOOMLY *and* DOROTHY.

Miss Gloom. Amazement! Mortimer arrived, and not yet sue for a divorce?

Dor. No, madam: not half an hour ago I met him coming out of the Red Lion, and though he thank'd you for your letter, and acknowledged the truth of its contents——

Miss Gloom. What! though he is convinced of his wife's falsehood?

Dor. Ay, madam: though he is satisfied she has elop'd with Mr Delville, yet, notwithstanding all this, Mr Mortimer won't hear of a divorce.

Miss Gloom. Brute! idiot! and did he send no message, Dorothy?

Dor. None, madam: and when I ask'd him if this was treatment for the author of Artemesia, the Victim of Sensibility, and the Confusions of the Soul—

Miss Gloom. Effusions, girl! how often must I correct you?—Effusions of the Soul, besides elegies, sonnets, and other pathetic and moral publications! —Well! and what did he say then, Dorothy?

Dor. Nothing, ma'am: he turned upon his heel and left me.

Miss Gloom. Did he?—In addition to my other wrongs, did he treat my writings with contempt? Then I'll be reveng'd—Delville has ruin'd him in

love, and I'll ruin him in fortune !—I'll marry his
uncle directly.

Dor. What, marry the rich stock-broker, ma'am ?

Miss Gloom. Yes: I'll break through my awful
vow of celibacy, and accept the long-proffer'd hand
of Mr Bonus—go, while I'm in the humour, Dorothy—go, find him, and be the herald of approaching
love !

Dor. Oh ; this will put Mr Mortimer for ever in
your power—I'll go find the little citizen directly.

Miss Gloom. Citizèn, Dorothy?

Dor. Nay, don't be angry, ma'am ! but you must
acknowledge, though Mr Bonus professes to be a
complete country 'squire, yet, in fact, he is as arrant
a cockney as ever heard Bow bells !

Miss Gloom. Nonsense, girl ! isn't Mr Bonus always
abusing the thick fogs of Cheapside, and praising the
pure breezes of Surry ?

Dor. Yes: and, when in Surry, where does he enjoy those pure breezes—where, but in card-rooms,
billiard-rooms, and ball-rooms ?—Except in the road
to his villa, does he ever see a green tree ; or, what's
worse, though he has liv'd ten years at the bottom
of Richmond-hill, has he once been on the top of it ?
—No, no—he is one of those who lead a London life
in the country :—and see ! here he comes, warm from
the Stock Exchange ! Now, now you may disclose
the welcome tidings yourself, madam.

Miss Gloom. I disclose !——oh fie, fie, Dorothy !
Have you no pity for a tender spinster ? Have you
no mercy on my maiden blushes ?—No : be you my
herald, whilst I'll go home and prepare for his reception : but observe, Dorothy, I will accept him only
on condition that he never forgives, or even sees
Mortimer, but at my express desire: tell him this,
and then, as Artemesia says—who, by the by, is in
her thirtieth edition—tell him,

To-morrow's sun gives Dian to his arms,
For rage has triumph'd over love's alarms!

[*Exit.*

Enter BONUS *and* COSTLY.—DOROTHY *retires up the Stage.*

Bon. Now, why, Costly—why will you be asking questions about stocks and the Stock Exchange, when you know I come out of town to be quiet and rusticate, and, in short, to pass my time in a pastoral, shepherd-like manner ?

Cost. Well, but I want to buy some long annuities, Mr Bonus.

Bon. Psha! we're not in 'Change Alley—not in that feverish, shop-keeping place, London, now :—no, we're in the country: and now for rural intelligence—first, the assembly—what sort of a ball had you last Monday ?

Cost. Cramm'd—overflowing, sir :—and so hot, that several ladies fainted.

Bon. There now ! and I not amongst them !—I all the time snuffing the smoky air of London :—plague on it!—and cards—Had you many card-tables, Costly ?

Cost. Above a dozen, sir :—and the quadrille party didn't break up till six in the morning.

Bon. There again ! not till six in the morning ?—Now, do all I can, there's no keeping these delightful hours in the city !—and Miss Gloomly—that cruel unrelenting maiden——was Miss Gloomly amongst them ?

Dor. (*Advancing and courtseying.*) Nay, if you knew all, Mr Bonus, you wouldn't call her cruel, I'm sure.

Bon. Not cruel, Dorothy !—why, hasn't she for ten long years been the omnium of my affections ?—haven't I doated on her for her love of retirement ?

—adored her for her unexampled chastity?—But where is she?—will she take a rural walk with me? —will she go shopping, or to the library, or to the box-office of the theatre?

Dor. Theatre!—ah! you're a happy man, Mr Bonus—she'll not only accompany you to the theatre, but to church!

Bon. A church!

Dor. To relieve you at once from your suspense, she relents!

Bon. Relents, Dorothy?

Dor. Yes: partly in consideration of your long attachment, but chiefly at my instigation, she consents to become Mrs Bonus whenever you please.

Bon. Become Mrs Bonus!—ti di di, ti di—(*Pulling out his chitterlin, drawing up his head, &c.*)—Am I at last the chosen shepherd?—ti di di di!

Dor. Stop: there is a condition annex'd—your nephew Mortimer is arrived, and has behaved so ill to my mistress, that she insists you never receive him without her permission?

Bon. Granted—he had before offended me by marrying a woman without stock; but now, Costly, we'll have such a wedding—such a *fête champêtre!* —I'll invite the whole county: and may I buy in at ninety, and sell out at fifty, if I ever enter the bills of mortality again.

Dor. That's right, sir: and also give up your summer excursions to Margate:—for my part, I can't bear the sea.

Bon. No more can I: but when I go to Margate, it's for the sake of the raffling, the dancing, and the card-playing!—and what with being in the rooms all the morning, and in the libraries all the evening, curse me if I think I ever saw the sea!

Cost. Go to Margate and not see the sea!—— ha! ha!

Bon. No: if a man want salt-water, can't he have

it in London? isn't there sea-bathing in the Thames,
you blockhead?—But shew the way, Dorothy—shew
me to your divine mistress: and when we're married,
how the cards of invitation will fly about!—" Mr
and Mrs Jenkins's compliments!"—and " Mr and
Mrs Bonus's compliments!"——nothing but routes,
balls, and galas:—oh! who would live in London,
when such are the joys of the country!—Lead to
Diana!—" Guardian angels," &c.

[*Exit singing*—DOROTHY *and* COSTLY *following*.

SCENE II.

A View near Richmond.

Enter MRS MORTIMER, EMILY, *and* CHARLES.

Emi. Avoid, forsake you!—why, Mr Gossamer
assured me you had escap'd from that wretch Delville, and were now safe under Mortimer's protection.

Mrs Mort. And so I hoped to be: but when I
arriv'd at the inn, where Sambo expected to find
him, he was gone!—and, would you believe it, Emily?—all the consolation that a long-lov'd husband
left me was this letter:—read, read, and pity me.

Emi. (*Reads.*)

" Madam,
" The circumstances under which I found you
with Mr Delville, and the acknowledgment of your
guilt made by honest Sambo, has so confirm'd the
charges in Miss Gloomly's letter, that you must be
sensible we can never meet again."

What, she has slander'd and defam'd you?

Mrs Mort. She has : she wrote to him at Gibraltar :—but go on.

Emi. (*Reads.*)

" And as the sight of our child would only heighten my affliction, and you are no longer in a situation to educate him, let Miss Gloomly fulfil her promise made to your father on his death-bed—' Should Mortimer and his wife be reduced to distress or separation, I solemnly pledge myself to become a parent to their child :'—these were her words, and that hour is now arriv'd!—I would say more, but 'tis impossible.

HENRY MORTIMER."

Here's blindness and credulity !—and Miss Gloomly —this censorious, slanderous—but it's always the case—out of ten scandalous stories, nine are sure to be invented by old maids.

Mrs Mort. And Sambo too !—he to take a part against me !—but I suppose he dar'd not vindicate my character, for fear of criminating his master's— Then should Delville imprison Mortimer for the debt I owe him, or should a duel be the result——

Emi. Nay, don't make it worse than it is—let's go directly in search of Mortimer.

Mrs Mort. Alas ! I know not where to find him —and, therefore, to shew I'm not the disobedient wife he thinks me—to give the strongest proof of duty and affection, I'll instantly obey his orders— I'll deliver my boy to his new parent—I'll part with this, the only comfort that is left me.

(*Kissing* CHARLES.

Emi. How ! part with him ?

Mrs Mort. Ay, Emily : is it not enough to separate me from himself, but he must also tear me from his image !—Ungenerous Mortimer !—but, when we do meet, he shall at least acknowledge I can remember him, though he has forgotten me.

Emi. Nobly resolv'd—and, in the mean time, if Mortimer can be found——

Enter GOSSAMER.

Goss. Mortimer found!—that's out of the question—he's elop'd—he's run away now, and the claret and the red sea flow'd for nothing!—but that's for future thought—Bonus's marriage! there's the first object.

Emi. My guardian's marriage!

Goss. Yes; he has consented: and Miss Gloomly —the crying philosopher—she has consented—but mum!—the most material thing is wanting—I haven't consented.

Emi. (*To* MRS MORTIMER.) Now, my life on't, she marries him on purpose to make you and Mortimer bankrupts in fortune as well as in love.

Goss. That's it—that's the condition in the settlement—Mortimer and his family are never to get a shilling!—and you, Emily—she is such an enemy of yours, that you are never to get a husband.—Dorothy told me the whole business—but, as I said before, George Gossamer hasn't consented.

Emi. Psha! what signifies your not consenting?

Goss. What! every thing—hark ye!—hasn't Miss Gloomly depriv'd this lady of her husband, by writing a most slanderous letter?

Emi. She has.

Goss. Very well: then if I deprive her of her husband by writing another slanderous letter, won't it be a fair retort, and prove that the laughing philosopher is a match for the crying one?

Emi. It will: but you don't understand scandal well enough——

Goss. Don't I?— can't I write old Bonus word, " that there are certain reasons for a certain marriage—and that at a certain little cottage, there's a

certain little chubby, rosy, sturdy"——hem!—oh—
leave me alone for hoaxing the old maid!——and
now, Emily—now for the little vulgar citizen.——
(*Going.*)

Emi. Vulgar citizen!—nay, Mr Gossamer; please
to recollect I was born and educated in the city—

Goss. Well, and suppose you were, Emily?

Emi. Then say what you like, sir; but I'm sure
there are a great many fashionable people who live
the other side Temple-Bar.

Goss. True: so there are; for the Fleet, the Poul-
try-Compter, and most of the spunging-houses are
on the other side of Temple-Bar!——but now to dip
my pen in scandal—now to fight Miss Gloomly with
her own weapons—and, that victory secure, depend
on't, I'll find Mortimer, and laugh him out of his suspicions.

Mrs Mort. Generous man! I wish I knew how to
repay your kindness.

Goss. Do you?—it's easily done: the next time
we meet, let me see the smile on my countenance
reflected on yours; for so far from wishing to have
the joke to myself, believe me, I'm never grave but
when my friends are so.—So adieu.   [*Exit.*

Mrs Mort. Pray Heaven he may succeed, for this
marriage will undo us all!—but yonder I see Miss
Gloomly entering her house—Come, Charles, let us
lose no time in executing your father's wishes.——
Sweet boy! and shall we meet no more?—am I in
a little hour to lose both child and husband?

Emi. Don't, don't despair:——I'll go and make
every inquiry after Mortimer, and when I find him,
I'll so lecture him——

Mrs Mort. Nay, do not blame him—he is deceiv'd,
my friend—and, though the cause of my unhappiness,
I still must feel for his—yes, Emily, spite of his
cruelty—though he for ever shuns me—yet shall my

constancy be so exemplary, that I will rather welcome poverty or death, than wound his honour, or
disgrace my child.   [*Exeunt.*

SCENE III.

An Apartment at MISS GLOOMLY'S—*Glass Doors
leading to a Garden—an Arm Chair turn'd half
round—a Settee, and a large Table.*

Enter MRS MORTIMER, CHARLES, *and a Servant.*

Serv. Madam, I'll deliver your message to Miss
Gloomly immediately.   [*Exit into garden.*
Mrs Mort. Well, Charles, do you know that we
must part?—do you know that you are to live here,
now?
Charles. Live here, ma'?
Mrs Mort. Alas! 'tis your father's orders—he
thinks me unworthy of so dear a charge, and Miss
Gloomly is bound by a solemn vow to be a mother
to you.
Charles. How! Miss Gloomly my mother?
Mrs Mort. Ay: 'twas her brother's dying request
—she is pledg'd to adopt you; and that tender appellation, which hitherto alone belonged to me, must
now be transferr'd to my enemy.
Charles. What! and must I call her mother then?
Mrs Mort. Your father wills it so; and, spite of
his unkindness, we must have no wish or thought
that is not his.

Re-enter Servant.

Serv. Madam, Miss Gloomly says she is much surprised at your visit, and, I'm sorry to add, declines
the pleasure of seeing you.

Mrs Mort. How! can she——

Serv. That was her message, ma'am!

Mrs Mort. Unfeeling, persecuting woman! does she thus fulfil her promise—and to such a benefactor? —my father left her all that he possess'd; and though he died in anger with his daughter, yet for this little one, who never wrong'd him, he charg'd her to adopt him when requir'd—and is this her gratitude?—I'll not believe it!—I'll hear her refusal from her own mouth!—Shew me to her—nay, I insist.—(*Going.*)

Charles. What! sha'n't I go with you, ma'?

Mrs Mort. No, my child; your state of health will little bear fatigue.

Charles. Dear! I'm so sorry, and so weary—indeed and indeed I may call Miss Gloomly mother, but I shall never love her half so well as I do you.

Mrs Mort. Sweet boy! sit there, and be composed.—(*Kisses him.*)——Don't be unhappy, Charles; for though the world deserts us, whilst I have hands to labour, spirits to assist, and pride to encourage me, you sha'n't want protection or support, I promise you.—(*Places* CHARLES *in the arm chair, and exit with servant.*)

Enter GOSSAMER.

(CHARLES *falls asleep in the chair, which being turn'd round, he remains unseen.*)

Goss. So, through Dorothy's interest, here I am! and if I don't break off this detestable marriage, the Mortimers lose their fortune, Emily loses her husband, and I lose thirty thousand pounds—but here it is—(*Producing a letter*)—here's slander for slander, Miss Gloomly; and I defy all the old maids in Europe to stuff more scandal into one epistle—I'll drop it in the little stock-broker's way, and if I can but get him *tête-à-tête*—here he comes, and only Dorothy with him!—now for it—(*Drops the letter*)—

there it is!—and I'll bet any gentleman a hogshead
of claret, that the Sons of Friendship didn't make a
greater laughing-stock of Delville, than this letter
will of the crying philosopher!—but mum—I must
observe.   (*Retires up the stage.*

Enter BONUS *and* DOROTHY.

Bon. I tremble as I tread on this chaste ground!
—but go and announce me—say the fond shepherd
is come to give her his hand, his heart, his fortune!

Dor. I will: but remember the condition—you
are to disinherit Mr Mortimer——

Bon. Granted—any thing—every thing—only let
me be lord and master of the saint-like Miss Gloomly!
(DOROTHY *exit.*)   Ah! this it is to marry out of
London—to select a sweet innocent country maiden,
who is as much a pattern of rural simplicity as myself!—(*Kicks against the letter.*)—What's here?—
(*Takes it up.*)—A letter directed to Miss Gloomly!
and open!—All her correspondents must be people
of sense and morality!—I've a great mind to take a
peep at it!—I will!—for I'm sure it will instruct and
improve me.—(*Reads.*)

" My divine Dian!—my angelic Miss Gloomly!"

Oh, from a female I suppose?—(*Reads on.*)

" I have just received your letter, informing me of
your fatal marriage with an old waddling stock-
broker, call'd Bonus!"

Upon my word, whoever you are, I'm very much
oblig'd to you.   (*Reads on.*)

" and if the postscript hadn't convinc'd me that our
former intimacy was to continue, I'd have blown
him, you, and myself into a thousand atoms!—My
soul's in a conflagration!"

And so is mine, I'm sure.   (*Reads on.*)

" But that satisfies me ; and though Fortune crosses
us, and Hymen parts us, yet Venus, Cupid, and
another little boy, will for ever bind us in adamantine
chains !"

Venus, Cupid, and another little boy!—mercy on
me !—who can write such.—(*Looks at the letter.*)—
" George Gossamer."—Bless my soul !—Why, can
Miss Gloomly be acquainted with such a——surely
she could never admit him under this immaculate
roof.——(*Here* GOSSAMER *steals towards stage door,
and tries to open it*—BONUS *sees him, and* GOSSAMER
assumes much embarrassment.)—Heaven defend me !
—why there he is, and trying to steal off unperceiv'd !
—Very well, Mr Gossamer—I see you, sir—I see
you.

Goss. No, you don't ! you don't see me. (*Trying
to escape,* BONUS *lays hold of him.*)

Bon. Hark ye, sir ;—pheugh !—I'm as hot as if
I were in the Stock Exchange !—in one word—what
brought you here, sir ?

Goss. (*Still assuming embarrassment.*) Not the
divine Dian, sir—upon my honour, not the divine
Dian.

Bon. There ! he denies it, and that only doubles
my suspicions !—and this letter, sir—to whom did
you write this letter ?—and how dare you call me an
old waddling stock-broker ?

Goss. That letter, sir !—I didn't write—that is, I
did write, but—but——

Bon. But what, sir ?

Goss. It's a joke—only a joke, upon my soul, sir.

Bon. D——n me if I think it is a joke—and were
I not convinced that Miss Gloomly was as innocent
and chaste as—(GOSSAMER *laughs, and pretends to
conceal it by putting his hand before his mouth.*)—
Why, what do you grin at, you chuckling ?—Is she
not all maiden purity—all rural simplicity ?—all——

(Gossamer *laughs, and pretends to conceal it again.*)
—Oh ho! then the divine Dian shall herself give
me an explanation!—I'll go and——

Goss. (*Stopping him.*) Don't—stay where you are.
——Zounds! if they meet, all's ruin'd—(*Aside.*)

Bon. Stand off—I'll bring her to confront you; and
if I find you have belied her—if your insinuations
about Venus, Cupid, and another little boy, prove
false and slanderous, your life—your life—(*Here, in
his rage, he runs against the arm chair, and* CHARLES
tumbles out of it.)—Now who the devil's this?

Goss. Mum!—it's Cupid.

Bon. (*Laying hold of* CHARLES.) Speak directly,
you young——what do you do here?

Char. Oh Lord! don't hurt me—I'm waiting for
my mother.

Bon. And who is your mother?

Char. Who?----why——oh, I recollect——Miss
Gloomly is my mother.

Bon. There! there's rural simplicity for you!—
Now, sir---do you call it a joke now?

Goss. No—now I see it's no joking matter.—D—n
me, I've been hoaxed myself here. (*Aside.*)—But
she comes!—now behave like a gentleman—recollect the delicacy of the subject, and say nothing,
but retire with dignity.

Enter, from the garden, MISS GLOOMLY *and* MRS
MORTIMER.

Miss Gloom. (*Speaking to* MRS MORTIMER *as
she enters.*) It don't signify---I'll never forgive Mortimer, befriend you, or adopt the boy!---so the sooner you leave my house——oh, my dear intended!---
(*Seeing* BONUS, *then looking at* GOSSAMER)---some
friend I suppose---Sir!

[*Courtesies to* GOSSAMER, *who bows in return.*

Mrs Mort. Madam, I shall not intrude——

Miss Gloom. (*Stopping* MRS MORTIMER.) No;

---pray stay and witness my triumph, and your perfidious husband's ruin!---now observe---first, Mr
Bonus, here's my picture!---a pledge of future affection and——spare a maiden's blushes—I declare I'm
so asham'd!—*(Holding up her fan.)*

Goss. (Whispering her.) There's no occasion!—
he won't expose you.

Miss Gloom. Not expose me!—oh—he won't have
the wedding public, I suppose—well! as you please,
Mr Bonus, since those irresistible powers, Hymen
and Cupid, have decreed it.—(BONUS *looks up at
her, and moves towards door*—BONUS *looks at her,
then at* GOSSAMER, *who holds down his head, pretending shame and confusion.)*---Why, the sooner the marriage takes place the better for us both—(BONUS
exit)—and therefore, Mr Bonus, if you——*(Looks
up, and, seeing he is gone, lets the picture fall)*—
Mercy!—why, where is he gone?

Goss. (Pointing to CHARLES.) Ask Cupid—ha!
ha! ha!

Miss Gloom. Why, what is all this? Do you know
who I am, sir?

Goss. The crying philosopher!

Miss Gloom. And who are you, sir?

Goss. The laughing philosopher!

Miss Gloom. Oh, this is some trick—some imposition! and I'll follow him, and have it all explain'd
before he leaves the house—Mrs Mortimer, you'll
not forget the debt I told you of; and for your son
—and you also, Mr Laughing Philosopher—unless
you can leave off grinning and smiling——

Goss. Excuse me—it's impossible.

Miss Gloom. Impossible!—read my works, and
then see if it's impossible.   [*Exit.*

Goss. Is that your son?

Mrs Mort. Yes, sir, this is the deserted Charles
Mortimer.

Goss. Mortimer! why, he said he belong'd to Miss

Gloomly—'egad! you begin hoaxing by times, my little hero.

Mrs Mort. That fault is mine—I bid him call her by the tender name of parent—but this debt—should she as well as Delville persecute Mortimer—

Goss. And this wedding!—this most tragical wedding!—She'll explain every thing to Bonus—he'll find out the boy is young Mortimer, and then he'll return—and then—*(Treads on picture, and picks it up.)*—Her picture here—ay: he'll not refuse this vinegar-faced picture a second time.

Mrs Mort. No: all's lost! for ever lost!

Goss. Lost!—s'life!—rouse, Gossamer, rouse! are you to be beat by novices?—and if ever two characters deserv'd to be trick'd and outwitted, it is an old maid, who invents false reports, and a stock-broker, who lives by them!—Let me see—his suspicions are already rais'd, and if I can but confirm them——

Mrs Mort. 'Tis all in vain—let us be gone.

Goss. I've hit it!—hit it already—*(Takes a picture out of his pocket.)*—Here's my own picture, painted for Emily ; and look—*(Tries it in the case which holds* Miss Gloomly's *picture)*—it's the same size—it fits exactly.

Mrs Mort. So I perceive—but will that avail?

Goss. Every thing! every thing! and you, Mortimer, and my little crying philosopher here, shall all laugh and be happy still!—come, I'll see you down stairs, and then return and make that settee my place of meditation!—there I'll stay, till the marriage is dissolv'd or celebrated—and they may abuse me if they like—they may say I'm a mountebank——a Merry Andrew—a buffoon!—while I can laugh and serve my friends, I care not what they call me.

[Exeunt.

ACT THE FOURTH.

SCENE I.

View of RICHMOND, *the Hill, River, Bridge, &c.*

Enter DELVILLE *and two Bailiffs.*

Del. So, you've got the warrant, you say——a warrant to arrest Henry Mortimer for five hundred pounds, at the suit of Edward Delville.

Bailiff. Here it is, sir.

Del. Away then, and imprison him, and I'll make one more effort to secure his wife :—whilst I can keep them separate, the chance of my success is tenfold :—away !—and yet, I don't know why, but I'm so tortur'd with contending passions, that——

Bailiff. Look, sir! Mr Mortimer is coming this way.

Del. He is : my happy and triumphant rival comes! — hat thought alone removes my scruples—love bears down all before it, and therefore do your duty, fellows :—Stay—Miss Gloomly's with him ;—this way, and watch your opportunity—quick—quick—(*They retire up stage, and exeunt.*)

Enter MORTIMER *and* MISS GLOOMLY.

Miss Gloom. I adopt him !——a little impudent urchin — declare, when I think of his and that wretch Gossamer's scandalous insinuations——

Mort. No matter—will you be a parent to my boy?

Miss Gloom. I a parent! there again—all in the same scurrilous story I find!—but know, to your confusion, Mr Bonus is satisfied; and the marriage, which will for ever ruin you and your runaway wife, is to take place this very night.

Mort. Have a care, madam: no reflections on Mrs Mortimer—I am the person she has wrong'd, not you; and I'll suffer no one to reproach her but myself!

Miss Gloom. So—I thought this would be the case—like other fond easy husbands, you'll forgive the pretty penitent, and take her home again.

Mort. Forgive her!—never:—think me not so lost to every delicate and manly feeling!—A daughter or a sister, after long penitence, may for an indiscretion be forgiven—but a wife! a mother! shall she be pardon'd, and partake a husband's blessing and a child's embrace?—no; the virtuous wife can have no more: and if all good and evil is confounded thus, how can we hope for innocence?

Miss Gloom. The very words my Artemesia says, and I'm glad you profit by my writings, and reflect and discriminate——

Mort. I do discriminate: and were it only for example sake, I'd scorn to countenance such growing evils!—but much is to be done, and that most speedily:—My boy! he first must be disposed of—and for this dastard Delville, who has detain'd me in this neighbourhood, and cowardly declines an answer to my challenge, of him I'll think no more—there is another and more certain remedy—farewel!

Miss Gloom. Why, where are you going, sir?

Mort. First to my uncle:—not to implore assistance for myself, but for that child, whom you so cruelly desert: and since your hour of compunction will arrive, let me point out how you can make atonement!—Your niece—(*Taking her hand*) my poor unfortunate Maria! you may pardon her, though her husband never can. (*Weeping.*)

Miss Gloom. I pardon her!

Mort. Yes: and should she fly from her betrayer, or should he, villain-like, abandon her, don't let her again want an asylum, I implore you! and when she asks what was the fate of her once happy Mortimer, tell her he sought the only consolation that was left him, and died, forgiving and adoring her!—I can no more—farewel!   [*Exit.*

Miss Gloom. Stay, stay, Mr Mortimer!—mercy on me!—gone to his uncle!—why, if any interview takes place, my former love, my offer of marriage, my proposal about the divorce—all, all will be divulg'd, and this will so confirm Gossamer's insinuations, that Mr Bonus will break off the match in reality.—Lord! I'll follow Mortimer——

Enter DELVILLE.

Del. Follow Mortimer!—you must follow him to prison then, Miss Gloomly.

Miss Gloom. To prison, Mr Delville!

Del. Ay: he is arrested, and at the suit of a villain!—but that's all past—'tis too late to retract; and therefore let love and Mrs Mortimer——— (*Going.*)

Miss Gloom. Stay: are you sure he is arrested, Mr Delville?

Del. I am—I am.

Miss Gloom. Then all's safe—he cann't see his uncle, and my marriage is secure.

Enter SAMBO.

Sam. Oh, sir! such news!—such an adventure! —This moment, as I was talking with Mr Mortimer at the bridge foot, two bailiffs came up and arrested him, and—ha! ha! ha! I beg pardon for laughing—

but haven't I often told you I should profit by my
Temple education?

Del. What! did you interfere, sir?

Sam. To be sure I did: but the bailiffs told me
law business was so scarce, that when they got a job
they must make the most of it now!—They said the
attorneys had push'd the joke too far, and the profession was so completely found out, that Westminster-Hall had no customers!—I could not help
laughing at that, you know, sir: but my joy was soon
check'd, by their laying forcibly hold of poor Mr
Mortimer; and they were taking him away, when an
odd thought, a sort of legal quibble, coming into my
head, I ask'd them what sheriff they belong'd to!—
and—ha! ha! ha!—it prov'd as I expected—there
was a flaw in the indictment—they arrested him in
the wrong county!

Del. In the wrong county, sirrah!

Sam. Yes:—the writ was made out into Middle-
sex, and we being the other side the bridge, were in
Surry, you know!—so we snapp'd our fingers, and
defied them!—and then they call'd me an outlandish
monster, and wonder'd where such a savage could
get any legal knowledge!—on which I pointed to
my face—" Look," says I, " don't you see by my
complexion that Nature designed me for one of the
profession?"

Del. S'death! and what became of Mortimer?

Sam. What!—why he walk'd off!—went to his
uncle's—ha! ha!

Miss Gloom. To his uncle's!

Sam. Ay: that he did! and I nonsuited the bailiffs!—I quash'd the pleadings! and if all Temple
students would turn the law to as good advantage,
what a glorious profession it would be!—But that's
not all—there's worse to come—you'll hardly believe
it, sir; but one of the fellows had the audacity to say
that the arrest was by your orders!—I bid him take

care, and just shew'd him this bit of ebony—(*His fist*)—but persisting in the falsehood, and offering to shew the writ, I—I—I hope you'll not think I did wrong, sir——

Miss Gloom. Why, what did you do, sir?

Sam. I knock'd him into the river, and so I'd serve every man that dare accuse my master of such a 'dishonourable action!

Del. Fool!—blockhead!—then know, it was by my orders.

Miss Gloom. There!—do you believe it now, sir?

Sam. No---though he'll take his oath of it, I won't believe it!—he who knows the blessings of liberty, he send a man to prison!—and for money lent to his wife!---no, no—he jests, ma'am—I'm sure he jests.

Miss Gloom. Mighty well!—but I suppose, Mr Delville, you don't mean to be outwitted in this manner; of course you'll employ the proper officer, unless, indeed, the servant is to prove the master?

Del. He the master!—no, no—'tis ever thus—he but adds fuel to the flame!—he but augments my desperation!—and, thus provok'd, I'll see myself to Mortimer's arrest:—Come, madam, you shall find I'm not the pliant fool you think me.

Sam. Don't, sir, for Sambo's sake——

Del. Away, sir: and d'ye hear, as Mortimer still thinks his wife criminal, mind you don't undeceive him—I have reasons for keeping them apart:—remember, sir!

Miss Gloom. And the next time you're in my company, remember we're not only in different situations, but of different complexions—you understand?

Sam. I do——(Miss Gloomly *and* Delville *exeunt*)—and thank Heaven we are of different complexions!—(*Putting his hand to his heart.*)—What! Mr Mortimer still think his wife criminal, and he

see to his arrest!---Can this be Mr Delville!—can
this be the same master who—(*Bursts into tears.*)—
I can't bear it!—I wish I were in my grave!—but I
will undeceive Mr Mortimer, though—I'll go directly and convince him of his wife's innocence!—
for as it is my duty to serve my master in a good
cause, so it is my duty to oppose him in a bad one!
[*Exit.*

SCENE II.

A View near Richmond.

Enter MRS MORTIMER *and* EMILY.

Emi. I tell you I can gain no intelligence of Mortimer; but I've heard that Delville means to throw
him into prison.

Mrs Mort. Ay : this, this is what I dreaded!—
Oh, Emily! is there no way to save him?

Emi. I know of none but applying to Mr Bonus ;
and since Gossamer has fail'd in breaking off the
marriage, of course, by this time, all his fortune is
at the disposal of Miss Gloomly.

Mrs Mort. Nay, perhaps not yet: and if he were
reminded that we might one day be reconcil'd——

Emi. Reconcil'd! for my part, I don't see how it's
ever to be brought about:—Mortimer seems so obstinate and so credulous, that when we do find him,
how is it to be accomplish'd?—who can convince
him of your innocence?

Enter SAMBO.

Sam. I can.—Oh, madam!—till this moment I
thought, when I left you at the inn, that Mr Morti-

mer had flown to your embrace; but since I find
there is still a misunderstanding, do, pray, make a
poor fellow happy :—I'm quite wretched; my heart
keeps sinking and sinking; but I think if I could see
you restor'd to your husband, it would jump into its
right place again.

Emi. What, will you avow her innocence?

Mrs Mort. And in defiance of your master, Sambo?

Sam. Why not, ma'am! it's a negro's business to
mind he goes to heaven as well as a white man's,
and we who have so much of the black gentleman in
this world, I'm sure must be heartily glad to keep
clear of him in the next: besides, though my master
gave me liberty, Mr Mortimer gave me life; and
surely liberty's nothing without life!—so come, let's
go to him directly.

Mrs Mort. Kind, generous Sambo!—but where,
where are we to find him?

Sam. Oh, I know——*(Produces a letter.)*—Look,
this challenge has inform'd me.

Mrs Mort. Challenge!

Sam. Ay, by this it appears he has been waiting
at old Blackbrook's, a farm-house about a mile off,
on purpose to shoot, or be shot by my master :—but
don't be alarm'd; I've intercepted the letter, and
there shall be no fight, depend on't : in my country
it isn't the etiquette to fight duels, and I'm too much
a man of fashion to suffer them to do an ill-bred thing,
you know.

Emi. Honest creature!—but don't wrong yourself—you haven't one fashionable requisite.

Sam. Yes, one at least, ma'am:—I never blush!
—*(Pointing to his face.)*

Mrs Mort. Heav'ns!—where is this to end!—he
challenge Delville, and Delville imprison him!—Oh,
my friend!—*(Falling on* EMILY.)

Sam. Nay, don't think of the challenge:—but for

the imprisonment---oh ! neither my hand or head will
save him a second time.

Mrs Mort. No: and the place of our reconciliation will be a prison!---Go, Emily---intercede with
Mr Bonus---though Miss Gloomly won't allow him
to assist Mortimer, yet for the sake of a child——

Emi. That's true; pity for the son may induce him
to befriend the father :---I'll go, and the child shall
be the string I'll play upon——

Mrs Mort. Do; describe his innocent and helpless state——

Emi. I will: and if the marriage has not taken
place, hope for my success.

Mrs Mort. Come, Sambo :——now then to this
farm-house; and if, tir'd of your master's bad conduct, you would forego his service, and share our
fallen fortunes——

Sam. Thank you, madam: but my master's bad
conduct makes it more incumbent on me to stay with
him.---Who else will bear with his follies, and labour
to correct them ?---And spite of all, I know he's still
so sound at the core, that I feel I couldn't exist
without him!---But come to Mr Mortimer; and though
I prevent quarrelling and fighting, it isn't the fashion
of my country to interrupt kissing and making it up
again !---no---that, I hope, is good breeding all the
world over !   [*Exeunt.*

SCENE III.

An Apartment at Miss Gloomly's—*The same
Scene as in Third Act.*

Gossamer *discovered lying on the Settee.*

Goss. So—though a lawyer is in the next room
with the settlement, and a parson with the licence,
here I am, and here I'll remain, till the old maid is
hoax'd out of her husband.—(*Gets off settee.*)—Let
me see, though—is all right?—have I made no mistake in changing the pictures?——First, here's Miss
Gloomly—(*Taking a picture out of his pocket*)—here's
the portrait of the crying philosopher, safe in my
pocket—(*Puts it back*)—and next, here's George
Gossamer—(*Taking up red case which lies on the
stage, where* Miss Gloomly *dropp'd it*)——here's
the laughing philosopher, safe in her case—(*Leaves
it on the stage*)——so if she again offer old Bonus
this pledge of affection, she'll give him my picture
instead of her own :——d—n me there'll be more
rural simplicity——but they come—I must lie snug
and observe.—(*Draws the table before settee, and then
lies upon it as before.*)—And now, oh, Momus, look
down on thy facetious votary!—though he be merry,
let him be wise, and——but they're here!—Amen!
—good night.

Enter Bonus *and* Miss Gloomly.

Miss Gloom. To suspect me of an amour, and with
such a profligate as that Mr Gossamer——

Bon. Spare me——spare an unfortunate country
gentleman, who has no wish but to pair off with his
fond turtle for life—From this hour we'll chime to-

gether like omnium and the consols! and, since the
lawyer and parson are waiting, why——

Miss Gloom. I understand: I'll see if they're ready:
---Look---here lies my picture, just where I dropt it
---(*Takes picture up*)—let me a second time present
you the portrait of one who has nothing but innocence
and purity of soul to recommend her.

Bon. (*Kissing her hand.*) Go—don't lose a moment—I'm all impatience—I declare I can't stand
still till I call this virgin hand my own!——(MISS
GLOOMLY *exit, kissing her hand to him—he kissing
his to her.*)—Cupid and Gossamer, indeed! pa! pa!
—(*Snapping his fingers.*)—How could I for an instant believe?—But it's all London!—that smoky
place husks the understanding!—however, she has
forgiven me; and now to gaze on the image of all
my soul adores '—now for the resemblance of that
innocence and purity—(*Opens the case, and looks at
the picture.*)—Why, what's here?—zounds!—it's a
man!—a d—d impudent, grinning, bearded rascal!
and more like Gossamer than—it is!—'tis my rival's
portrait; and now may Cupid fly away with me if I
don't believe that that boy——

Enter EMILY *hastily.*

Emi. Oh, my dear guardian!—I'm so glad I've
found you—Are you married?

Bon. No.

Emi. Are you sure of it?—quite sure?

Bon. Why, I think I am:—(*Putting his hand to
his head.*)—But what makes you ask?—have you too
heard any thing?

Emi. Every thing—I'll tell you all about it :——
They sit :)---In the first place, I've seen the boy!—
the sweet innocent that Miss Gloomly has so shame-
fully deserted.

Bon. What!

Emi. And I've taken quite a fancy to the little

cherub---and for the strangest reason---he's so like
my dear Mr Gossamer---(BONUS *makes for the stage
door.*)---Why, what's the matter?---(*Following and
stopping him.*)---'Tis on Mortimer's account I've been
speaking thus much of his son.

Bon. His son!

Emi. Ay: 'tis young Mortimer that Miss Gloomly
has deserted; and I hope pity for the boy may induce you to assist the father.

Bon. What! and it's young Mortimer that's like
Gossamer, is it?

Emi. To be sure---why, who else———

Bon. Who! oh, nobody, nobody:---then perhaps
it's all a mistake---perhaps my fears made me fancy
it a likeness---I'll ask her---Hark ye, Emily,---is
this picture like Gossamer?

Emi. (*Looking at it.*) That!---Lord! it isn't half
young or half handsome enough---that!---I'm sure I
should be very sorry if that resembled my lover.

Bon. And so should I, I'm sure:---So---so---stocks
are up again!---No doubt she gave it me by mistake
---it's a portrait of some friend or relation, and my
foolish apprehensions———and yet---(*Looking at picture again*)---it has certainly that fellow's brass, Lon-
don-looking countenance!

Re-enter MISS GLOOMLY.

(BONUS *keeps looking at the picture.*)

Miss Gloom. Now, Mr Bonus, the lawyer and
clergyman are quite prepar'd---What! haven't you
found out the likeness?

Bon. No: that's what I want to find out---I think
it a very formidable one, but Emily says it isn't half
young or handsome enough.

Miss Gloom. Oh, she flatters---she flatters!---but
come---come---I shall be mortified, if you gaze so
much on the copy while the original is so near you.

—(BONUS *can't take his eyes off.*)——How !—I hope
you don't mean to throw away a second opportunity ?

Bon. No : Hymen forbid !—'gad !—I'd better say
nothing, for fear of knocking all up at the critical
minute.—(*Aside, and putting picture in his pocket.*)—
Come, Dian, come—you also, Emily—come and be
bride's-maid——

Emi. Stay, sir, and before you dispose of all your
fortune to that lady, pray reflect on the distresses of
your unhappy nephew.—Mr Mortimer is about to be
reconcil'd to his wife ; but if you don't befriend him,
they will meet but to perish in a prison !

Bon. In a prison !—hang it, I don't like to hear
of that either.

Emi. 'Tis too true, sir :—Mr Delville means to
arrest him for five hundred pounds, and Mrs Mortimer has already combated so much misfortune, that
I'd rather sacrifice every shilling I possess, than see
their domestic happiness again interrupted !—Oh, sir !
if you won't take pity on them, let me advance the
money.

Bon. You ! no—why should you have——Poor
Harry !---he has suffer'd for marrying a woman without money, that's certain—and the air of a jail is
almost as bad as that of London, that's certain—and
sparing him five hundred pounds won't make a
stock-broker a lame duck, that's certain—and so—
(*Taking out his pocket-book*)—here, give him these
bannk-otes——

Miss Glo m. Hold, Mr Bonus—recollect the clause
in our marriage-settlement.

Bon. I do ; but though I shut my doors against
him, I'm not bound to shut the doors of a prison
upon him—so take it, Emily——

Miss Gloom. Mighty well, sir !—this is your love
for me, is it ?—you'll lavish your favours on the man
who has insulted me :—but I see it all—I am to
possess your hand, and your ward is to govern your

heart?—Ungrateful, barbarous man!—(*Crying ve-
hemently.*)

Bon. What, does she weep?

Emi. Never mind, give me the money.

Miss Gloom. (*Still crying loudly.*) Go, sir :---go,
give your fortune to your nephew, your affections to
your ward, and forget her who, spite of your cruelty,
still loves, still adores you!——Oh, I can't bear it!
—I faint!—I—(*Faints, and falls on the sofa ;* Gossamer *catches her in his arms.*)

Bon. (*To* Emily.) Let me go; I'll give her all I
possess :---(*Breaks from* Emily.)—Here, take this
pocket-book, thou lovely, thou angelic!

(*As* Bonus *offers the pocket-book to* Miss Gloomly,
Gossamer *snatches it out of his hand, and rises
from the settee.*)

Goss. That I will, and give it Mortimer! Damme,
here's a hoax for you!——I say, Emily, which cuts
the best figure now, the laughing or the crying philosopher?

Miss Gloom. Heaven defend me!—Why, where did
you come from?

Goss. From the moon, most divine Dian; from
the moon—but don't let me interrupt the ceremony
—marry her, Bonus—marry her——

Bon. (*Looking at the picture.*) Never saw a finer
likeness in all my life!---never saw a more innocent
pledge of affection!---so give me back my pocket-
book, and let the stock-broker once more waddle to
his villa.

Goss. Your pocket-book! that's very well—you
gave it me---it's mine by law, and if it save an unfortunate couple from prison—if it light up sunshine in
two faces long clouded by sorrow, why, you'll smile
—(*To* Bonus)—and you'll smile—(*To* Emily)---
and you'll—(*To* Miss Gloomly)—no—till you get
rid of your bad habits, you'll never smile.

Miss Gloom. Bad habits !--- Answer me ; how dare you slander an innocent woman ?

Goss. (*Aside to* MISS GLOOMLY.) How dare you slander an innocent woman ?—Remember Mrs Mortimer.—(MISS GLOOMLY *holds down her head.*) Ah ! this is paying you in your own coin—and for young Mortimer—you ought to have been a mother to him, and therefore I've done you the favour to prove you one !———Adieu, Emily :---there's an end of this marriage, and the next trick we play them, shall be to bring about our own.

Miss Gloom. Stay, and let me advise you, sir—

Goss. And let me advise you, ma'am—give up your own system and take to mine---make people happy, not miserable—promote laughing, not crying ; and if you don't prove more pleasant to yourself, and more useful to society, say Gossamer's not the first and wisest of philosophers !——Now to the Mortimers---now to make them happy---I say---(*Shewing pocket-book to* BONUS)---you take the joke, old Cupid, don't you? [*Exit.*

Bon. Come, Emily, let's breathe the pure air.

Miss Gloom. How ! have you nothing to say, Mr Bonus?

Bon. Nothing—I wish you happy—I wish you and all your family happy.———

Miss Gloom. Mighty well !---I leave you for the present---but remember your promise—recollect the settlement of your estate.

Bon. Settlement !——look ye—sooner than settle my fortune on you, or any of the Diana breed, hang me if I wouldn't sink it in the sinking fund.—— Come along, Emily, and if the pocket-book relieve the Mortimers, I feel it will relieve me ; for when a man is self-dissatisfied, not all the scrip, omnium, consols—no—not even rural life can afford satisfaction ! [*Exeunt.*

ACT THE FIFTH.

SCENE I.

BLACKBROOK's *Farm-House.—A Garden before it, and a Chair at the Side.—Moonlight.*

Enter MRS MORTIMER, CHARLES, *and Farmer* BLACKBROOK.

Mrs Mort. Go on; relieve me from this torturing suspense!—Meditate self-destruction, do you say?

Farm. Be patient, lady, and you shall hear all. You may be sure Mr Mortimer was a welcome visitor at my humble farm; for when he was no bigger than that young gentleman, many and many's the time I've fondl'd him on this knee—and, alas!—little did I think to see him grow up to such misery and desperation!

Mrs Mort. Desperation!—oh! do not distract me —is Mortimer living?

Farm. I hope so, lady: but you shall hear and judge:—To-night, as I was returning home through yonder wood, a man darted across me, and rush'd into the thickest covert: I follow'd him, and found 'twas Mr Mortimer! and observe—in his hand he held a phial, which, from what I over-heard him say, contained poison——ay! poison, lady—and when I advanc'd to seize him, he fled wildly from me, and, alas! I've neither seen nor heard of him since.

Mrs Mort. Not seen him!—perhaps, then—Where is the place?—conduct me instantly.

Farm. Most willingly: I'd traverse the world to
save him, and I've already sent my servants.

Mrs Mort. Come: lose not a moment!—enter the
house, my child; (*To* CHARLES) and should Sambo,
who, fearing his single evidence might not confirm
my innocence, is gone to intercede with his master
—should he return, bid him wait my coming :——
Lead on.

Farm. Nay, nay, your cares I hope will soon be
at an end.

Mrs Mort. They will—they will!—for if it be as
I suspect——oh, Mortimer! we'll meet where slander cannot part us!   [*Exit with Farmer.*

Enter MORTIMER *(through the Garden.)*

Mort. So—I am watch'd, pursued :——at every
turn my persecutors meet me ;——but I've escap'd
their observation, and here at length I may complete
the fix'd and settled purpose of my soul :—Harassed
by my enemies, forgotten by my friends, and forsaken by her who was the very stream and essence
of my life !—this friendly passport to another world
alone can snatch me from the fiends of this !—from
penury, despair, and jealousy. (*Produces phial.*)

Charles. (*Observing him.*) Bless me! who is that
gentleman ?

Mort. And yet, when I look back on my past
happiness, and think the source of it is still existing !
—that she and her dear image might still console—
still wipe away my sorrow, I grow irresolute, and
sigh for life ! (*Throws himself into the garden chair.*)

Charles. (*Walking towards* MORTIMER.) Lord !
I'm so happy—it's my father !

Mort. Life ! what, when she loves another ! when
at this moment she lavishes those smiles which——
Distraction! that thought is past all bearing, and thus
I bury in oblivion !—thus these poisonous drugs !—

(*As he raises his arm to drink,* Charles *lays hold of it, and kneels to him.*)

Charles. My father! (Mortimer *looks, and trembles violently.*) Oh! I'm so glad you're come home —I hope you'll go no more long journies now.

Mort. My child! my child! (*Embracing him.*)

Charles. Why, what's the matter?——how your hand trembles!—and this—(*Pointing to the phial;*) what's this, father?

Mort. That!—a toy!—a mere toy, Charles.

Charles. A toy!---Fie, fie, father!---you a man and play with toys?—nay, that belongs to me.---(Mortimer *bursts into tears, and catches him in his arms.*)

Re-enter Mrs Mortimer.

Mrs Mort. 'Tis all confirmed---he's no where to be heard of, and ere this, the dark deed——

Charles. Look, mother—look who's come home.

Mrs Mort. (*Looking sometimes at* Mortimer— *then running and falling at his feet.*) My Mortimer!

Mort. (*Rising and crossing her.*) Away! contaminate me not!---let me be gone.

Mrs Mort. (*Holding him.*) Stay: spare me but a moment—you've been deceiv'd.

Mort. I have!——I have!——and lest I should relapse, and be again deluded——But see! an evidence appears, to rouse my pride, and to confirm your guilt.

Enter Sambo *hastily, and with a paper in his hand.*

Sam. Oh, ma'am!—I'm just come from my master, and---pheugh! (*Fanning himself with his hat.*)

Mort. Speak, Sambo---were you not witness of her falsehood?

Sam. Softly, sir, and I'll tell you all about it—— Pheugh!—You must know my master was taken suddenly ill, and sent me for a physician---but I refused to go.---Says I, " Sir, the natives of my country are all very healthy, and for two simple reasons—first, because we've no doctors ; and next, because we've no such enlighten'd disorders as ingratitude, false friendship, seduction !—these," says I, " play the devil with a man's constitution."

Mort. Well ! and what then, sir ?

Sam. Then he grew worse, and asked me to prescribe for him ; and I did !—Doctor Sambo drew up this prescription, and the pulse mended, fever lessen'd, and the countenance exhibited that florid bloom which ever results from those excellent medicines, honesty and a good conscience—There, sir, read, only read. (*Giving the paper.*)

Mort. (*Reading.*) " Sir, Mrs Mortimer is innocent—she has fallen a victim to my vanity, and her aunt's slander—Miss Gloomly wrote you a most calumnious letter, and I, believing that she lov'd me, made others believe it !—but when you arrived at the inn, she not only avowed her love for you, but fled in pursuit of you.—Sambo will confirm these facts, and I am ready to make a public acknowledgment of them, or atone for my crimes in any other way you think proper.   EDWARD DELVILLE."

Sam. There ! there's a noble medicine ! and having established myself both as physician and lawyer, now for the third character—now to play the part of parson—May'nt I join your hands?—Oh ! had I such a wife, I'd hug her into atoms !

Mort. It is ! it must be so !—and had we sooner met——Maria !—my recovered wife !—(*Embracing her—then falling at her feet*)—can you pardon my suspicions ?

Mrs Mort. Rise, I entreat you.

Sam. (*Stopping her.*) Don't, ma'am—don't forgive him till he takes his oath he'll forgive my master !

Mort. (*Rising.*) Never ! Hark ye, Sambo—(*Aside to him*)—is this an answer to a challenge ?

Sam. He never got it!—I intercepted it!—but don't—don't persist—you can't wound him worse than he has wounded himself!—For my sake—for her's—for your child's!—Speak---intercede for my master, ma'am!——

Mrs Mort. Nay, I beseech you, Mortimer——

Mort. Well! since I believe his penitence is sincere——

Sam. What! you forgive him!—you won't hurt him! and you and Mrs Mortimer are man and wife again, and I live to see it!—" Dear Yanko say, and true he say" (*Singing and dancing, and catching* CHARLES *up in his arms.*)—Come along—you and I will so sing dance, and play battledore and shuttlecock together!—And for the falsehood I told about you, ma'am,—why, 'twas but a white one, and we blacks tell lies of no other colour.

Mort. Delville I pardon—but for Miss Gloomly —for this accomplished slanderer——

Sam. Oh! challenge her—shoot her, and welcome.

Mrs Mort. She has indeed been most vindictive; and last night renewing her application for the debt I owed her, and fearing it might involve you in new difficulties, I sent her all that I possess'd—my few trinkets, and even the lottery ticket you wrote to me to purchase; but her marriage with your uncle is broke off.

Mort. Indeed!—then we may apply to him.— Come, (*Taking* MRS MORTIMER'S *hand*) and if he still avoid us, here is enough to combat against adversity :—blest with thee, and this my young preserver——

Mrs Mort. How, Mortimer?

Mort. Nay, you shall know all in calmer moments :—and you, faithful Sambo—you who have sav'd us all, and in an age of dissipation and deception——

Sam. Nay, don't abuse the age—we're certainly improving every day, sir :---for instance, there's less law, less fashion, less faro ;—faro !---oh, one oughtn't to speak ill of the dead !—and if every woman would prove a Mrs Mortimer, there'd soon be less seducing, and then—saving your presence—I don't think the devil would have a disciple on earth.---But lead on, sir ; and I and your little papa, as you call him, will trot on merrily after you !—" Dear Yanko say," &c. (*Singing and dancing, and making* CHARLES *dance with him in imitation.*)   [*Exeunt.*

SCENE II.

A Street in Richmond.

Enter GOSSAMER *and* EMILY.

Goss. Nay, don't be alarm'd, Emily—though I haven't seen Mortimer, the pocket-book and Bonus's bank-notes have still been a friend to him.

Emi. Well !—but how—in what manner ?

Goss. You shall hear : Just now, who should I meet in a rage but the crying philosopher—she said Mrs Mortimer had sent her some trinkets and trifles in payment for a hundred pounds—but she wasn't to be defrauded in that manner—she would return them, and arrest Mortimer instantly :---on which I whipped out the pocket-book—paid the debt with Bonus's bank-notes, and redeem'd the trifles !—and look— here they are—a watch, a ring, and a lottery ticket ! (*Producing them.*)

Emi. A lottery ticket !

Goss. Ay; she gave me joy of my bargain with all my heart.   I'll surprise her—I'll give her joy of this with all my soul.

Emi. Well, but about Delville.

Goss. Oh! Delville has not only repented and cancell'd his debt, but has sent the tragic muse to bring about a comic catastrophe.

Emi. Indeed! Then the Mortimers are once more restor'd to each other!

Goss. They are: and now, when shall we be restor'd to each other?

Emi. Nay, what signifies asking?—when you know very well we shall never get my guardian's consent.

Goss. (*Smiling.*) Sha'n't we?

Emi. No—and what's the use of marrying without it, when I lose all my fortune?

Goss. And suppose your fortune were already lost —would the old stock-broker consent then?

Emi. That he would:—he'd then think me such a burden to him, that I do believe he'd marry me to——

Goss. To his clerk, or his butler, or your humble servant! Then be happy—make yourself perfectly easy, for I've the pleasure to inform you, that at this moment you're as poor as I am.

Emi. As poor as you are!

Goss. Ay; thanks to good fortune and a lucky hurricane, your whole property's blown into the sea —all your estate is whisk'd off in a whirlwind. (*Giving her a newspaper.*) There—in this newspaper, read the glorious, joyous tidings!

Emi. Why, surely it can't be.—(*Reads the newspaper.*)—" Accounts were yesterday received from Barbadoes, that on the 28th ult. a dreadful hurricane destroyed most of the property on the east part of the island, and particularly that beautiful estate called Mount Columbo!"——Dear, dear Mr Gossamer—that's mine, sure enough!

Goss. I know it! I know it!—and the best of the

joke is, Delville, who has property in the island—he
will confirm the fact.

Emi. You may laugh, but 'tis no laughing matter
to be ruin'd—reduc'd to dependence—beggar'd---
(*Weeps.*) No—say what you please, Mr Gossamer,
love can't exist without money, and now I've none,
and you've none!

Goss. (*Laughing.*) What! did you think I was in
earnest?

Emi. To be sure I did.

Goss. Ha! ha! ha! there's a hoax for you!

Emi. What! didn't this account come from the
West Indies?

Goss. No; but it came from a place as full of
warmth and fire! (*Pointing to his head.*) I'm sole
inventor and proprietor of this facetious hurricane!
I inserted it in that and other papers: I got Delville
to write this corroborating letter. (*Shewing one.*)

Emi. What, and all to trick my old guardian out
of his consent?

Goss. Yes, all to trick old Cupid!—Go—follow
up the blow—shew him Delville's letter directly—
(*Giving it to her*) and if we succeed, we gain thirty
thousand pounds by the frolic, and if we fail—why,
we've had a hearty laugh, which, speaking philoso-
phically, is perhaps worth all the money.

Emi. Delightful! I'll go to him instantly—To-
night he gives a ball, and before it begins he generally reads the evening papers.

Goss. Does he! then by this time he is in the
heart of the hurricane!—go, and if we should but
be married, why, then, Emily— then for Venus, Cupid,
and another little boy.   [*Exeunt.*

SCENE III.

A Room leading to a Ball-Room in BONUS'S *House.*

BONUS *discovered sitting at a Table, drinking Tea and reading Newspapers ; Servant waiting.*

Bon. (*Reading newspaper.*) " *Last night the oratorios overflowed.*"—Oratorio!—now there's the extravagance of these Londoners—they won't go to church, where they can have sacred music for nothing, but because it is in a theatre, they'll pay to hear it.—" *Plymouth !*"—ay, this is in my own way— this is country news.—" *Yesterday a celebrated lottery-office keeper stood in the pillory---Wind east.*"--- Now what the devil has wind east to do with it ?— but at Portsmouth or Plymouth, if a man is robb'd or murder'd, the account is sure to conclude with wind east.---" *Barbadoes.*"---Oh, this concerns my ward Emily—" *Barbadoes.—On the* 28*th ult. a dreadful hurricane*"—what's here ! a hurricane!—" *swept away—east part of island—particularly—estate call'd Mount Columbo !*"—Zounds ! here's wind east with a vengeance ! Why, the girl's ruin'd—she's a lame duck !

Enter EMILY, *weeping.*

Bon. Well ! have you heard, Emily ?
Emi. I have, sir :—Yesterday I was worth thirty thousand pounds—to-day I'm a beggar !
Bon. What !—it's confirm'd, is it ?
Emi. Yes, sir ; Mr Delville, whose estate adjoins mine, you know, has sent me this note.
Bon. (*Taking note from her, and looking over it.*) Oh, if Delville believe it—(*Reads.*)—" Hurricane—

tornado—whirlwind !"—Yes, yes—it's all over—the
estate's off!—Mount Columbo is gone on a salt-
water excursion, and you are left to——Zounds!
I wish you had been married—I wish you had a husband to maintain you.

Emi. Nay, sir, I hope my poverty will make no
difference.

Bon. Why, no—but women live high, and stocks
are low, and—s'life! if we had but caught some gud-
geon-heade . Londoner!

Emi. Ah! that's all past, sir—nobody'll marry a
pauper.

Bon. No—-the scoundrels are all so cunning—
and yet the news isn't known—the story can't be
blown upon ; and for early intelligence—'gad! how
often have I work'd them in the Stock Exchange by
early intelligence ?

Enter GOSSAMER.

Goss. How d'ye do, Cupid, how d'ye do?—What,
in tears, Emily ?—Haven't I told you, whenever you
were melancholy, to look full in your guardian's
face ?—Look, and you'll laugh directly—won't she,
sir ?

Bon. (*Smiling.*) She will, she will!—Damme,
here's the very gudgeon-headed Londoner I was
wishing for. (*Aside.*)—Mr Gossamer, I'm glad to see
you----I am under great obligations to you----you
sav'd me from a bad wife, and the least return I can
make, is to help you to a good one.

Goss. Sir!

Bon. 'Tis even so, sir :---and I can't reward your
deserts better than by giving you Emily, with a fortune of thirty thousand pounds!—(*Laughing aside.*)

Goss. Come, come, you forget—I'm an old hand.

Bon. An old hand!

Goss. Ay, you're joking, you comical rogue ; I see
you're joking.

Bon. No, I'm not—upon my soul, I'm not joking!
—so take him, Emily——

Emi. No, sir: you refus'd him when I was rich,
and now——

Bon. (*Aside to her.*) Be quiet—To use his own
words, I'm hoaxing him now!—You see how it is,
Mr Gossamer!—the girl's shy; so carry her over the
way to Parson Suttle's; and as I can't leave the ball,
do you go with them, Gregory---(*To Servant*)—be
witness I give consent, and see them married directly!—There! do you understand me now?

Goss. I do—damme, I take the joke now!—Come
along, Emily---come along, Gregory—I've got the
licence, and you are witness he gives consent——

Bon. Yes, yes—he's witness—Stop—stop, though
—one thing I must premise to you—as the estate is
in the West Indies, and now and then there are such
things as hurricanes——

Goss. Hurricanes!—oh, I don't mind hurricanes!
---if her estate was blown into the skies, I'd be bound
to whistle it all back again!

Bon. Would you?

Goss. To be sure I would:—besides—a word in
your ear---it's an ill wind that blows nobody good,
you know—Mum!—Lead on—Hey for matrimony
and thirty thousand pounds!---You take, don't you---
ha! ha! ha!

Bon. I do; ha! ha! ha! (Gossamer, Emily, *and*
Servant exeunt.) There! there! I've hoax'd him at
last!—The old maid too! I've robb'd her of her lover! Oh! here's contrivance.

Enter Mr *and* Mrs Mortimer, *and* Miss
Gloomly.

Miss Gloom. (*Speaking as she enters.*) Don't talk
to me---I keep no such company---Mr Bonus, I beg
you'll not suppose we came here together.

Bon. Not come together!—zounds! I wonder how

any of you came here at all !--First, you, sir---(*To*
MORTIMER)—what brought you here?

Mort. I came once more to entreat your pity and
protection ; and since you are no longer under the
influence of that lady——

Bon. That lady !—what's that lady to you, sir ?—
When you married a woman without stock, didn't I
swear I'd never forgive you ?

Mort. You did, sir.

Bon. Then, however I may be inclin'd, Harry, I
will not break my word.

Miss Gloom. That's some comfort, however. [*Aside.*

Bon. And now, most divine Dian !——but I know
what brings you here ?

Miss Gloom. Well you may, sir :—I came to afford you an opportunity of apologizing for your blindness and credulity.

Bon. Me an opportunity !—Hark ye—you came in
search of Gossamer---but the bird's flown !—he has
pair'd off with another mate !—and mine—it's all my
contrivance !

Miss Gloom. Your contrivance ?

Bon. Yes : in London I grant you I'm confus'd,
but the keen air of the country quickens the understanding !—and I've made such laughing-stocks of
you and your lover !—But observe—observe my contrivance !

Re-enter GOSSAMER, EMILY, *and Servant.*

Bon. Well ! is it all over?---are they married,
Gregory ?

Serv. They are, sir.

Bon. Toll de roll loll ! (*Singing and dancing.*)---
Now listen—only all of you listen !—(*Turns to* GOS-
SAMER.) You think your wife is worth thirty thou-
sand pounds, don't you?

Goss. I do.

Bon. There—there's a gudgeon-headed Londoner

for you!—She's not worth sixpence! her whole property is destroy'd by a hurricane!

Miss Gloom. By a hurricane!

Bon. Ay, all blown into the skies—But never mind—(*To* GOSSAMER)—you can whistle it all back again, you know—can't you, you comical rogue?

Goss. Yes, that I can, you comical rogue! Wheugh —(*Whistling.*)

Bon. Pooh! what signifies wheugh!—(*Mimicking him.*)

Goss. I'll tell you—It signifies that I wrote that account in the newspapers—that I persuaded Delville to confirm the fact—and at this moment Mount Columbo is worth thirty thousand pounds—and that, as I told you before, it's an ill wind that blows nobody good!—Mum!—You take, don't you?

Miss Gloom. I say, (*To* BONUS) who's the laughing-stock now?—and the keen air of the country quickens the understanding, does it?—Oh! the next time you want to outwit this mighty conjuror, apply to me.

Goss. To you!

Miss Gloom. Ay:—Now all of you listen to my story —On a debt of a hundred pounds, contracted by Mrs Mortimer, I charged him fifty for interest, and made him pay all these bank-notes for a paltry watch and a lottery-ticket—Look, Laughing Philosopher—here are a hundred and fifty proofs of my victory!—— (*Holding up bank-notes.*)

Goss. And look, Crying Philosopher!—(*Holding up lottery-ticket*)—here are five thousand proofs of mine!

Miss Gloom. Five thousand! Why, the watch, sir—

Goss. Wasn't worth five pounds, I grant you—but the lottery-ticket was yesterday drawn a prize of five thousand pounds!—Gregory there will attest the fact!---and now both of you take the advice of an old

5

proficient, and whilst you're hoaxing others, mind you're not hoax'd yourselves.

Bon. Why, Dian—here's another hurricane!

Miss Gloom. Psha! this is an imposition:—Give the ticket to the right owner.

Goss. I will give it to the right owner—(Miss Gloomly *is going to take it*—Gossamer *crosses her.*) —There, Mrs Mortimer!—there's a fortune of five thousand pounds for you, and if that isn't enough to make your fire-side happy, apply to me and Emily: whilst Columbo nets a guinea, you and your family shall never want a part of it.

Bon. (*To* Miss Gloomly.) I say—who's the laughing-stock now!—But don't think to have all the pleasure to yourself, Mr Gossamer—no—I may forgive you, Harry, without breaking my word now; so, in the first place, I'll make that five thousand ten! —in the second, instead of giving all my fortune to a hypocrite, I'll settle it on you and young Mortimer! —and, in the third place, give me both your hands— (*To* Mr *and* Mrs Mortimer)—and henceforth we'll be as happy as good-humour, a country life, and plenty of long annuities will make us.

Goss. Bravo, old Cupid! you're ɾ fine fellow; 'egad I think I'll be a stock-broker myself.

Bon. No, no—yours is the system, Gossamer— laugh is the staff of life!

Goss. It is: and since our smiles are nothing without yours—(*To the Audience*)—

May Gossamer diffuse his joy around—
Cloud not the sunshine that's so seldom found;
For if misfortune be the lot of man,
Laugh when you may—be happy when you can.
                                        [*Exeunt omnes.*

FORTUNE'S FOOL,

A

COMEDY,

IN FIVE ACTS.

AS PERFORMED AT THE

THEATRE-ROYAL, COVENT-GARDEN.

BY

FREDERICK REYNOLDS.

DRAMATIS PERSONÆ.

AP-HAZARD,	Mr Lewis.
SIR CHARLES DANVERS,	Mr Middleton.
ORVILLE,	Mr Macready.
TOM SEYMOUR,	Mr Fawcett.
SIR BAMBER BLACKLETTER,	Mr Quick.
SAMUEL,	Mr Abbott.

SERVANTS,—*Messrs Blurton, Wilde, Street, and Lee.*

MRS SEYMOUR,	Miss Morris.
MISS UNION,	Mrs Mattocks.
LADY DANVERS,	Miss Wallis.

ORANGE-WOMEN,—*Mrs Norton, Miss Leserve, and Mrs Walts.*

SCENE—London.

FORTUNE'S FOOL.

ACT THE FIRST.

SCENE I.

An Apartment in an Hotel—on one side of a Table,
Sir Charles Danvers *discovered asleep—on the*
other side, Lady Danvers, *reading.*

Lady Dan.—*(Putting down her book.)* Heigho!—If
this be the beginning of a runaway match, what will
be the end of it?—Here am I but just return'd from
Gretna-Green, and there's the loving partner of my
joys.—(Sir Charles *wakes, and looks at her.)—*
How the man stares?—It's very odd with what astonishment we always look at one another!—as much
as to say, how, in the name of Hymen, did we two
come together?——My life!

Sir Char. My soul!

Lady Dan. Come, come—it's time to reflect—now
we're married and return'd to London, 'tis fit you
should leave this hotel, and think of an establishment.

—How much did you say your fortune was, Sir Charles?

Sir Char. Fortune!—that depends on my uncle; and perhaps he is offended.—How much did you say yours was?

Lady Dan. That depends on my mother; and perhaps she is offended.

Sir Char. Indeed! What's to be done then?—Pray, Miss Seymour—Lady Danvers, I mean—what induc'd you to elope with me?

Lady Dan. I don't know—My mother wanted me to marry Mr Orville, whom I hated—you made love to me—told me matrimony was Elysium; and so, without thinking——

Sir Char. Without thinking!—ah! that was my case—Restless in my disposition—tir'd of dissipation, I thought to find happiness in domestic life—Well, well—we had a pleasant journey to Scotland, however.

Lady Dan. Very—but coming back, Sir Charles—Oh! what an alteration!

Sir Char. Alteration!—how?

Lady Dan. How!—why, the whole way to Gretna-Green, were you not all love, adoration, and attention; and in a little hour after the blacksmith had received his fee, didn't you become a different man? —before we re-cross'd the Tweed, you amus'd yourself by yawning—at Newcastle you talk'd of the expences of travelling—at York you forgot to hand me out of the carriage—at Doncaster, when I order'd your favourite dinner, you said there was'nt a dish you could eat—at Grantham, I saw you throw glances at the chamber-maid—from Stamford to London you wrangled with the drivers, and groan'd at the turnpikes; and from the time we arrived, till now, have you opened your eyes?—No—if you are my partner, you're a sleeping one, I'm sure, Sir Charles.

Sir Char. Lady Danvers, I confess the truth of all this, and sincerely ask your pardon ; but the fact is, I found that we had rush'd precipitately into marriage, without considering the consequences—too late I found it; for if our friends desert us, how are we to live ?—I spent all my fortune on the road.

Lady Dan. (*Agitated.*) You don't say so !

Sir Char. The last shilling went to the last post-boy—You don't know the expences of a family—A man may steer his own vessel through the storms of life, but if he takes another in tow——

Lady Dan. Down they both go to the bottom.—Upon my word, we're in a very pleasant situation—but you forgot what you said, Sir Charles: you vow'd that you could live with me on a crust in a cottage—light a fire with me under a hedge—beg—starve with me——

Sir Char. Did I ?—I'm sorry for it.—I can encounter poverty myself, but to make an innocent girl partake of it !—No, no—I have been dissipated —not dishonest.

Lady Dan. Then you wouldn't starve with me—now that's unfair, Sir Charles ; for I think I could undergo a great deal for you. I'm not sure that you love me, nor indeed have I had time to ask my heart whether it loves you ; but something tells me (and don't think me romantic) that your distresses have excited sensations towards you which your riches might never have inspir'd.

Sir Char. Generous girl !—Come—Fortune still may aid us—your mother may forget—my uncle may forgive—by this time they know of our return, and —heh !—who's here ?

Lady Dan. Miss Union, the match-maker, and her nephew, Mr Orville.

Sir Char. That Orville !—Was he to be your husband ?——Zounds ! how the plot thickens !—I owe his uncle ten thousand pounds, and if the old colonel approved of his marrying you——

Lady Dan. He approved of it so much, that, on the match taking place, he meant to settle on Orville all his large Cornwall estate.

Enter MISS UNION *and* ORVILLE.

Miss Uni. Welcome from Scotland, my pretty runaways.——Now answer me, miss—What is your apology for refusing my nephew—what right had you to marry—or what right has any body to marry without consulting me?—A'n't I the first of match-makers—don't I make it my profession? and if that barbarous blacksmith is to rob me of my greatest pleasure——

Sir Char. Your pardon, Miss Union—but what is your business here?

Miss Uni. My business is to inform Lady Danvers, that, in consequence of her Gretna-Green excursion, her mother hopes for the honour of never seeing or hearing from her again.

Sir Char. (*To* ORVILLE.) And now, sir, what is yours?

Orv. To inform you, sir, that, for the same reason, your uncle, Sir Bamber, disinherits you, and hopes for the honour of adopting a new heir.

Miss Uni. Yes: the young Welchman has cut you out in both places.—The son of a poor parson, and the awkward beau of Langothlen, is the new heir to Sir Bamber, and shall be the new husband to Mrs Seymour.

Lady Dan. Husband to my mother!

Miss Uni. To be sure—hasn't she often told you, that if you married any body but Orville, she would marry too? and when she was pursuing you, and her carriage broke down, didn't the young Welchman come up and save her life?

Orv. And hasn't she given him her picture as a proof of her affection?

Sir Char. I'll not believe a syllable of it—at least, I'll have better authority than your words for it.— Lady Danvers, do you make a personal application to your mother—I'll do the same to my uncle, and if they persist in deserting us, I know the worst.— Mrs Seymour cannot refuse her daughter mainte- nance, and I'll seek my fortune singly.—Come.

Lady Dan. Who can this obtruder be?—perhaps, though, he is not attach'd.

Miss Uni. He not attach'd!—What then? Can't I shew Mrs Seymour how to decoy him into the snares; how to manage her words, her eyes, her sighs; how to excite his affection by concealing her own?

Lady Dan. Conceal affection!

Sir Char. Yes: conceal affection, annihilate pas- sion, extirpate sensibility—in short, turn robber— footpad—and by the fire of the eye, instead of the flash of the pistol, defraud the artless and unthinking of their fortune, health, and happiness! This is Miss Union's road to matrimony—we have chosen a dif- ferent one, and if our friends forgive us——Come, Juliana; we won't despair.

[*Exit with Lady* DANVERS.

Orv. So far, so well! Distress will make them quarrel—then comes a separation—then, perhaps, a divorce; and then my dear aunt, Lady Danvers, and the large Cornwall estate, may be mine still: besides, I love her more than ever—But about the young Welchman—about Ap-Hazard—how has he got into favour with his godfather, Sir Bamber Blackletter?

Miss Uni. I'll tell you—You know the old book- worm is so fond of ancient authors, that he is about to publish a new edition of Chaucer—now you un- derstand I have some hope of making him my hus- band, by persuading him I am in possession of a sup-

posed manuscript of that poet;. and Ap-Hazard has
a stronger hold on his affections—he has brought to
town a bust—an original bust of Geoffery Chaucer!
—think of that, nephew.

Orv. Excellent!—And how did he come by it?

Miss Uni. It has long been in possession of his
father, who is a first cousin of Sir Bamber's, and
knowing his character, thinks this present will prove
a rare introduction for his son—and so it will!—The
baronet is but just returned to town, and hasn't
seen it; but he writes me word he is so delighted
with the account of the old head, and so out of humour with Sir Charles, that he shall turn his thoughts
entirely to his godson.—The Welchman's a lucky
creature.

Orv. He lucky!—Why, he's Fortune's Fool!—When
I knew him in Wales, one continued series of ill luck
pursued him:---if he touch'd china, it broke; if he
went shooting, his gun burst; if hunting. there was
no game: if he play'd at whist, his partner could neither trump nor follow suit; if he fell in love, his mistress married somebody else; and he told me himself, if he'd been a physician, as his father wish'd
him, every body would have enjoyed high health,
and he been the only sick man in all Wales.—Oh!
as the success of our scheme depends on him, I dread
a return of his bad fortune.

Miss Uni. Do you? then find him out directly—
instruct, advise him—Stay, Mrs Seymour is waiting
to consult me on the old topic, so I'll go with you.—
I shou'dn't think of Sir Charles finding fault. indeed!
—Where's the great harm in being a match-maker?
—We women have few occupations; and it lawyers
and proctors are paid for dividing people, why mayn't
I be fee'd for uniting them? Then if you talk of
physicians, Orville—they're fee'd for providing one
article of intelligence for a newspaper---I another;

and I leave you to judge whether marriage or death
is the pleasantest piece of information.   [*Exeunt.*

SCENE II.

*View of the Thames, the Bridges, Surry Hills; a
shewy Sailing Boat at Anchor.*

Enter AP-HAZARD.

Ap-Haz. There's the river and the bridges—
yonder's a chapel—next door's a billiard-table—here
comes a funeral—there goes a wedding.—Oh! it's a
rare town—Get on though, friend Ap-Hazard—remember you're only come for a fortnight's pleasure,
and so where next?—(*Looks in his pocket-book.*)

Enter ORVILLE.

Orv. There he is! and, wonderful to say, not in a
scrape yet!—Mr Ap-Hazard, welcome to town.

Ap-Haz. What! my old Welch companion, Mr
Orville! (*They shake hands.*)

Orv. Well! how much do you know of London?
—Have you seen the Squares—the Parks—the City
—St Paul's?

Ap-Haz. I have; and the Bank, and the Tower---
Apothecary's-Hall, and the Burying-Grounds—the
Gaming-Houses in St James's-street, and the Spung-
ing-Houses in Chancery-lane——the Bears in the
Stock Exchange, and the Beasts in Exeter Change
—Last night I went to the Theatres: they were so
full I couldn't get in—This morning I went to the
Prisons: they overflow'd too.—Oh! what a cruel
town, Mr Orville, when, if a man wants to go to
jail, there isn't room to admit him.

Orv. True; it's very hard—but where else have you been?

Ap-Haz. Every where—I've been in London only two days, and I know more of it than half the cockneys who were born in it—Oh! it's a glorious place! —they said I should find the streets pav'd with gold, and I have!—Mrs Seymour means to make me her husband—Sir Bamber his heir—ay, none of my old ill luck now—I've got my equivalent.

Orv. Have you?—then keep it—remember you were born under an unlucky planet, and from the day of your birth, to the present hour, your life has been one catalogue of cross accidents.

Ap-Haz. I know it; but here I breathe a lucky air, and if I do get into a scrape, I know how to get out of it—" What's to pay?"

Orv. What's to pay!

Ap-Haz. Yes; what's to pay!—In this town I find every body, as well as every thing, has its price —men of fashion, and men of no fashion—high ladies, low ladies—authors, Jews, beaus, pigs, sheep, and monkeys, are all to be bought and sold; therefore if my evil genius should rise again, here is a little gentleman that will soon lay him. (*Pulls out a purse of uncommon length.*) Ay; they'll not easily get to the bottom of it---so " what's to pay?" damme, " what's to pay" is my watch-word while I stay in London.

Orv. What! you think money an excuse for every absurdity?

Ap-Haz. To be sure—If I knock a man down —" what's to pay?"—if I kiss a married woman— " what's to pay?"—if I marry myself—" what's to pay?"—if I come into parliament—" what's to pay?" Money will mend crack'd heads, broken hearts, and wounded reputations—therefore I say again, " what's to pay" is my motto in the hour of danger.

Orv. Well, but take notice; mine and your friend Miss Union's schemes depend on your success. Sir Charles and Lady Danvers are our enemies; and if you marry Mrs Seymour, and are adopted by Sir Bamber, they meet the ruin they merit; if you fail, they triumph: recollect Fortune's a slippery jade.

Ap-Haz. Oh! curse her; I know her; she has led me such a life of it—but now I defy her—she can't dash the cup from my lip now—no, no—Mrs Seymour has given me her picture, and the bust secures old Blackletter. I tell you what—life's a lottery—I've hitherto had ten blanks to a prize—and now—I'll go buy the thirty thousand.

Orv. No; go and have your first interview with your godfather—Heh! who's landing from that boat? —as I live, Tom Seymour.

Tom. (*Without.*) Row back, I tell you.

Orv. If he should find out his mother is about to be married to this fellow—however he don't meddle in family affairs. (*Aside.*)

Tom. (*Without.*) Pull hard, my lads.

Ap-Haz. (*Looking out.*) What smart sea captain's this? I'm a bit of a sailor myself, and as I should like to hear about the dock-yards, and the late sea engagements, I'll talk to him—by his appearance he must be a very great naval character.

Orv. (*Aside.*) Great naval character! ha! ha! Poor Tom Seymour!—he never saw the sea in his life—never was below Gravesend—he is a fresh-water sailor.

Enter TOM SEYMOUR, *dressed in white trowsers, &c.*

Tom. (*Speaking as he enters.*) Pull hard, I tell you—save as much of the wreck as you can; and, d'ye hear, look out sharp for the log-book—— Zounds! what a tempest! and what a profession!

We sailors are always exposed to peril, while these
land lubbers here—What, Orville! never off shore.

Ap-Haz. Stormy weather, noble captain!

Orv. (To TOM, *who stares at* AP-HAZARD.*)* He's
a friend of mine, from Wales.—But what's the matter? You seem agitated.

Tom. Well I may—I've been shipwreck'd.

Orv. Shipwreck'd!—where?

Ap-Haz. Ay, where, sir?—where? Oh, how I
like to hear about a shipwreck! When did it happen? Where was it, captain?—In the Channel?

Tom. No; in Chelsea Reach.

Ap-Haz. Chelsea Reach! Why, what new ocean's
that? But tell me, did the ship founder, or did she
drive against a large ridge of barbarous rocks?

Tom. Neither: she drove against a little arch of
Battersea bridge—off Milbank we lost our mainmast
—at Vauxhall we sprung a leak—and at Ranelagh
we threw overboard————

Ap-Haz. All your live stock, stores, and provisions?

Tom. All our umbrellas, spencers, and opera-
glasses.

Ap-Haz. Umbrellas and opera-glasses!——Why,
what fantastic jackanapes is this? Fortune's at her
tricks again, I see, but let what will be the consequence, I'll ask him one more question.—Sir—captain, if the ship was lost, how came you not to sink
with it?

Tom. I did sink with it.

Ap-Haz. What, you were drown'd, were you?

Tom. No, not exactly; because when she came to
the bottom, I stood on the deck, and was knee high
in the river. Drown'd! bless your fat head—how
can a man be drowned in seven inch water? Oh,
you'll never be of service to your country.

Ap-Haz. No; but you shall; for I'll fetch a press-
gang——I'll——(*Going.*)

7

Orv. (*Stopping him.*) Softly : Will you force your ill-luck—purposely get into a scrape ? Consider, the cards are in your own hands.

Ap-Haz. They are.

Orv. Would you throw them away then ?

Ap-Haz. No, thank ye—thank ye—What's to pay, sir ? (*To* TOM.)

Orv. (*To* TOM.) You'll excuse my friend, Mr Sey-mour—he's a strange creature. Come, never mind the loss of your ship ; you have more than one, you know.

Tom. To be sure I have. There's the Sprightly Kitty ! (*Pointing to the vessel at anchor.*) Cleopa-tra's galley was but a coal barge to it—she's my fa-vourite, because my sister furnish'd the cabin for me : and, now I think on't, Orville, what's all this hurri-cane in my family ? I'm told Juliana has put to sea with Sir Charles Danvers—Mess! I must keep a good look out—that is, when the sailing match is over.

Orv. You'll find your sister has behaved very ill, sir.

Tom. Shall I ? I don't think it : more likely I shall find others have behav'd ill to her ; and if that's the case, she shan't want a friend, I promise you—while I can swim, my sister shan't sink——What say you, Mr——

Ap-Haz. Say ! that since I came to London, it's the only sensible speech I've heard. Sir, I beg par-don for hinting at a press-gang—you *are* a great na-val character, and I'll sail with you—at the risk of my life I'll sail with you.

Tom. So you shall—not to-day though—I'm go-ing to dine at La Fleece'em's club.

Ap-Haz. Then I'll go and dine at La Fleece'em's along with you.

Tom. Why, your friend's a strange creature in-deed, Orville ; however, I like his familiarity——so you shall go and dine with me ; and, what's more,

I'll make you one of the squadron, and you shall wear the uniform.

Ap-Haz. So I will—I'll wear the uniform.

Tom. And you shall be in my set—the aquatic set—all as great naval characters as myself—and you shall hear of nothing but rowing, sailing, fishing—and you shall play a rubber.

Ap-Haz. Stop there—I'm tied up.

Tom. Tied up! What, you lose now and then?

Ap-Haz. Lose now and then! If you'll believe me, I never turned up an honour in all my life. However, Fortune smiles at present, and there's nothing like pushing it: So come, Orville—come, my noble captain——(*Aside to* ORVILLE.)—I feel my ground, and you and Miss Union may count the game your own——I'll beggar the club, marry the widow, bamboozle old Blackletter, and then we'll all take such a sea-voyage in the Sprightly Kitty—

Tom. No, no; no salt water for me—let me encounter the billows of the Thames, not be tossed on the tumultuous ocean—give me a sailing-match, not a sea-fight—a trip to Richmond, not a voyage to China—and, instead of being shipwrecked on rocks and quicksands, Battersea Bridge and seven inch water for Tom Seymour.—Come, my boys, come to the club, and I'll shew you how to hold honours, and sail against wind and tide !   [*Exeunt.*

ACT THE SECOND.

SCENE I.

SIR BAMBER BLACKLETTER'S *Library.*

SIR CHARLES DANVERS *discovered writing at a Table.*

Sir Char. So——there's a match for the match-maker, however—trick for trick, Miss Union!—Let me see—(*Reads.*) " Matrimony—A lady, who has a heart to dispose of, would be happy to unite to a man of sense—of honour. She is indifferent about fortune, as she has two thousand a-year in a brass manufactory. Apply to Miss U——, No. 402, Grosvenor-street.—N. B. She would prefer an officer in the army or navy."——Ay, ay, that's touching Miss Union on her sore subject ; and if this advertisement don't torment her, I'll try something else—I'll teach her to busy herself with other people's affairs.

Enter SAMUEL *with the Bust of Chaucer—he puts it on the Table.*

Sir Char. There's the bust of Chaucer, I suppose, —the celebrated treasure that is to turn me out of this house, and fix the young Welchman in my place—Samuel, who gave you this curiosity ?

Sam. Mr Ap-Hazard, sir : He is now below with Miss Union, waiting to be introduced to master.— Icod! he comes at a bitter bad time ; for Sir Bamber is so bad with the gout——

Sir Char. The gout, has he?—Very well!—Leave me——I too am waiting to see Sir Bamber; for I won't lose my rights without struggling hard for them, I'm determined——(SAMUEL *exit.*)——In the mean time, I'll copy this matrimonial advertisement for Miss Union. (*Sits at table, writing.*)

Enter AP-HAZARD *and* MISS UNION.

Ap-Haz. I tell you I've relapsed——the disorder has-returned, and in London, as well as Wales, Fortune will whirl me into scrapes—Oh! that great naval character!—to decoy me to the club—win my money—my trinkets—get my note for fifty pounds, and then challenge me!

Miss Uni. Challenge you! Why?

Ap-Haz. Because, when I found that debts of honour were now-a-days no more thought of than other debts, I snapped my fingers in his face, called him a fresh-water pirate, and said I'd pay him in opera-glasses and umbrellas! On this he challenged me—then I run—for there's my luck again!—I daren't fight a duel—no, I daren't—unless it could be managed in an amicable way, by calling in the constables, or firing at fifty paces—at fifty paces, 'sblood! I could exchange fifty shots!

Miss Uni. Well!—but how did this end?—Did the captain overtake you?

Ap-Haz. No; I got the start, and kept it; and now my only chance is never seeing him or the Sprightly Kitty again——If he catches me, I'm a drowned man——Oh! I've got into my old train of ill luck—I shall trip every step I take, and you and Orville will tumble along with me!——(*Sees* SIR CHARLES DANVERS *at the table, and goes up to him.*) What fine fellow's this?—a servant, I suppose; for in this town they dress so smartly——Well, I don't blame them—when masters dress like pick-pockets,

servants may dress like gentlemen——Holloa! you
sir!

Miss Uni. I see there's no keeping him out of a
scrape!—Come here—that's your competitor, Sir
Charles Danvers: he is waiting to contest the point
with you; and, if you don't get in favour with Sir
Bamber, he'll still be his heir, and I shall lose my
revenge—Hush! here is the old commentator—Now
remember, on this interview depends your inheriting
five thousand a-year.

Enter SIR BAMBER BLACKLETTER *and* SAMUEL.

Sir Bam. (*To* SAMUEL.) Blockhead! to push a-
gainst me when I have the gout so bad in this hand,
that I can't even write my notes on Chaucer!—Go;
and when the bookseller comes, call me—(SAMUEL
exit.)——Ha! my intended wife!—My sweet Miss
Union!—Well!—where is he?—where's my godson?—where's my new heir?

Miss Uni. Here, sir—here is Mr Ap-Hazard—
here is the owner of the celebrated bust!—Now put
on your best manners—nothing like a first impression. (*Aside to* AP-HAZARD.)

Ap-Haz. I know it; and there I'm always lucky.
(*Aside to* MISS UNION.)—Oh, Sir Bamber! if you
knew the pleasure I feel in giving you this hearty
shake of the hand——(*Shakes his gouty hand very
hard.*)

Sir Bam. And if you knew the pain I feel——
wheugh!

Ap-Haz. What's to pay?

Miss Uni. He is Fortune's fool indeed——Make
amends by praising his library. (*Aside to* AP-HA-
ZARD.)

Ap-Haz. I will—What a superb library, Sir Bamber!—what a choice collection of ancient and modern publications!

Sir Bam. Modern!—Sir, there's no such trash

here. I haven't a book published within the present century, except John Gilpin, in four volumes.

Ap-Haz. John Gilpin, in four volumes! Pooh! he wouldn't fill the column of a newspaper.

Sir Bam. No; but I make him fill four octavos—Why, it isn't the original author now-a-days—he's never thought of—'tis the notes, alterations, illustrations, emendations—

Ap-Haz. And botherations——I beg pardon; I mean commentations.

Sir Bam. Yes, sir, and commentations—Look at that folio now—it's Gilderoy—that bonny boy, Gilderoy. The poem originally consists of about eighteen stanzas; but my notes swell it to eighteen hundred lines!—and I haven't done yet—I'll have a new edition, with additions and revisions, and I'll amplify the bonny boy into two thousand.

Miss Uni. Ay, and perhaps make two thousand by it, Mr Ap-Hazard—Chaucer most likely didn't get fifty pounds by his poems; but Sir Bamber, with my manuscript, and a print from your bust, will make a fortune by his new edition—Then his dress, —isn't it so classical—This coat was once worn by the immortal Dryden.

Sir Bam. The shoes were Rochester's, the waistcoat Wycherly's, and the wig my old friend Hudibras's—They say I'm like Hudibras—Isn't curious?

Ap-Haz. Curious!—Since I came to town, Sir Bamber, you are by far the greatest curiosity I've seen——(*Sir* CHARLES DANVERS *advances.*)—What do you want, sir?

Sir Bam. Ay, what do you want, sir?—Haven't I told you that your marriage has undone you?—that you are a dead letter, sir?——This is my heir now.

Sir Char. I hope not, sir: When you consider that in my ruin an innocent lady is involved, I think you will renew your protection, and be as you have ever been—a friend—a father to me.

Miss Uni. What right had you to marry that lady, when you knew she was betrothed to my nephew, sir?

Sir Char. No reflections on her, madam—censure me as you please; but Lady Danvers has behaved so generously, that if I've not a fortune to reward her virtue, I'll prove I have the spirit to defend it—Well, sir, what is your determination?

Ap-Haz. (*To* SIR CHARLES.) Ask old Geoffery Chaucer—(*Pointing to the bust.*) Ask him if the godson won't cut out the nephew.

Sir Char. 'Tis too plain : I see I am deserted; and Lady Danvers and myself must part!——Mrs Seymour no doubt will receive her daughter home again; and from this hour I'll trouble you no more. Farewell, sir! An unhappy marriage has been my ruin—may yours be more fortunate!

Sir Bam. What do you say, Charles?—Stay.

Sir Char. I forgot—If Colonel Orville should arrest me for the large debt I owe him, may I ask your assistance in confinement?—I never had any thing but what resulted from your bounty; and it will not be robbing a new heir to support an old friend in a prison !—Now to Mrs Seymour; and if she will but soften the afflictions of her daughter, I'll bear my own with patience !   [*Exit.*

Sir Bam. What, is he gone !—I've a great mind to call him back and correct the press——Holloa, Charles!

Miss Uni. (*To* AP-HAZARD.) Now's the critical minute—Shew him the bust—describe its value—its beauties—put him in a good humour, or it's all over with you——Come, Sir Bamber—never think of an ungrateful nephew—look at the bust—look at the image of immortal Chaucer !

Ap-Haz. (*With the bust in his hand.*) Ay, here's

old Geoffery !—here's the father of English poets !—
Look, sir—doesn't this remind you of Palamon and
Arcite ?—the Flower of Curtesye ?—the Assembly
of Fools ?

Sir Bam. The Knyght's Tale, and the Canterbury
Tales, and the money I shall make by my new edition ?—Oh ! that for Charles!—(*Snapping his fingers.*)—you're my heir !—The possession of it will
make me the envy of the literati ! the wonder of
the cognoscenti !—the delight of the dilletanti !—the
——I'm in an ecstacy !—Let me—let me touch it.

Miss Uni. Don't, for Heaven's sake—consider its
antiquity !—the least touch will crumble it to atoms.
——The day's our own ! (*Aside to* AP-HAZARD.)

Ap-Haz. (*The bust still in his hand.*) I defy Fortune now—(*Aside to* MISS UNION.)—What poetry
flowed from this mouth !—What genius flashed from
these eyes !—What fancy revell'd in this brain !—Ay,
ay : this is none of your modern paper-skull'd authors
—old Geoffery's head is sound—sound as—(*Here he
lets his hand fall on the head, and part of it breaks to
pieces.*)—Damnation ! What's to pay ?

Miss Uni. Pay !—the value of his estate, for
you've lost it.—Don't say a word, the more you talk,
the worse you'll make it.

Sir Bam. Finis !

Miss Uni. Go to Mrs Seymour, and leave me to
compose him—What do you gape at ? Run down
stairs as fast as you can.

Ap-Haz. Run down stairs !—I'm in such high
luck, that I shou'dn't be surprised if I tripp'd at the
top step, and, without touching a single stair, shot
headlong into the street !—It's an unlucky house,
and the sooner I'm out of it the better—Pacify him
—try to make peace for me ; and don't fear my success with the widow ; for if getting a wife be getting
into a scrape, I shall be married before the day's

out.—Oh Fortune! Fortune! wilt thou never smile
on me?　　　　　　　　　　　　　　　　[*Exit.*

Sir Bam. Was there ever such a hopeful heir!—
On his first introduction, he squeezes my gouty hand
—calls me a curiosity—breaks old Geoffery's head,
and then asks what's to pay?

Miss Uni. Nay; it's all accident; and you should
rather pity than condemn his bad luck—Give him
another trial—Besides, though the bust is broke,
there's still the manuscript.

Sir Bam. True; there's still Trickarinda—still
that ancient poem written by Dan. Chaucer, of which
you are now mistress, but which I shall possess the
day you become Lady Bamber Blackletter.

Enter MRS SEYMOUR.

Mrs Sey. A bookseller is waiting in the hall,
sir.

Sir Bam. Oh! I'll come to him.—At your intercession, Miss Union, I'll try a second edition of this
godson; but if he don't improve in his style, Charles
will get into my books, I promise you—Mrs Seymour, good morning.　　　　　　　　　[*Exit.*

Mrs Sey. My good friend, I've just met Sir
Charles Danvers—he tells me he is compell'd to
part with my daughter, and begs me to take her to
my house again—I cannot encounter it—indeed I
cannot—the sight of her was once so dear to me,
that——

Miss Uni. Can I assist?—You know I am devoted
to your service.

Mrs Sey. I'm sure you are; and as I cannot at
present receive her under my roof, will you give her
an asylum under yours?—It will prevent her being a
wanderer, and prove, though she has forgotten her
mother, I can still remember her.

Miss Uni. Most willingly:—I'll go to the Hotel,
and take her to my house this instant—Come, don't

fret about it, my dear friend—recollect you always said, if she married against your consent, you'd marry too—Think of Mr Ap-Hazard—nay, I'm sure he's a favourite.

Mrs Sey. He is indeed—I respect him so much for his generous conduct towards me, and also for his artless, uncontaminated mind, that if I do marry again, Miss Union, he is the man of all others I shall select for my husband.

Miss Uni. And you'd be right—He is the prettiest piece of pure innocence! Oh! if you had seen how the simple swain described your charms to me!—how he kiss'd the picture you gave him!—how he swore if you didn't have him, he'd take away his own life on the spot where he saved yours!—Come, come—Men are of some use in the creation, and widows can't marry too often—for if matrimony be a happy state, you ought to prove, to us spinsters, that you can't have enough of it.   [*Exeunt.*

SCENE II.

An Apartment in MRS SEYMOUR'S *House.*

Enter LADY DANVERS.

Lady Dan. Oh, Sir Charles!—when I left this house for Scotland, what pleasures did I not anticipate?—And now to return and find the doors shut against me!—However, the servants have kindly admitted me, and here I will remain till my mother comes home; then if Mr Ap-Hazard hasn't entirely supplanted me—but he has!—I know her heart is so full of love for him, there isn't room left for her unhappy Juliana!

Enter Ap-Hazard, *hastily.*

Ap-Haz. (*Fastening the stage door.*) So—I've outrun him again—I've beat this great naval character a second time—He was the last man I wish'd to see—of course the first I met—full butt, face to face —and if he isn't drown'd or press'd, I must leave London directly.—Never had man such infernal luck —(*Draws a chair and sits in it.*)—Yes, yes, you're in the old way, Master Ap-Hazard.

Lady Dan. Ap-Hazard!—this is the very gentleman.

Ap-Haz. I can't pay him, and I daren't fight a duel!—(*Sees* Lady Danvers.)—By St David, a divinity!—Oh! here's trumps at last! (*Rises.*)—Madam! (*Bowing.*)

Lady Dan. Sir! (*Curtsying.*)—He seems good tempered, and if I apply to him, perhaps he may befriend me.—Sir, I am the unfortunate daughter of Mrs Seymour, and as you are now so high in her favour——

Ap-Haz. Lady Danvers!—More hot water, by Heavens!—My dear girl, I wou'dn't have Mrs Seymour suppose us tête-a-tête together—No—not to be friends with the fresh-water captain—not to have Chaucer's head whole again—not——

Lady Dan. Nay, sir, I only ask to live and die under my mother's roof; and if I were in your situation—and once I was so happy, sir—I would not refuse to assist you.—Come, come—I know you have a humane heart, and I see—I see you will make interest for me! (*Laying hold of him.*)

Ap-Haz. Fortune's at work again!—She's a syren!—I'm now on a trap-door, and in ten seconds I shall shoot down amidst ten thousand furies—Pity a poor traveller, and let me go—Consider, if I get you into favour with Mrs Seymour, I shall kick myself out of it—so I won't—I won't interfere for you.

Lady Dan. (*Still laying hold of him.*) You must—
you shall.—I am parted from my husband, and if my
mother doesn't receive me, who will ?—Think how
critical, how delicate, how terrible is my situation !—
Oh ! you shall not leave me—Look, on my knees I
entreat you !—(*Kneeling to him.*)

Ap-Haz. Damme, there's no standing kneeling.
[*Kneels by her.*) O you angel !—if at this moment I
don't love you far, far beyond your mother——

Enter MRS SEYMOUR.

Holloa !—What's to pay ?

Mrs Sey. Lady Danvers ! Ap-Hazard !—First inform me, madam, what brought you here ?

Lady Dan. Ask your feelings, madam.

Mrs Sey. And now, sir, what brought you here ?

Ap-Haz. Ask Fortune, madam.—Indeed it's not
my fault, for she knelt to me ; and then when I look'd
in her face, and saw it was so handsome—that is, so
like her mother's—you comprehend——

Mrs Sey. I do, sir—She has art enough to corrupt
the most artless.—Lady Danvers, an asylum is found
for you—my friend Miss Union's carriage is waiting
to conduct you to her house, where you will meet
with that protection you chose to forsake in mine.

Lady Dan. To Miss Union !—Trust me with my
enemy !—Place me in the same house with Mr Orville !—Oh, my mother !

Ap-Haz. I'm out of one scrape at last !—so while
the mother's lecturing the daughter, I'll read what
accidents have befallen other unlucky dogs !—(*Takes
a newspaper out of his pocket—goes to the back part of
the stage—takes a chair, and sits with his back turn'd
to the audience.*)

Mrs Sey. I am determined—The servant will shew
you to the carriage—Who waits there ? (*Enter* TOM
SEYMOUR.)—What do you want, sir ?

Tom. I'll tell you when I've breath—that Welch

smuggler has so winded me with chasing him—I won
his money fairly, and if he don't pay and apologize,
I'll burn, sink, and destroy him, whenever I come
up with him.—Juliana!—my sister!

Lady Dan. Brother, intercede for me—I only ask
for shelter under my mother's roof, and she refuses
me!

Tom. I know the reason—She is going to be married.

Mrs Sey. No matter, sir—I will be obey'd.

Tom. Then look ye, Juliana; you shall turn sailor,
and live with me—we'll steer through life together,
and you shall share my honours and my profits!
(MRS SEYMOUR *smiles.*)—Ay, my profits, madam!
—I'd have you know, next week I'm going a voyage
of discoveries—all along the coast, from Whitehall to
Windsor.

Mrs Sey. Perhaps I don't mean to marry at all,
sir—if I do, I hope I shall make a better choice than
your sister has done—not unite myself to a ruin'd
gambler, like Sir Charles Danvers! No, the man I
shall select will boast a pure uncontaminated mind,
a faithful and an innocent heart, and one who never
saw a gaming-table in his life.

Tom. Mess! I'd be glad to see such a fellow! But
I suppose it's like a faster sailer than the Sprightly
Kitty—a thing not to be found.

Ap-Haz. (*Still in the chair, with his back towards
audience.*)—Trumps!—Trumps!

Tom. What's this the uncontaminated gentleman?
Mrs Sey. It is, sir.

Ap-Haz. (*Not regarding them.*)—Oh! Game!
Game!

Tom. Why, wind and tide seem both in his favour!—Holloa! father-in-law!

(*Tom smacks him on the back*—AP-HAZARD *jumps
up, and they meet face to face.*)

Ap-Haz. What's to pay?

Tom. What, is it you?—is this the innocent faithful creature that never saw a gaming-table?—ha! ha! He is really the most unlucky lubber living—Do you know, mother, last night, at hazard, he took twelve back hands running, and threw crabs to every one of them! and tossing up for guineas, he called tails, and it came heads twenty times following—Damme, never call tails, papa—never!

Mrs Sey. This is very extraordinary—Mr Ap-Hazard, I had the highest opinion of your honour; and when I gave you my picture——

Tom. Gave him your picture!

Ap-Haz. To be sure she did—Look at it, my undone son-in-law—(*Putting his hand in his waistcoat pocket*)—No, it's not there—Hang me, if ever I put my hand in the right pocket in my life—It's here.

Tom. No, it's here!---(*Taking the miniature out of his pocket, and holding it up.*)---Look at it, my undone father-in-law—I won it of him last night at La Fleece'em's, and never thought of looking at it before; but now I see the family likeness—There, take it, mother, and let it remind you that parents oughtn't to turn their children adrift for chusing a bad pilot, till they're sure they could have found a better for them themselves.

Mrs Sey. I see, and am asham'd of my credulity. —Mr Ap-Hazard, I desire we may never meet again. —Come, Juliana—I'll go with you myself to Miss Union's, where if you conduct yourself with propriety for a few weeks, I will recal you to my house—to my heart!—banish from my memory the errors of Lady Danvers, and once more be alive to the virtues of my long-lov'd daughter.

Lady Dan. Can you be so generous?—I'll die ere I a second time forsake you—and yet, my mother—

Mrs Sey. Nay, nor you, my son; neither of you must doubt Miss Union.

Tom. Not doubt her!—for my part, I don't know her, for except when the Thames is froze over, I am never at home.

Mrs Sey. She is my dearest friend, and is so fond of your society (*To* LADY DAN.) that I must keep my word with her—Come.—Mr Seymour, let me see you to-morrow—For you, Mr Ap-Hazard, the only reparation you can make me is to quit my house this instant.   [*Exit with* LADY DANVERS.

Tom. (*After a pause.*) Papa.

Ap-Haz. Tommy,—was there ever such luck?

Tom. Luck! ascribe it to luck! it's all owing to impudence, vice.

Ap-Haz. There now! this is always the way. When one man gets down in life and another gets up, the world exclaims, " it's all owing to good or bad conduct." I say, it's owing to good or bad luck; and I ask you candidly, when you were shipwreck'd on the coast of Battersea, was it good luck or good management that made you land in seven inch water, noble captain?

Tom. Come, there's a great deal in chance, to be sure; and as the tide is against you, its unsailor-like to add to your distress—so forget and forgive, my boy! Nay, you were merry enough just now—What was the good news that made you cry—" Trumps! trumps!"

Ap-Haz. I forgot that—there's a card yet— (*Kisses newspaper.*)—Sweet creature, I'll go to her directly—Look, captain, read that advertisement.

Tom. (*Reading newspaper.*) " Matrimony!—A lady, who has a heart to dispose of, would be happy to unite herself to a man of sense and honour."

Ap-Haz. That's me.

Tom. (*Reads.*) " She is indifferent about a fortune, as she has two thousand a-year in a brass manufactory—Apply to Miss U——, No. 402, Grosvenor-street.—N. B. She would prefer an officer in the army or navy."—Ay, that's me.

Ap-Haz. You see—I'll go directly.

Tom. No—you don't—I'll go.

Ap-Haz. You go!

Tom. Yes, I'll go—Don't you see she prefers an officer in the navy; and do you think I'd suffer my honour'd father to marry a woman made of brass?— No, no—I'll go; and if I succeed, I'll not only return all the prize I took from you, but give you a third of her booty beside.

Ap-Haz. Will you? Gad! I want the money, not the wife, and as you're so fortunate a fellow—

Tom. And you so unfortunate a one, that you'd sink a ship.

Ap-Haz. A navy, by Heavens!—So it's a bargain, captain—We'll go to La Fleece'em's, where I'm to take my seat in my new uniform, and then you shall visit the lady.

Tom. No, not till to-morrow—This is the most important day in the whole year—the Vauxhall sailing match, you rogue—the Sprightly Kitty is sure of the cup, and then think what eclat it will give my introduction. (*Looks at his watch.*) Oh! it's time to be on board—so go to La Fleece'em's alone—put on your new uniform—here's something to warm the pockets with—(*Giving him money*)—and now, if you get into a scrape—

Ap-Haz. (*Putting money in his long purse.*) I know how to get out of it—What's to pay, noble captain; what's to pay?   [*Exeunt.*

ACT THE THIRD.

SCENE I.

An Apartment in MISS UNION'S *House.*

Enter SIR BAMBER BLACKLETTER *and* LADY DAN-
VERS.

Sir Bam. Send for a proctor, did you say ?—Have
you applied to Mrs Seymour ?

Lady Dan. I have, sir, but there is no end to my
mother's credulity—This morning I informed her
that Miss Union wish'd me to gain a divorce from
Sir Charles, in order that I might marry Mr Orville
—nay—that she had even sent for a proctor to
consult on the subject, and consequently that while
I remained in this house, I knew I should be expos'd
to one continued scene of danger and of insult.

Sir Bam. Well !—and what was Mrs Seymour's
answer ?

Lady Dan. That she disbelieved the whole story,
and bid me beware how I accus'd Miss Union falsely.
—Stay here I will not—I'd rather die than pass another night under this roof—Oh, sir !—you were once
a friend to me.

Sir Bam. So I am still—I'm a friend to the whole
sex—that is, to the young part—for though I'm very
fond of old books, because they sometimes fetch a
great price, I've no attachment for old women, for
they never fetch any price at all.—I tell you what—

though I dare say Miss Union and Mrs Seymour
have both good reasons for their conduct, yet there
shall always be a place in my library for such a beautiful octavo as your ladyship—You shall come to my
house.

Lady Dan. Will you be so generous ?

Sir Bam. To be sure I will—Od!—Charles is
somewhat in my books again, and if I could find the
young runaway—where can he have hid himself?

Lady Dan. I have not heard from him since we
parted, and if he knew how I regarded him—Ah,
sir!—but for Miss Union's influence, we might be
still united—I not suffering separation—nor he in
danger of a prison.

Sir Bam. Not a word against Miss Union—she
possesses the Chaucerian Manuscript—the dear delicious Trickarinda!—and, now I think on't—if I'm
found decoying you from her house, she'll be so offended—Oh Lord! I shall lose the darling treasure.

Lady Dan. Nay, sir!—Miss Union needn't know
where I'm gone, nor that you are concern'd in my
escape.

Sir Bam. True :—if it could be manag'd—Let me
see—now for a plot—I'm well read in old plays and
——I have it—Are you not going to the opera to-
night ?

Lady Dan. I am—I sit in Miss Union's box.

Sir Bam. Then I'll meet you there, and find a way
to get off unseen—It's a modern plot, but so much
the better—like the plots in modern plays, it's not
likely to be found out—(*Knocking at the door.*)—
This is the proctor, perhaps.—(*Enter a Servant.*)—
Who is it ?

Serv. A strange gentleman, who wants to see my
mistress, sir.   [*Exit.*

Sir Bam. Ay, ay :—it's the proctor—Let us get
out of the way—Till we meet at the opera, farewell !
—I'll secure your escape ; and if this godson—this

what's to pay Welchman, at our next meeting, squeezes hands and break heads, Charles shall be my heir
still.

Lady Dan. Sir, I am all gratitude—Adieu!

Sir Bam. Adieu!—It's very odd what makes all
the women so fond of me? No—it isn't—my literary
reputation compells them to adore me—I'm the English Ovid!—I'm a new edition of the Art of Love—
" Sigh no more ladies," &c.

[*Exit singing*—LADY DANVERS *exit.*

Enter MISS UNION *and Servant.*

Miss Uni. No doubt it's the gentleman from
Doctors Commons—shew him up directly.—(*Exit
Servant.*)—Poor Mr Ap-Hazard! I declare I quite
pity him for his bad fortune, and pity is so nearly al-
lied to love—heigho!—Oh! here's the proctor—
Now if we can bring about a divorce between Sir
Charles and Lady Danvers, she and the large Corn-
wall estate may be Orville's still.

Enter TOM SEYMOUR *and Servant.*

Tom. (*The newspaper in his hand.*)   This is No.
402, and that's your mistress, you say?

Miss Uni. Yes, sir,—you're quite right—Pray be
seated.

Tom. Ma'am! (*Sitting.*)—It's her—it's the brass
lady!—now to strike her at once. (*Aside.*)—I gain'd
the cup, ma'am! the Sprightly Kitty won easy—I'll
tell you how it was, ma'am.

Miss Uni. Sir!

Tom. Six vessels set sail for the prize—the Nep-
tune got the start, and kept it—that is, as far as Milbank—there the Sprightly Kitty came up with her;
and then, ma'am, had you seen me at the helm!—
laid her close to the wind—kept between my antagonist and the shore—got the weather-gage—caught
a breeze—shot over to the Lambeth coast—tack'd—

upset a boat-full of common-council-men—dash'd
through the middle arch—brought her about—dropt
anchor off the proprietor's barge—received the cup
—guns firing—drums beating—the crew huzzaing!
—Oh, damme, ma'am, if you like officers in the navy,
I'm the man.

Miss Uni. This is very extraordinary—but now-a-
days men of business are all men of pleasure—however, to the point if you please—I sent for you about
a divorce.

Tom. What!

Miss Uni. I say, I sent for you about a divorce.

Tom. And I came to you about a marriage.

Miss Uni. Marriage!—Lord help you!—it's a
proctor I want.

Tom. No, no—it's a parson you want.

Miss Uni. Me! 'Tisn't of myself I'm talking—'tis
of a young couple who have lately parted—Sir
Charles and Lady Danvers.

Tom. Sir Charles and Lady Danvers!

Miss Uni. Yes: I want my nephew to marry the
lady, and therefore if you can put me in a way to
manage a divorce—Look!—(*Holds up a purse.*)—I
understand feeing!

Tom. Pray, does Lady Danvers wish this?

Miss Uni. No—to be sure she doesn't—but what
signifies that?—Here—(*Offering a purse.*)—Nay,
nobody will know or blame you for it.

Tom. (*Rising.*) Yes, there is one person who
will both know and blame me for it.

Miss Uni. Who?

Tom. Myself!—Hark ye:—I don't care a rope's
end for Sir Charles—but for Lady Danvers—for my
poor Juliana! I wouldn't add to her distress, if you'd
give me a three-decker, and ballast it with your own
brass!—So that (*Snapping his fingers*) for your two
thousand a-year: and as for your heart—miss!—I
don't wonder you want to dispose of it, for at night-

time it must be a damn'd troublesome messmate to
you.

Miss Uni. Why, what does the brute mean?

Tom. Mean!—that you may advertise for a husband every day in the week, and not even my cabin-
boy will have you—There—there's your hand-bill—
(*Giving her the newspaper.*)—You may keep it for
Tom Seymour—yes, for the brother of Lady Danvers.

Miss Uni. The brother of Lady Danvers!—What!
are you the famous sailor I've heard so much of?—
the mighty navigator, who annually costs his mother
three hundred pounds, for damage done the shipping,
in running foul of them!—Sir, I am Mrs Seymour's
dearest friend, Miss Union, and I'll inform her——

Tom. You her dearest friend!—Then bless the
Sprightly Kitty for keeping me clear of the family acquaintance!—You inform her!—I'll go to her directly—I'll tell her about your proctors, parsons, and divorces; and if I've not got a wife by the interview,
I'll prove at least that I have sav'd a sister,—ay,
and expos'd a false friend by it!—Your servant.

Enter Servant.

Serv. Sir, Mr Ap-Hazard is below—he desir'd me
to inform you that he is in a hurry to go to the opera;
and as he is in want of ready money, he begs you or
the lady will let him have a hundred pounds on account.

Tom. What, he expects to finger the brass, does
he? Tell him the lady means to keep it all to herself
—Stay—I'll tell him myself.—Look ye; if my mother don't remove you from the command of Juliana,
I will!—she is my sister—and may I never fire a
cannon, find an island, or make a fortune by prize-
money, if she shall be run a-ground, while her brother has an arm to steer with!   [*Exit.*

Miss Uni. I defy him: Mrs Seymour will believe

nothing to my disadvantage, I'm sure.—But what is all this? (*Looking at the newspaper.*) I advertise for a husband! I who never pass a day without an offer! —that have a list of discarded lovers as long as Pall-mall!—that can marry Sir Bamber at a moment's notice!—and here—to be stuck up here amongst Picture Galleries, Poney Races, Quacks, Conjurors ——Ha! I begin to suspect now—it's a trick—a stratagem of Sir Charles or Lady Danvers.

Enter ORVILLE.

My dear nephew, I'm so glad you're come—I've received such a new provocation from Sir Charles, or his wife, that I have now no longer any motive for restraining your conduct towards the lady—you may act as you please.

Orv. May I?—Then I'll compel her to sue for a divorce—Once in my power, I'll answer for forcing her to consent to a final separation from her husband:—She is now in the next room, and——

Miss Uni. Hold—this house is sacred, on Mrs Seymour's account. To-night you will find her at the opera; but remember, whatever are your plans, I have nothing to do with them.

Orv. I understand—I'll not involve you.—Oh! at the opera—I'll take care to secure her—(*Knocking.*) What's that knocking?—In the passage, too, when I enter'd, there was such a crowd of strange figures— However, I must repair to the opera—till we meet there, good night.

Enter Servant.

Serv. Ma'am, here's a Scotch gentleman says he comes according to advertisement.

More knocking, and enter another Servant.

Serv. Ma'am, here's a Frenchman asking for the lady who wants a husband.

10

More knocking, and enter another Servant.

Serv. Ma'am, here are six young Irishmen.

Miss Uni. Six young Irishmen! Mercy! here'll
be the whole town presently—Lock the doors—shut
up the house, and, d'ye hear, tell the gentlemen I
don't want a husband—Yes, tell them I do—but that
instead of having two thousand a-year, I owe thirty
thousand pounds—Come, Orville—Oh! if I don't
match them all, say I'm no match-maker. [*Exeunt.*

SCENE II.

*The Coffee-room at the Opera House—the Bar, with
Women behind—Fruit, Ice, Lemonade, &c. on it.*

Enter three Orange Women.

First Wom. (*Speaking to the woman at the bar.*)
A tumbler of water for General Symphony—he was
seized with hysterics during the last song.

Second Wom. A glass of pine ice for the Duchess
of Prattle—she has talk'd herself into a high fever.

Third Wom. Some jellies for Lord Totter—and
here—some hartshorn for Lady Danvers, who has
fainted away at the door of the coffee-room.

Enter ORVILLE.

Orv. Be quick, be quick, I tell you, or Lady Danvers will die—Curse old Sir Bamber—to be handing
her out of Miss Union's box at a moment—However,
I tripp'd up his heels—took her from him, and if she
hadn't fainted with apprehension, by this time she
had been safe on the road to my country house—

(*Woman gives him hartshorn.*)—Now to revive her,
and then——Zounds! Sir Bamber again!

Enter SIR BAMBER BLACKLETTER.

Sir Bam. This opera house is no house for us literary characters—Oh, Mr Orville! I've been so
insulted—This instant, as I was conducting Lady
Danvers out of Miss Union's box, a bullying fellow
seiz'd me by the arm—twirl'd me round like a T
totum, and sent me head foremost to the ground, as
dead as old Chaucer.

Orv. Well, sir, I hope you don't suspect me?

Sir Bam. Suspect you!—what, the nephew of my
dear Miss Union?—No, no—and yet it's well I know
your regard for me, for the fellow was dress'd in a
similar coat to yours—though the passage was dark,
and we commentators are very short-sighted, yet I'll
swear the rascal had on the uniform of La Fleece'em's
club.

Orv. Very likely—I'm not the only person here
in the uniform—There's Sir Charles Danvers.

Sir Bam. Charles in the uniform!—he, the ruffian!
—Oh, the desperado!—Well! whoever it is, Mr
Orville, he has not only taken from me the sweetest
girl in England, but also the greatest curiosity in the
whole world—my snuff-box!—my invaluable snuff-
box! which Charles the Second gave Killigrew for
his jokes, and which a pawnbroker gave me for sixty
guineas—Help me to search for him.

Orv. Excuse me—I'm engaged—Now to carry
Lady Danvers to my villa, and then she's mine for
ever! (*Aside.*) Good night, Sir Bamber; and, depend on't, Sir Charles was your assailant.   [*Exit.*

Sir Bam. Charles my assailant!—then Ap-Hazard
is my heir, and I'll leave Lady Danvers to starve
with her husband. I could forgive his taking his
wife from me, but to knock me down, and steal my
Killigrew!—Oh!—they may both go to Scotland

again—I've done with them—I've—Hah! who comes
here?—another man in the uniform! (*Stands aside.*)

Enter Ap-Hazard *in the Uniform.*

Ap-Haz. Bravo, Mr Ap-Hazard!—since you've
put on this uniform, you've come on amazingly—
Miss Union has exchang'd such glances with me,
that there's no doubt I shall finger the brass yet;
and crossing the passage, I found such a valuable
curiosity—such a divine snuff-box—(*Takes a pinch
of snuff out of it, and puts it in his pocket.*)—Ha! Bam!
how are you, Bam?

Sir Bam. Bam!—Surely he can't be the ruffian—
What brought you here, sir?

Ap-Haz. I came to see the opera, sir—but the
thing's impossible—I haven't had a glimpse of a single
dancer or singer.

Sir Bam. And why, sir?

Ap-Haz. Because the audience are the performers,
and there's nothing to be seen on the stage but soldiers, scene-shifters, prompters, and those pasteboard
figures stuck on to the scenes, call'd men of fashion
—Do you know, Bam, in Wales we us'd to pay but
sixpence to look at a waggon-full of wild beasts—
but here, at the opera house, you pay half-a-guinea
to peep only at monkeys.

Sir Bam. Hark ye, sir—did'nt you assault me just
now?

Ap-Haz. Me assault you?

Sir Bam. Yes, sir—Did'nt you take Lady Danvers
from me?

Ap-Haz. Me!—No, no—I was rather unfortunate
in the morning, but now I'm in better luck, and we'll
be better friends—Give me your hand—no—not the
gouty one—there—And now I'll make you amends
for fracturing old Geoffery's skull—Here—(*Pulling
out a paper*)—here's such a literary treasure!

Sir Bam. Is there?—let's see it.

Ap-Haz. Gently—no hurry—I look upon you as the father of the literati—the chief of commentators—the king of blue stockings—and therefore I'll read to you an original stanza, written by Shakespeare—written for one of the witches in Macbeth.

Sir Bam. An original stanza for one of the witches! —Oh! let me hear.

Ap-Haz. Ay—never, never publish'd———Listen. —(*Reads.*)

> Hinx, spinx, the devil winks,
>   The fat begins to fry;
> Nobody at home but jumping Joan,
>   Father, mother, and I.
>
>
> O, U, T,
> With a black and a brown snout,
>   Out! Pout! Out!

There!—isn't that genuine?

Sir Bam. Genuine! I'll take my oath it's Shakespeare's!—Yes, yes, Charles was the ruffian—Repeat it, my dear boy, repeat it.—" Hinx, spinx"—

Ap-Haz. (*Taking snuff.*) " The devil winks"— Take a pinch. (*Offering him his own snuff-box.*)— Why, what do you stare at?—Take a pinch, I say.

Sir Bam. (*Snatching the box from him.*) It is! no it isn't—yes, it is—my own dear Killigrew—Oh, you accomplish'd villain!

Ap-Haz. Villain!—I found it—I——

Sir Bam. It's all out now!—He was the assailant, and Charles is innocent. Now ar'n't you a pretty scoundrel!—At our first interview you break old Geoffery's skull, and at the second you crack mine! —Look ye; you may return to Wales, for I'll adopt a printer's devil——a compositor—a fly-boy——any body, in preference to such a hinx-spinx impostor!

Ap-Haz. What!—you give me up, do you?

Sir Bam. Give you up!—If it weren't for Miss Union, I'd have you hang'd!

Ap-Haz. Well!—what then?

Sir Bam. What then!

Ap-Haz. Ay, what then?—when a man has no luck in one world—Damme, it's insupportable! I'm tir'd out: and at this moment I'm in such a conflagration, that I could burn the theatre myself, and all the people in it.—Here—give me something cooling —ice—lemonade—vinegar!—(*Goes up to the bar, and in his hurry breaks three or four glasses.*)———— Very well!—" What's to pay?"—Curse it!—"What's to pay?"

Sir Bam. Poor Lady Danvers!—I wonder what's become of her: if I could find her, and make her amends———Heh! here she is, and Orville with her!

Enter LADY DANVERS, *struggling with* ORVILLE.

Lady Dan. (*Speaking as she enters.*) Sir, I insist —nay, I must—I will be heard!——Gentlemen, if you have any pity, protect me from this hypocrite.— Sir Bamber!—Mr Ap-Hazard, you once sav'd my mother in distress, now extend your gallantry to her unfortunate daughter!

Orv. Psha! they'll neither of them interfere for you: one's too old—the other too dastardly.

Ap-Haz. Who's dastardly!——I'll interfere for her—or for any body—or for every body!

Orv. Indeed!—What makes you so mad-headed?

Ap-Haz. What makes one man a highwayman?— another a suicide?—a third a duellist?—Why, desperation!—desperation!—I'm chuck-full of it at this moment! I can't be worse off than I am; so yield up the lady, or else take hold of the corner of that handkerchief—we'll fight across it, muzzle to muzzle, Mr Orville!

Orv. This interruption's tedious——Lady Danvers, I insist————(*Laying hold of her.*)

Ap-Haz. (*Standing before them.*) Stop, sir! I see you're one of those puppies who, having lost all character, try to relieve it by robbing women of their honour and men of their lives—(*Here* ORVILLE *produces pistols.*)—If so, there's my card—here's my pistol—(*Taking one from* ORVILLE)—and, unlucky as I am, I'll bet twenty to ten my shot against yours —(*Presents pistol.*)—Out of the way, Bam,—out of the way!

Orv. This isn't a proper place to adjust these matters in; you'll bring the audience to see you.

Ap-Haz. So much the better: I like to bring an audience to see me: and the fuller the house, the more my acting will be applauded.—However, if we can't fight here, we can fight elsewhere:—Come over the way to my lodgings—(ORVILLE *pauses.*) What! does Fortune leave you in the lurch?—Look, ma'am —look at the losing hero!

Orv. Don't fancy I'm afraid, sir: I don't like to leave the lady, that's all.

Sir Bam. (*Aside to* ORVILLE.) Oh! I'll take care of her, upon my honour.

Orv. What, you'll keep her safe till I return?— then I'll go with him—there is no other way; and, after all, I don't think he'll fight.—Come, sir, no delay——Madam, I'll make an example of your champion; and when I come back——

Ap-Haz. Madam, he shall never come back again! ——There's no danger: if he will fight, I won't: and the man who makes up his mind to one or to the other is equally determined—(*Aside.*)——Come along, sir.——Bam, I'm resolv'd——Madam, he's a dead man!   [*Exit with* ORVILLE.

Sir Bam. There they go—and now, my sweet octavo, we'll go too. I forgive the fellow every thing —I do; because he has saved you from Orville, who, I now see, was the real villain, after all.

Lady Dan. Ah, sir !—but if Mr Ap-Hazard should lose his life ?

Sir Bam. Lose his life !—Bless you ! when a quarrel takes place at a.theatre, it's five to one they don't fight ; and if they do, it's ten to one neither of them are wounded.   But come, let's to my house directly, and leave the people of fashion to sleep over the opera by themselves.—Do you know, Juliana, I've a great mind to give up literature, and learn to caper ? I have, for this reason—Now-a-days, the worst dancer makes more by his heels than the best author does by his head !   [*Exeunt.*

ACT THE FOURTH.

SCENE I.

Outside of SIR BAMBER's *House, in Grosvenor Square.*

Enter SIR BAMBER *and* LADY DANVERS.

Sir Bam. Ay, ay, I told you how the duel would end.

Lady Dan. Hadn't we better enter your house, sir ?—we may be pursued.

Enter, from the House, SAMUEL.

Sam. Oh, sir !—I'm glad you're come home.

Sir Bam. Why, what's the matter, sirrah ?

Sam. There's been such a rumpus, sir !—Mrs Seymour's butler has been here, asking after your honour and Lady Danvers.

Sir Bam. Indeed !

Sam. Yes.--They have been informed that you

had carried off the lady from the opera.—There'll be
blood spilt, I'm sure, for Mrs Seymour and her son,
Miss Union and her nephew, all vow revenge; and
if Lady Danvers is found in our house——

Sir Bam. None of your illustrations, sirrah! (*Exit*
SAMUEL.)—What's to be done?—Mrs Seymour will
persecute, Orville and her son insult me; and Miss
Union——'Sdeath! I shall lose both her and Trickarinda——No, no, she mus'n't be found in my house.

Lady Dan. I'm sorry to perplex you, sir; and if
I knew how——

Sir Bam. There is only one way—You must return to Miss Union's; for I'd rather be accus'd of
having written all the new novels of last year, than
prov'd to be author of your present elopement——
Mercy on me! here's one of our pursuers. (*They go
up the stage.*)

Enter AP-HAZARD, (*the flap of his coat torn.*)

Ap-Haz. Here's luck now!—I receive an assignation from Miss Union—keep on my best dress——

Sir Bam. Oh, it's only you, is it?

Ap-Haz. I receive an assignation, I say—knock
at the lady's door—all joy and expectation—when a
little, square, terrier-faced fellow seizes me by the
flap of the coat, tears it asunder, calls me a money-lender, himself a coach-maker, and swears I
swindl'd him out of a chariot worth three hundred
pounds—I explain, and he coolly walks off, saying
he never saw one man more like another than I am
to the notorious A. B.——Curse him! I must go
home and refit myself for the assignation.

Sir Bam. (*Stopping him.*) Don't you see Lady
Danvers?—she's all gratitude for your gallantry;
and, between ourselves, she has made notes on your
figure: She likes your title-page—your frontispiece
—mum—she's fond of you.

Ap-Haz. They all are!—Oh, with the women I'm

always fortunate!—Bless them! they never got me into a scrape.

Sir Bam. Didn't they?—You're a luckier fellow then than I thought you.

Ap-Haz. Never: they never lead any body into mischief.

Sir Bam. No!—Why, here's one of them has put a full stop to all my flights in love and literature.— The sex never get you into difficulties, you say?—— I've a great mind to fix him with the care of Lady Danvers—(*Aside.*)—I will.——Hark ye!—she's in a particular situation—she wants a protector.

Ap-Haz. A protector!

Sir Bam. Ay: Don't you know what a protector is?

Ap-Haz. Oh!—a man who takes care of himself.

Sir Bam. Come, that's a new reading.——She has no home, I tell you; and as I heard you say you were going to your lodgings, will you take her under your arm?

Ap-Haz. Will I not!——My dear Bam, always put yourself in Fortune's way.——Madam!

Sir Bam. Hush! I'll speak to her.——What a nanny-goat it is!—(*Aside.*)——Juliana——I can't keep my countenance—(*Laughing.*)——As you see the danger of going to my house, and object to return to Miss Union's, I've thought of a snug shelf for you:—A female relation of mine lives in the next street, and this favourite of the ladies (*Smiling at* AP-HAZARD) here will conduct you—nay, he'll fight for you, I warrant: though not a profess'd duellist, he can crack a skull as well as any cudgeller in England.

Lady Dan. Sir, I have no reason to think Mr Ap-Hazard will lead me into danger.

Ap-Haz. There you're wrong, madam: I never take a step without getting into danger: and since

I entered this inauspicious town, I've got into every
scrape a man can get into—except one.

Lady Dan. And what is that one?

Ap-Haz. A law-suit!—I've had no commerce with
the lawyers; although I have heard there are two
hundred thousand, I've escaped them all; and that's
an equivalent for most of my bad fortune.—Come,
let's be gone, madam.——I say, don't you envy me?

Sir Bam. I do : John Gilpin was nothing to you.—
Stop though :—Treat her kindly—behave like a man
of honour.

Ap-Haz. Honour!——Now I think on't, what's
become of Miss Union?—she's waiting all this time,
and——Well, I'll see her safe, *(Pointing to* Lady
Danvers*)* and then once more for the assignation.
——Lady Danvers, I've an arm to fight for you, a
head to plot for you, and a heart to feel for you!—
and——Oh, Sir Bam! " there is a tide in the affairs
of men, which, taken at the flood, leads on to fortune :" I'm now at high-water mark, and this pilot
will steer me into such an ocean of luck, that henceforth my watch-word shall be " what's to receive?"
—never will I ask " what's to pay ?" again.

[*Exit with* Lady Danvers.

Sir Bam. Ha, ha, ha!——Good luck to you.——
Now there'll be no blood spilt : I can triumph over
Mrs Seymour and her son, and preserve Miss Union
and Trickarinda.

Enter Tom *and* Mrs Seymour.

Tom. Where is my sister, sir?—You have decoy'd
her from the opera, and taken me from a harpoon-
ing party at Putney, where the fish are now waiting
for me—Deliver her up this instant, or, by the regatta,
I swear——

Sir Bam. None of your pitch and tar here, sir !
——Mrs Seymour, least this libellous report should
injure me in Miss Union's good opinion, I am com-

pelled to give up the real author at once—My hopeful heir is the gentleman—Lady Danvers is this instant gone with Ap-Hazard to his lodgings.

Tom. Oh, you old marauder !—What ! follow the track of Munchausen ?—try to outsail that great discoverer on the marvellous ocean !——All I know is, if Ap-Hazard has steer'd off with the Juliana brig, there'll be a pretty smart engagement between her and the Union fire-ship.

Mrs. Sey. Hold, sir !—haven't I told you not to reflect on that good woman ?

Tom. And haven't I told you to reflect on that good woman ?—I say Miss Union is a crazy vessel ; and as a proof of it, she sent Ap-Hazard a love-letter—he shew'd it me ; and may I never set the Thames on fire, if I don't think she is now in his cabin.——Juliana's a good girl, and takes too much after her brother, to act in an unsailor-like or dishonourable manner.

Sir Bam. This isn't to be borne !——Mrs Seymour, that you may be eye-witness of mine and Miss Union's innocence, will you go with me to Ap-Hazard's lodgings ?—In the mean time, your illiterate, amphibious son here may examine my house.

Mrs Sey. With all my heart.—Come, sir.

Sir Bam. (*To* TOM.) Mind though—when you enter the library, don't steal any of the manuscripts.

Tom. I steal them !—Pooh ! they're too heavy for the Sprightly Kitty : one cargo of Black-letter ballast would sink her and the whole crew.

Mrs Sey. Will you never forego this aquatic mania ?—will you never be creditable to your family, or useful to your country ?

Tom. Useful to my country !——I never had an opportunity of proving it. But I'll tell you what— if an enemy's fleet appears off our coast, I'll not trouble myself about the salt-water, because there are tight lads enough to take care of the Channel ; but for fresh-water, if they venture above bridge, only let me catch them in Chelsea Reach, and I and the Sprightly Kitty will give them such broadsides— Oh ! we'll assert the dignity of old Thames, and, while we have a plank to stand on, protect its fish- eries, coal-barges, navigation, and trade.   [*Exeunt.*

SCENE II.

AP-HAZARD's *Lodgings ; a Table with Wine ;
two Chairs.*

Enter AP-HAZARD *and* LADY DANVERS.

Ap-Haz. (*In another coat.*)   Now to meet Miss Union—Good b'ye :---Order what you want.

Lady Dan. Don't leave me, I entreat you.

Ap-Haz. Not leave you !—I'm sure you'll pardon me when I confess I've an assignation : the lady has been waiting these two hours : and no wonder at it; for when I set out for one place, I'm so sure of ar- riving at another, that the other day, when I meant to dine at Hyde-Park Corner, the drunken hackney- coachman set me down at Shoreditch church.

Lady Dan. I only ask you to remain till the mis- tress of the house comes home.—Pray have you ever seen or convers'd with her ?

Ap-Haz. Saw her this morning : she brought me my bill ; and because I was not fortunate enough to pay her, she bid me quit my lodgings.

Lady Dan. Your lodgings !—Surely I'm not de- ceiv'd.——Pray, sir, whose room is this ?

Ap-Haz. Mine, ma'am : these are my apartments. In the next room there lodges a dashing young ba- ronet : nobody knows his name, because he is so afraid of being tapp'd on the shoulder, that he hasn't stirr'd out since he came.—Over head is an old lady, who is all day fencing—underneath is a young one learning to play on the trumpet—in the garret is a spouting author—and over him is a nightly concert of mewing, caterwauling lovers.

Lady Dan. Sir, answer me this question—Is the mistress of this house a relation of Sir Bamber's?

Ap-Haz. No, to be sure she isn't—hang it, she may though; for, now I recollect, I've seen her roll up butter of her own making in manuscripts of his writing.——Well, it's too late for Miss Union now: no doubt she has given me up: and since you've been the cause of my disappointing one dear creature, make me amends, by allowing me to make love to a dearer—One kiss.

Lady Dan. Don't come near me, sir!

Ap-Haz. I thought you'd prove a lucky star; and you have: my heart forbodes such a scene of good fortune—*(Offers to kiss her.)*——Nay, if I don't behave like a gentleman, may I never turn up an honour as long as I live!

Lady Dan. Keep off, I insist, sir!—Is this your generosity? Oh, Sir Charles Danvers!—Sir Charles Danvers!—what misery has our union entailed upon me!—What have I suffered by forming an alliance, without considering whether there was fortune or affection to support it!

Ap-Haz. Sir Charles Danvers!—Pooh!—I don't care *that* for him: I've turn'd him out of one house already; and if he were here at this moment, I'd say to him——

Enter SIR CHARLES DANVERS.

Sir Char. Well, sir—what would you say to him?

Ap-Haz. What's to pay?—Nothing more, upon my word.

Sir Char. Being in the next room, and hearing my

name, I came to see who utter'd it——Lady Danvers!—alone—and in the apartments of my enemy!
——What! because he has supplanted me in my
uncle's affections, does he rival me in yours?—because he is heir to a large fortune, is he more worthy
your regard than a ruin'd, lost, unhappy husband?
——Speak!

Lady Dan. Sir Charles, your former good opinion
I do not wish to forfeit; and if not lov'd, I cannot
bear to be despis'd. I have been betray'd here; first,
by the artifices of Miss Union and Orville; and next,
by the treachery of your uncle and his friend.—This
is my justification: and now judge whether he can
atone for the loss of a husband, whom, till this hour,
I honour'd and esteem'd.

Sir Char. Hear me, sir!—What ill intentions
urg'd you to attempt such daring villainy?

Ap-Haz. Ill luck, not ill intentions, I assure you,
sir.—A woman never led me into a scrape before:
and I thought by sticking close to an angel, to keep
the devil at an agreeable distance.—But I see Love,
as well as Fortune, makes a fool of me—they're both
blind to my merits——and so good night.

Sir Char. Hold, sir!—stir not a step!——Lady
Danvers, misfortune, not hatred, parted us; and with
my life I'll guard you from your enemies—Give me
your hand——Ah! you once gave it me.

Lady Dan. I did; and if it be worth keeping, take
it again, Sir Charles. I've bought experience since
you left me; and I feel a pleasure in declaring, that,
were I single to-morrow, there is but one man on
earth should have my hand and heart—and that one
is Sir Charles Danvers.

Sir Char. Is it possible?—You transport me!

Ap-Haz. So she did me just now.——Take care,
my fine fellow—take care!—A man never has a cup-
full of joy in one hand, but presently pops a pail-full
of sorrow in the other.

13

Lady Dan. I'll make one more appeal to my
mother : I have now a new tale to unfold to her : and
if we can but convince her, and your uncle, of Miss
Union's duplicity, we may be happy still.——Why
that sigh, Sir Charles ?

Sir Char. My debts have fallen into other hands :
Old Colonel Orville is dead ; and my greatest foe is
now my chief creditor.——Orville is determined to
throw me into prison ; and on his account I was
driven to those rooms ; for which I have now reason
to thank him, since this interview has prov'd, my
Juliana, that though divided by necessity, we're still
united by dearer ties than matrimonial bonds—by
mutual inclination—by disinterested love.

Lady Dan. We are ; and, but for our enemies, Sir
Charles——

Sir Char. Ay, but for them !——'Sdeath ! when
I think how you have been treated !——However,
let me lose no time in conducting you to your mother's. I'll make at least one example amongst them
——And you, sir !—mark me, sir ! wait till I return ;
and then be prepared to give me such satisfaction as
the honour of an injur'd husband demands !

[*Exit with* LADY DANVERS.

Ap-Haz. An injur'd husband demands !—Very well
—Fire away, gentlemen !—If I had ten thousand lives,
I dare say you'd take them all—They sha'n't though
—(*Draws a chair, and sits in it.*)—Here I perch for
life !—from this chair I never stir—here I'll wrap
myself up like an owl in an old tree, and then—let
the tempest bellow round me—Heigho ! (*Looks at
the wine on the table*) I should like to drink a glass of
wine to raise my spirits ! (*Gets half up.*)—No—I
won't budge—if I stir, I know I shall tread on that
infernal piece of orange peel, slip down, and break
my neck !—Plague on't !—will there never come a
turn in my favour ?—will Fortune never—I'll sit
cross'd-legg'd for luck——Ha !—I have it—If my
pocket-book isn't stolen, there's a bill of my father's

in it now due—Here it is !—I'll touch the cash directly—set off for Wales to-night—leave these cockneys
to fight it out by themselves—laugh at having trick'd
them, and so—*(As he is going, enter* MISS UNION.)

Miss Uni. And so—make appointments with one
lady, only to keep them with another !—let me
bite my fingers for two hours, and be the whole time
sighing here with Lady Danvers !—What have you
got there ? a list of assignations I suppose—*(Snatches
the pocket-book from him)*—I'll teach you how to
keep them ! There !—*(Tears leaves out of the book,
note, &c.)*

Ap-Haz. You've torn my father's note ! O Lord !
What's to pay ?

Miss Uni. (*Knock at the door.*) Mercy! who's here ?

Enter a Servant.

Serv. Sir Charles Danvers has just sent, sir, to
desire you'll follow him to Hyde Park, and bring
pistols with you, directly.   [*Exit.*

Ap-Haz. I'll come. Now I can get rid of this
plague—and if I go near the Park——Oh ! I'll slip
thro' all their fingers yet.

Enter another Servant.

Serv. Mr Orville and his second are at the door
in a post-chaise, sir—and he swears, if you don't instantly set out for Hamburgh, he'll post you for a
coward.   [*Exit.*

Ap-Haz. It never rains but it pours.

Enter another Servant.

Serv. Mrs Seymour and Sir Bamber Blackletter,
sir—They say you have carried off Lady Danvers,
and if you don't instantly restore her to her mother,
your life must answer for the consequences.

Ap-Haz. Very well :—Shew them up—Only say,
my life is bespoke by so many people, that if they

don't make haste, I sha'n't have a bit of flesh left to peck at—*(Servant exit.)*—This is the crisis !

Miss Uni. Heavens !—if they should find me here—Mr Ap-Hazard—my dear Mr Ap-Hazard—only get me out of this scrape—Where shall I hide myself ?

Ap-Haz. (In a reverie.)—In a brass mine ;—for me—I'll consult the stars.

Miss Uni. Consult the stars, and let me be discovered!—Here they come, and I know they'll search every hole and corner to find Lady Danvers !—Where shall I go ?—Ha !—a window with a balcony !—I shall conceal myself in that balcony, and if you betray me—— [*Exit into balcony.*

Enter SIR BAMBER *and* MRS SEYMOUR.

Sir Bam. Now, sir, produce the lady—restore her to her unhappy mother.—Why, what's the fool staring at ?—Look at me—look in my face.

Ap-Haz. I do—and a more ill-omen'd visage never cross'd me—There's fatality in every furrow—a scrape in every wrinkle, and a devil—O, U, T,—out, with a black and brown snout—out ! pout ! out !

Enter TOM SEYMOUR.

Well, sir—have you seen your sister ?

Tom. I have—I acquit you, Sir Bamber—You are innocent—But O ! you fountain of all iniquity—*(Laying hold of* AP-HAZARD*)*—you rock—you quicksand—you whirlpool !—how dare you decoy my sister to these lodgings ?

Ap-Haz. The stars foretel a watery grave—and lo !—here comes the mighty master of the art of sinking, to shew me to the bottom—How did you feel when you were drown'd ?

Tom. Not half what you will when I shoot you on my quarter-deck—Lady Danvers is in this house—I have seen her.

Sir Bam. There !—Now, haven't I been libell'd ?—

hasn't Miss Union been lampoon'd?—and won't I
have you pilloried, sir, for saying that volume of virtue was in these apartments?

Tom. I said she sent this tornado a love-letter—
(Pointing to AP-HAZARD)—and I am sure she has
brass enough to—Mess!—don't weep so, mother:—
I'm not us'd to salt-water, and you'll make me cry
too.

Mrs Sey. I could have borne any thing but this
—to see my child disgrac'd!—her reputation sullied!
—Oh, my son!

Tom. (Crying.) Hang it!—I'm sorry I said I saw
her, now; but looking up to see if the wind blew fair
for Putney, I spied her in the balcony.

Sir Bam. In the balcony!—What! there?

Tom. (Still crying.)— Yes, there that pirate has
conceal'd my lost—unhappy sister.

Sir Bam. I'll have her out.

Tom. No—you sha'n't expose her.

Sir Bam. I will—to vindicate my own and Miss
Union's character—*(Throws up window, and leads
on* MISS UNION.)—This way, Lady Danvers.—The
devil!—my intended wife!

Ap-Haz. What's to pay?

Tom. There's brass for you!

Ap-Haz. Ha! ha! ha!—am not I the only unlucky one?—have I got a companion in my misfor
tunes?—Ha! ha! till this moment I stood alone—
now here's a joint paymaster!—*(Sees* SIR BAMBER
looking melancholy.)—What! another unlucky one!
Mrs Seymour too!—Oh!—if I go to the bottom
here'll be a jolly party to sink with me.

Mrs Sey. I'm so overjoy'd to find my daughter innocent, I have not pow'r to censure my false friend
—*(To* TOM.)—How came you, sir, to take this lady
for your sister?

Tom. That's what puzzles me—Mess!—I don't
know whether it was the front of her I saw—for

now-a-days women are so bamboozled in their rig-
ging, there's no telling the stem from the stern.

Ap-Haz. Your sister is gone to Mrs Seymour's
with her husband; and Miss Union—

Miss Uni. Sir—I'll speak for myself—Sir Bamber—Mrs Seymour—I came to these apartments in
search of Lady Danvers, and hearing music in the
street, I stept into the balcony to listen to my favourite tune—an old song of Chaucer's—the night-
ingale and——

Sir Bam. The cuckoo!—Oh! oh! oh!

Tom. Come, papa—as we're once more friends,
let's bear a hand together—let's steer to the club, and
drink Juliana's health in a thousand bumpers.—Good
night, mother—and to speak authorically, don't you
think Sir Bamber and Miss Union will bind up neatly together?

Ap-Haz. Yes; and if he means to have prints in
his edition of Chaucer, let me recommend for the
frontispiece a view of the balcony!—Mrs Seymour,
you're always welcome to your husband's apartments
—Bam, yours.—Come, my noble son-in-law—henceforth I'll not be troublesome to you, for now Fortune
has found somebody else to make a fool of, I hope
she'll give me a holiday!—she'll forget me; but,
damme, I'll remember her as long as I've a memory!

[*Exit with* TOM.

Miss Uni. There's nothing else, I believe, so I'll
follow.

Mrs Sey. Stay, madam—I deserve what I have
suffered for my credulity, but my daughter has merit-
ed a happier fate: and I hope this lesson may be
learnt from your conduct and my own—that to make
love a trade—to convert marriage into merchandize,
and dispose of a child to the highest bidder, is pro-
stituting the noblest passion of the human heart.

Sir Bam. Finis.   [*Exeunt*

ACT THE FIFTH.

SCENE I.

An Apartment at MRS SEYMOUR'S.

Enter MRS SEYMOUR *and* AP-HAZARD.

Mrs Sey. Lady Danvers to go out without seeing me ! to quit my house so soon after her return
to it, and then be found at Mr Orville's alone, and in
close conversation with him!—Tell me, sir ;—you say
you saw her there.

Ap-Haz. I say, my luck has turn'd.—Adieu !

Mrs Sey. Nay, are you going ?

Ap-Haz. Directly—I want a second, and as the
noble captain's not within, I must seek one elsewhere—I am a man of honour now—I have fought
Sir Charles—mean to fight Orville—so good day.

Mrs Sey. Fought Sir Charles Danvers !

Ap-Haz. To be sure—Why, you know nothing—
I'll tell you how it was.—He followed me to La Fleece-
'em's, and insisted on immediate satisfaction.—Not being in luck—that is, my courage not coming when I
call'd it, I demurr'd—then the members rose, lock'd
the door, and call'd me a shy cock !—forced this pistol into my hand—When I found there was nothing
else left for it, I fought like a lion ; and now I am
ready to fight any body—man, woman, and child—
but first I'll shoot your friend Orville.

Mrs Sey. He is no longer a friend of mine—

his persecution of Sir Charles, whom he means to arrest for the debt of ten thousand pounds due to his
uncle, would alone make me shun him.—But about
my daughter, sir—did you see her at Mr Orville's?

Ap-Haz. I did—I call'd to give him a hint, and
seeing her alone with him, I retir'd.—But I can't stay
—I must keep fighting while my hand's in.—Adieu!
—London improves—Fortune takes a turn; and come
what will—exit a man of honour!   [*Exit.*

Mrs Sey. Last night I did not see her, and this
morning she rose so early—What's to be done? I'll
go to Mr Orville's house—I'll—Hold—here she is—
I'll observe. *(Stands aside.)*

Enter LADY DANVERS—*(her hat and cloak on.)*

Lady Dan. Mr Orville has behav'd as I expected
—he us'd to profess regard for me, but now I have
put him to the proof.

Mrs Sey. (*Behind.*) To the proof!

Lady Dan. He treats me like an enemy. (MRS
SEYMOUR *advances.*)—My mother!—Oh! thank you
for restoring your protection to me—thank you for
the happiest night I have pass'd since I left you—
and yet there is one thing—I'm just come from Mr
Orville, and he has us'd me most unkindly.

Mrs Sey. Indeed!

Lady Dan. You us'd to praise him, mother, and
wish me to return his love.

Mrs Sey. I did—My weakness is no apology for
yours.

Lady Dan. No—but I thought, by reminding him
of former days—by saying that on your account I
would try to regard him——

Mrs Sey. Juliana, you'll break my heart—After
the struggles we have both encountered, I did expect we should part no more.

Lady Dan. And shall we, mother?

Mrs Sey. What can I do?—I could forgive you

any thing, for life is agony without you—but your husband—how shall I tell Sir Charles?

Lady Dan. Tell him!—what?

Mrs Sey. Of your imprudence, your unfeeling conduct.

Lady Dan. What conduct?

Mr Sey. Have you not been alone at Orville's house?—confess'd—

Lady Dan. Were you not my mother, I would not condescend to answer you.—Yes, madam, tell Sir Charles, at the risk of being insulted, I went alone to Mr Orville's—tell him I entreated, knelt, and wept to him—and if he asks the motive for all this, remind him of his own conduct last night at Mr Ap-Hazard's, and tell him, that as you've ever taught me one act of generosity deserves another, your daughter scorn'd to be ungrateful or outdone.—There, madam—read that paper.

Mrs Sey. (*Reading the paper.*) " Receiv'd of Lady Danvers, jewels to the value of five hundred pounds; in consideration of which, I promise not to take legal measures against Sir Charles Danvers for one month from this day.—HENRY ORVILLE."—My child! my child! (*Embracing her*) was this the motive?

Lady Dan. I had no more to offer; but if my life would save him from a prison, I'd lay it down with pleasure.

Mrs Sey. Exalted girl!—And does he know your friendship?

Lady Dan. He does, and will soon call to take leave of me—He is going abroad; and I hope Mr Orville will have no right to complain, since, by his exertions in another country, he will be more able to pay the debt, than by his being imprison'd in this.—Will you see him, mother?—Won't you part friends with him?—Consider, one kind word will cheer him

in his solitude, and 'tis the last time he'll ever intrude
upon you.

Enter SIR CHARLES DANVERS.

Sir Char. Juliana, the carriage is now waiting that
conveys me perhaps for ever from you.—Mrs Seymour here !—I beg pardon.

Mrs Sey. Sir Charles, where are you going ?

Sir Char. Abroad, madam—That lady has set me
a bright example ; and the hope that I may one day
repay her generosity drives me to another country,
where, by industry and economy, I may so adjust
my affairs as to return to this country with wealth
and honour.—Farewell.

Mrs Sey. Stay, Sir Charles.—My daughter has
indeed set a bright example !—an example which
not only you, but her mother may be proud to imitate !—I parted your hands—the least amends I can
make is to join them ; and if I've not the pow'r, I'll
prove I have the wish to serve you—I'll apply to
your uncle—exert myself every way in your interest,
and, in atonement for my past unkindness, I'll henceforth know no happiness but in promoting yours.

Lady Dan. Will you ? can you ?—We shall not
then be parted.

Mrs Sey. Never—I'll go instantly to your uncle,
and since Miss Union and Mr Ap-Hazard no longer
engross his attention—Ha ! here's my son and Mr
Orville ! You had better not be seen, Sir Charles :
step into the next room : we'll soon return, and bring
you welcome news.   (SIR CHARLES *exit.)*

Enter ORVILLE *and* TOM SEYMOUR.

Tom. Mum ! he's gone into dock, I see.

Mrs Sey. Mr Orville, I'm this moment going to
Sir Charles's uncle, and if you'll wait here till I return, all may be instantly adjusted.—Come, Juliana
—if I should fail, we'll join him in retirement, and

all that I possess shall be devoted to my children's welfare.   [*Exit with* LADY DANVERS.

Tom. She settle Sir Charles's affairs !—Why, these women chop about like weather-cocks; but I'm steady; firm as my own main-mast !

Orv. He has broke his agreement, and I'll break mine—If I once get him under lock and key, Lady Danvers may be mine at last.— Sir Charles ! (*Opens door.*)—Nay, we have seen you, sir. (SIR CHARLES *enters.*) Come, sir, pay me the whole debt, or the bailiff below stairs——

Sir Char. You can't be so ungenerous :—Mrs Seymour is now gone to my uncle.

Tom. Pooh ! he's still steer'd by Miss Union ; so call up the bailiff.

Sir Char. How ! are you against me ? The brother of Lady Danvers !

Tom. 'Tis on her account I am against you, sir.— Since you put to sea with Juliana, I and the Sprightly Kitty haven't sail'd ten leagues together; therefore, put him under hatches, Orville ; then one may fish or fight, or go on a voyage of discoveries, as it suits.

Sir Char. Hear me a moment: not on my own, but her account I speak :— We lately united again, and if our next meeting is to be in a prison—

Orv. United again ! Don't believe it, Mr Seymour. ——Without there.

Enter AP-HAZARD.

Ap-Haz. Oh ! have I found you, Mr Orville—Hah ! take your ground.

Orv. Blockhead ! are you come to get into a new scrape.

Ap-Haz. I get into a scrape ! Pheu ! my luck has turn'd.—Will you fight? (*To* ORVILLE)—or will you? (*To* TOM)—or you? (*To* SIR CHARLES.)—No, I know you will, so we'll shake hands.—Last night it was my destiny to have no courage; now it is my good fortune to have an overflow; therefore dispatch:—There's your second, here's mine.—As I thought, you're a shy cock.

Tom. Why, father, you're a different man.

Ap-Haz. I'm not; I'm the same man with different fortune. Do you suppose Alexander wasn't sometimes a shy cock? Yes, he had his nervous days, and I've had mine; haven't I, Sir Charles? But now, fight me; do; pray, some of you fight me: here, I'll give any man ten guineas that will fight me!

Orv. You interrupt us, sir.——Where are these bailiffs?

Ap-Haz. Bailiffs! Oh! dammc, they'll fight me.

Orv. (*At stage door.*) Come up stairs, and arrest Sir Charles.

Ap-Haz. Arrest Sir Charles!

Orv. Ay, Sir Charles Danvers, sir; have you any objection?

Ap-Haz. To be sure I have——What's to pay?

Orv. Pay!—Ten thousand pounds.

Ap-Haz. Is that all?—only ten thousand!—Psha!—when a man's in luck, thousands are units.—I'll pay it.

Orv. You!—ha! ha!—how?

Tom. Ay, how?—in paper or gold?

Ap-Haz. Neither.—In lead!—(*Presents pistols*)—by shooting off the five fingers of the first hand that offers to touch him.—Lay hold of my arm, brother hero—When I had bad luck, I made the bad share it, now I have good, the unfortunate shall partake of it; and there's such a charm about me at this moment, that only touch me, and you'll be invisible to all bailiffs, bullies, and black-legs.—I behav'd ill to your wife, and you fought me——

Tom. Mess! how's that?—Did he fight for his wife?

Ap-Haz. He did; and I fought for her too—so here's a pair of us.—Keep off.

Tom. (*Standing before the stage door.*) No—you don't—you sha'n't quit the room.

Orv. (*Standing by* TOM.) No—that you sha'n't—shall they, my friend?

Tom. No—for you shall, my friend—(*To* ORVILLE.) —Look ye, sir; in my mother's absence, I am master of this house, and while I thought Sir Charles was no friend to my sister, I was none to him; but now I find I've been on a wrong tack, I'll stick to him, as long as the Thames flows, and I'm lord-high-admiral of it!—so d'ye hear—cut—brush—scud—set sail —sheer off, or——

Orv. Sir, I shall persist.

Ap-Haz. Persist!—Oh!—he pushes his bad luck, does he?—Here—(*Putting money in his hand, and shutting it*)—odd or even, for a hundred.

Tom. I tell you what—if you don't weigh anchor this moment, I'll force you and your bailiffs into my long boat—heave you to leeward of the Sprightly Kitty, and open a broadside upon you, that shall blow you all from Chelsea to the Red Sea.

Orv. Very well, sir,—you shall hear from me, depend on't.—For you, Sir Charles, you are my prisoner to a certainty—To-morrow morning Sir Bamber marries Miss Union, and she'll take care that neither you nor this booby shall ever see one shilling of his property—so now your luck's turn'd again.   [*Exit.*

Sir Char. How! after the affair at Mr Ap-Hazard's, will my uncle marry Miss Union?

Tom. It's all owing to the Chaucerian Manuscript —to gain that he'll marry her, though it were as certain she'll steer him to Cuckold's Point, as that Columbus fish'd out America, and I won the Vauxhall cup.—She swore she came to your lodgings in search of Juliana; and as to the assignation, she threatens to have you hang'd for forging it.

Ap-Haz. I forge it!—Here it is—read—(*Gives them the letter.*)

Tom. Why this is in black-letter!—Pooh!—this is more like my old boatswain's hand than Miss Union's.

Sir Char. That's her usual trick—she writes in a disguis'd hand to avoid detection.—'Sdeath! is there no way to put a stop to this marriage? 'twill doom me to perpetual imprisonment, involve Mrs Seymour, and break the heart of Juliana.

Tom. There is no way—I'll bet ten to one.

Ap-Haz. I'll take any odds on any event, to any amount, in fifties, hundreds, thousands, millions!

Sir Char. You'll lose, I'll risk my life, sir.

Ap-Haz. Will you risk your money, sir?—will you lay the long odds?—'twill be a noble hedge for you:—and if each of you will bet me a hundred to ten—

Tom. I'll bet you a hundred to ten, you don't upset the marriage.

Sir Char. So will I.

Ap-Haz. Done! done!—Now then it's settled—Bam loses his wife, and I win the long odds. Farewell! Follow me to old Blackletter's, and I'll shew you what's to pay, my boys!   [*Exit.*

Tom. Brother, I hope you'll forgive me—I'm sorry I took part with that villain; for though not a saltwater sailor, I wish to be as like one as I can—I make voyages and sleep in a hammock, like a sailor; I drink grog and chew tobacco, though I hate it, like a sailor; I make love, tho' I'm not over-fond of that, like a sailor; I sing, dance, and spend my money foolishly, like a sailor; and after copying them in all these things, shall I do a dishonourable action?——No, damme, that would not be like a sailor.

[*Exit with* SIR CHARLES.

SCENE II.

A Room at Sir Bamber's.

Enter Sir Bamber *and* Miss Union, *followed by a Servant with a small green box—*Sir Bamber *is trying to lay hold of the box,* Miss Union *preventing him.*

Sir Bam. Do I behold thee ?—Does that angelic little box contain my Trickarinda ?

Miss Uni. Fie ! don't be so impatient, Sir Bamber.——(*Servant puts it on a table, and exit.*) Gently—before we open it, let me remind you of the terms—the only terms on which you are to become master of this immortal manuscript.—First, you are to sign an agreement—

Sir Bam. I know it :—I am to marry you to-morrow, and settle on you half my estate.—Now do let me have a peep—I wonder how she's dress'd—in black leather and gold facings !—or in sheets, perhaps.

Miss Uni. Secondly, you are to bind yourself not to pay Sir Charles's debts—Thirdly, not to give your godson—(Sir B. *tries to open the trunk*)—Nay, you wouldn't look at the manuscript before the settlement's sign'd—Consider the lawyer is in the next room.

Sir Bam. Oh ! if you wait for lawyers it's all over with me—I shall die—expire, in all the agonies of an expecting lover—Do—pray, let me—

Miss Uni. Well, to save your life—and I've no reason for distrusting you—here—(*Opening trunk, and taking out M.S. in a black binding*)—here is the

Chaucerian Manuscript, found at Union Castle, in Cumberland.

Sir Bam. Never mind where it was found—I've got it—Oh! how the touch thrills me!—Now for the title page.—(*Reads.*)—" Trickarinda—A Poem, full of witty and conceited mirth, written by Geoffery Chaucer."—That's it—that's the true old style—" witty and conceited mirth!"

Enter SAMUEL.

Sam. Lady Danvers and Mrs Seymour are coming up stairs.

Miss Uni. Coming up stairs!—Here's effrontery! —They want to break off the marriage—to persuade him to pay Sir Charles's debts.—Sir Bamber, as you're busy, shall I give them your answer?

Sir Bam. Do—say what you like.—Now for the contents.

Miss Uni. And now for my triumph—though I could not bring about a match for Mrs Seymour, she shall see I can make one for myself.—Shew me to them, sir.   [*Exit with* SAMUEL.

Sir Bam. (*Sitting at the table.*) Now for it— (*Reads.*)—" On yon green bank where Trickarinda sleeps."—There's a subject for a painter—I'll have such a picture gallery—such an exhibition—I'll begin advertising and puffing this very night—(*Sits reading.*)

Enter AP-HAZARD.

Ap-Haz. Don't tell me—I will speak to him.—How my luck is turn'd!—Coming here I saw a woman standing in the pillory—a female faro banker, who had cheated me out of thirty guineas—there was luck.—Then I call'd in at Westminster, to hear a great debate—that was over before I came—there was luck!—So, Bam—I fought at last, you hear.
                        (*Sits by him.*)

Sir Bam. (*Not regarding him.*) " The wind laughs round her, and the water weeps !"—The water weeps —there's an original thought !—What modern author would have hit on such a sympathetic—such— What brought you here, sir ?

Ap-Haz. The long odds.—I've taken two hundred pounds to twenty but I break off your match with Miss Union—Now, as I know the manuscript is your object, I'll shew you how to get it without having a wife for the appendix !—Hark ye—to save your head —risk your neck—steal it.

Sir Bam. Steal it !

Ap-Haz. Ay ; it's all in the way of your profession—Now-a-days all authors are thieves ; and if you're detected, 'twill be only call'd a plagiarism, you know —so put it in your pocket—go with me to Sir Charles—pay all his debts, and buy me a lottery-ticket— only buy me a lottery-ticket, and it's the thirty thousand, to a certainty.

Sir Bam. Why, what is all this ?—Leave the room, sir—be gone directly, or I'll order the servants to throw you out of the window.

Ap-Haz. Bless you !—I'm in such a train of luck, that if you were to chuck me from the top of Westminster-Abbey I should only light on the Treasury, and walk off with my pockets full.—But since you persist in marrying Miss Union, I'll shew you another manuscript. Look here ; here's the letter that brought her to my lodgings.

Sir Bam. Letter of Miss Union's !

Ap-Haz. Ay,—read, Bam—read that assignation.

Sir Bam. Assignation !—Oh dear !—she convinc'd me that she went to your lodgings in search of Lady Danvers.—(*Reads letter.*)—" Miss Union requests the company of Mr Ap-Hazard"—I'm easy—I'm satisfied—she's innocent, and you'll be hang'd for forgery, sirrah.

Ap-Haz. Forgery !

Sir Bam. It's not her writing—it's more like my

grandmother's hand than Miss Union's—I'll send for a peace officer—I'll——No—1 won't—I'll go on with the poem.—(*Returns to table, and reads.*)

Ap-Haz. Fortune's at work again—I shall lose the long odds after all.—Now, my dear god-father, pray think of Sir Charles—pray think of his poor wife—and, above all, pray think of the balcony.

Sir Bam. (*Reading.*)

" And, lo ! a monk, all hallowed from the cloister,
Grey as the morn, and white as any oyster."

There again !—white as any oyster.—What a melting thought !—I'm so transported——(*Here a leaf falls out of manuscript.*)

Ap-Haz. (*Picking it up.*) Give me leave, Sir Bamber—I'll do any thing, if you'll only take pity on your nephew, and——(*Looks at the leaf, then at the letter, and compares them together.*) It is !—no !—yes !—Ha ! ha ! ha ! (*Laughing loudly.*)

Sir Bam. Why, what's the matter ?——what's the fool laughing at ?

Ap-Haz. You were right—the letter is a forgery ; and the best of the joke is—ha ! ha !—I've found out who forged it.

Sir Bam. Who ?

Ap-Haz. Chaucer !—Geoffery Chaucer !——If he penn'd that poem, he penn'd this letter ; for damme but they're both written by one and the same person !—Look—every syllable—every letter is in the same hand.

Sir Bam. How ? in the same hand ! (*Compares.*) So they are—the P's, Q's, O's—they're all the same. —Why, what does this mean ?

Ap-Haz. Mean !—that you're imposed on, either by Chaucer or Miss Union ; and I think it's more likely that a live woman should forge Trickarinda, than that a dead man should send me a love-letter.

Sir Bam. I see it all—I'm bamboozled—Tricka-randa's a trick.

Ap-Haz. And Miss Union is—

Sir Bam. An impostor—a juggler—worse than the bottle-conjuror—she's lost my estate.

Ap-Haz. And I've won the long odds.—Oh, luck! luck! luck's every thing.

Enter MISS UNION, MRS SEYMOUR, *and* LADY DANVERS.

Miss Uni. Well, ladies, if you insist on seeing Sir Bamber, I can't prevent it——So you really believe that we're not going to be married?

Mrs Sey. Why, after what has pass'd, madam—

Miss Uni. Very well——then be satisfied——with your own eyes behold him sign an agreement that gives me his hand, and ruins Sir Charles Danvers for ever.—Here, my life, (*To* SIR BAMBER;) here is the settlement.

Sir Bam. Indeed!

Miss Uni. Yes, my chuck——it only wants your hand to finish it.—Pray observe, ladies.

Sir Bam. Ay, pray observe, ladies—see how my chuck's hand will finish it!—Thus I put an end to it—(*Tearing settlement*)—thus I destroy one most nefarious manuscript.

Ap-Haz. And here goes another——here goes Trickarinda. (*Tearing Trickarinda.*)

Sir Bam. You're found out, madam—You and old Chaucer write the same hand, do you?——(MISS UNION *holds down her head.*) Ay, ay, you overshot the mark there—so now " you may go sleep, while winds laugh round you, and the waters weep."

Enter TOM SEYMOUR *and* SIR CHARLES DANVERS.

Tom. Bear a hand, I tell you—the moment such a stout vessel comes in sight, I know the old ship

will strike.—Sir Bamber, I've brought him here to
engage with you.

Sir Bam. You've done right, and I strike my colours, my boy.——Charles, I'll pay your debts—I'll
settle a third of my estate on you and Juliana—and
here, Mr Hinx Spinx, (*To* AP-HAZARD) that Fortune may no longer make a fool of you, I'll make
you a recompence for winning the long odds, as you
call it—I'll give you a handsome annuity during my
life, and double it after my death.

Ap-Haz. An annuity!—give me an annuity!——
Damme, what's to pay?

Tom. I say, Miss Brass-mine—here's a divorce in
reality.

Miss Uni. Don't talk to me, sir.

Tom. Mess!—hadn't you and the proctor better
take a voyage together? I'll lend you the Sprightly
Kitty—she has a nice little balcony; and if you think
you shall be tired of each other, take me to steer
you, that's all——I'll upset a vessel with any man in
London.

Lady Dan. Miss Union, don't you see Mr Orville beckoning to you?

Miss Uni. I do; and I'll go make him join with
all the lovers in my list to see justice done me.——
Don't think I'm sorry, Sir Charles, that you and
your dear Juliana have made it up again——No——I
know what marriage is; and the more matches there
are amongst you, the more——Oh! I wish you were
all married.   [*Exit.*

Sir Bam. Holloa! hadn't you better take Trickarinda along with you? (*Throws the binding after
her.*)

Mrs Sey. Juliana, this is a happy hour.—My son,
let me congratulate you—you too, Mr Ap-Hazard:
the reward you have received is no more than your
merit deserves.

Ap-Haz. Merit!—it's luck, ma'am.

Mrs Sey. No, sir ; much as we are ruled by chance, we are govern'd more by conduct.

Ap-Haz. Indeed ! and must we stand upon our merit ? Not altogether, I hope. " Use every man after his desert, and who shall 'scape whipping ?" The less we deserve, the more merit is in your bounty. I'm in high favour with Fortune at present ; but—

Lest this propitious chance be but ideal,
I wish our friends around could prove it real :
Shew, by your smiles, a kind reward is nigh ;
Call me not Fool, and Fortune I defy.

[*Exeunt omnes.*

FOLLY AS IT FLIES:

A

COMEDY,

IN FIVE ACTS.

AS PERFORMED AT THE

THEATRE-ROYAL, COVENT-GARDEN.

BY

FREDERICK REYNOLDS.

DRAMATIS PERSONÆ.

SIR HERBERT MELMOTH,	*Mr Murray*
LEONARD MELMOTH,	*Mr H. Johnston.*
TOM TICK,	*Mr Lewis.*
PETER POST OBIT,	*Mr Munden.*
SHENKIN,	*Mr Knight.*
DR INFALLIBLE,	*Mr Simmons.*
CURSITOR,	*Mr Waddy.*
PINCHWELL,	*Mr Atkins.*
CAPIAS,	*Mr Beverley.*
MALCOUR,	*Mr Whitfield.*
LADY MELMOTH,	*Miss Murray.*
GEORGIANA,	*Mrs Gibbs.*
DAME SHENKIN,	*Mrs Powel.*

Servants, Creditors, &c.

SCENE—London.

FOLLY AS IT FLIES.

ACT THE FIRST.

SCENE I.

An elegant Apartment at SIR HERBERT MELMOTH'S.

SIR HERBERT *and* CURSITOR *discovered at a Table, with Writing Materials upon it.*

Cur. (*Writing.*) Well, well, that's sufficient, Sir Herbert; (*Putting paper in his pocket ;*) I'll draw the deeds of conveyance according to these instructions——(*Rises, and takes out his watch.*) Bless me, past four in the morning! Why, my lady is as late as usual.

Sir Her. Past four! and not yet come home!—— Oh, Ellen! Ellen!

Cur. Nay, fretting won't bring her. I'll warrant she won't return from Lady Malcour's assembly these two hours—and I ask you again, Sir Herbert, after getting rid of one troublesome wife, what could induce you to marry your own ward—a girl not twenty years of age?

Sir Her. That which, even now, makes me endure her dissipation and extravagance—affection—uncontroulable affection—My former marriage was against my choice, and yielded me no happiness.

Cur. No!—Why, it gave you a son, as noble a youth as any in the service of his country.

Sir Her. Yes; and love has not so amply filled my heart but there is room for Leonard. Yet, in Ellen—in her disinterested, artless mind—I thought to find unceasing consolation. I offered her my hand; and she, regardless of the difference of years, preferred her guardian to unnumbered suitors.

Cur. She did—even to the son of the lady she is now visiting——the handsome, the honourable Mr Malcour.

Sir Her. Yes, she chose me as her friend—protector—husband.

Cur. Granted——and a lucky preference it was; for in the two years you have been married she has been uncommonly active and industrious. Let me see—she has got through the fifteen thousand in the funds—run you in debt as many more—and compelled you to send for your son Leonard, to cut off the entail of the finest estate in all Pembrokeshire.

Sir Her. Sir, I am the person to condemn her, not you.

Cur. Nay, I am, perhaps, somewhat blunt; but I remember there was a time when Sir Herbert Melmoth would have blushed to owe any man a shilling, and would have perished rather than have asked an affectionate son to sign away his inheritance.

Sir Her. Why, yes, there was a time—Oh, how narrow are the bounds 'twixt virtue and disgrace! One crime so rapidly begets another, that he who, by extravagance, is the author of his own poverty, will climb, by any guilty steps, till he ascend the height from whence he fell.—What would you have me do?

Cur. What?—Controul your wife; insist on her retrenching.

Sir Her. I will; I'll talk to her——(*Knocking at the door.*) And, hark!—most opportunely she's arrived—I'll go, and——

Enter SHENKIN.

Shen. Look you, Sir Herbert—there be my lady, and Miss Georgiana, and Mr Malcour.

Sir Her. Mr Malcour with them!

Cur. Ay, there!—do you mark that?

Sir Her. I do—and she shall find—Fear not—I'm resolute—determined.　　　　　　　　　[*Exit.*

Cur. So you think now——but one of her smiles will undo all.

Shen. Inteed, and, upon my life, so it will, Mr Cursitor—Oh tear! tear! 'tis now only eight months since I did disgrace the noble race of Shenkins, by putting on a livery—and what I would give to be safe back at Abarathgwilly!

Cur. Abarathgwilly! What! then you come from Sir Herbert's neighbourhood?

Shen. Iss; and though I do not like my place, I do still like my master; for there is strong similarities between us. We are both fine scholars, you do know; both of noble families, you do know: To be sure, the Shenkins are older than the Melmoths by some centuries; but I do never mention it; because a man is not to be insulted for the blunders of his grandfathers and grandmothers, Mr Cursitor.

Cur. Right—and if you knew Sir Herbert and his son in Wales——

Shen. Knew him!—Pless my soul! my poor dead father was one of Sir Herbert's tenants——He did keep a great pig Latin school in the mountains; and, before he did die, Caractacus was his under-master.

Cur. Caractacus!—and, pray, who was he?

Shen. I—I'm Caractacus ; I'm the last prop of
the pedigree : and, you must know, my learned father had great griefs and troubles about his other
children ; for my brother, Alcibiades, did rob an orchard.

Cur. Alcibiades !——Oh, I begin to comprehend
now—As a schoolmaster and a man of learning, your
father was above giving his children such common
names as William, Thomas, John.

Shen. Inteed, I cannot say—but my brother Alcibiades did run away, and soon after Ajax Telamon
did die of the hooping-cough, and the youngest of
all did join a puppet-shew, and, in fording a small ri-
vulet, Punch, his wife, and little Junius Brutus, all
went down together.

Cur. Indeed!—great losses!—But your mother—is
she still living ?

Shen. To be sure—and, blessed be Saint David !
for I do love the good old lady better than chis and
pippins. I did come to town with her to open a school,
and teach English—but, somehow, no scholar did
come near us—and then I did go out for usher—
but, somehow, the boys did laugh at me. I do find
there is great difference between English-English
and Welch-English—and so I did hire lodgings for
the old lady, and a place for myself—and if wearing
a livery is beneath me, supporting a mother isn't
beneath me—And in her son Caractacus I do hope
she will forget Alcibiades, and Ajax Telamon, and
little Junius Brutus.

Cur. Hush—Sir Herbert returns—Now observe.

Enter Sir Herbert, Lady Melmoth, *and*
Georgiana.

Lady Mel. Nay, now I am angry in my turn, Sir
Herbert.—Suspect me of coquetting and flirting with
any man but my husband ! Come, cousin, you who
so oft take part against me, can vindicate me now.

Geor. Oh yes, Sir Herbert; though lur'd by fashion into follies numberless, her heart is still at home; and if you've rivals to contend with—'tis in two infant pledges of your mutual love, whom she the more adores, because they so resemble you.

Sir Her. Well, well—'tis ever thus—her magic power disarms me of my anger—I'll think on't no more.

Lady Mel. In truth, you have no cause;—for, since the day you proferred me this ring, my heart has never wandered, never—But don't now, don't mention it; for if the people I visit were to know how much I love my husband, they'd so torment and ridicule me!

Sir Her. And why—why dread their ridicule?

Lady Mel. I don't know—I'm a sad coward, I believe.—But remember the ball we are to give to-morrow in the eastern style.—I shall want plenty of money to finish the preparations; for my pride is concerned, and I'm sure you wou'dn't like to see me mortified or humbled, Sir Herbert.

Sir Her. No, not a wish shall be ungratified that I have power to grant you.——Mr Cursitor, that money may be raised, prepare the deeds instantly—I expect my son from his ship this very day.—But come, Ellen, you want repose.

Lady Mel. Yes, I'm so fatigued, but not sleepy. —Cousin, this is a very restless life.

Geor. Then why pursue it? Why leave the certain treasures that your home contains for such precarious and disgusting scenes?

Lady Mel. Well, after this winter—but, positively, I must go through with it this winter—I will not, to appear happy, make myself miserable—No—I'll retire with my husband and my children—that is, if you'll all stand by me; for to do such old-fashion'd

deeds requires more assurance than even a modern
fine lady possesses.

[*Exit with* SIR HERBERT *and* GEORGIANA.

Shen. Pless my soul, this is marrying for love, is
it? And they do say his last match, which was to
please his father, and for money, didn't answer either

Cur. No, monied matches never answer—there
the parties commence enemies—for, what with settlements, pin-money, attorneys, and trust deeds, they
go to law before they go to bed—and instead of bride
and bridegroom entering a church, it's like plaintiff
and defendant coming into Westminster-hall—So no
wife at all is my motto. (*Going.*)

Shen. And mine also. But, look you, Mr Cursitor, I do want your advice about finding my lost
brother, Alcibiades. I do somehow think you might
bring a sort of bill in Chancery for a discovery :—
But I peg pardon—This way : and as an honest lawyer will not disgrace the pest pedigree, Caractacus
will open the door in person.

[*Exit, showing out* CURSITOR.

SCENE II.

Outside of Melmoth-House, Lodge, Gateway, &c.

Enter MALCOUR *and* CURSITOR *from Gateway.*

Mal. Come, now inform me, Cursitor—Wasn't Sir
Herbert goaded to the soul to find me with his wife
at this late hour ?

Cur. Good morning, Mr Malcour. (*Going.*) I
see what you are aiming at. But if you think I'll

aid you in betraying Lady Melmoth, or any other married woman, you mistake your man.

Mal. Betraying!—S'death! he was the betrayer. Long ere Sir Herbert gained her hand, he knew that she encouraged my addresses—and yet most artfully seduced her from me.

Cur. That I deny—He fairly won her: and, for the encouragement you talk of, why, young ladies will have admiration, and young gentlemen will have vanity. So, once more, good morning, Mr Malcour.

Mal. 'Tis well—but he shall repent his treachery. Oh! if I forgive him!

Cur. That's not my affair—only don't involve me. Though an attorney, I mean to do my best towards going to heaven; and if you gallant, seducing gentlemen are of service to our tribe in this world, I don't think you'll help us in the next—So, a third time, good morning, Mr Malcour.   [*Exit.*

Mal. Mean, conscientious fool!—But here comes one who may be useful to my purpose. Leonard is my friend—we have already met—and if hereafter I can work on his ingenuous mind—

Enter LEONARD, *dressed in a Naval Uniform.*

So—here ends your journey, Leonard.—After an absence of two tedious years, once more welcome to your father's house. Does not the sight transport you?

Leo. It would; but I've a thousand fears—The letter which he wrote me—the business which demands my presence here—and, above all, this marriage with his ward. I know her, Malcour—'tis now six years since, with her cousin Georgiana, she was placed under my father's guardianship.

Mal. Ay, and that of Mr Post Obit:—Curse the old legacy-hunter for not opposing the match.

Leo. He dared not. He is wholly influenced by Sir Herbert—And now, Malcour, if she should involve this hitherto exalted man——Georgiana too! I still must feel for her, for she was born to smile away misfortune, and is the noblest prize a lover can contend for.

Mal. Like father, like son—Here'll be another thoughtless marriage, I see.

Leo. Nay, she knows not of my love, or if she did, have I the vanity to think she ever would return it? No, surrounded as she is by all that wealth and fashion can display, how can a rough, unpolished sailor hope success? Besides, the ocean has so much divided us, that we have seldom met.

Enter SHENKIN *from the Gateway.*

Shen. Pless my soul, I did think so—I did think I did hear your voice in the lodge—Tear! tear! how you to do, Mr Leonard? How you to do?

Leo. What, my old Welch companion? Hey-day! how's this? A livery, Shenkin?

Shen. Iss—You do see what we great men do come to :—but of that by and by. Walk you in, Mr Leonard.

Leo. Stop—Before we enter I would know something about my father and his bride—Is Lady Melmoth, in the character of wife, less extravagant than in that of ward?

Shen. (*Whispering.*) More, a great deal.

Leo. Indeed!

Shen. Don't you say I did tell you—but every day she do lay out hundreds on things she never uses; and I do verily think she do cost Sir Herbert the rent of all Abarathgwilly to dress herself like a druid. To be sure, they do say these muslins are so thin and unwholesome, that soon after the wife do wear white, the husband do wear black, and therefore that married men ought not to grudge this expence, do you see.

Leo. And does Sir Herbert thus submit?—But,

perhaps, she makes amends by a well-ordered and well-managed house.

Shen. Pless you—the house has no manager; for there is Sir Herbert paying twelve servants, and waiting on himself—sleeping in a pig canopied bed, in sheets as damp as the Severn—sitting in a great gold chair, with only a little chop for his dinner— master of the rarest horses and carriages, and pad- dling into the city with an old umbrella, to try to raise money to pay for them : but, however, if it be likely to end the sooner, I am not sorry she do dress herself like a druid.

Leo. 'Sdeath! 'tis unbearable—But, since I must, let me at once encounter it.—Malcour, good day; and, when convenient, make my father's house your home. (SHENKIN *laughs.*) Why, what do you smile at, Shenkin?—You know he's famed for hospitality.

Shen. Iss, in Wales; but Mr Malcour do know there be nothing of the kind here—for, inteed, and upon my life, you'll get nothing to eat but canopied beds gold chairs, and white muslins.—This way— Follov you Caractacus.

Mal. I'll see you in the evening—and be assured, let Forune treat you as she will, you'll find a friend in Malcour. (*Exeunt* LEONARD *and* SHENKIN *at Gate.*) So far, so well—The fickle Ellen thinks me still her friend; and, aided thus by Leonard, my hopes of vengeance will be tenfold.

DR INFALLIBLE *sings without.*

Heh? What fine gentleman have we here? Surely I recollect that face.

Enter DR INFALLIBLE, *and* EDWARD, *his Servant.*

Dr Inf. " Ti di diddle liddle."—What, Mr Mal- cour! My old acquaintance, Mr Malcour!

Mal. Why, it can't be! You the half starved journeyman to the half starved apothecary, who used to bring me medicines at Gloucester—You Tom Drudgewell!

Dr Inf. Mum—Not Tom Drudgewell now—Ever read the newspapers? (*Taking snuff affectedly.*)

Mal. Constantly.

Dr Inf. Recollect Dr Infallible?

Mal. To be sure—the fellow's always puffing himself.

Dr Inf. Be quiet—I'm Dr Infallible.

Mal. You!

Dr Inf. Yes, I'm sole proprietor and ingenious inventor of that immortal medicine call'd Radix Rheno—to be sold at my own house, price eight shillings and sixpence a bottle, stamp inclusive. N. B. No cure no pay—And a lamp over the door, to show the doctor don't practise in the dark.

Mal. Bravo! And, pray—for I forget—what is this Radix Rheno a cure for?

Dr Inf. Every thing.—Chirosis, polypus, ophondria, astherea, dyspepsia, atrophy, notophry, and that worst of all disorders, poverty.

Mal. So I see,—and that's a complaint I'm acquainted with; but curse me if ever I heard of the rest.

Dr Inf. Nor I, till I turn'd quack.

Mal. What the devil! Do you invent these disorders?

Dr Inf. No—our medicines invent them. We give the remedy, and that gives the disease.

Mal. Indeed! And don't the town find you out?

Dr Inf. Can't—dead men tell no tales.—But excuse me one instant.—Edward, take this letter—Compliments to Sir Herbert, and best love to Georgiana. [*Exit* EDWARD *at Gateway.*

Mal. To Georgiana! Why, zounds! have you the audacity to aspire——

Dr Inf. Hush—say nothing—I'll buy her. (*Ta-*

king snuff.) Cupid's a quack medicine, pleasant, pernicious, corrupt, and damn'd expensive.—I'll buy her.

Mal. Ridiculous! Do you suppose Sir Herbert
will consent?

Dr Inf. Not yet—but his wife must have money,
and that letter offers him a friendly loan of some
thousands—You understand—And now come home to
dinner.—My chariot there shall take you.—Look—A
carriage makes a doctor, you know. (*Looking out.*)

Mal. (*Also looking out.*) Your carriage! Why,
that's a hearse.

Dr Inf. So it is.—Well, that's also my carriage;
for if chariots set the doctors going, damme, but the
doctors set the hearses going.

Mal. True; but I must visit an old friend, at that
house yonder; so adieu.

Dr Inf. That! What, that house where the
knocker's tied up!—Dear delicious sight!—Oh! Turtle to an alderman—gold to a miser—a mistress to
her lover, isn't half so gratifying as a tied-up knocker
to a medical man. But adieu! and when you want
a dinner you know where to find one—and sure of
the best company, that is, sure of venison, turbot,
Burgundy, and Champagne. (*Going, stops.*) I say
though—that tied-up knocker! Cou'dn't you recommend?—No—don't trouble yourself.—Dare say
my Radix Rheno has been there already. [*Exeunt.*

SCENE III.

An Apartment at SIR HERBERT'S.

Enter LEONARD *and* GEORGIANA.

Geor. Yes, Mr Leonard, had it been otherwise,
none had more welcomed your return than Geor-

giana—But when you quit a station you so honour,
to be the victim of unequall'd folly, can she rejoice
to see you? No, no—indeed I am not so selfish.

Leo. I cannot understand you—I was sent for
home to join in selling my paternal land.

Geor. And do you mean to comply?

Leo. Most cheerfully—'twill be the proudest moment of my life, when I can prove to such a father
I am deserving of the name of son.

Geor. Then all is lost! This money will be squandered like the rest, and no resource remains. Oh!
be resolute—do not a deed he will hereafter curse
you for, but, by opposing, save him.

Leo. Oppose him! oppose my father! This is the
first request he ever made me; and if *I* e'er ask'd,
did *he* refuse? No—he gave the life that animates
this arm, and, till life ceases, it shall move as he di-
rects! And yet—for such a suppliant I could do
much—I'm sure you have no motive but our mutual
welfare.

Geor. Indeed I have not—I could not bear to see
you both involv'd in misery and ruin. But look—
we are interrupted—my other guardian comes.

Leo. What! Post Obit! Why, what at last brings
him to London?

Geor. He comes to take possession of a legacy—
is on a visit here—and more than ever governed by
Sir Herbert.—But go—your father waits for you;
and thus far indulge me—at least reflect on what I've
said.

Leo. I will, with gratitude; for if there be a joy
beyond all others, it is to know that such a heart as
yours takes interest in my fate. Thanks, thanks!
(*Kisses her hand.*)   [*Exit.*

Geor. Oh yes, you little think how deep the interest it takes. But what avails it? Sir Herbert coun-
tenances other lovers, and while I stay in this detested house, each moment teems with danger.

7

Enter POST OBIT (*in deep mourning.*)

Post Ob. Oh, my dear girl! your poor guardian
can scarce speak for vexation.

Geor. No Why, what has happened, sir?

Post Ob. What? Why, didn't I for the first time
in my life visit London, in order to take possession
of a large legacy left me by my East Indian neighbour; and didn't I purchase a new villa, a new farm,
and this new suit of mourning on the strength of it?
—And now, when I wait on the executor, to touch
the cash, they tell me the will has got a flaw.

Geor. A flaw, sir!

Post Ob. Yes, a cursed flaw! They say the East
Indian forgot what they lawyers call an appointment
—but what I call a disappointment, for here am I
with all these new expences, and, thanks to this Bengal blunderer, not a shilling left to pay for them.

Geor. It is very unfortunate, sir; but I hope you
will find a recompence in the two letters of recommendation you brought with you from Devonshire—
the one to the rich old widow in Pall Mall.

Post Ob. Why, there again—the rich old widow's
carried off.

Geor. Carried off! by whom, sir?

Post Ob. Why, by the late hard frost. She died
and made no sign, or, in plainer words, departed
without a will.

Geor. Well, but the other person, sir.

Post Ob. Ay, there we live again. This letter,
(*Producing it*) to a cousin I have never seen—to
the rich Thomas Tick, esquire—proprietor of a great
castle in the north—Hark ye—quarrelled with all
his other relations, and, owing to town dissipation—
feverish, rheumatic.——Oh! London is the place to
form friendships in—There they've bad health and
sound lawyers—But in the country! curse 'em—
they've no flaws but in their wills—And yet Lon-

don has one inconvenience—I don't like Sir Herbert's house.

Geor. No more do I, sir.—And if you would but remove me from his protection, and place me under your own—

Post Ob. I'm afraid.

Geor. Nay, if you knew the perils I'm exposed to. This very hour he received an offer of five thousand pounds, from one whose hand I have rejected— And to a man involv'd and harassed as Sir Herbert is,—Oh! my friend, protect me.

Post Ob. I would, but I cannot screw myself up to it. 'Sdeath! from a boy he has turned me round his finger—And, after all my submission, when I found out he had only bequeathed me a hundred pounds, and spoke my mind to him—Gad! he sent me a challenge—invited me to Hyde Park; yes, he did; and I, being of a good natur'd turn, and rather wishing other people to die than myself, declined the invitation.—But come, Georgiana, I must go change my clothes, and put by my mourning in lavender for the great Thomas Tick, esquire;—and if at present my good nature keeps me under, this you may depend on,—I'll stand up for you the moment I have got in all my legacies.   [*Exeunt.*

ACT THE SECOND.

SCENE I.

An Apartment at SIR HERBERT'S.

Enter SIR HERBERT *and* DR INFALLIBLE.

Sir Her. Yes, sir; I thank you for the offer of your friendly loan; but the arrival of my son makes it unnecessary.

Dr Inf. Very well, Sir Herbert—but money's no object to me, and if at any time you will condescend to be my banker—

Sir Her. Sir, again I thank you---but with regard to Georgiana, this is my fixed intention---gain her consent, and I will give you mine. But, anxious as I am to see her married, I wou'dn't barter her for all the gold that even you can offer.

Dr Inf. What! you are anxious to see her married!

Sir Her. Yes; she loves my son, for whom I've higher views: therefore, address her, for, as i know your character is unimpeached, and in the way of settlement—

Dr Inf. Ay, Radix Rheno for that, Sir Herbert. I'll go make love to her directly; and as for my patient, Mr Post Obit—

Sir Her. Oh, he moves as I direct.—Success attend you. At present I'm engaged on business with my son—and if in marriage Georgiana emulates her

cousin, your present wealth will seem contemptible—
for you'll have gain'd a treasure worth the world.

[*Exit.*

Dr Inf. Bravo! this is the age for quacking, and
all clever fellows are at it, from the Merry Andrew
on his rostrum to the doctor in his chariot. [*Going.*

Enter Post Obit (*newly dress'd.*)

Post Ob. Oh doctor! my dear doctor! is this Bedlam, or is it Sir Herbert Melmoth's? I thought to
pass a quiet month here; and after enduring insult
upon insult, what do you think? I am now to be shot
at.

Dr Inf. Shot at!

Post Ob. You shall hear.—Just now, after dinner,
the captain and Sir Paddy began talking of duelling.
—The former boasted he had lately wing'd a brother
officer, for traducing his dear love of a waistcoat;
(*Mimicking*) and Sir Paddy lamented he hadn't
fought for a whole month, tho' he had every where
offered five pounds for an affront.—This, you may be
sure, somewhat alarm'd me; and on their asking me
if I had ever fought, I replied, " No, not that I recollect;" on which Mr Jerry Cursitor observed,
" Recollect indeed! Why, he never has, and never
will, unless some of you leave him a thumping legacy;
then, of course, he'll try to blow your brains out."
This nettled me a good deal; and one word bringing
on another, says I, " I ask your pardon, Mr Cursitor,
but that's a lie."—Says he, " I hope no offence;"
and he knock'd me down.

Dr Inf. Indeed! and what followed?

Post Ob. What! Why, the captain and Sir Paddy
instantly rang the bell, called for horse-pistols, and
swore only one of us could leave the room alive!
But Cursitor and I were of a different opinion—we
wished the matter to drop, and said it was a joke.
" Joke," says the captain, forcing a cock'd pistol

into my hand—" Poltroon, did he not give you a
blow?" " No," says I, " he did not; did you, my
dear Cursitor? And if he did, I dare say I deserved
it, and therefore I'm ready to apologize."—" Pooh!"
says Sir Paddy, " it's no longer their affair—people
don't fight to please themselves; they fight to please
the town."—" Damn the town," said we; " our honour is completely satisfied: I've given him the lie,
and he has knocked me down: and if we fire away
till doomsday, how can we have more satisfactory
satisfaction?"

Dr Inf. What! and did they let you off?

Post Ob. No—only gave us leave of absence till
we made our wills, and then they are to come and
cane us if we don't go back and be killed. But,
doctor—my dear doctor—you, who understand life
and death,—can't you contrive——

Dr Inf. Contrive! What, make me a party in your
cowardice! Go, sir, go fight directly, and at least
once in your life give proofs of personal courage.

Post Ob. Once in my life! Come, that's not handsome, sir. You know very well I have given proofs
of personal courage.

Dr Inf. When? on what occasion, my little——

Post Ob. When! Why, if you will have it, when I
drank a bottle of your Radix Rheno. If that isn't
giving proofs of personal courage, the devil's in't.
And, now I think on't, you are the last man I shou'd
have applied to——for Alexander himself wasn't a
greater warrior than a quack doctor; so I'll go talk
to somebody else.

Dr Inf. Adieu! and if you wish to please the
pretty creatures, be yourself another Alexander.
Honour is the true love powder, and we heroes are
elixir vitæ to the ladies.   [*Exit.*

Post Ob. Puppy! if I must turn out, take care I
don't pick my man. But yonder I see an old friend
in the ball-room—and if he won't intercede for me,
and I can't get rid of my good nature, why, I'll re-

turn to these ferocious seconds—say I can't bear to have the thing upon my mind, and fairly beg that they'll cane me directly. [*Exit.*

SCENE II.

A magnificent Room, fitted up in the Eastern style.
(Music heard.)

Enter LEONARD.

Leo. This Sir Herbert Melmoth! this the idol of his tenantry! of the poor, and of his country! this my father! herding with people he has ever scorned, mixing in scenes as opposite to him as to right feeling and to nature. Oh, Georgiana! I will indeed reflect.

Enter SHENKIN.

Shen. How you to do, Mr Leonard? How do you like all this revelling and tevelling; this mobbing and robbing?

Leo. Tell me, Shenkin, have all these visitors been long Sir Herbert's friends?

Shen. Friends! pless my soul, he do not know 'em, nor do they know him.—My lady do want a great pig crowd, you do see; and so she do peg and pray of any pody to ask any pody.—Then she do hire some visitors by the night.

Leo. Hire visitors!

Shen. Iss, sure. Do you think, Mr Leonard, people would come, and be smok'd and smother'd, and ramm'd and jamm'd, and hear such noise and nonsense without being paid for it? Look you,—those foreign singers yonder—(*Pointing to the supper room*)

there—eating like vultures—they are not only paid,
but they will not open their mouths to sing, till they
have opened their mouths to eat. No song no supper, that is their way, Mr Leonard.

Leo. Indeed!

Shen. Then some do come without any invitation at
all; for I did hear that tall gentleman there—(*Pointing again*)—him with the rough lion head, and the
thin putterfly pody—says he, " Aw! aw! demme!
I always go uninvited to married people's houses;
for man and wife never speak—and therefore each
supposes the other has asked you—aw—aw—demme." Oh! 'tis sad work—sad work.

Leo. Disgusting sight! Lavish his fortune on a des-
picable set, who, if he died to-morrow—

Shen. Died! tear! tear! they do never know when
one another die, never; for inteed, and upon my
life, my lady did send me with cards of invitation to
her friend Captain Humdrum the whole winter long:
and she would have gone on till now, only the widow
did call one day, returned Lady Melmoth thanks for
her many polite invitations, and extremely regretted
it was not in the captain's power to accept them, as
he was buried six months before, in St Ann's Church-
yard.—But look you—I do forget my message—Sir
Herbert do wait for you, about cutting off your tail,
you do know.

Leo. I will see more before I come—I would observe this Lady Melmoth. (*More music.*)

[*Exit* SHEN.

Enter LADY MELMOTH *and* GEORGIANA.

Lady Mel. Come, Mr Leonard, why stand frowning there? Why don't you join in our pleasures?

Leo. Simply, madam, because I take no pleasure
in them.

Lady Mel. Indeed! Why, now, perhaps, if I were

to think a good deal, that might be my case also—
but no—one dare not be old-fashioned, you know.

Leo. I dare, madam. I can prefer real happiness
to artificial pleasure.—I do not game, because it don't
please me—I do not drink, from the self-same motive
—and I am not extravagant, because I feel more gratification at paying the tradesmen who supply my
table, than in entertaining a million of sycophants a-
round it.

Lady Mel. Nay, now you are too severe, Mr Leonard—One must keep up appearances ; and if, now
and then, one didn't entertain sumptuously, the world
would call one selfish, prudent—

Leo. Let them call you so. Who can be honest that
is not prudent ? Ay, you may smile ; but whilst I am
prudent, I can smile too ;—and I hope there are still
thinking beings in the world, who will not call me
narrow-hearted, because I am not expensive, or a
hypocrite, because I am not a profligate.

Lady Mel. Come, Georgiana, let us go to the ball-
room. I dare say I ought to reflect on all this ; but
reflection produces vexation, and vexation hurts the
complexion, and so—you had better follow, Mr Leonard.

Leo. No, madam, I can stay alone.

Lady Mel. Adieu, then ; and I wish you much
pleasure from your company. *(Going, returns.)* Oh,
I forgot—If you see Sir Herbert, do tell him to make
haste with those tiresome parchments; for I want to
pay Mr Malcour two or three hundred pounds I've
just lost to him at piquet. I also want money for
Cassino, and a thousand things. Adieu !—You had
better follow, Mr Leonard.   [*Exit.*

Geor. Now, are you satisfied ?

Leo. I am :—To sign will ruin, not relieve him !
And yet—look there—it is my father comes ! Alas !
my heart is so entwined with his—he has been so
kind a parent—so sincere a friend—

Geor. How! still irresolute! (*Takes his hand.*) For his sake! for your own! nay, for my thoughtless cousin's here, who is not now the mistress of her reason;—oh, then, for mine! I have a strong and secret motive here—and if I ask it as the first request—

Leo. (*Pressing her hand.*) 'Tis granted—'tis unalterable—your wishes triumph over his.

[*Exit* GEORGIANA *at the back scene, and*

Enter SIR HERBERT *from the wing.*

Sir Her. So, sir, as I thought,—'tis Georgiana keeps you from your duty.—S'death! why stand loitering here, when the deeds wait your signature? Come, come, no more delay.

Leo. Stay, sir—one word—When these conveyances are executed, is there an acre of paternal land left to support you?

Sir Her. No—but what of that? We've an equivalent in thirty thousand pounds.

Leo. True; and that expended, no resource remains.

Sir Her. None; you know there is no other.

Leo. Farewell, sir—spare me the conflict; pity and forgive me.

Sir Her. What! would you sacrifice your father?

Leo. No, sir—I would save my father.

Sir Her. Away! mean—selfish—

Leo. Selfish! Oh! you should know me better, sir. Place me at the lighted cannon's mouth, and say my death will ease you of a momentary pang, and I, with joy, will meet it.—But this—what is it you ask me? You bid me forfeit those hereditary claims which, for whole centuries, have been our family's support, and in old age had still been yours and mine—not to relieve you from misfortune—not to expend in honourable uses, such as to cheer the poor, and wipe away the widow's and the orphan's tear—No—but to waste in prodigality, and by indulging an unthinking woman, to ruin her, destroy your son, and in eternal sorrow plunge yourself.

Sir Her. Have a care, sir—recollect who you are.

Leo. Oh ! would I could forget ! for sure 'tis time, when I am reduced to speak such words to such a father.—But observe me, sir—I sign these deeds— the money they produce is lavished on your wife— in a few months 'tis squandered all in vanity and vice —the hour of distress ensues—despair, penury, imprisonment awaits you! And then, when Leonard should come forth and serve you, he too is destitute and lost ! and love, which palliates your crime, only encreases his—for he beholds you on a precipice— blinded by passion and bereft of thought, and has not courage to oppose and save you.

Sir Her. Peace, I command you—I will hear no more. (*In great agitation.*)

Leo. Now mark the other picture—(*Taking hold of his arm.*)—I decline the execution—for the first time I dare to disobey you—I leave your house—I am despised—disgraced—and your embarrassments commence—money cannot be raised without security ; and the day of extravagance ceases—your wife loses her fashionable friends—she is compelled to domesticate—she reflects—she sees the comforts of connubial love—she repents—you are beloved and happy —but money is still wanting to ensure that happiness. —You send for Leonard—he flies to meet you—you tell him what has past—tears of joy a-while choke his utterance ; he falls at your feet, and exclaims, " Take the estate ; the whole is yours : and, thank Heaven ! I have preserved it for my father." Now, sir, which conduct is most noble ? which is the most worthy of a son ?

Sir Her. This is all artifice—evasion—and I would hail with joy the ills you talk of, rather than be indebted for a moment's safety to an ungrateful, avari=

cious son. Be gone; return whence you came, and
to your country prove your duty, better than you
have proved it to your father.

Leo. Yes—let me go.—I still have ample consolation; for when next we meet, those frowns will be
converted into smiles.—Farewell! farewell! And yet
—our parting once was different—if I left you for a
day, you used to speak such tender and endearing
words!

Sir Her. Away! If you would please me, leave
me.

Leo. Well, well, I will obey, and cheerfully—for
if I stay I shall relapse, and grant him all he asks.
Once more, farewell—and though your thoughts are
all devoted to another object, mine still are fix'd upon the same—yes, for myself I care not. But bless
him, Heaven! bless the best of fathers!   [*Exit.*

Sir Her. 'Tis plain—'tis evident.—This is the
work of Georgiana; they parted as I entered, and
with these emphatic words, " Your wishes triumph
over his." Oh! she would keep the fortune for herself—she'd see the lovely Ellen ruin'd—beggar'd!
But I will disappoint her sordid views—I'll banish
hence all conscientious scruples, and give her to the
man who offers me that aid my worthless son denies
me.—So shall I save myself, and punish her.—Shenkin.

Enter SHENKIN.

Shen. Sir!

Sir Her. Go instantly to the ball-room, and watch
Georgiana—prevent her leaving the house.—I suspect she will elope with my son.

Shen. Elope!

Sir Her. Yes; and therefore this night shall make
her another's.—And mind, now, whilst I go myself for Dr Infallible, do you take care she don't

escape.—Mind, and be wary.—Oh, now comes my
triumph!　　　　　　　　　　　　　　　[*Exit.*

Shen. Pless my soul! I do think I will elope myself; for, inteed, 'tis time to go out of the house, now
the tevil has got into it.　Tear! tear! watch Miss
Georgiana—turn spy—gaoler!　Yes, I will watch
her, but it shall be to assist, not to oppress her ;—
and then, look you—good b'w'ye, Sir Herbert.　I
will not disgrace my ancestors, tho' you do yours—
No—I will go home to my poor mother, and tell her
I've not only maintain'd the pride of pedigree, but,
what is dearer to us both, the pride of conscience and
of virtue.　　　　　　　　　　　　　　[*Exit.*

SCENE III.

An Apartment at SIR HERBERT'S—*Folding doors in
Flat.*

Enter CURSITOR.

Cur. So the hour's out—the time allowed by these
bloody-minded seconds is expired, and I must return,
to be shot in that room, or submit to be posted and
disgraced.　Zounds! I offered fair enough—either to
take or to make an apology ;—or, if that wou'dn't
do, I offered to fight him at forty yards.—But no,
nothing will satisfy these savages.

Enter POST OBIT.

Post Ob. Mr Cursitor—my dear Mr Cursitor! do
you wish to die?

Cur. Not I, upon my honour.

Post Ob. That's a good fellow—And I've enquired, and there's no occasion.　The barbarians of old

used to shed blood, but the moderns———Hark ye—.
We certainly don't fight to please ourselves, you
know.

Cur. No—As Sir Paddy says, 'tis to please the
town.

Post Ob. Yes, we fight to support our credit with
Mr Jenkins and Mr Tomkins, and other busy neighbours, who will turn up their noses if they don't see
us act like men of honour—for this you may depend
on, Mr Cursitor, many a great hero would take a
kick quietly, if he thought nobody saw it—at least I
know I would—wou'dn't you?

Cur. No—not a kick—I might put up with the lie.
But go on—What are your intentions?

Post Ob. Listen.—Calling in constables would be
useless, for our sanguinary seconds would smuggle
us abroad. Fighting without ball is hopeless, for they
load the pistols—But there is a third way—mark
—Measure ground—eight paces—toss up for first
fire—I win—shoot at random—twenty yards over
your head—you fire in the air—seconds interfere—
—shake hands—Mr Jenkins and Mr Tomkins are
completely satisfied, and Jerry Cursitor and Peter Post
Obit are both men of honour as long as they live.

Cur. So we are.—S'blood! who's afraid?

Post Ob. Ay, damme, I'll fight you directly. Oh,
I thought I should get rid of my good nature at last!
Come along.

Cur. Ay, let's shew them what we're made of.——
But I say, I don't like your having the first fire.

Post Ob. Nonsense! If I hit you, upon my honour I'll make you any apology you think proper.—
Come—and we'll spur like game-cocks.

[*Exeunt at door in flat.*

Enter GEORGIANA (*hastily.*)

Geor. Not here either! no where to be found!
Heavens! what a moment of anxiety! By my advice

the generous Leonard disobeyed Sir Herbert, and now, as he left the house, was grateful for my counsel, and swore he felt such pleasure in obeying me, that he almost forgot the anger of his father.—And this friend I am to lose! Nay, if my guardian, Mr Post Obit, will not have the courage to protect me, I shall be torn from him I love to marry him I hate.

Enter Shenkin.

Shen. Inteed, and upon my life, so you will, Miss Georgiana; and therefore I do come to offer to run away with you myself, or to find Mr Leonard, and bring him to run away with you.

Geor. Generous fellow! There is no hope but one. Yet go to Mr Post Obit.

Shen. Do, and make you haste; for if he do not get you out of the house before Sir Herbert do return with the parson, and the doctor with the licence —Tear! tear! why not go home with me? Tho' we be poor in fortune we be rich in kindness, and Dame Shenkin will be a mother, and Caractacus a father to you.

Geor. It is in vain—My guardian only can protect me—I'll once more beseech, implore him. Oh! this it is to be deprived of parents—to be left a helpless orphan, to the sport of those who have no feeling or compunction.

Shen. Go you---and quick, quick---for, look you, —here is the enemy.

Geor. Farewell, thou honest creature! And if you see Mr Leonard, tell him I am gone to entreat the protection of him who can best afford it; and if I am successful, we may still meet, and still be happy ---but if I fail, and this detested marriage be the consequence, tell him to banish from his mind all memory of her who died regretting and adoring him! Farewell! (*Weeping.*)   [*Exit at door in back scene.*

Enter DR INFALLIBLE.

Shen. (*Weeping*) Good b'w'ye!----How you to
do, doctor? I do want you to do something for me.
---I do want you not to marry Miss Georgiana, and
she, too, do want you not to marry her—because,
look you, she do love an officer and a gentleman.

Dr Inf. Very likely; but she must love a doctor
and a gentleman---and so I'll inform her.

Shen. Stop you---She is with Mr Post Obit.

Dr Inf. With him! With that coward! What!
Does she hope he'll be her champion? Ha! ha!
See how I'll cool his courage. Come forth, my little
legacy-hunter---deliver up my prize this moment,
or, by the laws of honour————

Shen. Look---I do think it is the duty of your profession to take away pain, not to give it : and no medicine can do so much good as relieving a helpless
woman; therefore I'll be your doctor.--- Take you
the physic that is good for you, or, by the beard of
St Taffy, I must force it down your throat.

Dr Inf. Stand off, sir! I see you are set on to harass and insult me, and therefore let me seize my
victim, and chastise this dastardly————

(As he is trying to shake off SHENKIN, *two pistols are
fired off in the adjoining Room---then*

Enter POST OBIT, *with* GEORGIANA *under his arm,
from door in flat.*

Post Ob. " See the conquering hero comes!"

(*Going.*)

Dr Inf. S'death, sir! where are you going? Dare
you at such a moment remove her from Sir Herbert's
power?

Post Ob. (*Snapping his finger.*) That for Sir Herbert and his shabby legacies!—that for you and your
paltry Radix Rheno! And if either of you want satisfaction—there's my card—Hyde-Park—eight pa-

ces---And talk of five pounds, curse me if I wouldn't
give five hundred for an affront! Open the door,
Taffy. *(To* SHENKIN, *who obeys.)* You see, brother Alexander, honour is the true love powder, and
we heroes are elixir vitæ to the ladies. " None but
the brave deserve the fair."

[*Exit, handing out* GEORGIANA, SHENKIN *going before, and* DR INFALLIBLE.

ACT THE THIRD.

SCENE I.

An Apartment at PINCHWELL'S—*small—poorly furnished, &c.*

Dame SHENKIN *discovered sitting in an arm-chair,
weeping—*PINCHWELL *rising from another to go—*
SHENKIN *stopping him.*

Shen. Come, you—do not leave us till you be more
tender-hearted, Mr Pinchwell—Wait you now but a
day.

Pinch. I say, my rent—that's all; pay me my
rent.

Shen. Nay, look you, I have just come away from
my place, and how can I pay you for my poor mother's lodgings here, till Sir Herbert do pay me my
wages? He do put me off, and bid me call again

when he be at home—And do you, do you the same,
will you? Call you again when I be at home.

Pinch. No trifling, but in an hour's time pay me
down the sum of eleven pounds, or her next lodging
is a prison.

Shen. Pless my soul!—You cannot——

Pinch. Yes, that is my final determination.—And
now I'll go down to my lodger on the first floor—
now to the shuffling Mir Thomas Tick.—Plague on
ye—I don't know which is the worst of ye; for, what
with his duns, bailiffs, notaries, and attorneys, I and
the knocker are so continually going, that, curse me,
if we ar'n't both become thin in the service.—And
then there's no moving the rascal; for, amidst all
his difficulties, he contrives to pay his rent—and
here he'll remain a fixture for life. But your case
is different; so remember, my money, or a prison.

[*Exit.*

Shen. To prison! Send my poor, aged, widowed
parent to—Well, well—do you, Mr Landlord, send
her to prison—send her to be dead and buried—
but, by Saint David, there is a place where I will
send you, to be made as pretty toasted chis of—(*Advances to* DAME SHENKIN, *and takes her hand.*)
Mother, come you—don't you sit sobbing, and—Nay,
nay, is this like an ancient Briton, now?

Dame Shen. No—(*Rising*)—and since you've laboured to support me, I will endeavour——I can work
still.

Shen. And so can I—And I will get a new place,
mother. But the eleven pounds!—to raise them in
an hour, without friends, without——Tear! tear!
what will become of us? (*Noise at the door.*) Hey!
Who is coming? Pless my soul! I do fear it is a bailiff already. Iss, it is certainly a bailiff.

Enter TOM TICK *hastily, shutting the door after him.*

Tick. So I'm safe—I've outrun them. (*Leans a-*

gainst the door.)   Peugh ! How are you ? How are
you ? (*Nodding to* SHENKIN.)

Shen. (*Alarmed.*) How you to do ? How you to
do ?

Tom. Sorry to break in so abruptly—Afraid I take
you by surprize.

Shen. Not at all—We did expect you. Mr Pinchwell did threaten us with an officer.

Dame Shen. (*Aside to* SHENKIN.) Be quiet, son ;
'tis the gentleman who lodges on the first floor ; and
when I tell you that his debts were almost all incur-
red in trying to relieve a friend, you'll not affront—

Shen. Affront ! Tear I be very sorry, sir—And
yet, somehow, I be monstrous glad you be not a bailiff.

Tom. What ! you, too, a shy cock—you, too, afraid
of these agreeable——My dear fellow, give me your
hand.—Here's a pair of us.—My name is Tom Tick,
and just now the rascally landlord purposely let three
officers into the passage. I heard them, and had no
other way of escape but jumping up the chimney, or
flying into this garret : And here I am, and if you
will but shelter me till I hear from my banker—But
don't suppose I have change for sixpence there—only—mum—coax'd him with a present yesterday—
two Leicestershire pigs, aged six weeks or so ; and
to-day draw a bill on him dated six months or so—
You comprehend—one good turn—

Shen. No, I cannot guess—can you, mother ?

Dame. No, I can't conceive.

Tom. Can't you ? Then I'll tell you. I am owner
of an inn, call'd the Castle, on the north road ; and
my tenant, who is famous for his Leicestershire hogs,
now and then indulges me with a breed. Very well !
Then I send a couple to my banker, which he can't
refuse, you know, and a day or two after I draw a
bill on him, which he likewise can't refuse, you
know ; for, having accepted the pigs, of course he

accepts the bill; and before now, I have actually raised two hundred pounds by a single litter. There, that's the way to borrow money.

Shen. So it is—and, i'cot! it's dear pork for the banker—unless you pay it at last.

Tom. And if I don't, the banker can afford the loss: And for my other creditors, holders of bills I have been swindled of—why, they know my hand, but not my face.

Shen. Not know your face!

Tom. No—I sign'd to serve a friend, who pass'd away my notes to common usurers : and last week, but for a fortunate circumstance—do you know, sir, one of these fellows called a meeting of the whole body, and advertised it to be held in a room that projected over the new river; when, luckily, the crowd was so immense, and the parties so enraged, that, at the moment they vow'd eternal vengeance, whiz ! crack went the floor ! and souse they all tumbled into the water ! The Jews and money-lenders being used to ducking, got no damage, but the lawyers and annuity-brokers lost their securities—For notes and bonds not being water-proof, my name got soaked out through their pockets, and so far I was completely white-washed.

Shen. He ! he ! And your other creditors did get cool'd, and now you do start fair again.

Tom. Ay; but how long will it last ? For if my banker and another resource fails me—See—(*Taking out an empty purse*)—not enough for a dinner.

Shen. Tear ! That is our case; and we be so hungry—and look, look you—here comes the devil, to claw my poor mother for the eleven pounds.

Tom. Only eleven pounds !

Shen. No more: And if she do go to gaol, we shall both lie down and die together. (*Turns to* DAME SHENKIN, *and weeps.*)

Enter PINCHWELL *(hastily.)*

Pinch. Zounds! I thought so—Slipt through their fingers again, and you help to conceal him! (*To* SHENKIN.) Death and fire! Shall I never, never get rid of you?

Tom. Why wish it? Don't I pay my rent, Mr Landlord?

Pinch. Yes, and be hang'd to you. If you didn't, do you think I'd let you stay here and ruin my trade? Don't your duns stop up my shop-door; and, because they're not acquainted with your person, don't they seize my customers—cram them with bills—threaten them with bailiffs—hunt—drive——

Tom. Well—and haven't your customers cause to thank me? Hadn't they better pay my bills than yours? For don't you treble the price of ev'ry article—manufacture it of bad materials; and from the earnings of the laborious poor, haven't you set up a gig—and a bit of blood—and a straw-bonnet?

Pinch. I tell you what, curse me if I wou'dn't give ten pounds never to see your face again.

Tom. Would you, upon your soul?

Pinch. That I would—and say I never laid out money to better advantage.

Tom. Then I'll tell you what, make it twelve, and I'll take it.

Pinch. Twelve! Done—there's the cash—and now away with you, and I'll go get officers to take them away. (*Pointing to* SHENKIN *and* DAME.)

Tom. Stop—I'm off directly—but for these poor people, they may stay.

Pinch. Stay! Why, how will they pay their debt?

Tom. How! why, with your own money.—There —there's eleven pounds to stop your mouth, Mr Pinchwell—and there is the odd one to stop yours, my honest Welchman.—You need not examine them —they are very good—I took them just now;—and

I perfectly agree with you, (*To* PINCHWELL) you never laid out money to better advantage—and take my advice; go and continue the recreation; you'll find it more wholesome than the gig and the straw-bonnet.   [*Exit* PINCHWELL.

Shen. Pless you—pless you—My poor mother is free, and Caractacus is so grateful——

Tom. For what? Didn't you protect me? And therefore I but repay you what I owe you—and I wish from my soul I could do the same by all my creditors. I hate this shifting life—and did I not reflect misfortune first involv'd me——But psha! moralizing won't help me—I must to action.

Shen. So must we—we must look out for a new place, you do know.

Tom. Come on then.

Enter Servant.

Well, sir, what says the banker?

Serv. Sir, I am sorry to inform you he will neither accept the bill nor the present.

Tom. What! don't he bite at the pigs?

Serv. No, sir—and Doctor Infallible won't advance you another shilling.

Tom. Ungrateful, shuffling scoundrel!—Is this—But no matter—I'll first visit my friend Leonard—and then to the Temple—I'm sure the lawyers will discount for me.

Shen. Come you—then the lawyers have not heard you do not pay your notes, I am sure.

Tom. Yes, they have—and that's the reason they advance money upon them.—If a note be punctually paid, there can be no action, you rogue; but if unpaid, think of the glorious cannonade against drawer, acceptor, and indorsers.—These are their valuable bills; and the family of the Ticks are the best friends the lawyers have upon earth.—Where are the pigs?

Serv. Below, sir.

Tom. Give them to the Welchman, and he'll bite at them—I'll be damn'd if he don't.   [*Exeunt.*

SCENE II.

An Apartment at POST OBIT'S.

POST OBIT *and* GEORGIANA.

Post Ob. Was there ever any thing so ungrateful? Hav'n't I fought for you, and conquered? Hav'n't I rescued you from a bullying guardian and a mountebank lover?

Geor. You have, sir---I own the obligation, but---

Post Ob. But you still love Leonard Melmoth--- you would still unite yourself with that haughty, ruined family.   But take notice, I have forbid Leonard this new house of mine,---and as a proof that I mean to select a respectable husband for you, no man shall marry you that can't leave me a thumping legacy. This is the reward I expect as conqueror, and shall enforce as guardian.

Geor. Enough, sir :---I cannot marry without your consent.

Post Ob. Yes, you may---but you lose your whole fortune---you forfeit eighteen thousand pounds---and stripp'd of every shilling, will Leonard so offend his father?

Geor. And if he would, do you think I'd suffer him? No, sir---I have sufficiently involved him--- and not for the world shall he a second time oppose his father---therefore your triumph is complete; for till you consent, Leonard is lost to Georgiana.

Post Ob. Then he is lost for ever.---And now for my unknown cousin, the great Thomas Tick, esquire

---now to look out my letter of recommendation ; and then for a will without a disappointment.——But, plague on it---how shall I find him out ? Do you know that London is such a confus'd scene, that I can't tell one street, place, or house, from another ?

Geor. Indeed, sir !

Post Ob. No---to me they are all alike---and yesterday morning I saw no more difference in the bulls and bears in the Stock Exchange, and the lions and tygers in Exeter Exchange, than I did yesterday evening between the wranglers for fish at a lady's card party, and the criers of the same article at Billingsgate.---But keep up your spirits ; and while I go to Mr Tick, remember, in this house you're safe from all lovers but the one who will leave me a thumping legacy. [*Exit.*

Geor. And this is the asylum he affords me---this the protection I so long implored! But whither can I go ? Return to Melmoth House is hopeless---is impossible ;---and to apply to Leonard---No, no, turn not a thought that way.

Lady Mel. (*Without.*) Let me pass---I must and will see her---(LADY MELMOTH *enters.*) Georgiana !

Geor. My cousin ! *(Partly turning from her.*)

Lady Mel. Nay, it is not now the gay and haughty Lady Melmoth that addresses you, but a poor penitent, who sees her errors are beyond all pardon--- not you alone and Leonard are the victims of my folly---No---an indulgent husband——

Geor. What! the dreaded hour is come !

Lady Mel. Even so.---The house so lately decorated with all that art and fancy could suggest is now one naked ruin---All, all is seized---not e'en a bed is left, to yield repose to him who, till he knew a dissipated wife, ne'er felt the loss of it. And yet he forgives the wretch who, from the height of fortune and of fame---Oh, that he had but censured and reproached me!---It is his kindness cuts me to the heart.

Geor. Be pacified. Leonard will now come forth to succour and preserve him.

Lady Mel. No----his father will not hear him named, and vows to welcome ruin, ere ask of him assistance. Besides, it seems that Malcour has the ear of Leonard, and that he listens to the slanderous tale of that vain, boasting, and unfeeling man—when, Heaven's my witness! till yesterday I thought him still my friend--- But when he openly avowed his love, I scorn'd his bold, presumptuous offers, and had proclaim'd him to the world, but that I prized my husband's life beyond a villain's shame.

Geor. Oh yes! my life upon your innocence : and, could I talk with Leonard---but, by my guardian's orders, we are for ever parted.

Lady Mel. This I had heard, and therefore came to tell you that Sir Herbert and myself mean to seek out some distant and sequestered spot.---Come, go with us. He'll bury in oblivion all that's past, and I, repentant and reclaimed---

Geor. No---let me stay here ; and if my guardian will relax, and his consent be gained, Leonard may still be mine---and then I'll join you in retirement. ---And now return to him who anxiously expects you. Oh, may you be happy, cousin!

Lady Mel. And may the hour be not far off when this consent is gain'd---till then, farewell---and sure I must be happier than I have been---for I know not why, but the forc'd smile of dissipation ne'er yielded half the joy these tears of penitence afford.

Geor. No, because their fountain is the heart, and nature bids them flow, to moisten and revive those seeds of virtue long deadened in the heated soil of error and of fashion. Farewell! and to re-

ward a generous husband's love, be henceforth Ellen
Arundel, the child of feeling and simplicity.

[Exeunt.

SCENE III.

The Street. Outside of POST OBIT'S *House.*

LEONARD *and* TOM TICK *discovered near the Door.*

Leo. You see my fears were right. I am denied
admittance to Post Obit's house ; and if you are serious in your offer to assist your old school-fellow and
college friend, now, now is the moment.

Tom. My dear fellow, ask me to shoot the guardian, burn the house, fly away with the girl----in
short, ask me to do any thing, but lend you money,
and Tom Tick's responsible.

Leo. Then observe---I'm now call'd away to watch
over the fate of my father : his dissipated wife has
not only ruin'd him in fortune, but in love ; and her
attachment to Malcour shall convince him of his er-
ror---therefore, whilst I seek him, do you get sight
of Georgiana, as a person unknown to her guardian.

Tom. I may gain admission, and wheedle him out
of his consent.

Leo. That hope is vain. No longer influenced
by my father, he will indulge his hatred to our family ; and Georgiana is too proud to be Sir Herbert's
daughter, without a fortune to support her; but if
you'll tell her that the time may come, and that I
still adore---still——

Tom. Go along---I'm used to flourishing speeches
---I practise them every day for my duns : and ere
next we meet, I'll lay you all I'm worth---no, that's

a bubble bet—I'll lay you all I owe, that I secure the prize.

Enter Dr Infallible *behind ; seeing* Tom, *he stops, and listens.*

Leo. Kind, generous fellow ! you'll find me at our friend Malcour's.   But remember there are rivals as well as guardians to contend with, particularly one Dr Infallible.

Tom. He ! that rascal one of her lovers ! O ho ! then I've a double motive for serving you ; and I'll see you married to Georgiana, if it is only to out-quack that Radix Rheno mountebank :---So away--- go to your father, and let me commence operations.

Leo. Adieu ! success attend you---and if I could but describe to you how much I feel indebted---

Tom. And if you can't, I know very well what it is to be indebted, without troubling you or any man to explain it. [*Exit* Leonard.]   And now, take notice, my little doctor——

Dr Inf. (*Meeting him.*) And the little doctor does take notice, you see.   And after my advancing you such large sums of money, how dare you---

Tom. And after my advancing you to your present situation, how dare you refuse me more money, sir ?

Dr Inf. You advanced me ! Zounds, sir, 'twas genius, application.

Tom. No, sir, 'twas puffing, advertising ! Didn't I, at your own desire, insert a letter in all the news-papers, dated Monmouth, though I never was there in my life, stating, I had been worn to a skeleton with a confirm'd ophondria, though I don't know what the disorder means ; and that, as a last hope, I flew to your immortal medicine ; when, wonderful to tell ! and joy to my disconsolate friends ! the first glass warm'd the viscera, the second braced the nerves, the third enliven'd and electrified the whole

system ? And so far I spoke truth—To do you justice,
Radix Rheno is a delicious dram ; and after half a
bottle, I never was so jollily drunk in all my days.

Dr Inf. Dram! call my Radix Rheno a—fire and
fury ! if it were, who do you suppose wou'd take it ?

Tom. Who ? ask the ladies.

Dr Inf. Psha! all scurrilous alike---and long---
long before I knew you, I made as much noise as
any medical man in London.

Tom. I can't tell whether you made a noise, but
I know your patients did :---And if by accident your
name was seen at the bottom of a prescription, why,
'twas like my name at the bottom of a note---damme,
nobody took it.

Dr Inf. No matter, sir---I laugh at you, and defy you. And to prevent your effecting a marriage
between Leonard and Georgiana, by imposing on
Post Obit, I'll go directly, and lay a train to expose
you. I'll inform him of your debts, of your keeping
the Castle inn on the north road, of your whole family being compos'd---

Tom. I grant it. My father, uncle, and grandfather were all inn-keepers ; and I see your sneaking
motive for traducing them.---They lower'd the market ; for they called drams, drams, and, at a tenth
part your profit, sold Radix Rheno under its proper name—British spirit.—But to battle, for I'm on
fire till the war begins.

Dr Inf. And so am I ; for I'm secure of victory ;
and dub me coward, if Georgiana be not still the
doctor's.

Tom. And dub me coward, if she be not Leonard's. (*Exit* DOCTOR.) And now to sound the
trumpet of defiance---now to rap that little knocker
---and then, inspir'd by gallantry and friendship—

[*Going to door.*

Enter Post Obit, *from the House, meeting* Tom.

Your servant, sir, your servant---but as these lodgings are to be let, and I'm in haste to look at them
---(*Crosses* Post Obit, *who pulls him back by the
coat.*)

Post Ob. Softly---not so fast, if you please, my
young spark.----No man enters that house till I know
his name and business ;---and you, sir---

Tom. And I, sir ! My name is Tom Tick, sir.

Post Ob. What ! Thomas Tick, esquire, of the
north !

Tom. To be sure, I'm of the north !

Post Ob. And owner of the Castle ?

Tom. To be sure, I'm owner of the Castle !

Post Ob. Ten thousand pardons. You are the
very gentleman I was going to, my dear sir. (*Pulling off his hat, and bowing with great humility.*) I've
brought this letter of recommendation from your
friend, Robert Whimmy of Devonshire, who informs
me we are cousins. You know facetious Bob, sir ?

Tom. Know him! yes ; and by that smiling, smirk-
ing countenance, I know you to be one of his comical choice spirits---But cousins ! I doubt about cousins.

Post Ob. Don't---pray don't---Yours is a very uncommon name, and my mother---But, with submission, the letter will explain---only Bob has such a
regard for poor Peter Post Obit, that you mus'n't
believe all.

Tom. (*Snatching letter, and opening it.*) Post
Obit ! here's luck ! (*Aside.*)—" Dear Tom"—(*Reading letter.*)

Post Ob. Softly---to yourself, if you please---I'm
too modest to hear my own praises. (*Turning away
his head.*)

Tom. (*Turning away also, and reading the letter.*)
" Dear Tom——The bearer, Peter Post Obit, is

such a notorious legacy-hunter, and has so persecuted me to give him letters to opulent people in London, that, at once to punish and get rid of him, I have recommended him to you. His mother's name being Tick, I have easily convinc'd him you are cousins, and have also told him you are lord of a great castle in the north—have bad health, and, in consequence of a quarrel with your other relations, will very probably select him for your heir. Adieu! And by making as much of the credulous old blockhead as you can, you will oblige, ever truly yours, R. WHIMMY." (*Here they both turn round, and bow to each other.*) Oh, oh, I see it now. My dear, dear cousin! (*Shaking his hand.*)

Post Ob. That's right—You see I'm a true Tick.

Tom. I do—and to use Bob's words, upon my honour, I'll make as much of you as I can. (*Shaking hands with him.*) To be sure, I've no house in town to invite you to—at present—only elegant lodgings. But if you'll take a trip to the Castle, I'll give you such a reception—such dinners—such wine—such beds;—and then, fancy (*Counts with his fingers*) six servants out of livery—seven chamber-maids,—thirty horses—eight post-chaises.

Post Ob. Eight post-chaises!—Bless my soul! and how many coaches?

Tom. None. I've done with flies and dillys, and slapbangs, and——that is, I mean I always travel in my own carriage.——But it grows late, and I'm an invalid, you know, and particularly ordered by my physician to avoid the night air : So, with your leave, we'll talk further in your house. (*Taking his arm.*)

Post Ob. Come along—and don't—don't now, fret about your ungrateful relations.

Tom. No, sir—There is such a thing as a will ; and if I can find a respectable——But I feel flying pains, particularly in my back and my shoulder.

Post Ob. What! are you subject to attacks in the shoulder?

Tom. Continually, and chiefly in the open air: So, allons—and, as wine is the best restorative, over a bottle we'll drink Bob's health.

Post Ob. So we will, cousin.

Tom. And success to our better acquaintance.

Post Ob. So we will, cousin.

Tom. And confusion to all graceless relations.

Post Ob. So we will, cousin.—Huzza! there'll be no flaw or disappointment here!

[Exeunt into the house.

ACT THE FOURTH.

SCENE I.

Outside of POST OBIT'S *House—Night—Stage somewhat darkened.*

Enter DR INFALLIBLE *and* EDWARD, *meeting.*

Dr Inf. 'Sdeath! I shall lose the battle.——Well, Edward, what success have you met with?

Edw. None, sir: Mr Post Obit's doors are not only shut against you, but against your servants.

Dr Inf. Ay, ay; at present the enemy carries all before him; for, just now, when I met the old legacy-hunter, and told him Mr Tick was owner of the Castle on the north road, he said he knew he was owner of the Castle, and that made him so fond of

him.—And when I added that he was over head and
ears in debt, he fairly laughed in my face, and ex-
claimed, " Good evening, Mr Hocus Pocus."

Edw. Dotard!—But don't, sir, don't yield so easily.

Dr Inf. Yield! No, I'll shew him I'm indeed an
Alexander.——Hark ye; half measures never yet obtained a victory; and therefore, at once to strike
the grand decisive blow, this night I'll carry off
Georgiana.

Edw. That's right—But how will you secure her?
You can't get inside the house, you know.

Dr Inf. No; but, by making use of my antagonist's name, I may get her outside of the house, you
know—You comprehend?

Edw. I do, sir—You'll pass for Mr Tick.

Dr Inf. Yes he has often borrowed my name,
now I'll borrow his—and then, Edward——

Edw And then, sir, you'll bear her off in triumph.
—Let's about it instantly.

Dr Inf. Stay—we must first make preparations.
Go order horses and assistants to be ready to convey
her to my lone villa on the Downs, and then return
to the enterprise. Come.—Oh! there's an end of
Leonard and his champion.——And for you, Miss
Georgiana, once in my power, I'll serve you as I
serve my patients—death alone shall part us.

[*Exeunt.*

Enter TOM TICK *and* GEORGIANA, *from the House.*

Tom. Huzza! The victory is mine!

Geor. Oh! I'm most grateful. Till you arrived,
my guardian was inexorable. I had no hope of gaining his consent, and Leonard was for ever lost to
me—But now——

Tom. But now, thanks to Bob Whimmy, I'm your
guardian. I'm to nominate your husband; and don't

be afraid of my choosing Tom Tick.—No; if I trust myself with a wife, who the devil will trust me?

Geor. But the conditions—I heard you talk of an agreement and a will; and Mr Post Obit is now gone to his lawyer's. Alas! I fear you forfeit much to gain this power.—What, what is the sacrifice?

Tom. Sacrifice! Ha! ha!—Why, we're cousins. —He is a true Tick, I tell you; and so I am to make a will in his favour, and bind myself in a heavy penalty not to revoke it, provided he agrees—In short, he gives me the controul of you—the finest property under heaven; and I, in return, bequeath him the Castle, and all those magnificent apartments, the Sun, the Bear, the Lion.

Geor. There! 'tis as I dreaded.----And you are bound not to revoke this will?

Tom. And why should I revoke it? The Castle don't net the value of its sign, and is so involved in executions, mortgages, and Chancery suits, that there can't be a fitter legacy for my dear cousin: So, while I inform Leonard, return to your apartment.

Geor. Oh, dispatch!----I dread his meeting with his father. His fixed dislike to Lady Melmoth may tempt him to propose a separation; and, desperate as Sir Herbert is become——

Tom. Fear not---I'll dispatch; for if Radix Rheno should expose me before the will's signed---not that there's much danger; for Post Obit forbids him his house; and, for once, a legacy-hunter is uncivil to a doctor.----Adieu!----and, depend on't, in Leonard your fortune and your person shall find a brave protector; for matrimony, which endangers our persons, protects yours.---Oh! if I had the privilege of a petticoat! if I were a married woman!----Bless 'em! they are Sunday-men all the week. (*Going.*)

Voices without. Come along---come along.

Tom. (*Looking out.*) Zounds! who are all those people coming out of that tavern? What an infernal crowd? Surely they can never——(*Listens at the side.*)—Yes, I hear them buz about my name.----By Heaven! my creditors in a body, and with bills as long as their faces!---So, so, they have had another meeting----are on the look to lay hold of me----and Georgiana will be the victim of Peter Post Obit----and I of John Doe and Richard Roe.——The only chance is, these money-lending note-holders don't know my person; and, that they never may, I'll---- Here they come.----Curse ye! I wish I had ye over the new river again.

[*Exit up the stage, and stands aside.*

Enter Ten Creditors, with Papers in their hands.

1st Cred. Stop---Before we separate, suppose we once more read the resolutions.---(*Reads.*) " At a second meeting of the creditors of Mr Thomas Tick, held this day, it was proposed and unanimously a- greed to, 1st, To identify his person; 2dly, To dis- cover his place of residence; 3dly, To seize him and every item of his property."

2d Cred. Ay, that's right.---But how to set about it.---Zounds! isn't it strange none of us know him?

1st Cred. No, not at all.----We lenders of money do all our business in the dark. The sight of a man's hand-writing is enough for us----and if we knew all our creditors, gad! we should have the most nume- rous and fashionable acquaintance in London.

2d Cred. So we should.----And, as his new haunt is somewhere hereabouts, suppose we keep a sharp look out---Hush! somebody's coming---Who knows ---Stand aside. (*They go up stage----*Tom *remains concealed.*)

Enter Dr Infallible, *muffled in a great coat.*

Dr Inf. (*In a low voice.*) Now for it----now for my experiment---And if, by means of this contri- vance, I can lure her into my snares——(*Crossing stage.*) Soft!---(*Knocks at the door.*) Oh! be propitious, Fortune!

Serv. (*Opening a window over the door.*) Who's there?

Dr Inf. It's I---I want your young mistress.

Serv. You! Who are you?

Dr Inf. Why, don't you know?---Are you near-sighted, or is it so dark, that you can't see I'm Mr Tick?

Serv. What, master's new acquaintance, the great Thomas Tick, esquire?

Dr Inf. Yes, I'm the great Thomas Tick, esquire. (*Here the Tradesmen stare at each other, and begin to move forward.*)
And, d'ye hear, tell Miss Georgiana, I and Mr Leonard are waiting at the corner of the street in a hackney-coach, and beg to speak to her directly.

Serv. Mr Leonard with you!---I warrant she'll come directly.   [*Exit from window.*

Dr Inf. Bravo! the day's my own!----Poor Leonard! Poor Tommy Tick!
    [*Exit, walking on tip-toe, and rubbing his hands. Tradesmen exeunt after him, likewise walking on tip-toe, chuckling, and rubbing their hands.*

Tom. (*Advancing.*) Ha! ha! poor Tommy Tick!---Damme! now he's taken the name, I hope he'll stick to it; and I defy him to choose a more popular one---for see what crowds he draws after him!---No man living is more sought after: and if I were an actor, what houses I should bring!----But where, where will all this end?----I'll peep----'Sdeath! Post Obit is coming!---Now I'm down again; for if he has met them, and, after all, the real Simon Pure should be detected---

Enter Post Obit.

Post Ob. Here's pretty work!----Mr Tick, I'm astonished.----Going out, I met Dr Infallible, and he talks to me of your debts, and his own riches---And, coming home, I see this same monied man actually jump into a hackney-coach, to avoid a dozen duns! And, after in vain denying his name, and trying other hocus-pocus arts to get rid of them, he bade the coachman drive for it; and away they all went after him, like so many bull-dogs.----Gad! I hope, with all my heart, they won't quit him till he has paid every shilling---don't you, cousin?

Tom. That I do, with all my soul, cousin.----But enough of him, and his Radix Rheno.----Have you seen your lawyer?

Post Ob. I have---and the agreement, giving you the nomination of Georgiana's husband, will be ready to sign this very night, and the will also: So, whilst I go reconcile her, do you inform your friend.

Tom. I will----and, from this hour, keep in mind the lordly Castle.

Post Ob. And do you keep in mind your state of health----Don't stand chilling in the night air.——— Adieu!---and, d'ye hear, take care and keep off the attack in the shoulder, cousin.

Tom. Thank ye, cousin.---The doctor has kept off that already.   [*Exeunt*---POST OBIT *into the house.*

SCENE II.

An Apartment at SIR HERBERT'S, *stripp'd of its Furniture.*

Enter LADY MELMOTH *and* DAME SHENKIN.

Dame Shen. Come, come; why accuse and reproach yourself, my lady, when Sir Herbert has forgiven and forgotten every thing?

2

Lady Mel Yes ; but can I forget, when, in each room of this once splendid mansion, I trace the progress of extravagance and guilt—when, in my husband's wan and frenzied look I read distrust and desperation ?—You know not half the misery I dread. Deserted by his friends, bankrupt in fortune and in hope, may he not fly to self-destruction for relief ?—Nay, I have cause to think it—And now !—Why, wherefore does he not return ?

Dame Shen. Be patient :—Isn't he gone to borrow a small sum ? And, sure, amidst so many wealthy friends—

Lady Mel. No ; when winter comes, these summer insects are beheld no more : and for your sake —yes, yours and poor Shenkin's sorrows heighten mine.—Oh ! would I could relieve you.

Dame Shen. Nay, don't mind us, my lady —Had I a thought to see you so griev'd and so distress'd, I'd have died before I'd have applied for my son's wages ;—but we were in bitter want---out of place, and no means of subsistence.

Lady Mel. And I the author of your ruin. I have not the power---Merciful forgetfulness ! come to my aid --befriend---compose me. (*Throws herself in a chair, weeping.*)

Dame Shen. Poor lady ! She almost drives my own troubles out of my head---though, to be sure, if my son don't shortly get employment, and, some how, his simple manners are against him---A-lack ! go where he will, they dismiss,—and—

Shen. (*Without.*) " Oh the noble race of Shenkin." (*Singing.*)

Dame Shen. Bless me ! What noise is that ?

Shen. (*Without.*) " Oh the noble race of Shenkin."

11

Enters, in a new suit of clothes.

Mother! My tear, tear old mother! (*Embracing her violently.*)

Dame Shen. Mercy on me! Why, what's the matter?---What---

Shen. (*Putting his hand before her mouth.*) Stop ---Do not you put me out.— Look you.—I did hear of a place at Dr Infallible's, and so I did go to his great house to offer---And so, as I did stand in the hall, with the butler and the servants laughing at me, the doctor did push in with three or four companions, and being in a great haste and bustle, did order a fine supper to revive him---And this did remind me of your wants, mother; and so I did hold him by the arm, and swear he shou'dn't stir, till he did hear and relieve me; but instead of doing either, he did say I was another of the villains, and did send for a warrant, and then the constable did come, and then he did read aloud the doctor's description, and then— he! he!---Give me another hug, mother.

Dame Shen. Why, the boy's wild, distrac---

Shen. Stop you---do not you interrupt ---The constable did read at full length the doctor's name, and was going on, when, at one spring, I did rush into the supper-room. "Look you," said I, "three questions, doctor, before I be committed.—Were you born at Abarathgwilly?" "Ha!" said he.--- "Have you a mole on your left breast?" "Heavens!" said he.---" Is your Christian name Alcibiades?" "Oh, iss," said he. "Then," said I, "you did rob an orchard, and are my brother---I be little Caractacus---you lost Alcibiades—and, plessed pe Saint David, you have brought your cotlings to such a good market."---And then, for his own credit sake, he did order me these beautiful clothes—And then he did give me this beautiful gold watch, which did cost thirty guineas---And then I did run to tell you---

And then---" Oh the noble race of Shenkin." (*Kissing watch, and strutting.*)

Dame Shen. Thank Heaven for the joyous, welcome news! But how was it? Did you ask him how he got all these riches?

Shen. Iss---and there I did mistake.---You do know, we did always fear he wouldn't stop with the pippins; and so, when he did boast he had made his fortune by the coinage of his own brain, by Radix Rheno, I did think he said, by coining ready rhino ---and so I did tell him.—But come, he have ordered supper for us also---and the next time we do want eleven pounds, this little gentleman (*Kissing watch*) will pay it three times over, mother. (*Singing.*)

Dame Shen. Stay, my son---in our own good fortune let us not forget the distresses of others. (*Pointing to* LADY MELMOTH.)

Shen. Oh ho! What, she do begin to feel at last, do she?---Come---

Dame Shen. For shame! Is this the way you bear prosperity? Poor soul! the creditors have seized on all she has---have left her nothing but the humble dress she wears.

Shen. Inteed!

Dame Shen. Nothing---and we who've known such bitter want ourselves---

Shen. Want! Pless my soul! My mistress, wife of a Pembrokeshire baronet, want---Look you---I've no more money than this poor half guinea, and take it! Take it, while 'tis of its full value---for my fingers do wax so hot and melting, that it will be stew'd to a seven shilling piece before you can say Dim Sarsenid.

Dame Shen. My child! Still the same generous heart.

Shen. Iss; and if I thought altering my dress would alter my disposition, I would walk straight to Abarathgwilly, climb up into the tall cherry-tree, and change clothes with the sly old scarecrow.---But what will this small sum avail? Where are all their visitors—their friends?---Oh! I see now---Gone after the dinner tables---gone to leave cards at the next house their mahogany friends do put up at.---Let them---but let me show a different——Come along, mother---I have it.

[LADY MELMOTH *rises and listens.*

Dame Shen. Dear! dear! What do you mean?

Shen. Mean!—To let this watch point out to my poor lady hours, minutes, and seconds of peace, plenty, and happiness---to change it into money, and give it all to her.---And never say the rich are not happy---for all the kids on all the mountains can't skip more than my heart does at doing one small charitable action. [*Exit with* DAME SHENKIN.

Lady Mel. Generous creature! I'm most grateful; nor will his former situation make the gift less welcome; for he's ennobled who's benevolent, whilst they who are callous to the voice of charity sink to the lowest rank of poverty and vice. Oh! now here are the means, Sir Herbert.---But why—why does he delay? Sure, had all been well, long, long ere this he had returned. Alas! My heart's so full of fears and of forebodings.---Hark! what was that? The report of a pistol, and so near as the court-yard!— Merciful powers! 'Tis past! It is confirmed! (*Approaches door and listens.*) Yes, they utter forth the dreadful sound---Murder has been committed.---Oh, I've no hope but to rush forth and perish with him.

As she is going, enter SIR HERBERT, *in great agitation.*

Alive! In safety! My husband! (*Falling on his shoulder.*)

Sir Her. Hush! Guard the door. I'm known— I'm pursued—but I am innocent—I am no murderer.

Lady Mel. Speak! What has happened?

Sir Her. I know not. His piteous agonizing look still glares before me, and, coward like, I dared not to meet it. Could I behold those eyes that have so beamed pleasure for the life I gave them—Could I, when I destroy'd—Oh, Leonard! Leonard!

Lady Mel. Leonard! Speak, I implore you.— Where, where is your son?

Sir Her. I have no son: But now, he proffer'd me the whole estate, provided I would part with you. He said that Malcour would receive you. This, knowing of your innocence, enraged and maddened me. Words begat words, and seizing the pistol which I bore about me, I swore that moment I would perish at his feet, ere owe my safety to a presumptuous, disobedient son. He tried to force the weapon from my hand, and in the struggle—Oh, have mercy Heavens!—his breast receiv'd the fatal ball, and, staggering to the earth, he groan'd, and——

Lady Mel. No—not died—he did not, shall not die! (*Knocking at door.*) Hark! You're discovered.

Sir Her. I? What am I?—My son is sinking to the grave, and perhaps a father's tears might balm ——I'll go, and——No—no—it will not be——My wound is deadly as his own. (*Falls into a chair.*)

Lady Mel. And—this—this havoc is my—— (*Pointing to* SIR HERBERT.) Look here, ye votaries of dissipation! See if a life of gay, licentious pleasure, can compensate for such an hour as this! —I know, I'm sure, that in the splendid equipage and dazzling dress ye never taste one moment of substantial joy.—Then seek it in your husbands' and your childrens' hearts—make home a shelter 'gainst the storm ; and, let it roar around, still shall you find domestic life the scene of peace !—Oh ! do, do you not curse—despise me ?

Sir Her. No—In spite of all sorrow, still there's solace here.——(*Rises, and embraces her.*) But my son—Let us go make enquiry.

Lady Mel. No—to your chamber—I'll seek, assist him.—Come, come, retire while there's safety.
—Oh! that the death-blow had been all my own!

[*Exeunt.*]

ACT THE FIFTH.

SCENE I.

The Street.—Scene of Lincoln's Inn.

Enter MALCOUR *and* TOM TICK.

Mal. Yes, the hour of retribution is arrived—and in Leonard's wounds all Malcour's wrongs shall be revenged.

Tom. Nay, but where is he?——where is my dying friend?

Mal. In my house—under my protection.—And be his vile assassin who he may, I will detect and punish him.

Tom. And do you as yet suspect——

Mal. I do——I much suspect his father.——(TOM *starts.*) Aye; like you I am amazed, and shudder to have cause for my suspicion. But when I find my friend assassinated in the dark—hear him exclaim, "My cruel, cruel father!"—and, by his side, behold an instrument of death, marked with Sir Herbert's name——

Tom. Indeed!

Mal. Aye ; and, as corroborating proofs, when I
reflect on the late quarrel, and that the estate was
wholly his on Leonard's death——Oh ! if that dread
event takes place, think you he shall escape from
justice ? No—I will instantly accuse him. (*Going.*)

Tom. And I'll gain Post Obit's consent, and return to your house with Georgiana.

Mal. Hold—She must not see him—If he's disturbed, his death is certain.—Now, haughty Ellen,
we'll see how much you prize a favoured husband's
life : for there's a way to save it.   [*Exit.*

Tom. Not disturbed ! Nonsense !—I'll to Lawyer
Cursitor's directly, make my will in Post Obit's favour, and return with his preserving angel.——And
now, thou blind goddess ! keep others blind but for
a few minutes longer, and I and Leonard will be
happy, in spite of duns, death-hunters, devils, and
doctors !   [*Exit.*

Enter (*immediately*) Dr Infallible *and* Capias.

Dr Inf. There he goes—that's him !

Cap. Bless you. I know Tom Tick as well as he
knows Lenitive Capias—Why, we're so familiar, that
he always calls me by my Christian name.

Dr Inf. Very well, then arrest him instantly on
that warrant for two hundred pounds—Away !—Yet
stop.—As I mean Post Obit should see the great Thomas Tick in a spunging-house, what is your direction ?

Cap. (*Pointing off the stage.*) There, number 197,
Carey Street :—And shew me a smarter mansion than
Lenitive Capias's.

Dr Inf. Away—take the enemy prisoner. (*Exit*
Capias.) And now to send Post Obit to see his rich
friend in all his glory ; and then, Georgiana, left to
herself, will be completely in my power. Ha! ha!
There's a dose for the whole trio.   [*Exit.*

SCENE II.

An Apartment at CAPIAS'S *Spunging-house, very
elegantly furnished.—Table, Chairs, &c., all modern and handsome.—Window-Curtains up, and
Bars seen at the Window.*

Enter CAPIAS, *with Candles, followed by* TOM TICK,
in great agitation, looking pale.

Cap. Walk in, Mr Tick, and be composed. (*Putting down candles.*) I declare you'll fret yourself
quite ill.—Come, come. You know there's nothing
like a prison about my spunging-house. To be sure,
the bars are a little awkward ; but we'll let down the
curtains, and then you may fancy yourself in your
own lodgings. (CAPIAS *lets down the curtains, and
bars are concealed.*)

Tom Plague on't ! Nicked at such a moment !
Defeated by that rascally doctor !—My good fellow
—my dear Lenitive—I've an appointment with a
lady—And, as a man of gallantry, I'm sure now—
Do, do let me out for half an hour, will you ?

Cap. Psha ! Why don't you apply at once to your
wealthy friend, Mr Post Obit ? I told you before, if
he'd pass his word for you, I'd take it—and you'd
better make haste ; for I'm afraid there'll be plenty
of detainers.

Tom. I know it.—I lose my liberty, Georgiana
her lover, Leonard his life, and all——My good,
sweet Lenitive, this is the last place in which I would
wish to see Mr Post Obit—and if you won't let me
out for half an hour—do now—do lend me two hundred pounds for half an hour—Upon my honour—

Cap. What! you think you're likely to pay in half an hour?

Tom. As likely as in half a century, Lenitive.

Cap. True; but there's an end of your art here—there's no borrowing or spunging in a spunging-house.

Tom. No!—(*Knocking heard.*) Go, sir; go and attend to your customers.

Cap. Well, good night.—And, to shew you I bear you no ill will, I once more offer to let you out, if Mr Post Obit will be answerable: If not, don't stand fretting there, looking as pale as a ghost.—Psha! Why, there's nothing to remind you of a prison here; for, what with the genteel company, the elegant rooms, and the polite conversation, shew me the difference between Lenitive Capias's and a fashionable lodging-house, that's all.   [*Exit.*

Tom. Dished!—In for life!—Not for myself I feel: I deserve my fate—But to involve the happiness of others—to think that' my imprisonment devotes to misery, perhaps to death, two as generous and as noble hearts——Well, well—drooping won't save them.——Come, rouse, and exert yourself——And look! there's cause for it already; for here comes Post Obit, to vent forth all his anger and reproaches. —No matter—he shall see I'll carry it off with gaiety and spirit.

Enter POST OBIT, *hastily.*

Post Ob. So, Mr Tick, I've found you out at last. —And who do you think I've to thank for it?

Tom. The quack, sir—of course, the quack.

Post Ob. Yes: I'll tell you how it was. Not seeing you at Lawyer Cursitor's, I went out to look for you, and meeting the doctor, I asked him if he knew where you lodged? He told me at Mr Capias's, No. 197. Carey Street; and that, if I'd go there, I should see you in all your glory.—Very well! So,

owing to the darkness of the night, and my ignorance
of London, 'twas some time before I found the house;
and then, to be certain I was right, I said to Mr Capias's servant, " Are you sure Mr Tick lodges here ?"
" Oh yes, sir," says he ; " I'm sure Mr Tick is one
of Mr Capias's lodgers."—And then he smiled, and
I smiled :—and, upon my word, I envy you these
beautiful apartments.——But come ; I've done the
agreement : So go, go sign your will.

Tom. What ! at your old facetious tricks, I see—
That's a good joke to a man that's confined.

Post Ob. Confined ! What the devil——(*Getting
close to* TOM, *and looking in his face*)—is it so bad
with you, that you are confined ?

Tom. Pooh ! you see it is.

Post Ob. What ! and by the doctor's orders ?

Tom. Why, you know it's by the doctor's orders.

Post Ob. Not I——He only told me where you
lodged.—Bless me ! he does look charmingly ill indeed !—(*Aside.*) How was it ? Were you taken suddenly ?

Tom. Very—and in the old place too—in the
shoulder.

Post Ob. And if you stir out without the doctor's
leave, will the consequences be dangerous ?

Tom. Fatal, you comical rogue, fatal.

Post Ob. Bravo !—If I can but get him into the
night air, he'll make his will in one hour, and take
to his bed the next. (*Aside.*)——Nonsense !—Go to
Cursitor's—I'll stay and satisfy the doctor.

Tom. Will you ?—Lenitive ! (*Going to the wing,
and calling.*)

Post Ob. Heh ! who's Lenitive ?

Tom. The doctor's agent.——Lenitive ! (*Calling
again.*)

Post Ob. The doctor's agent ! Ag——Oh ! Oh ! I
understand—the apothecary. (*Aside.*)

Re-enter CAPIAS.

Tom. Here, my boy—here's Mr Post Obit!—and I don't know whether he is in jest or earnest, but he says he'll be answerable to the doctor.

Post Ob. Yes, yes; you may let him out: I'll stay, and be answerable to the doctor.

Cap. I'm satisfied.—This way, Mr Tick.

Tom. Ha! ha! this is the best joke I ever heard; but it won't be complete till I'm fairly out of the house: So good night.—It cost me some money to get into these beautiful apartments, as you call them, and if it costs you any to get out of them, you'll say it's one of Tom Tick's legacies, you know.—— Come, Lenitive.—But stay—stay—(*Speaking as if alarmed.*) Suppose I'm detained?

Post Ob. Psha! don't let them detain you: Say I'm answerable.

Tom. Better and better! Ha! ha! you are indeed a damned comical dog.—He! he! you'll kill me with laughing.   [*Exit with* CAPIAS.

Post Ob. Ha! ha! So I kill you, curse me if I care how it's done.—What a fool it is!—The Castle and all its magnificent appurtenances are mine.—— Gad! I hope it's a fine foggy night!—I'll see—I'll peep out of the window. (*Goes up stage.*)

Enter SHENKIN.

Shen. How you to do, Mr Post Obit?

Post Ob. (*Not regarding him, but undrawing curtains.*) Why, what's here? Bars! What does he do with bars? Surely he has no children! no infernal little heirs-at-law! (*Coming down the stage, and meeting* SHENKIN)—nor is he mad, nor—Zounds! 'tis very odd!—Taffy, do you know Mr Tick?

Shen. Iss, sure, I do know he did save my poor mother from prison, and so I did come here to shew

my gratitude! But, plessings on you! you were be-
fore-hand with me.—I do find you are answerable for
all the debts and detainers—And therefore well may
you peep through the iron bars. Tear! tear! having let the bird out of the cage, what joy must you
feel to see it hop away in health and liberty!

Post Ob. Cage! (*Looking round at the window.*)

Shen. Iss, cage, or spunging-house—'tis one and
the same thing, you do know. (*Here* POST OBIT *is
in great agitation.*) And how do I envy you these
ecstacies? Oh! what I would give to have taken the
weight off his shoulders!

Post Ob. Damn his shoulders, and you, and—Yes,
yes, I see it now—the lodgings—the confinement
—the apothecary!—Well—well—but perhaps—yes
—this distress may be only temporary—and his property in the north—Hark ye, sir—you know he's
owner of a castle. (*Shaking* SHENKIN.)

Shen. Owner of a castle!—Oh, I do recollect now
—Iss, sure—And by the price he do get for his Leicestershire pigs, I do think it be an inn of some consequence.

Post Ob. An inn! the Castle an inn!

Shen. Ay, it be no castle in the air, I assure you.
[POST OBIT *going.*

CAPIAS *without, to* DAME SHENKIN.

Cap. Here's the person you enquired after. (*Enters
with* DAME SHENKIN, *who takes* SHENKIN *aside.*)
And now, if you please, Mr Post Obit, you may as
well pay what you are answerable for.—The plaintiff's debts, you see, (*Shewing account*) are two hundred pounds, and the detainers already four hundred
—and then there's the costs and the fees. (POST
OBIT *rushes out behind him.*) What! an escape! Oh
ho! Stop the prisoner there! Stop the prisoner!
[*Exit after him.*

Shen. (*Coming forward with* DAME SHENKIN.)

Tear! tear! what sad doings? But perhaps you did not hear right, mother; perhaps you do mistake.

Dame Shen. (*Weeping.*) Oh, that I did! for I have lived too long—yes, I have lived too long.

Shen. Pless my soul! Mr Leonard dying!

Dame Shen. Yes, I tell you his wounds have proved fatal. And Mr Malcour, in whose house he is now breathing his last, not only won't let any of his family come near him, but actually threatens to lay a charge against Sir Herbert for wilfully destroying him.

Shen. Mr Leonard given over—and Sir Herbert accused—and—Lord! Lord! at such a moment we mus'n't forsake my old master, mother.

Dame Shen. Forsake him! No—We'll go directly, and find out the real culprit; for I am sure Sir Herbert's innocent.

Shen. Sure! I'll take my oath of it.—Come this moment:—and as his other friends have forsaken him —you shall be his nurse, Alcibiades his physician, and Caractacus again his servant.—Yes, mother, this hand shall work for him—and since rough misfortune has beat my old master down, it shall be found strong and willing to lift him up again.   [*Exeunt.*

SCENE III.

An Apartment at MALCOUR'S---*Folding Doors in back Scene.*

Enter SIR HERBERT *and a Servant.*

Sir Her. Let me pass—let me once more enfold within my arms the wrong'd, the dying Leonard.

5

Serv. Sir, 'tis too late : my master just now told us the fatal hour was approaching, and therefore his assassin should be seized.

Sir Her. Look at me—I am his father.—Have you the heart, at such a moment, to separate son and parent ?

Serv. His father !

Sir Her. Ay, that culprit Mr Malcour is in search of—that hapless wretch, 'gainst whom the proofs are most demonstrative and strong ; for I've no evidence of innocence, but here—but my boy ! Let him not curse me with his parting breath—and then conduct me where you please—I will surrender to my fate.

Serv. Indeed I know my master will condemn me, but for my life I cannot now resist a father's claim.—You may go in, sir—yonder is the chamber.

Sir Her. Thanks, thanks ! (*Stops, and trembles.*) There ? Did you say there ?—Heavens, was ever guilt so bold ? But let me implore his pardon and his pity —and then, most welcome my accuser !—Death has to me no terrors—No ; existence is the villain's punishment.   [*Exit at door in back scene.*

Enter MALCOUR.

Mal. How, sir, why don't you attend the door ? Go, shew up Lady Melmoth ! (*Exit Servant.*) Oh, this is beyond my hopes ! The humbled fair already in my house to sue for mercy ! Already !—But she comes.

Enter LADY MELMOTH.

Lady Mel. Oh, spare him, Mr Malcour—Not for poor Leonard I implore you—I know too well you can't avert his fate, but spare my husband.

Mal. Nay, madam, when I was suitor, did you shew me mercy ?—or am I so indebted to Sir Herbert, as to connive to serve him ?

Lady Mel. Ah ! think of two tender ones who

never wrong'd you.—I am unfit to guard so dear a
charge, and now you'd rob them of their father. For
their sake accuse him not. I see them now with supplicating hands entreating me to save their only hope
—and you consent—they are made happy; and I,
inspired by returning virtue, may be to him a wife,
to them a mother !

Mal. And what avail these promised joys to me ?
I share not in them—therefore observe—one only
way can save him.

Lady Mel. Name it.

Mal. (*Taking her hand.*) You well remember, that,
by every base and treacherous art, he tore this hand
from him who fairly won it. Then restore it, give it
to me, its rightful owner, and I'll withdraw the accusation.—Why, what alarms you?—Do you not understand me ?

Lady Mel. I do.—You'd have him purchase life
at the expence of a weak woman's honour.

Mal. No—I would have him give me restitution.

Lady Mel. 'Tis well—I have deserved this treatment. But think you this sacrifice will save Sir Herbert ?—think you he will survive the loss of honour ?
—No—virtue is the soul that animates his frame,
and that destroyed, he'll perish with it !—And see
the difference 'twixt his love and yours.—He'd welcome death ere I shou'd forfeit that which, if I do
not forfeit, you will betray the father of your friend !
—Oh, shame, shame ! Fallen as I am—sure, when
the heart is breaking, 'tis time to pity, not insult me.
(*Weeping.*)

Mal. Have a care—think of the awful proofs
against him—The previous quarrel; the estate so need-
ful to repair his fortune ; the instrument of death
marked with his name.—Remember, there is no other
hope.

Lady Mel. There is, thank Heaven ! Before it
dawn'd, and now it glares upon me.—Who urged

the unhappy Leonard to dispose of this estate?—
Who drove him from a doating father's arms?—Who
caused the quarrel that produced the fatal blow?—
And who will now most publicly acquit Sir Herbert
of the charge—acknowledge all the crime—and, in
the presence of surrounding witnesses, make Leonard, with his dying breath, confess the true, the
only culprit?—I, Ellen Melmoth!—I, that guilty
wife, who, amidst unnumbered crimes, has still the
pride to scorn a base seducer's arts, and die to save
a dear-lov'd husband's life! (*Going towards a chamber.*)

Mal. (*Stopping her.*) Hold, you will not be so
rash?

Lady Mel. Sir, I will be so just; and if his future
days pass on in peace, an ignominious death will
yield that joy a splendid life ne'er gave me! (MAL-
COUR *still holds her.*) Oppose me not.—A while ago I
was as cowardly as fear could make me, but conscious virtue once more warms my veins, and I've a
giant's strength.

Mal. Nay, then, suppose this boasted courage is
in vain.—What if I tell you Leonard is no more?

Lady Mel. You cannot—will not——

Mal. I would avoid the melancholy theme, but---
(*Holding down his head.*)

Lady Mel. Oh, speak it not!—I see—I read it in
your looks! Great Heaven, hide me from myself!
(*Falls on the ground.*)

Enter SIR HERBERT, *from the Chamber, leading on*
LEONARD, *with his arm in a black sling.*

Sir Her. He lives—we have witnessed his returning health.—We know the ball, which lodged but in
his arm, was instantly extracted; and the exaggerated story of his dangerous state was propagated by
that artful fiend, to shake the virtue of a matchless
wife.—But you are baffled, sir—He has heard all,

and comes to punish perfidy, and to reward the exalted Ellen's truth.

Lady Mel. Can you forgive me, Leonard?

Leo. Forgive you!—Oh! if my sufferings deserve
a recompence, let me receive it here, from one who,
while she sought applause from folly and from pomp,
forgot she had a heart that might have won e'en
Heaven's own praise.—And now, sir, (*Taking* SIR
HERBERT'S *hand,*) this is the happy hour I predicted.—Connubial blessings wait you!—And I may
exclaim, with joy and exultation, " Take the estate;
the whole is yours; and, thank Heaven, I have preserved it for my father!" Mr Malcour, we quit your
house, never to meet again.

Tom. (*Without.*)   This way, and don't believe a
word on't.

Enters, with GEORGIANA.

There—as I told you, only a slight scratch—alive and
merry, you see.

Leo. Georgiana! Why, how's this? Has Post Obit
consented?

Tom. No—but I have.—This paper, (*Gives it to*
LEONARD, *who reads it to himself,*) sign'd with his
own comic hand, gives me power to name her husband; and I don't know how you feel, brother guardian, (*To* SIR HERBERT,) but I nominate Leonard
Melmoth—I give him Georgiana, with charms to the
tune of eighteen thousand.

Leo. (*Having read paper.*) Astonishing! Why,
what could induce—

Tom. Curse me, if I can tell you—All I know is,
a quack threw me into a spunging-house, and a legacy-hunter took me out of it—that by his orders
I signed my will at the lawyer's, and by his orders
the lawyer gave me that agreement—that I'm free,
Georgiana safe, Leonard happy! and if the joke
prove a dear one to Post Obit, it's no fault of mine—

He would have a legacy ; and hang me, but I've left him a thumping one.

Sir Her. Generous friend ! You shall partake of our prosperity ; and in my son may Georgiana find atonement for all the wrongs committed by his father.   And now, Ellen, ere we commence our new career, let us remember that moderate pleasures are the most complete, and that extravagance, which takes its root in indolence and pride, concludes its fleeting life in fraud, in ruin, and disgrace !

Tom. So it does—And let no man run out—And for the future I'll pay punctually—but still—

> One debt there is, which we can never clear—
> The debt of gratitude that's owing here.
> Lend us your smiles once more—for my sake, do.

Enter SHENKIN.

Shen. And also for Caractacus, look you.

Enter DOCTOR.

Dr Inf. And for poor me—though driven from the plain,
> If you'll stand by me, I may fight again.

Enter POST OBIT.

Post Ob. And so may Peter.
Tom. ——————— Nay, adjust affairs,
> Give me your hand, and hope that they
> give theirs.

(TOM *shakes hands with* DOCTOR *and* POST OBIT.)

> You want no fee, if they support your
> cause,   (*To* DOCTOR.
> And you no legacy, but their applause.
>   (*To* POST OBIT.

END OF VOLUME SECOND.